# Programming Right from the Start with
# VISUAL BASIC .NET

# Programming Right from the Start with
# VISUAL BASIC .NET

THAD CREWS

CHIP MURPHY

Upper Saddle River, NJ 07458

Library of Congress Cataloging-in-Publication Data information is available.

**Executive Editor:** David Alexander
**Publisher:** Natalie E. Anderson
**Project Manager (Editorial):** Kyle Hannon
**Editorial Assistant:** Robyn Goldenberg
**Media Project Manager:** Joan Waxman
**Senior Marketing Manager:** Pamela Hersperger
**Marketing Assistant:** Barrie Reinhold
**Managing Editor (Production):** John Roberts
**Production Editor:** Renata Butera
**Production Assistant:** Joe DeProspero
**Manufacturing Buyer:** Diane Peirano
**Design Manager:** Maria Lange
**Art Director:** Pat Smythe
**Interior Design:** Jill Little
**Art Studio:** Matrix Art Services
**Cover Design:** Marjory Dressler
**Cover Collage/Illustration:** Marjory Dressler
**Manager, Print Production:** Christy Mahon
**Composition/Full-Service Project Management:** Pre-Press Company, Inc.
**Printer/Binder:** Von Hoffman Press

Credits and acknowledgments borrowed from other sources and reproduced, with permission, in this textbook appear on appropriate page within the text.



Pearson Education LTD.
Pearson Education Singapore, Pte. Ltd
Pearson Education, Canada, Ltd
Pearson Education–Japan
Pearson Education Australia PTY, Limited
Pearson Education North Asia Ltd
Pearson Educación de Mexico, S.A. de C.V.
Pearson Education Malaysia, Pte. Ltd

10 9 8 7 6 5 4
ISBN 0-13-141696-0 (Student)

# Dedication

*To my wife Tammy, and our children Reed, Noah, and Elizabeth.*

—Thad

*To my mother, Milbrey.*

—Chip

# Brief Table of Contents

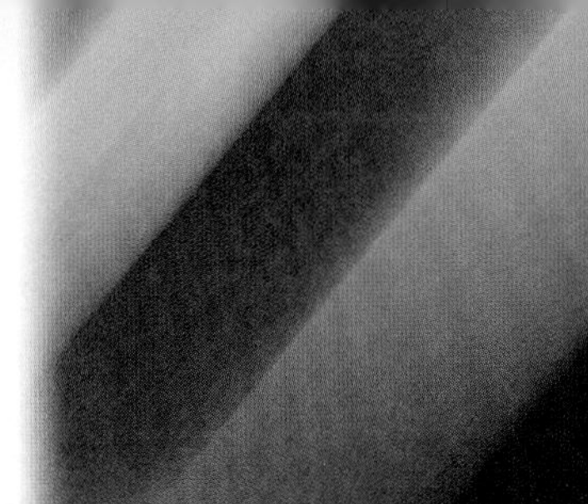

# Contents

# Preface

*Programming Right From the Start with Visual Basic .NET* emphasizes design over syntax, using an innovative pedagogy and the latest Visual Basic .NET technology. This comprehensive book uses a unique modular approach. Unit 1 uses the **Visual Logic** flowchart simulation tool to provide a minimal-syntax introduction to essential programming concepts, including variables, input, assignment, output, conditions, loops, procedures, functions, arrays, and files. Unit 2 provides conventional programming activities using Visual Basic .NET syntax, with an emphasis on designing and developing graphical, event-driven programs. Unit 3 provides advanced coverage of the .NET Framework, including chapters on ADO.NET database programming, ASP.NET web applications, and object-oriented programming. Unit 3 also contains two detailed case studies, one involving a complete Shopping Cart implementation (using ASP.NET and ADO.NET) and a second detailed case study of a working machine learning program.

*Programming Right From the Start with Visual Basic .NET* is consistent with national curriculum models. **IS'97 (revised as IS 2001)** provides model curriculum and guidelines for undergraduate degree programs in Information Systems. IS'97 topics for the programming course (IS'97.5) include "algorithm development; objects and event driven representations; data flow notation; programming control structures; program correctness, verification, and validation." It is interesting to note that no specific language syntax is mentioned. This is consistent with our philosophy that skills, not syntax, should be the focus of an introductory programming course.

A second national curriculum model is the **Computing Curricula 2001** (www.acm.org/sigcse/cc2001/). Thad Crews worked with the CC2001 Task Force as part of the Introductory Course Pedagogy Focus Group. The CC2001 report includes a call for course designs of various types, including a minimal-syntax approach.

> By introducing students to basic algorithmic concepts and constructs apart from any particular executable language, this approach minimizes the preoccupation with syntactic detail that demands for successful program execution typically engender among students. Instead, it requires that students reason about and explain the algorithms they construct . . .
>
> Once students have a solid grasp of the algorithmic foundations and the range of data and control structures . . . they can then move on to a more conventional language, either partway through the first course or, at the latest, the beginning of the second course. Because students have experienced a wider range of both data and control structures early, their later progress through conventional programming work can occur more rapidly and class time can be more explicitly focused on issues of effective programming practices and systematic debugging skills.

*Programming Right From the Start* gives students exposure to essential programming concepts before introducing the full power of Visual Basic and the .NET Framework.

## The Visual Logic Flowchart Simulation Tool

One of the groundbreaking features of this book is the Visual Logic Flowchart Simulation Tool (included free with this book). Visual Logic allows students to develop minimal syntax flowcharts that incorporate fundamental programming concepts, including variables, input, assignment, output, conditions, loops, procedures, functions, arrays, and files. Visual Logic flowcharts are **executable**, providing immediate and accurate feedback to the student. Visual Logic has been classroom tested with amazing success.

One instructor working with Visual Logic shared the following:

> The consensus among students was that Visual Logic is a very intuitive and effective tool for learning the basic logic structures. The students were unanimous in their recommendation of Visual Logic. Students were particularly impressed with the power of "instant" feedback to show the results of a logic structure.
>
> Our faculty was more than impressed with the Visual Logic application. Our former College of Business dean who has returned to full-time teaching mentioned that he considered it one of the most significant developments in the area of logic and design and problem solving that he has encountered. Needless to say, there was a consensus from the programming faculty on the benefits the tool and texts could have on our curriculum as a whole.

## Organization

- Proven classroom pedagogy for teaching introductory programming concepts. Material is presented in a clear and illustrated manner. Concepts are presented in an appropriate problem-solving context, empowering rather than overwhelming the student.
- The text is written to emphasize logic and design throughout all activities. Numerous case studies emphasize programming opportunities in the information age.
- Database programming with ADO.NET is explained clearly and simply from an information technology viewpoint.
- Web applications are presented from the ground up, ensuring that even novice students can understand and create client-server applications using ASP.NET Web forms.
- The power of the .NET Framework is demonstrated through a detailed Case Study implementation of a three-tier Shopping Cart Web application using ASP.NET and ADO.NET.
- Object-oriented programming is presented in a manner that emphasizes the role of object reuse.
- A rich collection of end-of-chapter features includes a chapter summary, key terms, review questions, and programming exercises.

# Supplements

## Visual Logic CD-ROM

A textbook version of Visual Logic comes FREE with the book! Visual Logic is a simple but powerful simulation tool that supports programming logic and design without traditional high-level programming language syntax.

## Instructor's Resource CD-ROM (0-13-141698-7)

The instructor support materials described in this section are available for adopters on the Instructor's Resource CD-ROM. The CD includes the Instructor's Manual, Test Item File, TestGen, and the helpful lecture tool Image Library, and PowerPoint slides (also available on the text's Web Site).

## Instructor's Manual

The Instructor's Manual features not only answers to all end-of-chapter material, but also teaching objectives and teaching suggestions. This supplement can be downloaded from the secure faculty section of the Crews Web site and is also available on the Instructor's Resource CD-ROM.

## Test Item File

The Test Item File, by Mark Alan Segall of Metropolitan State College of Denver, is a comprehensive collection of true–false, multiple-choice, fill-in-the-blank, and essay questions. The questions are rated by difficulty level and the answers are referenced by page number. An electronic version of the Test Item File is available as TestGen on the Instructor's Resource CD-ROM.

## Image Library

The Image Library is an impressive resource to help instructors create vibrant lecture presentations. Nearly every figure in the text is provided and organized by chapter for convenience. These images and lecture notes can be easily imported into Microsoft PowerPoint to create new presentations or to add to existing ones.

## PowerPoint Slides (on Instructor's Resource CD-ROM and Web Site)

Electronic color slides, by Paula Ruby of Arkansas State University, are available in Microsoft PowerPoint. The slides illuminate and build on key concepts in the text. Both student and faculty can download the PowerPoint slides from the web site, and they are also provided on the Instructor's Resource CD-ROM.

## Companion Web Site (www.prenhall.com/crews)

The password protected instructor Web site contains source code for all projects and case studies, as well as PowerPoint presentations for each chapter. The iWeb site also contains an abundance of reinforcement handouts for each chapter, designed to strengthen student understanding of material covered in the text. Each handout contains a student version (ready to copy and distribute) as well as an instructor master that includes solution and lecture suggestions.

# Acknowledgments

This was a large and complex publishing project, and it is our pleasure to acknowledge the many people who have contributed to its success. We would like to thank our reviewers, each of whom provided helpful suggestions that have improved this book.

Kevin Brunner, Graceland University
Belva Cooley, University of Montana
Mayur Desai, Indiana University-Kokomo
Nancy Herman, Pennsylvania State University-Harrisburg
Eli C. Minkoff, Bates College
Olga Petkova, Central Connecticut State University
Jerry Ross, Lane Community College/Linfield College
Glenn T. Smith, James Madison University
Charles Watkins, Villa Julie College
Karen Watt, Mount Aloysius College
Todd Whittaker, DeVry University
Bruce White, Quinnipiac University
Susan E. Yager, Southern Illinois University-Edwardsville

We want to thank Jen Carley and her colleagues at Pre-Press Company who did a great job with the numerous figures and visual elements of this text. We are extremely grateful to the tireless efforts of the extraordinary team of publishing professionals at Prentice Hall. Vanessa Nuttry and Debbie Hoffman provided timely assistance and were invaluable in getting the project started in the right direction. Senior Art Director Pat Smythe did a wonderful job coordinating the many design elements. Special thanks go to Kyle Hannon for her expert supervision. Her dedication to the project never wavered. Renata Butera was the production supervisor whose leadership was critical to the timely publication of the text.

We would like to extend a special note of thanks to David Alexander, Acquisitions Editor, for his encouragement and support. His vision allowed us to break new ground with this book, and achieve heights that would otherwise have been unattainable. Many different problems needed to be solved to get this book published, and David solved each one responsibly, quickly, and professionally. It has been a privilege and a pleasure to work with him on this project.

We would like to thank the various instructors who have worked with pre-print drafts of the book and shared their experiences with us. Their feedback has not only improved the quality of this book, but also contributed to the quality of the instructor's web site. It is our goal to provide the most helpful instructor support material possible. We welcome your feedback as well. You may contact us at http://www.prfts.com/contact.

We would like to thank our families for their unfailing love and support. Writing this book took far more time and energy than we ever imagined, but our families gave us the support and encouragement we needed. Their strength allowed us to give our very best, and the result is a better book for you, the reader.

Finally, we acknowledge God and thank Him for His many blessings.

Thad Crews
Chip Murphy

# Features

## Visual Logic

The Visual Logic program comes FREE with this book! Visual Logic is

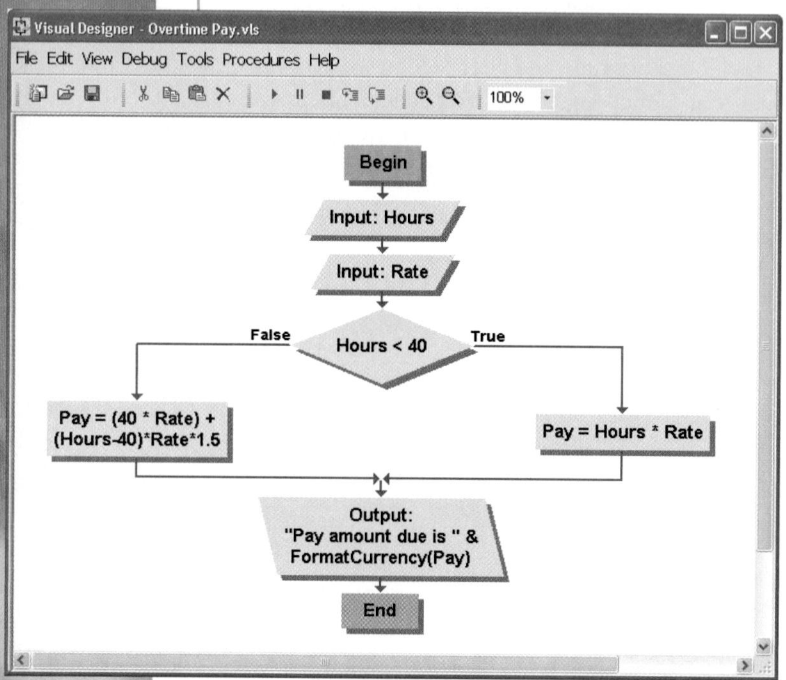


a simple but powerful tool for teaching programming logic with minimal syntax. Visual Logic uses flowcharts to explain essential programming concepts, including variables, input, assignment, output, conditions, loops, procedures, functions, arrays, and files.

## Executable Flowcharts

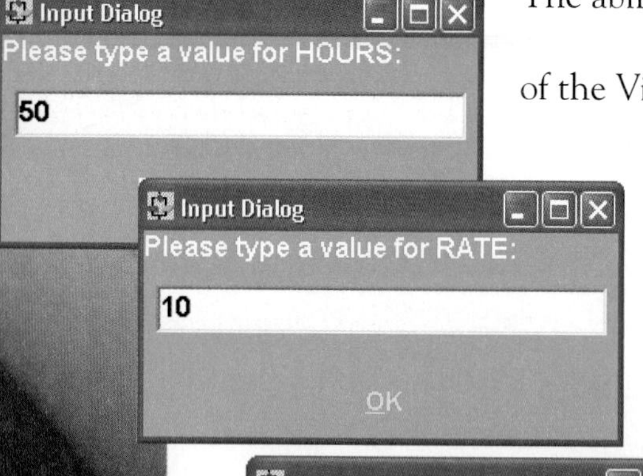


The ability to interpret and execute flowcharts is a unique feature of the Visual Logic program. It makes Visual Logic distinct as a tool for students learning to program. Visual Logic provides immediate and accurate feedback to the student, combining the power of a high-level language with the simplicity of flowcharts.

## ▶ Chapter Opening ◀

A two-page chapter opening contains an outline of chapter topics and a list of specific learning objectives that tells students what they will be able to do after completing the chapter.

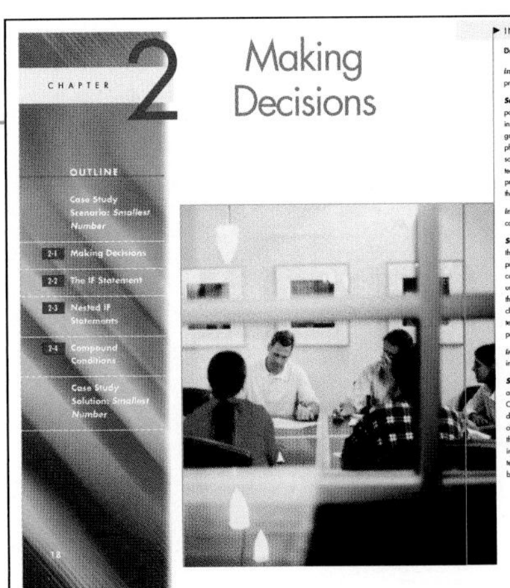

CHAPTER 2

Making Decisions

OUTLINE

Case Study Scenario: *Smallest Number*

2-1 Making Decisions

2-2 The IF Statement

2-3 Nested IF Statements

2-4 Compound Conditions

Case Study Solution: *Smallest Number*

18

▶ INTERVIEW

**Devinder Sud, Instructor, DeVry University**

***Interviewer:*** Please tell us how you got involved in your current IT profession.

***Sud:*** I have worked both in industry/business as well as teaching at the postsecondary level for the last twenty-two years. I was a math/physics instructor at a college in Canada. My fascination with technology was so great that I decided to complete my master's in computer science. My philosophy is to not only teach students the facts but also apply the facts to solving business problems. I can combine my business knowledge with technical know-how. My students learn the business requirements from their prospective senior project coordinators and use their IT backgrounds to solve the business problems presented.

***Interviewer:*** What is important for students to learn in a first programming course?

***Sud:*** Learning the first programming language is extremely important. Even though computers are being used in almost every home in America, programming computers is still not very easy to learn. Students must learn the content of their programming courses, but it's more important that they understand the concepts and gain the skills to readily upgrade the how with the newer toolsets. They should not just memorize the syntax in programming classes, but understand how all the components logically fit together. Today's technology will quickly become outdated, so learning must be a continuous process.

***Interviewer:*** What advice do you have for students preparing for a career in the IT industry?

***Sud:*** Students entering the information technology field must be prepared for a lifetime of learning as technology and processes continue to evolve. Colleges are only the first step. The knowledge gained in acquiring a college degree provides the entry point to the work world, but the long-term success of the IT professional will depend on the individual continuing to understand the new technology and the continually changing business issues. The individual must also have good communication skills and be able to work in teams. A person must be flexible to adjust to the continually changing business and technical environment.

OBJECTIVES

At the completion of this chapter, you will

- Understand how relational operators are used to create a condition
- Understand and use IF statements, including nested IF statements
- Understand and use compound conditions
- Develop and evaluate multiple solutions to the same problem
- Successfully write program solutions that require decision making

19

## Interview ◀

Each chapter opening also contains an interview with an IT professional. The persons interviewed have jobs ranging from entry level to CIO. They also represent the diversity of the IT workforce in terms of race, gender, and age.

## Case Study Scenario ◀

The Case Study Scenario is a unique feature for promoting *problem-based learning*. Each chapter begins with an interesting scenario that presents the student with a challenging programming problem. The knowledge required to solve the problem is presented in the chapter material.

142 Unit 2 Programming with Visual Basic .NET

CASE STUDY SCENARIO:

Home Mortgage Planner

Dr. Jenny Curan's personal finance course is one of the most popular in the business school. Her emphasis on practical applications of personal and family financial planning regularly causes students to rethink their approaches to buying, borrowing, and investing. Jenny often gets letters from students years after they have graduated thanking her for the valuable information they learned in her course.

Jenny begins class this day by asking, "How many of you presently own a home or plan on owning a home in the future?" Hands rise all across the room in response. "Great! Can someone tell me for how many years a home loan is typically financed?" A student replies 30 years, and heads nod in agreement. Jenny continues, "Correct. Most home loans are for 30 years. Of course, many people finance their homes over 15 years or 20 years instead. This makes the monthly payments higher, but they pay off the loan sooner and save quite a bit of money on interest charges. How much money is saved depends on the loan amount, the length of the loan, and the interest rate." Jenny then projects a spreadsheet on the overhead and enters some numbers to compare loans of different amounts with different interest rates over various lengths of time. The spreadsheet is a bit cumbersome, and at one point, Jenny types a value in an incorrect cell and the problem goes unnoticed for a few minutes, resulting in confusion for the entire class. When the problem is found, Jenny makes the appropriate corrections and jokes about bugs in the system.

Forrest walks up to her, as students are heading out the door. "Dr. Curan, that spreadsheet is nice, but if you were interested, I think I could write a Windows application that would do a better job. It would have a much nicer user interface, and you wouldn't have to worry about the formulas in the cells being acci-

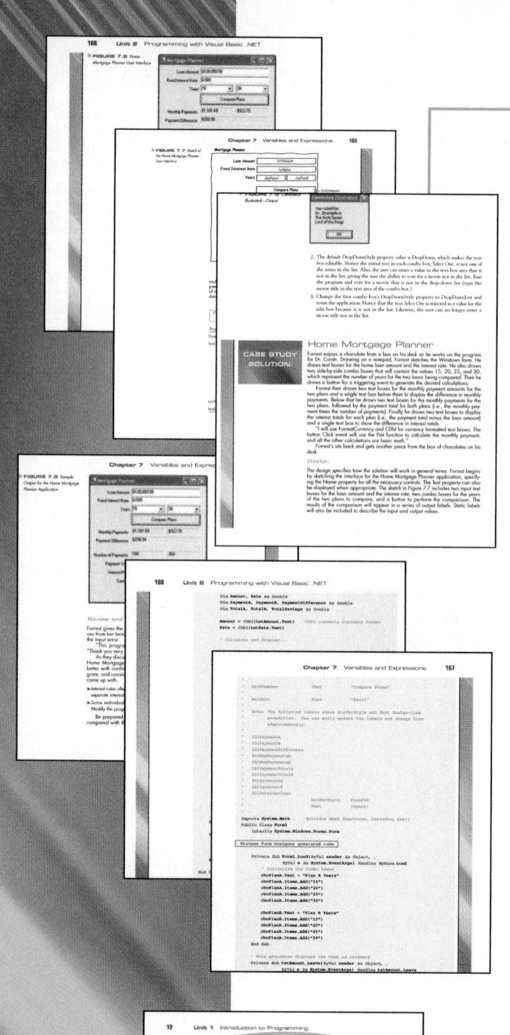

## ▶ Case Study Solution

The chapter concludes with the Case Study Solution that solves the Case Study Scenario problem using a *consistent programming methodology*.

a. Problem analysis

b. Design of the solution interface

c. Design of the solution code

d. Implementation of the solution interface

e. Implementation of the solution code

f. Testing of the solution

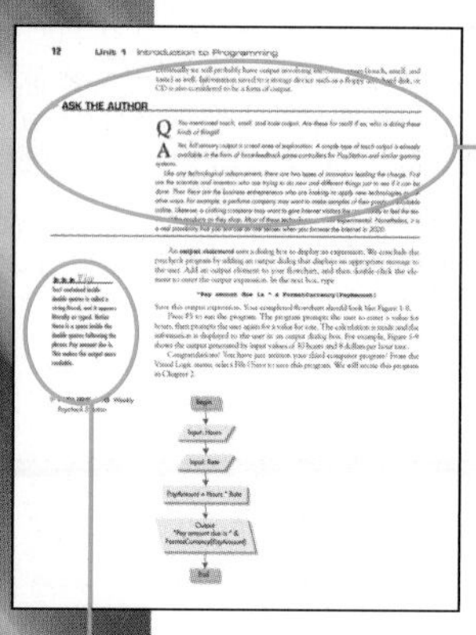

## ▶ Ask the Author

Ask the Author is another unique feature of *Programming Right From the Start*. Common student questions have been captured and embodied in the narrative, along with the author's answer. The purpose is to identify and dispel common areas of confusion.

## ▶ Tip

Tips appear in the margin to present students with valuable information that will improve their learning experience.

## Mentor

Mentor comments represent the voice of an experienced IT professional. Mentor comments provide the insight of an experienced professional's deeper understanding of the basic material and its relevance.

> **MENTOR**
>
> During the first Gulf War, a Patriot missile defense system operating at Dhahran, Saudi Arabia, was providing an antimissile shield against Iraqi Scud missiles. On February 25, 1991, the missile defense system failed to track and intercept an incoming Scud. This Scud subsequently hit an Army barracks, killing twenty-eight Americans. The error occurred because of a small timing inaccuracy (one-tenth of a second every thirty hours).
>
> A report to the General Accounting Office of the U.S. Congress contained the following summary.
>
> > The Patriot battery at Dhahran failed to track and intercept the Scud missile because of a software problem in the system's weapons control computer. This problem led to an inaccurate tracking calculation that became worse the longer the system operated. At the time of the incident, the battery had been operating continuously for over 100 hours. By then, the inaccuracy was serious enough to cause the system to look in the wrong place for the incoming Scud.
> >
> > The Patriot had never before been used to defend against Scud missiles nor was it expected to operate continuously for long periods of time. Two weeks before the incident, Army officials received Israeli data indicating some loss in accuracy after the system had been running for 8 consecutive hours. Consequently, Army officials modified the software to improve the system's accuracy. However, the modified software did not reach Dhahran until February 26, 1991—the day after the Scud incident.
>
> The full report can be found at http://www.fas.org/spp/starwars/gao/im92026.htm

## Manager

Manager comments represent the voice of an experienced project manager. Manager comments are not technical. They represent the business perspective, including project management, cost/benefit tradeoffs, teams, and end users.

> **MANAGER**
>
> Both reuse and reliability have significant financial benefits. Reuse is valuable because an object created in-house is created once and used again in future projects. This reduces the time, and therefore the cost, of the second project. The time benefits are even greater if the original development occurs by a third party. This is analogous to outsourcing in that general, time-consuming tasks are handled by a third party while the organization's developers concentrate on their core business goals.
>
> Testing and reliability potentially can generate even greater cost savings. Remember that corrective maintenance is expensive. Hard-to-find errors often cannot be identified without significant testing. Objects developed in-house cannot be tested to the same degree as a third-party object that has been extensively tested by the third-party provider and all organizations that have themselves adopted and tested the technology.

## Quick Check

Quick Check problems appear throughout the chapters to provide readers with an opportunity to apply their knowledge.

> *Quick Check 2-B*
>
> Evaluate each of the following compound conditions. Assume X = 3, Y = 7.
>
> 1. `(X = 1) AND (Y = 7)`
> 2. `(X = 1) OR (Y = 7)`
> 3. `(X < Y) AND (Y > 10)`
> 4. `(X ^ 3 = 27) AND (Y Mod 2 = 1)`
> 5. `(X ^ 3 = 27) XOR (Y Mod 2 = 1)`

## Topic Summary

Topic summaries appear within the chapter to recap important concepts. They improve readability and provide an excellent means of quick review.

> *Input Statement Summary*
>
> - Input statements are used to get data into variables.
> - In Visual Logic, the input flowchart element is a parallelogram with the keyword *Input* followed by the variable name.
> - When the input statement is executed, the user is prompted to enter a value using the keyboard. The value typed is then stored in the variable for later use.
> - String input must be placed inside double quotes.
> - Numeric input must contain only digits and possibly one decimal point. Percent symbols (%), dollar signs ($), and commas (,), among other symbols, are not allowed.

## ▶ Enhanced End-of-Chapter Content

Each chapter concludes with extensive activities, including a detailed chapter summary, list of key terms, challenging review questions, and an impressive collection of interesting programming activities.

242 **Unit 2** Programming with Visual Basic .NET

### ▶ Chapter Summary

- A procedure is a set of instructions that perform a specific task. Procedures make code easier to read and easier to maintain.
- An argument is a means of sharing information between the calling program and a procedure. A ByVal parameter creates a local copy of the formal argument. A ByRef parameter is a pointer to the formal argument, meaning any changes to the parameter will also update the argument.
- Modular programming involves breaking your application into procedures of logical units. Developing applications this way results in more readable code, improves your debugging process (because errors can be fixed once at the logical source), and provides a better environment for future maintenance.
- There are three types of procedures: event procedures, sub procedures (or subroutines), and function procedures (or functions).
- Event procedures contain code for responding to user or system events. Event procedures have the default naming convention *object_event* and handle the *object.event* signal.
- Sub procedures (or subroutines) are created by the developer to perform a logical series of actions. A subroutine is invoked by a statement containing the name of the subroutine and the actual parameter list (the keyword Call is optional). When the subroutine is finished, control returns to the line following the calling statement.
- Functions are identical to subroutines, except that functions return values. A function call usually appears as part of an expression, either on the right side of an assignment statement or as part of a condition. When a function procedure is finished, a value is returned and control continues with the calling statement.
- A variable declared in a procedure has local scope and can only be referenced

## ▶ Programming Exercises

Programming activities include a rich collection of programming exercises at the end of each chapter. These exercises range in complexity and are designed to reinforce important skills and ideas presented in the chapter.

**Chapter 10** The Professional Touch 281

### ▶ Programming Exercises

**10-1. Just a Prototype.** Write a program with an elaborate menu structure. However, the only menu item that works should be File | Exit. All other menu items should generate a message box indicating that the feature is not currently available or under development or the like.

**10-2. Fonts R Us.** Modify the Print and PrintPreview Illustrated example by adding a button that generates a font dialog. The selected font should become both the text box font and the printing font.

**10-3. Declaration of Independence.** Modify the Print and PrintPreview Illustated example by reading the entire Declaration of Independence from the text file Declaration.txt included on the student CD.

**10-4. Save Your Work.** The Text File I/O illustrated example loads a new text file over the current text file even if changes to the current text have not been saved. An improvement would be to notify the user with a message like "Changes to the current text will be lost! Do you wish to continue?" before loading the new file. If the user selects Yes, then the new file should load and the changes will be lost. If the user selects No, then the file load should be aborted. (Another option would be to save the

## ▶ Extended Case Studies

Additional programming opportunities appear in Units 2 and 3 in the form of two extended case studies. These case studies illustrate the power of Visual Basic .NET programming through the eyes of two students (**Singing Mimes**) and the owner of a small business (**Pizza and a Movie**).

208 **Unit 2** Programming with Visual Basic .NET

### ▶ Extended Case Studies

**Pizza and a Movie**

Business is booming at Pizza and a Movie, and with growth, there are growing pains. Because the business combines two different product types (rental and consumable), Noah is having problems finding packaged software that meets his business needs. For example, he needs a checkout application that handles his business logic. Movies rent for $2.99 each. Pizzas come in three sizes: medium ($8.99), large ($11.99), and gigantic ($13.99) with cheese. Each topping costs $0.99. The delivery fee of $3 is waived for orders totaling $20 or more (before tax). Furthermore, Noah provides a 10% pretax discount on orders containing both a pizza and a movie.

Create an application that serves as a checkout program for Pizza and a Movie. The application should allow the customer to check out up to three movies and purchase up to three pizzas on a single order. For each pizza ordered, the application should specify the size (medium, large, or gigantic) and also the number of additional toppings (up to 6). When the order is complete, the employee should press the Calculate Order Total button that generates the subtotal (including any discounts for pizza and movie combinations), sales tax, delivery fee (if appropriate) and the total price.

**Singing Mimes**

In an effort to find out what kind of software would be useful to teachers, Reed and Elizabeth decide to visit a local elementary school. They call the school and set up a meeting with Ms. McPherson, the technology coordinator at Rich Pond Elementary. Reed and Elizabeth are both impressed by the number of computers available to students of all grades. There is a computer lab that each class visits at least once per week. Each classroom also contains a computer. Ms. McPherson explains that the main uses of the computers are the Accelerated Reader program and Internet searches for specific information.

"There are also quite a few drill and practice programs available for math, spelling, and typing," she says. "Only a few of those programs can hold a student's attention for more than a few minutes, however."

She then shows an available first-grade math practice program that asks students to add two numbers, each between 1 and 20. The program replies with a big green "Yes" or red "No" after the student types in an answer. After twenty problems, the program gives the student a score for the exam.

"This program is not great, but some teachers use it for math practice," says Ms. McPherson. "There are much nicer programs available, of course, but they often cost $10 or $20 for one copy of a single program. Also, those programs often have lengthy

# Programming Right from the Start with
# VISUAL BASIC .NET

# UNIT 1 Introduction to Programming



Programming is problem solving. Unfortunately, the burden of syntax often prevents novice students from focusing on logic and design. In Unit 1, students learn to program using Visual Logic™, a minimal-syntax flowcharting tool that supports fundamental programming concepts, including variables, input, assignment, output, conditions, loops, procedures, functions, arrays and files. Visual Logic™ flowcharts are executable, providing immediate and accurate feedback to the student. At the conclusion of this unit, students will have developed a solid understanding of programming fundamentals which will provide a foundation for success in future programming languages.

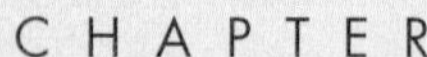

CHAPTER 1

# Input Process Output

## OUTLINE

## INTERVIEW

**Chris Sherman, Founder, Framework Development Group**

***Interviewer:*** Please tell us how you got involved in your current IT position.

***Sherman:*** After working in technology for 12 years, the last four as the CTO of two companies, I realized that one of the most significant gaps in business today is the lack of understanding and communication between technology and the other business units. While there are a number of reasons for this, it often starts because the person running technology is not, and does not want to be, involved with the business.

I started Framework Development Group to help companies bridge the technology–business gap. My goal is to work with senior management to help them understand their technology and how it is or isn't working towards the goals of the business.

***Interviewer:*** What is the project you are most proud of?

***Sherman:*** I was the technical lead for designing a results system that would take real-time information from the Olympic games and publish it to USATODAY.com. It gave me an opportunity to use my application architecture and programming skills to address a real-time, practical issue that was technically complex and critical to the business.

***Interviewer:*** What has been your personal key to success?

***Sherman:*** Surrounding myself with good people—no doubt about it. This doesn't always mean the brightest—I will take hard work and practical experience over bright any day. It means that you find dedicated and passionate individuals that share your drive in creating, building, and delivering effective technical solutions.

Working with (and later on hiring) the right people is the most important skill you can possess. Regardless of your individual talent, you cannot succeed alone—and it is much more rewarding to succeed as part of a team.

## OBJECTIVES

At the completion of this chapter, you will

- **Distinguish between logic and syntax**
- **Understand and use the input statement**
- **Understand and use the assignment statement**
- **Understand and use the output statement**
- **Understand and use arithmetic operators with precedence**
- **Successfully write program solutions that require input, processing, and output**

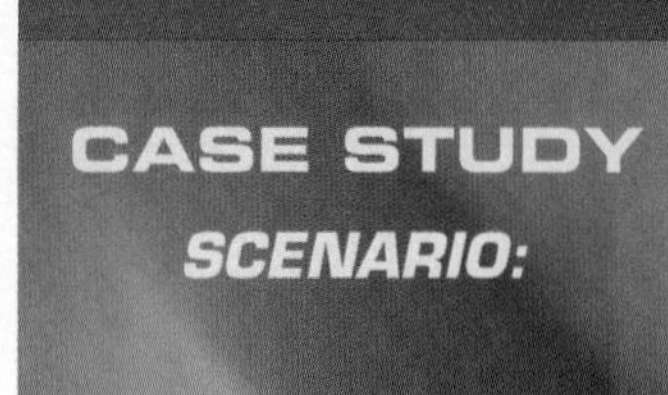


# Grocery Checkout

Dr. Marion Taylor's programming course is one of the most popular classes on campus: students appreciate Dr. Taylor's knowledge of the material and passion for teaching. In the minutes before the first class begins, Dr. Taylor and his students discuss movies, sports, and the parking problem on campus. As class begins, Dr. Taylor takes roll and hands out the syllabus, then asks, "How many of you have ever written a computer program before?" A few students raise their hands. "How many of you are ready to learn how to program?" Most of the class raises their hand. Looking around the room, Dr. Taylor smiles and says, "Well, the best way to learn programming is to program. Today we will cover input, processing, and output statements, the minimum functions necessary for a useful computer information system. After discussing these three statements, we will develop a working grocery checkout program. Our solution will input the purchase price of three items in the store. The program will determine the total price of all three items, add 6 percent sales tax, and display the resulting total." After a short pause for effect, he adds, "Oh yeah, and we will finish the program with enough time left in class for me to tell a bad joke."

Dr. Taylor's solution is presented later this chapter.

## 1-1 Logic and Syntax

A ***computer program*** is a solution to a problem, such as, "How can customers view and purchase products over the Internet?" or "How can sales representatives have immediate and accurate access to inventory data?" Each program (or solution) has two components, its algorithm and its syntax. An ***algorithm*** is the logical design used to accomplish a specific objective. Various tools for representing computing algorithms are available, the two most common being flowcharts and pseudocode. In this book we will use the ***Visual Logic***™, which combines the utility of flowcharts (graphical representations of algorithms) and pseudocode (a nontechnical description of an algorithm) with computer simulation. Using Visual Logic, computer algorithms may be written, saved, edited, executed, and debugged.

Once an algorithm has been developed, it must be communicated in an appropriate language. To communicate actions to a computer, developers use a programming language like Visual Basic, C#, C++, Java, Pascal, or Cobol (among others). ***Syntax*** refers to the specific rules of a programming language. There are literally hundreds of programming languages to choose from, each with its own unique syntax. Therefore, writing a computer program involves creating a logical design to solve a problem and then implementing that design in an appropriate syntax.

An ***information system*** is a combination of people and technology (computers) that collect, organize, and process data to produce information. For any information

**MENTOR**

A classic example of an algorithm is the directions for baking a cake. Information system algorithms, such as those used to sell products over the Internet, tend to be much more complicated.

It is important to realize that an algorithm remains the same, even though the language of implementation may be different. For example, "Add two eggs," "Agregue dos huevos," and "Ajouter deux oeufs" have the same meaning even though they are different languages. Likewise, the logic of an Internet shopping cart remains essentially the same regardless of its implementation language (Visual Basic, C#, C++, Java, Pascal, Cobol, etc.).

system to be useful, it must do at least three things: ***input*** data into the system, ***process*** data within the system, and ***output*** resulting information from the system. For example, an online catalog information system might have input that includes the product ID for the items a customer wishes to purchase, along with the customer's mailing address and credit card number. The processing could include referencing a database to determine the cost of each item, calculating the sales tax, computing the shipping charge based on the customer's mailing address, and billing the customer's credit card the appropriate amount. The output might include a customer receipt and reports for the sales department and the warehouse.

### ASK THE AUTHOR

**Q** What is the difference between data and information?

**A** From an information system perspective, ***data*** refers to numbers, characters, or images without context. Data by itself has no meaning. When data is processed in a context (either by a human or a computer system) it becomes ***information***. As information is collected, it can also be processed for patterns and insights, thus creating ***knowledge***. Finally, ***wisdom*** is appropriate behavior guided by knowledge. Consider the following example as it applies to a screen-printing company's online purchasing system.

"5000" is data.
"A 5000 percent increase in T-shirt orders by Gizmo Company" is information.
"A 5000 percent increase in T-shirt orders by any company is an unusually large increase" is knowledge.
"We had better confirm the numbers on this order before we manufacture and ship the T-shirts, just to make sure it was not a human or system mistake" is wisdom.

## 1-2 "Hello World"

It is a time-honored tradition that your first program in any language be the output message "Hello World." We will follow suit and write a Hello World program using Visual Logic.

Begin by running the Visual Logic program contained on the CD-ROM included with this text. When the program begins, you will see two flowcharting elements, *Begin* and *End*, connected by a flow-arrow. Click the left mouse button on the flow-arrow; the Flowchart Elements menu should pop up (Figure 1-1).

Select *Output* from the popup menu to add an output element to your flowchart. Then double-click on the newly added output element, opening the output dialog box. Type `"Hello World"` (make sure that you include the double quotes) in the text box, and then click the OK button. Figure 1-2 shows how your flowchart should look after closing the dialog box.

Press F5 to run the program. The program executes, generating an output dialog box that appears with the text "Hello World" (Figure 1-3). Congratulations! You have just written your first computer program!

### ASK THE AUTHOR

**Q** I know that there are many tools for drawing flowcharts, including Adobe Illustrator and Microsoft Visio. Can I run those flowcharts also?

**A** No. The ability to interpret and execute flowcharts is a unique feature of the Visual Logic™. It makes Visual Logic distinct as a tool for students learning to program. Flowcharts without feedback are of limited value because developers have no way of knowing if they are on the right track. Requiring the instructor to give feedback is problematic because of the time required to examine each flowchart, and the instructor's feedback is subjective. Visual Logic provides immediate and accurate feedback to the student, combining the benefits of a high-level language with the simplicity of the classic flowcharting tool.

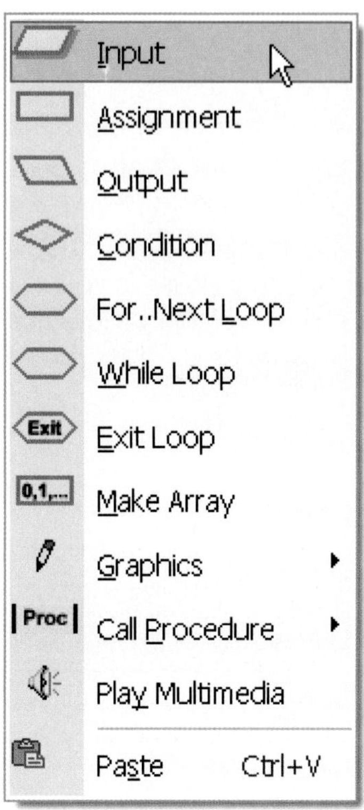


**FIGURE 1.1** *Flowchart Elements Menu*

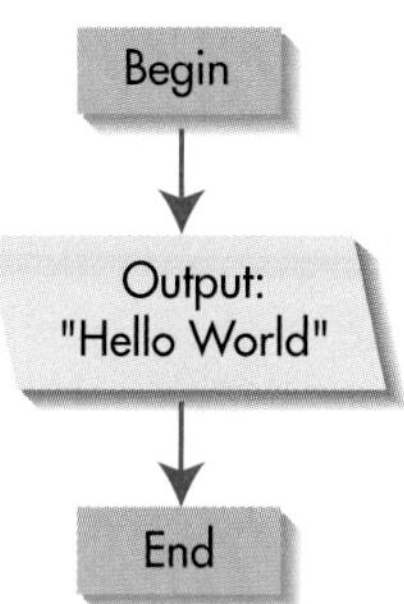


**FIGURE 1.2** *Hello World Solution*

**FIGURE 1.3** *Hello World Simulation Output*

## 1-3 Input Statements

Remember that an information system must *input* data into the system, *process* data within the system, and *output* resulting information from the system. The first of those three tasks, inputting data into the system, is accomplished by means of an input statement. An ***input statement*** accepts data from the user and stores that data into a variable. A ***variable*** is a storage location that can be accessed and changed by developer code. A variable has a name (which does not change) and an associated data value (which may change during execution).

To understand the input statement, consider the following modification to the Hello World program you just wrote. Click on the flow-arrow above the output statement and add an input element. Double-click on the input element, opening the input element dialog box. Type `Name` (without quotes) in the variable textbox and press OK. Then double-click on the output element and change the text in the dialog box to read `"Hello " & Name` (using quotes around "Hello " but not around Name). Your solution should now look like Figure 1-4.

▶▶▶ **Tip**

**The ampersand (&) is a concatenation operator, meaning it links items together.**

Run the program. You will be prompted to type a value for Name. Enter your name inside double quotes (e.g., "Dave"). The program will then display a message box with the appropriate greetings (e.g., "Hello Dave"; see Figure 1-5).

### Simple Programming Formats

The Hello Name program uses an input statement to prompt the user for a value that is stored and then reused in an output statement. The value entered at the input prompt can be either numeric (e.g., 42 or 3.14159) or a string (e.g., "Dave" or "Go Big Red"). Be aware that string input data must be entered within double quotes.

There are some constraints with numeric data as well. Most programming languages do not allow numeric input to include symbols such as the percent symbol (%)

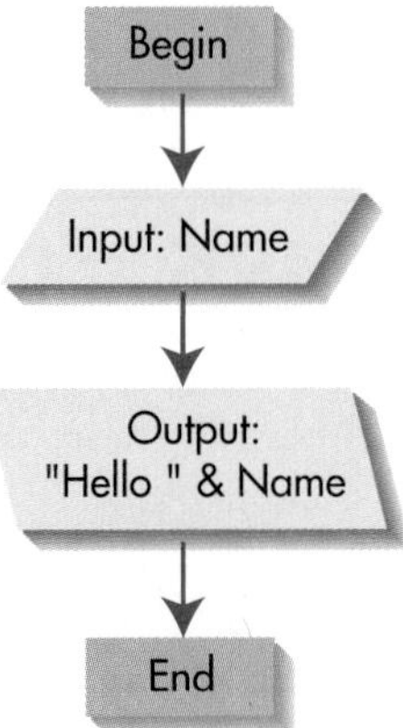


**FIGURE 1.4** *Hello Name Solution*

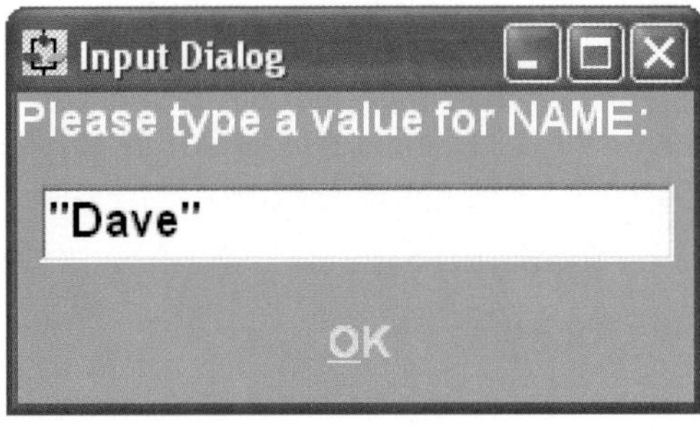

**FIGURE 1.5** *One Possible Output of the Hello Name Program*

**Table 1.1 Common Notations with Correct Programming Formats**

| Value | Written format | Programming format | Comment |
|---|---|---|---|
| String | Hello World | `"Hello World"` | Use quotes to delimit strings |
| Percent | 15% | `0.15` | Use decimal format |
| Dollars | $300 | `300` | Dollar signs not allowed |
| Large numbers | 12,345,678 | `12345678` | Commas not allowed |

or dollar sign ($) or even commas (,). Numeric input should consist of only digits and possibly one decimal point. You will quickly get used to using proper numeric notations for programming. Table 1-1 summarizes some common numeric notations and the correct programming format.

### *Variable Summary*

- Variables are storage locations used for holding data and information.
- Each variable has two components: its name (which does not change) and its value (which may change during execution).

### *Input Statement Summary*

- Input statements are used to get data into variables.
- In Visual Logic, the input flowchart element is a parallelogram with the keyword *Input* followed by the variable name.
- When the input statement is executed, the user is prompted to enter a value using the keyboard. The value typed is then stored in the variable for later use.
- String input must be placed inside double quotes.
- Numeric input must contain only digits and possibly one decimal point. Percent symbols (%), dollar signs ($), and commas (,), among other symbols, are not allowed.

## 1-4 Weekly Paycheck Program

You have now written your first two computer programs, Hello World and Hello Name. Your third program will be a bit more complicated. You will now write a weekly paycheck program that accepts the hours worked and the hourly rate for an employee, and the program will calculate and display the appropriate pay amount due to the employee for the current week. This weekly paycheck program will use all three basics of an information system—input, processing, and output—and will be developed in steps.

The weekly paycheck program has two input variables, *Hours* and *Rate*. Start the Visual Logic System. (If it is already running, under the menu click File, then New.) Click on the flow-arrow and select the input element. Repeat to add a second input element. Then double-click on each element to add the variable names **`Hours`** and **`Rate`** (Figure 1-6). The input for the weekly paycheck program is now complete.

**FIGURE 1.6** *Weekly Paycheck Program (Input)*

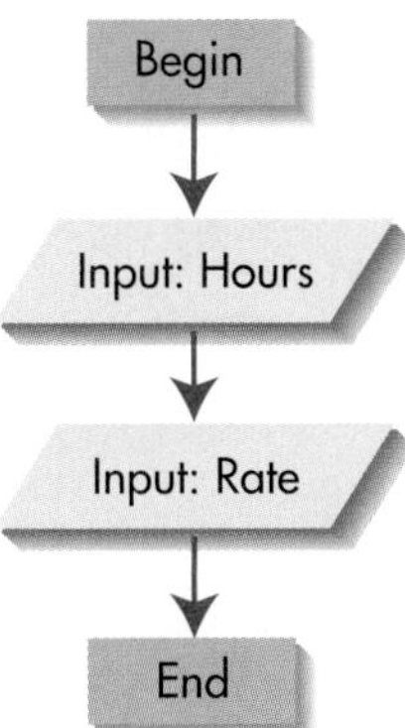


## ASK THE AUTHOR

**Q** You used **Hours** and **Rate** as variable names. Could you have chosen different names?

**A** Yes. You have a great deal of freedom when it comes to naming variables. However, there are some suggestions and rules you need to know.

1. A variable name should be descriptive of the data it holds.
2. A variable name must begin with a letter.
3. Only letters, digits, or the underscore character (_) may be used in variable names. Both Visual Logic and Visual Basic are case insensitive. This means that **HOURS**, **hours**, and **Hours** are all interchangeable. In this book we will use the convention of starting each word with an uppercase letter (e.g., **Cost**, **MailingAddressLine1**, **MailingAddressLine2**).
4. The variable name must not be a word that is reserved by the programming language for other special uses. A list of reserved words can be found in Appendix A.

## 1-5 Assignment Statements

The ***assignment statement*** can be used to perform a calculation and store the result. Addition (+), subtraction (−), multiplication (*), and division (/) are common arithmetic operations found in almost every high-level programming language. Note that the multiplication operator is typically an asterisk (*) rather than the traditional times operator (×), because X could be mistaken as a variable name.

To illustrate the use of the assignment statement, we return to the weekly paycheck program. You have already used two input statements to accept the data **Hours** and **Rate**. An assignment statement will be added to process that data. The required calculation is straightforward. Hours times rate produces the pay amount due.

Returning to Visual Logic, click on a flow-arrow below the two input statements, and then select an assignment element from the menu. Double-click the assignment element to open the assignment edit dialog. The text box on the left is labeled *Variable*, and the text box on the right is labeled *Expression*. An ***expression*** is a value-returning code element, such as a variable or mathematical formula. Most programming languages follow this tradition of specifying the expression on the right hand side (RHS) of the assignment statement, and the variable to store the result on the left hand side (LHS) of the assignment statement. When executed, the right hand side expression is evaluated first. The result of the expression is then stored into the left hand side variable.

Enter **Hours * Rate** in the right hand expression text box and **PayAmount** in the left hand text box. When finished, your solution should look like Figure 1-7. Your program now accepts two input values and performs an appropriate calculation based on those input values.

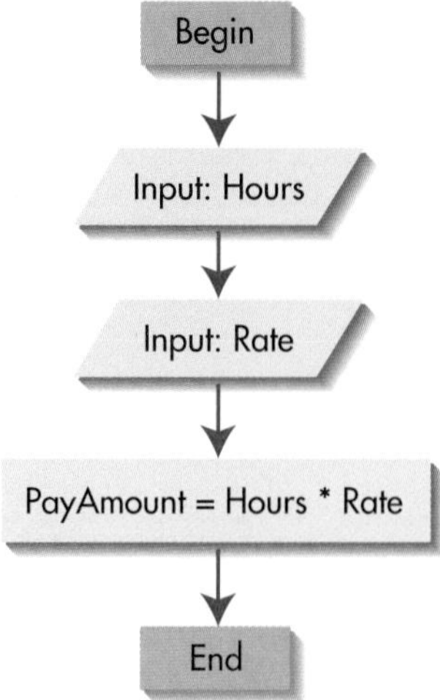


**FIGURE 1.7** *Weekly Paycheck Program (Input and Assignment)*

### *Assignment Statement Summary*

- Assignment statements are used to perform calculations and store the result.
- In Visual Logic, the assignment flowchart element is a rectangle with a variable on the left hand side (LHS) and an expression on the right hand side (RHS).
- When executed, the expression is evaluated, and the result is stored in the variable.

## How to Write Arithmetic Expressions

The calculation in the weekly paycheck program is rather straightforward (hours times rate). As a developer, you will often have to perform calculations that are significantly more complex. Visual Logic supports seven arithmetic operators, evaluated in the order of ***operator precedence*** shown in Table 1-2. Operators of the same precedence are evaluated left-to-right. Parentheses can be used to override the default precedence order.

There are three operators related to division. Regular division (/) produces a decimal value if necessary. Integer division (\) and integer remainder (Mod) require integer arguments and produce an integer answer. Integer division is the integer result, throwing away any remainder. Integer remainder is the amount leftover after taking out as many whole occurrences of the numerator from the divisor as possible.

**Table 1.2** Numeric Operator Precedence, Highest to Lowest

| Operation | Operator | Expression1 | Result1 | Expression2 | Result2 |
|---|---|---|---|---|---|
| Exponentiation | `^` | `5 ^ 2 + 1` | 26 | `5 ^ (2 + 1)` | 125 |
| Multiplication and division | `* /` | `1 + 3 * 7` | 22 | `17 / 3` | 5.667 |
| Integer division | `\` | `12 \ 4` | 3 | `17 \ 3` | 5 |
| Integer remainder | `Mod` | `12 Mod 4` | 0 | `17 Mod 3` | 2 |
| Addition and Subtraction | `+ -` | `4 - 5 + 2` | 1 | `4 - (5 + 2)` | -3 |

**MENTOR**

Integer division and integer remainder are new operators to most students. Once they are understood, however, they can be used in a variety of situations. For example, you can determine if N is even or odd using the integer remainder operator. If N Mod 2 is 0, then N is even. If not, then N is odd.

For another example, consider the everyday task of giving correct change. If you were owed 82 cents in change, you typically would not expect 82 pennies. Instead, you would expect 3 quarters, 1 nickel, and 2 pennies. A developer can use an expression like Amount \ 25 to determine how many quarters are appropriate, then another integer division expression for dimes, and then another for nickels. Pennies could be easily determined using the integer remainder operator.

**Table 1.3** Formulas and Expressions

| Mathematical Formula | Expression |
|---|---|
| $B^2 - 4AC$ | `B^2 - 4*A*C` |
| $\sqrt{A^2 + B^2}$ | `(A^2 + B^2) ^ (1/2)` |
| $P(1 + R)^N$ | `P * (1 + R) ^ N` |
| $\dfrac{1}{\dfrac{1}{R_1} + \dfrac{1}{R_2} + \dfrac{1}{R_3}}$ | `1 / (1/R1 + 1/R2 + 1/R3)` |

## Quick Check 1-A

Evaluate each of the following mathematical expressions. Assume A = 3, B = 5.

1. `A + B * 5`
2. `(2 * 3) ^ 2`
3. `11 \ A`
4. `2 * 3 ^ 2`
5. `11 / A`
6. `11 Mod A`

Table 1-3 illustrates how some well-known formulas can be written in computer program format.

## Quick Check 1-B

Write Visual Logic expressions for each of the following.

1. The average of Exam1, Exam2, and Exam3.
2. $1 + \frac{1}{2} + \frac{1}{4}$
3. $\dfrac{4A^2B}{C}$

# 1-6 Output Statements

Output can occur in many forms. Two common types of output are screen output and printed output, both of which are visual. Sound output is common through speakers.

Eventually we will probably have output involving the other senses (touch, smell, and taste) as well. Information saved to a storage device such as a floppy disk, hard disk, or CD is also considered to be a form of output.

## ASK THE AUTHOR

**Q** You mentioned touch, smell, and taste output. Are these for real? If so, who is doing these kinds of things?

**A** Yes, full sensory output is a real area of exploration. A simple type of touch output is already available in the form of force-feedback game controllers for PlayStation and similar gaming systems.

Like any technological advancement, there are two types of innovators leading the charge. First are the scientists and inventors who are trying to do new and different things just to see if it can be done. Then there are the business entrepreneurs who are looking to apply new technologies in creative ways. For example, a perfume company may want to make samples of their products available online. Likewise, a clothing company may want to give Internet visitors the opportunity to feel the texture of the products as they shop. Most of these technologies are still experimental. Nonetheless, it is a real possibility that you will use all five senses when you browse the Internet in 2020.

**Text contained inside double quotes is called a string literal, and it appears literally as typed. Notice there is a space inside the double quotes following the phrase *Pay amount due is.* This makes the output more readable.**

An ***output statement*** uses a dialog box to display an expression. We conclude the paycheck program by adding an output dialog that displays an appropriate message to the user. Add an output element to your flowchart, and then double-click the element to enter the output expression. In the text box, type

```
"Pay amount due is " & FormatCurrency(PayAmount)
```

Save this output expression. Your completed flowchart should look like Figure 1-8.

Press F5 to run the program. The program prompts the user to enter a value for hours, then prompts the user again for a value for rate. The calculation is made and the information is displayed to the user in an output dialog box. For example, Figure 1-9 shows the output generated by input values of 30 hours and 8 dollars per hour rate.

Congratulations! You have just written your third computer program! From the Visual Logic menu, select File | Save to save this program. We will revise this program in Chapter 2.

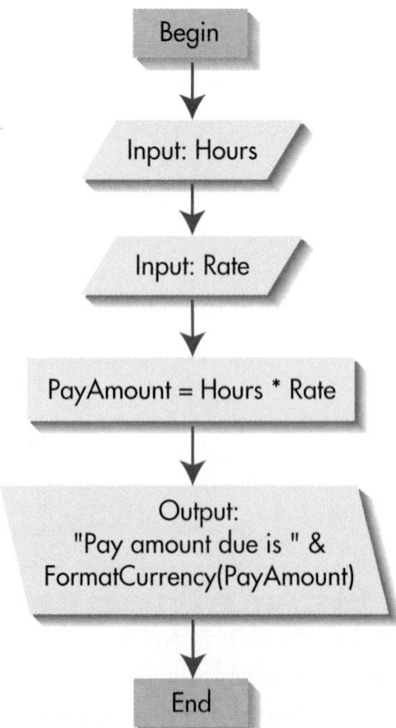


**FIGURE 1.8** *Weekly Paycheck Solution*

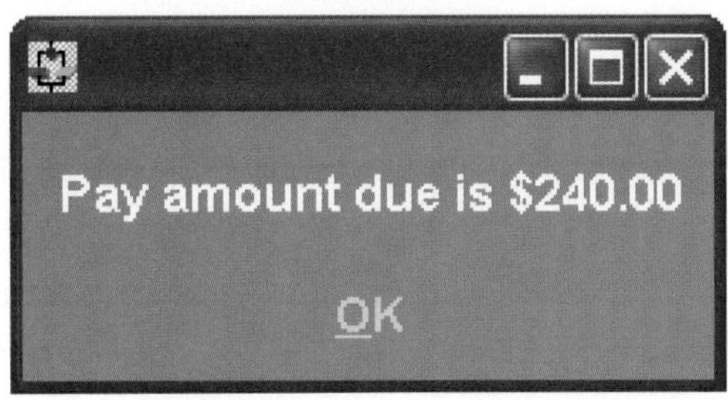


**FIGURE 1.9** *Weekly Paycheck Solution Output (Hours = 30, Rate = 8)*

## Intrinsic Functions

The Weekly Paycheck Solution uses the intrinsic function *FormatCurrency* to display a numeric value in a currency format, including a leading dollar sign, two decimal places, and delimiting commas as necessary. ***Intrinsic functions*** are predefined commands that provide developers with common, helpful functionality. Intrinsic functions are divided into several categories, including math functions, business functions, string functions, time and date functions, conversion functions, file access functions, and so on. Another intrinsic function is *FormatPercent*, which takes a decimal percent value and converts it to its equivalent value with a percent symbol and two decimal places. *Abs* accepts a numeric value and produces the absolute value equivalent. *Int* accepts a decimal value and produces the integer whole value. *Round* accepts a decimal value and produces the nearest integer value. Finally, *Random* accepts an integer value N and produces a random integer between 0 and (N-1). Table 1-4 shows examples of these intrinsic functions.

**Table 1.4** Intrinsic Functions for Visual Logic

| Example | Result |
|---|---|
| `FormatCurrency(12345)` | $12,345.00 |
| `FormatCurrency(.02)` | $0.02 |
| `FormatPercent(0.0625)` | 6.25% |
| `FormatPercent(0.75)` | 75.00% |
| `Abs(-3.3)` | 3.3 |
| `Abs(5.67)` | 5.67 |
| `Int(3.8)` | 3 |
| `Int(7.1)` | 7 |
| `Round(3.8)` | 4 |
| `Round(7.1)` | 7 |
| `Random(5)` | A random integer between 0 and 4 |
| `Random(100) + 1` | A random integer between 1 and 100 |

## *Output Statement Summary*

- Output statements are used to display information.
- In Visual Logic, the output flowchart element is a parallelogram with the keyword *Output* followed by an output expression.
- When executed, string literals are displayed exactly as typed inside the containing quotes.
- When executed, expressions are evaluated and the result is displayed.

- The ampersand (&) operator may be used to concatenate a series of string literals, variables, and expressions into one large expression.
- Carriage returns in the output expression appear as carriage returns in the displayed output.

## 1-7 Debugging with Visual Logic

Even the best developers will eventually make mistakes. A programming mistake is often called a **bug** (see Manager box, below), although the term *error* is probably more appropriate. Visual Logic provides debugging support to help you track down and fix your errors. Figure 1-10 shows the execution and debugging portion of the Visual Logic standard toolbar. Note that these functions are also available under the Debug menu item. *Run* is the command that executes the simulator. *Pause* stops the simulation on the current command. *Terminate* ends the execution of the current program.

The last two options, Step Into and Step Over, allow a paused program to execute one step at a time. When the program is paused, the Variable Watch window appears displaying the current values for all program variables. *Step Into* takes you to the next command, and will go into a structure like a condition or a loop (which we discuss in the following chapters). *Step Over* takes you to the next command at the same level as the current command. Using the step commands to study the program variable values as each statement executes can be helpful in determining why your program is generating an error.

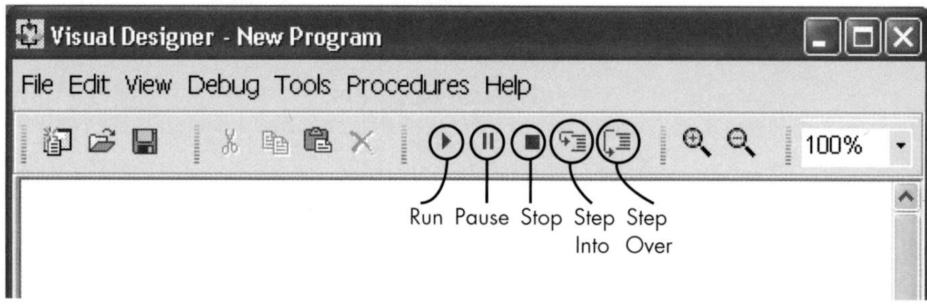


**FIGURE 1.10** *Execution and Debugging in the Visual Logic Toolbar*

### MANAGER

There is an interesting history behind the term *bug*. The term may have arisen as early as the fourteenth century to mean "an object of dread" derived from the Welsh word *bwg* for hobgoblin. Thomas Edison is quoted as using the term *bugs* for flaws in a system in 1878.

The term became particularly popular in 1947 when a moth was found in a relay of the Harvard Mark II machine. Grace Murray Hopper (who later helped design COBOL and is affectionately knows as the "Mother of Modern Computing") was involved in the project. She once related the events as follows, "Things were going badly; there was something wrong in one of the circuits of the long glass-enclosed computer. Finally, someone located the trouble spot and, using ordinary tweezers, removed the problem, a two-inch moth. From then on, when anything went wrong with a computer, we said it had bugs in it."

The moth was taped in the computer log, with the following entry: "First actual case of bug being found." The logbook, now in the collection of Naval Surface Weapons Center, still contains the remains of the moth.

(Additional Source: *The AFU and Urban Legends Archive.* "Have Some Grace and Don't Let it Bug You," *Does Not Compute.* http://www.tafkac.org/faq2k/compute_86.html)

# Grocery Checkout

"Now it's time to put our new knowledge to the test," Dr. Taylor says ten minutes before the class ends. "We have discussed how Visual Logic can be used to do input, processing, and output. Our grocery checkout problem requires three input values (the prices of the three items), three calculations (the subtotal of the three items, the appropriate sales tax, and the resulting total), and a single output (the resulting total). Let me show you how this can be done in Visual Logic." Below are the steps Dr. Taylor follows when demonstrating the solution for the class.

1. From the Visual Logic menu, select File | New to start a new program. Add three input elements to your flowchart. Enter the variable names `Item1`, `Item2`, and `Item3` respectively.
2. Add an assignment element to your flowchart. Enter `SubTotal` as the result variable, and enter `Item1 + Item2 + Item3` as the expression.
3. Add a second assignment element to your flowchart. Set the variable `SalesTax` to be the result of the expression `SubTotal * 0.06` .
4. Add a third assignment element that sets `Total` to be the sum of `SubTotal + SalesTax`.
5. Display the `Total` with an appropriate output statement. Your solution should look something like Figure 1-11.
6. Run your program to see if it works. If the input values are 10, 20, and 30, the output should be "Your purchase total is $63.60."

After finishing the program, a student asks "Dr. Taylor, there are three assignment statements in the solution. Can it be done with only one assignment statement?"

**FIGURE 1.11** *Grocery Checkout Solution*

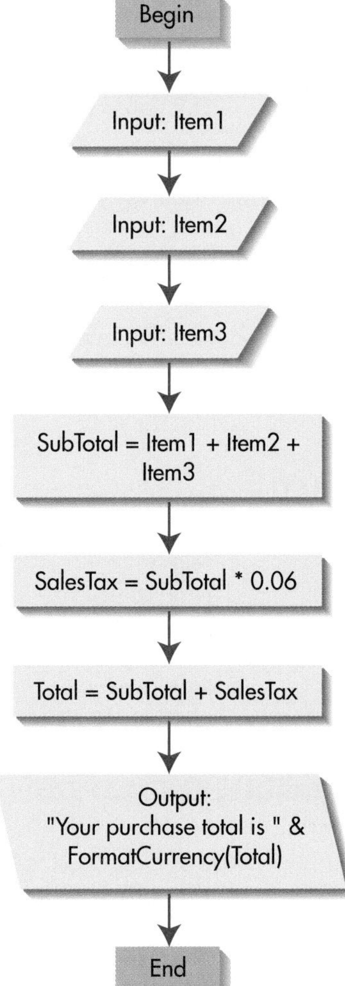

Dr. Taylor nods. "Yes. You could have set Total equal to the following:

```
Total = (Item1 + Item2 + Item3) * 1.06
```

Both solutions are right because they both produce the correct result. It is a subjective question as to which, if either, is the better solution.

"In conclusion, let me once again ask the question: How many of you have ever written a computer program?" All raise their hands.

A student from the back of the class shouts, "What about the bad joke?"

"Just remember, you asked for it." (Laughter) "What did the termite say when he went into the bar?" (pause) "Where is the bar tender?"

A couple of students chuckle and explain the joke to their neighbors. Most moan and roll their eyes, not sure if it was supposed to be funny or not. "Don't quit your day job," one student says.

"Don't worry," Dr. Taylor says, smiling.

## Chapter Summary

- Variables are storage locations used for holding data and information.
- Each variable has two components: its name (which does not change) and its value (which may change during execution).
- Input statements are used to get data into variables. When executed, the user is prompted to enter a value using the keyboard. The value typed is then stored in the variable for later use.
- Expressions are value-returning code elements, such as a variable or mathematical formula.
- Assignment statements are used to perform calculations and store the result. When an assignment statement is executed, the expression is evaluated and the result is stored in the variable.
- Output statements are used to display information. When an output statement is executed, string literals are displayed exactly as typed inside the containing quotes, and expressions are evaluated and the result is displayed. The ampersand (&) operator may be used to concatenate a series of string literals and expressions into one large expression.
- Input, assignment, and output statements are sufficient to write small but interesting computer programs.

## Key Terms

**algorithm** p. 4
**assignment statement** p. 9
**bug** p. 14
**computer program** p. 4
**data** p. 5
**expression** p. 9
**information system** p. 4
**intrinsic function** p. 13
**input statement** p. 7
**knowledge** p. 5
**output statement** p. 12
**operator precedence** p. 10
**syntax** p. 4
**variable** p. 7
**wisdom** p. 5

## Review Questions

1. Consider the similarities and differences between developing an algorithm and developing syntax. What skills are required for each activity? What is the added value for each activity?

2. Identify possible input, processing, and output for a video store's rental checkout system.
3. Imagine you are an entrepreneur with access to some of the innovative output technologies regarding smell, touch, and taste. Identify some business uses of these technologies that you think might become profitable.

## Programming Exercises

**1-1. Run the Numbers.** Write a program with two input values. The program should display the sum, difference, quotient, product, and average of the two numbers.

**1-2. A Rose by any Other Name.** Paulette has just planted a large rose garden that she wants to fertilize. She knows the area of her rose garden in square feet, but the fertilizer is measured by the square yard. Write a program that converts square feet (input) to square yards (output).

**1-3. "As I was going to St. Ives . . . "** Consider the following nursery rhyme:

> *As I was going to St. Ives, I met a man with seven wives. Every wife had seven sacks, every sack had seven cats, and every cat had seven kittens. Kittens, cats, sacks, and wives, how many were going to St. Ives?*

The question at the end of the rhyme is a trick question because only the narrator is going to St. Ives. Write a program to determine the total number of things (including people, animals, and sacks) that were met by the narrator.

**1-4. Twenty Thousand Leagues Under the Sea.** Jules Verne's *Twenty Thousand Leagues Under the Sea* is the story of Captain Nemo and his fantastic submarine Nautilus. The story is told from the perspective of Professor Aronnax, who entered the Nautilus as a prisoner but later is treated as a guest. It is a story of intrigue and suspense, of respect and revenge. At one point the professor writes, "I have crossed 20,000 leagues in that submarine tour of the world, which has revealed so many wonders." You can read the book online at The University of Virginia's Electronic Text Center, http://etext.lib.virginia.edu

Perform an Internet search to find the conversion ratios between leagues and nautical miles. Then write a program that converts leagues into nautical miles and run your program to see how many nautical miles Professor Aronnax traveled.

**1-5. Jake's Problem.** Jake has a car with an 8-gallon fuel tank. Jake fills his tank with gas and then drives 60 miles to a friend's house. When he gets to his friend's house, he has 6 gallons left in his fuel tank. Write a program that uses three input elements to enter values for tank size, miles traveled and gallons left. The program should calculate and display how many miles Jake can drive on a full tank of gas. (Note: Be sure to use input elements to accept the values 8, 60, and 6 rather than hard coding them into your solution.)

**1-6. Correct Change.** Write a program to assist a cashier with determining correct change. The program should have one input, the number of cents to return to the customer. The output should be the appropriate change in quarters, dimes, nickels and cents. *Hint*: Consider how integer division (\) and integer remainder (Mod) can be used as part of your solution.

CHAPTER 2

# Making Decisions

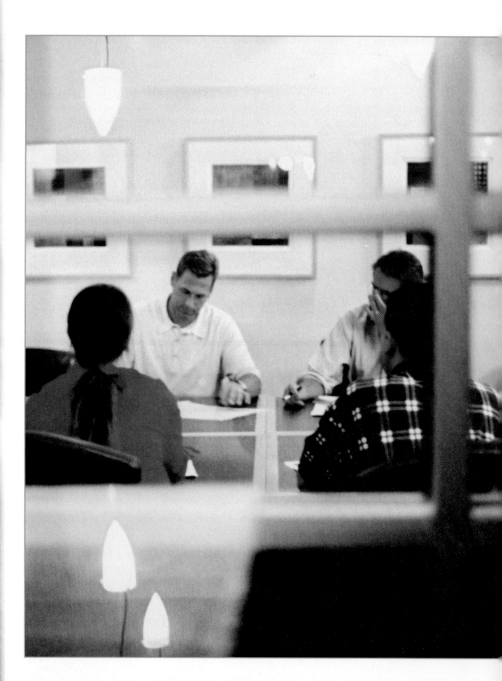

## OUTLINE

## ▶ INTERVIEW

**Devinder Sud, Instructor, DeVry University**

***Interviewer:*** Please tell us how you got involved in your current IT profession.

***Sud:*** I have worked both in industry/business as well as teaching at the postsecondary level for the last twenty-two years. I was a math/physics instructor at a college in Canada. My fascination with technology was so great that I decided to complete my master's in computer science. My philosophy is to not only teach students the facts but also apply the facts to solving business problems. I can combine my business knowledge with technical know-how. My students learn the business requirements from their prospective senior project coordinators and use their IT backgrounds to solve the business problems presented.

***Interviewer:*** What is important for students to learn in a first programming course?

***Sud:*** Learning the first programming language is extremely important. Even though computers are being used in almost every home in America, programming computers is still not very easy to learn. Students must learn the content of their programming courses, but it's more important that they understand the concepts and gain the skills to readily upgrade the *how* with the newer toolsets. They should not just memorize the syntax in programming classes, but understand how all the components logically fit together. Today's technology will quickly become outdated, so learning must be a continuous process.

***Interviewer:*** What advice do you have for students preparing for a career in the IT industry?

***Sud:*** Students entering the information technology field must be prepared for a lifetime of learning as technology and processes continue to evolve. Colleges are only the first step. The knowledge gained in acquiring a college degree provides the entry point to the work world, but the long-term success of the IT professional will depend on the individual continuing to understand the new technology and the continually changing business issues. The individual must also have good communication skills and be able to work in teams. A person must be flexible to adjust to the continually changing business and technical environment.

## OBJECTIVES

At the completion of this chapter, you will

- **Understand how relational operators are used to create a condition**
- **Understand and use IF statements, including nested IF statements**
- **Understand and use compound conditions**
- **Develop and evaluate multiple solutions to the same problem**
- **Successfully write program solutions that require decision making**

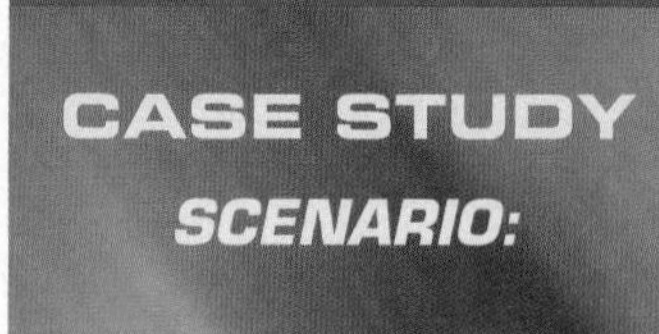


# Smallest Number

Dr. Taylor begins class by discussing some of the programs the students wrote as homework from Chapter 1. He presents a solution to Jake's problem (Chapter 1) that contains some unusual logic. This atypical algorithm triggers questions about the difference between a correct solution and a good solution. Dr. Taylor explains, "A correct solution generates the appropriate information, but a good solution is a correct solution that is also easy to understand and maintain."

A student sitting near the middle of the room raises her hand and asks, "Can there be multiple good solutions to the same problem?"

"Absolutely. Consider the problem of finding the smallest (or largest) value from a series of input data. Finding such a value is an essential step for many activities, including sorting or calculating weighted grades," Dr. Taylor explains. "Today we will consider multiple solutions to this problem, illustrating the importance of analyzing different program designs."

Dr. Taylor's solutions are presented later in this chapter.

## 2-1 Making Decisions

In the previous chapter we developed a program for calculating a weekly paycheck. The amount due was calculated using a simple assignment statement:

```
PayAmount = Hours * Rate
```

This calculation works fine under normal circumstances. However, it is a common practice for many businesses to give overtime pay to employees who work more than 40 hours in a week. The formula for calculating pay with overtime is 40 hours at regular pay *plus* hours over 40 at one-and-a-half times regular pay. This can be easily expressed in an assignment statement, as follows:

```
PayAmount = 40*Rate + (Hours - 40)*Rate*1.5
```

Unfortunately, neither assignment statement is correct all the time. If an employee works 50 hours at $10/hour, the first formula would underpay the employee by $50. However, if an employee works 30 hours at $10/hour, the second formula would then underpay the employee by $50. What is needed, therefore, is a way for the program to choose which formula is appropriate. In other words, the program needs to make a decision.

### ▶ ASK THE AUTHOR

**Q** What kind of decisions can a computer make?

**A** A computer's decision-making process is limited because each of the computer's possible actions must be specified in advance. Whereas a human can truly *decide* something, a computer in fact only *selects* between predefined actions based on the result of some evaluation. Those with an appreciation for the history of computing may find it interesting that Dijkstra used the term *selection* in his 1970 paper on structured programming when referring to a computer's decision capabilities (see the following Mentor Box).

**MENTOR**

Edward Dijkstra's article "Structured programming" (in *Software Engineering Techniques*, 1970) demonstrated that any logical programming solution might be expressed using only three control flow constructs: *sequential*, *selection*, and *repetition*. By using only these constructs, programmers can create code in which the logical design is evident on inspection, thus making solutions easier to develop, test, and maintain. These three fundamental control structures are the primary themes for the first three chapters of *Programming Right From the Start*.

## 2-2 The IF Statement

The most common decision structure is the ***IF statement***. The IF statement begins with a condition, followed by a block of statements that execute only when the condition evaluates to true, and a block of statements that execute only when the condition evaluates to false. The two blocks are called the true block and the false block (for obvious reasons). The IF statement ends where the two blocks reconnect.

A ***condition*** is a boolean expression that evaluates to either true or false. Conditions typically involve one of the six ***relational operators*** shown in Table 2-1.

**Table 2.1** Relational Operators

| Operator | Description | Expression | Result (*assume* x = 2, y = 3) |
|---|---|---|---|
| `=` | Equal | `x = 2`<br>`x = y` | True<br>False |
| `<>` | Not Equal | `y <> 5`<br>`y <> 3` | True<br>False |
| `>` | Greater Than | `x > 1`<br>`x > y` | True<br>False |
| `<` | Less Than | `x < y`<br>`x < 2` | True<br>False |
| `>=` | Greater Than Or Equal | `x >= 2`<br>`x >= y` | True<br>False |
| `<=` | Less Than Or Equal | `x <= 2`<br>`x <= 1` | True<br>False |

### Quick Check 2-A

Evaluate each of the following conditions. Assume A = 2, B = 6.

1. `A < B`
2. `A = B`
3. `17 Mod B <> 5`
4. `(A - B) = (B - A)`
5. `B + A * B = 18`

## Simple IF Statements

To understand how an IF statement is used in Visual Logic, consider the simple problem of reading two values and determining if they are equal or not. Our solution will use two input statements followed by an IF statement to compare the two values. Add an output statement inside the true branch to display the message **`The values are equal`**. Likewise, add an output statement inside the false branch to display the message **`The values are not equal`** (Figure 2-1). Run this solution multiple times with different input values to verify its behavior.

## Solving the Overtime Problem

An IF statement can be used to solve the overtime problem. Specifically, the solution will make a decision about which formula is appropriate based on the number of hours worked by the employee.

From the Visual Logic menu, select File | Open. Open the file containing the paycheck program you saved from the previous chapter (see Figure 1-8). Click on the flow-arrow above the assignment statement, and add a condition element to your flowchart. Then double-click the element to enter the condition. In the text box, type the following condition:

```
Hours < 40
```

Press OK to close the condition edit dialog. Drag the existing assignment statement to the true branch and drop it there. Click the false branch and add a new assignment statement with the overtime formula. Your flowchart should now look like Figure 2-2. Run the program multiple times to ensure that the condition is working properly.

**FIGURE 2.1** *A Simple IF Statement*

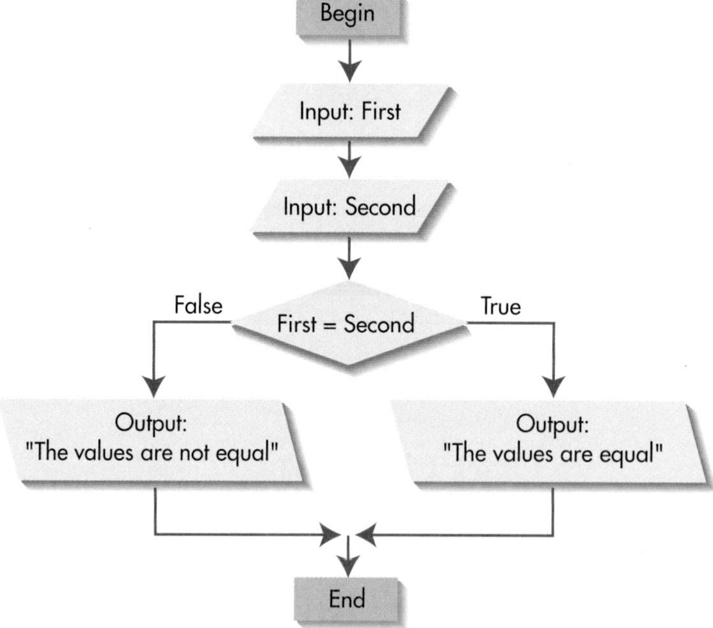

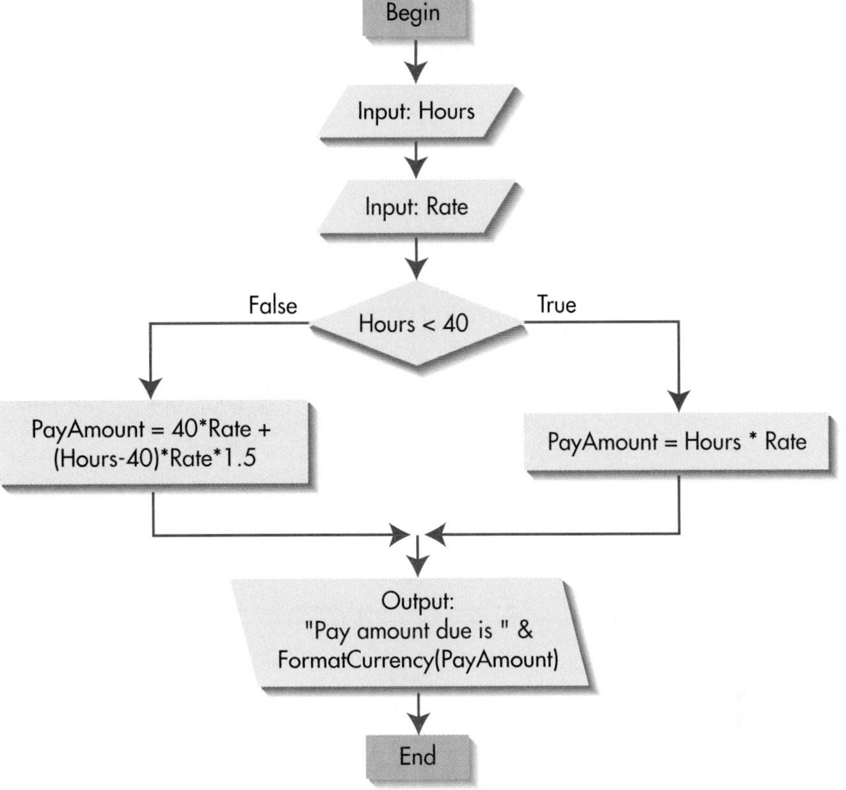


**FIGURE 2.2** *Weekly Paycheck Program with Overtime*

### *IF Statement Summary*

- IF statements are used to choose between actions.
- In Visual Logic, the IF flowchart element is a diamond containing a condition and two exit arrows labeled *True* and *False.*
- A condition is a boolean expression, typically involving one of six relational operators.
- When executed, the condition is evaluated. If the condition is true, control flows along the true arrow. If the condition is false, control flows along the false arrow.
- An IF statement ends where the true and false branches reconnect.

## 2-3 Nested IF Statements

The true and false branches of an IF statement may contain any number of statements of any type, including other IF statements. The term ***nested IF*** refers to an IF statement contained within the true or false branch of another IF statement.

To understand nested IF statements, consider the simple problem of reading two values and determining if they are equal, if the first is greater than the second, or if the first is smaller than the second. The three possible outputs are properly handled by the nested IF solution in Figure 2-3.

### Long Distance Billing Problem

Consider the example of determining the billing rate for a long distance phone call. According to one billing plan, if a call is made between 6:00 am and 6:00 pm, then the billing rate should be 10 cents per minute. Nights and mornings are free. One possible solution to the billing requirement is shown in Figure 2-4. The problem assumes a military time format is being used.

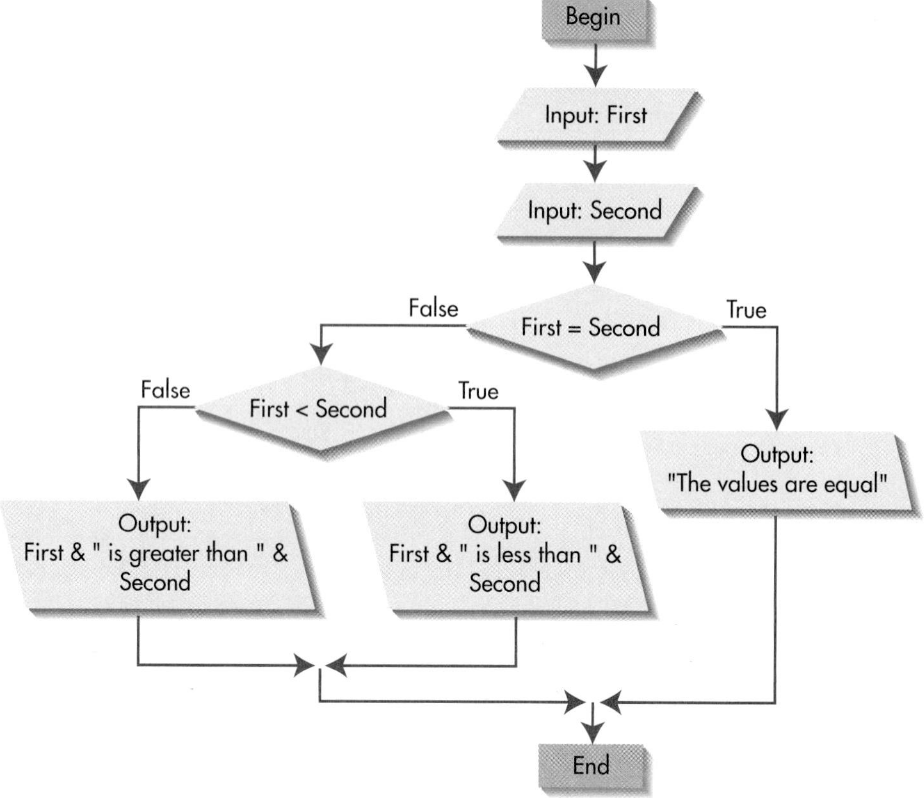


**FIGURE 2.3** *A Nested IF Solution*

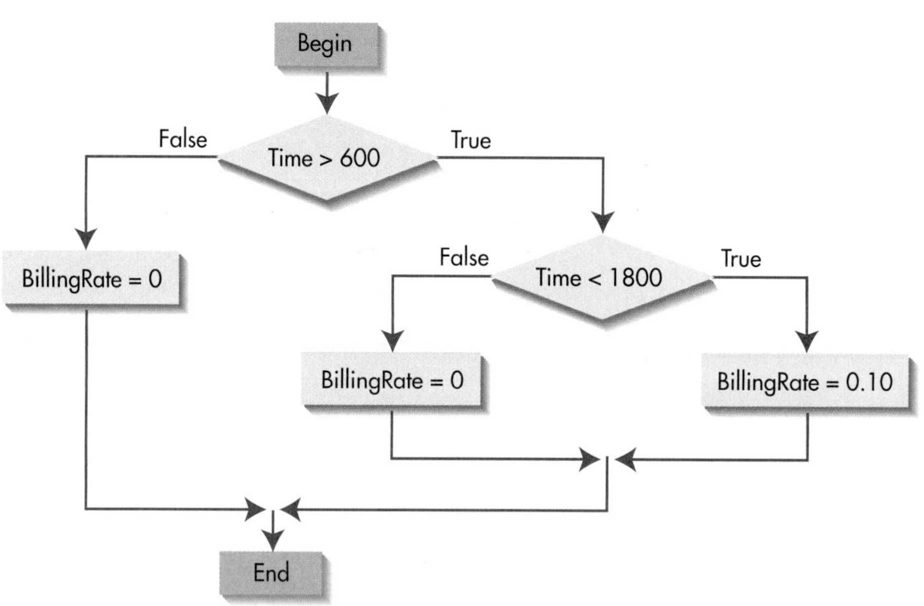


**FIGURE 2.4** *Nested IF Condition to Compute Long Distance Billing Rate*

## 2-4 Compound Conditions

When it comes to making decisions, developers are often faced with complex conditions that require multiple comparisons. A ***compound condition*** consists of two conditions within parentheses joined by a ***logical operator***. The four most common logical operators are NOT, AND, OR, and XOR. Table 2-2 illustrates these four logical operators.

**Tip**

**Parentheses are necessary around the conditions before and after logical operators.**

### Table 2.2 Logical Operators with Results

| Operator | Description | Example | Result (*assume* A = 5, B = 8) |
|---|---|---|---|
| `NOT` | Returns the opposite of the condition | `NOT (A < 3)` | True |
| | | `NOT (B = 8)` | False |
| `AND` | Returns true if and only if both conditions are true | `(A = 1) AND (B = 9)` | False |
| | | `(A = 5) AND (B = 9)` | False |
| | | `(A = 1) AND (B = 8)` | False |
| | | `(A = 5) AND (B = 8)` | True |
| `OR` | Returns true if at least one condition is true | `(A = 1) OR (B = 9)` | False |
| | | `(A = 5) OR (B = 9)` | True |
| | | `(A = 1) OR (B = 8)` | True |
| | | `(A = 5) OR (B = 8)` | True |
| `XOR` | Returns true if the conditions have opposite values | `(A = 1) XOR (B = 9)` | False |
| | | `(A = 5) XOR (B = 9)` | True |
| | | `(A = 1) XOR (B = 8)` | True |
| | | `(A = 5) XOR (B = 8)` | False |

To understand how compound conditions may be used, consider that automobile insurance companies charge a premium for male drivers under the age of 25. The gender and age requirements can both be tested with a compound condition:

```
(Gender = "Male") AND (Age < 25)
```

Another example would be a test to see if a student is a senior (90 or more hours) with a grade point average at or above 3.25:

```
(HoursEarned >= 90) AND (GPA >= 3.25)
```

There are times when a single compound condition can be used in place of a nested IF. For example, consider the long distance billing algorithm shown in Figure 2-4. This can be rewritten using a single compound condition, as shown in Figure 2-5. Both solutions are right because they both produce the correct result. It is a subjective opinion as to which, if either, is the better solution.

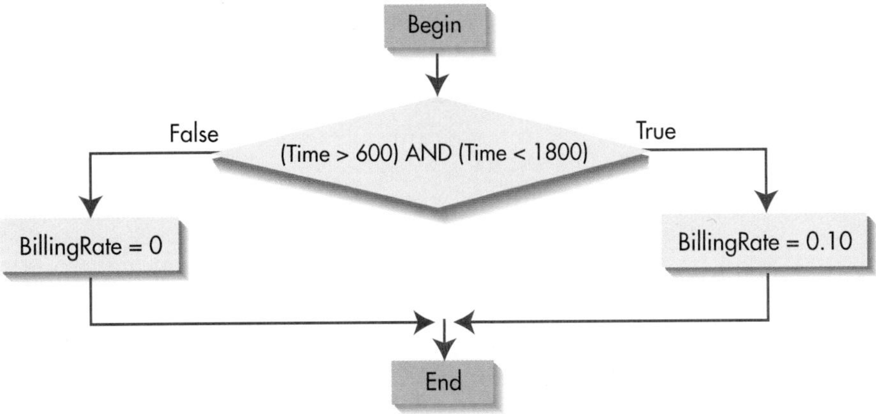


**FIGURE 2.5** *Compound Condition to Compute Long Distance Billing Rate*

## ASK THE AUTHOR

**Q** Are you saying there is no difference between the nested IF solution and the compound condition solution to the long distance billing problem?

**A** There are advantages and disadvantages with both. If the night and morning billing rate were to change, you would have to change two assignments in Figure 2-4 but only one in Figure 2-5, meaning the compound condition reduces the likelihood of a simple oversight error. On the other hand, using compound conditions requires caution because it is easy to use OR when AND is required and vice versa. What would happen in Figure 2-5 if the logical operator OR had been used instead of the AND? (*Hint:* Customers would be unhappy.)

Generally speaking it is a good idea to consider multiple solutions and choose the one that is clearest to you. The Case Study Solution will further illustrate this point.

## Quick Check 2-B

Evaluate each of the following compound conditions. Assume X = 3, Y = 7.

1. `(X = 1) AND (Y = 7)`
2. `(X = 1) OR (Y = 7)`
3. `(X < Y) AND (Y > 10)`
4. `(X ^ 3 = 27) AND (Y Mod 2 = 1)`
5. `(X ^ 3 = 27) XOR (Y Mod 2 = 1)`

# Smallest Number

"IF statements, nested IF statements, and compound conditions give developers a great deal of options when it comes to developing solutions. Consider the problem of inputting three unduplicated values and displaying the smallest value. We will examine four different solutions to this problem, all of which are correct. However, they are not necessarily equal."

Dr. Taylor recognizes the look of slight confusion on the faces of some students. He continues, "For example, you may find one of the solutions easier to understand than the others. Given the choice, you should use the algorithm you understand best. In addition, some solutions lend themselves to modification better than others. A good developer often spends a significant amount of time considering alternative solutions rather than always using the first idea that comes to mind."

## Solution 1: Nested Conditions

Dr. Taylor hands out the first solution (Figure 2-6). "This first solution uses nested conditions. The first condition determines which is the smaller of A and B. The smaller of A and B is then compared with C via a nested condition. The smaller value of the second comparison is then displayed."

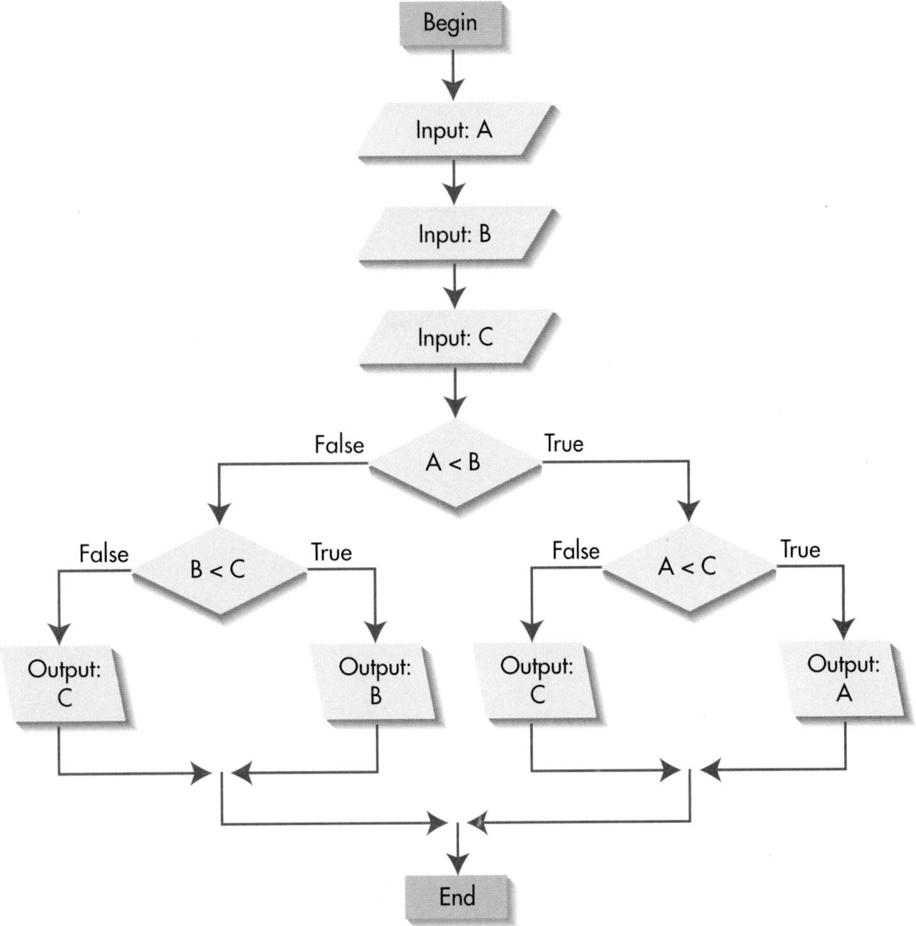


**FIGURE 2.6** *Smallest Number Solution Using Nested Conditions*

### Solution 2: Compound Conditions

"This second solution (Figure 2-7) uses a series of compound conditions. The first compound condition checks to see if A holds the smallest value and, if so, prints A. Similar compound conditions are used for testing B and C. These conditions are sequential (rather than nested)."

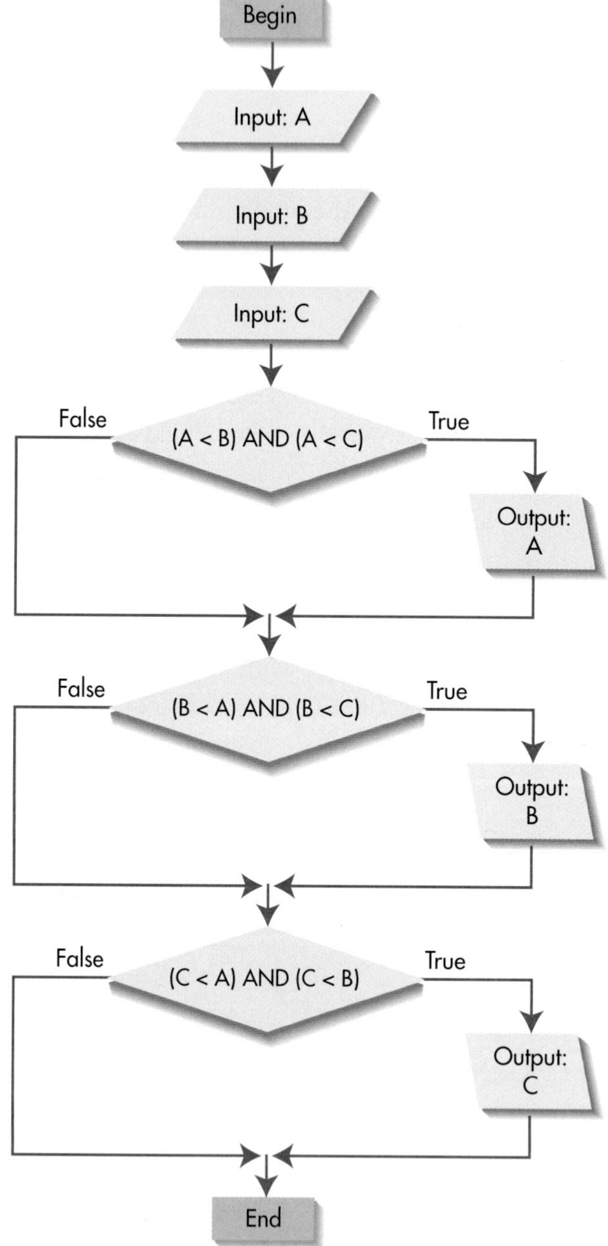


**FIGURE 2.7** *Smallest Number Solution Using Sequential Compound Conditions*

### Solution 3: Nested and Compound Condition

"The third solution (Figure 2-8) to the smallest number problem begins with a compound condition. In this case, however, the program contains a nested condition in the false branch. Since A is not the smallest, the nested condition need only compare B and C to determine the smallest value."

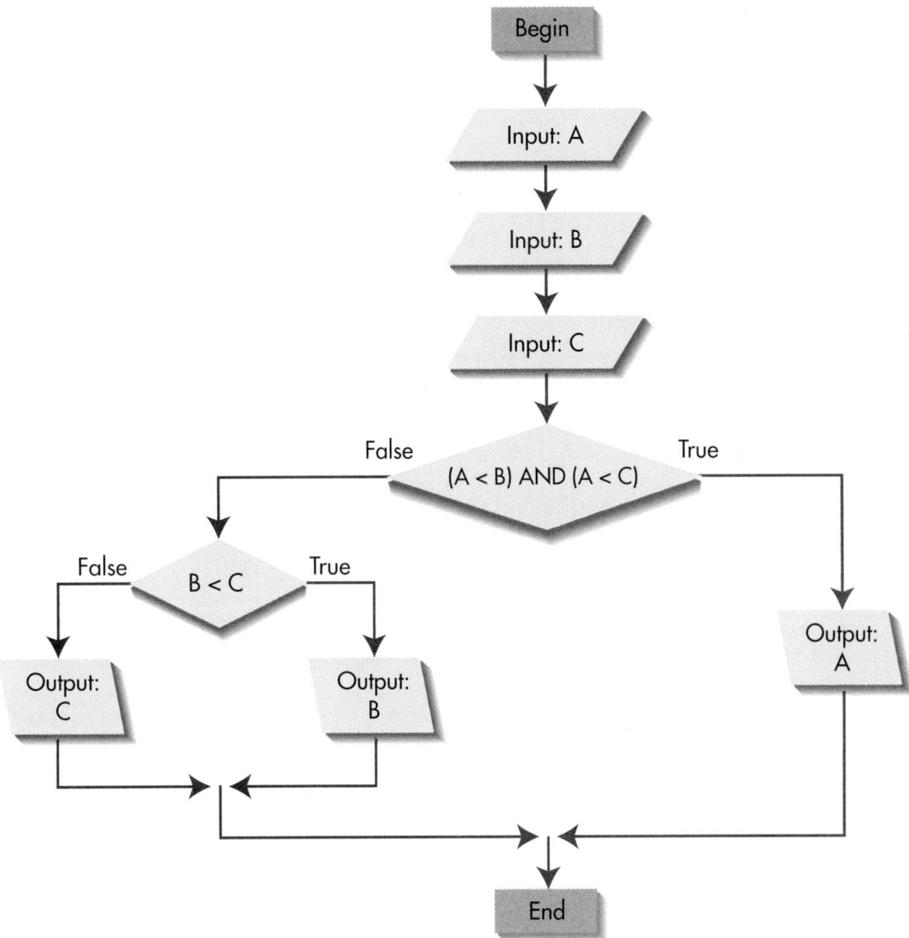


**FIGURE 2.8** *Smallest Number Solution Using Nested and Compound Conditions*

### Solution 4: Placeholder Variable

"Our fourth and final solution (Figure 2-9) takes a different approach than the first three. This solution makes use of a variable, `Smallest`, to serve as a placeholder for the smallest value. The placeholder is initially given the value of the first input number. Then each remaining input number is individually compared with the placeholder value. If a smaller number is found, the placeholder becomes the same as the newer, smaller value. After all values have been compared, the placeholder will hold the smallest of the input values."

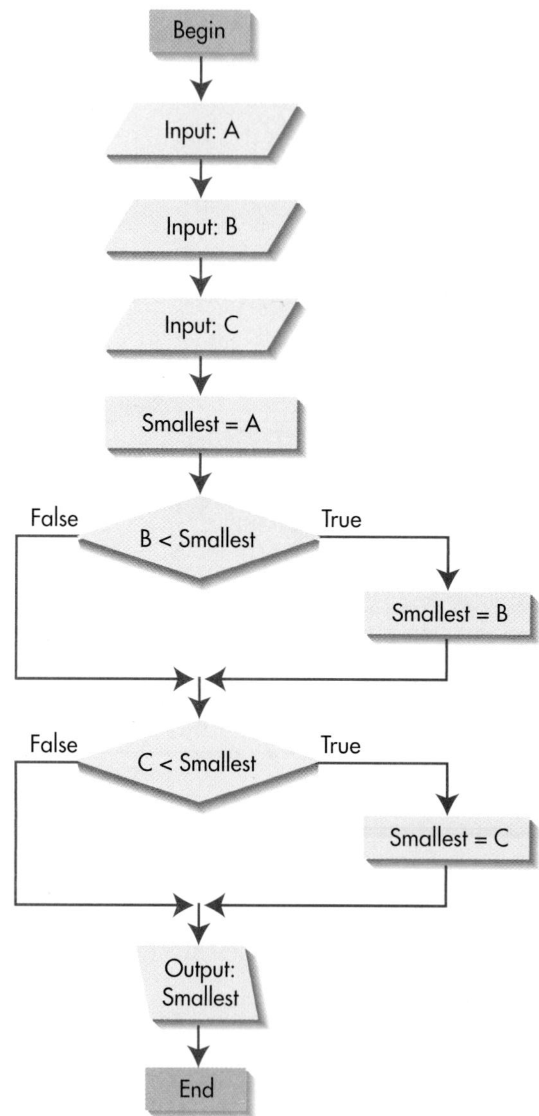


**FIGURE 2.9** *Smallest Number Solution Using a Placeholder Variable*

"All four of these solutions for finding the smallest number are correct. Which one is best?" The ensuing discussion is lively with a variety of opinions presented. The solutions are evaluated for how well they would handle slight variations on the problem. For example, what if duplicate values were allowed, or what if the middle value were required instead of the smallest value, or what if the size of the input were more than three values? The general consensus is that each solution has its advantages and that different solutions lend themselves better to different variations of the original problem. Looking at his watch, Dr. Taylor wraps up the conversation. "Comparing the strengths and weaknesses of multiple solutions is a key skill for a successful developer. I think you are all doing a very good job."

## Chapter Summary

- A condition is an expression that evaluates to either true or false. Conditions typically use one of six relational operators: =, >, <, >=, <=, or <>.
- IF statements use conditions to choose between actions. When executed, the condition is evaluated. If the condition is true, control flows to the true branch. If the condition is false, control flows to the false branch.
- The true and false branches of an IF statement may contain any valid statement, including other IF statements. An IF statement within the true or false branch of another IF statement is referred to as a nested IF.
- A compound condition is two or more conditions joined by a logical operator. The four most common logical operators are AND, OR, NOT, and XOR.

## Key Terms

**compound condition** p. 24
**condition** p. 21
**IF statement** p. 21
**logical operators** p. 24
**nested IF** p. 23
**relational operators** p. 21

## Review Questions

1. What is the difference between a correct program solution and a good program solution? Why is it important for solutions to be not only correct but also good?
2. Identify possible uses of decision statements (IF statements) for a video store's rental checkout system.
3. The long distance billing problem has a nested IF solution (Figure 2-4). This solution was rewritten as a compound condition solution (Figure 2-5). Can all nested IF solutions be rewritten as compound condition solutions? As part of your answer, consider the problem of inputting two values and displaying if the first is smaller than, equal to, or greater than the second (Figure 2-3). If it can be rewritten, include the new solution with your answer. If it cannot be rewritten, explain why not.
4. Consider the four solutions in Figures 2-6 through 2-9. These solutions assume the input data contains unduplicated numbers. Determine if each solution would work if duplicate input values were allowed (e.g., 3, 5, 3 as input).

## Programming Exercises

**2-1. Positive Difference.** Write a program that inputs two values and displays their positive difference. For example, if the first input is 6 and the second input is 9, then the positive difference is 3. Likewise, if the first input is 9 and the second input is 6, the output is still a positive 3.

**2-2. All's Well That Ends Well.** Write a program that inputs a number between 1 and 10 and displays the number with the appropriate two-letter ending (e.g., 1st, 2nd, 3rd, 4th, 5th, . . . ).

**2-3. Middle Value.** Write a program that displays the middle value of three unduplicated input values. Hint: Review the four solutions in the smallest number case study in this chapter. Consider how easy or hard it would be to modify each of those algorithms to find the middle value rather than the smallest value. Then modify the algorithm you consider most appropriate for this problem.

**2-4. Smallest of Five.** Write a program that displays the smallest of five input values that may include duplicate values (e.g., 6, 4, 8, 6, 7). Hint: Review the four solutions in the smallest number case study in this chapter. Consider how easy or hard it would be to modify each of those algorithms to find the smallest of five rather than three values. Then modify the algorithm you consider most appropriate for this problem.

**2-5. Grade Determination.** Write a program that will input three test scores. The program should determine and display their average. The program should then display the appropriate letter grade based on the average. The letter grade should be determined using a standard 10-point scale (A = 90 – 100, B = 80 – 89.999, C = 70 – 79.999, etc.)

**2-6. All's Well That Ends Well, Part II.** Write a program that inputs a number between 1 and 1000 and displays the number with the appropriate two-letter ending (e.g., 1st, 2nd, 3rd, 4th, 5th, . . . ). Hint: This problem is harder than it sounds. The most common ending is th, but there are many exceptions. You might want to start by finding all the exceptions and looking for patterns. You might then find integer division (\) and integer remainder (Mod) helpful in testing for those patterns.

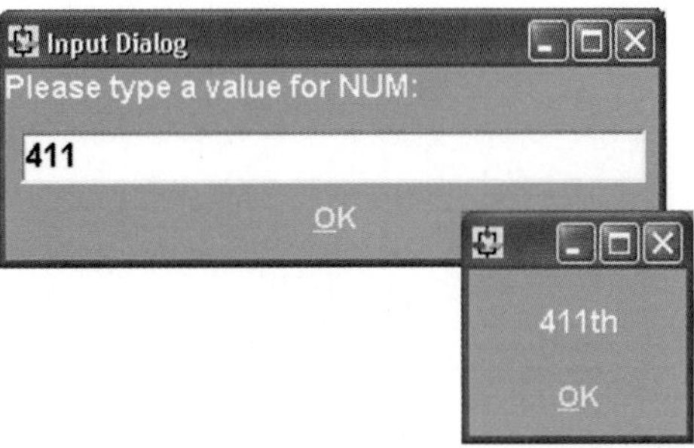


**2-7. The Perfect Fit.** Write a program with three input variables, RW (for rectangle width), RH (for rectangle height), and SS (for square side). The program should output two sentences. The first sentence will be one of the following.

"The object with the greatest area is the square."
"The object with the greatest area is the rectangle."
"The square and the rectangle have the same area."

The second sentence will be one of the following.

"The square fits inside the rectangle."
"The rectangle fits inside the square."
"Neither shape fits inside the other."

Note: A 5 × 3 rectangle does not fit inside a 5 × 5 square.

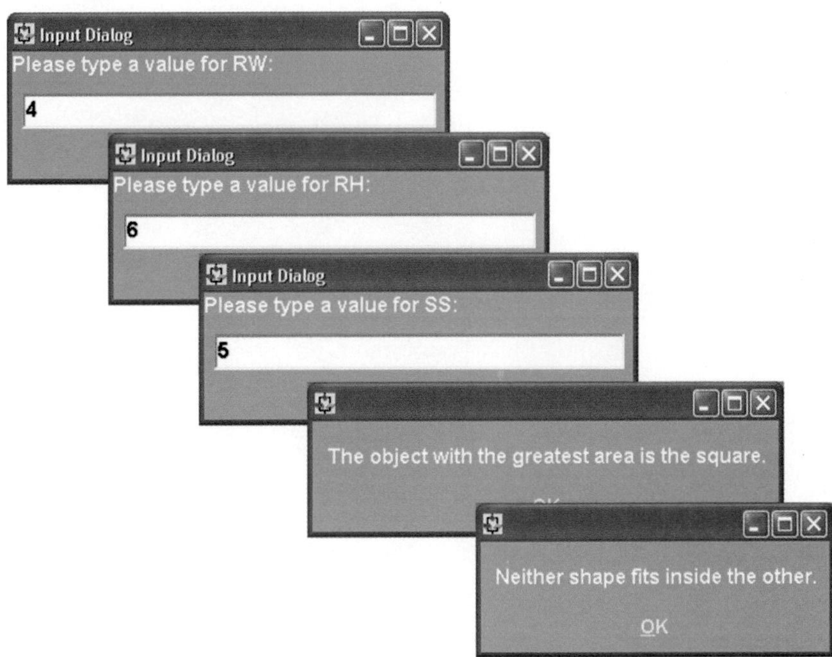

CHAPTER 3

# Repeating Actions

## OUTLINE

▶ INTERVIEW

**Christopher Malo, Supervisor of Web Design Department, GoInternet.net**

***Interviewer:*** Please tell us how you got involved in the IT industry.

***Malo:*** I started at GoInternet.net as a telemarketer and quickly found that I couldn't sell a glass of water in the desert. They had an opening in the web design department and gave me a shot because of my interest and capabilities in technology. At that time, we had three people in web design. Now we have over forty, and I supervise the department.

At times I felt like I didn't have much creative freedom, especially when GoInternet.net was exclusively focused on providing template web pages. Regardless, I'd take the time to learn new things on my own. As the company grew and as the sophistication of our customers grew, our customers no longer wanted cookie cutter templates. They wanted a more individual look and a more unique web presence. So I was ready to give our customers what they wanted, and GoInternet.net was only too willing to give me the opportunity.

***Interviewer:*** What kind of projects are you currently working on?

***Malo:*** We create customized, enhanced web sites for companies desiring a unique web presence. Two of the projects I am working on happen to be limousine sites. One is a Philadelphia-based limousine service, with partners in other countries, who plans to market worldwide. Some of the issues we're addressing include different language barriers, currency conversions, time differences, airport pickups, and flight schedules. The other limousine company is based in Florida and targets high-end entertainment, sports, and political figures. Not only do they offer car services, they can provide armed bodyguards! My challenge here is to reflect and appeal to the high-end, security-conscious clientele my client is trying to attract.

***Interviewer:*** What advice do you have for students entering the computer field?

***Malo:*** Computers and software are ever-expanding and changing. You must stay on top of the latest developments or you'll be left in the dust. Unless you're up-to-date, the competition will pass you by.

## OBJECTIVES

At the completion of this chapter, you will

- **Understand how console input and output (console I/O) work**
- **Understand and use the For loop statement**
- **Understand and use the While loop statement**
- **Understand and use the Exit loop statement**
- **Understand and use counters and accumulators**
- **Develop and evaluate solutions that require loops and nested loops**

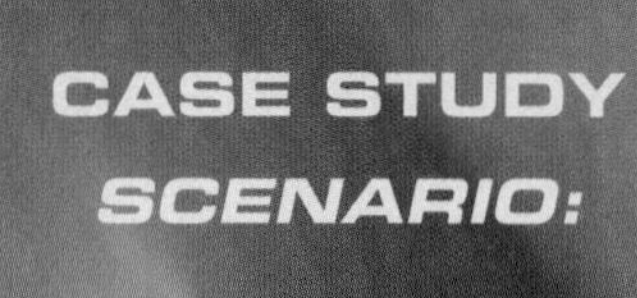


# High-Low Game

"I would like to begin today's class with a demonstration, and I will need the assistance of one student. Whose birthday is closest to today?" After a brief discussion among the students, it is determined that Gail's birthday in two weeks is closest. Dr. Taylor continues, "I am now going to perform a mind reading demonstration. Gail, I need you to think of a number between 1 and 1000, but do not tell me the number. I just need you to concentrate on that number."

"Okay, I've got it." Gail says. Dr. Taylor picks up a notepad and a marker, then shuts his eyes in concentration. After a few seconds he writes his answer on the notepad where the class cannot read it. "All right, I have recorded my answer. Gail, please tell the class, were you thinking of the number 836?"

"No." Gail says.

Dr. Taylor turns the notepad over and shows the class that he had written "No" as his answer.

A mixture of moans and laughter fill the air. Dr. Taylor continues, "Guessing a numeric value between 1 and 1000 in a single guess would indeed be very impressive. Today we are going to write a computer program that generates a random value from 1 to 1000 and asks the user to guess the number in as few guesses as possible. After every wrong guess, the program will tell the user if the actual number is higher or lower than the guess."

"Like the High-Low game on *The Price is Right*?" Kevin asks.

"Exactly! Given the High-Low feedback, a good guesser should correctly identify the number in about ten guesses."

Dr. Taylor's solution appears at the end of this chapter.

## 3-1 Console Input and Output

Sometimes you want the input and output interactions with the user to be maintained for later inspection. This can be done through the use of console input and output statements. Figure 3-1 shows the input edit dialog window with the console input option selected. A similar option exists inside the output edit dialog window.

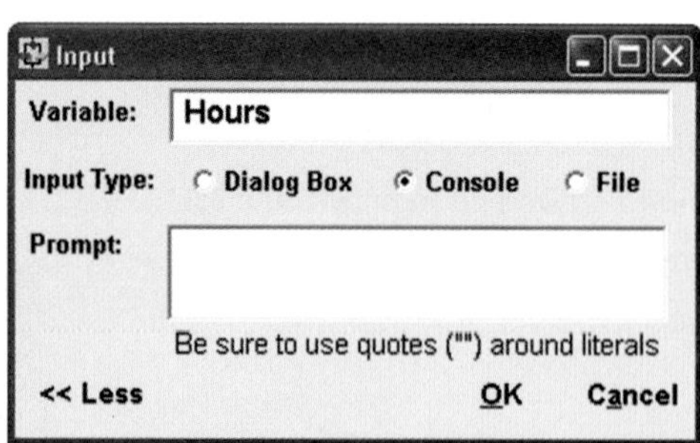


**FIGURE 3.1** *Input Edit Dialog Window with the Console Input Option Selected*

The flowchart elements for console input and output look just like the dialog I/O elements with a console screen icon at the top of the flowchart element (see Figure 3-2).

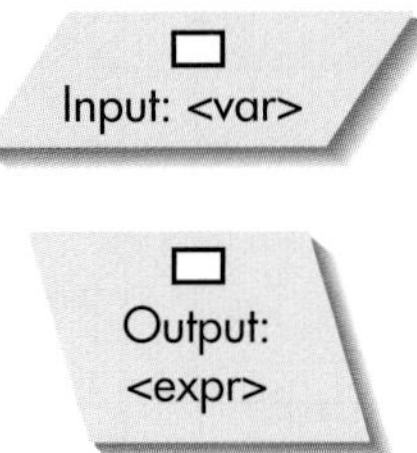


FIGURE 3.2 *Console Input and Output Elements*

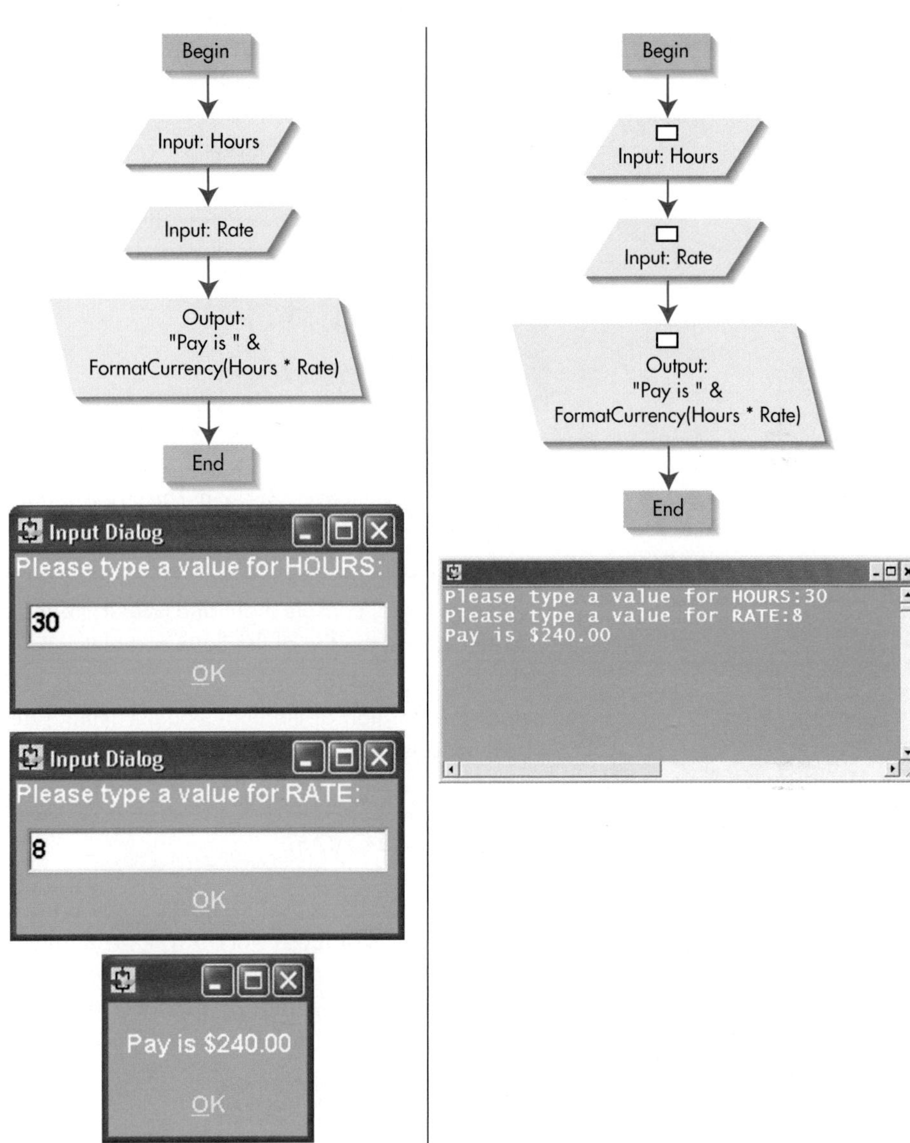


FIGURE 3.3 *Dialog I/O (left) Versus Console I/O (right)*

Console I/O is persistent, meaning each line of input and output remains in the console window for the lifetime of the program. The programs in Figure 3-3 illustrate the differences between Dialog I/O and Console I/O.

## Console End-of-Output Character

Because console output is persistent, multiple outputs can appear on the same line. The ending position of the current output (and therefore the starting position of the next console I/O) is indicated with the ***end-of-output symbol (§)***. Figure 3-4 illustrates the difference in how Visual Logic handles the end-of-output symbol. Note that the end-of-output symbol is only visible when editing the console output expression.

FIGURE 3.4 *The Console End-of-Output Symbol*

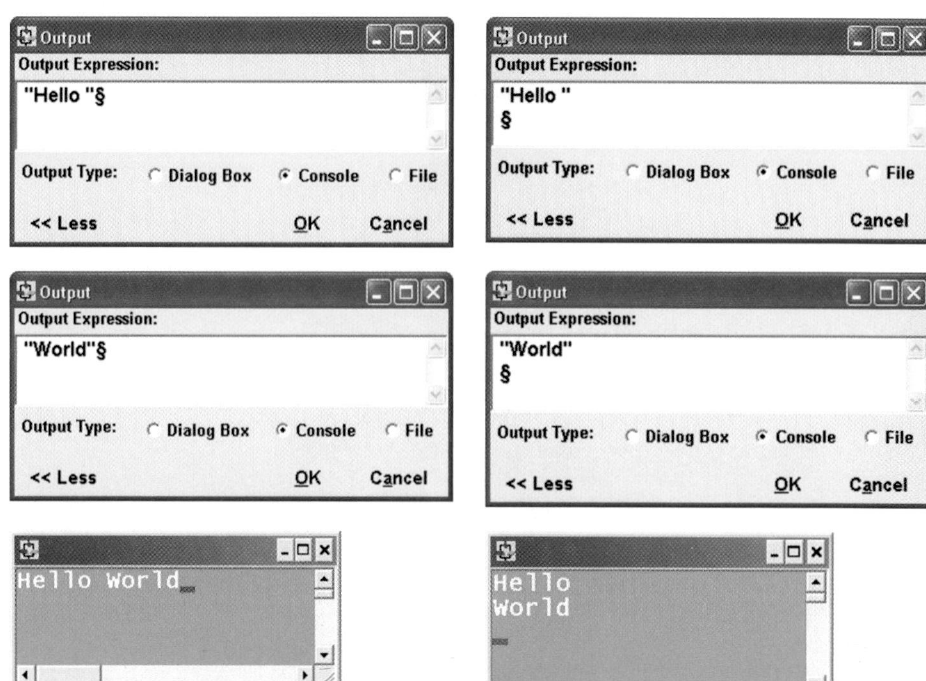


## *Console Input/Output Summary*

- Console input and output are recorded in the console window.
- In Visual Logic, console input and output are indicated by the presence of the console screen icon at the top of the flowchart element.
- The end-of-output (§) symbol always appears at the end of the console output expression. The position of the end-of-output symbol determines the starting location for the next console I/O.

# 3-2 For Loops

***For loops*** are used to repeat actions a predetermined number of times. The best way to understand how For loops work is to look at an example. Start a new solution and add a For loop element from the element menu. Double-click the element to open the edit dialog window containing four text boxes. Enter the following values as shown: variable name `Count`; initial value `1`; final value `5`; and step `1`.

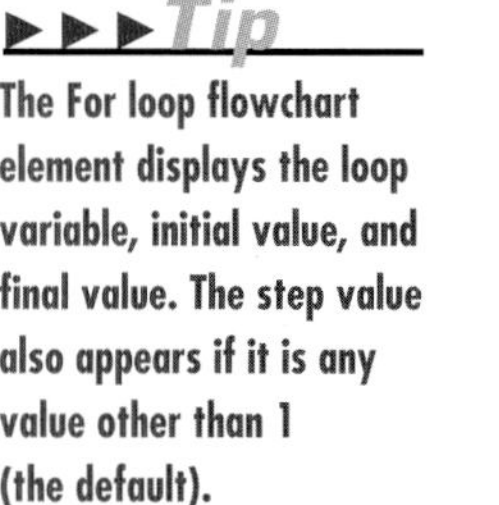

**Tip**

**The For loop flowchart element displays the loop variable, initial value, and final value. The step value also appears if it is any value other than 1 (the default).**

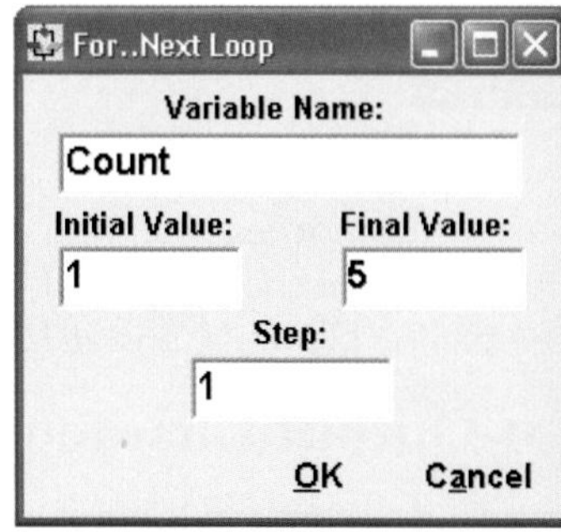


Close the edit dialog. The loop element displays the ***loop variable***, ***initial value***, and ***final value***. The ***step value*** is not displayed in this case because 1 is the default and is therefore assumed. The element has two exiting flow-arrows. The horizontal flow-arrow leads to the body of the loop and returns to the loop element. After each pass through the body of the loop, the loop variable is automatically updated by the step value. When the value of the loop variable exceeds the final value, control flows to the element below the loop element. Add two console output elements as shown in Figure 3-5.

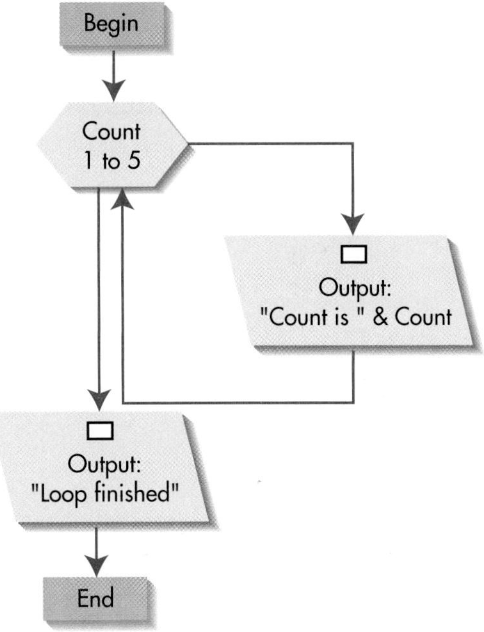


**FIGURE 3.5** *For Loop Program*

Press F5 to run the program. When control flows into the loop element, the loop variable is assigned the initial value of 1. Control then flows to the body of the loop, generating the output

```
Count is 1
```

Control then flows back to the For loop element, which causes the loop variable to automatically update by one. Because the loop variable (which is now 2) is still less than or equal to the final value, the body of the loop executes again, generating the output

```
Count is 2
```

This process of executing the body and then updating the loop variable repeats three more times, generating the following output:

```
Count is 3
Count is 4
Count is 5
```

After the fifth pass the loop variable is updated to the value 6. Because the loop variable is now greater than the final value, the loop is finished, and control leaves the loop and moves to the next element, which displays the message "Loop finished." The final output for the program is shown in Figure 3-6.

**FIGURE 3.6** *Output from Program Shown in Figure 3-5*

## Quick Check 3-A

Use a For loop for each of the following:

1. Display the squares of the numbers 1 to 10 (e.g., 1, 4, 9, 16, 25, etc.) in a console output window.
2. Display the numbers between 1 and 100 that are multiples of 5 (e.g., 5, 10, 15, 20, etc.) in a console output window.

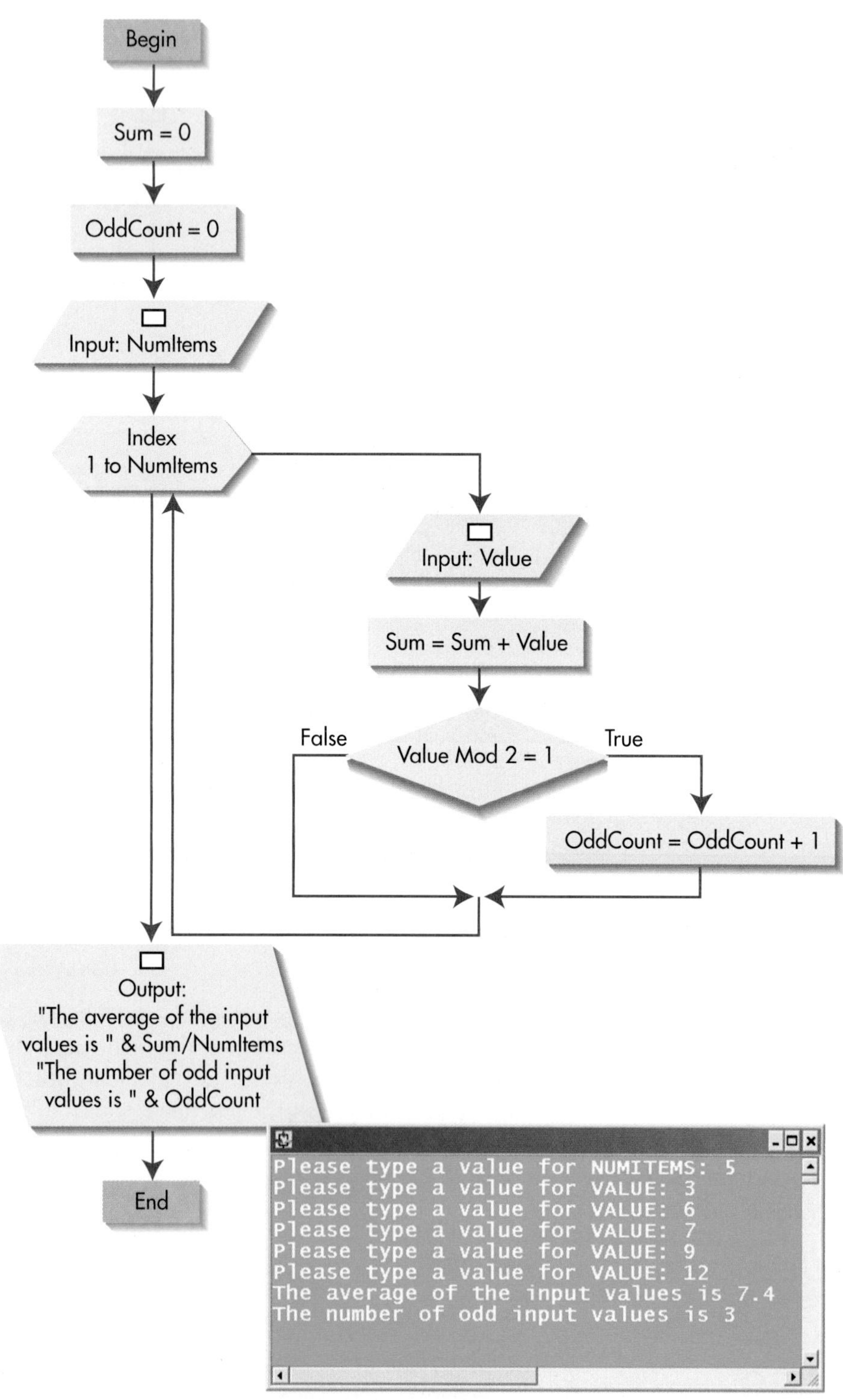


**FIGURE 3.7** *A Solution Using a Counter and an Accumulator*

## Counters and Accumulators

Counters and accumulators are often used inside loops to help perform common calculations such as counts, totals, and averages. ***Counters*** are variables that keep track of how many times a statement has executed. Typically a counter involves an assignment statement inside a loop with the format

```
Counter = Counter + 1
```

***Accumulators*** are variables that maintain a running total. Typically an accumulator involves an assignment statement inside a loop with the format

```
Accumulator = Accumulator + NewValue
```

Figure 3-7 illustrates the use of a counter and an accumulator. The solution begins by prompting the user for the number of values to be input. A loop is used to input and process the data. The body of the loop contains an input statement followed immediately by the Sum accumulator. The input value is then tested to determine if it is an odd value. If the value is odd, then the OddCount counter is incremented.

After the specified number of input values have been read and processed, the loop is finished and control flows to the output statement, which calculates and displays the average and also displays the number of inputs that were odd.

**MENTOR**

It may not be necessary to initialize an accumulator or counter variable because most languages (including Visual Logic and Visual Basic) assign a default value of zero to all numeric variables. However, it is considered good programming practice to initialize counters and accumulators directly before the loop where they are used.

## *Quick Check 3-B*

What is the output of the two programs shown in Figure 3-8?

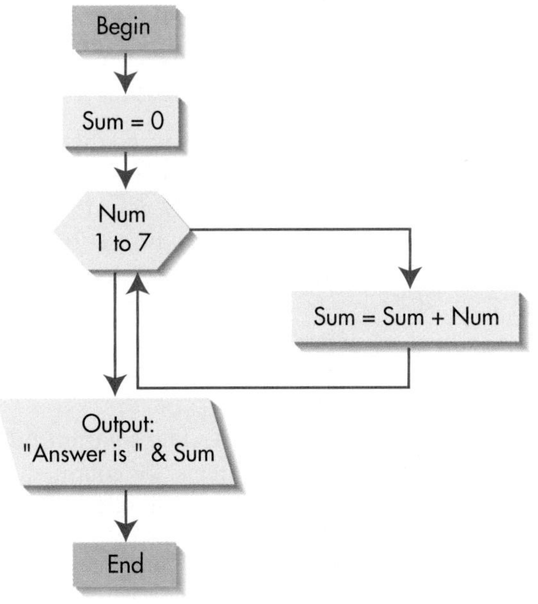


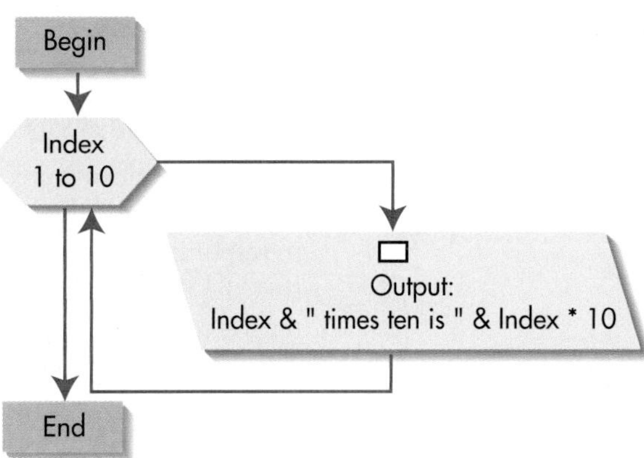


**FIGURE 3.8** *For Loop Quick Check Problems*

### FOR Loop Summary

- For loops are used to repeat actions a predetermined number of times.
- In Visual Logic, the For loop flowchart element is a six-sided figure with a loop variable, a start value, an end value, a step value (if not 1), and two exit arrows. The body of the loop is to the right and below the element.
- When executed, the first action is to initialize the loop variable to the start value.
- The body of the loop executes as long as the value of the loop variable does not exceed the final value. (Note: If the step value is negative, then the body of the loop executes as long as the value of the loop variable is not smaller than the final value.) After the body of the loop executes, the loop variable is updated by the step value, and the process is repeated.
- Counters and accumulators are variables typically used inside a loop to help calculate counts, totals, and averages. Counters are incremented by one, and accumulators are updated by the value of a variable.

## 3-3 While Loops

***While loops*** are used when an action is to be repeated an unknown number of times. For example, the number of employees in a company will change over time. A good payroll program will calculate employee paychecks one at a time until every employee has been processed.

A While loop contains a condition. Whenever the condition evaluates to true, the body of the loop is executed and control returns to the condition. When the condition evaluates to false, control flows to the element after the loop. In other words, the body of the loop repeats *while* the looping condition is true.

While loops come in two forms, ***pre-test loop*** and ***post-test loop***. The only difference is that a pre-test loop tests the looping condition before executing the body of the loop. If the condition is initially false, then the loop body is never executed. When using the post-test loop, the body executes one time before the looping condition is ever tested, thus guaranteeing at least one execution of the loop body regardless of the condition. After one pass through the loop, there are no differences between the pre-test and post-test forms.

### Validating Input

While loops have many uses, as you will discover. One such use is to ensure that a user has entered valid data. Consider the program shown in Figure 3-9, which asks the user to respond to a question by entering either 1 or 2. A While loop can be used to ensure that the user responds with a proper value (otherwise the loop forces the user to reenter the response). Figure 3-10 shows how the program makes as many requests as necessary to obtain a proper response.

### Grocery Checkout Revised

Consider again the grocery checkout program from Chapter 1. The solution presented there requires the customer to purchase exactly three items. Of course, customers may really purchase any number of items. Limiting the program to exactly three inputs is therefore not realistic.

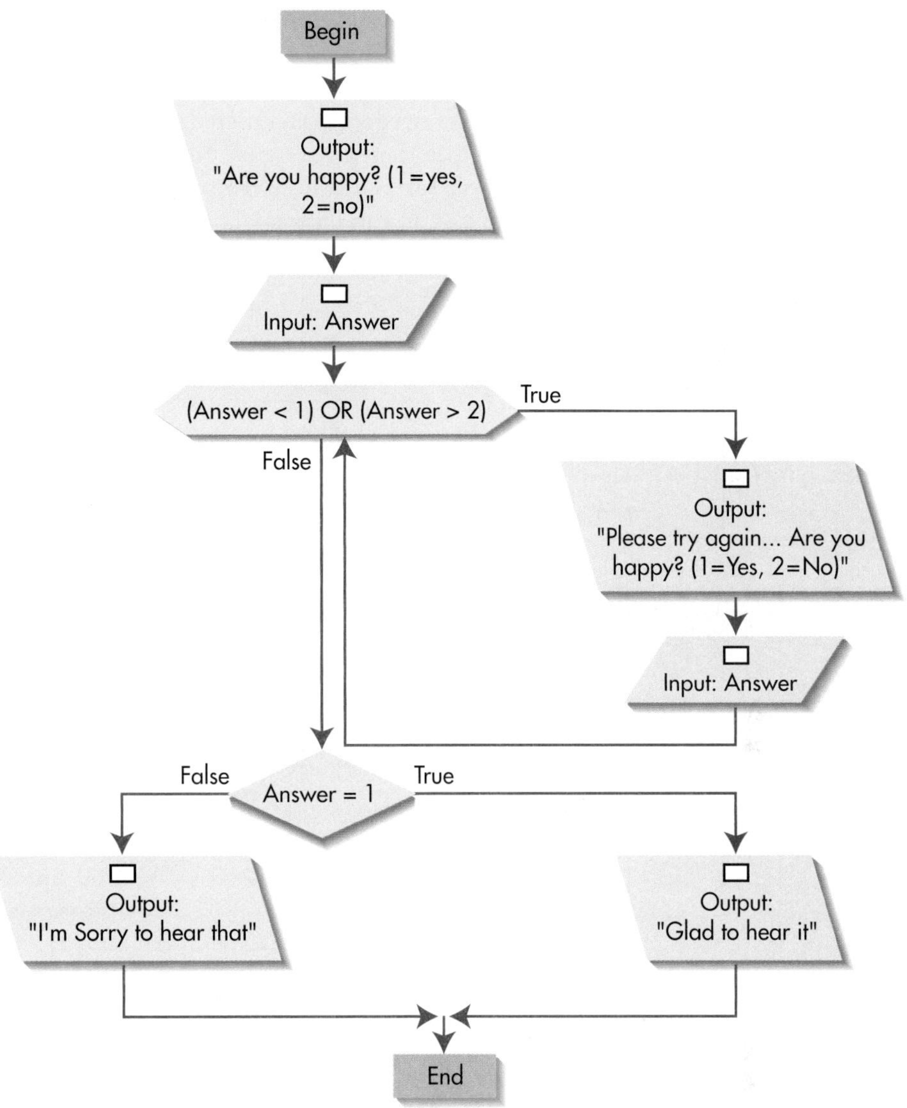


**FIGURE 3.9** *While Loop (Pre-test) Used to Verify Input*

```
Are you happy? (1=Yes, 2=No)
Please type a value for ANSWER: "Hello"
 Please try again... Are you happy? (1=Yes, 2=No)
Please type a value for ANSWER: 5
 Please try again... Are you happy? (1=Yes, 2=No)
Please type a value for ANSWER: 1
Glad to hear it
```

**FIGURE 3.10** *Output for Solution That Verifies Input*

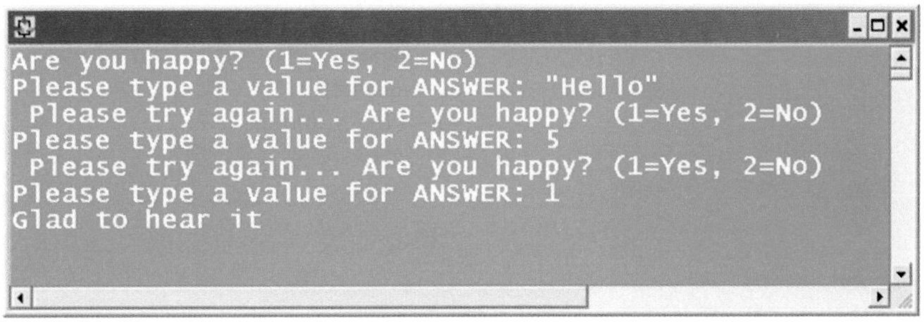

An improved solution algorithm would be to input (scan or keyboard) one item price at a time until all the item prices have been entered. The loop body would use an accumulator to keep up with a running total of all the prices entered. After the last item price had been entered, a ***sentinel value*** (or signaling value) would be used to indicate the end of input. Sales tax would then be added and the resulting total displayed just as it was in the original solution. The solution flowchart for this algorithm is shown in Figure 3-11. Notice that console input and output are used, creating a record of I/O activity in the console window (Figure 3-12).

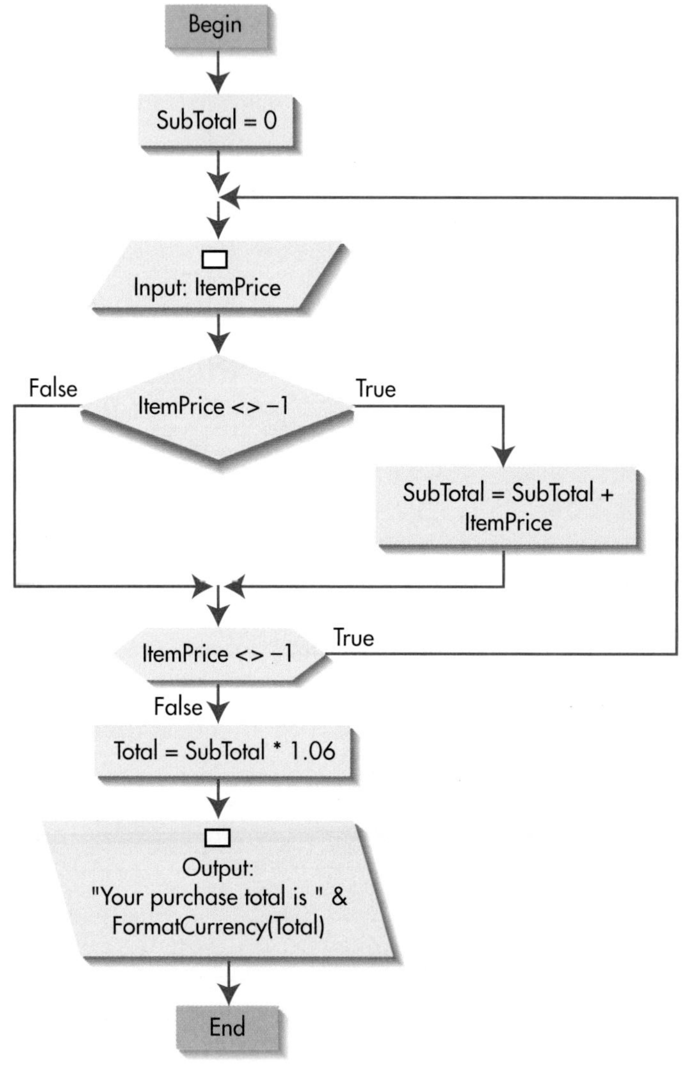


**FIGURE 3.11** *While Loop (Post-test) Used to Solve Grocery Checkout Problem*

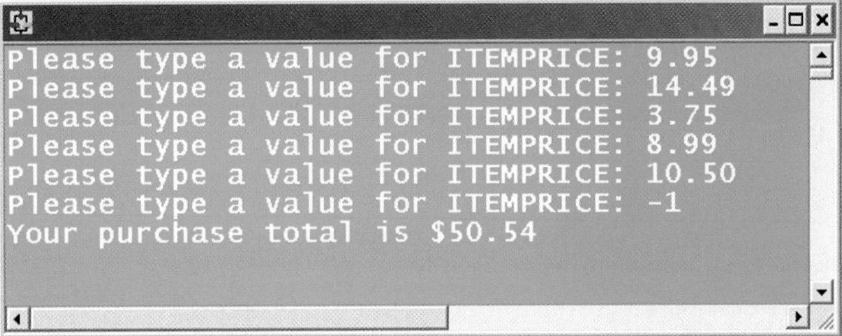
```
Please type a value for ITEMPRICE: 9.95
Please type a value for ITEMPRICE: 14.49
Please type a value for ITEMPRICE: 3.75
Please type a value for ITEMPRICE: 8.99
Please type a value for ITEMPRICE: 10.50
Please type a value for ITEMPRICE: -1
Your purchase total is $50.54
```

**FIGURE 3.12** *Console Output Window for Post-test Loop Solution*

**MENTOR**

Sentinel values are used to signal the end of input. Negative one (–1) is a common sentinel value, such as for item prices or exam scores. Negative one is an appropriate sentinel value in these cases because prices are never negative (if something costs a negative dollar, then you should buy a million of them and retire), and no matter how poorly a student does on an exam, the score will not be negative. However, –1 is not a good sentinel value if the input is outside temperature because that could be valid input (the temperature can easily be –1° Celsius in many places around the globe). When entering temperature, a good sentinel value might be 99999 or any other value that would not appear in valid input data.

## Exit Loop

Writing a sentinel loop requires a little extra effort. In addition to processing the valid data, the sentinel value must also be identified and handled. This is commonly known as the ***loop-and-a-half problem***. The extra processing often requires code duplication. For example in Figure 3-11 the sentinel value test is duplicated, once inside the body of the loop and again at the end of the loop.

In an effort to avoid code duplication, many developers use an Exit loop when processing sentinel values. An ***Exit loop*** causes control to jump out of the loop to the statement immediately below the loop. When using an Exit loop, the loop condition is typically set to true, making it a continuous loop. The body of the loop begins with an input statement followed by a test to see if the input is the sentinel value. If so, then the Exit loop statement occurs, terminating the loop. The remainder of the loop body is used to process nonsentinel values.

To illustrate how an Exit loop statement can be used, consider the alternative sentinel solution (Figure 3-13) to the checkout program. In this solution, only one element tests the sentinel value (rather than testing for the sentinel value twice as done in Figure 3-11). Both solutions produce exactly the same output, and there is no general consensus among developers about which sentinel solution is better.

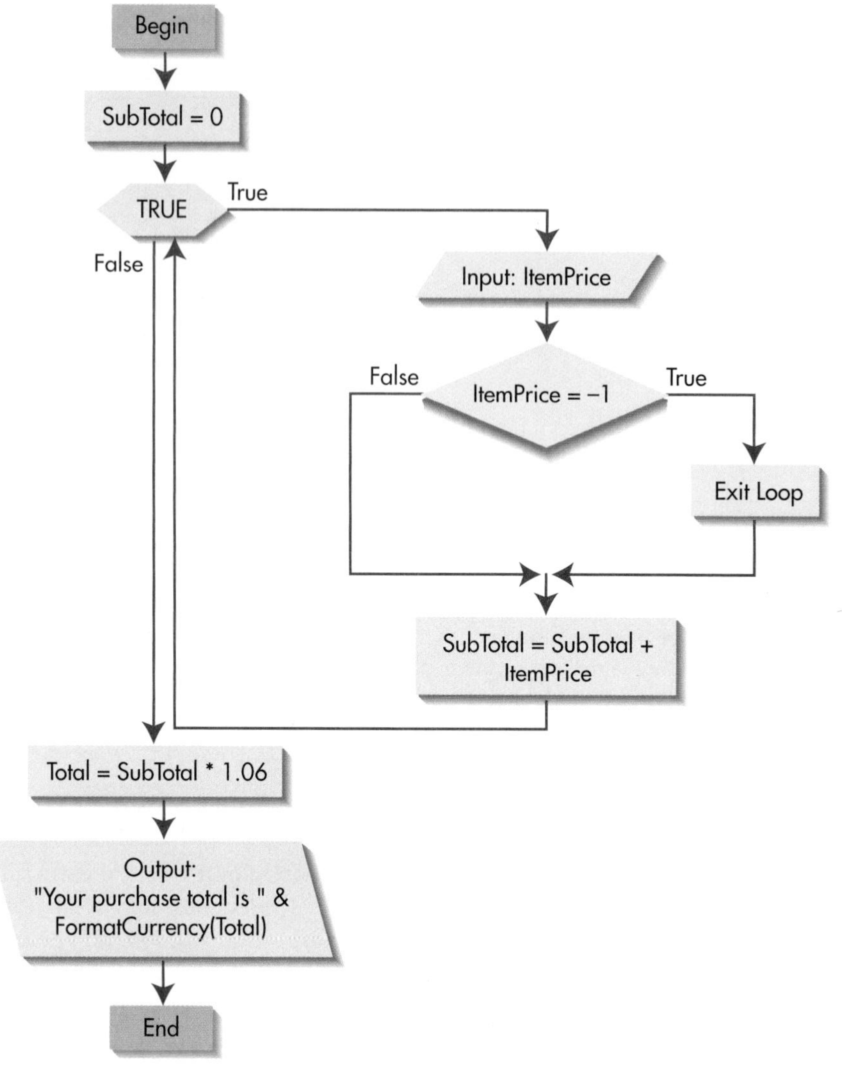


**FIGURE 3.13** *Alternative Grocery Checkout Solution Using Loop Exit*

## *While Loop Summary*

- While loops are used to repeat actions an unknown number of times. While loops have two forms, pre-test and post-test.
- When a pre-test loop is executed, the condition is tested immediately. When a post-test loop is executed, the body of the loop executes once before testing. In both cases, if the condition is true, the body of the loop executes and the process is repeated. In both cases, the loop terminates when the condition is false.
- The Exit loop statement causes control to jump directly to the statement following the current loop.

# 3-4 Nested Loops

For loops and While loops both allow code inside the body of the loop to be repeated many times. Any valid statements can occur inside the body of a loop, including input, assignment, output, conditions, and even other loops. A ***nested loop*** refers to a loop contained inside the body of another loop. An example of a

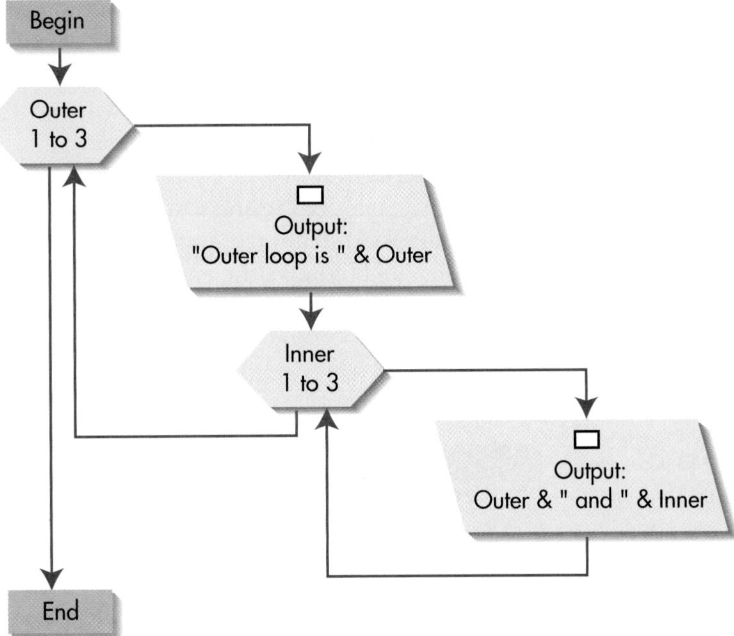


**FIGURE 3.14** *A Nested Loop Example*

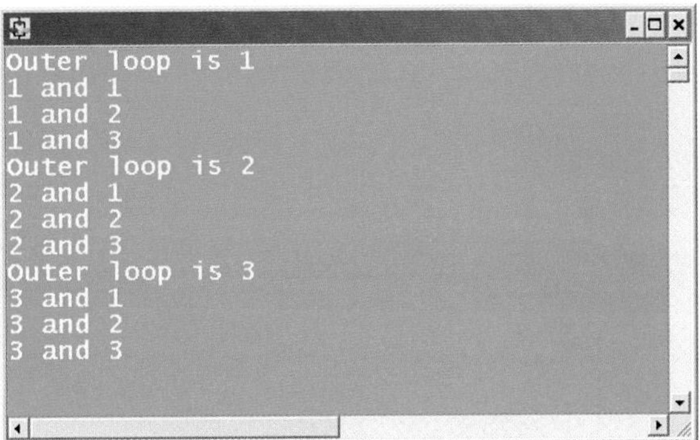

Outer loop is 1
1 and 1
1 and 2
1 and 3
Outer loop is 2
2 and 1
2 and 2
2 and 3
Outer loop is 3
3 and 1
3 and 2
3 and 3


**FIGURE 3.15** *Output for Nested Loop Example*

nested loop is shown in the Figure 3-14 solution. The output of this nested loop is shown in Figure 3-15.

## Triangle Problem

To illustrate the power of nested loops, consider the problem of displaying a series of circles that form a right triangle like the following:

```
o
oo
ooo
oooo
ooooo
oooooo
ooooooo
oooooooo
ooooooooo
oooooooooo
```

This triangle has ten lines of output. This suggests the solution should use a loop from 1 to 10 in which each pass through the loop generates one line of output.

When examining each line of output, we realize that each line contains the same number of circles as the line number (e.g., line four has four circles, line five has five circles, etc.). The solution therefore has an outer loop **`LineCount`** from 1 to 10 to print the ten lines of the triangle, with an inner loop **`CircleCount`** from 1 to **`LineCount`** for printing each line of circles.

Each horizontal line of circles can be generated by a series of console output statements, each containing a single circle followed immediately by the end-of-output symbol (§). After the final circle in a line, an additional console output statement is required to move the end-of-output symbol (§) to the beginning of the next line (Figure 3-16). Figures 3-17 and 3-18 show the final solution and the resulting output.

**FIGURE 3.16** *Console Outputs for Triangle Solution*

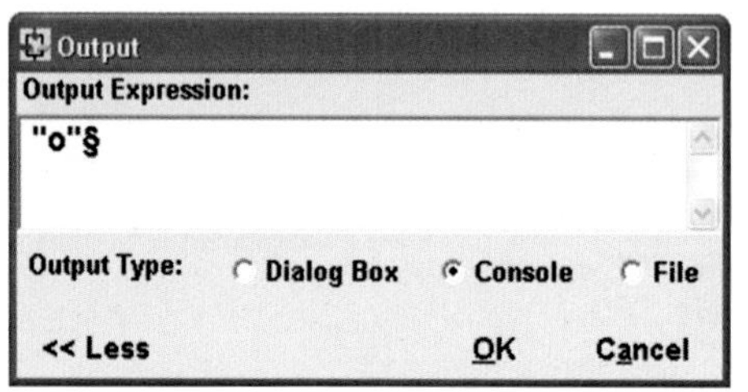


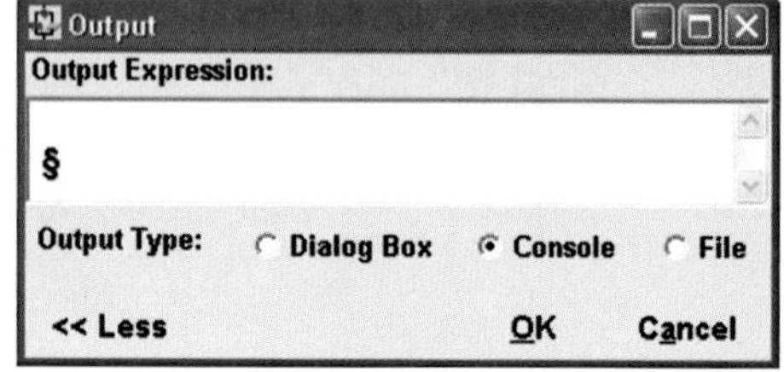


**FIGURE 3.17** *Solution to Triangle Problem*

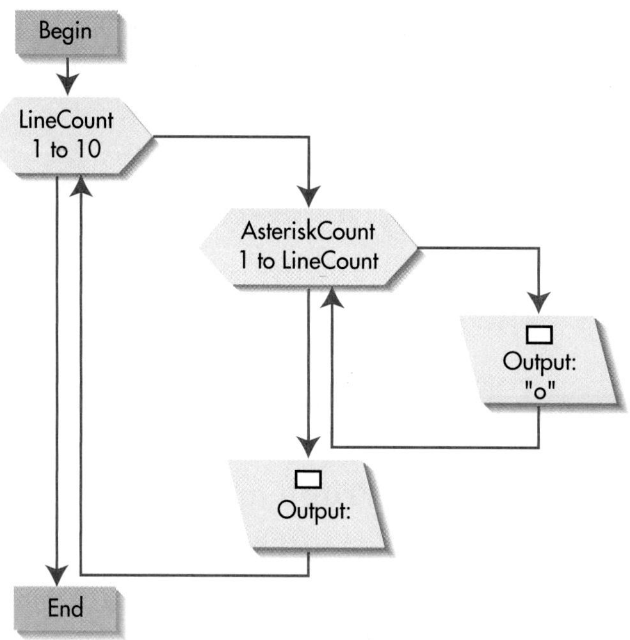

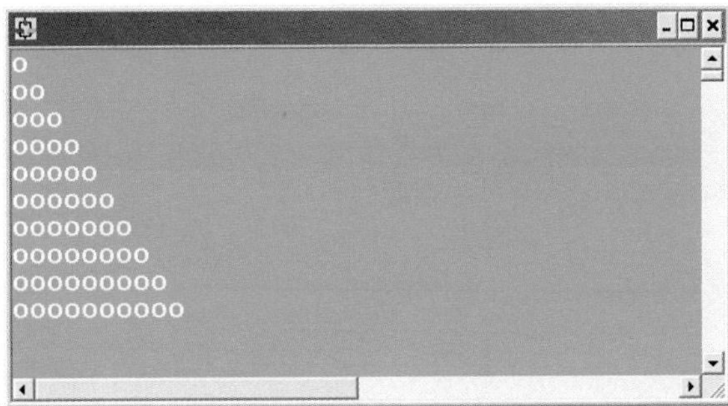
o
oo
ooo
oooo
ooooo
oooooo
ooooooo
oooooooo
ooooooooo
oooooooooo

**FIGURE 3.18** *Output for Triangle Problem Solution*

CASE STUDY
SOLUTION:

## High-Low Game

"Now let's try to develop a solution to the High-Low game. We can use the Random function to generate the secret number from 1 to 1000. Will our solution require the use of a loop?" Students nod in response to Dr. Taylor's question. "Which is more appropriate for this solution, a For loop or a While loop?" Multiple students call out "While loop," pointing out that the number of times the loop will repeat is not known in advance.

"Now then, what are some of the actions that will be repeated inside the body of the loop?"

"Typing in the user's guess," says Gail.

"An appropriate 'Higher' or 'Lower' message," says Kevin.

"Anything else?" Dr. Taylor asks. After a short pause Rachel suggests, "We probably need a counter to keep up with the number of guesses."

"Very good. Let's put all those pieces together." Dr. Taylor's solution appears in Figure 3-19.

**FIGURE 3.19** *High-Low Game Solution*

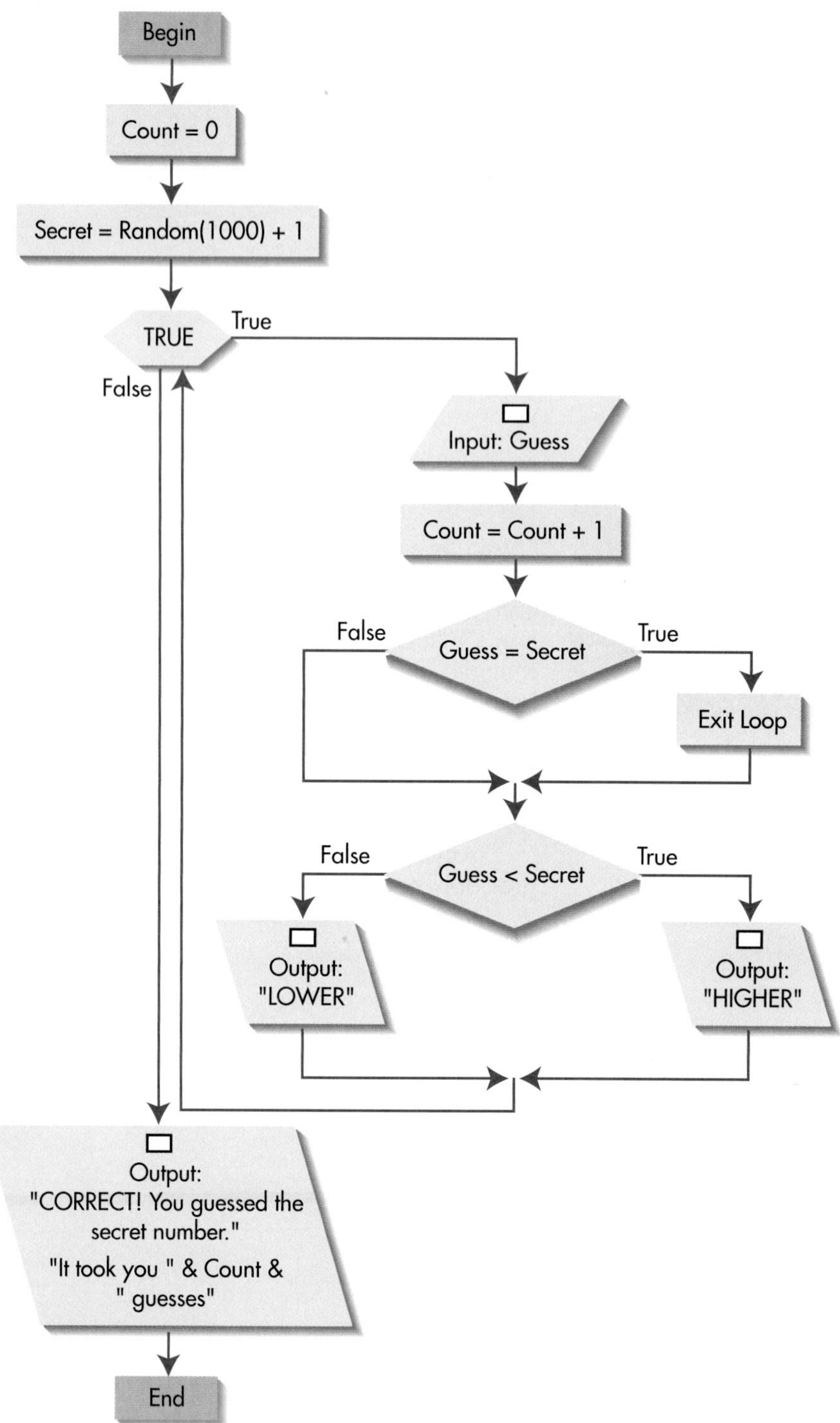

## CHAPTER SUMMARY

- Console I/O is persistent, meaning each line of input and output remains in the console window for the lifetime of the program.
- The end-of-output (§) symbol always appears at the end of the console output expression. The position of the end-of-output symbol determines the starting location for the next console I/O.
- For loops are used to repeat actions a predetermined number of times. When executed, the first action is to initialize the loop variable to the start value. The body of the loop then executes. After the body of the loop executes, the loop variable is updated by the step value, and the process is repeated as long as the value of the loop variable does not exceed the final value.
- While loops are used to repeat actions an unknown number of times. The body of the loop executes as long as the looping condition is true. When using the pre-test version of the While loop, the condition is tested first, and the loop body only executes if the initial test is true. When using the post-test version of the while loop, the loop body executes before the condition is tested; thus, the loop always executes at least one time. Both loops terminate when the condition evaluates to false.
- Counters and accumulators are variables typically used inside a loop to help calculate counts, totals, and averages. Counters are incremented by one, and accumulators are updated by the value of a variable.
- The Exit loop statement causes control to jump directly to the statement following the current loop.
- A nested loop refers to a loop that appears inside the body of another loop.

## KEY TERMS

accumulator p. 41
console input p. 36
console output p. 36
counter p. 41
end-of-output symbol (§) p. 37
Exit loop p. 45
final value p. 38
For loop p. 38
initial value p. 38
loop variable p. 38
loop-and-a-half problem p. 45
nested loop p. 46
post-test loop p. 42
pre-test loop p. 42
sentinel value p. 44
step value p. 38
While loop p. 42

## REVIEW QUESTIONS

1. What is the difference between a For loop and a While loop?
2. What is the difference between an accumulator variable and a counter variable?
3. What is the difference between a While loop with a pre-test and a While loop with a post-test?
4. Consider the solution to the High-Low game shown in Figure 3-19. If the assignment statement `Secret = Random(1000) + 1` was moved into the body of the loop, would the solution still work correctly?
5. Consider the solution to the High-Low game shown in Figure 3-19. If the assignment statement `Count = Count + 1` was moved to the top of the loop body, would the solution still work correctly?
6. Consider the solution to the High-Low game shown in Figure 3-19. If the assignment statement `Count = Count + 1` was moved to the bottom of the loop body, would the solution still work correctly?

## ▶ Programming Exercises

**3-1. Merry Christmas.** Write a program that uses a loop to display "Ho Ho Ho Merry Christmas" to console output. *Note:* Your program should use the word *Ho* only once.

**3-2. It's Hip to be Square.** Write a program that displays the squares of the numbers 1 to 10 to console output.

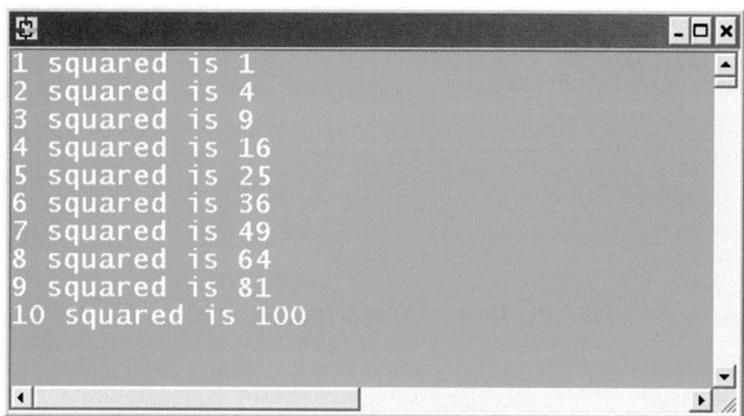


**3-3. Average I.** Write a program that uses a For loop to read exactly five values from the user and then display their average.

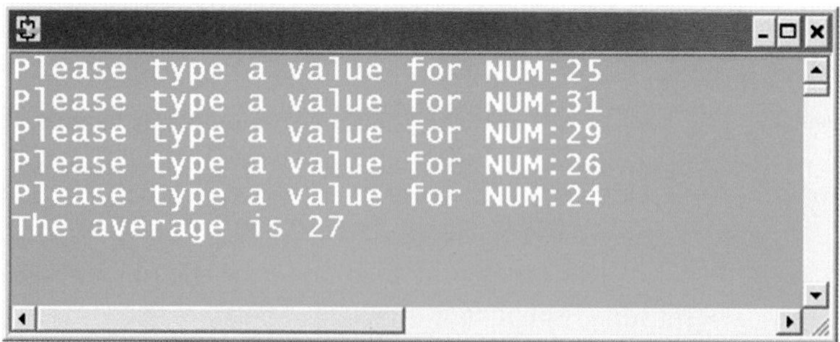

**3-4. Average II.** The solution to Average I only works if the user wants to input five values. Modify the previous program so it begins by asking the user for the number of values. The program then uses a For loop to read the specified number of values and then display their average.

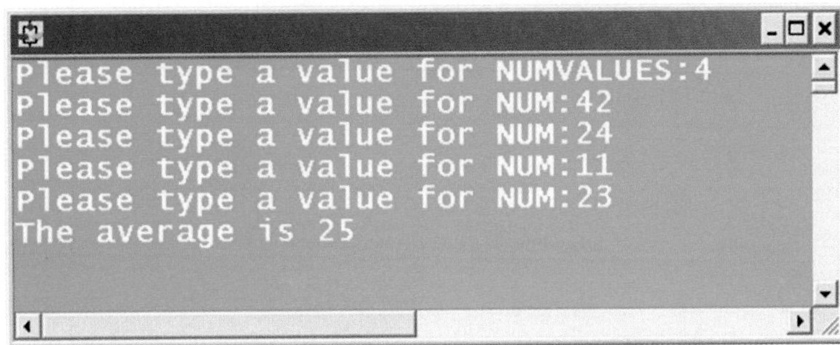


**3-5. Average III.** The solution to Average II works for any number of values. However, the user must know in advance how many values will be entered. Write a new program that reads a list of values from the user until the user enters the sentinel value -1. At that point the program should display the average of the values entered (not including the sentinel).

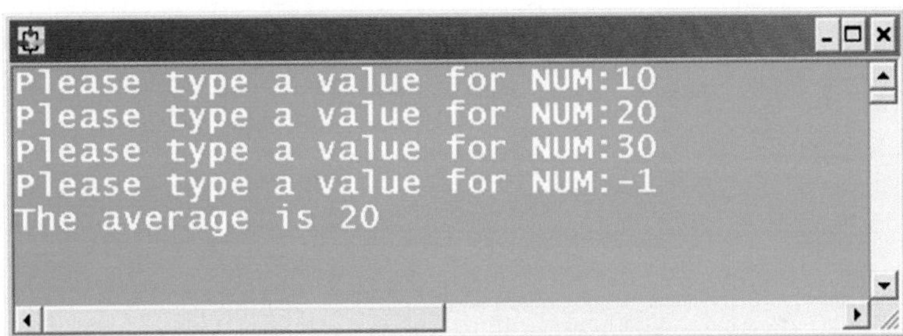


**3-6. The Two Step.** Write a program with only one loop that prints the even numbers from 20 to 60 (20, 22, 24, . . . , 58, 60). Then modify the program (still using only one loop) so that the number 40 does not print, but instead print two # symbols in its place (20, 22, . . . , 38, ##, 42, . . . , 58, 60).

**3-7. King of the Hill.** Write a program that reads in a list of positive integers from the user until the user enters the value –1 as a sentinel. At that time the program should display the largest value in the input list.

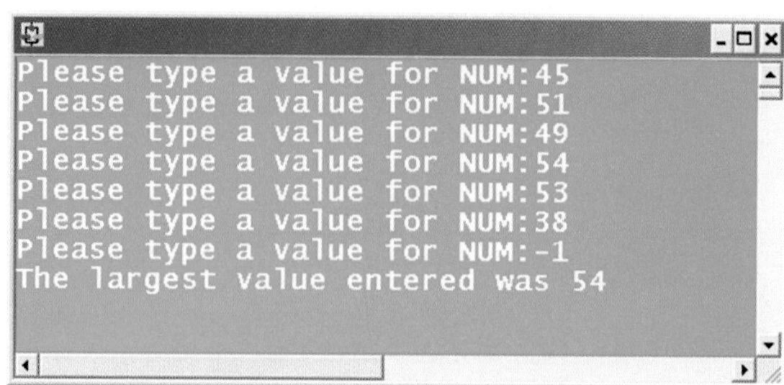

Please type a value for NUM:45
Please type a value for NUM:51
Please type a value for NUM:49
Please type a value for NUM:54
Please type a value for NUM:53
Please type a value for NUM:38
Please type a value for NUM:-1
The largest value entered was 54

**3-8. Right Triangle.** Write a program that generates the following triangle to console output. Note that the number of blank spaces decreases each line.

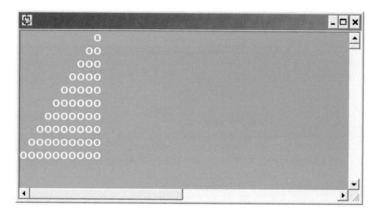

**3-9. Triangle.** Write a program that generates the following triangle to console output. Note that every line contains an odd number of circles.

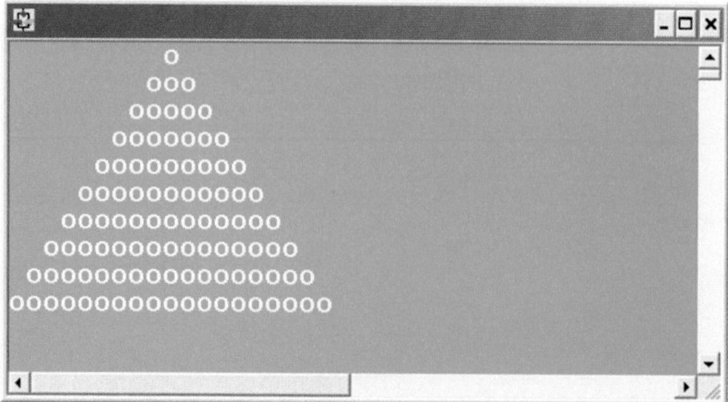

**3-10. Diamond.** Modify your solution to the triangle problem to generate the following diamond.

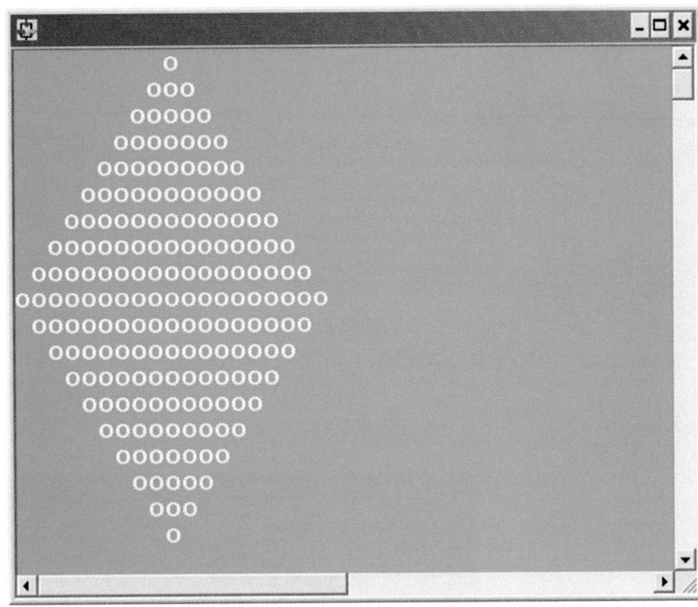

**3-11. High-Low Redux.** Write a solution to the High-Low game problem without using the Exit loop statement.

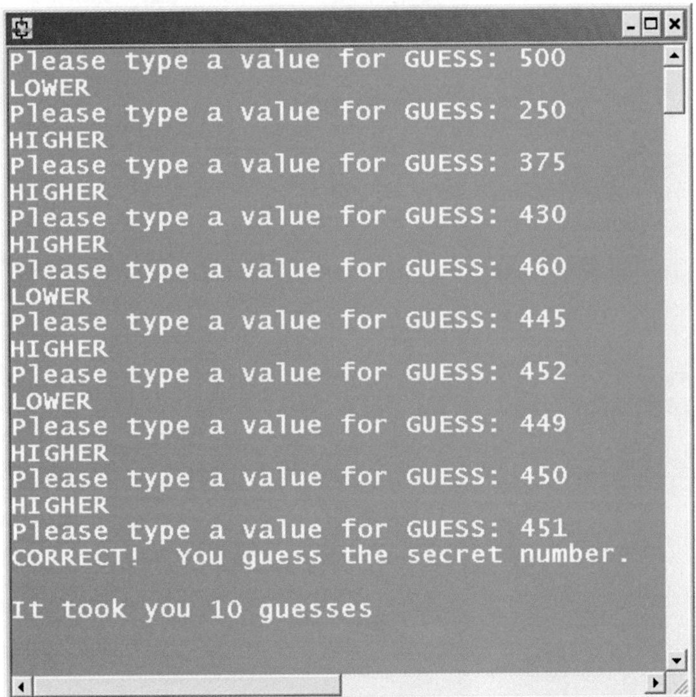

CHAPTER 4

# Arrays

## OUTLINE

▶ INTERVIEW

## Dave Moles, Prentice Hall

***Interviewer:*** Please tell us how you got involved in the IT industry?

***Moles:*** A few years after high school I found myself working in the college software department of Prentice Hall. It was a small department, but it handled all of the computer software, which at the time numbered in the low hundreds and was only available on media known as 5" diskettes. As the years passed, I was involved in many aspects of the IT industry, such as technical writing, object oriented programming, multimedia/web application development, digital video production, project management, process control, and so on.

***Interviewer:*** What is important for students to learn in a first programming course?

***Moles:*** Logic and decision mapping. It's key to helping a programmer create the flow of a particular application function and form good data structures.

***Interviewer:*** What is the best part of your job?

***Moles:*** Helping people meet a particular need or solving a problem related to computer technology. There are a lot of people out there who are uncomfortable using computer technology, and some of them will always be that way. So it's up to us, the computer professionals, to help them to use the technology to achieve a goal in a seamless fashion.

***Interviewer:*** What has been your personal key to success?

***Moles:*** My best friend once told me, "If you're not going to do something right, then don't bother doing it at all," and I have tried to keep that in mind whenever I've been working on a project. It's really a philosophical concept and one that speaks volumes, but for the sake of brevity, I'll just say that in respect to programming you will learn the right ways to do things, but somewhere down the line you'll probably learn about certain shortcuts that, at face value, appear to be cheap and easy substitutes but are not 100 percent effective, and you'll risk your credibility by using them.

## OBJECTIVES

At the completion of this chapter, you will

- **Understand the concept of an array**
- **Be able to declare arrays of various sizes**
- **Be able to populate and access the elements in an array**
- **Understand how to manipulate and process an array**
- **Consider multiple problems that benefit from an array solution**
- **Understand the Bubble Sort algorithm**

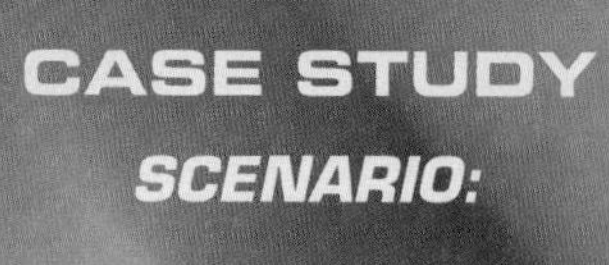


# Sorting Data

A dozen umbrellas lie on the ground just inside the classroom door when Dr. Taylor begins his lecture. "A cold, rainy day like today makes me want to stay in and order pizza for delivery rather than go out myself." Handing a phone book to a student in the front row, Dr. Taylor says "Gail, please look up the phone number for Domino's Pizza on Main Street, and if you don't mind, I will time how long it takes you to find the number." Gail flips through a few pages while Dr. Taylor looks at his watch. "Here it is . . . 555-8275," she says.

"Seven seconds. Thank you Gail." Dr. Taylor presses some keys on his cell phone while continuing his conversation. "Now please look up the name of the person with the phone number 555-5982, and again I will time you." Dr. Taylor's focus returns to his watch even as he speaks into the phone. Gail slowly flips a couple of pages, then stops just about the same time Dr. Taylor ends his call. "I assure you the number is in there, Gail. We will wait while you look it up."

"You will probably wait a long time," she says, "because there is no fast way to find a number."

"Why not? It's the same data."

"But the phone book is sorted by names, so finding a name is easy. Finding a number is very difficult because a phone book is not sorted by numbers."

Dr. Taylor takes the phone book from Gail. "Exactly! The sorting process does not change the data, but it organizes the data in a context, making it useful information. Sorting is a fundamental processing activity, and we will discuss it very soon.

"But first, we need to discuss arrays, which are a useful means to hold large amounts of data, sorted or unsorted."

Dr. Taylor's sorting solution is presented later in this chapter.

## 4-1 Arrays

Remember that variables are storage locations. Up to this point, we have only seen variables that can store a single piece of data. Sometimes it is beneficial for a variable to hold a collection of related data as a group. Examples of related data include the names of all the employees of a company, the batting averages of all the players on a baseball team, or the grade point averages of all the students in a graduating class. The easiest and most common way to store such related data is with an array.

> ▶▶▶ **Tip**
> **The array length for a zero-based array is always one more than the upper bound. For example, an array with four elements will have index values 0, 1, 2 and 3. This array therefore has a length of 4 and an upper bound of 3.**

An ***array*** is a variable that holds a collection of related data values. Each of the values in an array is called an ***element***. Each element in the array is identified by an integer value called its ***index***, which indicates the position of the element in the array.

Most modern programming languages implement ***zero-based arrays***, meaning that array index values begin with 0. The ***array length*** is the number of elements in the array. The ***upper bound*** of an array is the index of the last element.

Figure 4-1 shows an array named *Scores* with an upper bound of 8. There are therefore nine elements, Scores(0) through Scores(8). In many ways, each element is like a separate variable, capable of storing and recalling a value as needed. The array elements, like variables, have an initial value of 0 but should be treated as if they were unassigned and unknown.

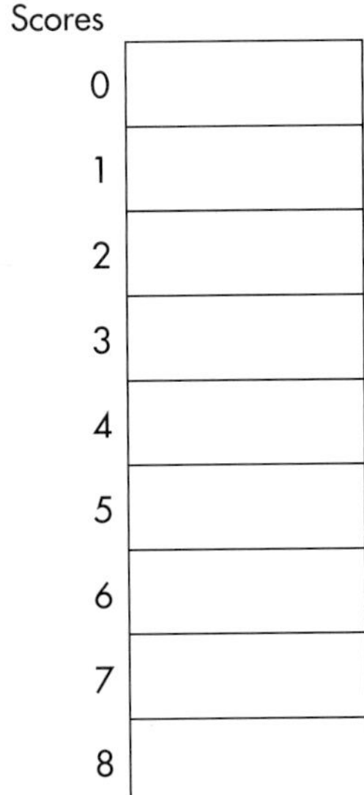


**FIGURE 4.1** *A Scores Array Structure with an Upper Bound of 8*

## Creating an Array

In Visual Logic you create, or declare, an array using the ***Make Array command***. The Make Array edit dialog contains a text box for entering the name of the array and its upper bound. Figure 4-2 shows the Visual Logic declaration for creating the array structure shown in Figure 4-1.

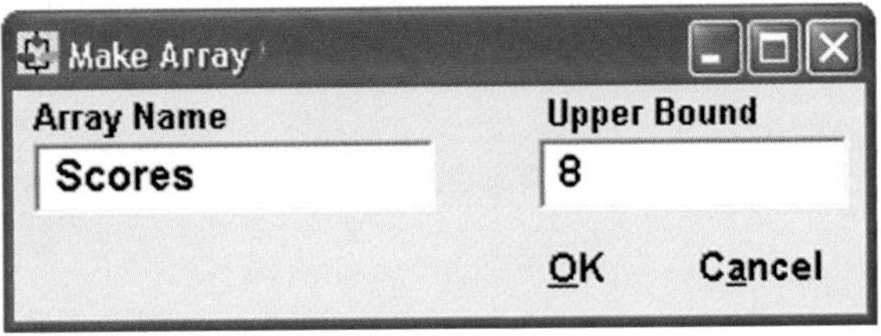


**FIGURE 4.2** *The Make Array Edit Dialog Box*

## Accessing Individual Elements of an Array

To access individual array elements, you specify the array name and follow it with an index expression enclosed in parentheses. The value of the expression determines which element to access. The index to an array can be an integer constant, an integer variable, or an integer expression. For example, Figure 4-3 shows the values in the Scores array after four elements have been referenced.

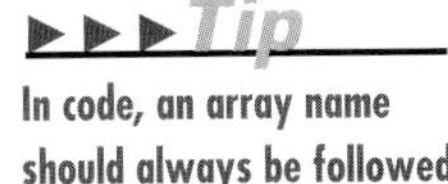

**In code, an array name should always be followed by an index value inside parentheses.**

A reference to `Scores(9)` would generate an out-of-bounds error. Arrays contain a finite number of elements, each of which is referenced by a unique index. If you attempt to reference an array with an index value greater than the upper bound of the array, the result will be an ***out-of-bounds error***.

Arrays are powerful tools for developers. In particular, it is common to use the For loop in conjunction with an array—the loop variable is used to index the array. For example, consider a flowchart that creates a Squares array with an upper bound of 10 and fills the array elements with the square of their index. Figure 4-4 shows the resulting contents of the Squares array.

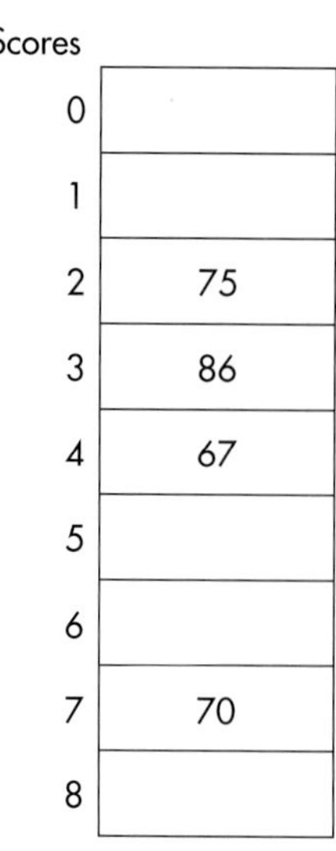


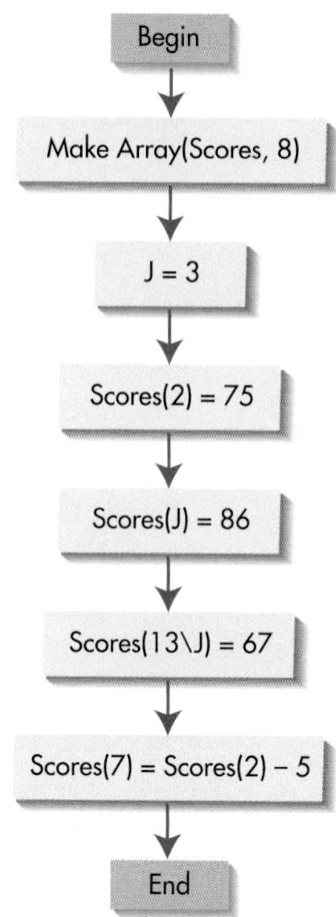


**FIGURE 4.3** *The Scores Array after Four Elements have been Referenced*

Squares

| | |
|---|---|
| 0 | 0 |
| 1 | 1 |
| 2 | 4 |
| 3 | 9 |
| 4 | 16 |
| 5 | 25 |
| 6 | 36 |
| 7 | 49 |
| 8 | 64 |
| 9 | 81 |
| 10 | 100 |

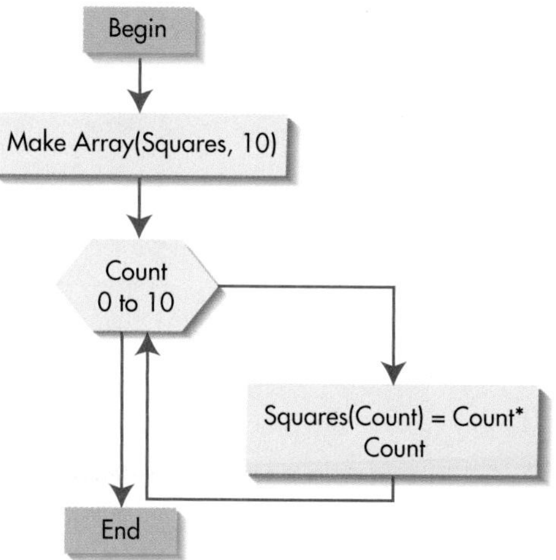


**FIGURE 4.4** *An Array with Eleven Elements*

**Tip**

**When working with arrays, make sure the index values used to select an element are within the range of the array bounds. Referencing an array element outside of the array bounds will either create an error or, in some languages, generate unpredictable results, neither of which is desirable.**

## When to Use Arrays

Arrays are useful when you are storing or processing large amounts of related data because all the values can be contained in a single array variable and accessed using a loop variable as the array index value. Arrays are also useful when information must be stored and processed twice. Consider the Reverse Order problem of reading ten values from the user and displaying those values in reverse order. An array-based solution for this problem is straightforward. First, you declare an array to hold ten values. Then you use a loop to read in the ten values. Finally, you use a second loop to display the values in reverse order. A flowchart for this solution follows.

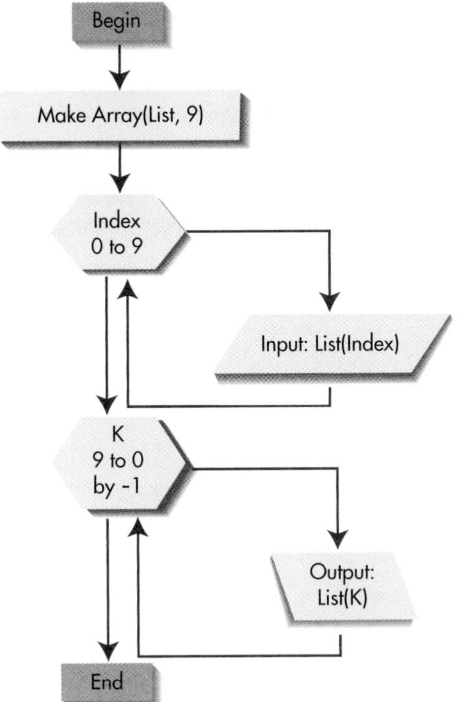


## Quick Check 4-A

Consider the preceding Reverse Order problem when answering the following questions.

1. Implement the flowchart solution shown above. Run the solution to verify that it works.
2. Write a Visual Logic solution to the Reverse Order problem without using an array.
3. Consider your Visual Logic solutions to problems 1 and 2. Which solution would be most easily modified to handle one hundred input values?

## Array Summary

- An array is a storage location that holds a collection of related data.
- The values in the array are called the array elements.
- Individual elements in an array are identified by means of an index. Index values are integer values from 0 to the upper bound of the array.
- When referencing an element of an array, the index is written in parentheses, as in A(5) or A(Count).
- The index value that references an array can be provided by an integer constant, an integer variable, or an integer expression. This gives a great deal of power to developers when using arrays.
- It is common to use the For loop in conjunction with an array—the loop is used to index the array.
- Arrays are useful when working with large amounts of related data or data that needs to be processed multiple times.

# 4-2 Above Average Problem (Mutual Funds)

Perhaps the best way to learn about arrays is to see them in action. Consider the following situation.

Jim is a financial analyst with many large investment clients. Each year Jim identifies ten different mutual funds that he shares with his clients for investing. At the end of each year he keeps the funds that performed better than the ten-fund average and replaces the others with new funds.

Write a program to input the annual growth rate for each of the ten funds in Jim's recommended fund list. The program should determine the average of the ten funds; it should then display all the funds that have a higher than average growth rate.

## Analysis and Design

This problem requires that the data be processed twice. First, all the data must be read to determine the average of the ten funds. Then all the data must be processed again to test each element against the average. Storing the data in an array makes the data available throughout the lifetime of the program. The solution is shown in Figure 4-5. A sample output is shown in Figure 4-6.

**FIGURE 4.5** *Solution for Mutual Funds Problem*

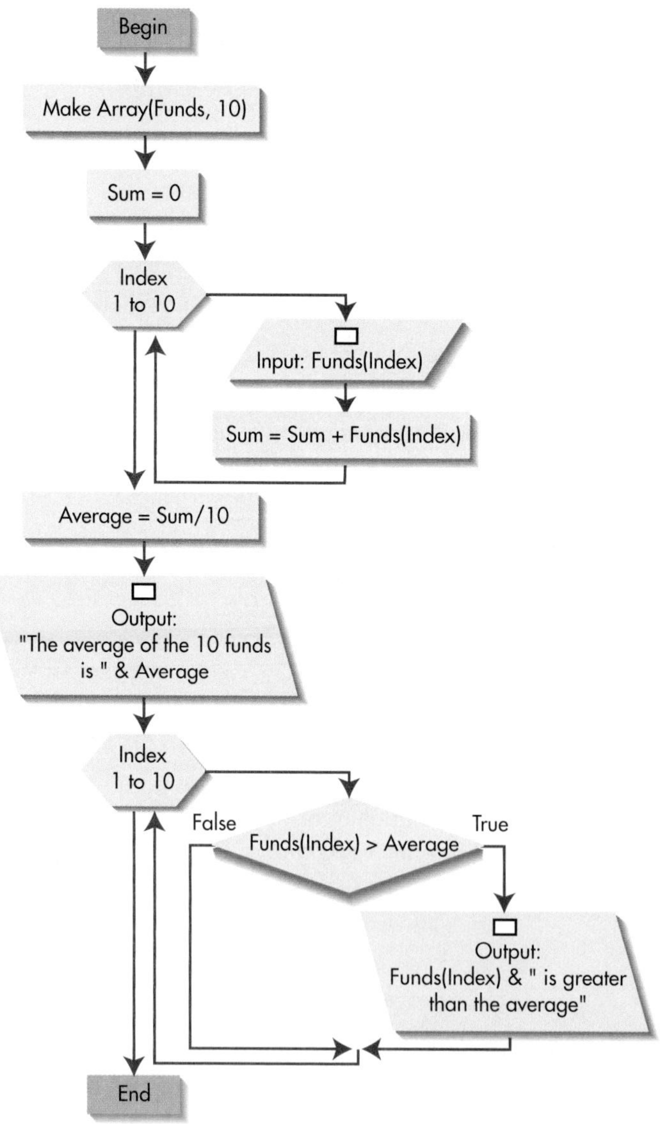

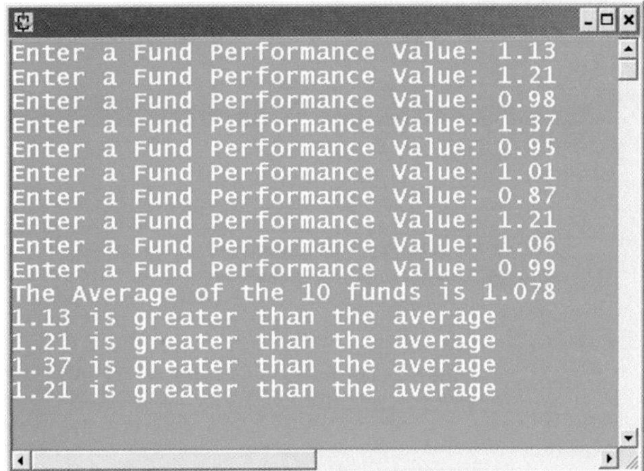

Enter a Fund Performance Value: 1.13
Enter a Fund Performance Value: 1.21
Enter a Fund Performance Value: 0.98
Enter a Fund Performance Value: 1.37
Enter a Fund Performance Value: 0.95
Enter a Fund Performance Value: 1.01
Enter a Fund Performance Value: 0.87
Enter a Fund Performance Value: 1.21
Enter a Fund Performance Value: 1.06
Enter a Fund Performance Value: 0.99
The Average of the 10 funds is 1.078
1.13 is greater than the average
1.21 is greater than the average
1.37 is greater than the average
1.21 is greater than the average


**FIGURE 4.6** *Mutual Funds Solution Output*

## *Quick Check 4-B*

The solution in Figure 4-5 stores values in array positions 1 through 10. Modify the program to store values in array positions 0 through 9, with an array upper bound of 9.

# 4-3 Largest Value Problem (Highest GPA)

Finding the largest or smallest value in a list is a fundamental activity for developers. Consider the following situation.

> The Alpha Beta Gamma fraternity is one of many popular Greek organizations on campus. Every semester, ABΓ recognizes the graduating brother who has the highest GPA. The number of graduates changes from semester to semester.

Write a program that accepts as input the number of ABΓ brothers graduating at the end of the current semester. The program then creates an appropriately sized array and reads the GPA values for each graduating brother. The program should determine and display the largest GPA value in the list.

## Analysis and Design

The solution will use an array whose upper bound is specified by an input variable. The solution is then simply a matter of finding the largest value in a list.

There are two common solutions to finding the largest value in a list. The first approach uses a *value* placeholder variable (Figure 4-7). The second solution uses an *index* placeholder variable (Figure 4-8).

Examine the solutions in these two figures—you will find they are very similar. In both cases, the first input value is used to declare the upper bound of the GPA array. Both solutions then read the first GPA value, store it into the array, and also store the placeholder variable. A loop is then used to read all the remaining values in the list.

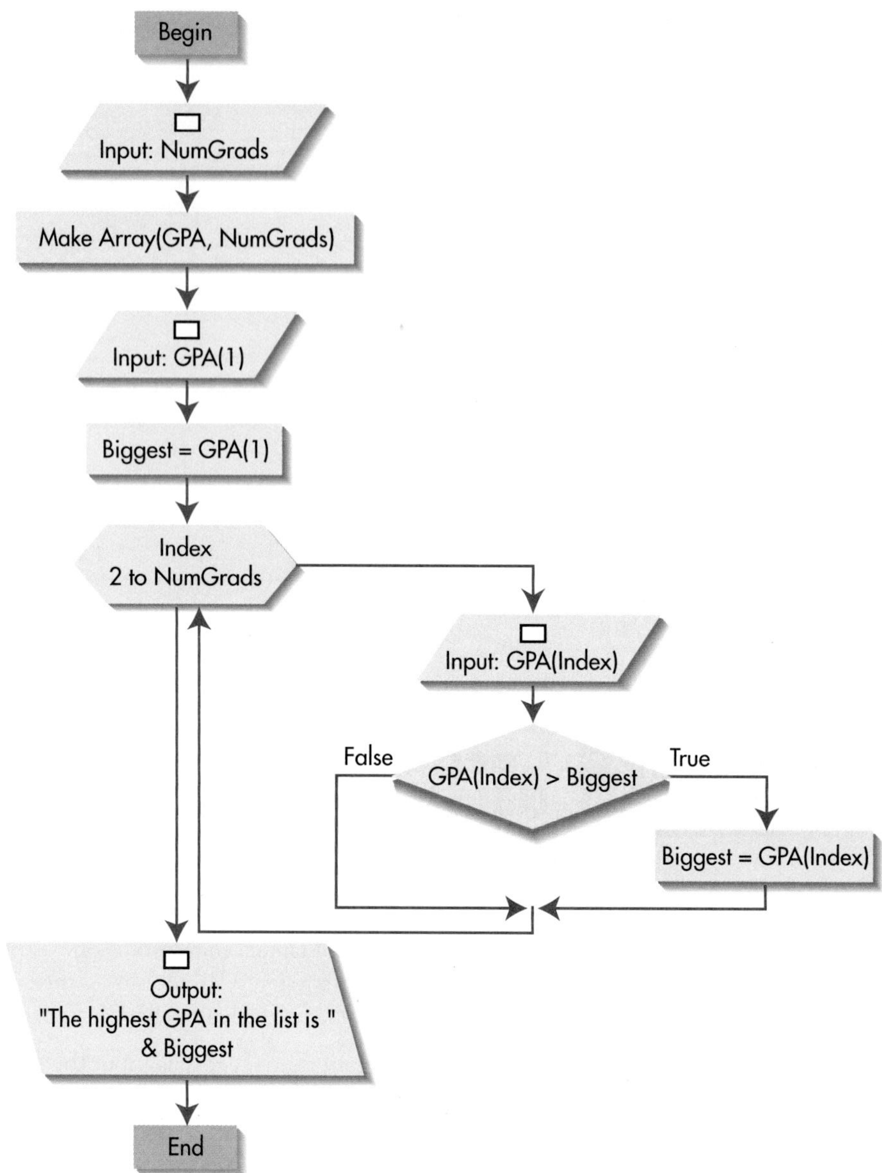


**FIGURE 4.7** *GPA Solution using the Value of the Largest Element*

After each remaining value is read, a comparison is made with the placeholder variable. If the new value is greater than the placeholder value, the placeholder variable is updated appropriately. Finally, after all values have been read and tested, the solution displays the appropriate placeholder value, which is the largest value in the list. The console I/O in Figure 4-9 could have been generated by either the Figure 4-7 solution or the Figure 4-8 solution.

## ASK THE AUTHOR

**Q** Why did you use an array in the GPA solution?

**A** I wanted to illustrate the difference between an index placeholder variable and a value placeholder variable. Experienced developers often write solutions that manipulate index values because those values provide the most power and flexibility. Given the index of an element, a developer can easily pull up the element's value. Furthermore, given an index value, the developer can also determine the previous index value and therefore the previous element value, the following index value and therefore the following element value, and so on.

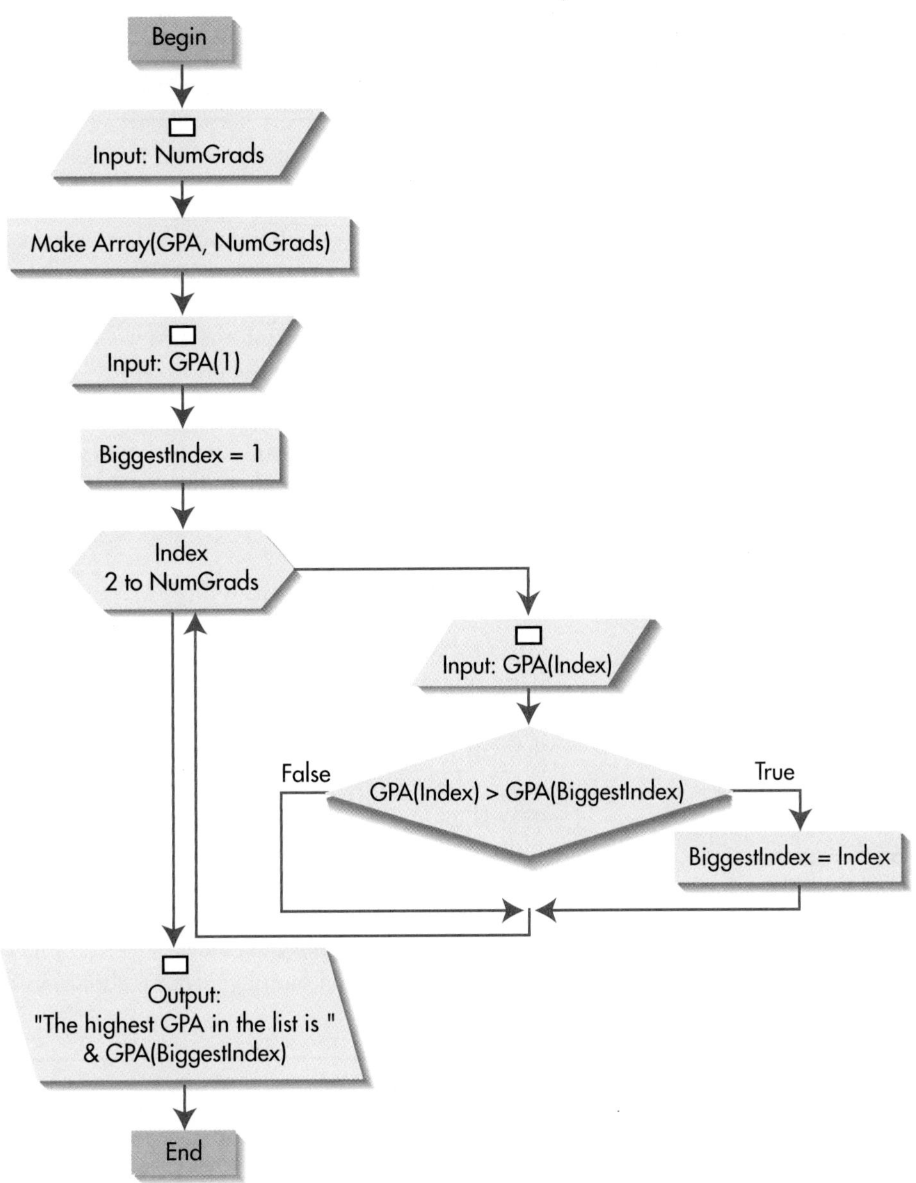


**FIGURE 4.8** *GPA Solution using the Index of the Largest Element*

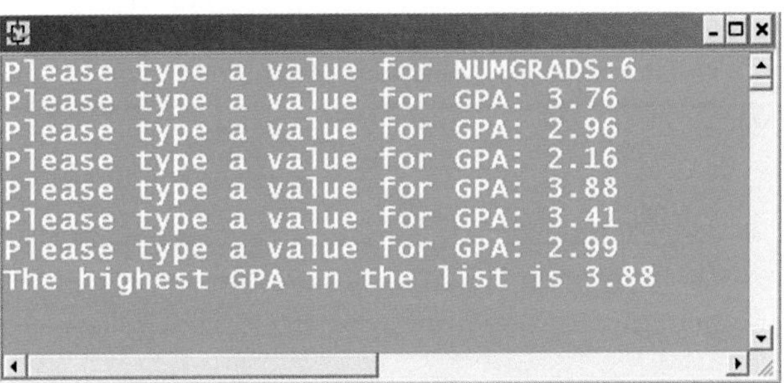

Please type a value for NUMGRADS:6
Please type a value for GPA: 3.76
Please type a value for GPA: 2.96
Please type a value for GPA: 2.16
Please type a value for GPA: 3.88
Please type a value for GPA: 3.41
Please type a value for GPA: 2.99
The highest GPA in the list is 3.88


**FIGURE 4.9** *Console I/O for GPA Solution*

## Quick Check 4-C

The solution in Figure 4-8 stores values beginning at index position 1. Modify the program to store values starting at index position 0.

# 4-4 Working with Index Values (Two-Week Totals)

In this section we look at a problem involving consecutive element values. Consider the following situation.

> Anthony owns a small business and plans to install new inventory hardware and software during the upcoming year. The installation process will require two weeks. To minimize the disruption that will occur during the migration, Anthony wants to deploy the system during the two weeks that had the lowest consecutive two-week total gross sales during the previous year.

Write a program that uses an array to hold the weekly gross sales for the fifty-two weeks of the previous year. The program should determine which two consecutive weeks have the lowest total, and it should display the index values that correspond to those two weeks.

## Analysis and Design

**Tip**

**Notice that the second loop in Figure 4-10 stops one element before the upper bound. If the loop variable were the upper bound (52), then Weeks(Index + 1) would be out of bounds, causing an error.**

This problem is similar to finding the smallest or largest value in an array. The primary difference is that you are looking for the smallest consecutive pair of element values. In addition, your final solution is the week, or index, rather than the gross, or element, values, so you must determine the index of the smallest consecutive values.

We have already seen a solution for finding the index of the largest element in an array (Figure 4-8). Finding the smallest two-week total is a slight variation on that solution.

In this case, the index placeholder maintains the first of two consecutive elements whose total is the smallest evaluated so far. When a smaller pair of consecutive element values is found, the placeholder variable is updated. The solution is shown in Figure 4-10. A partial sample output is shown in Figure 4-11.

### ASK THE AUTHOR

**Q** Do I really have to enter fifty-two input values every time I run this program?

**A** Manual data entry is one of your options, but it would be time consuming. A second option would be to generate random values for the weekly gross sales. This would be fast, but the data would be unpredictable. A third option would be to specify the file option within an input dialog. When an input file is specified, all input comes from the specified file rather than the keyboard. The file WeeklyGross.txt is provided on the student CD as an input file for this problem.

## Quick Check 4-D

The solution in Figure 4-10 stores the fifty-two weekly gross values in array positions 1 through 52. Modify the program to store values in array positions 0 through 51.

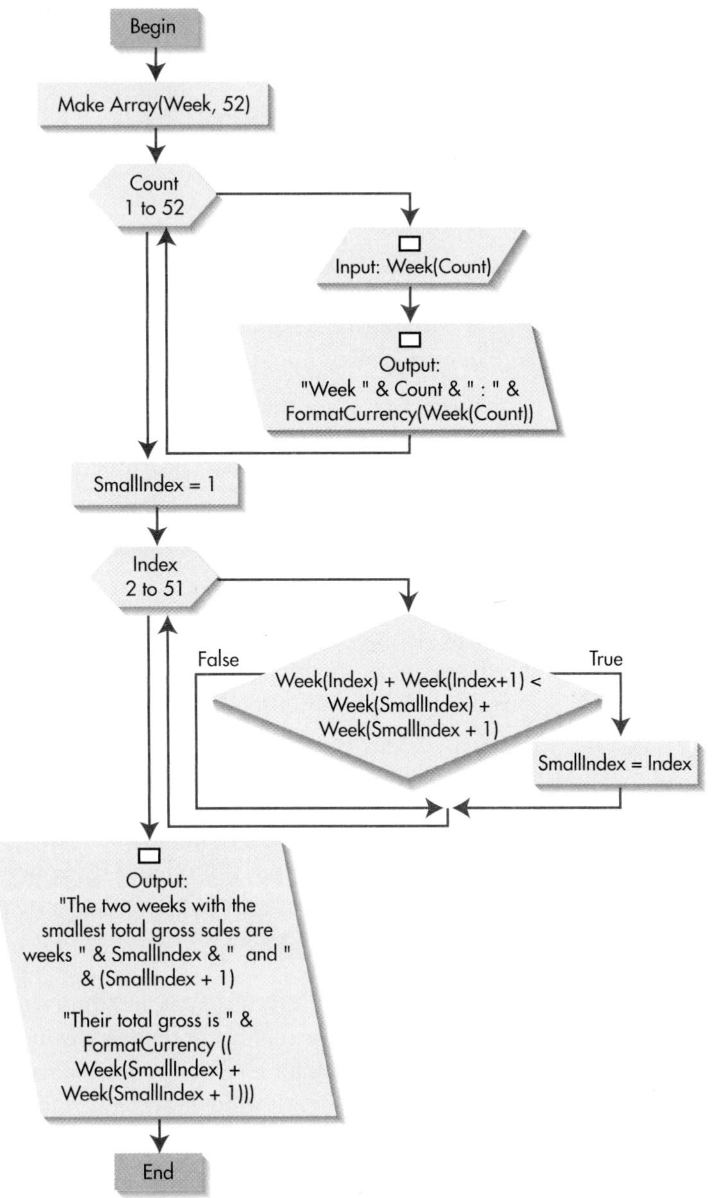


**FIGURE 4.10** *Smallest Consecutive Weeks Solution*

**FIGURE 4.11** *Output for Smallest Consecutive Weeks*

```
Week 40 : $235.00
Week 41 : $201.00
Week 42 : $232.00
Week 43 : $265.00
Week 44 : $252.00
Week 45 : $205.00
Week 46 : $209.00
Week 47 : $250.00
Week 48 : $206.00
Week 49 : $272.00
Week 50 : $275.00
Week 51 : $226.00
Week 52 : $211.00
The two weeks with the smallest
total gross sales are 45 and 46

Their total gross is $414.00
```

## 4-5 Simulation (Die Roll)

Simulations are powerful computing applications. Long before a satellite is launched or a new automobile design is moved into production, computer simulations have modeled its behavior and functionality. A less complicated simulation is presented as follows.

> A balanced die is equally likely to roll a 1, 2, 3, 4, 5, or 6. If a balanced die is rolled many times, the roll values should be evenly distributed. As the number of rolls increases, the distributions should become closer to one-sixth, or 16.67 percent. What are the percentages after forty rolls? What are the percentages after four hundred rolls?

Write a program that performs a simulation of a balanced die rolled many times. The program should use an array of counters to record the number of times each index value was rolled. The program should display the results visually as a histogram. The program should also calculate and display the percentages for each of the six roll values.

### Analysis and Design

A single die roll can be simulated using the expression Random(6) + 1. Random(6) produces one of six different values. However, the first possible value is 0, and the last possible value is 5. Adding 1 to the result produces random values between 1 and 6, which is our goal.

The solution is shown in Figure 4-12. The solution begins by creating an array to store counters for each of the six roll values. A loop is then used to generate one random roll and update the appropriate counter.

The histogram output is produced using nested loops. The inner loop generates a horizontal line of circles whose length is determined by the counter value, followed by a console output to start a new line. The outer loop repeats this process for each of the six roll values.

Finally, the solution calculates and displays the percentages for each of the six roll values by dividing the number of times a specific value was rolled by the total number of rolls. Sample outputs for forty and four hundred rolls are presented in Figure 4-13. Your histogram will be slightly different because random values will generate different totals.

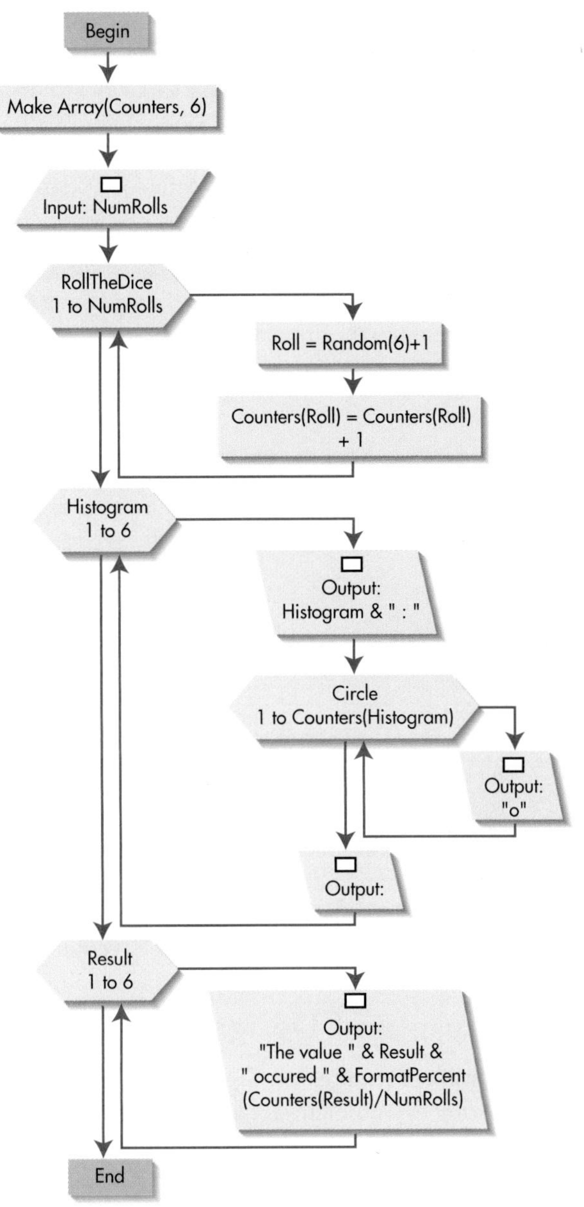


▶ **FIGURE 4.12** *Die Roll Simulation Solution*

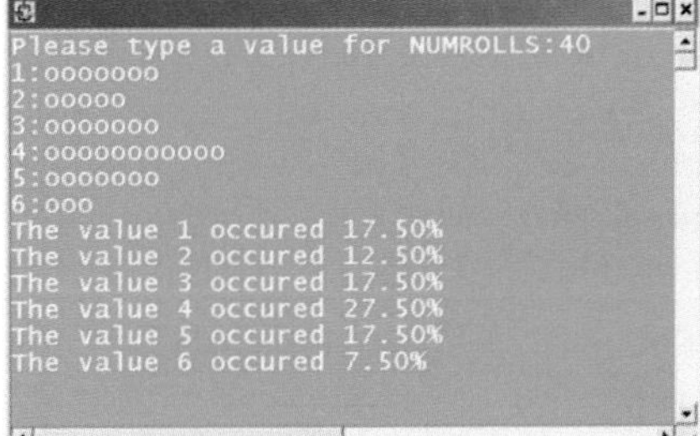


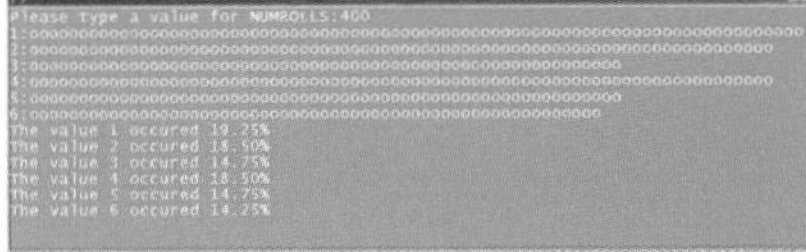

▶ **FIGURE 4.13** *Output for Die Roll Simulation*

## *Quick Check 4-E*

Run the solution in Figure 4-12 using 4000 and 40000 as the number of rolls. (Note: 40000 will take a minute or two to run, depending on the speed of your computer). What happens to the final percentages, as the total number of rolls increases?

## 4-6 Parallel Arrays (Girl Scout Cookies)

In this section we examine a problem that requires two arrays, one holding text data and the other holding numeric data. Consider the following situation.

> Every spring you look forward to buying a box of Caramel deLites Girl Scout cookies from your niece, Belinda. Her troop gives an award to the girl who sells the most boxes of cookies each year. They are looking to develop a software solution to assist in determining the annual award winner.

**Table 4.1** Girl Scout Data

| Girl Scout | Boxes Sold |
|---|---|
| Amy | 13 |
| Belinda | 51 |
| Cindy | 15 |
| Gail | 26 |
| Kelsey | 81 |
| Marilyn | 25 |
| Martha | 9 |
| Pam | 71 |
| Tammy | 43 |

Write a program that determines which Girl Scout sold the most boxes of cookies. The program should input the names of all the Girl Scouts and the number of boxes they sold this year. Table 4-1 shows a sample of this data. The program should output the Scout who sold the most boxes and the number of boxes she sold.

### Analysis and Design

This problem requires two lists, one for names and one for boxes sold. One approach for solving this problem would be to maintain these two lists in parallel arrays. ***Parallel arrays*** are two or more arrays whose elements are related by their position in the arrays. This means the fifth element in the first array is somehow related to the fifth element in the second array. For example, the data in Table 4-1 above can be represented in two parallel arrays. The first array holds the name of the person selling cookies, and the second array holds the number of boxes sold by that person (Figure 4-14).

The problem now can be viewed as a search problem for the index of the largest element in the Boxes array; that index is then used to determine the name of the girl who sold the most cookies. The solution is shown in Figure 4-15, and the output is shown in Figure 4-16.

**FIGURE 4.14** *Parallel Arrays, Names and Boxes Sold*

| Names | | Boxes | |
|---|---|---|---|
| 0 | Amy | 0 | 13 |
| 1 | Belinda | 1 | 51 |
| 2 | Cindy | 2 | 15 |
| 3 | Gail | 3 | 26 |
| 4 | Kelsey | 4 | 81 |
| 5 | Marilyn | 5 | 25 |
| 6 | Martha | 6 | 9 |
| 7 | Pam | 7 | 71 |
| 8 | Tammy | 8 | 43 |

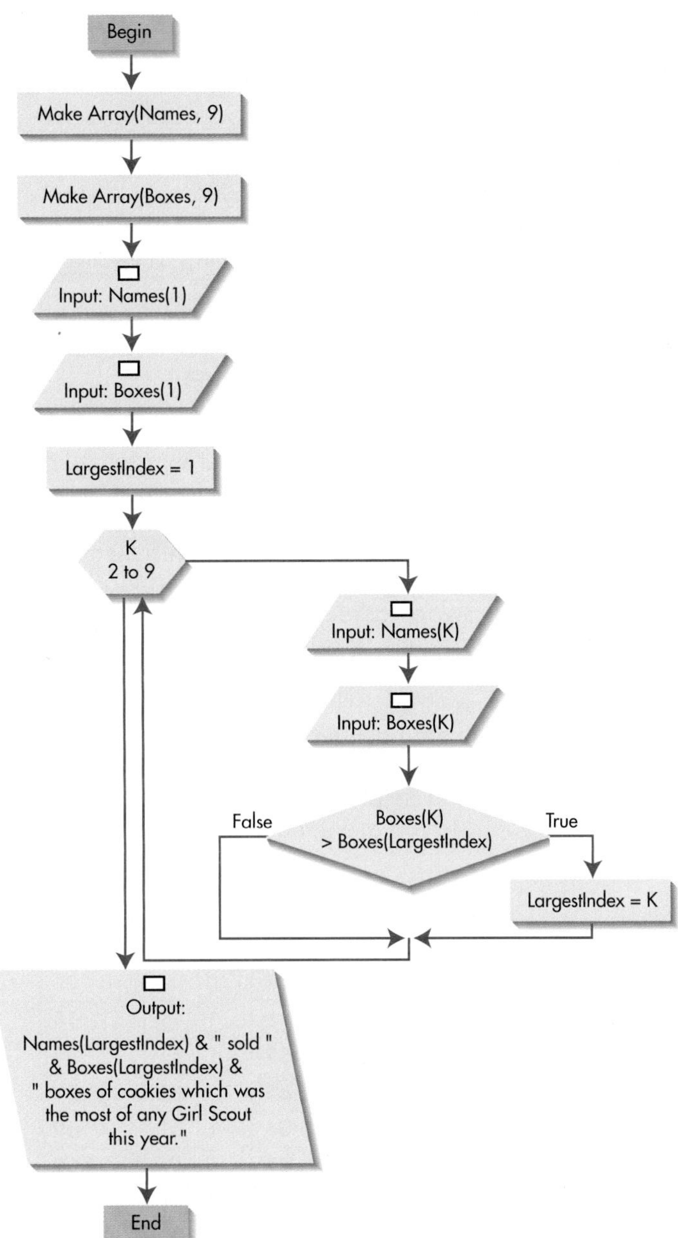


**FIGURE 4.15** *Parallel Array Solution to the Girl Scout Cookies Problem*

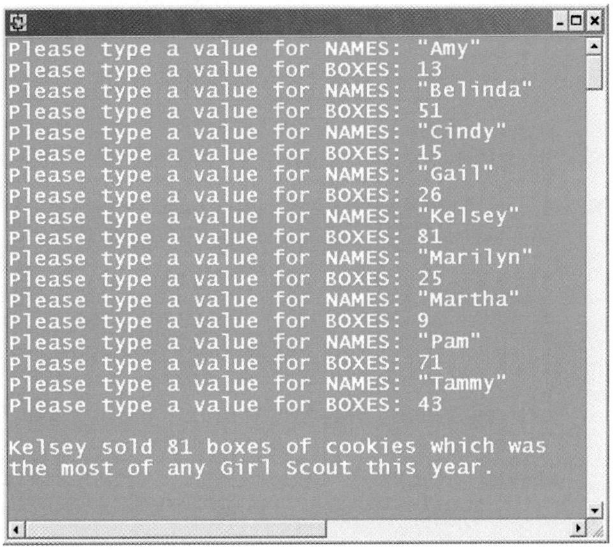

```
Please type a value for NAMES: "Amy"
Please type a value for BOXES: 13
Please type a value for NAMES: "Belinda"
Please type a value for BOXES: 51
Please type a value for NAMES: "Cindy"
Please type a value for BOXES: 15
Please type a value for NAMES: "Gail"
Please type a value for BOXES: 26
Please type a value for NAMES: "Kelsey"
Please type a value for BOXES: 81
Please type a value for NAMES: "Marilyn"
Please type a value for BOXES: 25
Please type a value for NAMES: "Martha"
Please type a value for BOXES: 9
Please type a value for NAMES: "Pam"
Please type a value for BOXES: 71
Please type a value for NAMES: "Tammy"
Please type a value for BOXES: 43

Kelsey sold 81 boxes of cookies which was
the most of any Girl Scout this year.
```

**FIGURE 4.16** *Output for Girl Scout Cookies*

## ASK THE AUTHOR

**Q** Why do you need a program to determine who sold the most cookies? I can just look at the data in the original table and figure it out in my mind.

**A** For only nine people a program is not really necessary. However, the solution works the same for nine people as it does for ninety thousand people. If you wanted to determine the highest volume seller at the national level, then a program would be essential. I used nine instead of ninety thousand to keep the data manageable. However, the solution would work equally well for either size data set.

**CASE STUDY**
***SOLUTION:***

## Sorting Data

"Probably the simplest way to sort an array is a technique called ***Bubble Sort***. The basic idea is to repeatedly compare two adjacent values and swap them if they are in the wrong order. The bigger values flow in one direction, and the smaller values flow in the other direction." Dr. Taylor turns to the blackboard, draws an array with nine elements, and fills them with apparently random values.

"The heart of the solution is a loop from the start to the end of the array. The loop swaps adjacent elements if necessary as it goes. After one pass through the array, the largest value will have moved to the end of the array." Dr. Taylor makes a few marks on the chalkboard to illustrate the eight comparisons needed to pass through the entire array and the resulting location of the largest element in the final position (see Figure 4-17).

"If you repeat the loop a second time, the second largest element will be placed in its proper location." Dr. Taylor makes additional marks on the chalk-board to represent the second pass through the array (see Figure 4-18).

**FIGURE 4.17** *Array After One Pass Using Bubble Sort (Largest value, 71, in proper location)*

| | K = 0 | K = 1 | K = 2 | K = 3 | K = 4 | K = 5 | K = 6 | K = 7 | DONE! |
|---|---|---|---|---|---|---|---|---|---|
| 0 | 24 | 24 | 24 | 24 | 24 | 24 | 24 | 24 | 24 |
| 1 | 52 | 52 | 15 | 15 | 15 | 15 | 15 | 15 | 15 |
| 2 | 15 | 15 | 52 | 52 | 52 | 52 | 52 | 52 | 52 |
| 3 | 62 | 62 | 62 | 62 | 31 | 31 | 31 | 31 | 31 |
| 4 | 31 | 31 | 31 | 31 | 62 | 52 | 52 | 52 | 52 |
| 5 | 52 | 52 | 52 | 52 | 52 | 62 | 62 | 62 | 62 |
| 6 | 71 | 71 | 71 | 71 | 71 | 71 | 71 | 44 | 44 |
| 7 | 44 | 44 | 44 | 44 | 44 | 44 | 44 | 71 | 38 |
| 8 | 38 | 38 | 38 | 38 | 38 | 38 | 38 | 38 | 71 |
| | No Swap | **Swap** | No Swap | **Swap** | **Swap** | No Swap | **Swap** | **Swap** | |

**FIGURE 4.18** *Array After Two Passes Using Bubble Sort (Largest two values, 62 and 71, in proper locations)*

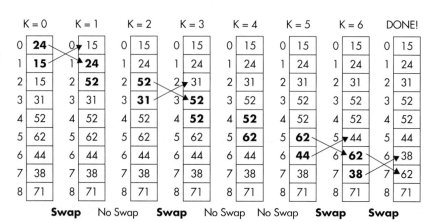

| | K = 0 | K = 1 | K = 2 | K = 3 | K = 4 | K = 5 | K = 6 | DONE! |
|---|---|---|---|---|---|---|---|---|
| 0 | 24 | 15 | 15 | 15 | 15 | 15 | 15 | 15 |
| 1 | 15 | 24 | 24 | 24 | 24 | 24 | 24 | 24 |
| 2 | 15 | 52 | 52 | 31 | 31 | 31 | 31 | 31 |
| 3 | 31 | 31 | 31 | 52 | 52 | 52 | 52 | 52 |
| 4 | 52 | 52 | 52 | 52 | 52 | 52 | 52 | 52 |
| 5 | 62 | 62 | 62 | 62 | 62 | 62 | 44 | 44 |
| 6 | 44 | 44 | 44 | 44 | 44 | 44 | 62 | 38 |
| 7 | 38 | 38 | 38 | 38 | 38 | 38 | 38 | 62 |
| 8 | 71 | 71 | 71 | 71 | 71 | 71 | 71 | 71 |
| | **Swap** | No Swap | **Swap** | No Swap | No Swap | **Swap** | **Swap** | |

Dr. Taylor continues, "After two passes, there are two elements that are certain to be in their proper locations. Three passes ensure three elements are in the proper location and so on. Sorting the array therefore requires N-1 passes where N is the number of elements in the array. If N-1 elements are in the proper location, the Nth element must also be in the proper location."

He then begins handing out a sheet with a solution similar to Figure 4-19 printed on it. "This handout shows a simple implementation of Bubble Sort. Notice the two loops we just discussed. The solution also includes code to display the sorted values." Figure 4-20 shows the output generated by the solution in Figure 4-19.

"Why is it called Bubble Sort?" Roger asks while examining the sheet.

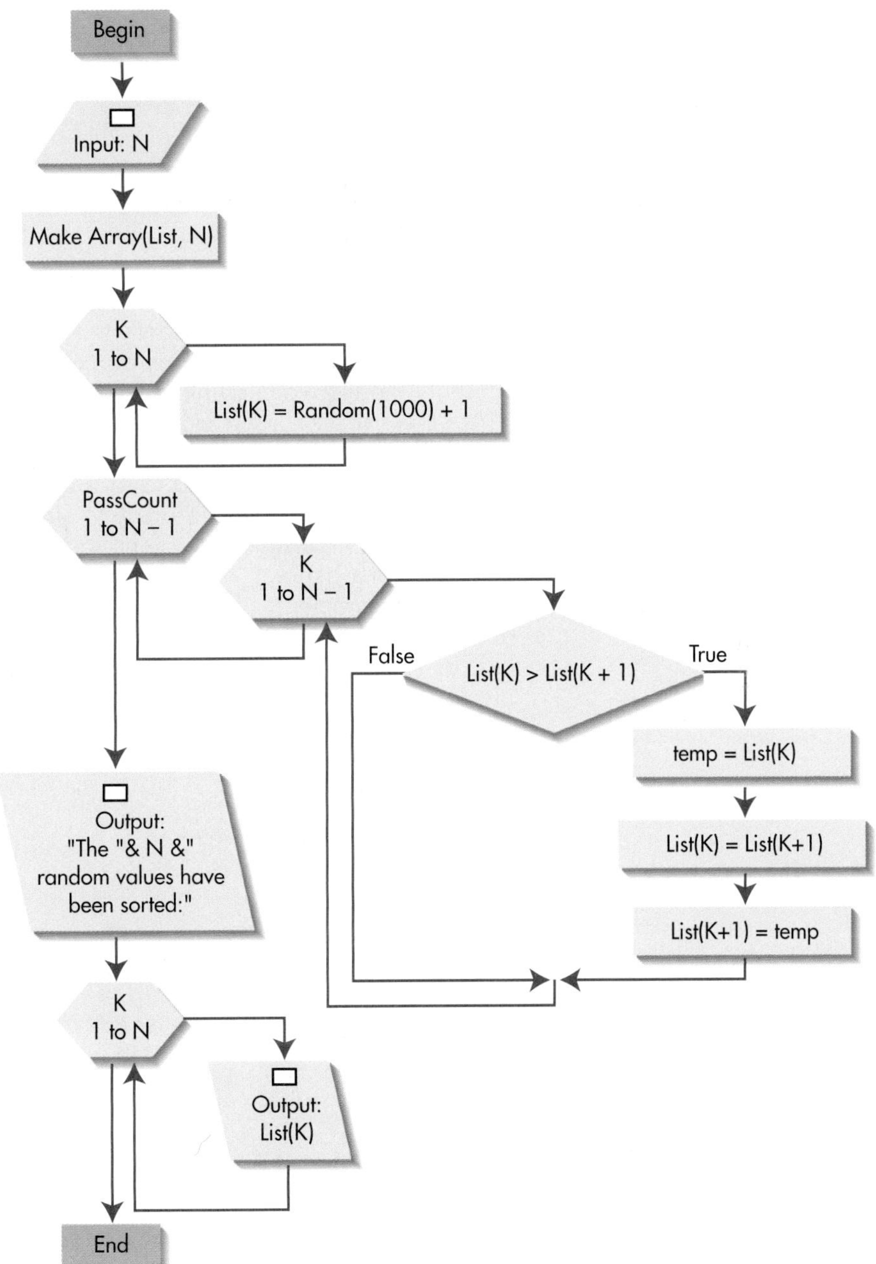


**FIGURE 4.19** *Bubble Sort Solution*

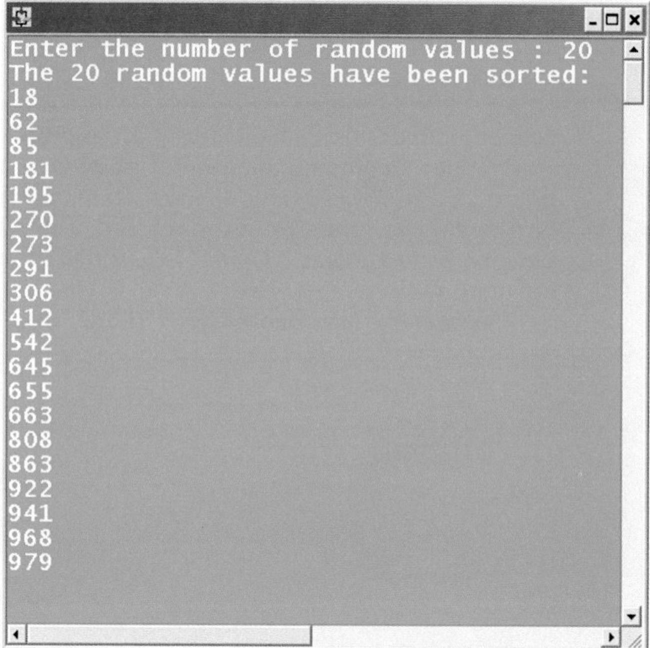

Enter the number of random values : 20
The 20 random values have been sorted:
18
62
85
181
195
270
273
291
306
412
542
645
655
663
808
863
922
941
968
979


**FIGURE 4.20** *Bubble Sort Output*

"Because the values move slowly to their final destinations like bubbles floating gradually through water. This algorithm is also sometimes called *sink sort* because the heaver values sink to the bottom."

"Are there other sorting algorithms?" Ed asks.

"Absolutely, and almost all of them run faster than Bubble Sort. But Bubble Sort is the easiest to understand, and it works fine with arrays of size five thousand or less. If the size of the array is significantly bigger than that, you will probably need to consider one of the faster, more complex sorting algorithms."

A few more aspects of the Bubble Sort algorithm are discussed in the remaining few moments of the class. Finally, there is a knock on the classroom door by a Domino's delivery person holding a flat, cardboard box. Dr. Taylor smiles, as the aroma of pepperoni and sausage pizza fills the room. Glancing at his watch, he announces, "My lunch has arrived with perfect timing. Class dismissed."

## Chapter Summary

- An array is a variable that holds a collection of related data values. Each of the values in an array is called an element. Each element in the array is identified by an integer value called its index, which indicates the position of the element in the array.
- Most modern programming languages implement zero-based arrays, meaning that array index values begin with 0. The length of an array is the number of elements in the array. The upper bound of an array is the index of the last element.
- To access individual array elements, you specify the array name and follow it with an index expression enclosed in parentheses. The value of the expression determines which element to access.
- Arrays contain a finite number of elements, each of which is referenced by a unique index. If you attempt to reference an array with an index value greater than the upper bound of the array, the result will be an out-of-bounds error.
- Parallel arrays are two or more arrays whose elements are related by their positions in the arrays.
- Bubble Sort is a simple sorting technique involving multiple passes through the array, each pass comparing adjacent elements and swapping them if necessary.

## Key Terms

**array** p. 58
**array length** p. 58
**Bubble Sort** p. 72
**element** p. 58
**index** p. 58
**Make Array command** p. 59
**out-of-bounds error** p. 59
**parallel arrays** p. 70
**upper bound** p. 58
**zero-based arrays** p. 58

## Review Questions

1. How is an array with five elements similar to five different variables?
2. How is an array with five elements different from five different variables?
3. What is the difference between an array index and an array element?
4. What is the difference between an array length and an array upper bound?
5. In Visual Logic, how is an array declared?
6. The index value that references an array can be a constant or a variable. Explain how this is helpful to developers.
7. Identify some general recommendations for when to use an array.
8. Consider the Bubble Sort solution in Figure 4-19. What is the purpose of the Temp variable? Explain why swapping two values could not be done without a third storage location.

## Programming Exercises

**4-1. Above Average.** Write a program that accepts five input values and stores them into an array. The program should display those five numbers in reverse order. The program should then display all the numbers in the array that are larger than the average of the five numbers.

**4-2. Target Practice.** Write a program that accepts ten input values and stores them into an array. The program should then input a target value and output how many times the target value appears inside the array.

**4-3. Password.** Write a program that maintains two parallel arrays. The first array holds five usernames, and the second array holds five passwords. The program should read the five username and password pairs, then store those values into the parallel arrays.

After the arrays have been loaded, the program should behave as a login screen, prompting for a username and a password. The program should respond appropriately with one of three output messages. If the username does not match one of the values in the username array, then the message should be "Username not found." If the username is found in the username array, but the password does not equal the parallel value in the password array, then the message should be "Username and password do not match." If the username is found and the password matches the parallel value in the password array, the message should be "Access granted."

**4-4. Two Dice Simulation.** Write a program that simulates the rolling of two dice four hundred times. Use the Random function twice to generate a separate random value from 1 to 6 for each of the two dice. Your program should maintain an array of counters with an upper bound of 12; index values 0 and 1 will be unused. The program should update the array counter with an index value equal to the sum of the two dice. (For example, if the random values were 3 and 4, then the dice total is 7, and the index 7 element should be incremented by one.) After the four hundred totals have been counted, the program should display the values in the array in a histogram format. The program should also calculate and display the percentages for each of the roll totals. The figure below shows a sample output. Your histogram will be slightly different because the random values will generate different totals.

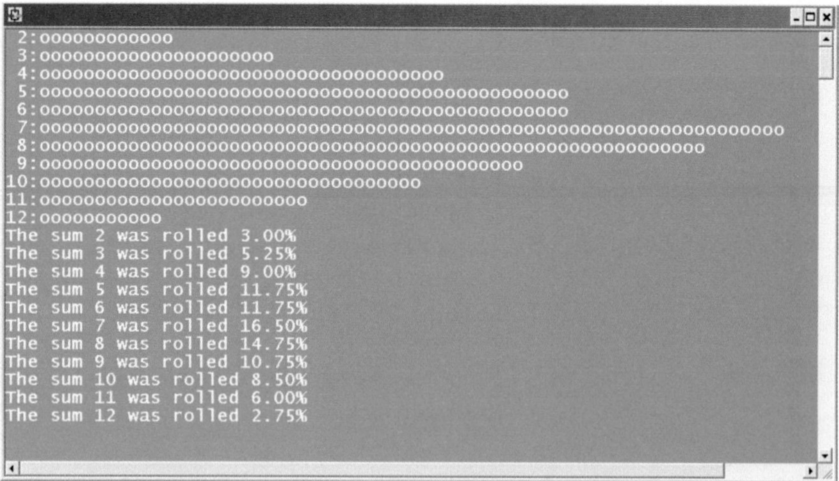

The sum 2 was rolled 3.00%
The sum 3 was rolled 5.25%
The sum 4 was rolled 9.00%
The sum 5 was rolled 11.75%
The sum 6 was rolled 11.75%
The sum 7 was rolled 16.50%
The sum 8 was rolled 14.75%
The sum 9 was rolled 10.75%
The sum 10 was rolled 8.50%
The sum 11 was rolled 6.00%
The sum 12 was rolled 2.75%

**4-5. Girl Scout Cookies Redux.** Consider again the Girl Scout Cookies problem presented earlier in this chapter. Write a program that fills the parallel arrays, one holding the names of the Girl Scouts and the other holding the number of cookie boxes sold by the girls. Write a program that sorts the Boxes array using Bubble Sort. To keep the array indexes coordinated, be sure to do a parallel swap in the Names array whenever you perform a swap in the Boxes array. The program should then print the names of the girls and the number of boxes sold by the girls in order, based on number of boxes sold.

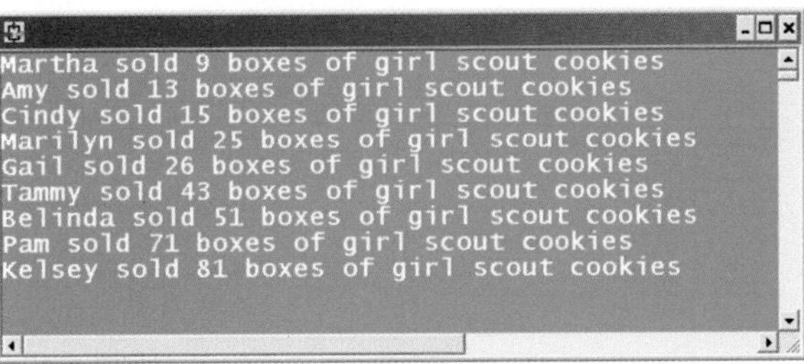

Martha sold 9 boxes of girl scout cookies
Amy sold 13 boxes of girl scout cookies
Cindy sold 15 boxes of girl scout cookies
Marilyn sold 25 boxes of girl scout cookies
Gail sold 26 boxes of girl scout cookies
Tammy sold 43 boxes of girl scout cookies
Belinda sold 51 boxes of girl scout cookies
Pam sold 71 boxes of girl scout cookies
Kelsey sold 81 boxes of girl scout cookies

CHAPTER 5

# Graphics and Procedures

## OUTLINE



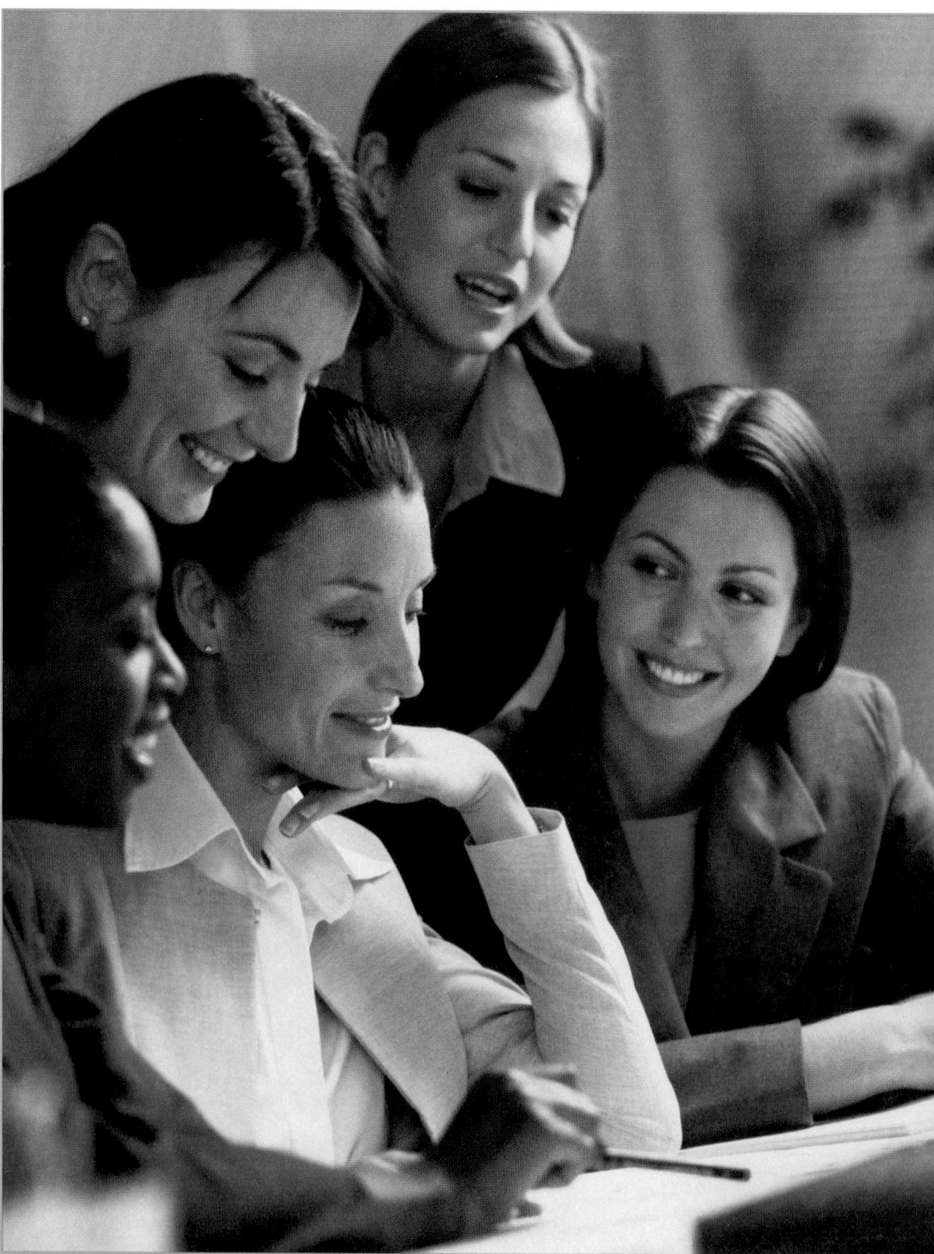

## INTERVIEW

### Jennifer Rakestraw, CIS major

***Interviewer:*** Why did you choose a computing major?

***Rakestraw:*** I originally was going to study secondary education with hopes of one day becoming a high school English teacher, but during my senior year in high school, I decided to pursue my passion for computers. I was definitely more interested in business than math and science, which guided me towards my current major of computer information systems.

***Interviewer:*** Have you seen the Visual Logic program?

***Rakestraw:*** Yes, I have. I took introduction to programming a few semesters ago. The tool was not available to us at that time, but I wish it had been. Visual Logic seems to be a dynamic program that makes programming logic clear without the details of a language. I think a strong feature of the program is its ability to actually generate a running program from a flowchart. I especially enjoyed its ability to create graphics with the use of simple, straightforward programs.

***Interviewer:*** Do you have any plans for the summer?

***Rakestraw:*** I sent off several applications this past year and finally decided on working for a company near my hometown. I will be performing first-level support for their IT department and working on computer hardware.

***Interviewer:*** Where do you see yourself in five years?

***Rakestraw:*** In five years, I hope to be working for a medium to large company, though I'm not sure what aspect of IT I want to focus my attention on. I performed very well in my database class this past semester, so I might consider that when trying to make my career choice. I also have a strong interest in web design and would love an opportunity to work in a position pertaining to it.

***Interviewer:*** Finally, what advice do you have for students preparing for a computing major?

***Rakestraw:*** A major in computers is obviously extremely hands-on, and it's important to take the extra time to practice what you learn on computers and not just read textbooks. A computer major is a challenge, but with the way the world is heading, it will definitely be a valuable major.

## OBJECTIVES

At the completion of this chapter, you will

- **Learn the Visual Logic graphics commands and how they work**
- **Appreciate the concept of structured design**
- **Know the process for creating procedures**
- **Understand the role of procedure arguments**
- **Realize the difference between formal arguments and actual arguments**
- **Develop and evaluate solutions that utilize graphics and procedures**

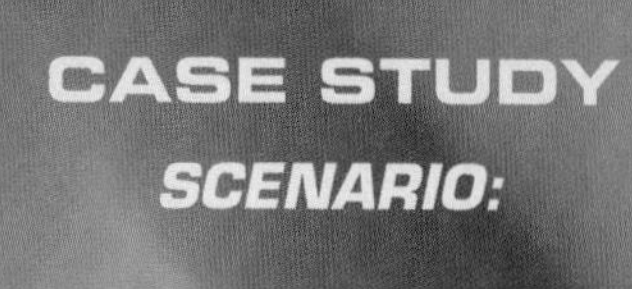


# Drawing Houses

"The materials we have covered so far in this course, including expressions, conditions, loops, and arrays are foundational concepts essential to most any programming language," Dr. Taylor says at the beginning of class. "Visual Basic, C#, C++, Java, Cobol, Pascal, and other popular languages all use these commands in their solutions. Even graphical languages use these commands."

"What's a graphical language?" one student asks.

"Graphical languages contain graphics commands that allow developers to create programs that generate a variety of interesting, pictorial outputs." Dr. Taylor turns on the overhead projector and shows a series of images, including geometric figures and colorful designs. "For example, all these images were created with Visual Logic graphics commands combined with expressions, conditions, and loops."

Dr. Taylor walks away from the projector to the desk at the front of the room. "In addition to graphics, we will also discuss a common strategy for solving complex problems, which is to break the problem down into smaller pieces, solve the smaller pieces individually, and then put the pieces back together to solve the original problem."

"Kind of like divide-and-conquer?" asks Emily.

"Yes, exactly. We write solutions to the small pieces in blocks called procedures. We then call the procedures as necessary to solve the original problem."

Jason raises his hand. "Did you say we will write programs that generate all those images?" he asks, pointing to the screen that is still showing various graphics outputs.

"Yes. We will soon be making the images you see on the screen. That last image, the one with multiple houses, requires both graphics and procedures. But we start with simple geometric shapes."

Dr. Taylor's solution to the house graphics appears later in this chapter.

## 5-1 Graphics

Visual Logic graphics are a variation on ***Logo Programming Language,*** which has been used in educational settings for over three decades. The graphics commands are based on the idea that a pen can be instructed to move over a drawing board, leaving a mark as it moves. The drawing board is illustrated in Figure 5-1. Note that the coordinates (0, 0) are at the center of the screen and that north, east, south, and west are 0 degrees, 90 degrees, 180 degrees, and 270 degrees respectively. These are absolute positions and directions that do not change.

The fourteen graphics commands available in the Visual Logic system can be accessed through the element menu, as shown in Figure 5-2. Each command is described in Table 5-1. These graphics commands can be combined with other Visual Logic commands to create many interesting programs, as we will see shortly.

### Forward and Turn Right

The first two graphics commands we examine are ***Forward*** and ***Turn Right***. The Forward command moves the pen a specified number of units. If the pen is down, a line is drawn. If the pen is up, it moves without making a mark. The Turn Right command rotates the drawing direction a specified number of degrees. The pen does not move and does not make any marks.

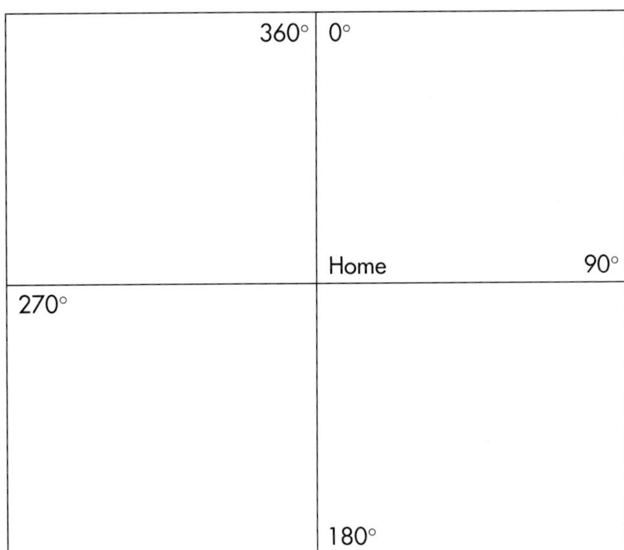


**FIGURE 5.1** *Absolute Graphics Positions*

**MANAGER**

In the early 1970s, Semore Papert and others at MIT developed Logo as an exploratory learning environment that would be understood by children and adults alike. The Logo Programming Language originally utilized a turtle-sized robot that moved around on the floor with a pen attached to its belly. As personal computers became available, the turtle and pen migrated to the computer screen. However, the idea of a *turtle* remains popular as a tribute to Logo's history. For more information about Logo, visit the Logo Foundation at http://el.media.mit.edu/logo-foundation/index.html.

**Table 5.1** Descriptions of Turtle Graphic Commands

| Command | Description |
|---|---|
| Forward **N** | Move the turtle N units forward (in the current direction) |
| Back **N** | Move the turtle N units backward (opposite the current direction) |
| Turn Right **D** | Turn the turtle D degrees to the right (clockwise) |
| Turn Left **D** | Turn the turtle D degrees to the left (counterclockwise) |
| Move to **X, Y** | Move the turtle to specified X, Y position |
| Go Home | Move the turtle to the center of the screen, facing up (north) |
| Set Color **C** | Set the pen color to the specific color C |
| Color Forward **F** | Step through a fixed color palette by F |
| Pen Width **N** | Set the pen width to N units |
| Circle **N** | Draw a circle with a center at the current location and a radius of N units |
| Fill Circle **N** | Draw a circle with a center at the current location and a radius of N units; fill the circle using the current pen color |
| Pen Up | Lift the turtle pen, so that no lines are drawn as the turtle moves |
| Pen Down | Lower the turtle pen, so that a line is drawn as the turtle moves |
| Set Direction **D** | Rotate the turtle so it faces D degrees |

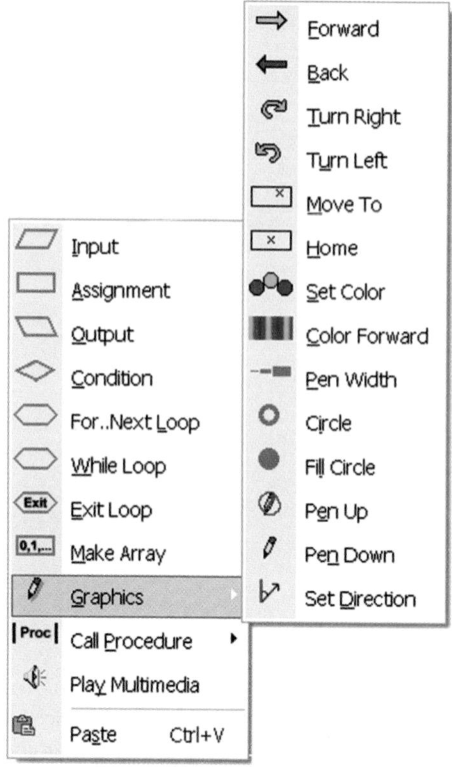


**FIGURE 5.2** *Visual Logic Graphics Commands*

Consider the graphics program shown in Figure 5-3a. By default, the pen begins at the home position, which is at the center of the screen facing north (the top of the screen). The first graphics command is Forward 100 which results in a line 100 units long drawn north, the initial drawing direction. The second command, Turn Right 90, turns the drawing direction right by 90 degrees. There is no movement, but its direction is now due east. The final command, Forward 50, causes the pen to move forward (in this case, east) 50 units. The exact length of the units will vary from screen to screen, but the second line should be half as long as the first line. The output is shown in Figure 5-3b.

> **Tip**
> The commands Turn Right and Turn Left do not move the pen. They only rotate the drawing direction.

Many interesting designs can be made using only the Forward and Turn Right commands. A program that draws a small square (sides 50 units in length) is shown in Figure 5-4a. Figure 5-4b shows the step-by-step actions of the turtle when following the commands. A small turtle icon has been included in the images to illustrate the

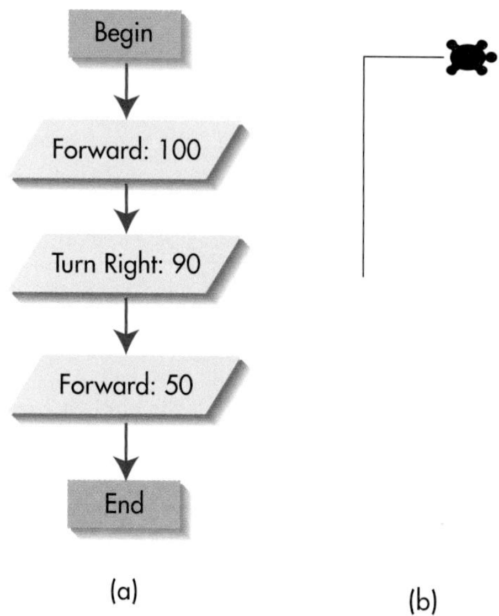


**FIGURE 5.3** *A Graphics Right Angle*

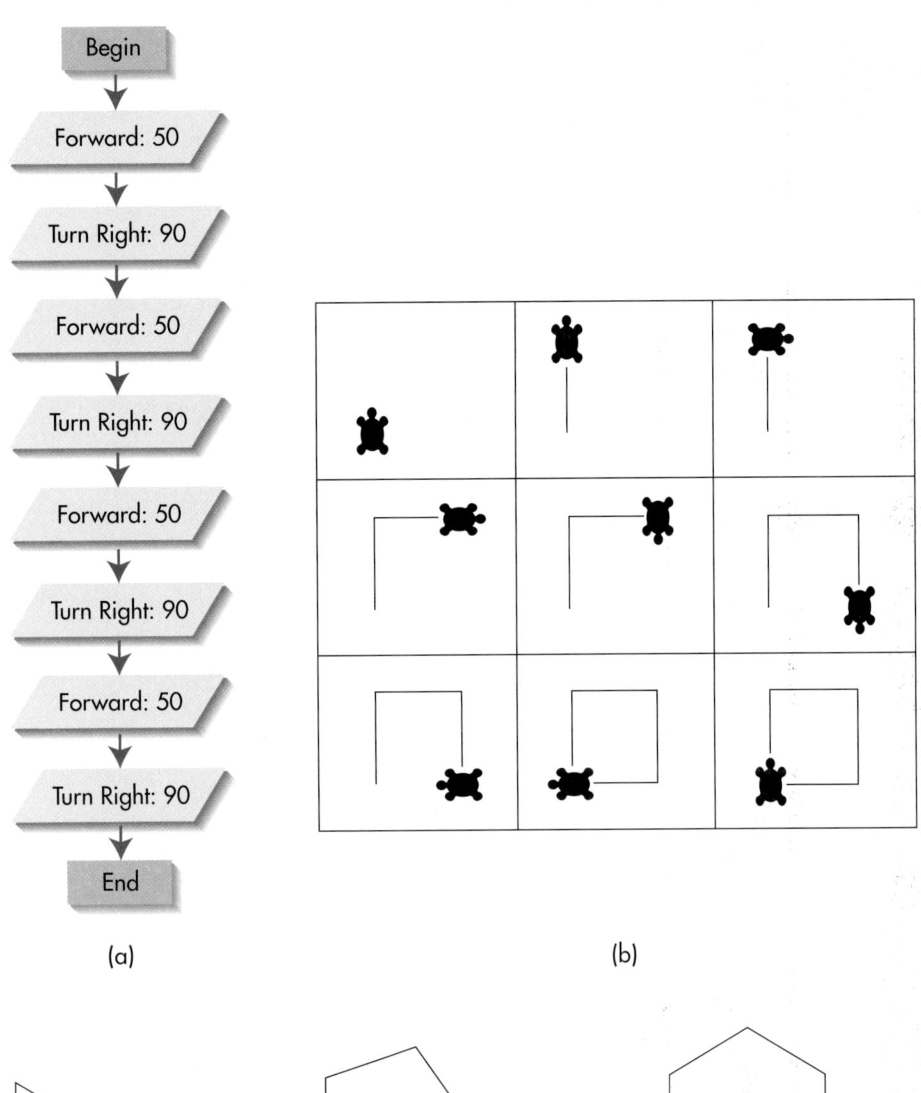


**FIGURE 5.4** *Drawing a Square with Visual Logic Graphics*

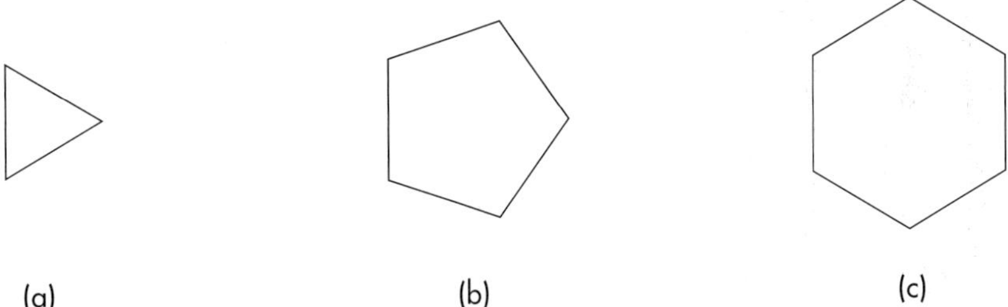


**FIGURE 5.5** Forward *and* Turn Right *Quick Check Problems*

drawing direction at each stage. Note that the last command, Turn Right 90, is not necessary for drawing the square. However, it does return the drawing direction to exactly where it started. This can be helpful when drawing multiple figures.

## Quick Check 5-A

Using only Forward and Turn Right commands, draw the shapes in Figure 5-5. (*Hint:* The drawing direction must rotate a total of 360 degrees to return to its original direction.)

## Using Loops

At this point you should have successfully drawn the four shapes (triangle, square, pentagon, and hexagon) from the previous section. In doing so, you probably noticed a couple of patterns about the shape drawing process. The first pattern is the repetition of the commands Forward and Turn Right. These two commands appear the same number of times as the sides of the figure. The second pattern is not so obvious.

The degrees the drawing direction must turn right are different for each shape and are based on the number of sides in the shape. Since the drawing direction will end up facing the same direction it started, the sum of all the right turns should be 360 degrees. The drawing direction should therefore rotate right 360 / N degrees after every turn, where N is the number of sides on the figure.

Determining patterns can make it easier to write programs because a pattern can be expressed once and repeated many times with a loop. The program shown in Figure 5-6a illustrates how a loop can be used to make a shape drawing solution. The user enters the number of sides desired for the shape, and then a loop is used to draw the sides of the shapes. Inputs of 3, 5, and 6 would draw the shapes shown in Figure 5-5. An input of 10 would generate a decagon (10 sides), as shown in Figure 5-6b.

When the loop variable is included inside the body of the loop, the output can be interesting. For example, Figure 5-7 creates a spiral by drawing increasingly longer lines after each turn. Figure 5-8 shows the same program with a 91-degree rotation.

**FIGURE 5.6** *A Shape Drawing Program with a Sample Decagon Output*

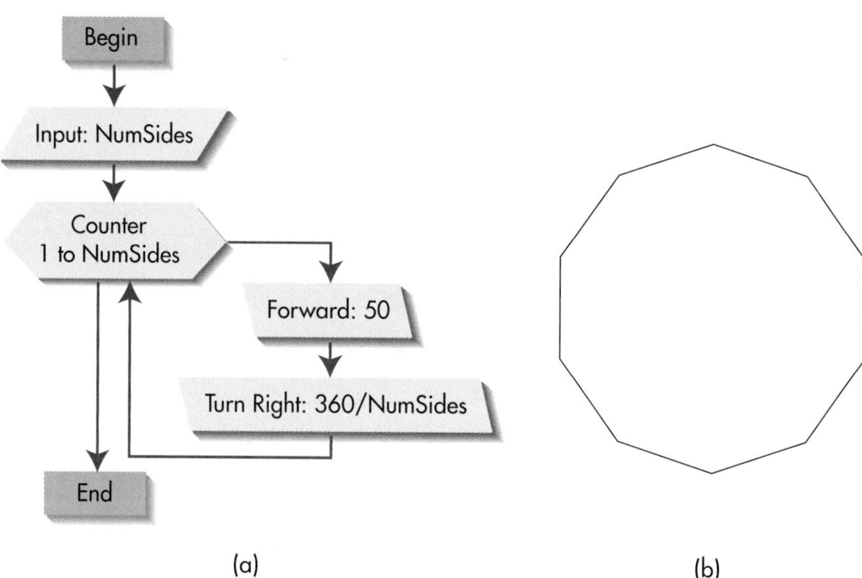


**FIGURE 5.7** *A Spiral Program*

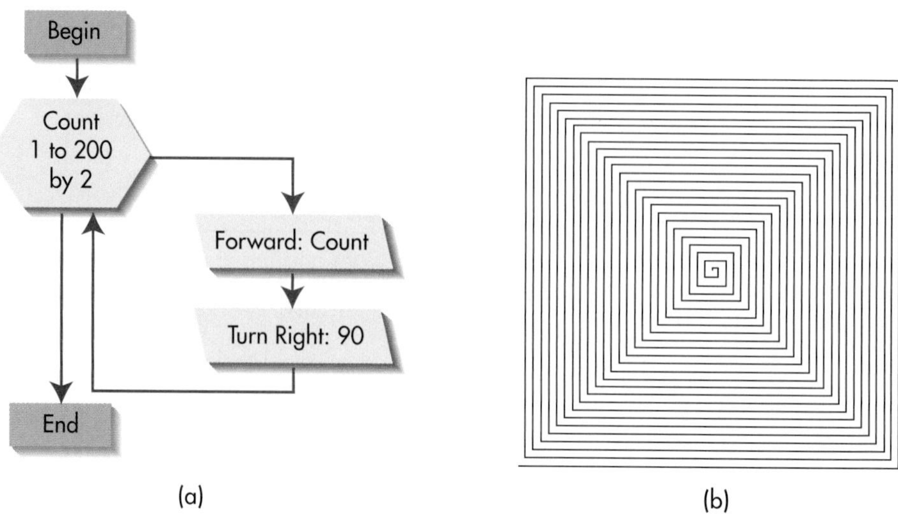

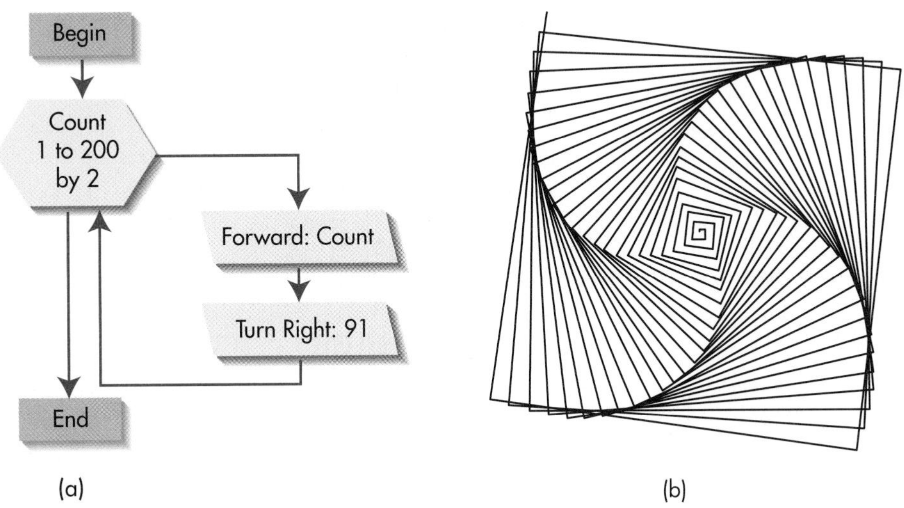


FIGURE 5.8 *A Spiral Program with a 91-degree Rotation*

## 5-2 Working with Color

By default, the pen draws with black ink and is 1 unit in width. Visual Logic provides commands for changing the pen's color and width. The ability to manipulate the pen gives developers even greater opportunity to be creative in their designs.

### Set Color and Pen Width

The ***Set Color*** command allows the developer to select any color from the standard color dialog box. Figure 5-9 shows the color dialog with custom colors expanded. The ***Pen Width*** command changes the thickness of the drawing pen.

A yellow circle and a series of thick yellow lines combine to look like a sun as shown in Figure 5-10. Notice that when the pen color is changed to yellow, it stays yellow for the rest of the program (or at least until it is changed again later).

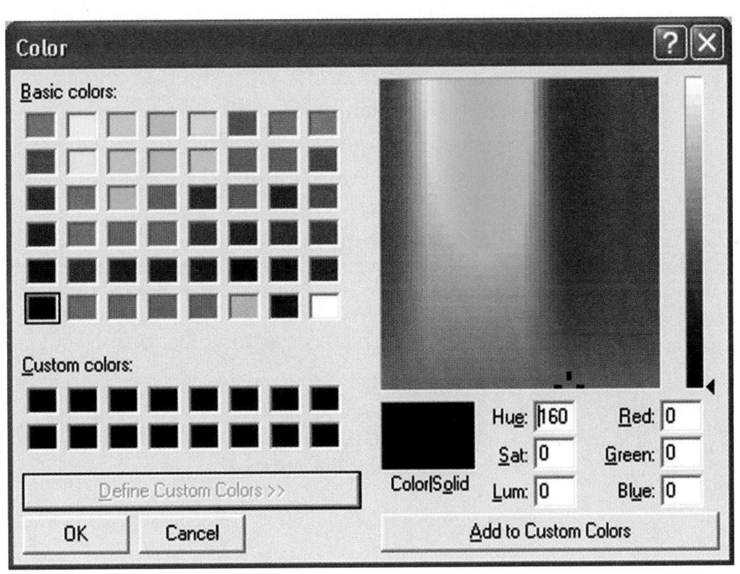


FIGURE 5.9 *The Color Dialog Box (expanded)*

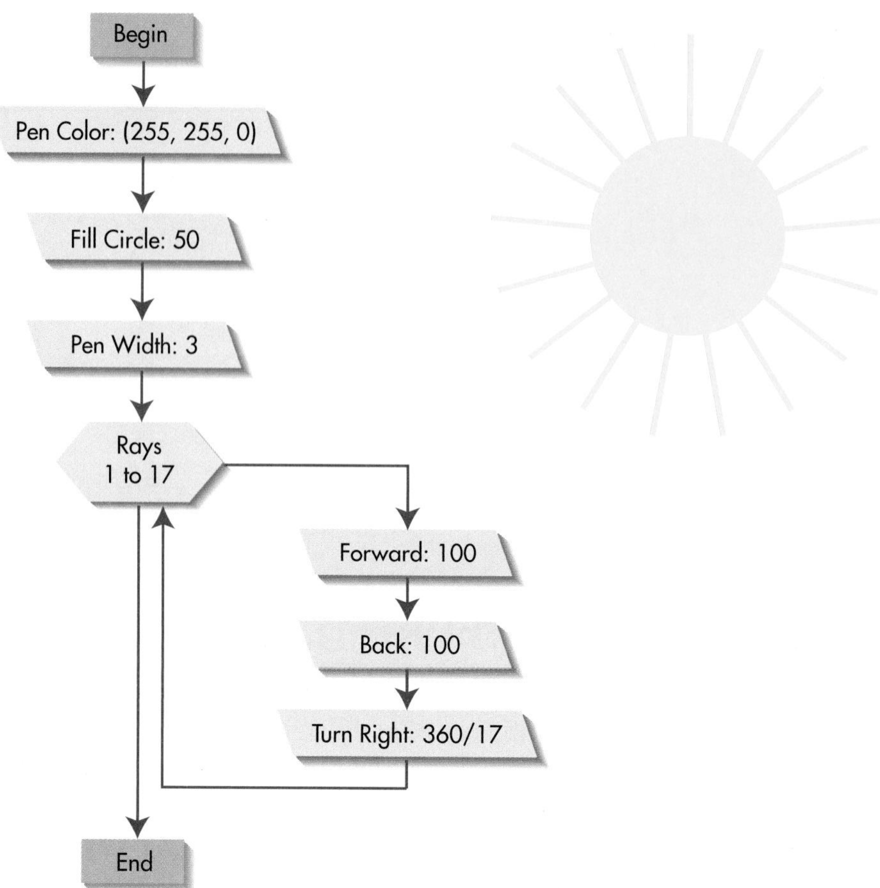


**FIGURE 5.10** *Sun Algorithm and Output*

## Color Forward

Another way of changing the pen color is to use the ***Color Forward*** command. This command moves the pen through the three base colors of red, green, and blue. There are 256 shades between blue and green, 256 shades between green and red, and 256 shades between red and blue, at which point the color cycle begins again. The Color Forward command typically occurs inside a loop.

Figure 5-11 shows one use of the Color Forward command. The program draws increasingly larger circles with the pen color rotating through shades of blue, green, and red. If the default pen width of 1 is used, some pixels are left uncolored because of mathematical rounding. The slightly thicker pen width of 2 makes the colors solid between the concentric circles.

## *Quick Check 5-B*

Modify the solution in Figure 5-11 in the following ways:

1. Change the Color Forward value to 5. How does this change the image?
2. Change the Color Forward value to 256. How does this change the image?
3. Change the pen width to the default value 1. How do the small mathematical rounding errors affect the image?

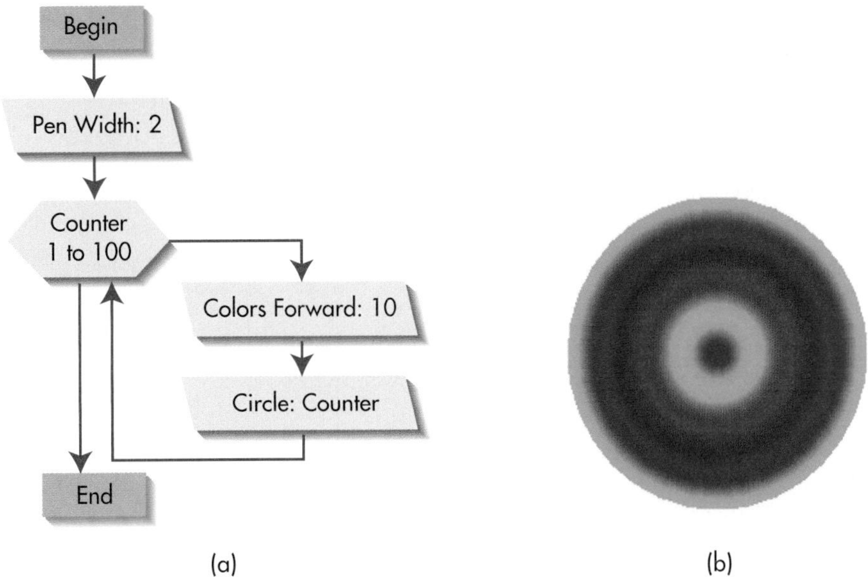


**FIGURE 5.11** *Colored Concentric Circles Program and Output*

## 5-3 Structured Design Using Procedures

As problems become larger and more complicated, it becomes necessary to design solutions in a systematic manner. One common approach is called ***structured design***. When structured design is used, a problem is broken into smaller pieces, each of which is solved individually. The solution to an individual piece of the problem is often stored in a procedure.

**Tip**

**A procedure is a series of instructions that are grouped together and treated as a single unit.**

A ***procedure*** is a series of instructions that are grouped together and treated as a single unit. The procedure can be called from elsewhere in the solution by referencing the procedure's name. When the procedure is called, control flows to the statements inside the procedure. When the procedure is finished, control returns to the calling statement (Figure 5-12).

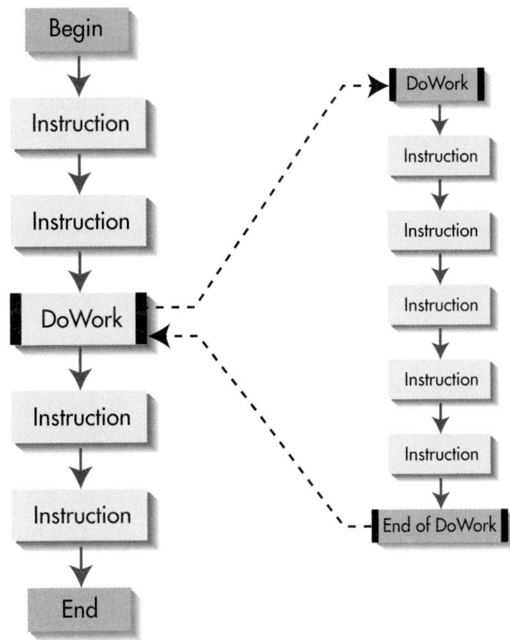


**FIGURE 5.12** *Flow of a Procedure Call*

## Rotating Flags Problem

To understand how procedures are created and used, consider the problem of drawing eight rotating flags, as shown in Figure 5-13.

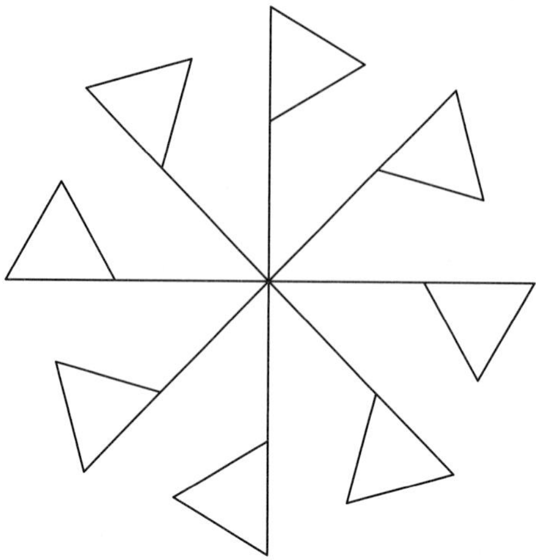

**FIGURE 5.13** *Rotating Flags Output*

The following flowchart shows one possible solution to this problem.

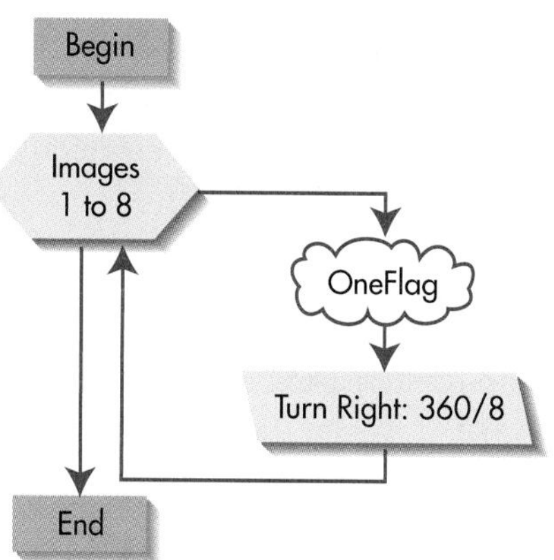


The flowchart illustrates the top level of our structured design. The details of how a flag is drawn are not important at this point. Of course, the details must eventually be specified, and that can be done in a procedure.

To create a procedure in Visual Logic, select "Procedures | Add New Procedure . . ." from the main menu (Figure 5-14).

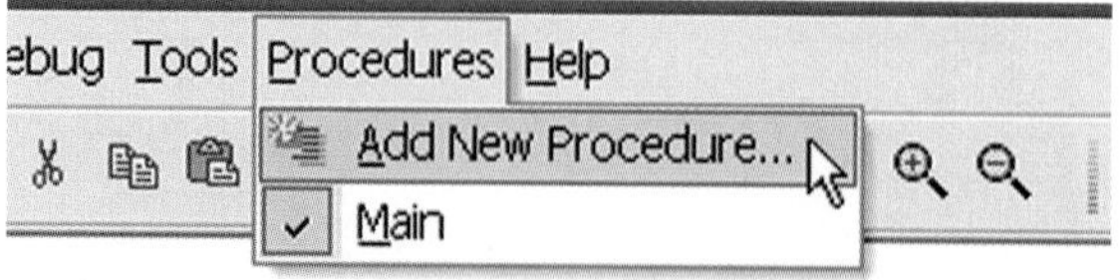


**FIGURE 5.14** *Showing Procedures and Variables*

The Procedure Edit dialog box appears, containing a text box for the name of the procedure and a list box for the arguments. (Arguments allow communication between the procedure and the calling program. Arguments are discussed later in this chapter.) Enter `OneFlag` into the text box (Figure 5-15) and press OK.

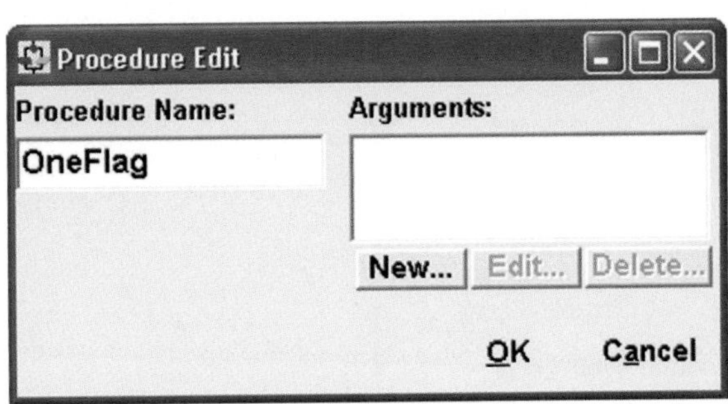


**FIGURE 5.15** *The Procedure Edit Dialog Box*

Visual Logic creates an empty procedure stub with the name you specified (Figure 5-16).

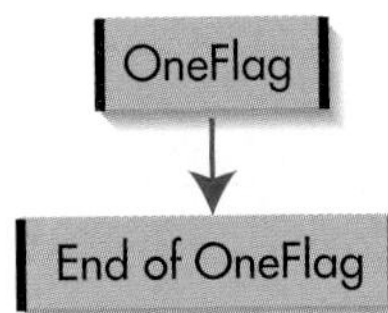


**FIGURE 5.16** *The OneFlag Procedure Stub*

**Tip**

**Procedure names cannot contain blank spaces.**

Commands are added to the procedure exactly the same as they are in the main routine. Drawing the flag begins by drawing the pole (70 units long) on which the flag flies. The flag itself is a triangle with sides of 50 units. After the triangle is drawn, the procedure moves the pen back to the initial starting location. The full implementation of the OneFlag procedure is shown in Figure 5-17.

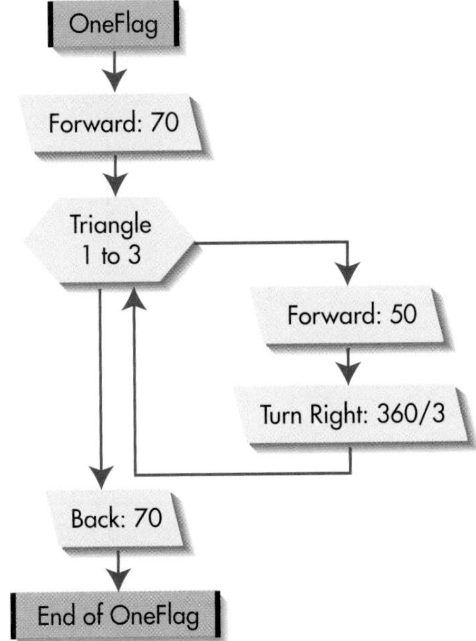


**FIGURE 5.17** *The Complete OneFlag Procedure*

Now that the OneFlag procedure has been written, it may be called as if it were an elemental action. The command menu contains a procedures option that has a submenu of all available procedures (Figure 5-18).

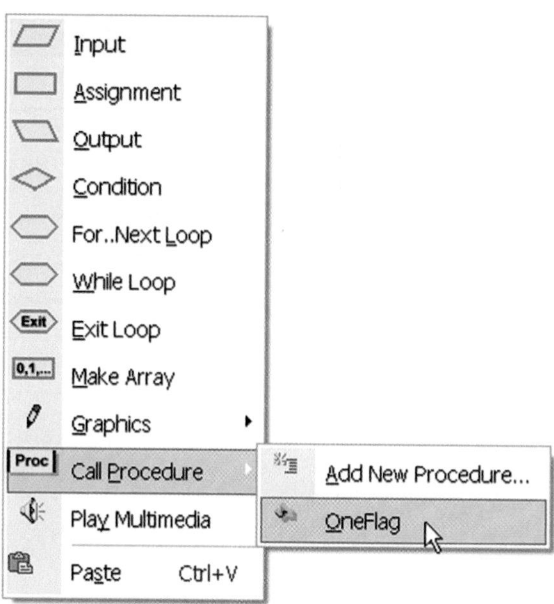


**FIGURE 5.18** *Calling a Flag Procedure*

Figure 5-19 shows the flowchart implementation of the rotating flags solution. The output of this program perfectly matches the desired output originally presented in Figure 5-13.

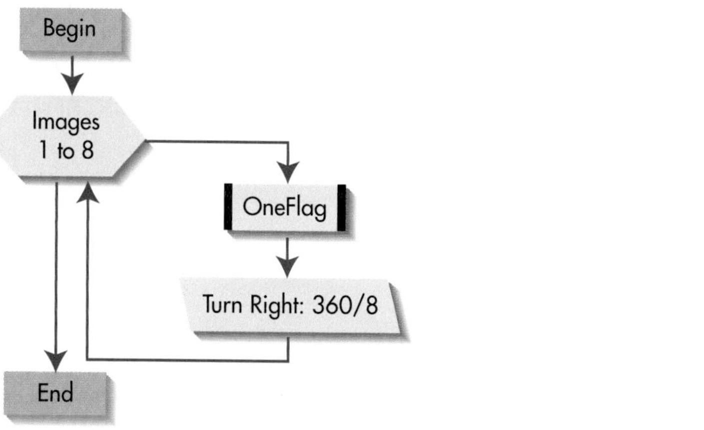


**FIGURE 5.19** *The Solution for the Rotating Flags Problem*

## Quick Check 5-C

Using the OneFlag procedure, write programs that generate the output shown in Figure 5-20.

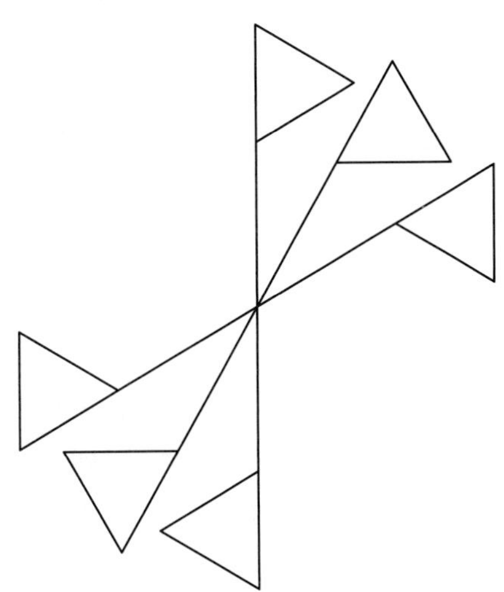

**FIGURE 5.20** *Output for Two Programs That Utilize the Flag Procedure*

## 5-4 Procedures with Arguments

**Tip**

**Formal arguments are also known as parameters.**

In the previous section, we demonstrated how to create and use a procedure. In this section, we illustrate how arguments can be used to make procedures more powerful. An ***argument*** (or parameter) is a piece of information that is communicated between the calling code and the procedure. The argument is referred to as an ***actual argument*** at the time of the call and as a ***formal argument*** in the called procedure. The difference between actual and formal arguments can be clearly understood in the rotating shapes program.

### Rotating Shapes Program

Figure 5-21 shows three different graphic outputs. All three were created by rotating a shape around 360 degrees. Figure 5-21a is easily recognized as being three rotated hexagons. Figure 5-21b looks like stacked blocks but actually is six rotated hexagons. (If you look closely, you can see that Figure 5-21a represents half of the lines in Figure 5-21b.) Finally, the intricate design of Figure 5-21c is the result of rotating ten pentagons.

Now consider the challenge of writing a single program to generate all three outputs in Figure 5-21. A solution that displays a user-specified number of hexagons could be used to generate Figure 5-21a (with an input value of 3) and Figure 5-21b (with an input value of 6). However, it cannot generate Figure 5-21c because that image is drawn using pentagons rather than hexagons. A more general solution is required.

The following flowchart provides a high level design of our solution. The DrawFigure procedure will be able to draw a shape with any number of sides. The number of sides to draw is passed to the procedure by means of a parameter.

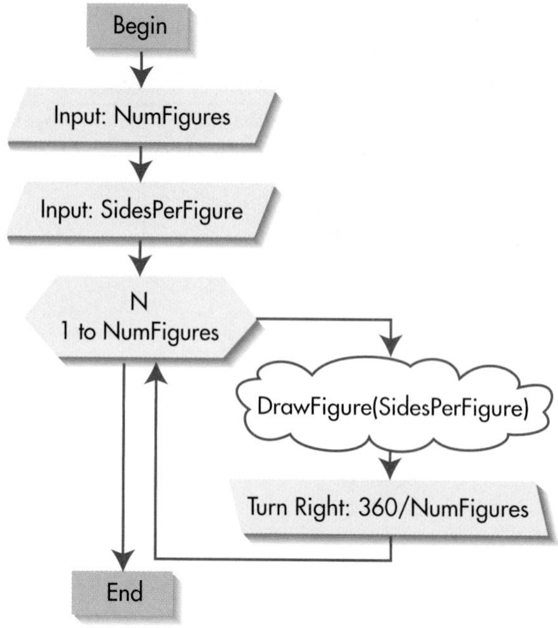


This algorithm can generate all the drawings in Figure 5-21 and many, many more.

**FIGURE 5.21** *Various Outputs Generated by Rotating Shapes Around 360 Degrees*

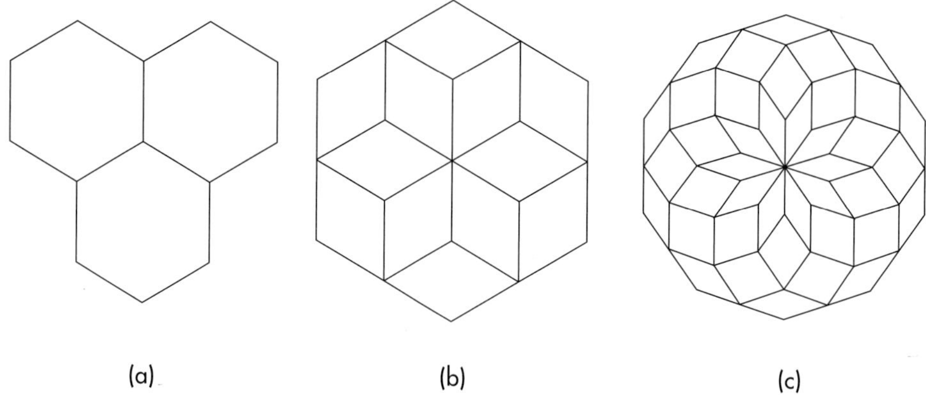


## Visual Logic Implementation

Now that the generalized algorithm has been developed, it can be implemented in a new Visual Logic solution. We begin by implementing the composite action DrawFigure(NumSides) as a procedure. Select Add New Procedure from the procedures menu. In the Procedure Edit dialog box, give the procedure the name `DrawFigure`. Then click the New button under the Arguments box, name the formal argument variable `NumSides`, and click OK. The Procedure Edit dialog box should look like Figure 5-22.

**FIGURE 5.22** *The Procedure Edit Dialog Box with one Formal Argument*

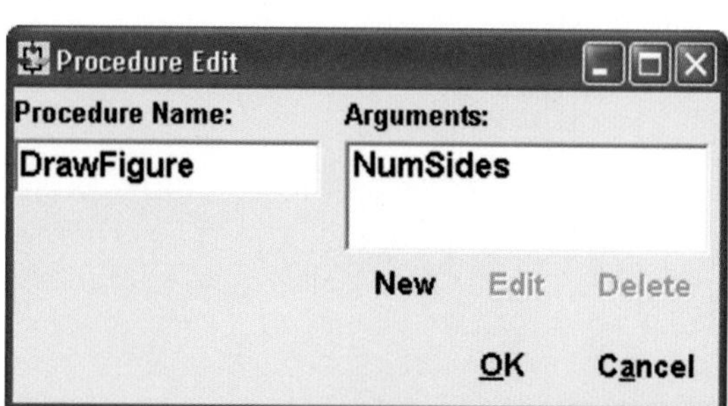

The procedure header and footer elements display the procedure name followed by all formal arguments in parentheses. Add a For loop to the body of the procedure. The loop should iterate from 1 to the value of the formal argument `NumSides`, with a loop body that draws a line and then rotates `360 / NumSides` degrees. Figure 5-23 shows the completed DrawFigure procedure.

**FIGURE 5.23**
*The DrawFigure Procedure*

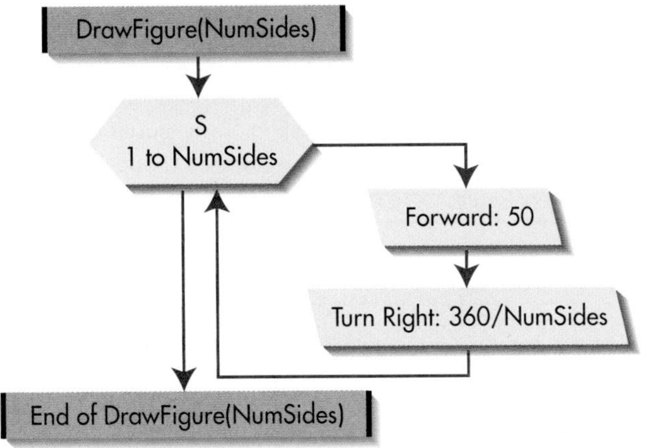


The DrawFigure procedure is now finished. Return to the main procedure, where you should implement the algorithm for this problem. Recall that the solution requires two input statements and a For loop. The body of the loop contains a call to the DrawFigure procedure followed by a Turn Right command.

Double-click on the DrawFigure element to open the Arguments dialog box. Notice that the procedure name cannot be edited in the procedure call. However, the actual argument can (and should) be specified at this time. Remember that the actual argument is an expression generated by the calling program, which determines the value of the formal argument inside the procedure code. In this case, the user's input becomes the actual argument (Figure 5-24).

Test the program by generating all three outputs shown in Figure 5-21. Continue running the program using different input values, and see what kind of interesting drawings you can create.

**FIGURE 5.24**
*Rotating Shapes Solution with SidesPerFigure as an Actual Argument*

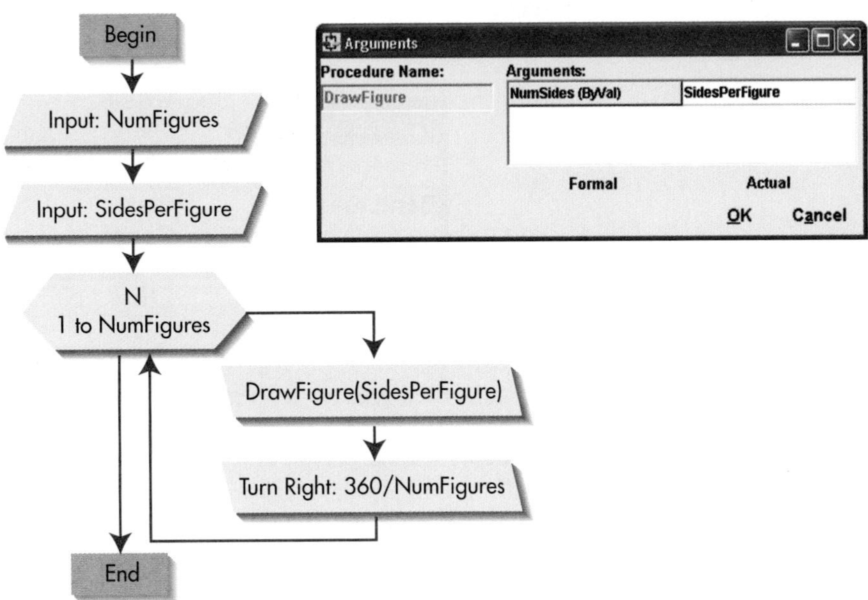

## ASK THE AUTHOR

**Q** Did we really have to use a procedure in the rotating shapes program?

**A** No. You never *have* to use a procedure. You could write any program as a single monolith of code. Procedures become more and more useful as programs get larger and larger.

**Q** Okay, I understand that procedures are helpful for breaking up large programs. But the rotating shapes program is not a large program. Why bother with procedures?

**A** Small programs are good for learning about procedures and parameters because they are easier to write and debug. If you master the idea of procedures and arguments when working with small programs such as rotating shapes, then you will be successful with procedures when writing larger, more challenging computer applications.

### *Procedures with Arguments Summary*

- An argument is a means of sharing information between the calling program and a procedure.
- Formal arguments are declared in the Procedure Edit dialog box at the same time as the procedure name. Formal arguments are displayed in parentheses after the procedure name in the procedure's header and footer elements.
- The calling program specifies the actual arguments at the time of the procedure call. Actual arguments are displayed in parentheses after the procedure name in the procedure call element.
- The order of the arguments matters. The first actual argument corresponds to the first formal argument, the second actual argument corresponds to the second formal argument, and so on.

## 5-5 Recursion

The rotating shapes solution from the previous section involved a procedure with a single argument. Procedures can contain as many arguments as necessary for passing all required information between the calling program and the procedure. To illustrate the use of multiple arguments, start a new application and create a procedure named **`BentLine`**. Under the Arguments list box, click the Add button to add the argument **`Size`**. Click the Add button again to add a second argument **`Count`**.

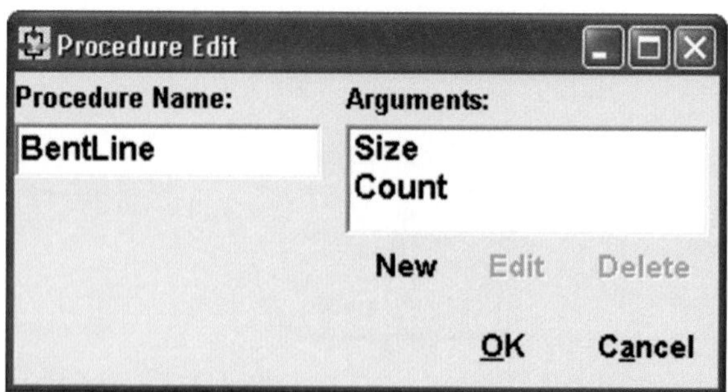


Close the procedure edit dialog box. Visual Logic creates a procedure stub for BentLine containing the two arguments Size and Count in the argument list. Add the code shown in Figure 5-25 to the BentLine procedure.

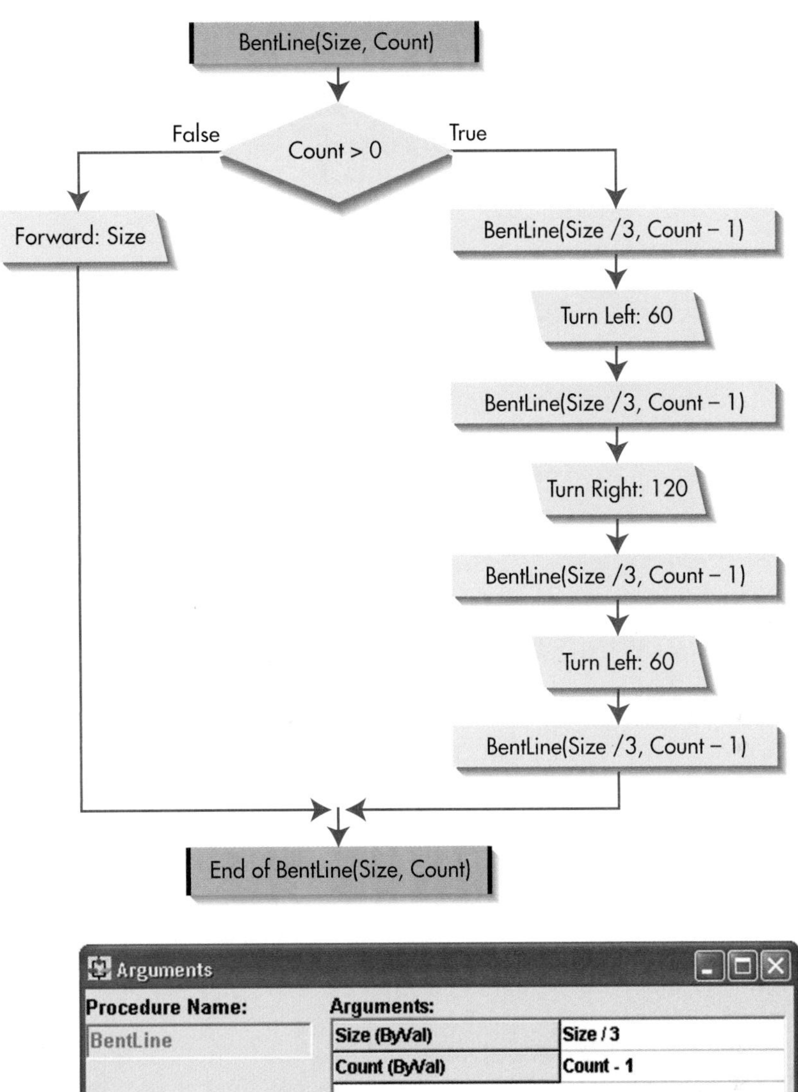


**FIGURE 5.25**
*A Recursive Procedure for Drawing a Bent Line*

You will notice that BentLine is a recursive procedure. A ***recursive procedure*** is a procedure that calls itself—it is similar to a loop in that the code will be repeated many times. To prevent infinite recursion, a recursive procedure typically first performs a test on one of its arguments to check for a base case. If the base case is satisfied, then the procedure does some processing without calling itself. If the base case is not satisfied, then the procedure does some processing that includes a recursive call.

After the BentLine procedure is complete, return to the main procedure and add a call to BentLine. Double-click on the procedure element and enter actual argument values of `200` and `1` to the formal arguments of Size and Count respectively.

When you close the Arguments dialog box, the main program will look like Figure 5-26.

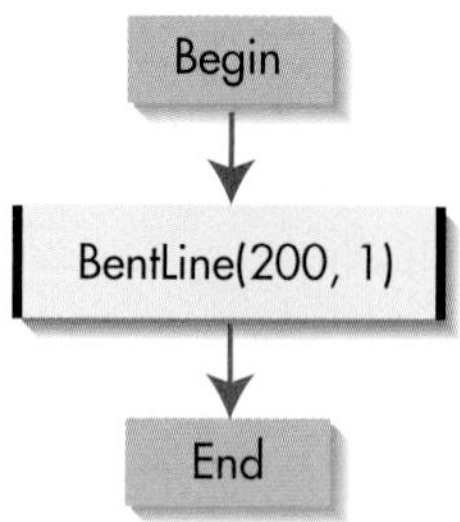


**FIGURE 5.26** *The Main Body with a Call to the Recursive BentLine Procedure*

Run the solution. You should get a line with a single bend. Edit the Count argument to 2 and rerun the solution. Then change the Count value to 3 and 4, running the solution after each change. You should generate outputs similar to Figure 5-27.

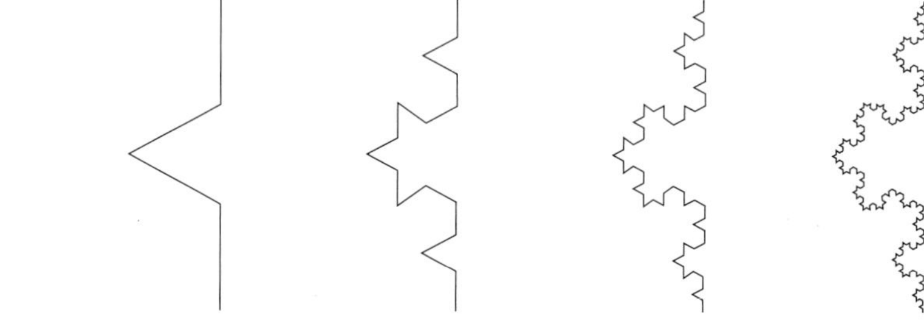

**FIGURE 5.27** *Bent Line Outputs for 0, 1, 2, 3, and 4 Bends*

## Quick Check 5-D

Modify the BentLine solution by changing the Size argument value to 400. How does that affect the solution?

**CASE STUDY SOLUTION:**

# Drawing Houses

### Problem

Write a program to generate a series of houses similar to the image shown in Figure 5-28.

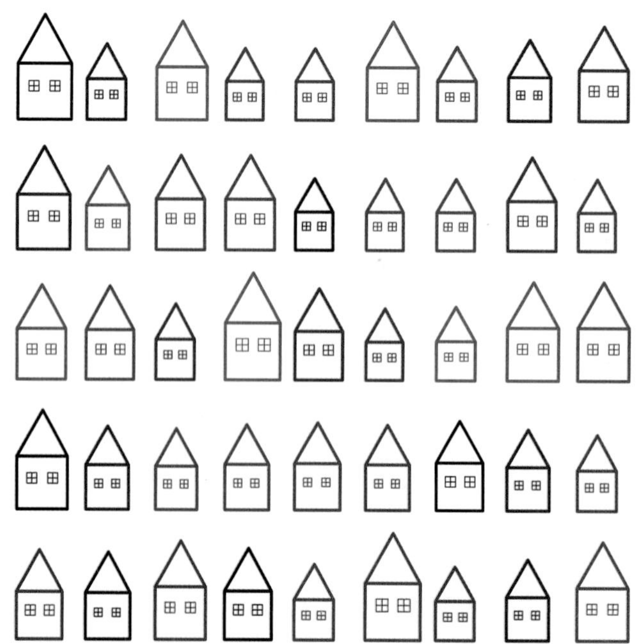

**FIGURE 5.28** *Houses Output*

## Analysis

The image contains forty-five houses, each drawn using a random pen color. The design for each house is the same: a square base with a triangle roof and two windows. This house design could be captured in a `DrawHouse` procedure with arguments for the screen position and size. The solution's main procedure would then call `DrawHouse` forty-five times using calculated values to determine the X, Y position of the house on the screen and the house size (Figure 5-29).

**FIGURE 5.29**
*The Main Procedure for the Houses Solution*

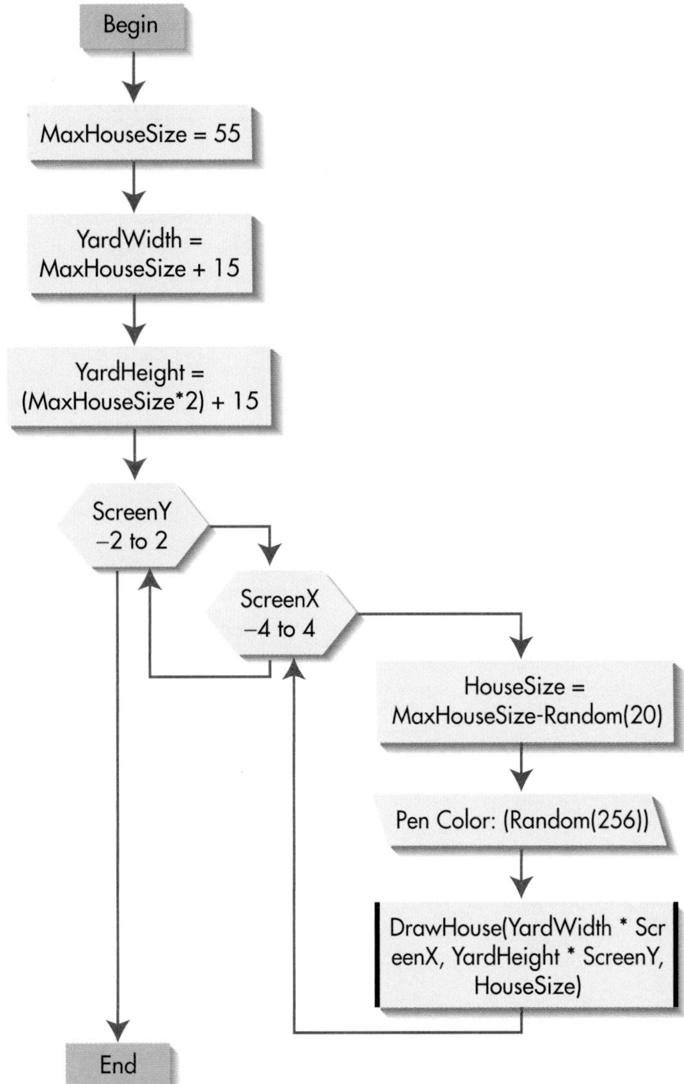


Drawing a house can be broken down into three smaller tasks: drawing the frame of the house, drawing the roof, and drawing the two windows. The frame is simply a square, and the roof is simply a triangle. The windows are a bit more complex, requiring the pen to move to a location where four contiguous squares are drawn. Furthermore, there are two windows for each house, which suggests the advantage of a single `DrawWindow` procedure that is written once and called twice using calculated values to determine the X, Y position of the window and the window size. The **DrawHouse** procedure appears in Figure 5-30, and the **DrawWindow** procedure appears in Figure 5-31.

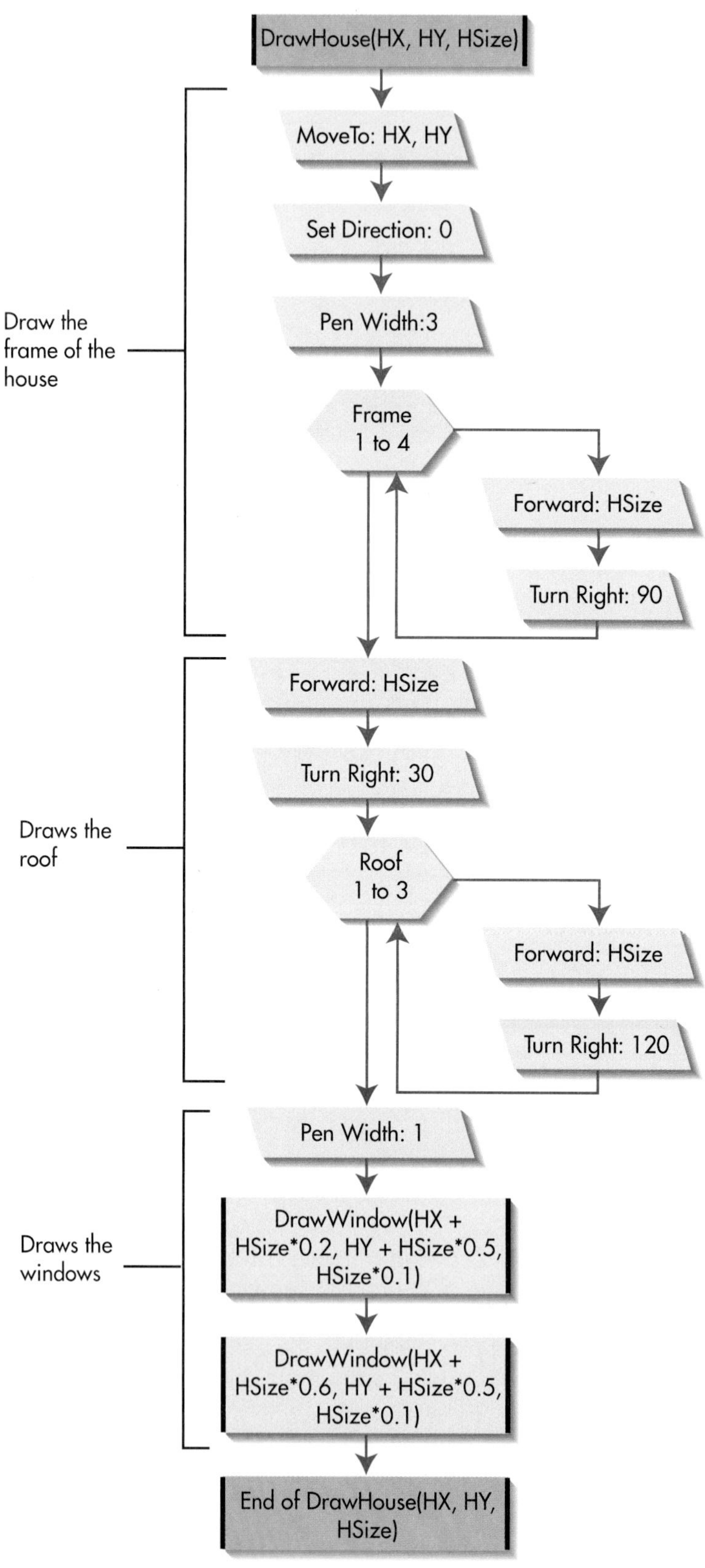


**FIGURE 5.30**
*The DrawHouse Procedure*

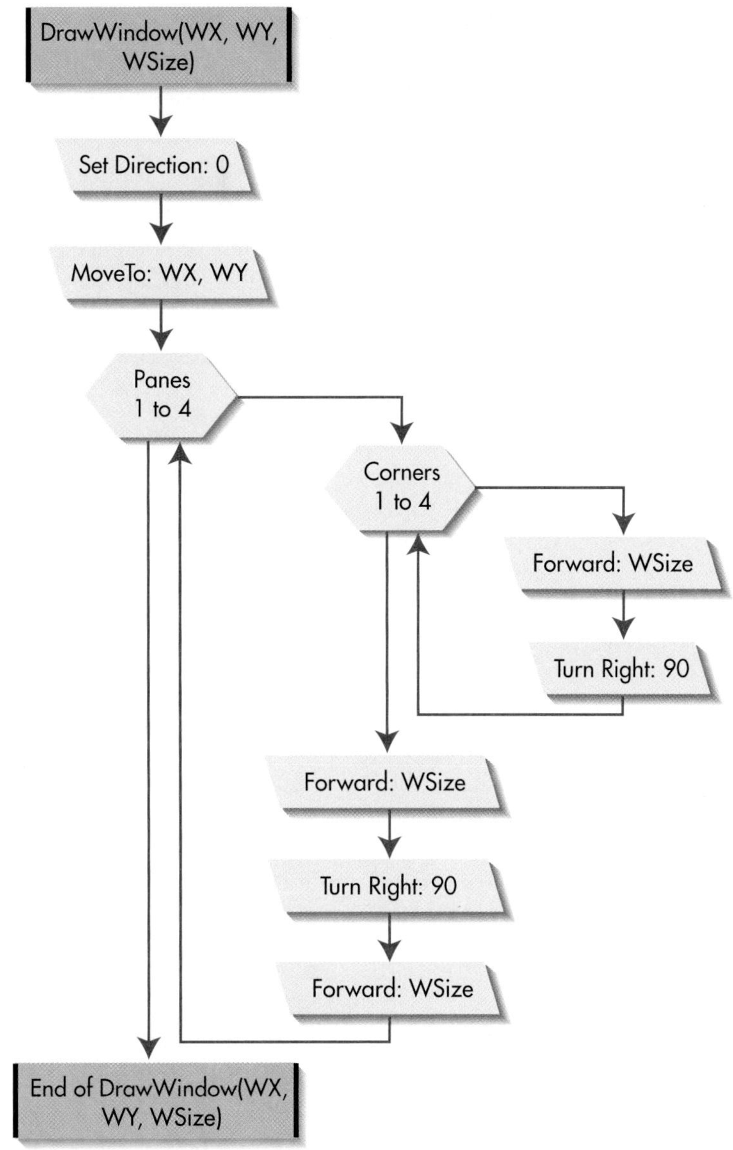


**FIGURE 5.31**
*The DrawWindow Procedure*

## Chapter Summary

- Visual Logic graphics include commands, such as Forward and Right, that move a virtual pen across the screen.
- Procedures allow code to be written once and called many times. Procedures also allow for code to be organized by logical function.
- An actual argument is a value or reference passed from the calling code to a procedure. A formal argument is the corresponding variable in the procedure that receives the value or reference.

## Key Terms



## Review Questions

1. What is the Visual Logic graphics pen, and how is it related to the Logo Programming Language turtle?
2. If the current pen drawing direction is north, and you want to draw a line from the current position to a point 100 units to the east, what graphics command(s) would you use?
3. Explain the difference between the Set Color command and the Color Forward command.
4. Explain the difference between the Circle command and the Fill Circle command.
5. What is structured design? How does it benefit developers when solving large problems?
6. What is a procedure? What happens when a procedure is called? What happens when a procedure is finished executing?
7. What is the purpose of an argument? What is the difference between a formal argument and an actual argument?
8. What is a recursive procedure? How does a recursive procedure avoid infinite recursion?

## ▶ PROGRAMMING EXERCISES

**5-1. Raising Flags.** Draw four flags of increasing sizes.

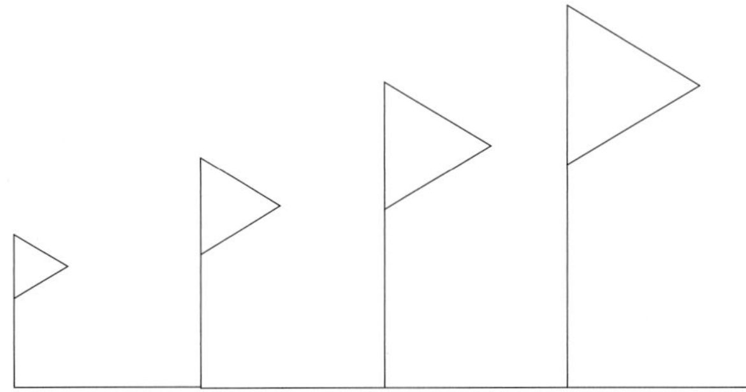

**5-2. Rotating Rectangles.** Write a graphics program with three inputs: rectangle height, rectangle width, and number of rectangles. The program should then display the specified rectangles rotated around a center point. Two outputs are shown below. In the first, the height is 100, the width is 50, and the number of rectangles is 5. In the second output below, the height is 50, the width is 200, and the number of rectangles is 7.

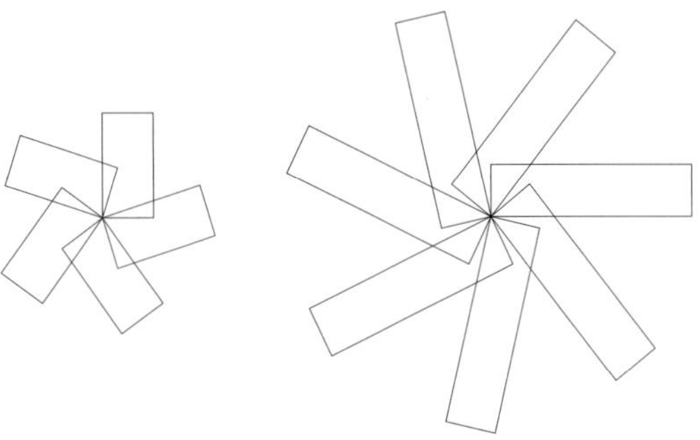

**5-3. Concentric Squares.** Use the Color Forward command to generate a series of concentric squares similar to the following figure.

**5-4. CD Burn.** It is always a good idea to back up your files on a regular basis, and this process has been made easier by affordable CD-burners. Generate an image similar to the following to remind others that frequently backing up your hard drive on CD is a good idea. Hint: This can be drawn similar to sun rays with color changes.

**5-5. Fireworks.** Consider the image of fireworks in a nighttime sky. Write a procedure called Burst with two formal arguments: Size and NumRays. The Burst procedure should move the pen to a random location on the screen, move the pen color forward 256, and then draw a firework burst with a size and number of rays specified by the arguments. The main procedure should assign random values for the two variables S and N, and pass those two values as actual arguments to the Burst procedure. The main procedure should repeat the random value generation and Burst procedure call using a loop to generate an image similar to the image below. Note: Because of the random values, your solution image will be different each time you run your program.

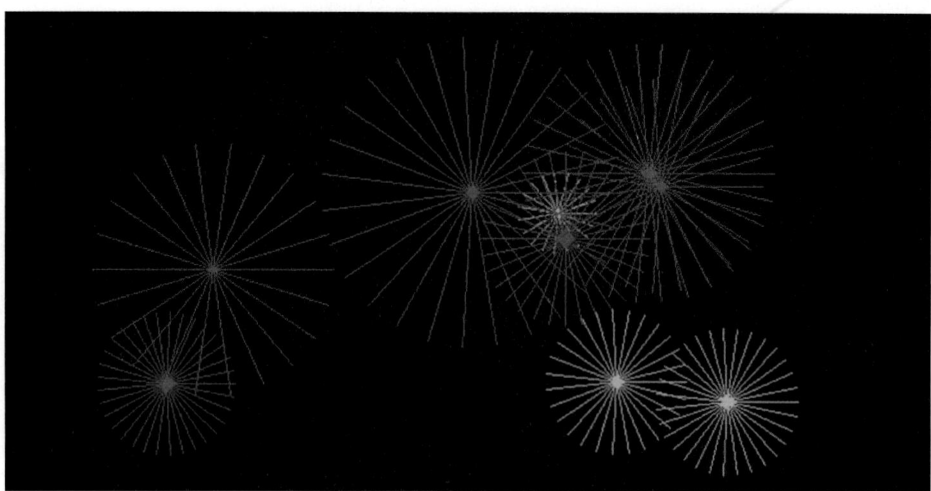

# UNIT 2 Programming with Visual Basic .NET



Introductory programming courses have evolved over the years to include a core set of programming activities. These activities provide sufficient skills for developing a wide range of interesting applications. Modern programming courses extend this historical core to include an emphasis on usability. The advent of graphical user interfaces and event-driven programming offers a consistent and predictable paradigm for modern application development. Unit 2 combines the rich historical tradition with the power of modern programming technology.

CHAPTER 6

# Hands-on Introduction to Visual Basic .NET

## OUTLINE

▶ INTERVIEW

**Leigh Anne T. Schory, Web Developer, EBSCO Industries, Inc.**

***Interviewer:*** What advice do you have for students in a programming logic course?

***Schory:*** Have a solid foundation in programming. You must understand technologies for what they are, what they do, and how they function. For example, learn how to use arrays and lists. Learn and understand how they are organized, how they are stored, etc. Understand what an object is, how its properties and methods relate to it, and how using stand-alone objects can benefit your code. Learn how to modularize your code by using include files, procedures, and functions. Keep your code modularized so that if you change any part of the underlying infrastructure, you do not have to recode the entire site. And most importantly, learn to comment your code well. More than likely, someone else will have to modify your code at a future date, or you will have to sift through someone else's code and try to determine the logic in order to modify, rewrite, or troubleshoot the code.

***Interviewer:*** How does your company use .NET?

***Schory:*** Recently, we launched an effort to rewrite all of our existing web sites and to develop all of our new web sites using .NET. Specifically, we will be developing all of our commerce and catalog sites in Microsoft's Commerce Server using a .NET architecture, and all of our brochure sites will be developed in Microsoft's Content Management Server, also using the .NET architecture. These implementations will allow us to utilize the functionality already built into these applications without having to reinvent the wheel every time by writing our own applications to accomplish the same tasks with less organization and less security.

***Interviewer:*** What is the project you are most proud of?

***Schory:*** I was the lead developer for designing and implementing a real-time eligibility inquiry system. This system allows providers to determine a patient's insurance information in real-time by converting it into the proper medical codes that represent that data, transmitting that information for processing, capturing the response sent back, and interpreting that response from medical codes back into readable English.

## OBJECTIVES

At the completion of this chapter, you will

- ▶ **Have hands-on experience developing applications with Visual Basic .NET and Visual Studio .NET**
- ▶ **Understand events and their relationships to the graphical user interface**
- ▶ **Explain the advantages of objects for developing applications**
- ▶ **Understand and effectively use the Button, Label, and PictureBox controls**
- ▶ **Successfully write Windows applications that modify properties at runtime**

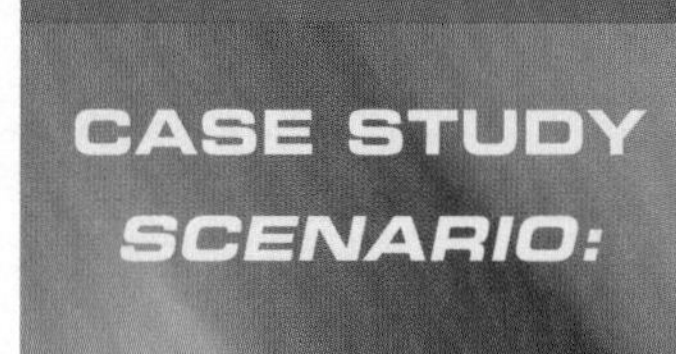


# Young Entrepreneurs

Reed and Elizabeth are business majors finishing their junior years in college. They also have started a small business called *Singing Mimes* in order to gain some practical experience and make some money. Elizabeth is a marketing major, and Reed is an information systems major. They have both had one programming course, and Reed plans on taking a second programming course in his senior year.

Elizabeth points out that computer software is a huge industry. One small but growing aspect of the software industry is gaming and educational software, which generated $12 billion in business last year alone. They do not have the skills to write any single application that would compete against the big-budget companies. Instead, their plan is to write Visual Basic .NET "edutainment" software, a combination of educational and entertainment software. They plan to include multiple programs on a single CD that they would sell at a low cost. They can produce 1000 CDs, including labels, cases, and case covers, for $1200. They hope to sell the CDs for approximately $5 each to local businesses, schools (as potential fund-raisers for school groups), and customers they attract on the Internet. They can break even if they sell 240 CDs and can raise almost $4,000 if they sell all the CDs. Most importantly, this project will provide them with valuable experience that will build their résumés in preparation for their graduations in twelve months.

Reed and Elizabeth's first Singing Mime program is presented later in this chapter.

## 6-1 What Is Visual Basic .NET?

In this chapter you will begin using Microsoft's ***Visual Basic .NET (VB.NET)***. VB.NET is a tool with many defining characteristics.

- VB.NET is a modern development language that shares a syntax heritage with the Beginners All-purpose Symbolic Instructional Code (BASIC) language. BASIC was developed in the 1960s to make fundamental programming constructs (conditions, loops, procedures, etc.) easy to learn and use. In 1991 the Microsoft Corporation developed Visual Basic, which became the world's most popular language for developing Windows applications. VB.NET is the seventh version of Microsoft's Visual Basic programming environment, the successor to Visual Basic 6.
- VB.NET maintains Visual Basic's tradition of excellence as the world's most widely used tool for developing Windows applications. Windows applications use a ***graphical user interface (GUI***, pronounced "goo-ey") that provides visual cues to the user, such as menus, buttons, and icons, that allow the user to work intuitively and efficiently.
- Unlike previous versions of Visual Basic, VB.NET was completely redesigned to be highly integrated with Microsoft's .NET Framework, a new platform that sits on top of the operating system and provides many capabilities for building and deploying desktop and web-based applications. VB.NET gives developers the tools they need to develop powerful web and e-business applications.

- Unlike previous versions of Visual Basic, VB.NET is a full-fledged object-oriented programming language, making it comparable to C++, Java, Delphi, and Microsoft's new C# (pronounced "C sharp") in terms of developing object-oriented systems.

In summary, VB.NET is an excellent choice for creating interactive business applications.

## 6-2 Using Visual Studio .NET

VB.NET applications are developed from within ***Visual Studio .NET (Visual Studio)***. Visual Studio is a single comprehensive environment that supports multiple programming languages and performs many common programming tasks automatically, including syntax checking, interpreting, compiling, debugging, and deploying applications.

**Tip**

**Setting the Profile to Visual Basic Developer will give Visual Studio a look and feel like previous versions of Visual Basic. This will also allow the online Help to give more appropriate information.**

If you do not already have Visual Studio.NET installed on your computer, install the version included with this book. To run Visual Studio, click Start, select Programs, select Microsoft Visual Studio .NET, and then select Microsoft Visual Studio .NET. The Visual Studio Development Environment window will open to the Start Page. If necessary, select the My Profile link, and change the Profile to Visual Basic Developer to make your screen look like Figure 6-1. The development environment contains multiple windows and multiple functionalities, and is therefore called an ***integrated development environment (IDE)***.

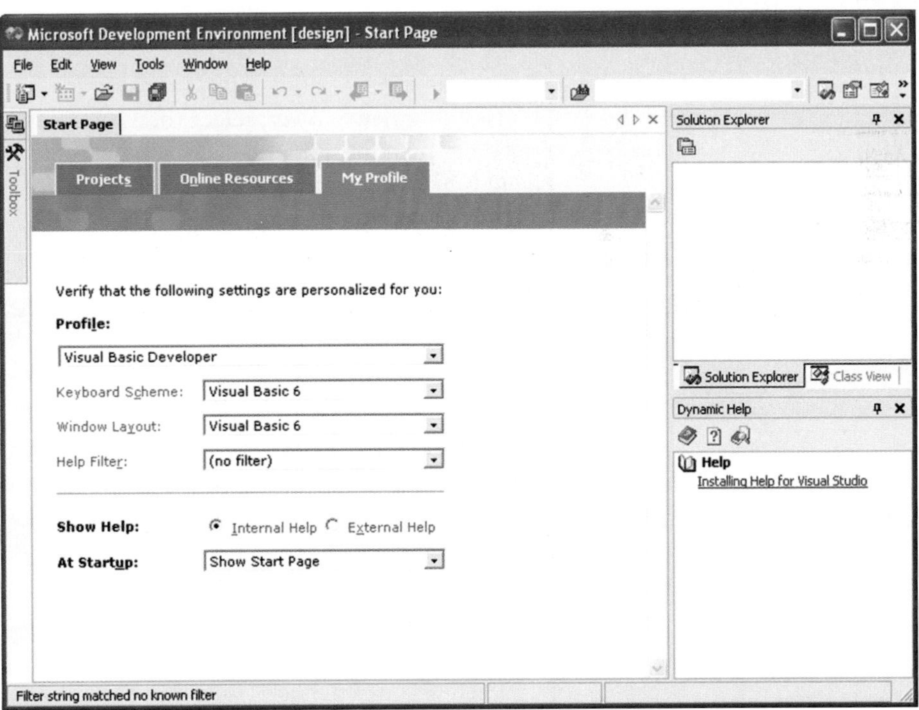


**FIGURE 6.1** *Start Page for the Visual Studio IDE*

## MENTOR

The IDE has two types of windows—tool windows and document windows. The tool windows can be rearranged to personalize your viewing and editing space. For example, tool windows have an auto hide feature that allows you to see more of your code at one time by minimizing tool windows along the edges of the IDE. When auto hidden, the name and icon of a window are visible on a tab at the edge of the IDE. When you move the cursor over the tab, the window slides back into view and is ready for use. When an auto hidden window loses focus, it automatically slides back to its tab on the edge of the IDE. The auto hide is set using the pushpin in the upper right corner of the window. The pushpin may be locked (vertical) or unlocked (horizontal). Figure 6-2 shows a tool window with a locked pushpin. If you click the pushpin to unlock it, the tool window will automatically hide when the cursor is moved away.

Another way to manage your IDE is to dock and undock the tool windows. Windows in the IDE start off docked, meaning one or two sides are locked to the boundary of another window. You can use drag and drop to change the docking boundaries. You can also double-click the title bar to free a docked window or restore a floating window to its previous location.

Finally, you can close a tool window by clicking the close button marked with an X in the window's upper right corner. Closed windows can be reopened by selecting the window from the View menu option.

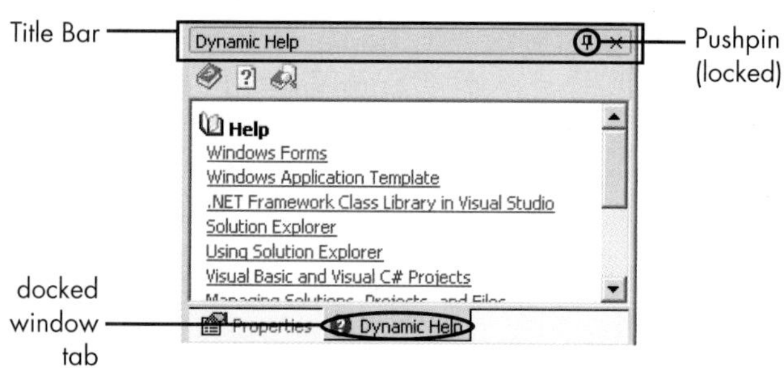


**FIGURE 6.2** *Tool Window*

To start a new project, select the Projects tab link. If this is the first time Visual Studio has run on this particular machine, then the Projects tab display will look like Figure 6-3. Future visits to the Projects tab link will contain Names and Modified dates of previous projects.

**FIGURE 6.3** *The IDE Projects Tab*

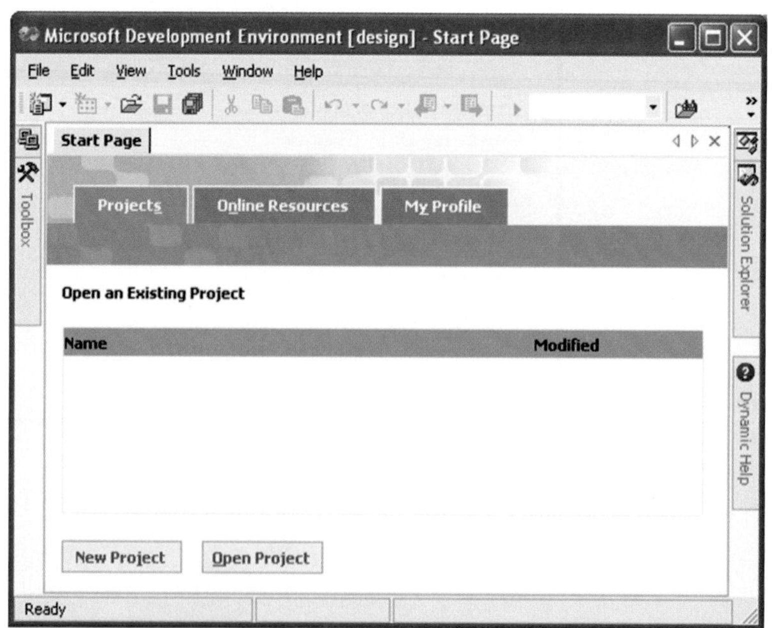

## ASK THE AUTHOR

**Q** What is the difference between a ***project*** and a ***solution***?

**A** For the most part, a project and a solution are the same thing. Visual Studio always opens a project within a solution, and most solutions contain only one project. However, there are times when many developers (and teams of developers) are working together on a single large solution. Visual Studio helps coordinate such large-scale solutions by allowing developers to work on separate projects that combine into a larger solution. In this book we will use the terms *solution* and *project* interchangeably because our solutions will typically have only a single project.

Click the New Project button, which will open the New Project dialog box (Figure 6-4). Because Visual Studio supports multiple project types, you must specify the type of project you will be creating. In this book we will always select Visual Basic Projects. Additionally, for each project type, you have a choice of application type. In Unit 2 we will always select the Windows Application icon. Set the Name text box value to **`Hello Project`**, which becomes the name of the project. Visual Studio will create a folder titled Hello Project at the location specified in the location text box.

Press OK to close the New Project dialog box. The Visual Studio IDE will appear. The IDE will look something like (but not necessarily exactly like) Figure 6-5.

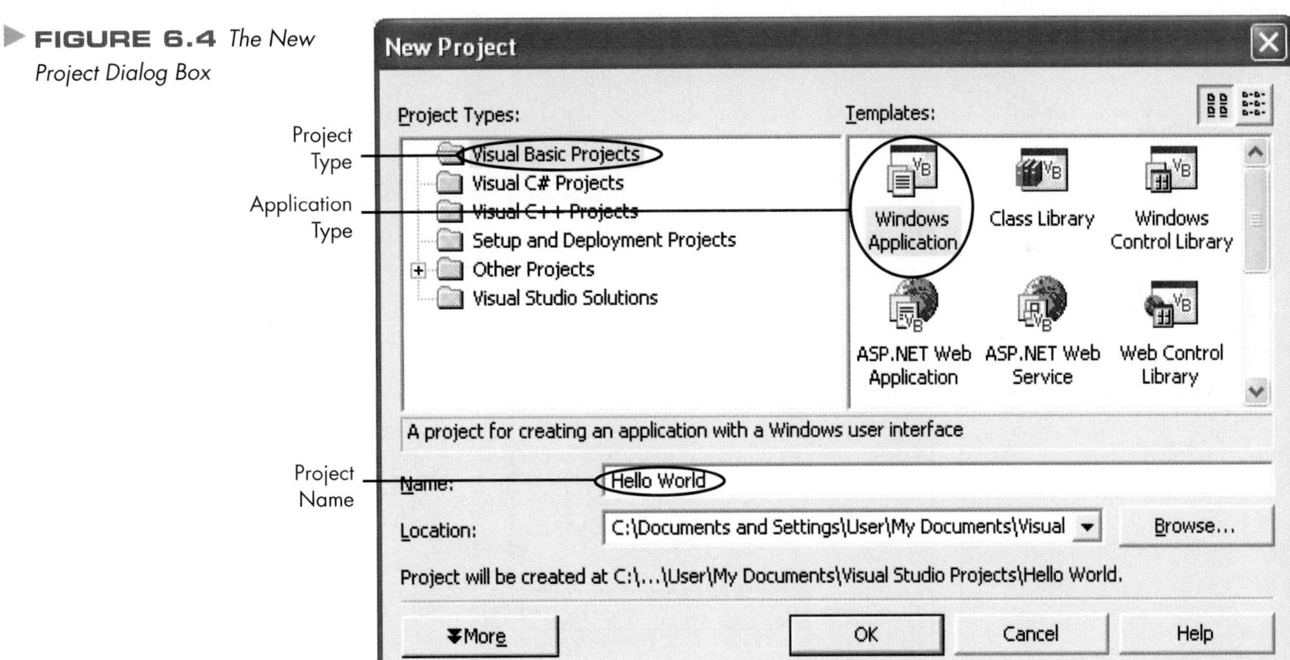


**FIGURE 6.4** *The New Project Dialog Box*

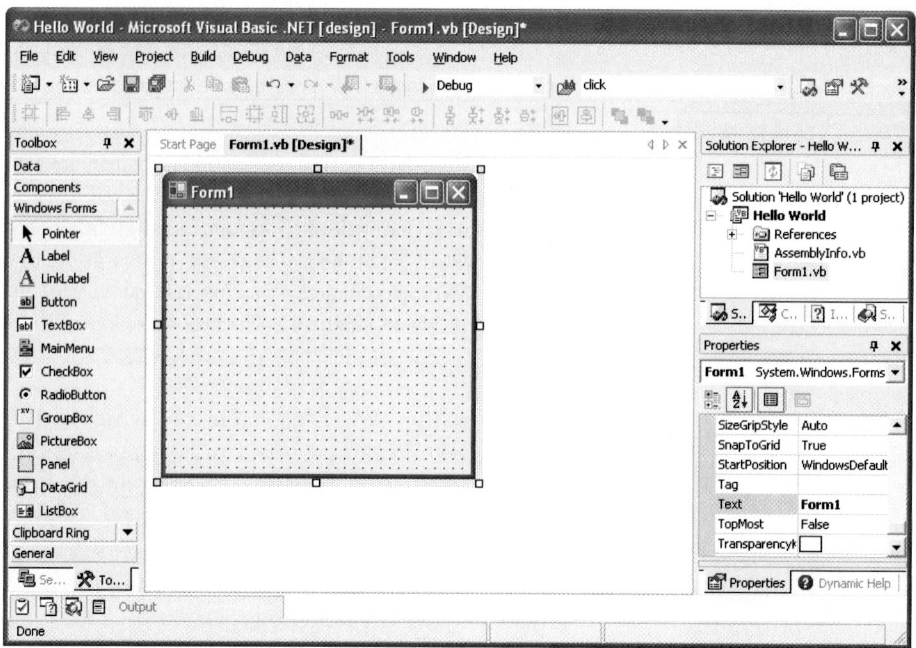


▶ **FIGURE 6.5** *The Visual Studio IDE for the Hello Project*

The Visual Studio IDE can be a bit overwhelming the first time you see it. After all, there are more than one hundred clickable elements on the screen! The best way to appreciate this IDE is to look at its main parts (see Figure 6-6).

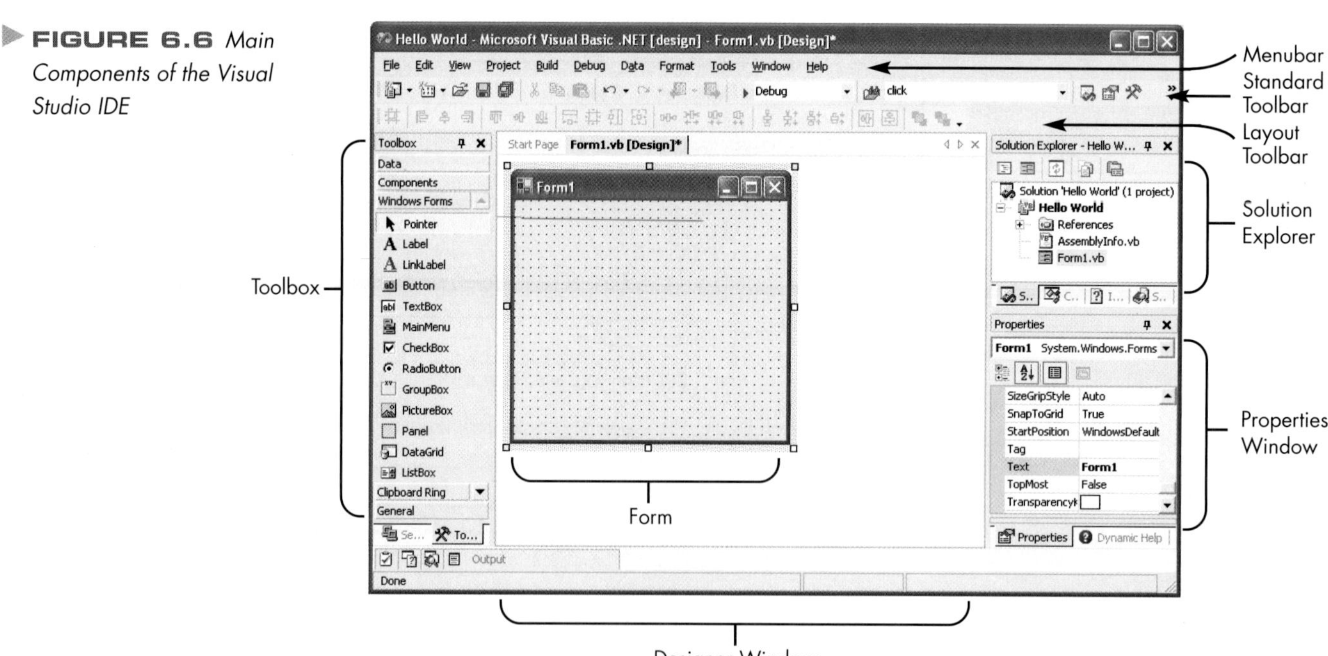


▶ **FIGURE 6.6** *Main Components of the Visual Studio IDE*

**Other toolbars, such as the debug toolbar, can be added and removed by right-clicking in the unused toolbar space .**

The top of the IDE looks similar to that of Word, Excel, and other Windows applications. The ***menubar*** contains File, Edit and Help plus some other options specific to Visual Studio. Directly below the menubar are the ***standard toolbar*** and the ***layout toolbar***. The standard toolbar gives icon shortcuts for frequently used menu commands, such as open, save, cut, copy, and paste. The layout toolbar provides icon shortcuts to commands for formatting the forms' and other objects' layouts, with such options as Align Left and Make Same Width.

The middle of the screen is the ***Designer window***, which contains forms being developed. The ***toolbox*** located on the left of the screen contains the controls you can add to the form. Forms with controls make up the GUI of your application.

**Even though *AssemblyInfo.vb* and *Form1.vb* share a common .vb extension, the Solution Explorer displays them with different icons to indicate their different purposes.**

The right side of the screen contains the last two windows in our overview. The top right window is the ***Solution Explorer***. Remember that a solution typically contains one project, but other projects can be added. Each Windows application project contains three items: a references folder, an assembly file, and a form file. The references folder and assembly file contain information necessary to run your .NET project. The form file contains information about the Windows Form, including the interface and the code behind the interface.

The bottom right window is the ***Properties window***. The Properties window contains three parts. The top part is a combo box that displays the name and class of the selected object. The middle part is the properties list, where the left column contains all the properties of the selected object, and the right column contains a settings box for viewing and editing the selected property's value. Finally, the bottom part of the Properties window is a description pane that provides a brief description of the selected property.

## 6-3 Your First VB.NET Program: Hello World

The best way to learn about a language is to write a Hello World program, the easiest possible program that contains developer code.

### Step 1: Add Button to Form

Our Hello World project will require one button on the form. Visual Studio makes it easy to add buttons and other controls to forms. Look in the toolbox for the control you want to add, and select it with a single click of the mouse. The control will remain depressed. Then draw a rectangular region by holding the mouse button down. When you release the mouse, the selected control (in this case, a button) will appear in the region you selected (see Figure 6-7). Adding controls this way is often referred to as *painting* the interface. You can also add controls by double-clicking the desired control in the toolbox, which creates a control on the form with a default size and location.

Repeat the process to create a second button in the lower right corner of the form (see Figure 6-8). Our project now has a form with two button controls.

**FIGURE 6.7** *Adding a Button Control to a Form*

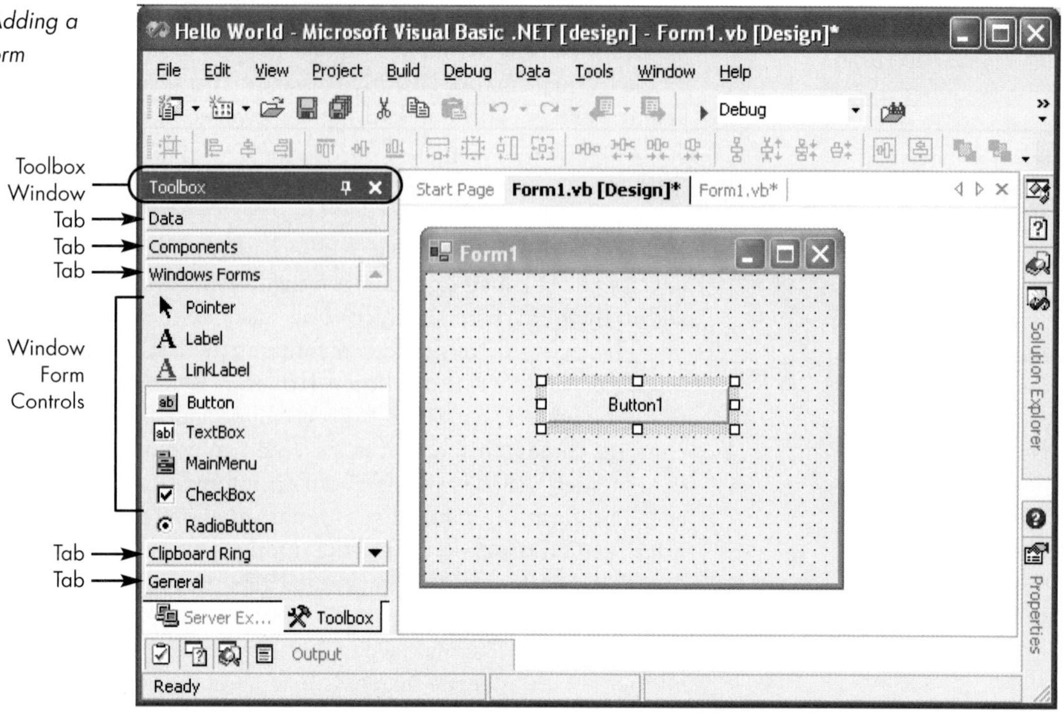

**FIGURE 6.8** *The Hello World Form with Two Button Controls*

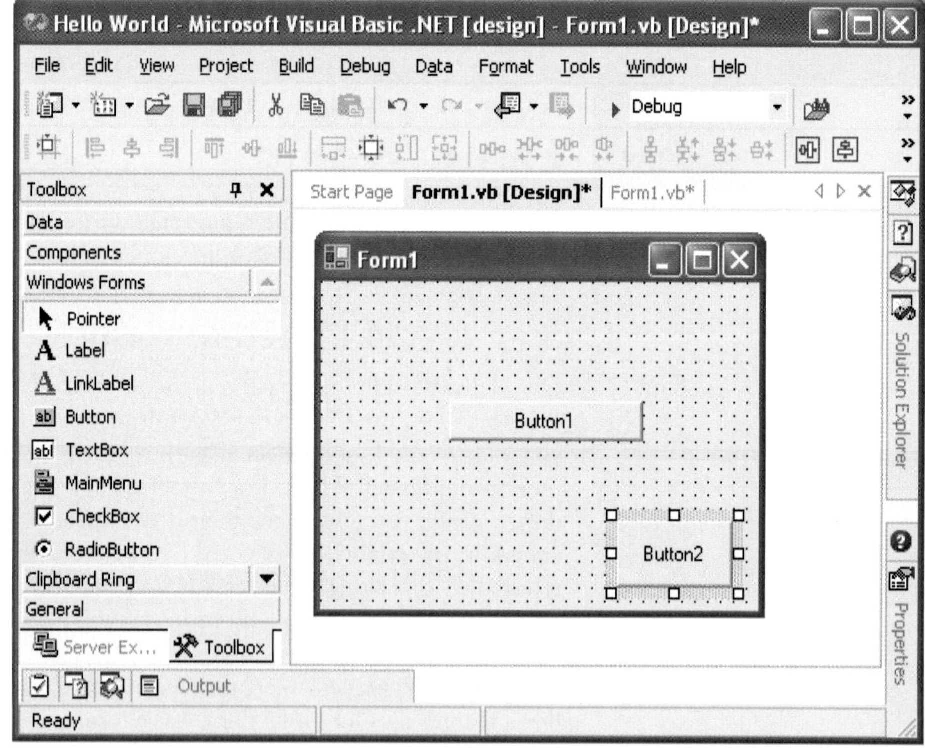


## Step 2: Set Properties

The look and feel of a control is determined by its properties. The first property you should set is the Name property to specify a unique and descriptive identifier for each control object. The name for each control should begin with a three-character, lowercase prefix followed by a descriptive mixed-case name.

Table 6-1 lists the standard naming conventions used in this book along with some sample control names.

**Table 6.1** Standard VB.NET Control Naming Conventions

| Control Type | Prefix | Example Name Property |
|---|---|---|
| Button | btn | **`btnCalculate`** |
| Label | lbl | **`lblDecription`** |
| PictureBox | pic | **`picImage`** |
| Timer | tmr | **`tmrDisplayAd`** |
| Text box | txt | **`txtNumDependents`** |
| List box | lst | **`lstTestScores`** |
| Combo box | cbo | **`cboSelectTopping`** |
| Checkbox | chk | **`chkRSVP`** |
| Radio button | rad | **`radPaymentMethod`** |

**Tip**

**The Properties window displays only one object at a time. It is a good habit to verify visually that you have the proper object selected before you change any property values.**

Single-click Button1 to select it. You can tell which object is selected because it is outlined by a thick gray border with eight handle boxes. The properties of the selected object appear in the Properties window. Find the Name property and enter **`btnHello`** as its value (Figure 6-9).

Even though the Name property has been changed, the button still shows the text *Button1*. The Text property determines the visible text on a button. Find the

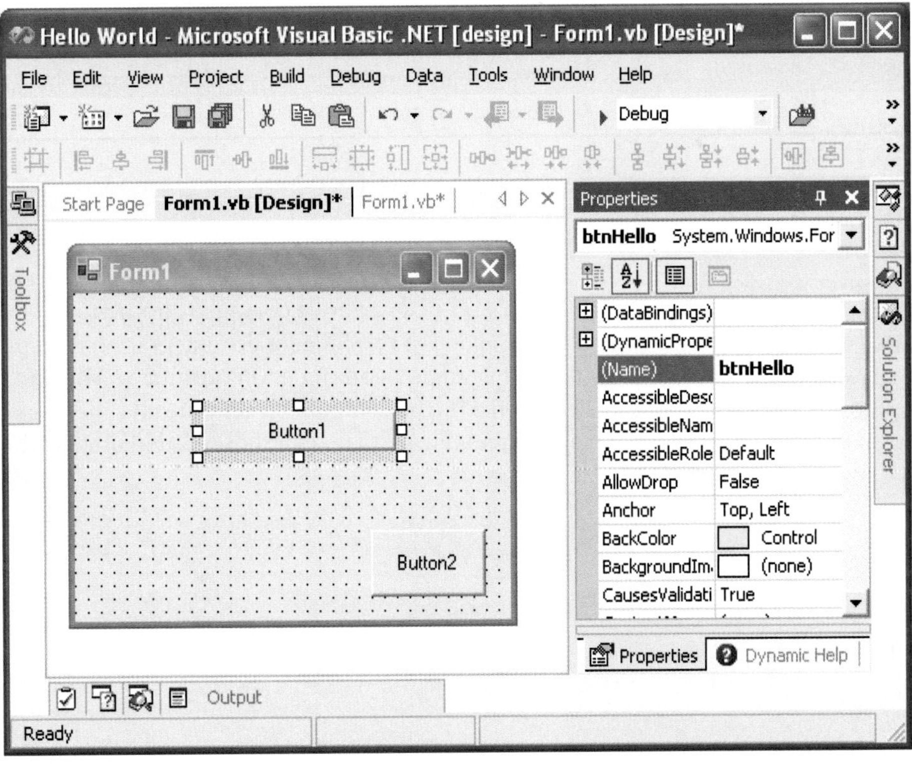


**FIGURE 6.9** *Setting the Name Property for a Button Control*

**FIGURE 6.10**
*Changing the Text Property of the btnHello Control*

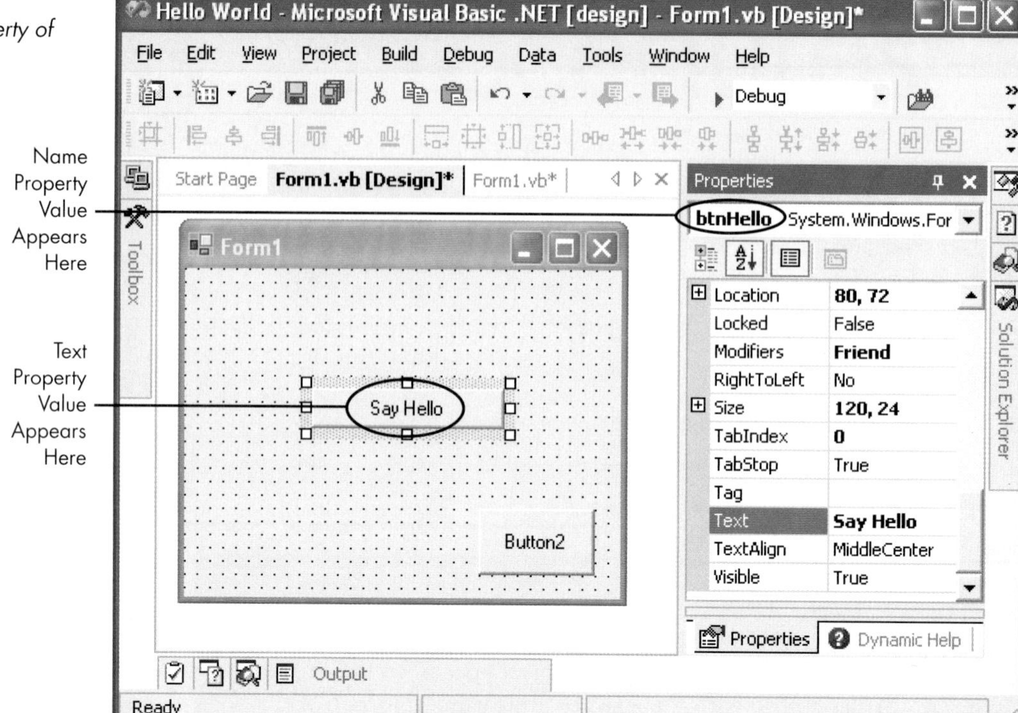


**Tip**

**Be careful not to confuse the Name property with the Text property. The Name property specifies the formal name of the control and should begin with a three-character prefix followed by a descriptive name without spaces. The Text property determines the text visible to the user and may contain spaces.**

**Tip**

**To create an access key, place an ampersand (&) before the letter that will be the access key. At runtime, you can select the control by pressing ALT + access key.**

Text property and enter **`Say Hello`** as its value. Notice that the Text property value appears on the face of the button in the form shown in Figure 6-10.

Repeat this process by selecting the Button2 control and setting its Name property to **`btnExit`** and its Text property to **`E&xit`**. The ampersand (&) in the Text property creates an access key. Finally, change Form1's Text property to **`Hello World Form`**.

## Step 3: Add Code

Press F7 or select View | Code from the menubar to open the ***Code Editor*** where you enter, display, and edit your code. It is good programming style to begin all projects with a set of descriptive comments at the top of the code. A ***comment*** is a descriptive note added to the code for documentation or explanatory purposes. Comments begin with a single quote (') and continue to the end of the line. Comments are totally ignored by the computer at runtime and therefore have no effect on how the program behaves. Figure 6-11 shows the Code Editor with a comment block at the beginning of the file.

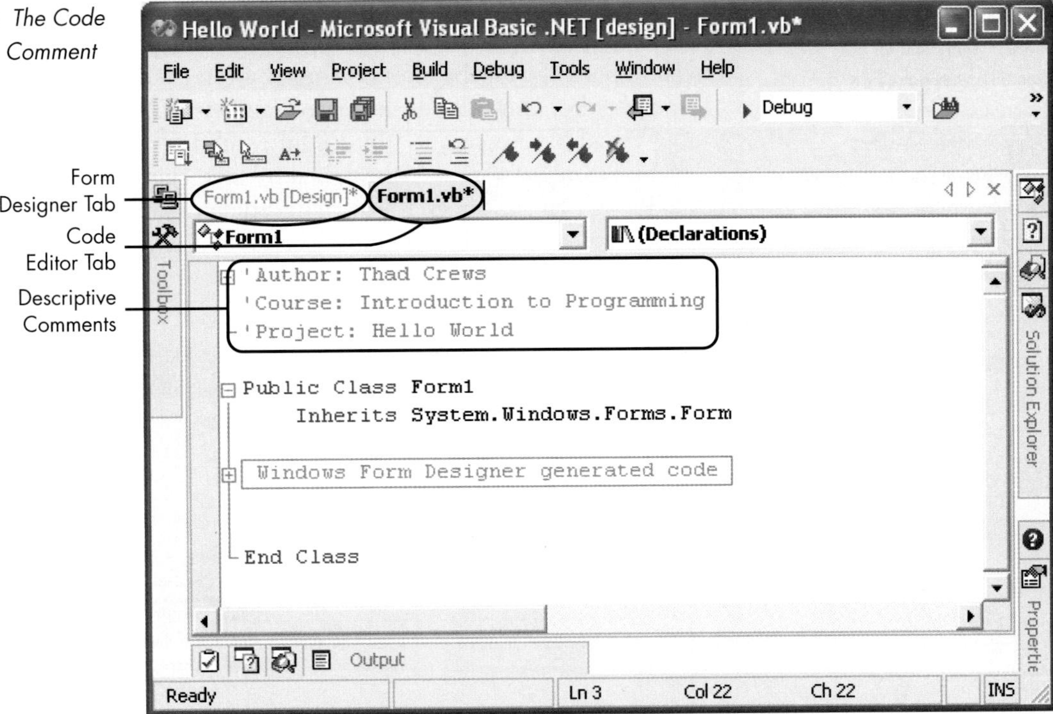


**FIGURE 6.11** *The Code Editor with a Leading Comment Block*

A major part of Visual Basic programming is writing event procedures. An event procedure is code that is called in response to an event, such as a mouse click. The Code Editor can create event procedure stubs (or shells) for you. To create an event procedure stub, you first must select the desired control from the Class drop-down list (Figure 6-12).

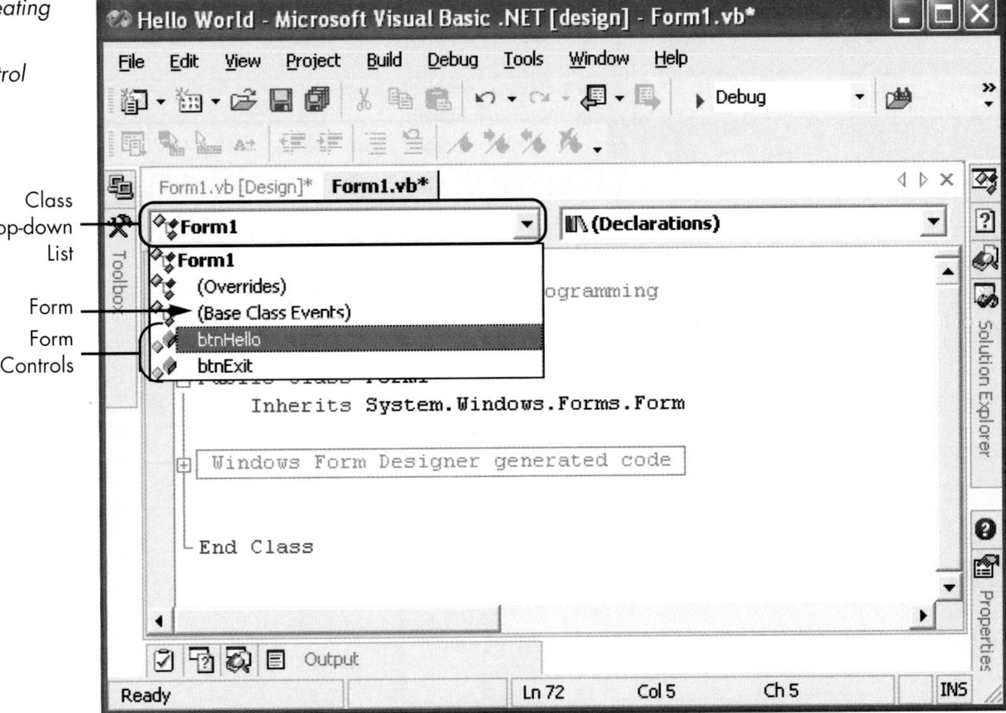


**FIGURE 6.12** *Creating an Event Procedure Stub, Step 1: Selecting the Control*

**Tip**

While it is possible to type the event procedure declaration yourself, it is highly recommended that you let Visual Studio create the stubs for you; you should then write the code that appears within the stub.

Depending on which control you select, Visual Studio will populate the method drop-down list appropriately. For example, a button has fifty-seven events to which it can respond. By far the most common button event is the click event. Select "Click" from the drop-down list as shown in Figure 6-13.

Visual Studio creates a procedure stub for the specified control and specified event. Figure 6-14 shows part of the btnHello click event procedure stub, which concludes well off the screen to the right. Students are strongly encouraged to use Visual Studio's procedure stub generation feature rather than typing stubs in manually.

**FIGURE 6.13** *Creating an Event Procedure Stub, Step 2: Selecting the Event*

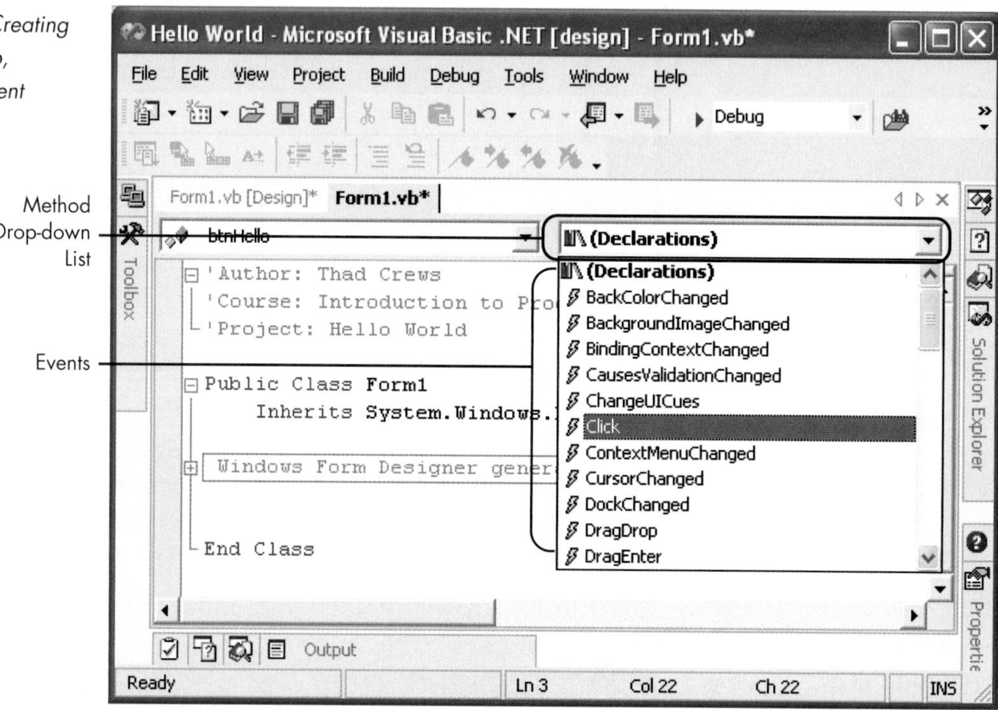


**FIGURE 6.14** *A Click Event Procedure Stub Generated by Visual Studio*

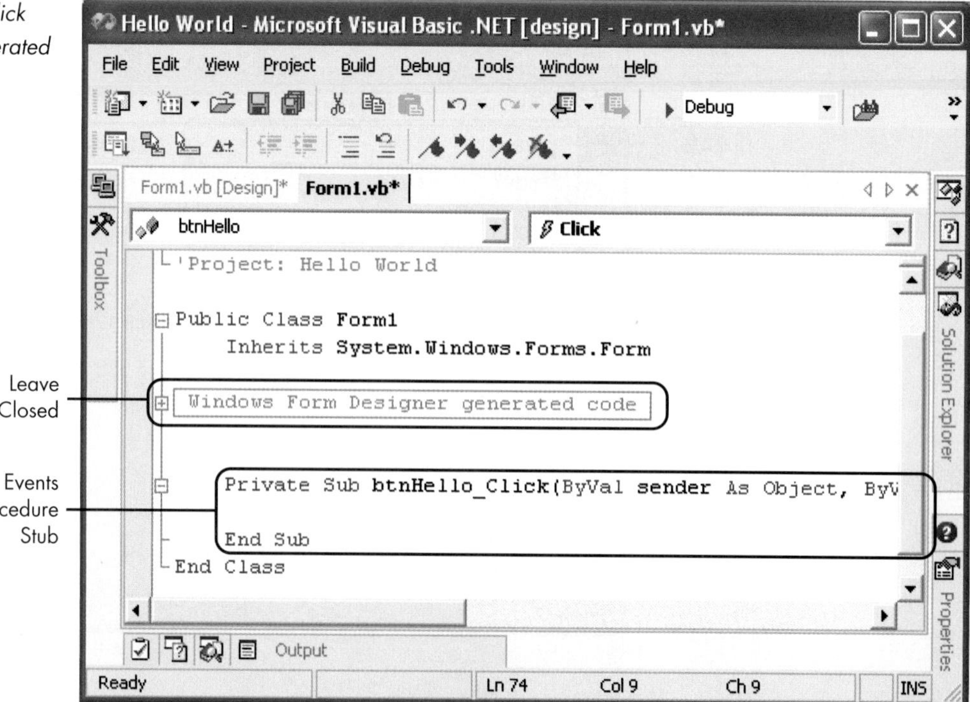

Any code written inside this event procedure will execute whenever the btnHello button is clicked. Position the cursor within the stub, and type **`MsgBox("Hello World")`**. Then create a click event stub for the btnExit button and type **`MsgBox("Goodbye")`** and then **`End`** inside that procedure. The End command causes the application to terminate. Figure 6-15 shows both event procedure stubs, including a descriptive comment for the End command.

**FIGURE 6.15** *Code for Two Click Event Procedures*

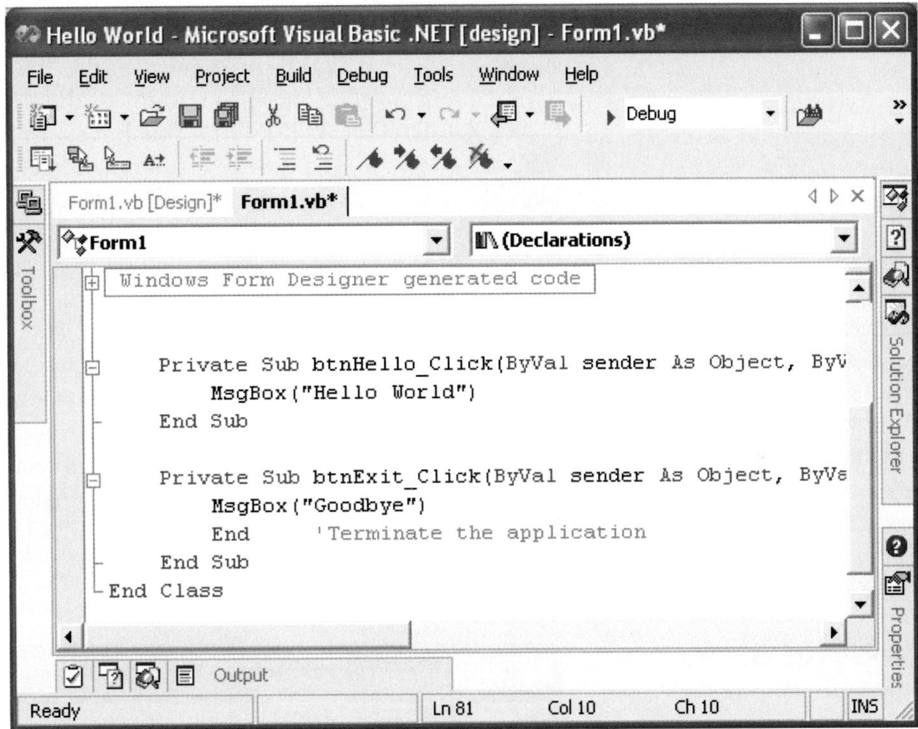


## Step 4: Run the Project

You are ready to run your project to see if it works. You can run the project by clicking the run icon in the standard toolbar or by pressing F5. If all is well, you will see quite a bit happening in the background followed by a window with a button like that of Figure 6-16.

**FIGURE 6.16** *Hello World GUI*

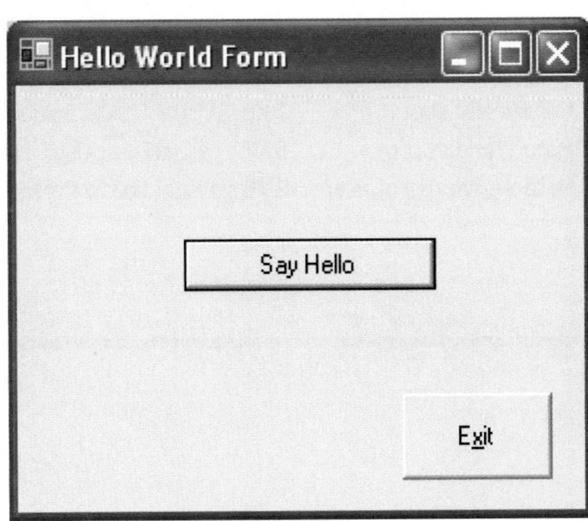

**FIGURE 6.17** *Message Box Output*

Pressing the "Say Hello" button generates a message box with the text *Hello World* as shown in Figure 6-17. Likewise, pressing the "Exit" button generates a message box with the text *Goodbye* and then terminates the application.

CONGRATULATIONS!!! You have just written and executed your first VB.NET program. The developers of Amazon.com started from humble beginnings like this.

## Step 5: Save the Project

**Tip**

**It is a good idea to save your work often, and especially before running a project.**

You always want to remember to save your work when you are finished. Be sure to select Save All rather than Save Form because even the simplest VB.NET project involves more than just a single form file. In fact, it is a good idea to find out where Visual Studio saved your Hello World projects. One common location is My Documents in a folder called Visual Studio Projects. Your machine might be different. Regardless of its location, the Hello World folder should contain the files shown in Figure 6-18.

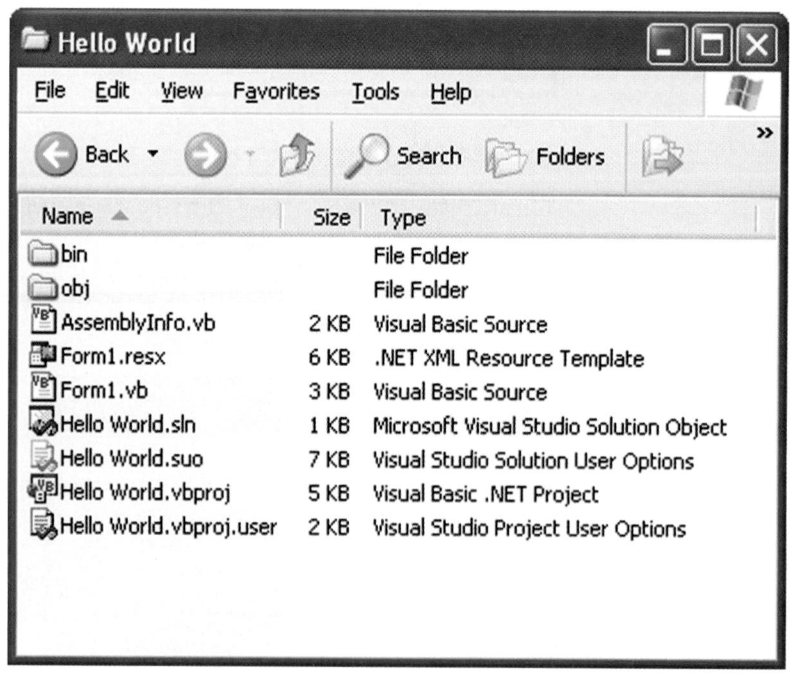


**FIGURE 6.18** *Files in the Hello World Folder*

## 6-4 Windows GUI

Visual Basic is the most widely used tool in the world for developing Windows applications.

Windows applications utilize a GUI that provides visual cues to the user, such as menus, buttons, and icons, that allow the user to work intuitively and efficiently. For example, the operating system command of deleting the widget.txt file can be accomplished by

1. dragging and dropping the file's icon into the trash can,
2. selecting the file and pressing the Delete key, or
3. right-clicking on the file and selecting Delete from the resulting pop-up menu.

All of these GUI commands are faster and more intuitive than typing the command line statement `del c:\windows\desktop\widget.txt`.

A GUI also makes applications like Word and Excel much easier for users. These applications contain WYSIWYG ("What You See Is What You Get") formatting, dialog boxes, menus, icons, and online help, which allow the user to be productive without memorizing hundreds of specific key strokes and commands. Because the GUI is common for all Windows applications, once you have learned one Windows application, you have a head start on the next one, and so on.

### ASK THE AUTHOR

**Q** Who invented the GUI, Microsoft or Apple?

**A** Neither. Early research on the GUI began at the Stanford Research Laboratory and at the Massachusetts Institute of Technology in the 1960s. In 1973 Xerox PARC developed the Alto computer containing all of the elements of the modern GUI. The GUI became widely available to the general public with Apple's Lisa (1983) and Macintosh (1984). The GUI became available for IBM-PC compatible users in 1987 when Microsoft released Windows 3.0, and it is now common for almost all operating systems, including Unix/Linux machines running X Window.

## 6-5 Working with Objects

Developing a Windows application with a GUI used to be a difficult task. Even something as simple as a GUI button required significant effort. Consider the following.

- The button must have the proper size (width and height).
- The button must be at the proper location (distance from the top and left margins of its container).
- The button must display text, such as *Click Me* or *Exit*, centered horizontally and vertically.
- The button should have a visual indication when it has the focus. Typically, this is a thicker border and a dashed line around the inside edge.
- The button must work with other GUI controls by receiving and passing the focus when the Tab key is pressed.
- The user should be able to select the button by either clicking it with the mouse or pressing Enter when the button has focus.
- The button should look pressed or pushed when the mouse is pressed with the cursor over the button; it should return to its normal state when the mouse is released.
- Clicking the button should trigger an appropriate action.

Multiply this complexity by all the GUI elements in a standard Windows application (resizable windows, text boxes, menus, scroll bars, etc.), and you can appreciate the work required to develop those first Windows applications.

This all changed when Microsoft released Visual Basic 1.0 in 1991. Visual Basic greatly simplified the development process by providing a collection of useful, reusable graphical interface control objects that made adding a button as easy as drag-and-drop. You could create great Windows applications quickly by simply combining pre-built components to create your finished application.

Pre-built GUI components are one example of objects. Generally speaking, an ***object*** is anything we might use in our application for acquiring, manipulating, or presenting data or information. An object contains both ***properties*** (data) and ***methods*** (actions for manipulating an object's data) that are appropriate to support the intended use of the object. An object is defined once (an object definition is called a ***class***), and then the developer creates as many ***instances*** of the object as necessary for the application.

Forms and controls are pre-built graphical objects used to create the GUI for your application. The use of forms and controls is what makes Visual Basic so popular for creating Windows applications. Rather than reinventing the wheel (or button) with every new application, a button control class has been defined once, and now developers can create instances of that button control with a simple drag-and-drop. Other controls include labels, picture boxes, text boxes, check boxes, radio buttons, timers, and many more. Because these controls have already been defined, they are easily used during development.

## ▶ ASK THE AUTHOR

**Q** Are all objects graphical, like forms and controls?

**A** No. As an illustration, consider a banking application. Some of the objects likely to be included in an object-oriented solution would be customers, accounts, and transactions. If the bank had one thousand live customers, the application solution would have one thousand customer objects. If a specific customer had three accounts (checking, savings, and car loan), there would be three corresponding account objects in the application. The application would call an appropriate method every time money was taken from an account, such as when a check cleared or a debit card purchase was processed. Likewise, anytime money was added to an account, in the form of a deposit or loan payment for example, there would be a corresponding method action. If the object classes were well made, a sophisticated banking application could be implemented as numerous objects interacting with each other in a manner that corresponded to the real actions of the bank customers.

Objects are essential to the .NET Framework. You use form and control objects to create the GUI. You use ASP.NET to create dynamic web applications. You use ADO.NET objects to connect to a database. In other words, developers of modern applications must know how to work with objects.

The ***.NET class library*** is a library of classes included in the Microsoft .NET Framework and is designed to be the foundation on which .NET applications are built. The .NET library contains a large number of classes with reusable code. To help manage this complexity, .NET uses ***namespaces***, which are collections of related classes. System.Windows.Form is the namespace containing classes for creating Windows-based applications.

## Reuse and Reliability

One of the most powerful features of object classes is that they are ***reusable***. Developers have spent thousands of hours designing and developing the classes for the forms and common controls we use in this book. Fortunately, we do not have to repeat their efforts. We simply use the classes and the objects they produce. This illustrates a key point: when working with objects, you should not reinvent the wheel with each new project. If an appropriate object class already exists to do the job, use that object.

**MANAGER**

Because so many classes are available for reuse, developers can quickly create a wide range of interesting applications. Visual Basic is therefore often called a ***rapid application development (RAD)*** system. Early RAD systems were limited in functionality and inefficient during execution. Such is no longer the case. Modern RAD systems like VB.NET are used to generate a broad range of professional applications. At the same time, many traditional programming languages like C++ are now supported by development environments with visual tools. Therefore, the line between traditional development languages and RAD environments is disappearing.

Objects can also enhance ***reliability***. Reliability is the result of good design and lots and lots of testing. The VB.NET class library is the result of thousands of hours of testing by developers. The combination of reuse and reliability makes predefined objects an attractive choice to developers.

**MANAGER**

Both reuse and reliability have significant financial benefits. Reuse is valuable because an object created in-house is created once and used again in future projects. This reduces the time, and therefore the cost, of the second project. The time benefits are even greater if the original development occurs by a third party. This is analogous to outsourcing in that general, time-consuming tasks are handled by a third party while the organization's developers concentrate on their core business goals.

Testing and reliability potentially can generate even greater cost savings. Remember that corrective maintenance is expensive. Hard-to-find errors often cannot be identified without significant testing. Objects developed in-house cannot be tested to the same degree as a third-party object that has been extensively tested by the third-party provider and all organizations that have themselves adopted and tested the technology.

## Consumers and Producers

All VB.NET developers *use* objects, but not all VB.NET developers necessarily *write* object classes. Stated in economic terms, all VB.NET developers are *consumers* of objects, but only some are *producers* of object classes. Any good VB.NET developer should know how to use (consume) the appropriate object in .NET. Writing (producing) object classes is often unnecessary.

## ASK THE AUTHOR

**Q** I want to learn how to write object classes and use objects. Which should I learn first?

**A** For multiple reasons, you should learn how to use objects before you learn how to write object classes. First, you will find object classes are easier to write (and you will write them better) if you already know how objects are used. Second, the number of high-quality objects available to developers is growing rapidly. You may find that objects for which you needed to write classes yourself five years ago are available today in a class library. For example, the .NET Framework class library contains the most extensive collection of objects for e-business applications development to date.

When you do start writing your own object classes, VB.NET will be helpful there as well. Key object-oriented features, such as inheritance, polymorphism, and late binding, are all supported by the .NET Framework, making VB.NET a viable language choice for developers interested in writing their own object classes. Chapter 14 explains how to write object classes in VB.NET.

### *Object Summary*

- An object is a self-contained entity that has both properties and methods. The properties of an object provide access to its data, and the methods of an object are the procedures used to manipulate the object and its data.
- Windows forms are objects. Visual controls, such as buttons, text boxes, menus, and scroll bars, are also objects as are nonvisual controls, such as timers.
- The .NET class library contains a rich set of classes. You may also write your own object classes, a topic discussed in Chapter 14.

## 6-6 Control Objects

As you design and modify the user interface of your project, you will find it necessary to add, align, and position controls. The ***Control class*** contains numerous properties and methods common to all controls for developing the user interface. A selected subset of the most commonly used properties and methods appears in Tables 6-2 and 6-3. These properties and methods are sufficient to write numerous interesting applications.

**Table 6.2 Common Control Properties**

| Property | Description |
|---|---|
| BackColor | Gets or sets the background color for the control |
| Bottom | Gets the distance between the bottom edge of the control and the top edge of its container's client area |
| Cursor | Gets or sets the cursor that is displayed when the mouse pointer is over the control |
| Enabled | Gets or sets a value indicating whether the control can respond to user interaction |
| Font | Gets or sets the font of the text displayed by the control |
| ForeColor | Gets or sets the foreground color of the control |
| Height | Gets or sets the height of the control |
| Left | Gets or sets the x-coordinate of a control's left edge in pixels |
| Location | Gets or sets the coordinates of the upper left corner of the control relative to the upper left corner of its container |
| Name | Gets or sets the name of the control |
| Right | Gets the distance between the right edge of the control and the left edge of its container |
| Size | Gets or sets the height and width of the control |
| TabIndex | Gets or sets the tab order of the control within its container |
| TabStop | Gets or sets a value indicating whether the user can give the focus to this control using the Tab key |
| Text | Gets or sets the text associated with this control |
| Top | Gets or sets the y-coordinate of the control's top edge in pixels |
| Visible | Gets or sets a value indicating whether the control is displayed |
| Width | Gets or sets the width of the control |

**Table 6.3 Common Control Methods**

| Method | Description |
|---|---|
| Focus | Sets input focus to the control |
| Hide | Conceals the control from the user |
| Show | Displays the control to the user |

The control class shares its behavior with more specific controls suitable for a particular purpose, such as buttons, labels, picture boxes, and timers. These four specific control classes are described in the following section.

## The Button Control

The ***Button control*** is considered to be the most basic graphical control. The user typically clicks a button to perform an action. When the button is clicked, it looks as if it is being pushed in and released. Selecting the button triggers the click event handler. You place code in the click event handler to perform an appropriate action.

The text displayed on the button is contained in the Text property. If your text exceeds the width of the button, it will wrap to the next line. However, it will be clipped (chopped off) if the control cannot accommodate its overall height.

A button's click event can be triggered by doing any of the following:

- Clicking the button with the mouse
- If the button has the focus, then pressing the spacebar or Enter key
- If the button's text property contains an access key, pressing ALT + the underlined letter
- If the button is the Cancel button of the form, pressing ESC
- Calling the button's PerformClick method to select the button programmatically

**Tip**
**A form's CancelButton property can be set to a specific button control. If the property is set, pressing the ESC key selects the button regardless of the focus.**

## The Label Control

The ***Label control*** is used to display text that cannot be edited by the user. The caption displayed in the label is contained in the Text property. The Alignment property allows you to set the alignment of the text within the label. The text can be displayed single-line or multiline, and the control can be either fixed in size or can automatically resize itself to accommodate its caption. If AutoSize is set to false, the words specified in the Text property will wrap to the next line, if possible, but the control will not grow.

Even though the user cannot edit the control, you can change the text programmatically. For example, if your application is processing a large file, you can write code to display and update a "percent done" message in a label.

## The PictureBox Control

**Tip**
**When using images in a program, it is a good idea to copy the images to the project's bin folder, which is the default file directory.**

The ***PictureBox control*** is used to display graphics in bitmap, GIF, JPEG, metafile, or icon file formats. The picture that is displayed is determined by the Image property, which can be set at runtime or at design time. You can load or change the image at runtime using the FromFile method of the Image class.

```
PictureBox1.Image = Image.FromFile("CompanyLogo.gif")
```

One of the main advantages of using a picture box for images is the SizeMode property that specifies how the image and control fit with each other. The SizeMode property can be set to do the following:

- Align the picture's upper left corner with the control's upper left corner
- Center the picture within the control
- Adjust the size of the control to fit the picture it displays
- Stretch any picture to fit the control

**MENTOR**

Stretching a picture, especially one in bitmap format, can produce a loss in image quality. Metafiles, which are lists of graphics instructions for drawing images at runtime, are often better suited for stretching than bitmaps are.

## The Timer Control

The ***Timer control*** is used to raise an event at user-defined intervals. The length of the intervals is defined by the Interval property, whose value is in milliseconds. When Enabled is true and the Interval is greater than zero, the Tick event is raised every interval. The key methods of the Timer component are Start and Stop, which turn the timer on and off. You may also start and stop the timer by changing the Enabled property value to true or false. When the timer is switched off, it resets; there is no way to pause a Timer control.

**MENTOR**

A timer is a nonvisual control and therefore does not need to be displayed on the Windows Forms Designer surface. When a nonvisual control (or component) is added to a form, the Windows Forms Designer shows a resizable tray at the bottom of the form where all components are displayed. Once a control has been added to the component tray, you can select the component and set its properties as you would any other control on the form.

# 6-7 Working with Events

Visual Basic supports ***event-driven programming*** in which the application recognizes and responds to events. An ***event*** is an action or occurrence recognized by some object and for which you can write code to respond. Events can occur as a result of a user action or a program calculation, or they can be triggered by the system. Common user events include clicking the mouse, moving the mouse, entering text, or pressing a key on the keyboard. Events may also be system generated, such as a timer Tick event.

**Tip**

**The Button control does not support the DoubleClick event. If the user attempts to double-click the control, it will be processed as two Click events.**

An ***event handler*** contains code that responds to a particular event. VB.NET developers carefully design their applications by determining the controls available to the user and the appropriate events associated with those controls. The developer then writes the code to implement the events consistent with the application's design. Common events associated with the Control class are presented in Table 6-4.

**Table 6.4 Common Control Events**

| Event | Description |
|---|---|
| Click | Occurs when the control is clicked |
| DoubleClick | Occurs when the control is double-clicked |
| MouseDown | Occurs when the mouse pointer is over the control and a mouse button is pressed |
| MouseMove | Occurs when the mouse pointer is moved over the control |

Some events are specific to certain objects. For example, the Tick event applies only to timers. The Form object has two unique events as well, Load and Activate. These object-specific events are presented in Table 6-5.

**Table 6.5 Object-Specific Events**

| Object | Event | Description |
|---|---|---|
| Form | Load | Occurs before a form is displayed for the first time |
| Form | Activated | Occurs when the form is activated in code or by the user |
| Timer | Tick | Occurs every Interval milleseconds when enabled |

**ASK THE AUTHOR**

Q What is the difference between the Click and MouseDown events?

A For some controls, the Click event can be raised by user actions other than clicking the mouse; for example, pressing Enter will execute the Click event for a button if it has the focus.

Another difference is that the MouseDown event includes additional information about the event, including which mouse button was pressed, and the x and y coordinates of the mouse click. Finally, the MouseDown event is triggered immediately upon a mouse press, whereas a Click event is only triggered by a mouse press and release on the same control.

**Tip**

**While it is possible to type event procedure stubs directly in the Code Editor, it is recommended that you let Visual Studio create the stubs for you using the pull-down boxes at the top of the Code Editor. This prevents the possibility of typographical errors and also ensures that the parameter list is correct.**

**Tip**

**Double-clicking a control creates a stub for its default event. The default event for Form, Button, Label and PictureBox controls is the Click event. The default event for a Timer control is the Tick event.**

## Event Procedures

As a developer, you can write event procedure code to make your application respond appropriately. The naming convention for an event procedure is the name of the triggering object followed by an underscore character followed by the name of the event. For example, the click event for a form named frmMain is frmMain_Click. Visual Studio will create a control's default event procedure stub if you double-click on the control during design time. You can also create an event stub by selecting the object and event from the Code Editor window.

## Rem Statement

A **Rem statement** provides an explanatory remark (or comment) in a program. You can also use an apostrophe (') to indicate a remark statement. If the Rem keyword follows other statements on a line, it must be separated from the statements by a colon. However, when you use an apostrophe, the colon is not required after other statements.

*Syntax:*

```
REM comment
' comment
statement ' comment
```

*Examples:*

```
' The line below changes the image for the PictureBox control
picLogo.Image = Image.FromFile("CompanyLogo.gif")
btnCalculate.Text = "Click Me!"   'Change the caption of the button
```

Remarks are totally ignored by Visual Basic; therefore, they neither speed up nor slow down the performance of the program. Remarks document your program's logic, making it easier for developers to understand and maintain the code.

Different organizations have different policies regarding documentation. Likewise, different instructors have different documentation expectations from students. As a general rule, there are three types of remarks.

***Header comments*** occur at the beginning of a project file. These typically include the name of the author, the purpose of the project, and the date created. When maintenance occurs, a new maintenance entry should be added to the header comment specifying the developer, modification description, and date of modification.

***Block comments*** appear above a block of one or more lines of code and describe the function or behavior of that code block within the larger algorithm.

***Inline comments*** typically appear on the same line as a statement. Inline comments are used to document and clarify non-obvious statements.

## Rnd Statement

Many applications, especially games and simulations, benefit from the use of randomly generated numbers. VB.NET provides the ***Rnd statement***, which generates a single precision random value between 0.0 up to (but not including) 1.0.

Simulations often require random integer values between 1 and some upper bound value, such as the roll of a die or the number of people waiting in line at a restaurant. The Rnd statement can also be used for this purpose.

*Syntax:* *value* = *Int*(**Rnd**() * *upperbound*)

*Examples:*

```
DiceRoll = Int(Rnd() * 6) + 1
XPos = Int(Rnd() * 200)
```

Notice the use of the intrinsic function Int, which accepts a numeric argument and returns the integer portion of the argument. Int and other intrinsic functions are explained in detail in Chapter 7.

Note that the random dice roll in the example above contains a trailing +1. This is because Int(Rnd() * 6) generates one of six integer values, 0, 1, 2, 3, 4, or 5. Adding one to this result generates the desired range of values.

Remember that the computer is not smart, and it cannot think of a number like a human can. Instead, the computer generates a sequence of random numbers by following a mathematical algorithm. The numbers in the sequence depend on the seed value. If a program uses the same seed value, it will generate the same sequence of numbers. The ability to create the same sequence of random numbers can be helpful when you're developing and debugging a program with random values. To change the random sequence, you need only change the seed value. The ***Randomize statement*** is used exactly for that purpose. The Randomize statement need only be called one time, and all the resulting random values will be different. Without the Randomize statement, there is the possibility that repeated executions of a program could yield the same results, which would be deterministic instead of the intended random behavior.

### Example Program: Jumping Button

The following program provides a simple illustration of an event procedure that uses the Rnd statement to change the position of a button every time it is pressed. Start a new project and add a single button to the form. Double-click on the button to pull up the Code Editor and add the appropriate code below to the Click event procedure.

```
Public Class Form1
  Inherits System.Windows.Forms.Form

Windows Form Designer generated code

  Private Sub Button1_Click(ByVal sender As System.Object, _
              ByVal e As System.EventArgs) Handles Button1.Click
    MsgBox("Hello World")
    Button1.Top = Int(Rnd() * 200)
    Button1.Left = Int(Rnd() * 200)
  End Sub
End Class
```

Run the program (F5) and see how changing the Top and Left properties of the button makes it move around the screen after each Hello World message.

### *Event Procedure Summary*

- An event refers to an action or occurrence detected by a program. Events can be user actions, such as clicking a mouse button or pressing a key, or system occurrences, such as opening or closing a window. Most modern applications, particularly those that run in Macintosh and Windows environments, are event-driven.
- An event procedure is the method that handles an event. Visual Studio creates the event procedure stub, and the developer writes the code that appears within the stub.
- Remarks, or comments, should be used liberally to document the logic of your solution.
- Random values can be generated using the Rnd statement. The sequence of random values will be the same unless the seed is changed by calling the Randomize statement.

## 6-8 Project Development Process

Building a software application is often compared to building a house. First you decide what kind of house you want (ranch, A-frame, tri-level, etc.) and what features you want (privacy, lots of sunlight, good for entertaining, etc.). Then you design a house blueprint that achieves all of the objectives. The blueprint design must be detailed, not only containing the entire floor plan down to the last inch, but also containing a description of all electrical and plumbing information. When the design is finalized, then the construction can begin. If you have a good design being worked on by skilled professionals (carpenters, plumbers, electricians, brick layers, etc.), the house should turn out great.

Of course, a house is never finished, not even after the construction is over and the owners have moved in. There is always work required to keep it well maintained, such as landscaping, decoration, and cleaning. There are also predictable modifications required to keep the house modern, such as repainting and refurnishing. And if the owners want to continue to live in the house, it is possible they will request a major renovation like an extension on the house so that they can increase their enjoyment and use of the house.

The process of building a house is indeed a good analogy to building a software application. The software project begins with the ***analysis stage***, in which the developer decides what kind of application and features he or she wants. In the ***design stage***, the developer plans out how to achieve the goals of the analysis stage. The design should be detailed, including an interface design to describe the layout of the GUI and a code design to describe the events and associated modules. When the design is finalized, then the developer begins the ***implementation stage***. If a good design is being implemented by skilled professionals (developers, programmers, etc.), the application should turn out great.

Of course, the application is not finished just because it has been delivered to the client. After delivery, the application enters the ***maintenance stage***. There are three types of maintenance. The first is *corrective maintenance*, whereby the clients report problems and the developers fix the problems. There is also *adaptive maintenance*, which involves predictable modifications required to keep the application modern, such as changes to support upgrades of the operating system or database. Finally, *enhancement maintenance* is necessary when the client requests a major renovation to increase the enjoyment and use of the application.

## The Cost of Poor Planning

It is well understood in the construction industry that potential problems must be identified and corrected as early as possible. Imagine a problem in the design of a house that results in an insufficient number of electrical outlets for a particular room. If the problem is detected during the design stage, then it is relatively easy to fix. However, if the same problem goes undetected until the implementation (building) stage when walls have been put up, then the time, effort, and costs required to fix the problem are all considerably greater.

Application designers must also realize the importance of finding problems early. Industry data suggests that fixing an analysis problem requires three times as much time and effort if the problem is not fixed until the design stage, about ten times as much if it is not fixed until the implementation stage, and fifty to two hundred times as much if it is not addressed until the maintenance stage. This means a problem that could be fixed in a day during analysis might require two hundred person-days to fix if not addressed until the maintenance stage.

## ASK THE AUTHOR

**Q** What is a person-day?

**A** A person-day is the amount of work one person could do in one day. A person-day is a measure of effort, not time. Two people working on the same task for an entire day would represent two person-days of work, even though only a single day of real time is involved. Likewise, person-week and person-month are also measures of effort rather than time.

## Testing and Documentation

You may be asking, *What about testing and documentation?* Some authors present testing and documentation as separate stages. In practice, both testing and documentation are essential activities for each stage of development. There should be testing in the analysis stage to ensure that the developer has identified what the client wants and needs. The testing at this stage could consist of a series of "What if . . .?" questions. It is also essential that there be documentation during the analysis stage indicating what the developer and the client have agreed on. The developer will need this documentation to provide guidance to the design activity. It is also helpful to have the analysis documentation in the event that the client tries to change the project objective during the development process. Without mutually agreed on analysis documentation, the client may try to grow the project in little increments that could result in the application becoming significantly more complex. There is nothing wrong with adding features and functionality at the client's request, but the developer should be compensated for those additions.

### *Project Development Summary*

- The analysis stage determines what the solution needs to do. The design stage determines how the solution will do it. The implementation stage involves writing code to implement the design. The maintenance stage begins when the product is delivered.
- For an industrial software solution, the maintenance stage consumes approximately 66 percent of the time and money spent on the project. Developers should always be aware of decisions that will impact maintenance, good or bad.
- Testing and documentation are essential activities of every development stage.

## Young Entrepreneurs

Reed and Elizabeth start by brainstorming about all the possible applications they can develop for their Singing Mimes Company. "For our first project, we should keep the code simple and let VB.NET do most of the real work," Elizabeth says. "Even something as simple as Hello World could be interesting if you clicked on a cool image instead of a button."

"We can get some animated gif images for free off the Internet," Reed explains. "You just have to make sure it is an image that you have permission to use. I know of one site that has animated dragons. Using timer events, we could make the dragon appear and disappear on the form."

"We can use timers to turn the image on and off, and move the dragon's position on the screen using the random function," Elizabeth continues. "We could write click event code that keeps up with the number of hits. Finally, we could have a third timer to indicate when the game is over."

Elizabeth and Reed name their game *DragonStryke* and record their design on notebook paper.

### Design

The design specifies how the solution will work in general terms. They begin by sketching the interface for the DragonStryke application, specifying the Name property for all the necessary controls. The Text property can also be displayed when appropriate. The sketch in Figure 6-19 includes a PictureBox control for the dragon image, two label controls to describe and display the number of hits, another label to display the final score, a button to start a new game, and another button to exit the application. The buttons and final score label will be hidden when the game is being played.

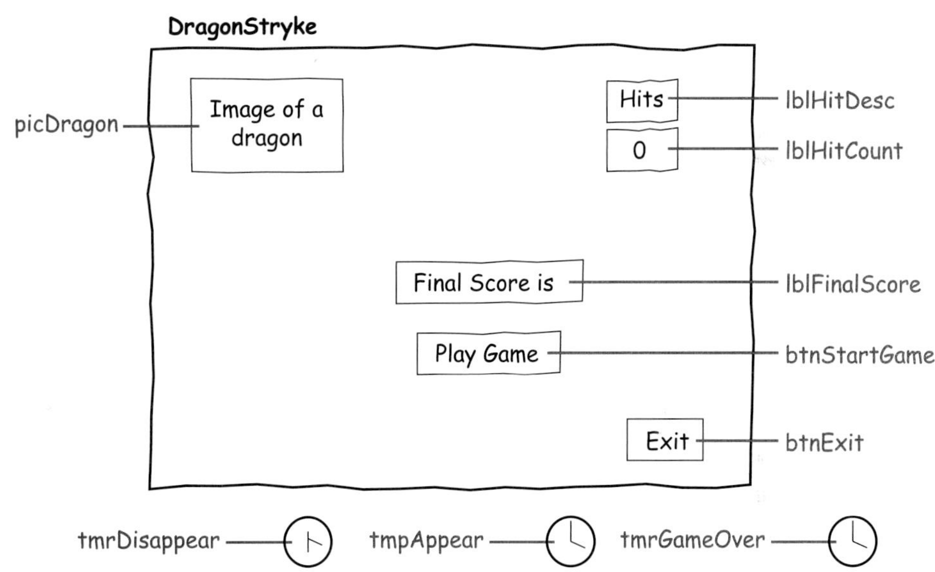


**FIGURE 6.19** *Sketch of the DragonStryke User Interface*

The design should also include a high-level specification of all the actions and behavior required by the project. This can be done using flowchart or pseudocode notation and should describe behavior without getting into details of implementation. Table 6-6 provides pseudocode descriptions of the procedures in the DragonStryke design.

**Table 6.6** Design Pseudocode for DragonStryke Application

| Procedure | Behavior |
|---|---|
| btnStartGame_Click | 1. Set game score label to zero<br>2. Hide buttons and final score label<br>3. Start disappear timer and game over timer<br>4. Show dragon |
| tmrDisappear_Tick | 1. Turn off disappear timer<br>2. Hide dragon<br>3. Turn on appear timer |
| tmrAppear_Tick | 1. Turn off appear timer<br>2. Move dragon to random location<br>3. Show dragon<br>4. Turn on disappear timer |
| tmrGameOver_Tick | 1. Stop timers<br>2. Hide dragon<br>3. Update and show final score label<br>4. Show buttons |
| picDragon_Click | Update game score label |
| btnExit_Click | End the application. |

### Implementation

After they complete the general design, they must implement the details. The first step of implementation is to build the GUI. Figure 6-20 illustrates the DragonStryke GUI.

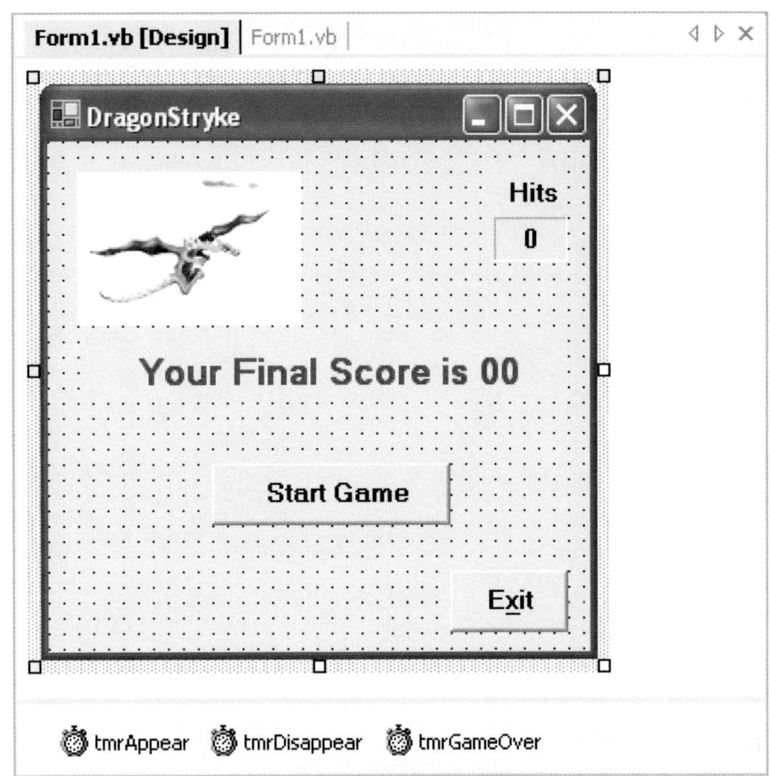


**FIGURE 6.20**
*DragonStryke User Interface*

The second step is to implement the functionality described in the pseudocode design. It is also a good habit to document important design time property values for the form and interface controls. The solution code with good documentation follows.

```
' Author: Reed & Elizabeth
' Project: DragonStryke
' Description: DragonStryke is a game in which the player attempts to click
'              a moving image. The image will appear and disappear at
'              random intervals. The number of times the image is "hit" is
'              maintained throughout the play. The game ends after a
'              predetermined amount of time.


' *** Design Time Properties ***
' OBJECT                      PROPERTY         SETTING
'
' picDragon                   Image            "dragon.jpg"
'                             SizeMode         StretchImage
'                             Visible          False
'
' lblHitDesc                  Font             10 point, Bold
'                             Text             "Hits"
'                             TextAlign        MiddleCenter
'
' lblHitCount                 BorderStyle      Fixed 3D
'                             Font             10 point, Bold
'                             Text             0
'                             TextAlign        MiddleCenter
```

```
' tmrDisappear                 Interval         1000
'                              Enabled          False
'
' tmrAppear                    Interval         2000
'                              Enabled          False
'
' tmrGameOver                  Interval         14500
'                              Enabled          False
'
' btnStartGame                 Font             10 point, Bold
'                              Text             "Play Game"
'                              Visible          True
'
' btnExit                      Font             10 point, Bold
'                              Text             "E&xit"
'                              Visible          True
'
' lblFinalScore                Autosize         True
'                              Font             14 point, Bold
'                              ForeColor        Red
'                              Visible          False
Public Class Form1
    Inherits System.Windows.Forms.Form

Windows Form Designer generated code

    Private Sub btnStartGame_Click(ByVal sender As Object, _
            ByVal e As System.EventArgs) Handles btnStartGame.Click
            ' Set the defaults before starting each game
            lblHitCount.Text = "0"               'Set hit count to zero
            btnStartGame.Visible = False         'Hide button
            btnExit.Visible = False              'Hide button
            lblFinalScore.Visible = False        'Hide label
            picDragon.Visible = True             'Show dragon

        ' Turn on appropriate game play timers
        tmrDisappear.Enabled = True          'Start timer to hide dragon
        tmrGameOver.Enabled = True           'Start timer to end the game
    End Sub

    Private Sub btnExit_Click(ByVal sender As Object, _
            ByVal e As System.EventArgs) Handles btnExit.Click
        MsgBox("Thanks for playing DragonStryke")    'Acknowledge Exit press
        End                                          'End application
    End Sub

    Private Sub picDragon_Click(ByVal sender As System.Object, _
            ByVal e As System.EventArgs) Handles picDragon.Click
        ' Convert label text to an integer value, then add one
        lblHitCount.Text = CInt(lblHitCount.Text) + 1
    End Sub
```

```
    Private Sub tmrAppear_Tick(ByVal sender As System.Object, _
              ByVal e As System.EventArgs) Handles tmrAppear.Tick
        tmrAppear.Enabled = False              'Turn off this timer
        picDragon.Top = Int(200 * Rnd())       'Move dragon to random position
        picDragon.Left = Int(200 * Rnd())      'Move dragon to random position
        picDragon.Visible = True               'Show the dragon
        tmrDisappear.Enabled = True            'Start timer to hide dragon
    End Sub

    Private Sub tmrDisappear_Tick(ByVal sender As System.Object, _
              ByVal e As System.EventArgs) Handles tmrDisappear.Tick
        tmrDisappear.Enabled = False           'Turn off this timer
        picDragon.Visible = False              'Hide the dragon
        tmrAppear.Enabled = True               'Start timer to show dragon
    End Sub

    Private Sub tmrGameOver_Tick(ByVal sender As System.Object, _
              ByVal e As System.EventArgs) Handles tmrGameOver.Tick
        ' Turn off all timers
        tmrAppear.Enabled = False
        tmrDisappear.Enabled = False
        tmrGameOver.Enabled = False

        ' Make sure dragon is hidden
        picDragon.Visible = False

        ' Show Final Score
        lblFinalScore.Text = "Your Final Score is " & lblHitCount.Text
        lblFinalScore.Visible = True

        ' Show Buttons
        btnStartGame.Text = "Play Again"       'Update start button text
        btnStartGame.Visible = True
        btnExit.Visible = True
    End Sub

End Class
```

### Testing the Solution

You can test Reed and Elizabeth's solution by implementing their design as shown in the previous section, and then running the application. Figures 6-21 and 6-22 show sample output for the DragonStryke Solution. If your solution does not run properly, review your work and make sure you have the proper controls and property values. Also verify that you typed the code in correctly. If you are having problems running your solution, you may want to read Appendix B: Debugging.

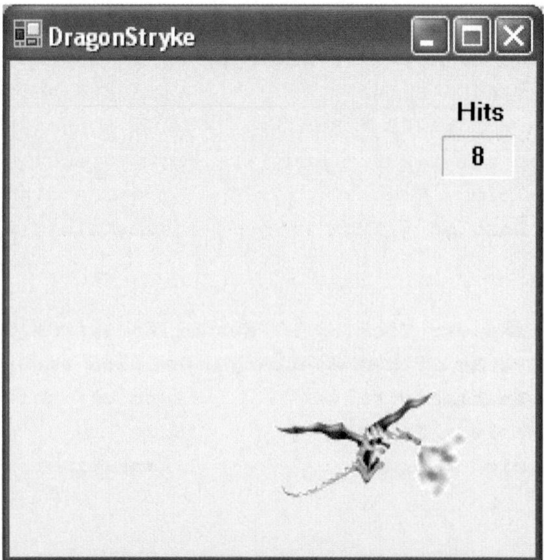


**FIGURE 6.21** *Sample Output for DragonStryke Solution (Game in Progress)*

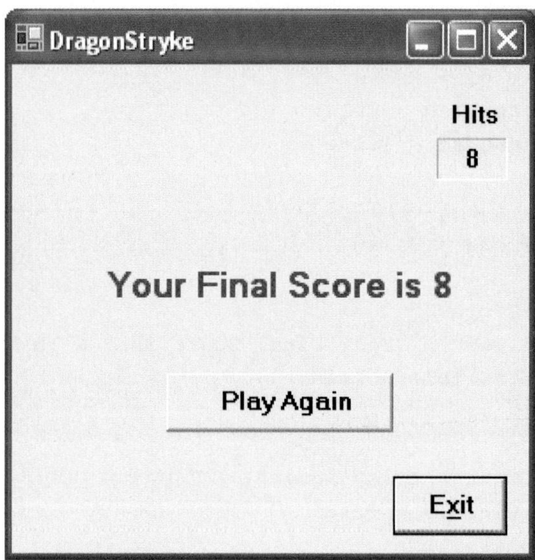


**FIGURE 6.22** *Sample Output for DragonStryke Solution (Game Over)*

### Review and Enhance the Project

Elizabeth and Reed are pleased with their DragonStryke program as a fun environment for practicing mouse movement and button clicking. They also realize that DragonStryke, like any software program, can be made better with continued time and effort. Review the DragonStryke program and consider ways it could be improved. Here are some of the ideas Reed and Elizabeth came up with.

- Add a background image to the form, perhaps a sky and clouds.
- Add labels to show the number of misses. When the game is over, display the user's hit rate as a percentage.
- Change the timer values so the dragon stays visible and invisible for random amounts of time.
- Add a second PictureBox and two more timers (tmrAppear2 and tmrDisappear2) to create a second dragon that appears and disappears separately from the first.

Try these or any other changes you think would be appropriate. Be prepared to discuss various modifications in terms of the work required and the resulting benefits.

## Chapter Summary

- Visual Basic is an object-oriented, event-driven language.
- An object is a self-contained entity that has both properties and methods. The properties of an object provide access to its data, and the methods of an object are the procedures that manipulate the object and its data.
- Windows forms are objects. Controls such as buttons, text boxes, menus, scroll bars, and timers are also objects.
- Most of the objects you will need are available in VB.NET. In the event you need an object that has not already been written, you can write your own object classes (the topic of Chapter 14).
- An event refers to an action or occurrence detected by a program. Events can be user actions, such as clicking a mouse button or pressing a key, or system occurrences, such as opening or closing a window. Most modern applications, particularly those that run in Macintosh and Windows environments, are event-driven.
- An event procedure is the method that handles an event. Visual Studio creates the event procedure stub, and the developer writes the code that appears within the stub.
- The analysis stage determines what the solution needs to do.
- The design stage determines how the solution will do it.
- The implementation stage involves writing code to implement the design.
- The maintenance stage begins when the product is delivered. There is more time and money spent during this stage of an industrial software solution than in all the other stages combined.
- Testing and documentation are essential activities of every development stage.

## Key Terms

## Review Questions

1. What are objects? How are objects and classes related? How are properties and methods related?
2. What is the difference between the Name property and the Text property?
3. What is the difference between the Enabled property and the Visible property?
4. What is the difference between the properties Top, Left, Width, and Height?
5. What is the difference between the TabStop and TabIndex properties?
6. What are events? How are events and objects related? What is the difference between an event procedure and an object method?
7. What is frmMain_Load? What is frmMain in this example? What is Load in this example?
8. What are the four stages of software development? What happens in each stage? Identify some possible testing and documentation that might be appropriate at each stage.
9. What are the two design activities within the design stage? Why are both important?

## Programming Exercises

**6-1. Excuse-o-Rama.** Design and implement a Windows application with four buttons and a label. Clicking each button should display an excuse in the label explaining why the student did not submit a homework problem on time. For example, the first button might display the message "My dog ate my homework," and the second button might display "My roommate ate my homework." Each of the four buttons should have a single, unique excuse. (The following figure has an answer label with BoardStyle = Fixed3D, Font = Bold, and TextAlign = MiddleCenter).

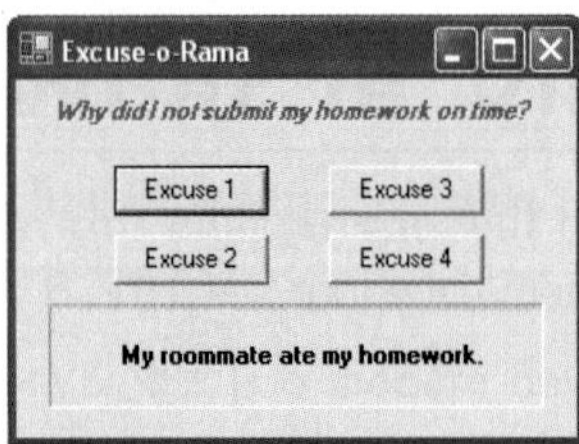


**6-2. Excuse-o-Rama Illustrated.** Modify the Excuse-o-Rama application by adding a picture box to illustrate each excuse. The image associated with each excuse should be unique and somehow related to the excuse. You may download images from the Internet, take pictures with a digital camera (if one is available), or draw images yourself with Microsoft Paint or a more advanced graphics program if available.

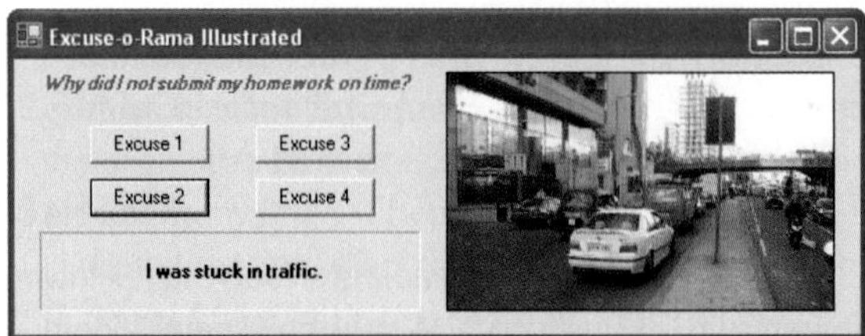


**6-3. Words to Remember.** Design and implement a Windows application with four buttons, a label and a picture box. The Text properties for the buttons should be the names of four individuals you personally admire. Clicking a button should display an image of the person and a quote from the person. Clicking a different button should cause the label text and image to change. You need only one image and one quote for each person.

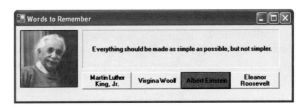

**6-4. DragonStryke 2.** Modify the DragonStryke application using at least two of the enhancements identified in the Review and Enhance the Project section.

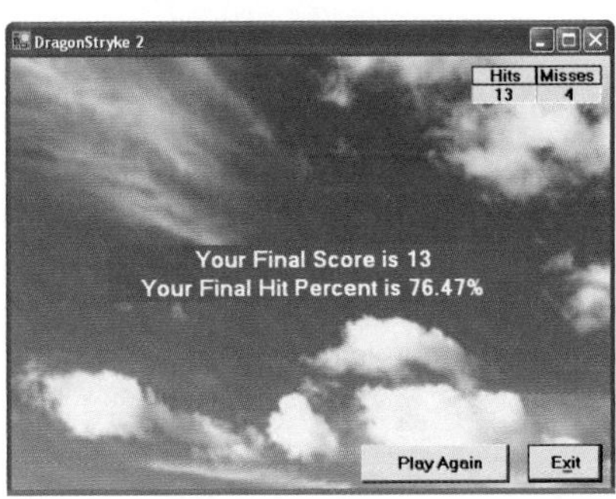


## ▶ Extended Case Study

### Pizza and a Movie

Pizza and a Movie is a small but growing business venture near campus. Pizza and a Movie is a combined video rental and pizza delivery store. You can browse for movies when picking up your pizza. You can also call the store and order a pizza and movie, and they will be delivered together to your apartment or dorm room. The store runs numerous specials for customers who get food and movies on the same order.

The store opened eighteen months ago and quickly established a loyal customer base because of the pizza quality and a large number of new release movies on video and DVD. Noah, the owner, has just increased his store floor space by 50 percent for more movies and a dine-in area. Noah is launching an advertising campaign to promote the store's growth in movies, floor space, and dine-in service. Noah has asked you to develop a Windows application to illustrate the growth of his small business. If Noah likes your application, he plans to incorporate it into the Pizza and a Movie Internet homepage.

Design and implement a Windows application to promote the growth of Pizza and a Movie.

### Singing Mimes

Reed and Elizabeth are encouraged by the success of their DragonStryke application. Reed enthusiastically informs his business partner of his next contribution to the Singing Mimes collection. "I am going to build a software version of Whack-a-Mole with four moles appearing and disappearing from holes in the ground," he says.

Elizabeth nods in agreement. "That sounds like fun. Would each mole appear and hide independently of the others?"

"Absolutely," Reed says. "It will require a few more timers, but that's not too much trouble. As for the mole images, I could probably find some free ones on the Internet, but it might be more fun (and funny!) if I just draw them myself."

Design and implement an application that plays Whack-a-Mole. There should be four moles that appear from holes at random times and remain visible for a short time. If the player clicks on a visible mole, then that is recorded as a hit and the mole image becomes "whacked" for the rest of the time it is visible. After twenty seconds the game ends and displays the player's score (1 point per hit).

CHAPTER 7

# Variables and Expressions

## OUTLINE





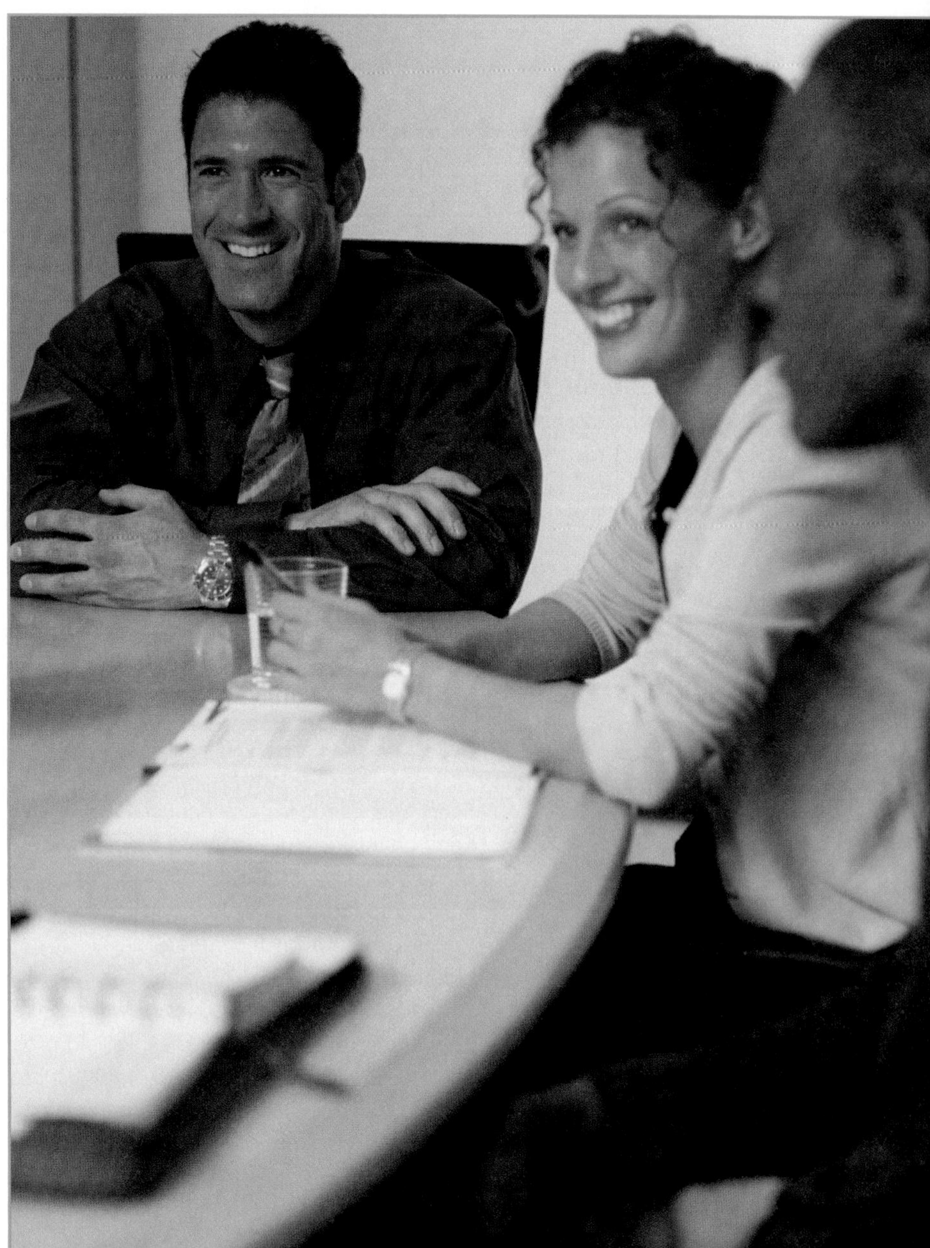

▶ INTERVIEW

## George R. Koscho, CDP, AITP Association President

***Interviewer:*** Please tell us how you got involved in the IT industry.

***Koscho:*** My background follows a rather nontraditional path. After I graduated from high school, I took a job in a plastics factory and went to computer school at night. When I completed my course work, I began looking for a job in the emerging data processing field. During one of my many job interviews, an interviewer advised me to enlist in the service and attempt to get in the data processing field in the military. I joined the Navy, and based on my computer training, they made me a machine accountant. I was assigned to the naval base in Norfolk, Virginia, and I have lived in this area ever since.

***Interviewer:*** What advice do you have for students entering the computer field?

***Koscho:*** Get as much education as you can and don't specialize too much in one area. Our field is constantly changing and what is in vogue today may not be in five years. In addition, include the people skills as part of your repertoire. Finally, I would recommend that students develop a "stick to it" attitude. I see many young professionals that seem to feel that if a program or a system runs, their job is done. What really counts is providing the user with the correct results, and this can sometimes take a lot of work beyond getting a program or a piece of purchased software running.

***Interviewer:*** What do you wish someone had told you when you were an undergraduate student?

***Koscho:*** The real world does not work like an educational institution. I found quickly that the grade I received in a college course was directly related to the amount of preparation I put into studying for an exam. That does not necessarily work in the real world. How technically qualified you are is only part of how successful you will be, because there are many other variables involved, such as politics and personality issues.

## OBJECTIVES

At the completion of this chapter, you will

- **Distinguish between Numeric, String, Char, Boolean, Date, and Object data types**
- **Explain the similarities and differences between variables and constants**
- **Understand and use the Dim and Const statements**
- **Understand and use arithmetic, comparison, and logical operators**
- **Explain the advantages of intrinsic functions for performing common calculations**
- **Understand and effectively use the TextBox, ListBox, and ComboBox controls**
- **Successfully write Windows applications involving calculations that require complex expressions and intrinsic functions**

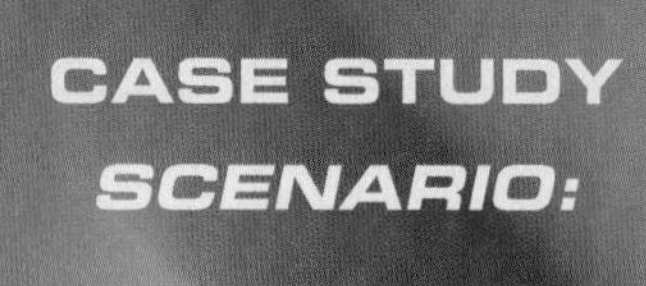


# Home Mortgage Planner

Dr. Jenny Curan's personal finance course is one of the most popular in the business school. Her emphasis on practical applications of personal and family financial planning regularly causes students to rethink their approaches to buying, borrowing, and investing. Jenny often gets letters from students years after they have graduated thanking her for the valuable information they learned in her course.

Jenny begins class this day by asking, "How many of you presently own a home or plan on owning a home in the future?" Hands rise all across the room in response. "Great! Can someone tell me for how many years a home loan is typically financed?" A student replies 30 years, and heads nod in agreement. Jenny continues, "Correct. Most home loans are for 30 years. Of course, many people finance their homes over 15 years or 20 years instead. This makes the monthly payments higher, but they pay off the loan sooner and save quite a bit of money on interest charges. How much money is saved depends on the loan amount, the length of the loan, and the interest rate." Jenny then projects a spreadsheet on the overhead and enters some numbers to compare loans of different amounts with different interest rates over various lengths of time. The spreadsheet is a bit cumbersome, and at one point, Jenny types a value in an incorrect cell and the problem goes unnoticed for a few minutes, resulting in confusion for the entire class. When the problem is found, Jenny makes the appropriate corrections and jokes about bugs in the system.

Forrest walks up to her, as students are heading out the door. "Dr. Curan, that spreadsheet is nice, but if you were interested, I think I could write a Windows application that would do a better job. It would have a much nicer user interface, and you wouldn't have to worry about the formulas in the cells being accidentally changed. We are doing programs similar to this in my Visual Basic course."

"Yes, Forrest, I would like to see that," says Jenny. "Thank you for volunteering your service."

Forrest's solution is presented later this chapter.

## 7-1 Data Types

Remember from Chapter 1 that a ***variable*** is a storage location that can be accessed and changed by developer code. A variable has a name (the identifier that distinguishes the variable) and an associated data value. A variable also has a data type that determines the kind of data values the variable can store. The most common VB.NET data types are explained in the following sections.

### Numeric Types

Visual Basic supplies several numeric data types for handling numbers in various representations. ***Numeric types*** can be broken into two broad classifications: integral and floating-point.

***Integral data types*** are those that represent only whole numbers. Table 7-1 shows the four integral data types. As you can see, the larger memory sizes allow larger values to be stored. ***Integer*** is the most common integral data type and will be used in this book except for the rare occasion when a value greater than 2 billion is necessary (in which case Long will be used).

**Table 7.1** Integral Data Types

| Integral Types | Memory Size | Value Range |
|---|---|---|
| `Byte` | 1 byte | 0 through 255 (unsigned) |
| `Short` | 2 bytes | −32,768 through 32,767 |
| `Integer` | 4 bytes | −2,147,483,648 through 2,147,483,647 |
| `Long` | 8 bytes | −9,223,372,036,854,775,808 through 9,223,372,036,854,775,807 |

**MENTOR**

If you are familiar with earlier versions of Visual Basic, you may know that the Integer data type was originally defined as a 16-bit data type (which holds numbers from −32,768 through 32,767). Integer is now defined relative to the current generation of processors. For the current generation of processors (32-bit), Integer is defined as a 32-bit data type (which holds numbers from −2,147,483,648 through 2,147,483,647). The Integer size has been changed because it is more efficient for a processor to operate on variables that are the same size as its internal registers. Soon 64-bit processors will be commonplace, and the Integer type will likely change to be 64-bit.

***Floating-point data types*** are those that represent numbers with both integer and fractional parts. In other words , floating-point data types have a decimal point. Table 7-2 shows the two floating-point data types. As you can see, the larger memory sizes allow larger values to be stored. ***Double*** is the most common floating-point data type and will be used throughout this book.

**Table 7.2** Floating-point Data Types

| Visual Basic Type | Storage Allocation | Value Range |
|---|---|---|
| `Single` (single-precision floating-point) | 4 bytes | −3.4028235E+38 through −1.401298E −45 for negative values; 1.401298E −45 through 3.4028235E+38 for positive values |
| `Double` (double-precision floating-point) | 8 bytes | −1.79769313486231570E+308 through −4.94065645841246544E−324 for negative values; 4.94065645841246544E −324 through 1.79769313486231570E +308 for positive values |

## ▶ ASK THE AUTHOR

**Q** Why not use Double for all numeric data, integral and floating-point?

**A** Two reasons. First, arithmetic operations are faster with Integer than with floating-point data types. Second, integral data types are precise values, but floating-point data types are approximations of real numbers, and rounding errors may occur. To consider an example of the potential damage that can result from a small numeric inaccuracy, read the following Mentor comment about the Patriot missile defense system.

**MENTOR**

During the first Gulf War, a Patriot missile defense system operating at Dhahran, Saudi Arabia, was providing an antimissile shield against Iraqi Scud missiles. On February 25, 1991, the missile defense system failed to track and intercept an incoming Scud. This Scud subsequently hit an Army barracks, killing twenty-eight Americans. The error occurred because of a small timing inaccuracy (one-tenth of a second every thirty hours).

A report to the General Accounting Office of the U.S. Congress contained the following summary.

> The Patriot battery at Dhahran failed to track and intercept the Scud missile because of a software problem in the system's weapons control computer. This problem led to an inaccurate tracking calculation that became worse the longer the system operated. At the time of the incident, the battery had been operating continuously for over 100 hours. By then, the inaccuracy was serious enough to cause the system to look in the wrong place for the incoming Scud.
>
> The Patriot had never before been used to defend against Scud missiles nor was it expected to operate continuously for long periods of time. Two weeks before the incident, Army officials received Israeli data indicating some loss in accuracy after the system had been running for 8 consecutive hours. Consequently, Army officials modified the software to improve the system's accuracy. However, the modified software did not reach Dhahran until February 26, 1991—the day after the Scud incident.

The full report can be found at http://www.fas.org/spp/starwars/gao/im92026.htm

## String and Char Types

The ***Char*** data type stores a single character in Unicode format. The ***String*** data type stores a sequence of Unicode characters. The maximum length for a String is around 2 billion, probably far more than you will ever need.

In the past, differences in culture and language resulted in different computer-based encoding standards for characters and symbols. These multiple standards made it difficult to develop applications that supported various cultures and languages. ***Unicode*** is a 16-bit international character encoding system that covers values for more than 45,000 characters (with room for more than another million). As a result, Unicode provides a single encoding standard that can support numerous cultural and language differences.

A Unicode character is stored as a 16-bit numeric value; this is true for 0 through 65535 (unsigned). The first 128 characters (0 through 127) of Unicode correspond to the ***ASCII (American Standard Code for Information Interchange)*** character set. Table 7-3 shows ASCII values 32 through 127, which correspond to the alphanumeric and symbol characters available on a standard U.S. keyboard. The second 128 characters (128 through 255) represent special characters, such as Latin-based alphabet letters, accents, currency symbols, and fractions. The remaining characters are used for language, mathematical, and technical symbols from around the world.

## Boolean, Date, and Object Types

The ***Boolean*** data type is an unsigned value that is interpreted as either true or false. If a value has only two states, such as true or false, yes or no, or on or off, then it may be stored in a Boolean variable.

**Table 7.3** ASCII Values 32 through 127

| Dec | Char | Dec | Char | Dec | Char | Dec | Char | Dec | Char | Dec | Char |
|---|---|---|---|---|---|---|---|---|---|---|---|
| 32 | <space> | 48 | 0 | 64 | @ | 80 | P | 96 | ‘ | 112 | p |
| 33 | ! | 49 | 1 | 65 | A | 81 | Q | 97 | a | 113 | q |
| 34 | “ | 50 | 2 | 66 | B | 82 | R | 98 | b | 114 | r |
| 35 | # | 51 | 3 | 67 | C | 83 | S | 99 | c | 115 | s |
| 36 | $ | 52 | 4 | 68 | D | 84 | T | 100 | d | 116 | t |
| 37 | % | 53 | 5 | 69 | E | 85 | U | 101 | e | 117 | u |
| 38 | & | 54 | 6 | 70 | F | 86 | V | 102 | f | 118 | v |
| 39 | ’ | 55 | 7 | 71 | G | 87 | W | 103 | g | 119 | w |
| 40 | ( | 56 | 8 | 72 | H | 88 | X | 104 | h | 120 | x |
| 41 | ) | 57 | 9 | 73 | I | 89 | Y | 105 | i | 121 | y |
| 42 | * | 58 | : | 74 | J | 90 | Z | 106 | j | 122 | z |
| 43 | + | 59 | ; | 75 | K | 91 | [ | 107 | k | 123 | { |
| 44 | , | 60 | < | 76 | L | 92 | \ | 108 | l | 124 | \| |
| 45 | — | 61 | = | 77 | M | 93 | ] | 109 | m | 125 | } |
| 46 | . | 62 | > | 78 | N | 94 | ^ | 110 | n | 126 | ~ |
| 47 | / | 63 | ? | 79 | O | 95 | _ | 111 | o | 127 | _ |

The ***Date*** data type stores a date and time value that includes second, minute, hour, day, month, and year values. The range of possible Date values includes 12:00:00 AM January 1, 1 AD through December 31, 9999 AD at 11:59:59 PM. Date values must be enclosed within number signs (#) and be in the format m/d/yyyy, as in #12/7/1941#.

The ***Object*** data type is the universal data type in VB.NET. It is also the default data type for a variable if no type is specified. An Object variable can hold data of any type.

## ASK THE AUTHOR

**Q** Would it be easier to declare all your variables as the generic Object data type?

**A** No. In terms of speed, the Object data type is inefficient because the program has to do the extra work to determine the proper data type each time the variable is referenced. In terms of space, it is also inefficient because the Object uses 4 bytes as a pointer in addition to the bytes necessary to hold the actual data.

I encourage you to use correct, specific data types for your variables whenever possible. First, it enables IntelliSense™ support for your variables, improving Visual Studio's feedback when you write code. Second, it reduces the likelihood of statements that generate runtime errors related to data type mismatching. Finally, it results in faster execution of your code.

## Quick Check 7-A

Consider the data associated with checking out books at the library. Indicate the most appropriate data type for the following data. In some cases, multiple data types may be equally valid.

1. Book title
2. Customer's Social Security number
3. Checkout date
4. Overdue? (yes or no)
5. Customer's age
6. Sales tax
7. Late fee
8. Type of checkout (book, video, audiotape)

# 7-2 The Dim Statement

A variable is a storage location that can be accessed and changed by developer code, but you must declare variables before you use them. Variables are declared with the ***Dim statement*** (short for Dimension statement). The Dim statement specifies the name of a variable and its associated data type.

*Syntax:*

```
Dim identifier [, identifier] [As datatype [= initialvalue] ]
```

*Examples:*

```
Dim VoteCount As Integer
Dim First, Second, Third As Integer
Dim ExamAverage As Double
Dim LastName As String
Dim KeyPressed As Char
Dim Graduating As Boolean
Dim VacationStartDate As Date
Dim Widget
Dim Age As Integer = 21
Dim LateFee As Double = 3.99
```

One or more variables can be declared with a single Dim statement. If a list of variables appears before the keyword *As*, then each variable in the list is declared to be the specified data type. If the keyword As is not used, then the default datatype (Object) is assumed.

You can also use the Dim statement to specify the variable's initial value by placing an equal sign after the data type. If you do not specify an initialization value, Visual Basic assigns the default value to each variable (e.g., Integer and Double variables are assigned 0, Boolean variables are initialized to False, String and Object variables are initialized to Nothing, and Date variables are initialized to 12:00 AM January 1, Year 0001).

## Naming Rules for Variables

When talking to another person, you can use a variety of words to refer to the same thing. For example, when referring to the president of the United States you can say *President*, *Commander in Chief*, or *Head of the Executive Branch*, and most people will understand that all three refer to the same person. Likewise, when checking out at a grocery store, you may use the terms *receipt*, *sales receipt*, and *sales printout* interchangeably.

Computers are powerful but not smart. The instructions you give a computer must be clear and unambiguous. You cannot refer to the same variable as *receipt* sometimes and *sales receipt* at other times. A variable must have a unique name, called an ***identifier***. VB.NET identifiers must be formed according to the following rules.

- Identifiers must begin with a letter or an underscore.
- Identifiers must contain only letters, digits, and underscores.
- Identifiers cannot be reserved words (see Appendix A).

The identifier rules are enforced by Visual Basic, and your program will not run if any of the rules are broken. In addition, there are strong recommendations for variable names that you should also follow.

- Variable names should begin with a letter.
- Variable names should be mixed case, with the first letter of each new word capitalized.
- Variable names should be long enough to be meaningful and short enough to be manageable.

**Tip**

**In VB.NET, identifiers are case insensitive, so HatSize, HATSIZE, and hatsize are all considered the same identifier.**

### ASK THE AUTHOR

**Q** Some Visual Basic books use data type abbreviations at the beginning of all variable names, for example, dblSalesTax for a sales tax variable of type Double. Why does this book not use them?

**A** Many professionals believe that data type prefixes are cumbersome and hurt readability. If you download the sample VB.NET programs from Microsoft, you will see that they do not use data type abbreviations. Likewise, introductory books in other programming languages (C++, Java, C#) typically do not use data type prefixes, and neither do advanced Visual Basic books. The naming rule conventions used in this book are based on the best practices most often used in professional settings.

### Quick Check 7-B

Consider each of the following potential variable names. First, determine if each follows the rules for a valid identifier. If it is valid, indicate whether or not it follows the recommendations for variable names.

1. first Place
2. 133tsp3ak
3. dim
4. LastName
5. 49ers
6. town&Country

## Working with Constants

A ***constant*** is a storage location whose value cannot change during the execution of the program. Constants are declared with the **Const** declaration. The value of a constant must be specified at the time the constant is declared.

*Syntax:*

```
Const identifier As datatype = value
```

*Examples:*

```
Const AGE As Integer = 21
Const LATE_FEE As Decimal = 3.99
```

Constant names are identifiers and therefore must conform to identifier rules. In addition, the following recommendations are used in this book regarding constant names.

- Constant names should begin with a letter.
- Constant names should be all uppercase, with an underscore between words.
- Constant names should be long enough to be meaningful and short enough to be manageable.

### ASK THE AUTHOR

**Q** Why bother with constants?

**A** Consider a program that references the value 52 in code. The value 52 could refer to the number of weeks in a year, the number of cards in a deck, the product of 26 times 2, or something else entirely. In other words, literal values have ambiguous meaning. Replacing literals with descriptive constants makes the code more readable. It also makes the code easier to understand and maintain when it is revisited weeks, months, or years later. That is why experienced developers make a habit of using constants rather than literals.

## *Quick Check 7-C*

Consider again the data associated with checking out books at the library. Write Dim or Const statements with appropriately named identifiers and appropriate data types for each of the following.

1. Book title
2. Customer's Social Security number
3. Checkout date
4. Overdue? (yes or no)
5. Customer's age
6. Sales tax
7. Late fee
8. Type of checkout (book, video, audiotape)

## 7-3 Operators and Expressions

One of the strengths of a computer is its ability to make calculations quickly and accurately. All calculations must be expressed clearly and unambiguously to ensure consistent, accurate results. An ***operator*** is a symbol that indicates an action to be performed. Value-returning code elements such as variables, constants, and expressions can be combined with one or more operators to form an ***expression***. It is essential that developers accurately understand the full range of operators and the values they produce.

### Arithmetic and String Operators

***Arithmetic operators*** require numeric operands and produce numeric results. The common mathematics operations of addition, subtraction, multiplication, division, and exponentiation are supported. In addition, there are two additional operators for integer division and integer remainder.

The string operator concatenation (&) requires String operands and produces a String result which is the first operand followed by the second operand.

Table 7-4 shows the mathematical and string operators and their effects.

**Table 7.4** Arithmetic and String Operators with Example Usage

| Operator | Description | Example | Result |
|---|---|---|---|
| `^` | Raises first value to the power of the second | `A = 7 ^ 2`<br>`B = 20 ^ 3` | A becomes 49<br>B becomes 8000 |
| `*` | Multiplies two values | `A = 7 * 2`<br>`B = 20 * 3` | A becomes 14<br>B becomes 60 |
| `/` | Divides first value by second value | `A = 7 / 2`<br>`B = 20 / 3` | A becomes 3.5<br>B becomes 6.667 |
| `\` | Returns the integer result for a division | `A = 7 \ 2`<br>`B = 20 \ 3` | A becomes 3<br>B becomes 6 |
| `Mod` | Returns the integer remainder for a division | `A = 7 Mod 2`<br>`B = 20 Mod 3` | A becomes 1<br>B becomes 2 |
| `+` | Adds two values | `A = 7 + 2`<br>`B = 20 + 3` | A becomes 9<br>B becomes 23 |
| `-` | Subtracts two values | `A = 7 - 2`<br>`B = 20 - 3` | A becomes 5<br>B becomes 17 |
| `&` | Concatenates two strings | `S = "sun" & "set"` | S becomes "sunset" |

## Comparison Operators

***Comparison operators*** require numeric operands and produce a logical (true or false) result. Greater-than-or-equal (≥) is created using a greater than symbol followed immediately by an equal symbol (>=). Not-equal (≠) is created using a less than symbol followed immediately by a greater than symbol (<>). Table 7-5 shows the comparison operators and their effects on numeric data.

**Table 7.5** Comparison Operators with Example Usage

| Operator | Description | Example | Result |
|---|---|---|---|
| > | Greater than | 5 > 7 | False |
| | | 5 > 5 | False |
| | | 5 > 3 | True |
| < | Less than | 5 < 7 | True |
| | | 5 < 5 | False |
| | | 5 < 3 | False |
| >= | Greater than or equal | 5 >= 7 | False |
| | | 5 >= 5 | True |
| | | 5 >= 3 | True |
| <= | Less than or equal | 5 <= 7 | True |
| | | 5 <= 5 | True |
| | | 5 <= 3 | False |
| = | Equal | 5 = 7 | False |
| | | 5 = 5 | True |
| | | 5 = 3 | False |
| <> | Not equal | 5 <> 7 | True |
| | | 5 <> 5 | False |
| | | 5 <> 3 | True |

## Logical Operators

***Logical operators*** require logical operands and produce a logical result. Table 7-6 shows the logical operators NOT, AND, OR, and XOR and their effects on logical data.

**Table 7.6** Logical Operators with Example Usage

| Operator | Description | Example | Result |
|---|---|---|---|
| `NOT` | Logical opposite | `NOT True` | False |
| | | `NOT False` | True |
| `AND` | Both values are true | `True AND True` | True |
| | | `True AND False` | False |
| | | `False AND True` | False |
| | | `False AND False` | False |
| `OR` | At least one value is true | `True OR True` | True |
| | | `True OR False` | True |
| | | `False OR True` | True |
| | | `False OR False` | False |
| `XOR` | Exactly one value is true | `True XOR True` | False |
| | | `True XOR False` | True |
| | | `False XOR True` | True |
| | | `False XOR False` | False |

## Operator Precedence

When several operations occur in an expression, each part is evaluated and resolved in a predetermined order called ***operator precedence***. A developer must know the order of operator precedence to properly understand and write expressions.

The arithmetic and concatenation operators have higher precedence than comparison operators, and comparison operators have higher precedence than logical operators. There is also precedence within the larger classifications. The complete operator precedence is presented as follows.

1. Evaluate all arithmetic/concatenation operators with the following precedence:

   Exponentiation (^)
   Multiplication and division (*, /)
   Integer division (\)
   Integer remainder (Mod)
   Addition and subtraction (+, –)
   String concatenation (&)

2. Evaluate all comparison operators as follows:

   All comparison operators (=), (<>), (<), (>), (<=), (>=) have equal precedence

3. Evaluate all logical operators with the following precedence:

   Negation (NOT)
   Conjunction (AND)
   Disjunction (OR, XOR)

**Tip**

**For complex expressions, it is a good idea to use parentheses liberally, especially when mixing logical and relational operators. This makes the expression more readable and avoids mistakes related to operator precedence.**

Multiple operators with the same precedence are evaluated left-to-right. Parentheses can be used to override the order of precedence and force some parts of an expression to be evaluated before others. Operations within parentheses are always performed before those outside. Within parentheses, operator precedence is maintained.

## Quick Check 7-D

Indicate the value of the following expressions. Assume A = 3, B = 5, X = 4.3, and Y = 7.0

1. A * B ^ 2
2. X / Y + 2
3. B * 3 Mod 4
4. X > Y
5. X * 2 > Y + 3
6. (X * 2 > Y + 3) OR (B < A)

# 7-4 The Assignment Statement

One of the common uses of an expression is to perform a calculation for an assignment statement. An ***assignment statement*** is used to store a value into a variable or an object property.

*Syntax:*

```
variable = expression
object.property = expression
```

*Examples:*

```
Pay = Hours * Rate
PersonCount = PersonCount + 1
txtResult.Width = 1000
lblHypotenuse.Text = (Width ^ 2 + Height ^ 2) ^ 0.5
```

The left side of an assignment statement is a variable or an object property. The right side of an assignment statement is an expression. When executed, the value on the right side of the assignment operator is assigned to the variable or property on the left side of the assignment operator.

### ASK THE AUTHOR

**Q** The equal sign (=) is used as an assignment operator, as shown in the preceding examples, and also as an equal comparison operator, as shown earlier in the chapter. How do I know if (=) means assignment or comparison?

**A** The meaning of the equal sign is determined by the surrounding context. For example, the statement

```
If A = B Then
```

uses (=) as an equality comparison to see if A and B are equal. On the other hand, the statement

```
A = B
```

on a line by itself is an assignment statement that takes the value of B and copies it into the variable A.

Here is an idea that might help you learn to distinguish assignment from equality. If you can replace the equal sign (=) with a greater than sign (>) and the statement still makes sense, then the equal sign is being used as an equality test rather than an assignment.

## Quick Check 7-E

Write VB.NET assignment statements for each of the following.

1. Determine the average of the variables ExamScore1, ExamScore2, and ExamScore3.
2. Determine the amount to pay for a meal using the FoodTotal variable plus 6.5 percent sales tax and an additional 15 percent gratuity.
3. Determine the area and perimeter of a rectangle using Length and Height variables.

# 7-5 Intrinsic Functions

VB.NET provides a large number of ***intrinsic functions*** to improve developer productivity. Intrinsic functions support a broad range of activities, including math calculations, business calculations, time and date functions, string formatting functions, and many more. Some of the common functions used in this book are presented in the following sections.

**Tip**

**CDbl stands for "Convert to Double". There are similarly named conversion functions for converting to Integer (CInt), String (CStr), etc.**

## Simple Functions

There are a number of simple yet powerful functions in VB.NET that provide great assistance to developers. For example, the **CDbl** function converts a numeric string into a double value. If the string has no numeric equivalent, then CDbl generates an error. The ***IsNumeric*** function returns true if a string has a numeric equivalent. Table 7-7 shows CDbl and IsNumeric along with a few other common functions.

**Table 7.7** Simple Intrinsic Functions Commonly Used in VB.NET

| Function | Description | Example | Result |
|---|---|---|---|
| `Val` | Returns the numbers contained in the argument; stops at the first nonnumeric character | `Val("23.5")`<br>`Val("$32")`<br>`Val("hello")` | 23.5<br>0<br>0 |
| `CDbl` | Returns a double value if the argument can be converted to double | `CDbl("23.5")`<br>`CDbl("$32")`<br>`CDbl("hello")` | 23.5<br>32<br>Type mismatch error |
| `IsNumeric` | Returns true if the argument can be converted to a double | `IsNumeric("23.5")`<br>`IsNumeric("$32")`<br>`IsNumeric("hello")` | True<br>True<br>False |
| `Rnd` | Returns a random value between 0 and 1 | `Rnd()`<br>`Int(Rnd() * 6)+ 1` | Double value between 0 and 1<br>Integer value between 1 and 6 |
| `Abs` | Returns the absolute value of a number (must import System.Math) | `Abs(16)`<br>`Abs(-16)` | 16<br>16 |
| `Int` | Returns the integer portion of a number | `Int(123.456)` | 123 |
| `FormatCurrency` | Returns a currency formatted string rounded to two decimal places | `FormatCurrency(4.5)`<br>`FormatCurrency(1234.5678)` | "$4.50"<br>"$1,234.57" |
| `Format(expr,str)` | Converts an expression value to a specific string format | `Format(6.6666, "0.###")`<br>`Format(1/2, "0.###")`<br>`Format(1234.588, "0.##")` | "6.667"<br>"0.5"<br>"1234.59" |

## ASK THE AUTHOR

**Q** What is the difference between CDbl and Val? Which is better for converting text box values?

**A** If the string value has no numeric equivalent, then Val returns 0, and CDbl generates an error. For example, assume a text box contains "hello". The Val of the text box will be 0, and the CDbl or the text box will crash the program. This means that Val is a good choice for working with text box values.

But that is not the end of the story. CDbl can handle text that is formatted as currency. If a text box contains "$12,345.89," then CDbl returns 12345.89, and Val returns 0. This means that CDbl is a good choice for working with text boxes that display currency values. In Chapter 8, we see how CDbl and IsNumeric can be used together to avoid the program crash scenario.

## Financial Annuity Functions

**Tip**

**An annuity is a series of fixed cash payments made over a period of time. An annuity can be a loan (such as a home mortgage) or an investment (such as a monthly savings plan).**

The functions in the previous section were rather simple, requiring either zero arguments or just one. VB.NET also provides some more powerful intrinsic functions that allow developers to solve more complicated problems, such as financial annuity calculations.

Suppose you go to your local bank to get a $5,000 loan in order to buy a used car. Your monthly payments on the car loan would be based on a number of factors, including the interest rate for the loan, the length of the loan, and the frequency of payments (semimonthly, monthly, quarterly, etc.). When these details are specified, you can determine what your payments will be. For example, if you get the loan at 8.5 percent over 3 years with monthly payments, you can calculate that you will owe the bank $157.84 each month for the next 36 months.

***Pmt*** is a function for determining monthly payments. The Pmt function returns the payment for a loan based on periodic, constant payments and a constant interest rate.

*Syntax:*

```
Pmt(Rate, NPer, PV)
```

*Example:*

```
Pmt(AnnualRate / 12, Years * 12, Amount)
Pmt(0.07083, 36, -5000)
```

The first argument, *Rate*, is the interest rate per period. It can be calculated by dividing the annual interest rate by the number of periods in a year. For example, an annual percentage rate (APR) of 8.5 percent with monthly payments has a rate per period of 0.085 / 12, or 0.007083.

**Tip**

**All payment periods should be expressed in the same units. For example, if Rate is calculated using months, NPer must also be calculated using months.**

The second argument, *NPer*, is the total number of payments in the annuity or the number of years times the number of payments in a year. For example, there are 3 * 12 (or 36) monthly payments on a three-year loan.

The third argument, *PV*, is the present value (or lump sum) that a series of payments to be paid in the future is worth now.

**FIGURE 7.1** *Monthly Payment for $5,000 Loan over 3 Years at 8.5 Percent APR*

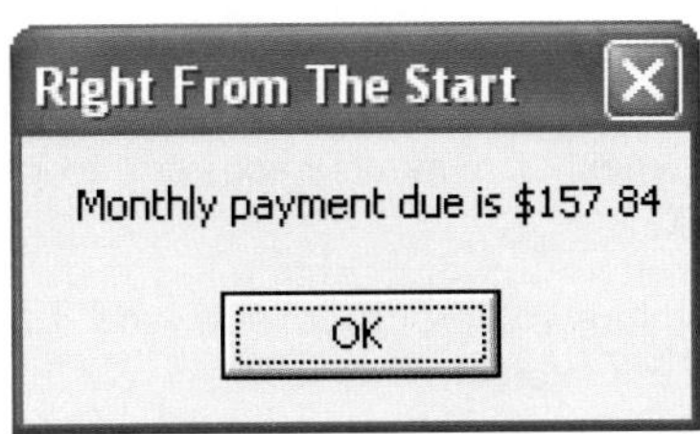


The following code calculates and displays the required monthly payments for a $5000 loan over 3 years at 8.5 percent APR. Figure 7-1 shows the payments for the loan.

```
Private Sub btnCalculate_Click(ByVal sender As System.Object, _
             ByVal e As System.EventArgs) Handles btnCalculate.Click
  Dim AnnualRate As Double
  Dim Years As Integer
  Dim Amount As Double
  Dim Payment As Double

  AnnualRate = 0.085        ' 8.5% as decimal value
  Years = 3                 ' 3 year loan
  Amount = -5000            ' $5000 loan amount (borrowed, therefore negative)
  Payment = Pmt(AnnualRate / 12, Years * 12, Amount)
  MsgBox("Monthly payment due is " & FormatCurrency(Payment))
End Sub
```

## ASK THE AUTHOR

**Q** Why did you use a negative value (–5000) for the amount in the preceding example?

**A** For all arguments, cash paid out (such as deposits to savings) and cash received (such as dividend checks) are represented by opposite signs (positive and negative). If you are making calculations based on borrowing an amount of money and then paying it back, the signs have to be opposite. Since I wanted the payback amount (seen by the user) to be positive, I made the borrowed amount negative.

**FV** is a function for determining the future value of an annuity based on periodic, fixed payments and a fixed interest rate.

*Syntax:* FV(*Rate, NPer, Pmt*)

*Example:* `FV(0.0725 / 12, 5 * 12, -50)`

**Tip**

**Pmt and FV functions are just two of the many intrinsic financial functions available to Visual Basic developers. You can use the online help to read about other financial functions available to developers.**

The preceding example calculates the future value of an annuity based on payments of $50 a month at 7.25 percent APR for 5 years. At the end of the 5-year period, the annuity would be worth $3,602.90.

## Quick Check 7-F

1. Determine the weekly payments necessary to pay back a $1000 loan in 1 year at 12 percent APR.
2. Determine the future value of a college fund if $100 is saved every 2 weeks for ten years at 8 percent interest.

# 7-6 InputBox and MsgBox

***InputBox*** and ***MsgBox*** are intrinsic functions that facilitate communication with the user by means of a dialog box. A ***dialog box*** is a pop-up window that informs the user of some information or accepts information from the user. A dialog box therefore allows the program to communicate (or dialog) with the user.

## The InputBox Function

The InputBox function is a simple means for prompting the user for keyboard input. The information entered by the user is returned to the program for processing.

*Syntax:*

```
result = InputBox(prompt[, title])
```

*Examples:*

```
Name = InputBox("What is your name?")
Age = InputBox("Please enter your age", "Data Request")
```

The prompt argument is a string expression displayed as the message in the dialog box. The second argument is an optional title string to appear in the title bar of the dialog box. If omitted, the application name is used for the dialog title.

When executed, InputBox displays a dialog box containing the specified prompt and a text box. The application waits for the user to enter text into a text box and then click the OK button. When the OK button is pressed, the information typed into the text box is returned for processing. If the user presses the Cancel button instead, an empty string is returned. The following section shows how a message box can be used to obtain input data for a program.

## The MsgBox Function

The MsgBox function displays a message in a dialog box.

*Syntax:*

```
MsgBox(prompt)
```

*Examples:*

```
MsgBox("Hello World")
MsgBox("The Result is " & Result)
```

The prompt argument is a string expression that gets displayed as the message in the dialog box. You can use the concatenation operator (&) to combine multiple values into a single string. The Visual Basic carriage return and line feed constant ***(vbCrLf)*** can be used to generate a hard return in your dialog output, as shown in the following example. Figure 7-2 shows the resulting output.

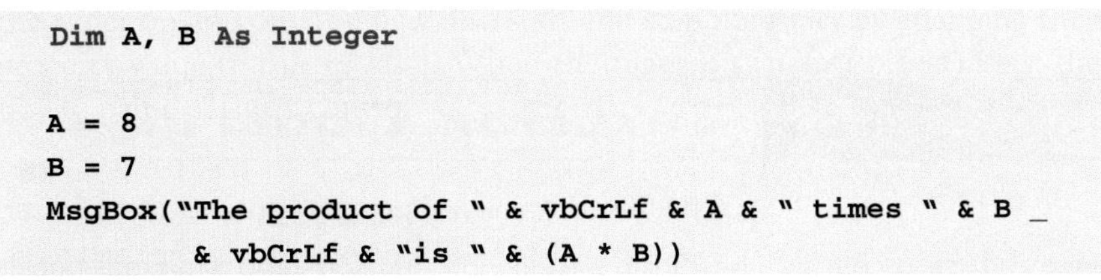

```
Dim A, B As Integer

A = 8
B = 7
MsgBox("The product of " & vbCrLf & A & " times " & B _
        & vbCrLf & "is " & (A * B))
```

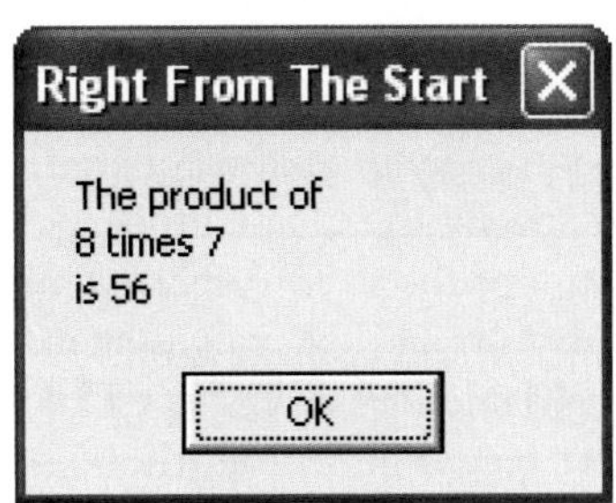


**FIGURE 7.2** *MsgBox Output with Line Feeds*

The following example illustrates the use of InputBox and MsgBox.

```
Dim Width, Height, Area As Double

Width = InputBox("Enter a value for Width")
Height = InputBox("Enter a value for Height")
MsgBox("Area is " & Width * Height)
```

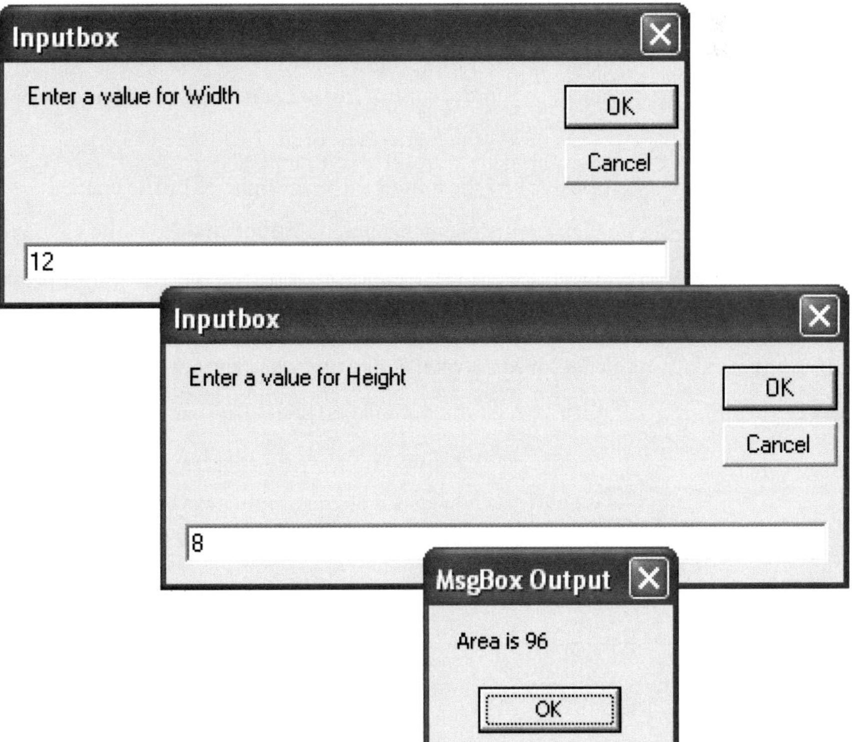


**FIGURE 7.3** *InputBox and MsgBox Combined*

### *InputBox and MsgBox Summary*

- The InputBox function displays a dialog box with a prompt to the user and a text box where the user can reply. The value typed in the text box is the value returned.
- The MsgBox function displays a dialog box with a message. The message can include any number of value-returning elements concatenated together.

## 7-7 TextBox Control

The ***TextBox control*** provides an area for the user to enter data while the program is executing. TextBox controls can also be used to display output on the form.

### TextBox Properties

Common properties of the TextBox control are shown in Table 7-8. As with all controls, you should first specify the Name property for referencing the control in code. The Text property contains the value displayed inside the text box. The Text property is a String. If you wish to treat Text values as numeric, you should either assign the values to a numeric variable or use Val or CDbl to convert the values to a numeric equivalent. If the text box is multiline, then appending the Visual Basic constant vbCrLf will cause a carriage return and line feed, similar to pressing the Enter key when typing.

**Table 7.8 Commonly Used TextBox Properties**

| Property | Description |
|---|---|
| `Name` | ("txt" prefix) Indicates an identifier name to reference the object |
| `AcceptsReturn` | Gets or sets a value indicating whether pressing Enter in a multiline text box creates a new line of text in the control or activates the default button for the form |
| `AcceptsTab` | Gets or sets a value indicating whether pressing the Tab key in a multiline text box types a Tab character in the control instead of moving the focus to the next control in the tab order |
| `BorderStyle` | Gets or sets the border type of the text box |
| `Font` | Gets or sets the font of the text displayed by the control |
| `MaxLength` | Gets or sets the maximum number of characters the user can type into the text box |
| `Multiline` | Gets or sets a value indicating whether this is a multiline text box |
| `PasswordChar` | Gets or sets the character used to mask characters of a password in a single-line text box |
| `ReadOnly` | Gets or sets a value indicating whether text in the text box is read-only |
| `ScrollBars` | Gets or sets which scroll bars should appear in a multiline text box |
| `Text` | Gets or sets the current text in the text box |
| `TextAlign` | Gets or sets how text is aligned in the text box |
| `TextLength` | (runtime only) Gets the length of text in the control |
| `WordWrap` | Indicates whether a multiline text box automatically wraps words to the beginning of the next line when necessary |

## TextBox Methods

Common methods of the TextBox control are shown in Table 7-9. The AppendText method adds text to the end of the existing text in the text box. The Cut and Copy methods place the currently selected text into the clipboard, and the Paste method copies the text from the clipboard to the text box. Visual Basic can access the Windows clipboard for the purpose of temporarily storing text.

**Table 7.9 Commonly Used TextBox Methods**

| Method | Description |
|---|---|
| `AppendText(text)` | Appends text to the current text of text box |
| `Clear()` | Clears all text from the text box |
| `Copy()` | Copies the current selection in the text box to the clipboard |
| `Cut()` | Moves the current selection in the text box to the clipboard |
| `Paste()` | Replaces the current selection in the text box with the contents of the clipboard |
| `Select(text)` | Selects text within the control |
| `SelectAll()` | Selects all text in the text box |
| `Undo()` | Undoes the last edit operation in the text box |

### *TextBox Control Summary*

- TextBox controls can be used to accept input and display output. When used for output, the ReadOnly property is often set to true.
- When inputting numeric values, save the text box values into appropriately typed variables or convert text box values using Val or CDbl.

# 7-8 ListBox Control

The ***ListBox control*** makes a visible list of items. The user can select items in the list using mouse clicks.

## ListBox Properties

Common properties of the ListBox control are shown in Table 7-10. As with all controls, you should first specify the Name property for referencing the control in code. The list box does not contain a Text property. Instead, items are displayed as part of the Items property, which is a list of items. The user can select zero, one, or multiple selections based on the SelectionMode property. If the list box will be used for output

**Table 7.10 Commonly Used ListBox Properties**

| Property | Description |
|---|---|
| `Name` | ("lst" prefix) Indicates an identifier name to reference the object |
| `Items` | Gets the items in the list box; this property is itself an object with its own set of properties and methods for managing the items that appear in the list box |
| `MultiColumn` | Gets or sets a value indicating whether the list box supports multiple columns |
| `SelectedIndex` | Gets or sets the zero-based index of the currently selected item; returns a value of −1 if no item is selected—only used when SelectionMode is set to One |
| `SelectedItem` | Gets or sets the currently selected item in the list box—only used when SelectionMode is set to One |
| `SelectionMode` | Gets or sets the method in which items are selected in the list box; possible values are None, One, MultiSimple, and MultiExtended |
| `Sorted` | Gets or sets a value indicating whether the items in the list box are sorted alphabetically (regardless of the order they are entered) |

►►► *Tip*

**The three-letter control prefix for a list box is L-S-T in all lowercase (lst). Students sometimes incorrectly think it is the number one ("1") followed by the letters *st*. Be careful to avoid this common mistake.**

purposes only, then the SelectionMode should be set to None so that no items may be selected. Setting the MultiColumn property to true enables the control to display items across the width of the control, which can reduce the need to scroll down to see an item.

## ListBox Methods

The list box provides methods that enable you to efficiently add items to the list and to find text items within the list. The Items.Add method is used to add items to the list. Other common methods are shown in Table 7-11.

**Table 7.11 Commonly Used ListBox Methods**

| Method | Description |
|---|---|
| **`Items.Add(`*`text`*`)`** | Adds *text* to the end of the list of items |
| **`Items.Clear()`** | Clears the list box, removing all items; Items.Count is set to 0 |
| **`Items.Insert(`*`index, text`*`)`** | Inserts *text* into the list at the location indexed by *index*; all items at that location and below are moved down one position |
| **`Items.Remove(`*`text`*`)`** | Removes all instances of *text* from Items |
| **`Items.RemoveAt(`*`index`*`)`** | Removes the item at the specified *index* from Items |

## ListBox Illustrated: Select Ice Cream Toppings

To demonstrate the functionality of a ListBox control, consider the task of selecting toppings for an ice cream sundae. The solution will contain two list boxes, the first with all the possible toppings, and the second with only the selected toppings. Double-clicking a topping in the first list box will add it to the second list box.

The toppings in the first list box can be added at design time (using the Properties window) or at runtime (using code). In this example we will use runtime code to fill the list box. In the Code Editor, select (Form1 Events) from the Class drop-down list. Then select Load from the Method drop-down list. Visual Studio will create a FormLoad event procedure stub. You should also create a Double-Click event procedure for each of the two list boxes.

Fill in the stubs with the following code, and then execute the program.

```
Private Sub Form1_Load(ByVal sender As System.Object, _
          ByVal e As System.EventArgs) Handles MyBase.Load
   lstChoices.Items.Add("Caramel")
   lstChoices.Items.Add("Hot Chocolate")
   lstChoices.Items.Add("Chocolate Fudge")
   lstChoices.Items.Add("Strawberry")
   lstChoices.Items.Add("Pineapple")
   lstChoices.Items.Add("Nuts")
   lstChoices.Items.Add("Cherry")
   lstChoices.Items.Add("Whip Cream")
  End Sub
  Private Sub lstChoices_DoubleClick(ByVal sender As System.Object, _
          ByVal e As System.EventArgs) Handles lstChoices.DoubleClick
   lstSelected.Items.Add(lstChoices.SelectedItem)
  End Sub
  Private Sub lstSelected_DoubleClick(ByVal sender As System.Object, _
          ByVal e As System.EventArgs) Handles lstSelected.DoubleClick
   lstSelected.Items.Remove(lstSelected.SelectedItem)
  End Sub
```

As you execute the preceding code, consider the following illustrating activities.

1. Notice the scroll bar is automatically created by VB.NET if the number of items in the list is too big for the display size of the list box.
2. Double-click on an item in the first list box. This triggers a Double-Click event that adds the selected item to the second list box.
3. Double-click on an item in the second list box. This triggers a Double-Click event that removes the selected item from the second list box.

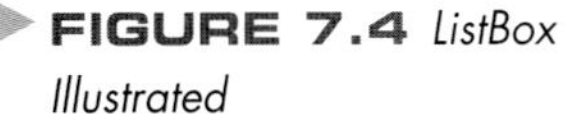

**FIGURE 7.4** *ListBox Illustrated*

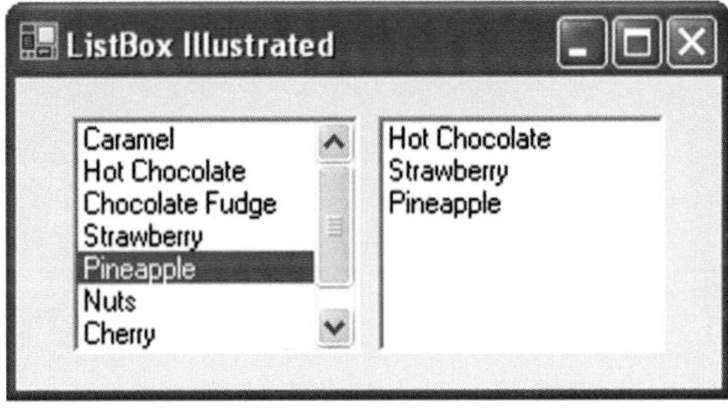

# 7-9 ComboBox Control

The ***ComboBox control*** combines the functionality of the TextBox and ListBox controls. The user can select values from the drop-down list or enter values directly into the text box area.

## ComboBox Properties

Most of the properties and methods of the ComboBox control are also found in the TextBox or ListBox controls. The Text property specifies the string displayed in the editing field. The Items property is an object representing the collection of the items contained in the drop-down list. The default behavior of the ComboBox control is to display an editable text field with a hidden drop-down list. Setting the DropDownStyle property to DropDownList makes the text portion accept only values from the drop-down list. Common properties of the ComboBox control are shown in Table 7-12.

**Table 7.12 Common ComboBox Properties**

| Property | Description |
|---|---|
| `Name` | ("cbo" prefix) Indicates an identifier name to reference the object |
| `DropDownStyle` | Gets or sets a value specifying the style of the combo box |
| `Items` | Gets an object representing the collection of the items contained in the combo box |
| `Text` | Gets or sets the text in the text box portion of the combo box |

## ComboBox Illustrated: Movie Voting

To demonstrate the functionality of a ComboBox control, consider the task of selecting favorite movies from three different categories. The solution will contain three combo boxes, each containing movies from three different classifications (comedy, mystery, series). The user may select a movie from each classification and then click a button to register a vote.

Start a new project with three combo boxes and a button. Type the code as follows, and then execute the program.

```
Private Sub Form1_Load(ByVal sender As System.Object, _
          ByVal e As System.EventArgs) Handles MyBase.Load
   cboComedy.Text = "Select One"
   cboComedy.Items.Add("Monty Python and the Holy Grail")
   cboComedy.Items.Add("Dr. Strangelove")
   cboComedy.Items.Add("Duck Soup")
   cboComedy.Items.Add("The Princess Bride")
   cboComedy.Items.Add("Waterboy")

   cboMystery.Text = "Select One"
   cboMystery.Items.Add("Citizen Kane")
   cboMystery.Items.Add("Memento")
   cboMystery.Items.Add("The Sixth Sense")
   cboMystery.Items.Add("Rear Window")
   cboMystery.Items.Add("Minority Report")

   cboSeries.Text = "Select One"
   cboSeries.Items.Add("The Godfather")
   cboSeries.Items.Add("Star Wars")
   cboSeries.Items.Add("The Matrix")
   cboSeries.Items.Add("Lord of the Rings")
   cboSeries.Items.Add("Harry Potter")

   cboComedy.Focus() 'give focus to the comedy combo box
End Sub

Private Sub btnVote_Click(ByVal sender As System.Object, _
          ByVal e As System.EventArgs) Handles btnVote.Click
  MsgBox("You voted for: " & vbCrLf & cboComedy.Text & _
  vbCrLf & cboMystery.Text & vbCrLf & cboSeries.Text)
End Sub
```

As you execute the preceding code, consider the following illustrating activities.

1. Select a movie from each combo box, then press the Vote button. The Click event procedure uses the Text property to display the selected value in each combo box (see Figures 7-5 and 7-6).

**FIGURE 7.5** *ComboBox Illustrated—Selection*

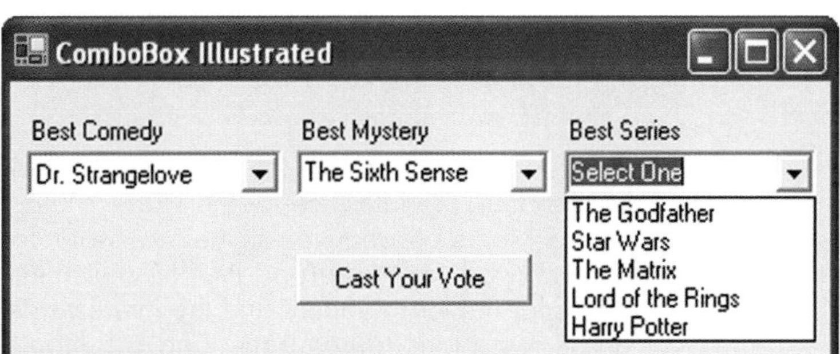

▶ **FIGURE 7.6** *ComboBox Illustrated—Output*

2. The default DropDownStyle property value is DropDown, which makes the text box editable. Notice the initial text in each combo box, *Select One*, is not one of the items in the list. Also, the user can enter a value in the text box area that is not in the list, giving the user the ability to vote for a movie not in the list. Run the program and vote for a movie that is not in the drop-down list (type the movie title in the text area of the combo box.)
3. Change the first combo box's DropDownStyle property to DropDownList and rerun the application. Notice that the text *Select One* is rejected as a value for the edit box because it is not in the list. Likewise, the user can no longer enter a movie title not in the list.

## Home Mortgage Planner

Forrest enjoys a chocolate from a box on his desk as he works on the program for Dr. Curan. Drawing on a notepad, Forrest sketches the Windows form. He draws text boxes for the home loan amount and the interest rate. He also draws two side-by-side combo boxes that will contain the values 15, 20, 25, and 30, which represent the number of years for the two loans being compared. Then he draws a button for a triggering event to generate the desired calculations.

Forrest then draws two text boxes for the monthly payment amounts for the two plans and a single text box below them to display the difference in monthly payments. Below that he draws two text boxes for the monthly payments for the two plans, followed by the payment total for both plans (i.e., the monthly payment times the number of payments). Finally he draws two text boxes to display the interest totals for each plan (i.e., the payment total minus the loan amount) and a single text box to show the difference in interest totals.

"I will use FormatCurrency and CDbl for currency formatted text boxes. The button Click event will use the Pmt function to calculate the monthly payment, and all the other calculations are basic math."

Forrest's sits back and gets another piece from the box of chocolates on his desk.

### Design

The design specifies how the solution will work in general terms. Forrest begins by sketching the interface for the Home Mortgage Planner application, specifying the Name property for all the necessary controls. The Text property can also be displayed when appropriate. The sketch in Figure 7-7 includes two input text boxes for the loan amount and the interest rate, two combo boxes for the years of the two plans to compare, and a button to perform the comparison. The results of the comparison will appear in a series of output labels. Static labels will also be included to describe the input and output values.

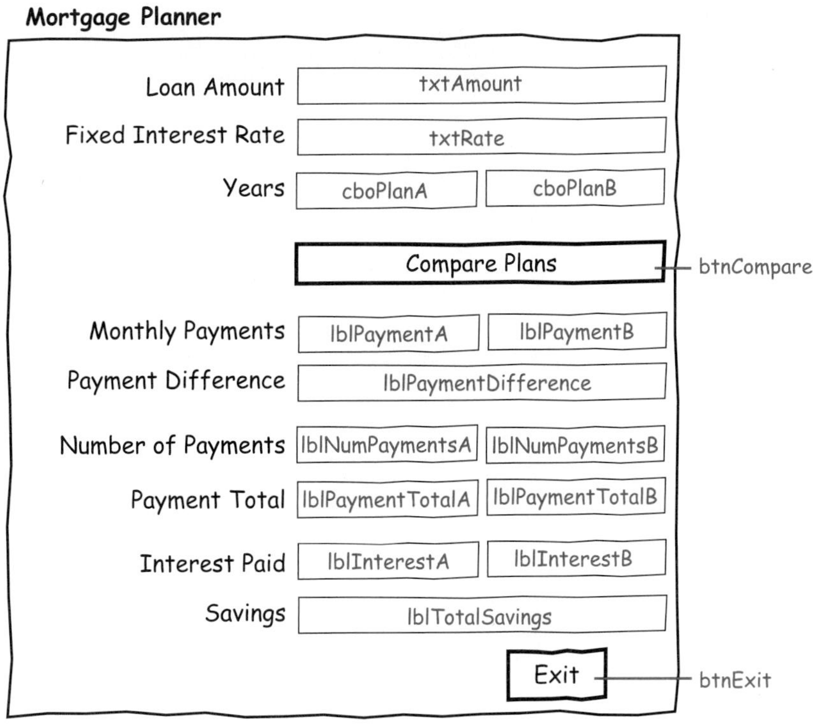

**Mortgage Planner**



**FIGURE 7.7** *Sketch of the Home Mortgage Planner User Interface*

The design should also include a high-level specification of all the actions and behavior required by the project. This can be done using flowchart or pseudocode notation and should describe behavior without getting into details of implementation. Table 7-13 provides pseudocode descriptions of the procedures in the Home Mortgage Planner design.

**Table 7.13** Design Pseudocode for Home Mortgage Planner Application

| Property | Behavior |
|---|---|
| Form1_Load | Populate combo boxes with values 15, 20, 25, and 30 |
| btnCompare_Click | 1. Use Pmt to calculate monthly payments for each plan and display result in output labels |
| | 2. Calculate monthly payment difference and display in output label |
| | 3. Calculate and display number of monthly payments per plan |
| | 4. Calculate and display sum of all payments for each plan |
| | 5. Calculate and display interest total (payment total minus principle) for each plan |
| | 6. Calculate and display difference in total interest between the two plans |
| txtAmount_Leave | Format loan amount value as currency |
| btnExit_Click | End the application |

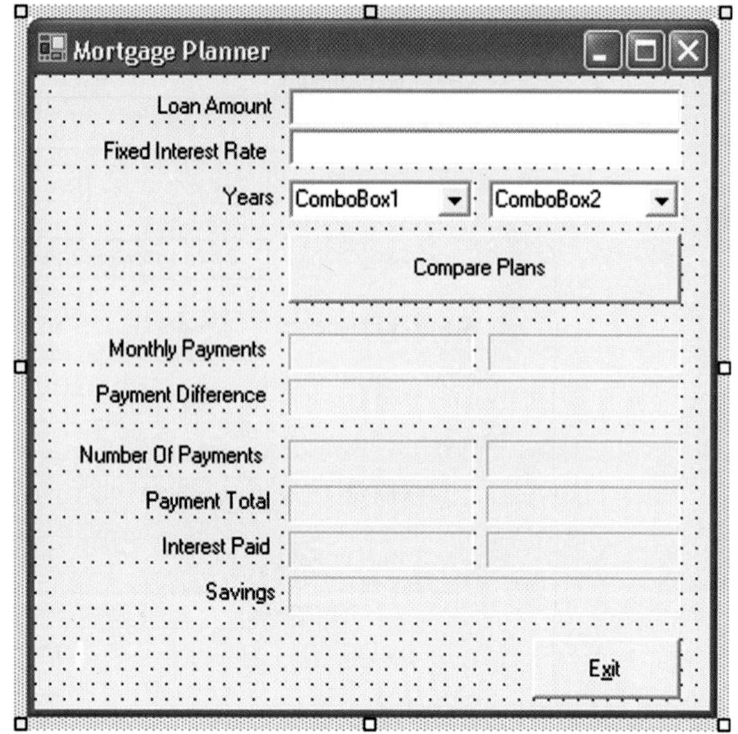


**FIGURE 7.8** *Home Mortgage Planner User Interface*

### Implementation

After Forrest completes the general design, he must implement the details. The first step of implementation is to build the GUI. Figure 7-8 illustrates the Home Mortgage Planner GUI.

The second step is to implement the functionality described in the pseudocode design. It is also a good habit to document important design time property values for the form and interface controls. The solution code with good documentation follows.

```
' Author: Forrest
' Project: Home Mortgage Planner
' Description:  Home Mortgage Planner is an application that compares two
'               plans for paying off a home mortgage over different
'               time periods.  It shows differences in monthly payments,
'               total amount paid over the life of the loan, and the
'               total savings for the shorter loan.
'
'
'    *********** Design Time Properties ***********
'   OBJECT                PROPERTY       SETTING
'
'   txtAmount             Text           (Empty)
'
'   txtRate               Text           (Empty)
'
'   cboPlanA              Text           "Plan A Years"
'
'   cboPlanB              Text           "Plan B Years"
```

```
'
'   btnCompare            Text            "Compare Plans"
'
'   btnExit               Text            "E&xit"
'
'   Note: The following labels share BorderStyle and Text design-time
'         properties.  You can multi-select the labels and change them
'         simultaneously.
'
'   lblPaymentA
'   lblPaymentB
'   lblPaymentDifference
'   lblNumPaymentsA
'   lblNumPaymentsB
'   lblPaymentTotalA
'   lblPaymentTotalB
'   lblInterestA
'   lblInterestB
'   lblTotalSavings
'                         BorderStyle     Fixed3D
'                         Text            (space)
'
Imports System.Math      'Provides Math functions, including Abs()
Public Class Form1
    Inherits System.Windows.Forms.Form

Windows Form Designer generated code

    Private Sub Form1_Load(ByVal sender As Object, _
            ByVal e As System.EventArgs) Handles MyBase.Load
        ' Initialize the combo boxes
        cboPlanA.Text = "Plan A Years"
        cboPlanA.Items.Add("15")
        cboPlanA.Items.Add("20")
        cboPlanA.Items.Add("25")
        cboPlanA.Items.Add("30")

        cboPlanB.Text = "Plan B Years"
        cboPlanB.Items.Add("15")
        cboPlanB.Items.Add("20")
        cboPlanB.Items.Add("25")
        cboPlanB.Items.Add("30")
    End Sub

    ' This procedure displays the text as currency
    Private Sub txtAmount_Leave(ByVal sender As Object, _
            ByVal e As System.EventArgs) Handles txtAmount.Leave
        txtAmount.Text = FormatCurrency(txtAmount.Text)
    End Sub
    ' This procedure handles all of the calculations and fills
    ' the labels with the results
    Private Sub btnCompare_Click(ByVal sender As System.Object, _
            ByVal e As System.EventArgs) Handles btnCompare.Click
```

```
        Dim Amount, Rate As Double
        Dim PaymentA, PaymentB, PaymentDifference As Double
        Dim TotalA, TotalB, TotalSavings As Double

        Amount = CDbl(txtAmount.Text)    'CDbl converts currency format
        Rate = CDbl(txtRate.Text)

        ' Calculate and display...

        '    ...monthly payments for both plans
        PaymentA = Pmt(Rate / 12, cboPlanA.Text * 12, Amount) * -1
        PaymentB = Pmt(Rate / 12, cboPlanB.Text * 12, Amount) * -1
        lblPaymentA.Text = FormatCurrency(PaymentA)
        lblPaymentB.Text = FormatCurrency(PaymentB)

        '    ...monthy payment difference
        PaymentDifference = Abs(PaymentB - PaymentA)
        lblPaymentDifference.Text = FormatCurrency(PaymentDifference)

        '    ...number of payments for each plan
        lblNumPaymentsA.Text = cboPlanA.Text * 12
        lblNumPaymentsB.Text = cboPlanB.Text * 12

        '    ...payment total for each plan
        TotalA = PaymentA * cboPlanA.Text * 12
        TotalB = PaymentB * cboPlanB.Text * 12
        lblPaymentTotalA.Text = FormatCurrency(TotalA)
        lblPaymentTotalB.Text = FormatCurrency(TotalB)

        '    ...total interest for each plan
        lblInterestA.Text = FormatCurrency(TotalA - Amount)
        lblInterestB.Text = FormatCurrency(TotalB - Amount)

        '    ...total difference between the two plans
        TotalSavings = Abs(TotalB - TotalA)
        lblTotalSavings.Text = FormatCurrency(TotalSavings)
    End Sub

    Private Sub btnExit_Click(ByVal sender As System.Object, _
                ByVal e As System.EventArgs) Handles btnExit.Click
        MsgBox("Thank you for using Home Mortgage Planner")
        End
    End Sub

End Class
```

### Testing the Solution

You can test Forrest's solution by implementing his design as shown in the previous section, and then running the application. Figure 7-9 shows sample output for the Home Mortgage Planner solution. Notice how the Amount value is automatically formatted to currency. If you are having problems, you may want to read Appendix B: Debugging.

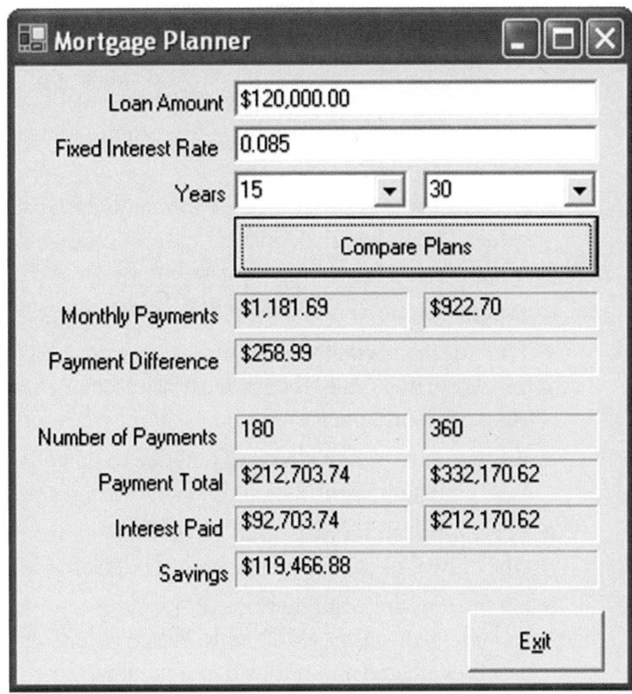


**FIGURE 7.9** *Sample Output for the Home Mortgage Planner Application*

### Review and Enhance the Project

Forrest gives the program to Dr. Curan, and she tries it out, using the input values from her lecture notes and generating the same results, only this time without the input error.

"This program is better than the spreadsheet I was using," says Jenny. "Thank you very much for your effort."

As they discuss the practical ways the program will be used, they realize the Home Mortgage Planner program, like any software program, can be made better with continued time and effort. Review the Home Mortgage Planner program, and consider ways it could be improved. Here are some of the ideas they came up with.

- Interest rates often differ based on the length of the loan. Modify the program to allow separate interest rate inputs for each loan.
- Some individuals prefer to make a larger down payment and borrow less money. Modify the program to allow two different loan amounts to be compared.

Be prepared to discuss various modifications in terms of the work required compared with the resulting benefits.

## Chapter Summary

- A variable is a storage location that can be accessed and changed by developer code. A variable has a name (the unique identifier that distinguishes the variable) and an associated data value.
- A constant is another type of storage location with a name and an associated data value. The value of a constant cannot change during execution.
- A data type specifies the kind of data that a storage location can hold. The data types used in this book are Integer, Double, String, Char, Boolean, Date, and Object.
- The unique name for a variable, constant, object, or subroutine is called an identifier. Identifiers must begin with a letter or underscore, must contain only letters, digits, and underscores, and must not be a reserved word.
- While not required, it is good practice to make variable names descriptive with mixed case. Constant identifiers should also be descriptive, but typically all uppercase.
- The Dim statement is used to declare a variable by specifying its name and data type. The Const statement similarly declares the name and data type of a constant.
- Expressions are combinations of operators and value-returning code elements such as variables, constants, and literals. When several operations occur in an expression, each part is evaluated and resolved in a predetermined order called operator precedence.
- One of the common uses of an expression is to perform a calculation for an assignment statement. The value on the right side of an assignment statement is stored into a variable on the left side of the assignment statement.
- The process of changing a value from one data type to another is called conversion. Some conversions are implicit and done automatically by Visual Basic. Other types of conversions require an explicit statement using an appropriate conversion keyword.
- Pmt is an intrinsic function that returns the payment for a loan based on periodic, constant payments and a constant interest rate.
- For a program to be useful, it must perform some type of input/output. The InputBox function allows the user to type input into a dialog box. The MsgBox function provides the user with an output message displayed through a dialog box.
- A TextBox control provides GUI form input by providing an area on the form where the user can enter data while the program is executing. A text box can also be used to display output on a form.
- A ListBox control provides GUI form input as a list of items that the user can select by clicking. A list box can also be used to display output on a form.
- A ComboBox control combines the functionality of the TextBox and ListBox controls. The user can select values from a drop-down list or enter values directly into a text box area.

## Key Terms

**arithmetic operators** p. 149
**ASCII (American Standard Code for Information Interchange)** p. 144
**assignment statement** p. 152
**Boolean** p. 144
**CDbl** p. 153
**Char** p. 144
**ComboBox control** p. 162
**comparison operators** p. 150
**Const** p. 148
**constant** p. 148
**Date** p. 145
**dialog box** p. 156
**Dim statement** p. 146
**Double** p. 143
**expression** p. 149
**floating-point data types** p. 143
**FV** p. 155
**identifier** p. 147
**InputBox** p. 156

## REVIEW QUESTIONS

1. What is the difference between a variable and a constant? What is the difference between a constant and a literal value?
2. How is an integral data type similar to a floating-point data type? How are they different? Explicit conversion is required when converting from which type to the other?
3. How is the String data type similar to the Char data type? How are they different?
4. Identify values that might be stored in Boolean or Date data types.
5. What are the naming rules for identifiers? What is the difference between identifier naming rules and variable naming conventions? What are the naming conventions for constants?
6. What is the purpose of the Dim statement? The Const statement?
7. What is an operator? What are the arithmetic operators? What is the precedence of those operators?
8. What are the comparison operators? What are the logical operators? What is the precedence for these operators?
9. What is the purpose of an assignment statement? What can appear on the right side of an assignment statement? What can appear on the left side of an assignment statement?
10. What is the purpose of the InputBox function? What is the purpose of the MsgBox function?
11. What is the purpose of the Pmt function? How is it related to the FV function?
12. How is a text box similar to a list box? How are they different?
13. How is a combo box similar to a text box and a list box? How are they different?

## PROGRAMMING EXERCISES

**7-1. Run the Numbers.** Write a program that inputs two numeric values and displays the sum, product, and average of the two values. The program should have two text boxes for input and three labels for output. The program should also have two buttons, one to perform the calculation and one to exit the program.

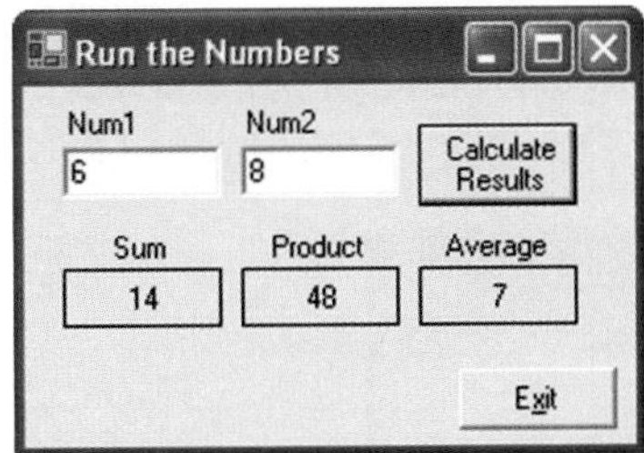


**7-2. Jake's Problem.** Jake has a car with an 8-gallon fuel tank. Jake fills his tank with gas and then drives 60 miles to a friend's house. When he gets to his friend's house, he has 6 gallons left in his fuel tank. Write a program with three input text boxes for tank size, miles traveled, and fuel left. The program should use those inputs to calculate and display how many miles Jake can drive on a full tank of gas. Run the program again with the following data: 9-gallon fuel tank, 120 miles traveled, and 6 gallons remaining. Which of Jake's cars can travel farther on a full tank of gas?

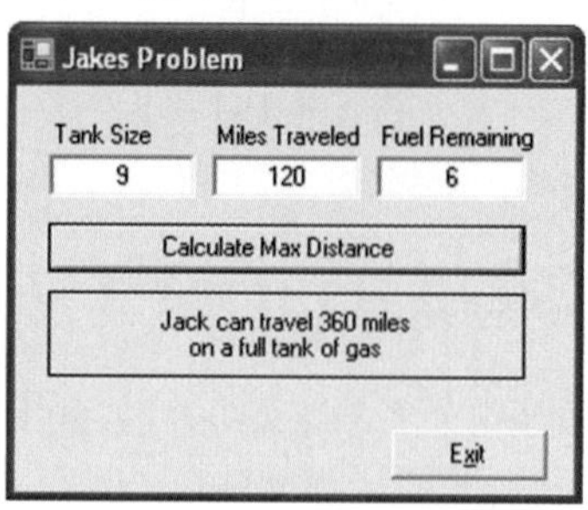


**7-3. Sales Receipt.** Write an application that adds items to a sales receipt one at a time using an input text box and a button. Each time the button is pressed, the new item price should be added to a list box control, which acts as a receipt. The program should also contain output labels for subtotal, sales tax, and total that should be updated whenever an item is added to the receipt. The program should use a constant SALES_TAX with a value of 0.065 (6½ percent). *Hint:* Use FormatCurrency and CDbl to create and read currency string values.

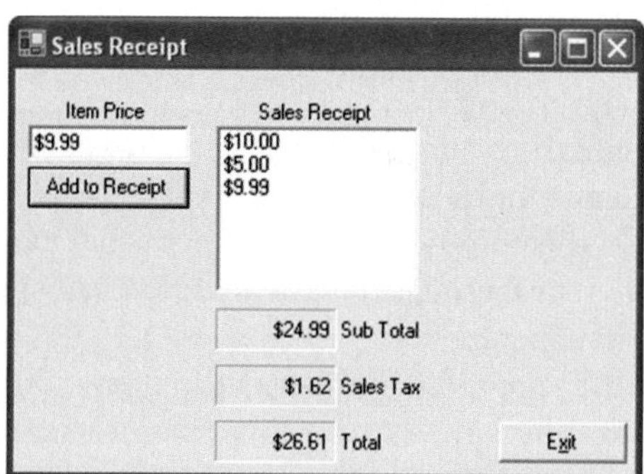


**7-4. Economic Order Quantity.** Business managers use inventory models for calculating optimal order quantities and reorder points. For example, *Economic Order Quantity* is an accounting formula that determines the point at which the combination of order costs and inventory carrying costs are the least. The result is the most cost-effective quantity to order. The basic Economic Order Quantity (EOQ) formula is as follows:

$$EOQ = \sqrt{\frac{2UR}{C}}$$

*where U = annual usage in units, R = order cost, and C = annual carrying cost per unit*

Write an application that calculates EOQ given the input values for annual usage, order cost, and annual carrying cost per unit. *Hint:* Use Format with a string value of 0.## to display the EOQ value to two decimal places.

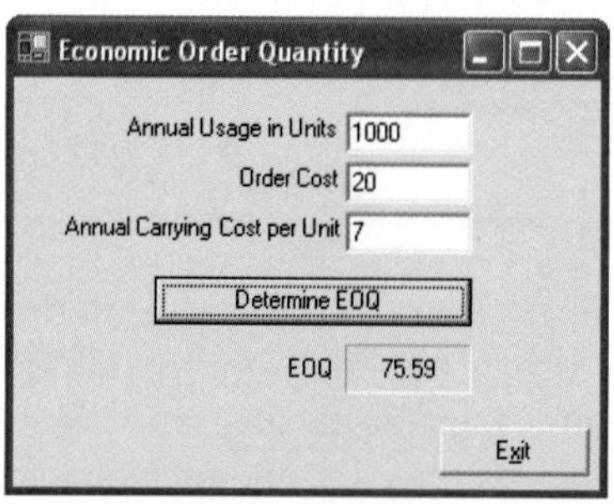

**7-5. Future Value.** "Spend less than you make" is a fundamental mantra of most financial planners. One activity that often helps motivate individuals to save money is to realize how valuable saving (and investing) can be over time. Write an application with three input text boxes that accept values for a monthly savings/investment amount, the average annual percentage rate of the investment, and the number of years the saving and investing takes place. Use your application to determine which of the following saving plans has the highest future value:

- Saving $100 a month at 10 percent APR for 10 years
- Saving $50 a month at 10 percent APR for 20 years
- Saving $50 a month at 7 percent APR for 30 years

**7-6. Home Mortgage Planner Redux.** Modify the Home Mortgage Planner application to include the two enhancements identified in the Review and Enhance the Project section.

## Extended Case Studies

### Pizza and a Movie

Business is good at Pizza and a Movie, and Noah has just purchased a touch-screen monitor that will eventually allow customers to make their orders electronically. He is creating a limited functionality prototype of the electronic order form. The prototype only allows one pizza per order. A combo box should be used to specify the size of the pizza (Medium = $8.99, Large = $11.99, Gigantic = $13.99). Toppings ($0.99 each) are selected using list boxes. The first list box contains the following six toppings: Pepperoni, Sausage, Ham, Onions, Green Peppers, Black Olives. The second list box contains the toppings selected for the pizza order. When the user double-clicks on a topping in the first list box, that topping is added to the second list box. Double-clicking on a topping in the second list box removes it from the user's topping list. The application should always display accurate subtotal, tax (assume 6.5 percent tax rate), and total values.

### Singing Mimes

Reed and Elizabeth are creating CDs containing various educational and entertainment software applications. They are selling the CDs for $5 each. In addition, they are creating a user's manual that contains documentation about each application on the CD. The user's manual is helpful for customers wanting detailed information about the various applications on the CD. Furthermore, the user's manual creates an additional revenue source for the company. Black-and-white copies of the manual will be sold for $3 each, and color copies of the manual will be sold for $5 each. Reed and Elizabeth expect some schools will buy multiple copies of the CD (to install on multiple machines) but only purchase one or two manuals. They need an order form that contains three input text boxes for purchase quantities of CDs, black-and-white manuals, and color manuals. There should be three adjacent output text boxes that display the group price (unit quantity times unit price) for each. There should also be an output text box that totals the three group price text boxes.

CHAPTER 8

# Controlling Execution

## OUTLINE



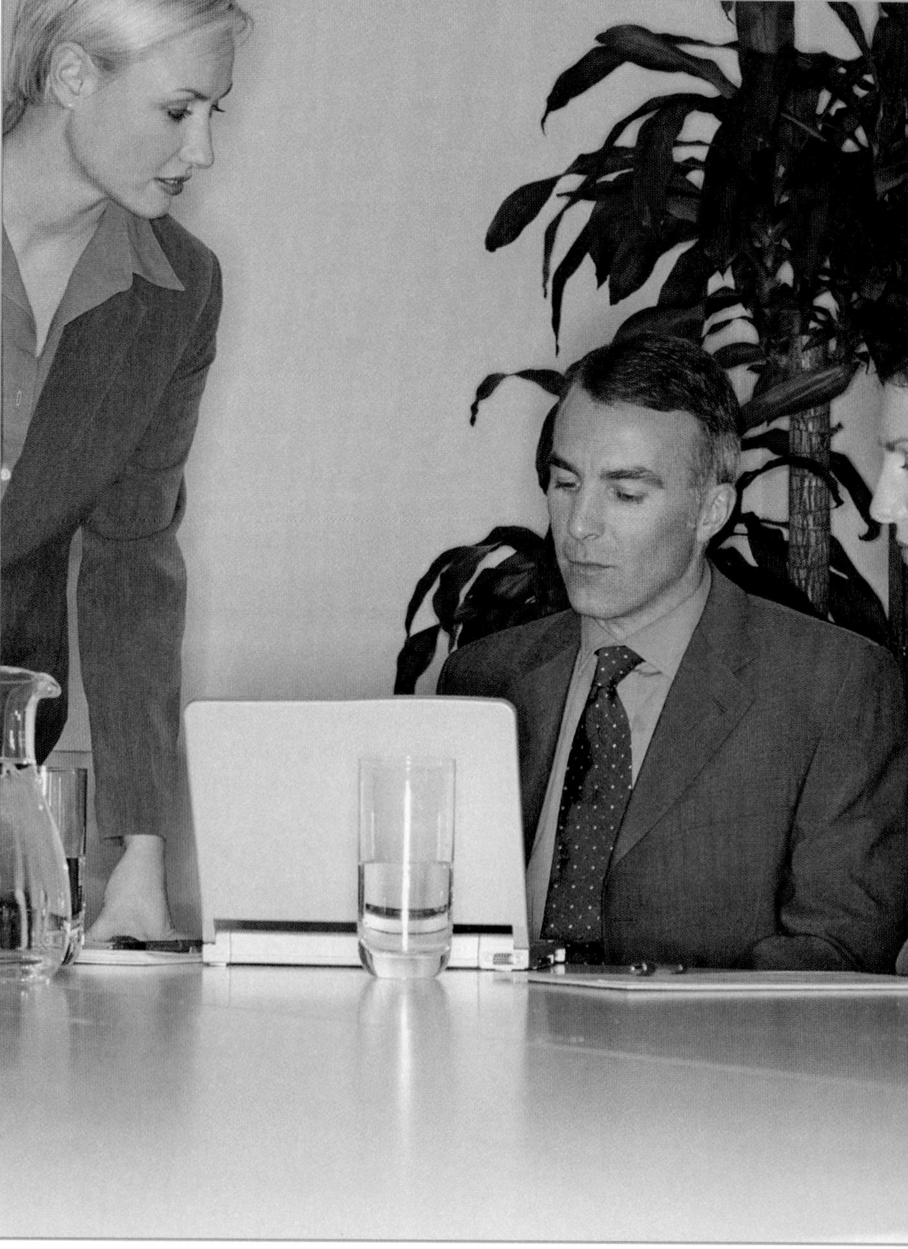

▶ INTERVIEW

**Brian McKim, Editor and Publisher, SHECKYmagazine.com**

***Interviewer:*** Please tell us how you got involved in the IT industry

***McKim:*** I got a part-time job as a software/hardware rep/merchandiser for a few months back in 1996. I hated it, but it forced me to tackle projects that I wouldn't have on my own. The position called for me to purchase a more powerful laptop, which in turn enabled me to learn web design. When we eventually purchased a scanner, we set about scanning the piles of comedy memorabilia we had accumulated over our nearly two decades of performing standup comedy. It evolved into a site that covered all of professional standup. I had newspaper, magazine, photography, and graphic design skills, so we automatically approached it as an online magazine that featured interviews, columns, listings, and other resources. We launched the magazine, appropriately enough, on April 1, 1999—ancient history in WWW terms.

***Interviewer:*** SHECKY is an unusual online magazine. Can you explain why?

***McKim:*** We're low-tech compared with most online magazines. We want the magazine to load quickly—so we have no Flash, no video clips, no audio. We currently feature ten columnists—all are standup comics. We're mainly focused on content. "Content is king," as they say.

We have no advertisers, which gives us total creative control but almost no revenue. In the midst of the dotcom heat, we were frequently asked, "Are you making any money?" Our standard response was "No, but we're not losing any either." And when the other ventures started hemorrhaging money and going bust, we were still standing because we hadn't overreached.

We're often asked if we plan on offering a print edition, a hard copy. We are horrified by the idea, since it would create a whole set of problems and considerations that we don't have right now as an electronic publication—ad sales, printing costs, distribution, hard deadlines, etc. That is very old school thinking. We fully appreciate the freedom, the ease, and the reach of an online magazine. Of course, there's the puzzle of figuring out how to generate revenue, but for now we are benefiting in many ways besides money.

## OBJECTIVES

At the completion of this chapter, you will

- **Understand and use multiple versions of the If . . . Then statement**
- **Understand and use the Select Case statement**
- **Understand and use the Do . . . Loop statement**
- **Understand and use the For . . . Next statement**
- **Understand and use the Exit statement**
- **Distinguish between syntax, runtime, and logic errors**
- **Explain the advantages of Try . . . Catch for structured exception handling**
- **Understand and effectively use the CheckBox and RadioButton controls**
- **Successfully write Windows applications where the flow of execution changes through conditions, loops, and error-handling structures**

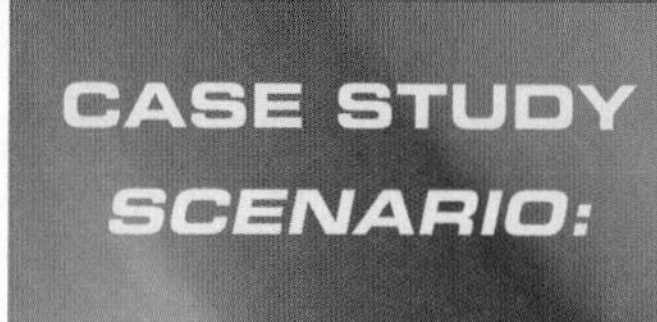


# Currency Conversion

Allen Bauer is the vice president of sales for the Pretty Fish Company in New York. Allen is a firm believer that technology should be used to empower his employees by making them more efficient in their jobs. He has scheduled a meeting with Madison, a bright, young systems analyst at Pretty Fish, to discuss an idea.

In his office with Madison, Allen explains, "I need the information systems department to develop a monetary conversion program. The program will be something for our sales representatives that they can load on their laptops and have readily available when traveling or working with international clients. The application should allow sales reps to select the conversion currency from a list to avoid the possible problem of misspelling Indonesia's Rupiah or forgetting that Somalia uses the Shilling."

"We should be able to do that for you without much trouble," Madison says, as she finishes writing down her notes about the new application. She then adds, "If you want, we can take it a step further."

Allen leans back in his chair and says, "I'm listening."

"We could make the application do more than simply calculate a single currency conversion. We could allow the salesperson to enter a range of U.S. dollar amounts and have the application display the resulting target currency amounts for each value in the range. The salesperson could even specify the size of the increments within the range. This could be very helpful to a salesperson who needs to discuss different sales amounts and pricing differences."

"Very good, Madison," says Allen. "I knew you were the right person for this project." Madison's solution is presented later this chapter.

## 8-1 If . . . Then Statement

The ***If . . . Then*** statement is one of the most important structures in any programming language because it gives developers control over the flow of execution and allows the software solution to support multiple possibilities. The simple If . . . Then structure contains a ***condition*** followed by a block of statements that execute only when the condition evaluates to true. The use of Else and ElseIf statements allows the condition structure to become more complex.

*Syntax:*

```
If condition Then statement

If condition Then
   statements
[ ElseIf condition Then
   statements ]
[ Else
   statements ]
 End If
```

*Examples:*

```
'*** Single Line If . . . Then
If IsNumeric(txtAmount.Text) Then Total = Total + txtAmount.Text

'*** Multi-line If . . . Then
If Average >= 90 Then
   MsgBox("Your grade is A")
   ACount = ACount + 1
End If

'*** Multi-line with Else
If Score >= 60 Then
    PassCount = PassCount + 1
Else
    FailCount = FailCount + 1
End If

'*** Multi-line with ElseIf and Else
If Hour(Now) < 12 Then
    MsgBox("Good Morning")
ElseIf Hour(Now) < 17 Then
    MsgBox("Good Afternoon")
Else
    MsgBox("Good Evening")
End If

'*** Nested Ifs
If cboStatus.Text = "Preferred" Then
    If cboVolume.Text = "High" Then
        Markup = 0.25
    Else
        Markup = 0.3
    End If
Else
    Markup = 0.4
End If
```

**►►► Tip**

**The single-line If . . . Then is useful when you are executing a single statement on a true condition. The single-line If . . . Then does not use an End If.**

You can use the If . . . Then statement to execute a single statement or a block of statements. To execute only a single command when the condition is true, you can use the *single-line format*. The more general *multi-line format* requires an ***End If*** and can be used to execute blocks of statements. The multi-line form may contain one or more ***ElseIf*** statements to test additional conditions if previous conditions are false. Finally, the multi-line form may have an ending ***Else*** statement containing code that executes when all previous conditions are false.

## If . . . Then Illustrated: Water Temperature

The following code uses a multi-line If . . . Then with ElseIf and Else to display "Solid," "Liquid," or "Gas" based on the degrees Fahrenheit for water. A quick reminder: water freezes at 32 degrees Fahrenheit and boils at 212 degrees Fahrenheit.

*Examples:*

```
If DegreesFahrenheit < 32 Then
    MsgBox("Solid")
ElseIf DegreesFahrenheit < 212 Then
    MsgBox("Liquid")
Else
    MsgBox("Gas")
End If
```

## Quick Check 8-A

1. Write an alternate solution to the water temperature problem using three single line If . . . Then statements.

2. Write an alternate solution to the water temperature problem using nested If . . . Then statements.

## If . . . Then Illustrated: Smallest Value

Assume there are three Integer variables A, B, and C. The following code uses a multi-line If . . . Then with ElseIf and Else to display the smallest of the three values. One possible solution follows.

```
If (A <= B) And (A <= C) Then
    MsgBox(A & " is the smallest")
ElseIf (B <= C) Then
    MsgBox(B & " is the smallest")
Else
    MsgBox(C & " is the smallest")
End If
```

## Quick Check 8-B

1. Write an alternate solution to the smallest value problem using three single line If . . . Then statements.

2. Write an alternate solution to the smallest value problem using nested If . . . Then statements.

## If . . . Then Illustrated: Exit Confirmation

The MsgBox function displays a message in a dialog box. Because MsgBox is a function, it also returns a value. Specifically, MsgBox returns the value of the button pressed by the user. You can use MsgBoxStyle to determine the buttons available in the dialog box; you can test the selected button using MsgBoxResult. The following click event procedure displays a message in a dialog box with two buttons, yes and no (see Figure 8-1). If the user clicks the yes button, then the program displays a closing message and ends the application. By confirming the user's intention to exit the program in this manner, you can avoid any problems related to an accidental program termination.

```
'This Exit button click event procedure uses MsgBox to confirm before exiting
Private Sub btnExit_Click( ByVal sender As System.Object, _
        ByVal e As System.EventArgs) Handles btnExit.Click
    If MsgBox("Exit Program?", MsgBoxStyle.YesNo) = MsgBoxResult.Yes Then
        MsgBox("Have a nice day!")  'Closing message
        End 'End the program
    End If
End Sub
```

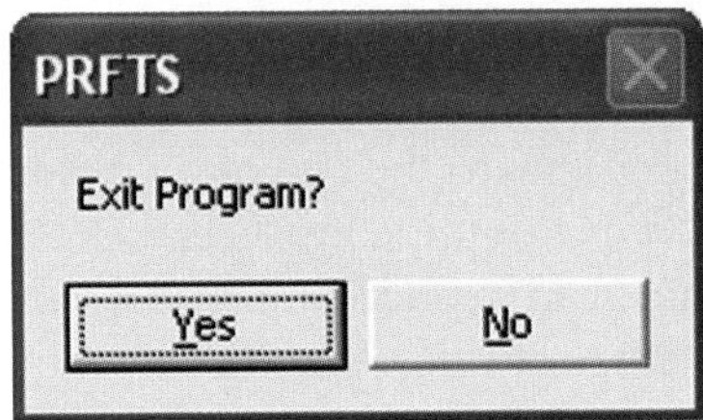


**FIGURE 8.1** *A Message Box with Yes and No Buttons*

## *If . . . Then Summary*

- The If . . . Then statement is the basic conditional statement.
- The single-line If . . . Then is useful when you are executing only one statement when a condition is true. A single-line If . . . Then statement does not use an End If.
- The multi-line form supports blocks of actions. If a condition is true, the statements enclosed by the Then block are executed. If a condition is false, any following ElseIf conditions are evaluated in order. If all conditions are false and there is an Else block, the Else block is executed. Once any block finishes executing, execution jumps to the statement immediately following the If . . . Then statement.

# 8-2 Select Case Statement

Many programming languages contain a statement that supports multiple branches for various values of a single expression. VB.NET supports this type of decision using the ***Select Case*** statement, a decision structure that executes statements based on the value of an expression.

*Syntax:*

```
Select Case test_expression
   [ Case test_value_clause
     statements ]
   [ Case Else
     statements ]
End Select
```

*Example:*

```
Select Case Val(txtScore.Text)
    Case 100
        MsgBox("A+ Perfect Score!")
    Case 98, 99
        MsgBox("Grade is A+")
    Case Is >= 90
        MsgBox("Grade is A")
```

```
    Case 88 To 90
        MsgBox("Grade is B+")
    Case Is >= 80
        MsgBox("Grade is B")
    Case Else
        MsgBox("Grade is C or lower")
End Select
```

When executed, the test expression is evaluated once, and each test value clause is then compared in order until a match is found. When a test value clause matches the test expression, the corresponding statement block is executed. The optional Else block executes if none of the test value clauses match. Once a block has finished executing, execution passes to the end of the Select statement.

There are three types of test constructs. First and most common is a simple value. Second, the test clause can include a relational value using the keyword Is. Finally, the test clause can be a range of values specified by the To keyword. A comma may be used to separate multiple test constructs in a single test value clause. The test expression and test clause must be of comparable types; otherwise, a compile-time error occurs.

## Select Case Illustrated: Water Temperature

The following code uses a Select Case statement to display "Solid," "Liquid," or "Gas" based on the degrees Fahrenheit for water.

```
Select Case DegreesFahrenheit
    Case Is < 32
        MsgBox("Solid")
    Case Is < 212
        MsgBox("Liquid")
    Case Else
        MsgBox("Gas")
End Select
```

## *Quick Check 8-C*

Write an alternate solution to the water temperature problem using the Select Case statement, but without using the less than (<) operator.

**▶▶▶Tip**

**You can use a colon (:) to place multiple statements on the same line. The colon's functionality is the compliment of the underline (_) used to write a single statement across multiple lines.**

## Select Case Illustrated: Digits as Text

The following code uses a Select Case statement that displays the appropriate text "zero," "one," "two," etc. based on the single-digit integer value of the variable Number. This solution places the test clause and the corresponding action on the same line, separated by a colon (:).

```
Select Case Number
    Case 1 : MsgBox("one")
    Case 2 : MsgBox("two")
    Case 3 : MsgBox("three")
    Case 4 : MsgBox("four")
    Case 5 : MsgBox("five")
    Case 6 : MsgBox("six")
```

```
    Case 7 : MsgBox("seven")
    Case 8 : MsgBox("eight")
    Case 9 : MsgBox("nine")
    Case 0 : MsgBox("zero")
End Select
```

## 8-3 Do . . . Loop Statement

The ***Do . . . Loop*** statement is the general iterative statement. The Do . . . Loop statement allows you to repeatedly execute a group of statements until a condition is true, until a condition is false, as long as a condition is true, or as long as a condition is false. There are therefore four versions of the Do . . . Loop statement.

*Syntax:*

```
Do While condition
   statements
Loop

Do Until condition
   statements
Loop

Do
   statements
Loop While condition

Do
   statements
Loop Until condition
```

*Examples:*

```
'Do While . . . Loop
Count = 1
Do While Count <= 7
    lstOutput.Items.Add(Count)
    Count = Count + 1
Loop

'Do Until . . . Loop
Count = 1
Do Until Count > 7
    lstOutput.Items.Add(Count)
    Count = Count + 1
Loop

'Do . . . Loop While
Count = 1
Do
    lstOutput.Items.Add(Count)
    Count = Count + 1
Loop While Count <= 7
```

```
'Do . . . Loop Until
Count = 1
Do
    lstOutput.Items.Add(Count)
    Count = Count + 1
Loop Until Count > 7
```

The Do . . . Loop statement repeats a block of statements an unknown number of times. The number of times the loop executes is based on a condition. If the While keyword is used, a condition value of true causes the loop to repeat. If the Until keyword is used, a condition value of false causes the loop to repeat. Therefore, the statement block will repeat either *while* the condition is true or *until* it becomes true.

The location of the test condition can appear above the loop following the Do keyword or below the loop following the Loop keyword. If the condition appears above the loop, then the condition is tested before the loop body executes. If the condition is at the bottom of the loop, then the loop body is guaranteed to execute once before the condition is tested. After one pass through the loop, the location of the condition makes no difference.

## ASK THE AUTHOR

**Q** What is the point of having four different versions of the Do . . . Loop?

**A** Understanding the subtle differences gives you increased flexibility in the code you write. You can interchange the While and Until keywords by negating the condition. For example, instead of saying, "While Counter <>−1," you may choose to say, "Until Counter =−1." Likewise, you can force one pass through the body of the loop by placing the condition at the bottom of the loop.

Which of the four versions is best in any particular case depends on the specific situation and which version is most clear in your eyes.

**Tip**

**To stop an endless loop when debugging a program, press Ctrl+Break.**

## Do . . . Loop Illustrated: Annual Withdraw

Consider the following problem. You have $15,000 in a savings account that earns 5 percent APR. At the end of the year, you withdraw $1,000 from the account, or, if the account contains less than $1,000, you withdraw the balance and close the account. Determine how many years the account will remain open and the total amount of money you will withdraw from the account. The following code solves this problem, and the resulting output is shown in Figure 8-2.

```
Dim Balance, Withdraw, WithdrawTotal As Double
Dim YearCount As Integer

Balance = 15000
Do While Balance > 0
    YearCount = YearCount + 1
    Balance = Balance * 1.05  'Earn 5 percent APR this year
```

```
    If Balance >= 1000 Then
        Withdraw = 1000
    Else
        Withdraw = Balance
    End If
    WithdrawTotal = WithdrawTotal + Withdraw
    Balance = Balance - Withdraw 'Make this year's withdrawal
Loop
MsgBox(FormatCurrency(WithdrawTotal) & " was withdrawn over " & _
        YearCount & " years")
```

**FIGURE 8.2** *Annual Withdraw Output*

## Do . . . Loop Illustrated: How Old are You?

Another use of a Do . . . Loop is to validate user input when using the InputBox function. Remember that InputBox prompts the user for a value and returns the result. The actual value entered by the user may be inappropriate for the application. A Do . . . Loop can used to reprompt the user again and again until valid data is finally entered.

The following code prompts the user for his or her age and then informs the user of a lower bound on the number of days the person has been alive. The solution uses the IsNumeric function to determine if the user's age input is a valid numeric value. If the input is not numeric, a Do . . . Loop is used to reprompt the user until valid numeric data is entered. Only after the input has been validated does the program calculate the number of days. Figure 8-3 shows the dialog boxes from a sample run of the code.

**Tip**

**The IsNumeric function determines if a value is a valid numeric.**

```
Dim Reply As String
Dim Age As Integer
Reply = InputBox("Enter your age")
Do While Not IsNumeric(Reply)
    Reply = InputBox("Invalid number.  Try again.  Enter your age")
Loop
Age = CInt(Reply)
MsgBox("You are at least " & 365 * Age & " days old")
```

**FIGURE 8.3** *How Old Are You Dialog Windows*

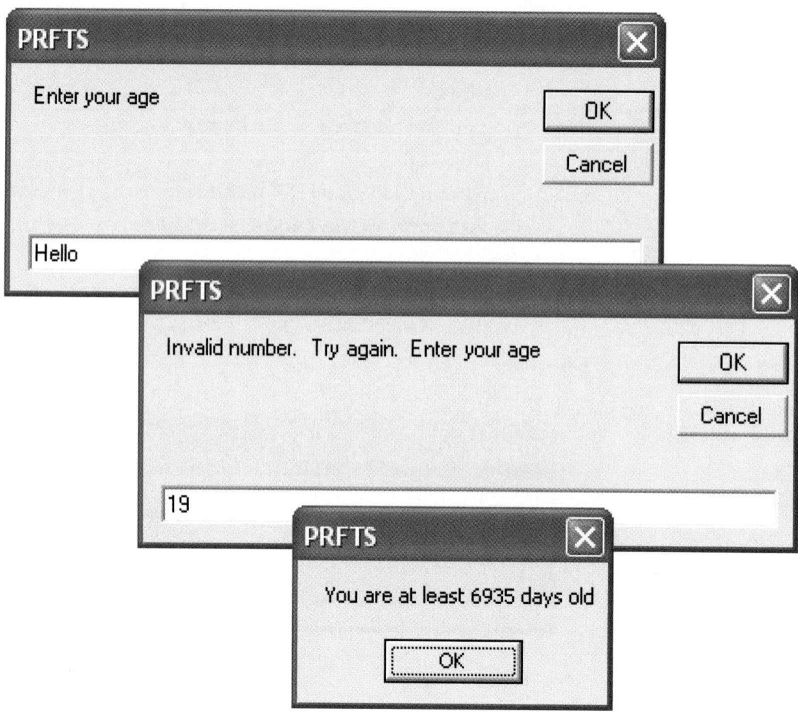


## 8-4 For . . . Next Statement

The ***For . . . Next*** statement is a loop that repeats a known number of times. Use the For . . . Next statement when you know in advance how many times the body of the loop will execute.

*Syntax:*

**For** *loopvariable* = *start* **To** *end* [ **Step** *stepvalue* ]
*statements*
**Next** [ *loopvariable* ]

*Examples:*

```
For Count = 1 To 7
    lstOutput.Items.Add(Count)
Next

For J = 2 To 100 Step 2
    Sum = Sum + J
Next J
MsgBox("The sum of the even numbers from 1 to 100 is " & Sum)
```

**Tip**
**Using the Step keyword, you can specify the value to increment or decrement the counter after each pass through the loop.**

The For . . . Next loop contains a *loop variable* whose values are determined by the loop's *start*, *end*, and *step* values. When the loop begins, the loop variable is assigned the start value. After each pass through the body of the loop, the loop variable is automatically updated by the step value. The loop repeats until the loop variable value exceeds the final value.

The step value is optional and defaults to 1 if unspecified. You can specify a different step value using the Step keyword. If the step value is negative, the end value should be less than the start value.

## ASK THE AUTHOR

**Q** It seems like any For . . . Next loop could be rewritten as a Do . . . Loop. Is this true? If so, then why have a For . . . Next at all?

**A** Yes, any For . . . Next loop can be rewritten as a Do . . . Loop. Having said that, let me also say that the For . . . Next loop is still valuable. For example, most infinite loops are Do loops where the developer forgot to properly update the loop condition variable inside the body of the loop. This is much less common with For loops because the loop variable is automatically updated after each iteration. It is also generally agreed that the For loop is easier to read, understand, and maintain. We have already pointed out how anything that improves understanding and maintenance is probably a worthwhile activity. Finally, For loops are great when working with arrays, as you will see in Chapter 9.

## For . . . Next Illustrated: Payment Plans

Assume you have been hired for ten days of work. Your boss gives you the option of getting paid $100 a day for all ten days or $1 for the first day, $2 for the second day, $4 for the third day, and so on with the amount paid doubling each day. The following code determines which payment plan is most profitable. The output is shown in Figure 8-4.

```
Dim Plan1, Plan2 As Double
Dim Day, P2Current As Integer

P2Current = 1
For Day = 1 To 10
  lstOutput.Items.Add("Day " & Format(Day, "00") & _
              "   Plan1=" & FormatCurrency(100) & _
              "   Plan2=" & FormatCurrency(P2Current))
  Plan1 = Plan1 + 100
  Plan2 = Plan2 + P2Current
  P2Current = P2Current * 2
Next
lstOutput.Items.Add("")
lstOutput.Items.Add("Plan1 pays " & FormatCurrency(Plan1))
lstOutput.Items.Add("Plan2 pays " & FormatCurrency(Plan2))
lstOutput.Items.Add("")
If Plan1 > Plan2 Then
  lstOutput.Items.Add("Plan1 pays better")
Else
  lstOutput.Items.Add("Plan2 pays better")
End If
```

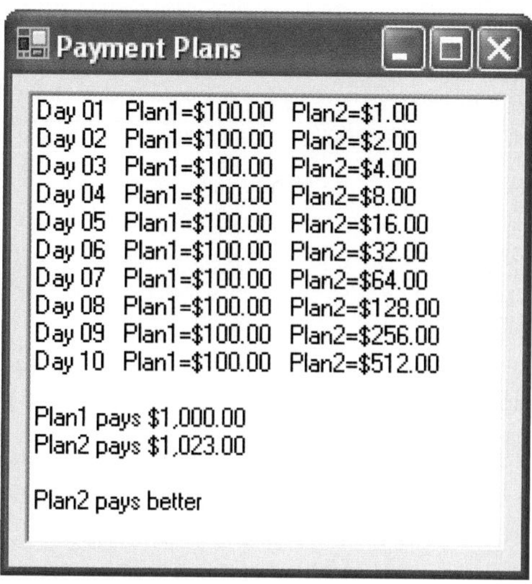
Payment Plans
Day 01 Plan1=$100.00 Plan2=$1.00
Day 02 Plan1=$100.00 Plan2=$2.00
Day 03 Plan1=$100.00 Plan2=$4.00
Day 04 Plan1=$100.00 Plan2=$8.00
Day 05 Plan1=$100.00 Plan2=$16.00
Day 06 Plan1=$100.00 Plan2=$32.00
Day 07 Plan1=$100.00 Plan2=$64.00
Day 08 Plan1=$100.00 Plan2=$128.00
Day 09 Plan1=$100.00 Plan2=$256.00
Day 10 Plan1=$100.00 Plan2=$512.00
Plan1 pays $1,000.00
Plan2 pays $1,023.00
Plan2 pays better

**FIGURE 8.4** *Payment Plans Output*

## For . . . Next Illustrated: Lifetime Earnings

The following code calculates a person's lifetime earnings. Assume the person receives a 4 percent raise every year until retirement at age 62. The program should input the person's name, age, and starting salary. The output should be the projected total amount earned before retirement. One possible solution is shown in the following code. You can test the solution by assuming the person starts working at age 23 with an initial salary of $25,000. That person would be projected to earn $2,375,637.89 before retiring (see Figure 8-5).

```
Private Sub btnLifeTime_Click(ByVal sender As System.Object, _
            ByVal e As System.EventArgs) Handles btnLifeTime.Click
    Dim Name As String
    Dim Salary, Total As Double
    Dim Count, Age As Integer

    Name = InputBox("Enter the person's name")
    Age = InputBox("Enter " & Name & "'s age")
    Salary = InputBox("Enter " & Name & "'s starting salary")
    For Count = Age To 62
        Total = Total + Salary
        Salary = Salary * 1.04
    Next
    MsgBox(Name & " will earn " & FormatCurrency(Total) & _
        " before retiring.")
End Sub
```

**FIGURE 8.5** *Lifetime Earnings Output*

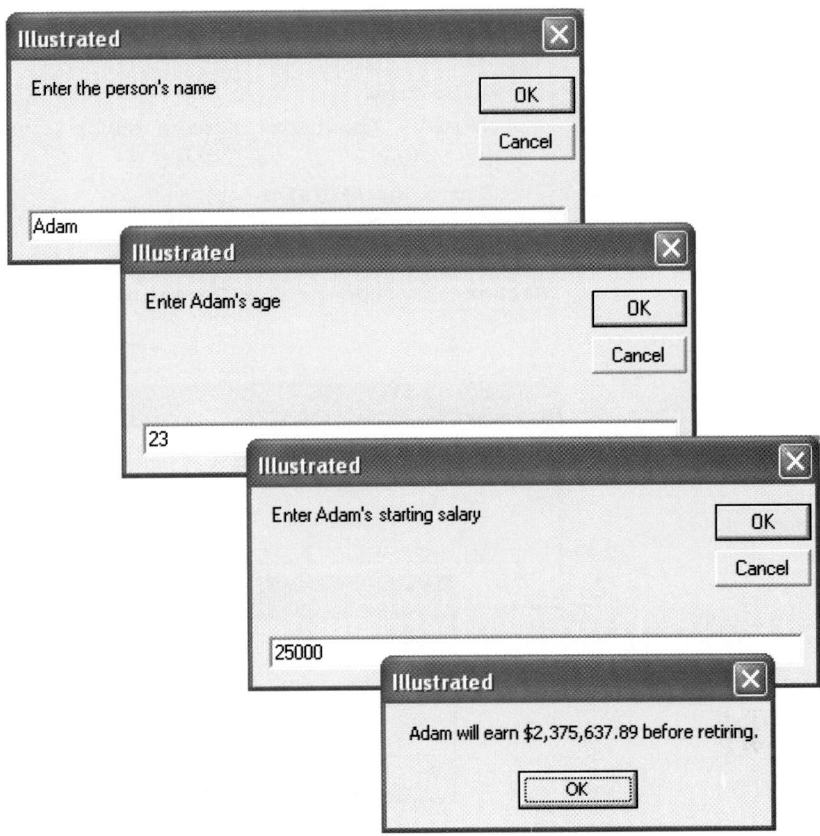


## 8-5 Exit Statement

The ***Exit statement*** allows you to immediately exit from a decision, loop, or procedure code block. The keyword Exit is followed by the block type being exited from, and execution continues with the statement immediately following the block of code.

*Syntax:* Exit *blocktype*

*Examples:*

```
Exit Do
Exit For
Exit Select
Exit Sub
```

The Exit statement in any of its forms can appear as many times as needed inside the specified block of code. If there are nested programming control statements, execution jumps to the end of the innermost control statement of the kind specified in the Exit statement.

### Exit Do Illustrated: Sentinel Value

A sentinel value is a special value that appears at the end of a list of data to be processed. The sentinel value itself should not be processed. Many developers find that a Do . . . Loop combined with an Exit statement make sentinel controlled loops easy to write and read. The following example code accepts input values from the user until the sentinel value –1 is entered. The solution then displays the average of the values entered (see Figure 8-6).

```
Dim Value, Sum, Count As Double

Do While True
    Value = InputBox("Please enter a value, or -1 to quit")
    If Value = -1  Then Exit Do
    Sum = Sum + Value
    Count = Count + 1
Loop
MsgBox("Average is " & Format(Sum / Count, "0.##"))
```

**FIGURE 8.6** *Sentinel Value Output*

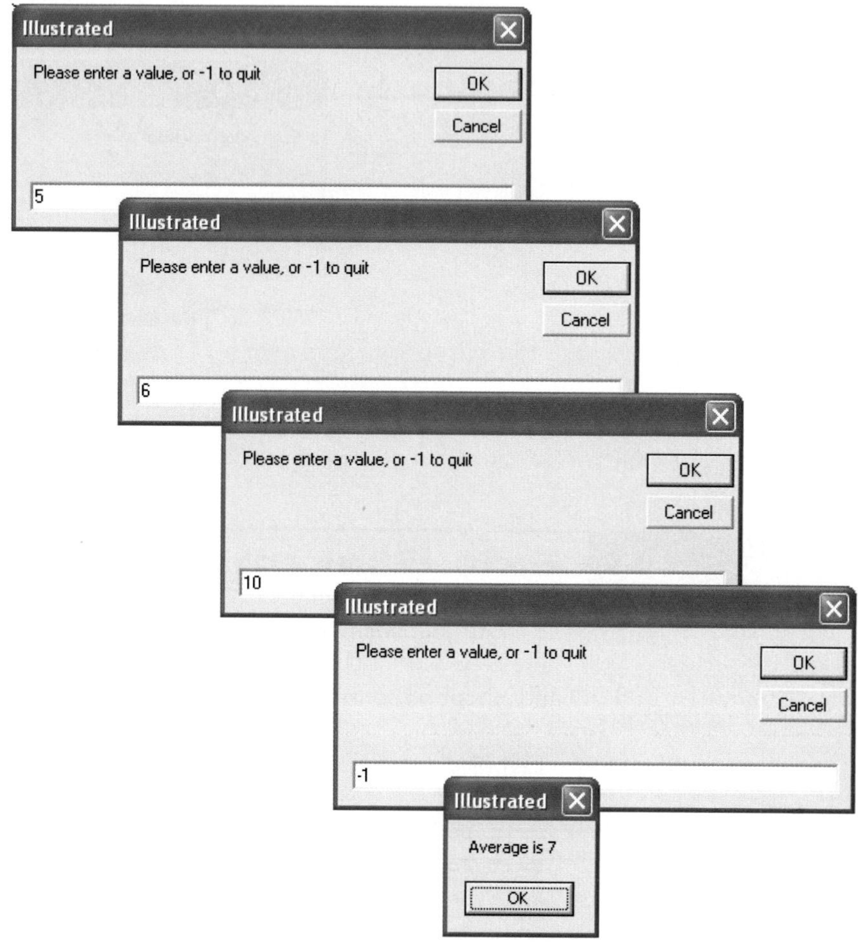


## Exit Sub Illustrated: Numeric Input Validation

The Exit statement can also be used to cause control to leave a sub procedure. Consider a program that multiplies two numeric values entered in a text box. If you assume the user enters valid data in the text box, the solution is simple, as shown in the following.

```
'This event procedure assumes numeric text box values, which is risky.
'It will crash if the text box contains a nonnumeric value.
Private Sub btnCalculate_Click(ByVal sender As System.Object, _
          ByVal e As System.EventArgs) Handles btnCalculate.Click
    MsgBox("The product is " & txtInput1.Text * txtInput2.Text)
End Sub
```

If the user enters valid data, then the code works fine. But what if the user leaves a text box blank or enters nonnumeric data in either text box (see Figure 8-7)? The program crashes when it tries to multiply the nonnumeric data (see Figure 8-8).

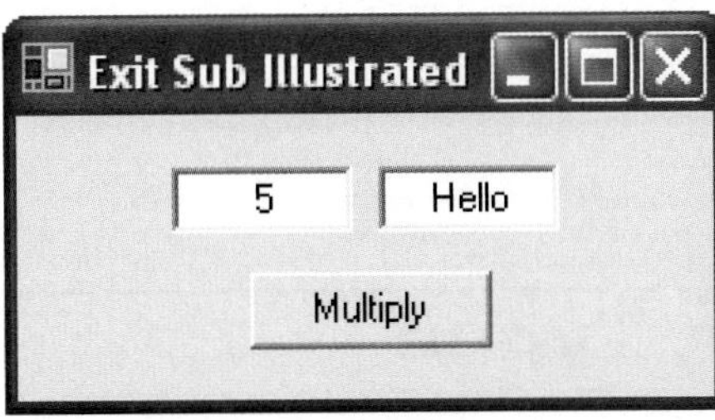


**FIGURE 8.7** *Example of Nonnumeric Data in an Input Text Box*

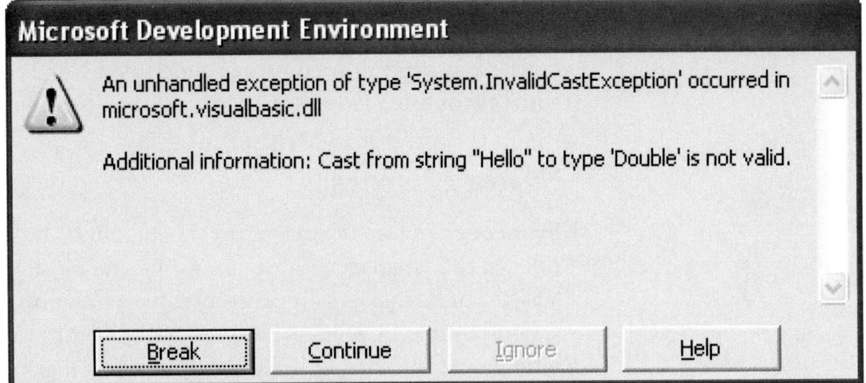


**FIGURE 8.8** *Multiplying Nonnumeric Data Causes the Program to Crash*

We can avoid this particular crash by verifying that the input data is numeric before attempting any multiplication. If the input data is not numeric, the user is informed of the problem (Figure 8-9), and control then leaves the calculation event procedure without attempting the multiplication operation. The user can then correct the input and retry the calculation. The following code illustrates this data validation process using the IsNumeric function to determine if the input data is numeric.

```
'This event procedure verifies the text box values are numeric.
'Any nonnumeric text box value is identified and handled properly.
Private Sub btnCalculate_Click(ByVal sender As System.Object, _
            ByVal e As System.EventArgs) Handles btnCalculate.Click

    If Not IsNumeric(txtInput1.Text) Then
       MsgBox("Please enter a numeric value in the first text box")
       Exit Sub
    End If

    If Not IsNumeric(txtInput2.Text) Then
       MsgBox("Please enter a numeric value in the second text box")
       Exit Sub
    End If

    MsgBox("The product is " & txtInput1.Text * txtInput2.Text)
End Sub
```

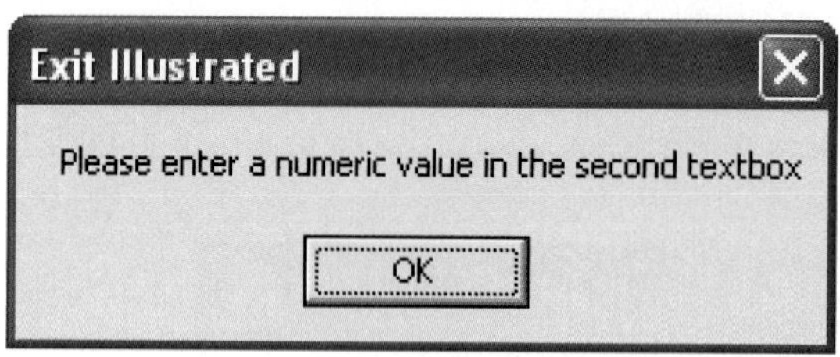
Exit Illustrated
Please enter a numeric value in the second textbox
OK

**FIGURE 8.9** *User Informed of Nonnumeric Input Data*

## 8-6 Error Types

Nobody writes a perfect computer program the first time, every time. When you program, you will create errors (or *bugs*). The process of identifying and fixing errors is called debugging. If you want to be good at fixing errors and avoid creating new errors, you need to spend some time understanding them. In Visual Basic, errors fall into one of three categories: syntax errors, runtime errors, and logic errors.

### Syntax Errors

***Syntax errors*** (or *compiler* errors) occur when you write code that does not follow the rules of the language. Syntax errors are the most common type of errors. Fortunately, Visual Studio makes syntax errors easy to find and fix. When Visual Studio recognizes a syntax error, it marks the error with a blue wavy line underneath. Moving your mouse over the marked code causes an error message to appear. If you try to execute a project with syntax errors, the Visual Studio compiler will give you a message saying there were build errors and list the errors for you as a task list in the output window. You can click on the errors in the task window, and Visual Studio will take you directly to the offending line.

### Runtime Errors

***Runtime errors*** are the result of syntactically correct code that cannot be executed. A runtime error generates an ***exception,*** which is an "exceptional situation" that requires special handling. If the exception is not handled, then the program will halt execution.

The following assignment statement is fine syntactically. However, a runtime error occurs if the value of Count happens to be 0 (because dividing by 0 is illegal).

```
Average = Sum / Count  'Runtime Error if Count is 0
```

The following code is also syntactically correct but can cause a runtime error if the user either leaves the text box blank or enters nonnumeric data, such as "Hello."

```
Dim Score As Integer
Score = txtScore.Text  'Runtime Error if txtScore.Text is "Hello"
```

Another possible cause of a runtime error is accessing a file on a floppy diskette. If the proper diskette is not inserted in the floppy drive, then a *file-not-found* exception will occur. That same exception will occur if you request a file from a network server when the network is down.

You should anticipate and handle code that may result in runtime errors. It is simply unacceptable for your application to fail every time a user types "Hello" in the wrong text box or the company's intranet server is down for a few minutes. The good news is that Visual Basic, using structured error handling, provides a means for catching and handling the exceptions generated by runtime errors. The ***Try . . . Catch*** statement allows for structured exception handling. You should use Try . . . Catch to protect blocks of code that may generate exceptions. Doing so allows your solution to recover from runtime errors without crashing.

*Syntax:*

```
Try
    statements that might cause a runtime error
Catch [ exception As type ]
    statements
End Try
```

*Example:*

```
'This code catches the runtime exception without crashing
Count = 0
Try
    Average = Sum / Count
Catch
    MsgBox("Caught a runtime error")
End Try
MsgBox("Program still running...")

'The following runtime exception crashes the program
Count = 0
Average = Sum / Count
MsgBox("Program never gets this far ...")
```

The Try block contains code where an exception can occur, such as accessing a file or a database. If an error occurs in the Try block, program control is passed to the appropriate Catch statement where the exception is handled (handling typically includes an informative message to the user) and processing continues. If there is no exception, then the Catch code is ignored.

In the preceding example, there are two division statements, each of which causes a divide-by-zero exception. The first division statement is handled within a Try block; therefore, the program continues to execute, displaying the "Program still running" message. The second division statement is not inside a Try block; therefore, the resulting runtime exception is not handled, and the program crashes and all unsaved data is lost.

Runtime errors can occur when a user enters bad data, when a database is unavailable, when files have been moved or renamed, and so on. It is important that these predictable problems be handled gracefully through structured error handling so that your application does not crash (losing all unsaved work) but instead informs the user of the situation and continues working. When implementing your code, try to think of ways where code could fail, and try to handle those exceptions.

## Logic Errors

The third type of error is the most problematic. ***Logic errors*** are mistakes in the solution design or implementation that cause incorrect behavior. A simple example of a logic error is the following statement.

```
Average = A + B + C / 3    'Logic Error (does not calculate average)
```

This assignment statement appears to have been written with the intention of calculating and storing the average of the three values A, B, and C. The line contains valid syntax (i.e., it runs), and it does not generate a runtime exception. Unfortunately, it is an incorrect implementation of the intended design. Instead of adding the three values and dividing by 3, the expression starts by dividing C by 3, then adds A and B to the quotient. Further, this miscalculated Average value may be used in future calculations, compounding the effect and masking the error's origin. This example shows why logic errors are the most problematic.

### MANAGER

Syntax errors are easy to find, easy to fix, and don't cause maintenance problems (because they must be removed before the product can be run, tested, and delivered to the client). On the other hand, logic errors are hard to find and fix and are potentially big maintenance problems. A logic error may go undetected until the software has been installed on a thousand client machines, which makes corrective changes a significant effort. Further, logic errors often appear as the result of changes to the system, meaning that maintenance changes might result in the need for additional maintenance. This is why companies look to hire developers who are good at both syntax and logic. In fact, because syntax changes over time, many companies are more concerned with their developers' logic and design skills than they are with their developers' syntax knowledge.

## *Error Type Summary*

- Syntax errors are violations of the rules of the programming language. Visual Studio identifies syntax errors for you (but you must fix them yourself).
- Runtime errors occur when an application attempts to perform an action that the system cannot execute, such as dividing by 0 or accessing a file on the A: drive when the floppy is not inserted. A runtime error will crash the program unless the exception is handled with Try . . . Catch.
- Logic errors occur when the program generates incorrect output or displays incorrect behavior. Unlike syntax and runtime errors, logic errors can go unnoticed, and even when they are detected, the sources of the errors can be difficult to diagnose.

## 8-7 CheckBox Control

The ***CheckBox control*** allows the user to specify values such as Yes/No, True/False, or On/Off. You can also use a group of CheckBox controls to display a set of options from which the user can select zero options, one option, or more.

### CheckBox Properties

The Image property allows for an image to be associated with the CheckBox. The Appearance property determines whether the CheckBox appears as a typical CheckBox or as a button. When appearing as a button, the button will be either pushed (checked) or normal (unchecked). These and other common CheckBox properties are described in Table 8-1.

**Table 8.1 Common CheckBox Properties**

| Property | Description |
|---|---|
| Name | ("chk" prefix) Indicates an identifier name to reference the object |
| Appearance | Gets or sets the value that determines the appearance of a CheckBox control |
| Checked | Gets or sets a value indicating whether the CheckBox is in the checked state |
| CheckedState | Gets or sets the state of the CheckBox |
| Enabled | Gets or sets a value indicating whether the control can respond to user interaction |
| Image | Gets or sets the image that is displayed on a button control |
| Text | Gets or sets the text associated with this control |
| ThreeState | Gets or sets a value indicating whether the CheckBox will allow three check states rather than two |
| Visible | Gets or sets a value indicating whether the control is displayed |

### CheckBox Illustrated: Express Yourself with Style

Create a form with a text box and three CheckBox controls as shown in Figure 8-10. The CheckBox values should turn on and off the bold, italic, and underline effects of the text box.

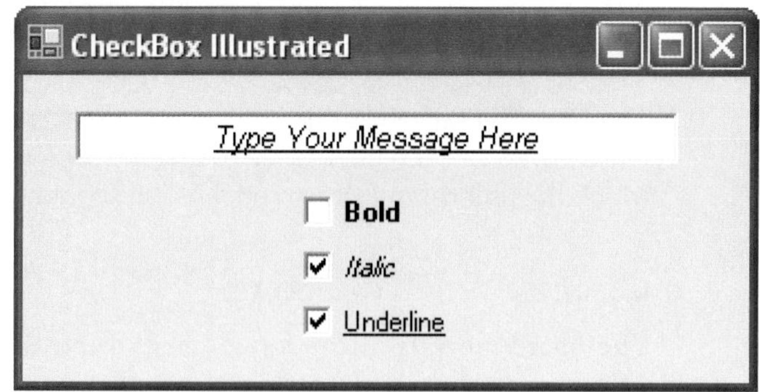


**FIGURE 8.10** *Express Yourself with Style Output*

In earlier versions of Visual Basic, the code for the chkBold change event would have looked something like the following.

```
'The following code was okay for VB6, but does not work for VB.NET
If chkBold.Checked = True Then txtMessage.Font.Bold = True
```

The preceding statement does not work with VB.NET because the Bold property of a Font object is read-only (meaning you cannot change its value using an assignment statement). The VB.NET code below changes the text box by creating a new Font object. The statement New Font has three arguments. The first two arguments are assigned the same font name and font size as the current txtMessage font. The third argument is a Style type, which contains information about bold, italic, underline, and more. The XOR operator is used to toggle only the selected style value while leaving the other style values unchanged.

```
'The VB.NET solution creates a new Font object for the text box
Private Sub chkBold_CheckedChanged(ByVal sender As System.Object, _
            ByVal e As System.EventArgs) Handles chkBold.CheckedChanged
    txtMessage.Font = New Font(txtMessage.Font.Name, txtMessage.Font.Size, _
        txtMessage.Font.Style Xor FontStyle.Bold)
End Sub

Private Sub chkItalic_CheckedChanged(ByVal sender As System.Object, _
            ByVal e As System.EventArgs) Handles chkItalic.CheckedChanged
    txtMessage.Font = New Font(txtMessage.Font.Name, txtMessage.Font.Size, _
        txtMessage.Font.Style Xor FontStyle.Italic)
End Sub

Private Sub chkUnderline_CheckedChanged(ByVal sender As System.Object, _
            ByVal e As System.EventArgs) Handles chkUnderline.CheckedChanged
    txtMessage.Font = New Font(txtMessage.Font.Name, txtMessage.Font.Size, _
        txtMessage.Font.Style Xor FontStyle.Underline)
End Sub
```

## 8-8 RadioButton Control

▶▶▶ **Tip**

**The RadioButton control can only select a single item from a group. The RadioButton should therefore be used when the options are mutually exclusive.**

▶▶▶ **Tip**

**The CheckedChanged event is called when a RadioButton is checked or unchecked. Note that checking a RadioButton also unchecks the previously checked RadioButton in the group, thus calling two events.**

The ***RadioButton control*** allows the user to select a single item from a list of mutually exclusive options. All RadioButton controls in a given container constitute a group. When the user selects one RadioButton within a group, the others clear automatically. To create multiple groups on one form, place each additional group in its own container, such as a GroupBox or Panel control.

### RadioButton Properties

The Appearance property of the RadioButton control can make it appear like a toggle button—depressed if selected. The Image property allows for an image to be associated with the RadioButton. These and other common RadioButton properties are described in Table 8-2.

**Table 8.2** Common RadioButton Properties

| Property | Description |
|---|---|
| Name | ("rad" prefix) Indicates an identifier name to reference the object |
| Appearance | Gets or sets the value that determines the appearance of the RadioButton control |
| Checked | Gets or sets a value indicating whether the control is checked |
| Enabled | Gets or sets a value indicating whether the control can respond to user interaction |
| Image | Gets or sets the image that is displayed on a RadioButton control |
| Text | Gets or sets the text associated with this control |
| Visible | Gets or sets a value indicating whether the control is displayed |

### RadioButton Illustrated: Express Yourself with Color

Create a form with a text box and two sets of RadioButton controls as shown in Figure 8-11. The first RadioButton set should determine the background color of the text box (white, yellow, or green). The second RadioButton set should determine the foreground color of the text box (black, blue, or red).

▶ **FIGURE 8.11** *Express Yourself with Color Output*

RadioButton Illustrated

Type Your Message Here

BackColor: White, Yellow (selected), Green

ForeColor: Black, Blue, Red (selected)

The code for the RadioButton click events follows.

```
Private Sub radWhite_CheckedChanged(ByVal sender As System.Object, _
            ByVal e As System.EventArgs) Handles radWhite.CheckedChanged
    If radWhite.Checked = True Then txtMessage.BackColor = Color.White
End Sub

Private Sub radYellow_CheckedChanged(ByVal sender As System.Object, _
            ByVal e As System.EventArgs) Handles radYellow.CheckedChanged
    If radYellow.Checked = True Then txtMessage.BackColor = Color.Yellow
End Sub

Private Sub radGreen_CheckedChanged(ByVal sender As System.Object, _
            ByVal e As System.EventArgs) Handles radGreen.CheckedChanged
    If radGreen.Checked = True Then txtMessage.BackColor = Color.LightGreen
End Sub

Private Sub radBlack_CheckedChanged(ByVal sender As System.Object, _
            ByVal e As System.EventArgs) Handles radBlack.CheckedChanged
    If radBlack.Checked = True Then txtMessage.ForeColor = Color.Black
End Sub

Private Sub radBlue_CheckedChanged(ByVal sender As System.Object, _
            ByVal e As System.EventArgs) Handles radBlue.CheckedChanged
    If radBlue.Checked = True Then txtMessage.ForeColor = Color.Blue
End Sub

Private Sub radRed_CheckedChanged(ByVal sender As System.Object, _
            ByVal e As System.EventArgs) Handles radRed.CheckedChanged
    If radRed.Checked = True Then txtMessage.ForeColor = Color.Red
End Sub
```

## Currency Conversion

Madison returns to her office and peers out the window that overlooks the company parking lot. She turns away and responds to a few phone messages, then pulls out her legal pad with the notes from Allen Bauer's requested Currency Conversion application. She considers the need to present choices of target currency to the user and draws a combo box for this purpose.

Next, she considers the need for the application to display a range of U.S. dollar amounts and the resulting amounts in converted currency. The first and last value in the range can easily be entered into two text boxes, with a loop used to display all the values between them. Madison pauses and considers that the user might be interested in conversion rates by the thousands or ten thousands and that the program will also need to allow the user to specify an optional increment. She draws a third text box for this purpose. She then draws a list box for showing each of the specific currency conversion amounts. Finally, she draws a button for a triggering event to generate the conversion calculations.

Madison puts her pen on her notepad and pulls out a large container of water to refresh herself. "I wonder what the currency conversion rate is between the U.S. dollar and Atlantis?" she says, laughing.

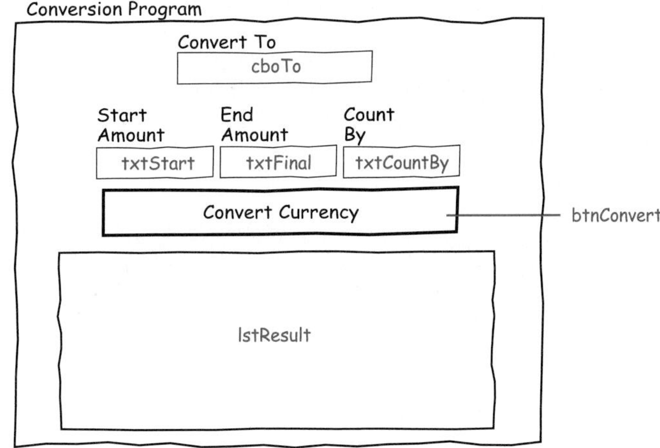


**FIGURE 8.12** *Sketch of the Currency Conversion User Interface*

### Design

The design specifies how the solution will work in general terms. She begins by sketching the interface for the Currency Conversion application; specifying the Name property for all the necessary controls. She also writes down the Text property when appropriate. The sketch in Figure 8-12 includes a combo box for the target conversion currency; three text boxes for the start, end, and step values of the conversion range; and a button to perform the conversion. The results of the conversion will appear in a list box. Static labels are included to describe the interface to the user.

The design should also include a high-level specification of all the actions and behavior required by the project. This can be done using flowchart or pseudocode notation and should describe behavior without getting into details of implementation. Table 8-3 provides pseudocode descriptions of the procedures in the Currency Conversion design.

**Table 8.3** Design Pseudocode for Currency Conversion Application

| Procedure | Behavior |
|---|---|
| Form1_Load | Populate the combo box with the names of the currencies for conversion |
| btnConvert_Click | 1. Validate the start value is numeric |
| | 2. Validate the final value is numeric |
| | 3. Validate the CountBy value is numeric (assume 1 if the CountBy is blank) |
| | 4. Verify the start value does not exceed the final value |
| | 5. Determine the appropriate conversation rate based on the selected value in the combo box |
| | 6. Add header to the output list box |
| | 7. Use a loop to make calculations and add results to the output list box |
| txtStart_Leave | Ensure input is formatted in dollars |
| txtEnd_Leave | Ensure input is formatted in dollars |
| txtCountBy_Leave | Ensure input is formatted in dollars |

### Implementation

After she completes the general design, she must implement the details. The first step of implementation is to build the GUI. Figure 8-13 illustrates the Currency Conversion GUI.

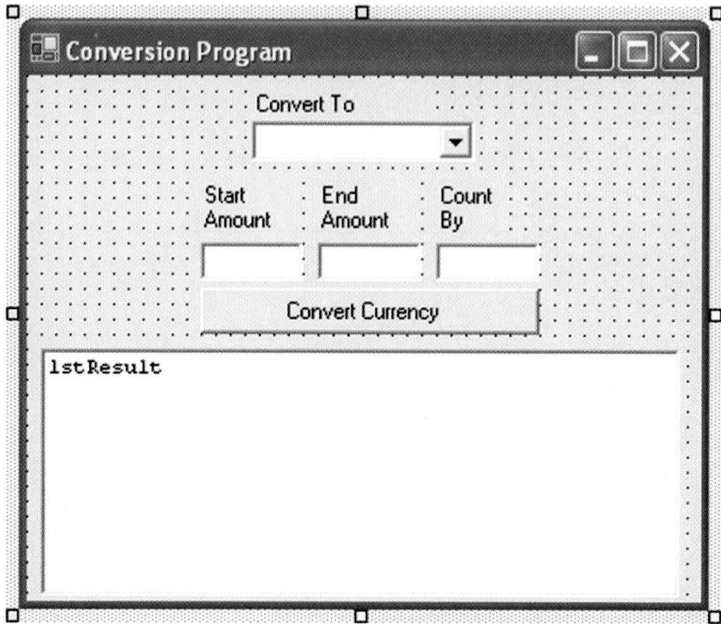


**FIGURE 8.13** *Currency Conversion User Interface*

The second step is to implement the functionality described in the pseudocode design. It is also a good habit to document important design time property values for the form and interface controls. The solution code with good documentation follows.

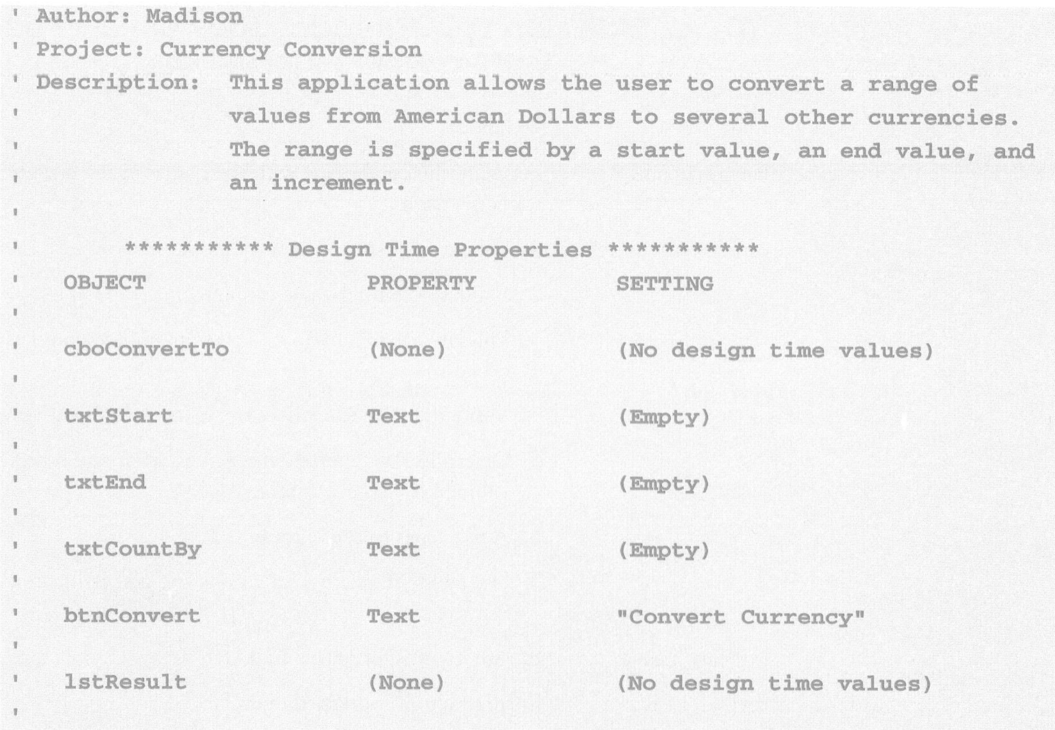

```
' Author: Madison
' Project: Currency Conversion
' Description:  This application allows the user to convert a range of
'               values from American Dollars to several other currencies.
'               The range is specified by a start value, an end value, and
'               an increment.
'
'        *********** Design Time Properties ***********
'   OBJECT                 PROPERTY          SETTING
'
'   cboConvertTo           (None)            (No design time values)
'
'   txtStart               Text              (Empty)
'
'   txtEnd                 Text              (Empty)
'
'   txtCountBy             Text              (Empty)
'
'   btnConvert             Text              "Convert Currency"
'
'   lstResult              (None)            (No design time values)
'
```

```
Public Class Form1
    Inherits System.Windows.Forms.Form
Windows Form Designer generated code
    Private Sub Form1_Load(ByVal sender As System.Object, _
            ByVal e As System.EventArgs) Handles MyBase.Load
        ' Initialize cboConvertTo with available currencies
        cboConvertTo.Items.Add("Mexico Pesos")
        cboConvertTo.Items.Add("U.K. Pounds")
        cboConvertTo.Items.Add("Euro")
        cboConvertTo.Items.Add("India Rupees")
        cboConvertTo.Items.Add("Japan Yen")
        cboConvertTo.Items.Add("Canada Dollars")
    End Sub

    Private Sub btnConvert_Click(ByVal sender As System.Object, _
            ByVal e As System.EventArgs) Handles btnConvert.Click
        Dim Amount As Integer
        Dim ConvertRate As Double

        ' Make sure the user has entered valid values
        If Not IsNumeric(txtStart.Text) Then
            MsgBox("Please enter a valid Start amount")
            Exit Sub
        End If

        If Not IsNumeric(txtEnd.Text) Then
            MsgBox("Please enter a valid End amount")
            Exit Sub
        End If

        If txtCountBy.Text = "" Then txtCountBy.Text = FormatCurrency(1)
        If Not IsNumeric(txtCountBy.Text) Then
            MsgBox("Please enter a valid Step amount")
            Exit Sub
        End If

        If Val(txtStart.Text) > Val(txtEnd.Text) Then
            MsgBox("The Start amount cannot exceed the End amount")
            Exit Sub
        End If

        ' Determine the appropriate conversion rate
        Select Case cboConvertTo.Text
            Case "Mexico Pesos"
                ConvertRate = 10.2365
            Case "U.K. Pounds"
                ConvertRate = 0.644405
            Case "Euro"
                ConvertRate = 1.02364
            Case "India Rupees"
                ConvertRate = 48.3854
            Case "Japan Yen"
                ConvertRate = 123.572
```

```
            Case "Canada Dollars"
                ConvertRate = 1.58326
            Case Else
                MsgBox("Please select a valid 'Convert To' currency")
                Exit Sub
        End Select

        ' Fill list box by first displaying the column headings and then
        ' the specified range of values and their converted equivalent
        lstResult.Items.Clear()
        lstResult.Items.Add("U.S. Dollars".PadLeft(20) & cboConvertTo.Text.PadLeft(20))
        lstResult.Items.Add("==========".PadLeft(20) & _
                            "==============".PadLeft(20))
        For Amount = txtStart.Text To txtEnd.Text Step txtCountBy.Text
            lstResult.Items.Add(FormatCurrency(Amount).PadLeft(20) & _
                    FormatNumber(Amount * ConvertRate, 2).PadLeft(20))
        Next Amount
    End Sub

    Private Sub txtStart_Leave(ByVal sender As Object, _
            ByVal e As System.EventArgs) Handles txtStart.Leave
        ' Ensure inputs are formatted in dollars
        If IsNumeric(txtStart.Text) Then
            txtStart.Text = FormatCurrency(txtStart.Text)
        End If
    End Sub

    Private Sub txtEnd_Leave(ByVal sender As Object, _
            ByVal e As System.EventArgs) Handles txtEnd.Leave
        ' Ensure inputs are formatted in dollars
        If IsNumeric(txtEnd.Text) Then
            txtEnd.Text = FormatCurrency(txtEnd.Text)
        End If
    End Sub

    Private Sub txtCountBy_Leave(ByVal sender As Object, _
            ByVal e As System.EventArgs) Handles txtCountBy.Leave
        ' Ensure inputs are formatted in dollars
        If IsNumeric(txtCountBy.Text) Then
            txtCountBy.Text = FormatCurrency(txtCountBy.Text)
        End If
    End Sub
End Class
```

### Testing the Solution

You can test Madison's solution by implementing her design as shown in the previous section, and then running the application. Figure 8-14 shows sample output for converting to U.K. Pounds. Run the program with invalid data in the three text boxes and the combo box to test the program's error-handling code. If you are having problems, you may want to read Appendix B: Debugging Techniques.

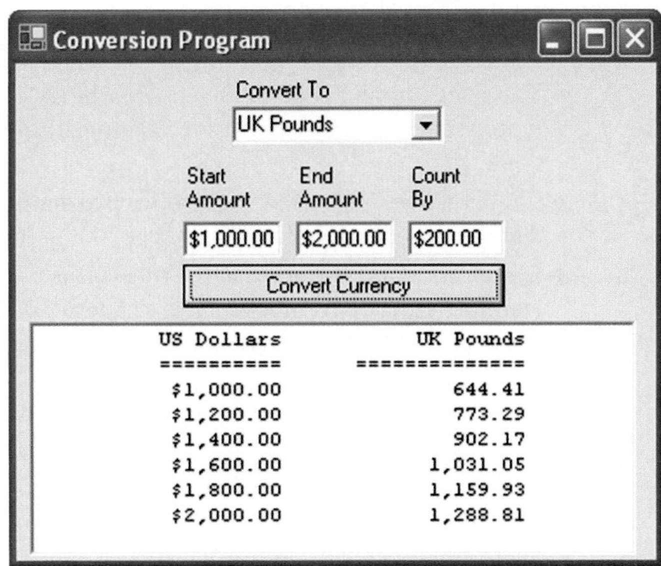


**FIGURE 8.14** *Sample Output for Currency Conversion Application*

### Review and Enhance the Project

"Very well done," Allen says, as Madison finishes demonstrating her solution. "This program should be a big hit for our international business sales reps." As they discuss the practical ways the program will be used, they realize the conversion program, like any software program, can be made better with continued time and effort. Review the conversion program and consider ways it could be improved. Here are some of the ideas Allen and Madison came up with:

- Add a picture box to display the national flag of the conversion country. Likewise, display an image of the currency itself.
- It is possible that one of the international Pretty Fish sites will do business with another international location, involving two different non-U.S. currencies. Add another combo box to allow conversions between any two currencies, such as yen to euro.

Try these or any other changes you think would be appropriate. Be prepared to discuss various modifications in terms of the work required compared with the resulting benefits.

## Chapter Summary

- A condition is an expression that evaluates to true or false or a data type that is implicitly convertible to Boolean.
- The If . . . Then statement can be single-line or multi-line. The single-line If . . . Then is used when executing only one statement when the condition is true. The single-line If . . . Then does not contain an End If.
- To execute blocks of statements, use multiple-line If . . . Then statements. In the multi-line syntax, the keyword Then should be the last thing on the line on which it appears. The keywords Else and End If should appear alone on a line. The keyword ElseIf may be used to create a nested If . . . Then.
- To support multiple branches based on the value of an expression, use the Select Case statement.

- The Do . . . Loop statement repeats a block of statements either while a condition is true or until it becomes true.
- The For . . . Next statement repeats a block of statements a specific number of times. The loop counter variable is automatically updated after each pass through the loop.
- The Exit statement allows control to pass out from a condition or loop or procedure.
- Syntax errors are violations of the rules of the programming language. Visual Studio identifies syntax errors for you (but you must fix them yourself).
- Runtime errors occur when an application attempts to perform an action that the system cannot execute, such as trying to divide-by-zero or accessing a file on the A: drive when the floppy is not inserted. If no provision is made, runtime errors crash the program.
- Logic errors occur when the program generates incorrect output or displays incorrect behavior. Unlike syntax and runtime errors, logic errors can go unnoticed for long periods of time. Even when they are detected, the source of the error can be difficult to diagnose.
- Runtime errors produce exceptions that can be handled through the Try . . . Catch structure. The Try block contains code that the developer knows may result in a runtime error. The Catch block contains code that is executed if the error occurs. A runtime error inside a Try . . . Catch block does not crash the program.
- The CheckBox control indicates whether a particular value is on or off. It can also be used to select multiple items from a list of options.
- The RadioButton control allows the user to select a single item from a list of mutually exclusive options.

## Key Terms

**CheckBox control** p. 193
**condition** p. 176
**Do . . . Loop** p. 181
**Else** p. 177
**ElseIf** p. 177
**End If** p. 177
**Exception** p. 190
**Exit statement** p. 187
**For . . . Next** p. 184
**If . . . Then** p. 176
**logic error** p. 192
**RadioButton control** p. 195
**runtime error** p. 190
**Select Case** p. 179
**syntax error** p. 190
**Try . . . Catch** p. 191

## Review Questions

1. What is a condition? How is a condition used with the If . . . Then statement? How is a condition used with a Do . . . Loop?
2. How is a single-line If . . . Then statement similar to a multi-line If . . . Then statement? How are they different?
3. How is an If . . . Then statement similar to a Select Case statement? How are they different? Can the "Smallest Value" If . . . Then solution be rewritten as a Select Case solution? Why or why not?
4. How many versions of Do . . . Loop are there? What is the difference between them?
5. How is a Do . . . Loop similar to a For . . . Next loop? How are they different?
6. What is the purpose of the Step value in a For . . . Then loop?

7. What is the purpose of the Exit statement? How many versions of the Exit statement are there?
8. What is a syntax error? How are syntax errors detected?
9. What is a runtime error? How are runtime errors detected?
10. What is a logic error? How are logic errors detected?
11. What is Try . . . Catch used for? When should it be used?
12. How is a CheckBox similar to a RadioButton? How are they different?

## Programming Exercises

**8-1. Middle Value.** Write an application with three input text boxes, two buttons, and one output text box. Clicking the first button should cause the middle value of the three input text boxes to appear in the output text box. Clicking the second button should terminate the application. Additionally, the output text box should clear when any of the input text boxes are changed, thereby avoiding an inconsistent state in the user interface. The program should also display an appropriate error message if the input text boxes do not have numeric values.

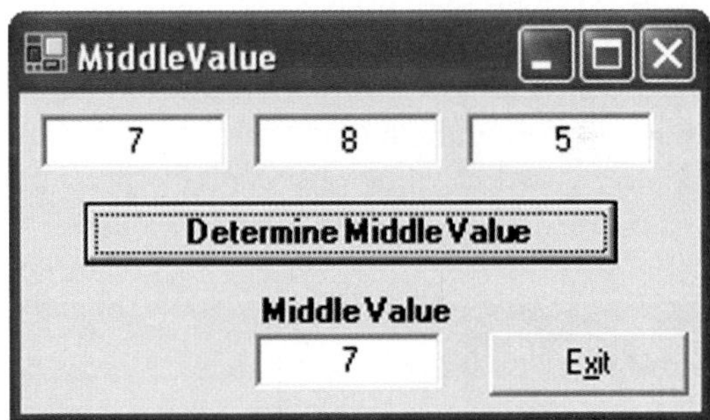


**8-2. Lifetime Earnings Redux.** Write a program to calculate a person's lifetime earnings, similar to the For . . . Next Illustrated solution earlier this chapter. In this version, there should be five input text boxes that specify the person's name, age, starting salary, annual raise, and retirement age. The program should also contain an output label that displays the projected total amount earned before retirement. (Do not use InputBox or MsgBox in your solution.) Your solution should also handle erroneous data—such as typing "hello" in the age text box—in an appropriate manner.

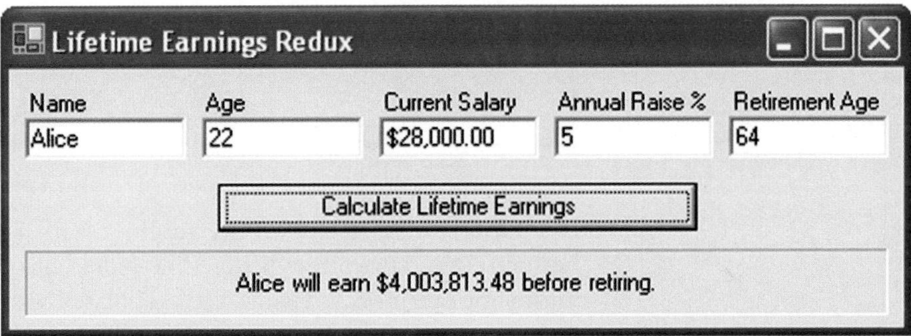


**8-3. Express Yourself.** Create a form with a text box, three CheckBox controls, and two sets of RadioButton controls. The CheckBox values should turn on and off the bold, italic, and underline effects of the text box. The first RadioButton set should determine the background color of the text box (white, yellow, or green). The second

RadioButton set should determine the foreground color of the text box (black, blue, or red).

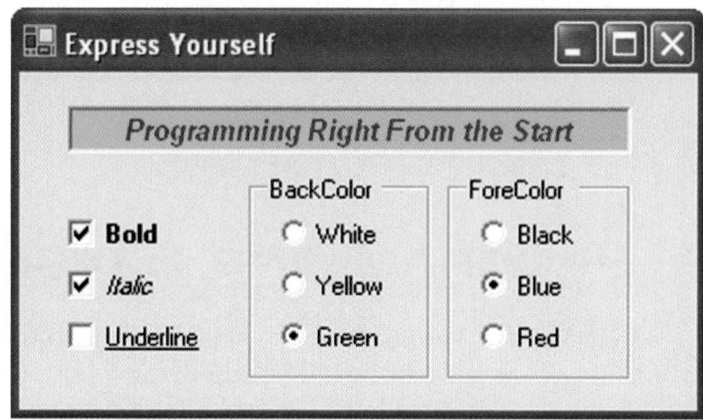


**8-4. Tax Exempt.** Write an application that adds items one-at-a-time to a sales receipt using an input text box and a button. Each time the button is pressed, the new item price should be added to a list box control, which acts as a receipt. The program should also contain output labels for subtotal, sales tax, and total along with a check box for "tax exempt." If the check box is checked, then tax should be excluded from the receipt (i.e., have a 0 value). The subtotal, sales tax, and total values should be updated whenever an item is added to the receipt. The program should use a constant SALES_TAX with a value of 0.065 (6½ percent). *Hint:* Use *FormatCurrency* and *CDbl* to create and read currency string values.

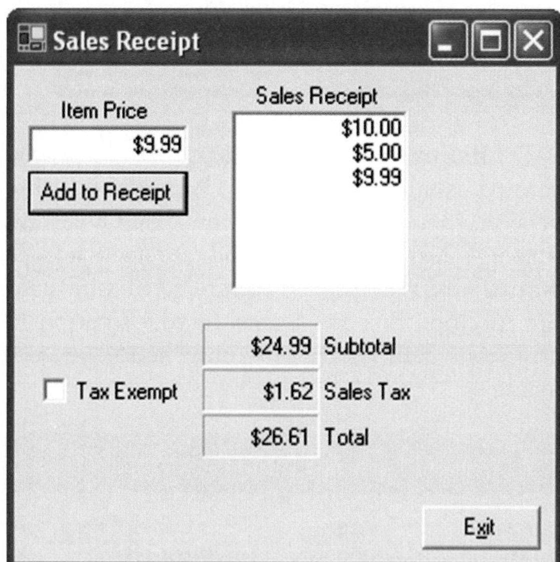


**8-5. Operator Assistance.** Create a form with a label, two buttons, and seven radio buttons between two text boxes. The radio buttons should be labeled to match the arithmetic operators. Pressing the "Calculate" button should apply the selected arithmetic operator to the values in the text boxes and display the output in the label.

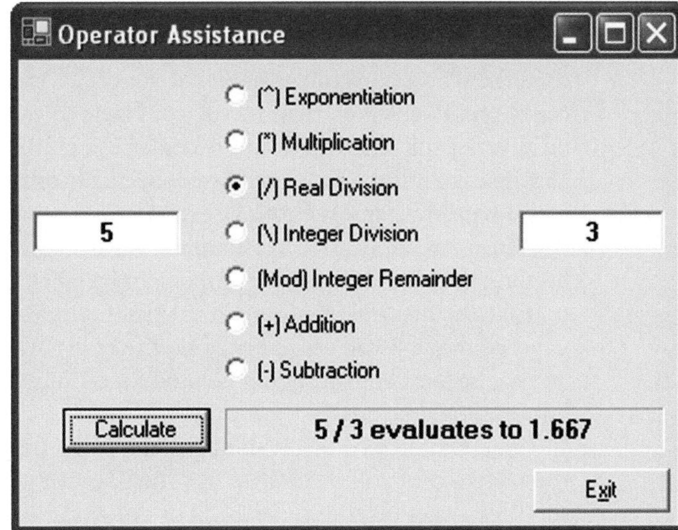


**8-6. Olympic Judges.** When an overall score during Olympic events is determined, the highest and lowest judges' scores are dropped, and the remaining judges' scores are averaged. Write an application with six input text boxes representing six Olympic judges and output text boxes to display the highest and lowest scores; these two scores are dropped, and the average of the remaining scores should be displayed in the Average text box.

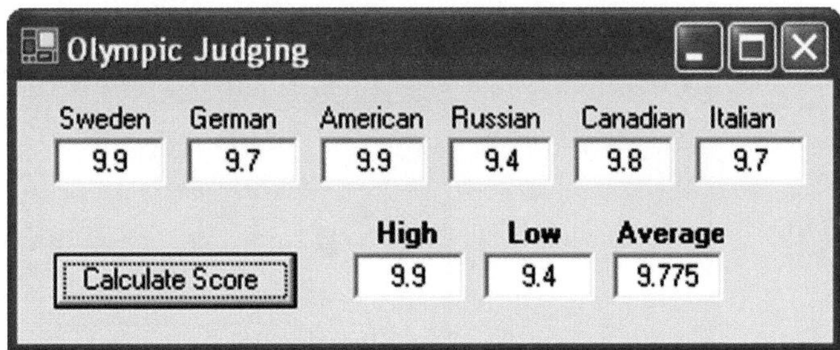


**8-7. Numbers to Text.** Develop an application in which the user enters an integer number from 1 to 9999 and presses a button to generate a text equivalent of the number. For example, if the user enters 11, the text displayed should be "eleven." If the user enters 421, the text displayed should be "four hundred twenty one." Your program should give an appropriate message if the input is not an integer between 1 and 9999.

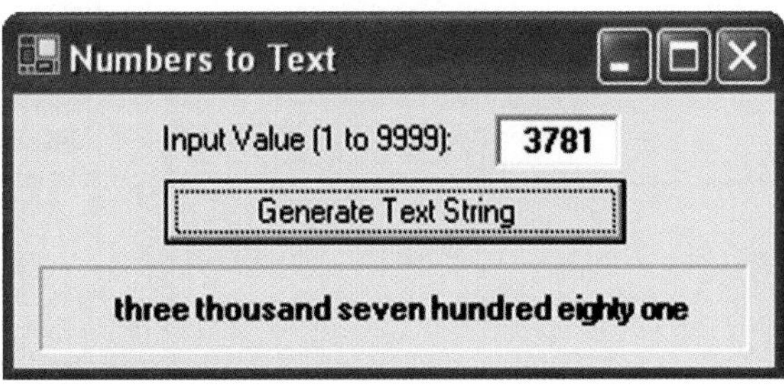

**8-8. Vegas Dice.** Vegas Dice (called *craps*) is played with two dice. The game begins when the player rolls the dice. If the sum of the two dice is 7 or 11 on the first roll, then the player wins the game. If the sum is 2 ("snake eyes"), 3 ("trey"), or 12 ("boxcars") on the first roll, then the player loses the game. If the sum is 4, 5, 6, 8, 9, or 10 on the first roll, then that sum becomes the player's point for that game. The player continues to roll the dice until he or she either rolls the point again (which means the player wins the game) or rolls a seven (which means the player loses the game).

Write an application to simulate Vegas Dice. Your program should contain two buttons, two picture boxes, a list box, and a label. One of the buttons should be used to make the first roll of a game. If the first roll does not win or lose the game, then the value of the first roll should become the point and should be displayed in the label, and the second button should be used for all subsequent rolls in the game. Only one button should be enabled at a time.

The two picture boxes should graphically display the values of the two dice for the most recent roll, regardless of which button generated the roll. You may use the six dice images on the student CD or draw your own. The results of each roll should be displayed in a list box followed by an appropriate message.

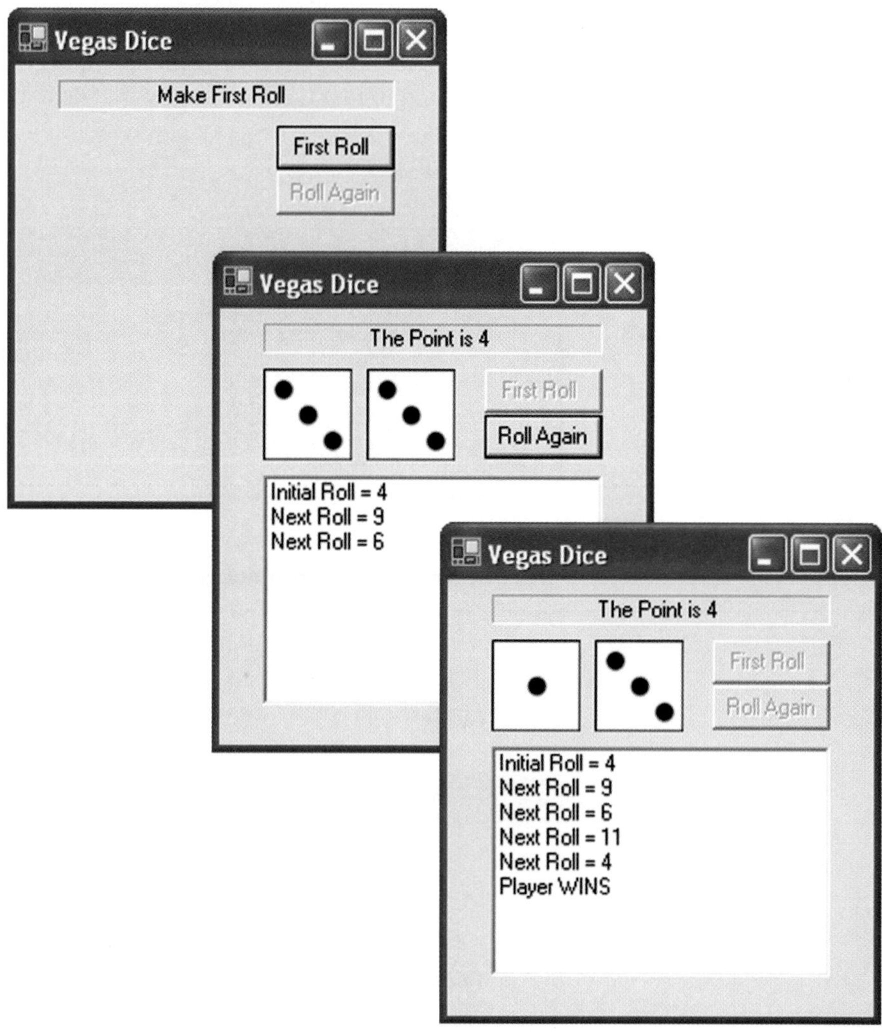

**8-9. Table Profit.** Casinos make money when gamblers play games that slightly favor the house (the casino). Vegas Dice is one such game (as explained in the previous question). Write a modified Vegas Dice application that plays games quickly and displays only the results of each game (and not the individual rolls). The new application should play a user-specified number of games and display the overall win/loss percentage. The following image shows a screen shot taken after a set of six games. (Because of random values, your win/loss sequence and percentages may differ.) Assume a single Vegas Dice table can host approximately four games per minute, or about five thousand games per day. Further assume the table either wins or looses $5 each game. What is the average daily profit or loss for a single Vegas Dice table?

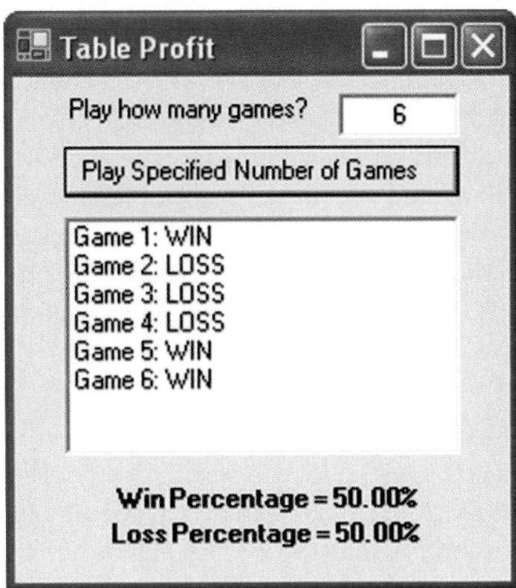


**8-10. Conversion Redux.** Modify the Currency Conversion program described in this chapter's Case Study Solution by adding a Convert From combo box so the application can be used to convert from any currency to any currency. You should also add code to verify that the start amount, end amount, and by-count amount are all valid numeric data and respond appropriately if the data is not numeric.

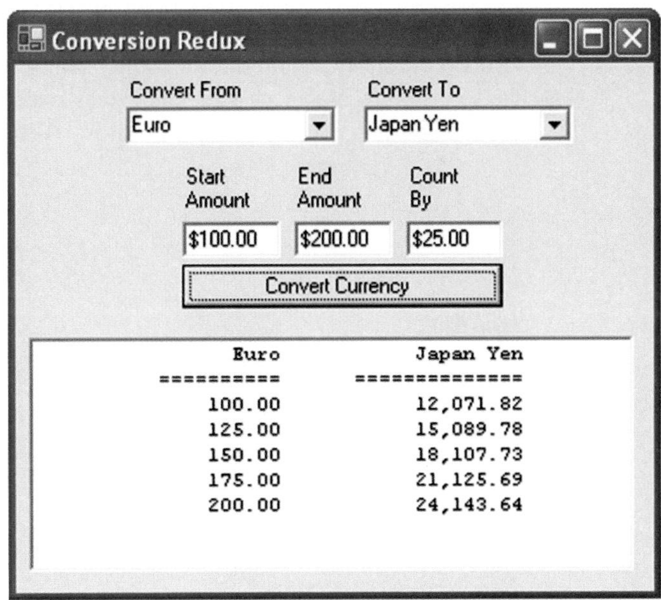

# Extended Case Studies

## Pizza and a Movie

Business is booming at Pizza and a Movie, and with growth, there are growing pains. Because the business combines two different product types (rental and consumable), Noah is having problems finding packaged software that meets his business needs. For example, he needs a checkout application that handles his business logic. Movies rent for $2.99 each. Pizzas come in three sizes: medium ($8.99), large ($11.99), and gigantic ($13.99) with cheese. Each topping costs $0.99. The delivery fee of $3 is waived for orders totaling $20 or more (before tax). Furthermore, Noah provides a 10% pretax discount on orders containing both a pizza and a movie.

Create an application that serves as a checkout program for Pizza and a Movie. The application should allow the customer to check out up to three movies and purchase up to three pizzas on a single order. For each pizza ordered, the application should specify the size (medium, large, or gigantic) and also the number of additional toppings (up to 6). When the order is complete, the employee should press the Calculate Order Total button that generates the subtotal (including any discounts for pizza and movie combinations), sales tax, delivery fee (if appropriate) and the total price.

## Singing Mimes

In an effort to find out what kind of software would be useful to teachers, Reed and Elizabeth decide to visit a local elementary school. They call the school and set up a meeting with Ms. McPherson, the technology coordinator at Rich Pond Elementary. Reed and Elizabeth are both impressed by the number of computers available to students of all grades. There is a computer lab that each class visits at least once per week. Each classroom also contains a computer. Ms. McPherson explains that the main uses of the computers are the Accelerated Reader program and Internet searches for specific information.

"There are also quite a few drill and practice programs available for math, spelling, and typing," she says. "Only a few of those programs can hold a student's attention for more than a few minutes, however."

She then shows an available first-grade math practice program that asks students to add two numbers, each between 1 and 20. The program replies with a big green "Yes" or red "No" after the student types in an answer. After twenty problems, the program gives the student a score for the exam.

"This program is not great, but some teachers use it for math practice," says Ms. McPherson. "There are much nicer programs available, of course, but they often cost $10 or $20 for one copy of a single program. Also, those programs often have lengthy storylines associated with them, which do not always work well when many students share computers. They are great for home use, but we need something different here in the schools."

Ms. McPherson shows some other programs to Elizabeth and Reed, but the comments are about the same. The computers are available, but teachers typically do not have the time or expertise to try out all the available programs. Some do not work on existing hardware, some are so poorly designed that they are useless, and many of the professional programs are expensive and better suited for home use.

On the drive back, Reed and Elizabeth discuss the wide range of program ideas they thought of during their visit. They agree to each develop a drill and practice program for first-grade math. The program will involve adding two digits from 1 to 20. They decide to create a race between the player and the computer. Both the player and the computer will have a picture box that sits on top of a racetrack (also a picture box). The picture boxes will move across a racetrack by increasing their Left property. The player's picture box will move whenever the player correctly answers a math problem. A new math problem will be automatically created and displayed after each correct answer. The computer's picture box will move at a speed determined by the player's selection. The user will be able to specify the computer's speed to be Turtle, Rabbit, or Road Runner. The race will end when either picture box crosses the finish line.

Design and implement a math drill and practice program based on the race theme described in this case study. The application should generate and display a random addition problem involving two digits, each between 1 and 20. The application should allow the user to enter an answer. If the answer is correct, the user's image should move across the racetrack. Regardless, a new addition problem should be generated and displayed. The computer opponent should move across the racetrack in response to a Timer's tick event. The user should be able to select between three speeds for the opponent, which result in appropriate interval values for the Timer. The program should end when either the user or the computer opponent crosses the finish line.

CHAPTER 9

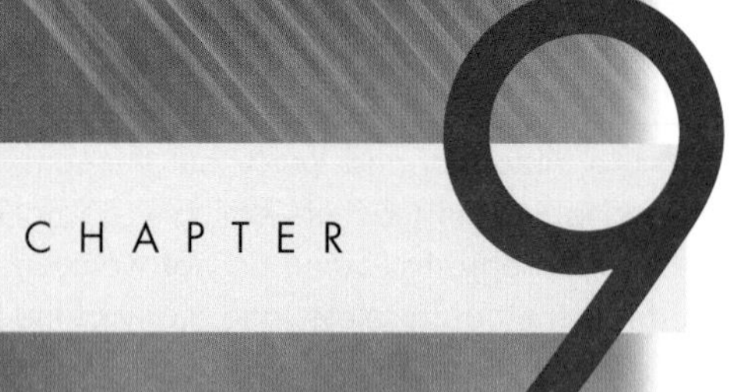

# Procedures and Arrays

## OUTLINE

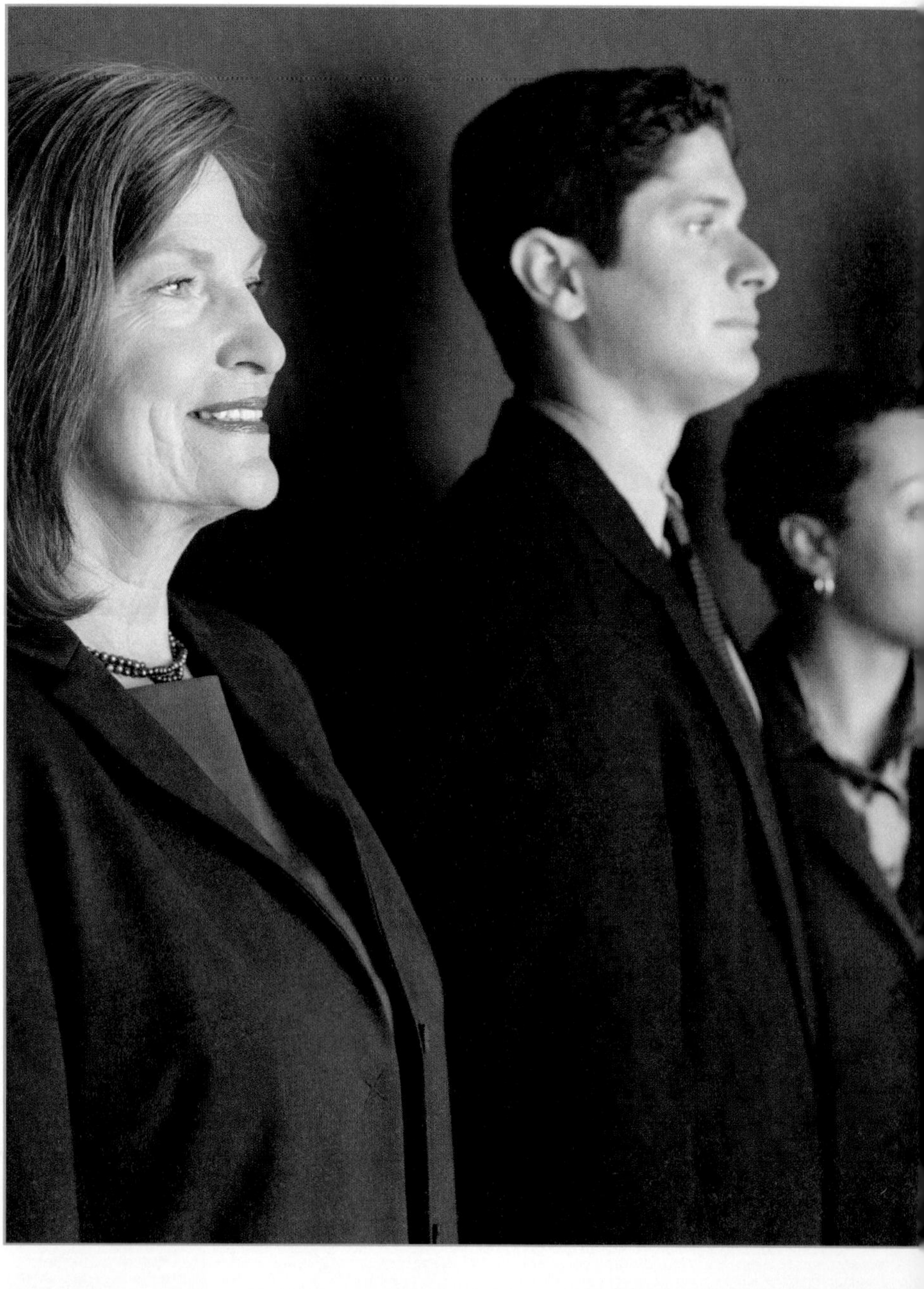

## ▶ INTERVIEW

### Robert Overdorf, President, Golf Mapping

***Interviewer:*** Please tell us how you got involved in the IT industry.

***Overdorf:*** Golf Mapping utilizes GPS, or Global Positioning Technology, to create a digital image of golf courses. My father is a golf course architect, so I started working on courses when I was thirteen by sitting on bulldozers while they were shaping courses to my father's specifications. As I got older and worked more closely with course design, I saw a need to simplify the process. Using computers and computer technology were the obvious choices. I've been the president and owner of Golf Mapping for the past eight years.

***Interviewer:*** What you are most excited about for the future?

***Overdorf:*** The fact that patience and perseverance have paid great dividends to me, and I will reap that reward in the near future. As I continue to grow, so does technology. The fact that what I am doing now could be obsolete in a few years forces me to always stay ahead of the curve.

***Interviewer:*** What is the best part of your job?

***Overdorf:*** The best part of my job is traveling to new places, meeting new people, and of course, playing new courses. I love watching a client get excited about what our technology can offer.

***Interviewer:*** What projects are you currently working on?

***Overdorf:*** Projects I am currently working on include an eighteen-hole golf course where I am controlling the design with GPS and creating a detailed digital image or map of the features as well as the components of in-ground products. By the end of the year, I will map more than forty courses.

***Interviewer:*** What advice do you have for students entering the computer field?

***Overdorf:*** Never underestimate the other person. People are amazing; they come up with and implement amazing ideas. Understand that a computer is a tool without emotions. Don't get emotional during the tough times—patience is a virtue.

## OBJECTIVES

At the completion of this chapter, you will

- **Understand the different types of variable scope**
- **Understand the three types of procedures in VB.NET**
- **Explain the similarities and differences between function and sub procedures**
- **Explain the relationship between arguments and parameters**
- **Distinguish between an array element and an array index**
- **Understand how to declare, reference, and resize an array**
- **Understand how to declare and use a structure array**
- **Understand how to declare and use a control array**
- **Understand how to work with KeyPress events**
- **Successfully write Windows applications involving procedures and arrays**

# Snakes Game

Chuck Noland is a first-year systems analyst working at a large, regional FedEx hub. Even though his background is C++ and Java, his strong analysis and design skills resulted in his assignment to work with a team on some cutting-edge projects that use VB.NET. His first six months on the job have been divided among three tasks: learning the nuances of VB.NET for his team project, collecting requirements specifications from FedEx employees for a new intranet (internal within the organization) web-enabled application, and providing maintenance support for a seven-year-old application that still has a significant customer base. He has also become good friends with "Wilson."

Chuck and Wilson work well together, demonstrating excellent creative synergy. Chuck has been learning VB.NET by reading books and writing a variety of applications. "Wilson, I just read about an application called *Snakes Game* that creates a game board using an array of controls. The basic idea is that the user moves a snake (or worm) around the board searching for food, and the snake grows longer when food is eaten. The game ends when the user accidentally runs the snake into a wall or wraps it into itself. The goal is to get the longest snake possible. This sounds like a pretty fun program, and I think it would be a great learning experience to write it. What do you say?"

Wilson's gaze remains directed toward the monitor, making no obvious response, but Chuck knows his friend and is sure they will have a good time writing the program together.

"Great," Chuck says, inferring support from Wilson's silence. "Let's get started!"

Chuck and Wilson's solution is presented later this chapter.

## 9-1 Understanding Procedures

**All Visual Basic code is written within procedures.**

A ***procedure*** is a block of statements that begins with a declaration statement and concludes with an End statement. Procedures are the building blocks of your application and are useful for performing repeated or shared tasks. You can call a procedure from many different places in your code, and a procedure can be executed multiple times throughout the program as necessary.

Procedures allow for ***modular programming,*** a methodology whereby long programs are divided into numerous small procedures that are based on logical activities. From a developer's perspective, breaking your application into logical units makes the code easier to read. Modular programming also makes your application easier to maintain. If a change is required, the change occurs only once in the procedure, and the effects of the change occur throughout the numerous calls to the procedure everywhere in the solution.

**Arguments and parameters are the preferred means of communication between the calling code and the procedure. When calling a procedure, the calling arguments should match the formal parameters in number, order, and type.**

Information can be passed to and from procedures by means of arguments and parameters. An ***argument*** is a value passed from the calling code to the procedure. A ***parameter*** is a variable listed in the formal procedure declaration that receives the argument. Passing data from actual arguments to formal parameters is a means of sharing information between the calling code and the procedure.

There are three types of procedures in VB.NET: *event procedures*, *sub procedures*, and *function procedures*.

## 9-2 Event Procedure

**Tip**
You have been writing event procedures since Chapter 6, so some of this material will be review.

An event is a signal that informs an application that something important has happened. An ***event procedure*** (or *event handler*) is a procedure containing code that is executed in response to an event. When the event is raised, the code within the event handler is executed.

*Syntax:*

```
[Private|Public] Sub Object_Event([parameters]) Handles Object.Event
   [statements]
End Sub
```

*Example:*

```
Private Sub btnSayHello_Click(ByVal sender As System.Object, _
        ByVal e As System.EventArgs) Handles btnSayHello.Click
    MsgBox("Hello")
End Sub
```

**Tip**
All Windows Form event procedures have two parameters. The first is a reference to the object that raised the event, and the second depends on the type of event.

For event handlers, Visual Basic uses a standard naming convention that combines the name of the object that signaled the event, an underscore, and the name of the event. In the preceding example, the button btnSayHello has a click event named btnSayHello_Click.

Each event handler provides two parameters. The first parameter, *sender*, provides a reference to the object that raised the event. The second parameter is an object whose type depends on the event that is being handled. The properties and methods of these parameters provide the developer with additional information that can be used when processing the event.

### ASK THE AUTHOR

**Q** The *sender* and *e* parameters have ByVal in front of them. What does ByVal mean?

**A** There are two conventions for passing arguments to parameters, ***ByVal*** and ***ByRef***. The default convention is ByVal, which means the parameter will be a local copy of the argument. Thus, any change to the parameter within the procedure will not affect the value of the passing argument.

If you declare a parameter as ByRef, the parameter will be a pointer to the actual argument. Any change to the parameter also changes the actual argument. When the argument is a large structure, ByRef is often used to avoid the significant time and memory necessary to make a local copy. You can also use ByRef when you want the parameter to pass back information to the calling code. However, you must be careful when using ByRef: an accidental change to the parameter will have a corresponding unplanned change on the value of the argument. An unexpected change to an argument is called a side effect and can cause serious problems in your solution.

### Event Procedure Illustrated

Create a form with a command button named btnHola. Double-click on the button to create a click event procedure stub in the Code Editor window. The event procedure stub should look like the following code.

*Example:*

```
Private Sub btnHola_Click(ByVal sender As System.Object, _
            ByVal e As System.EventArgs) Handles btnHola.Click

End Sub
```

The keyword Private at the beginning of an event procedure is an accessibility type that specifies what other solution code can access the procedure. Private is the default and is the safest and most common accessibility. Accessibility is explained in Chapter 14.

You can also create event procedure stubs by selecting the control and the desired event from the combo boxes at the top of the Code Editor. For example, to create a procedure stub for a button's mouse move event, select btnHola from the class name combo box, and then select MouseMove from the method combo box from within the Code Editor window. Visual Studio will respond by creating the following event procedure stub.

```
Private Sub btnHola_MouseMove(ByVal sender As Object, _
            ByVal e As System.Windows.Forms.MouseEventArgs) _
            Handles btnHola.MouseMove

End Sub
```

Notice the similarities between the Click and the MouseMove event procedure stubs. Both procedures begin with *Private Sub*. Both have two *ByVal* formal arguments: *sender* and *e*. Both have the *Handles* keyword at the end of their declarations. Both procedures end with *End Sub*. The differences between the two are the names of the procedures (btnHola_Click versus btnHola_MouseMove) and the corresponding Handles methods (btnHola.Click versus btnHola.MouseMove). It is helpful to become familiar with these similarities and differences.

If you double-click on a control in the Form Designer window, Visual Studio takes you to the control's default event procedure in the Code Editor window. The default event for a Button control is the click event.

Add two labels named lblXPos and lblYPos to the form. Then add the following code to the two event procedures.

```
Private Sub btnHola_Click(ByVal sender As System.Object, _
            ByVal e As System.EventArgs) Handles btnHola.Click
    MsgBox("Hola mundo")
End Sub

Private Sub btnHola_MouseMove(ByVal sender As Object, _
            ByVal e As System.Windows.Forms.MouseEventArgs) _
            Handles btnHola.MouseMove
    lblXPos.Text = e.X
    lblYPos.Text = e.Y
End Sub
```

Run the application. Clicking the button triggers the click event with a message box that displays the Spanish phrase for "Hello world." Moving the mouse over the button triggers the mouse move event that changes the label's text values based on the cursor's X and Y position. X and Y are properties of the MouseEventArgs object (which is the type of the *e* parameter in the MouseMove event procedure declaration.)

## 9-3 Sub Procedure

A ***sub procedure*** (or *subroutine*) contains developer code to perform a logical action. A sub procedure can make the solution easier to understand because it can break a large solution into smaller, coherent parts. A sub procedure can also be used as a container for code that is called multiple times, making it easier to debug and maintain.

*Syntax:*

```
[Private|Public] Sub ProcedureName([parameters])
   [statements]
End Sub
```

*Example:*

```
Private Sub Greeting()
      Dim Name As String

      Name = InputBox("What is your name?")
      MsgBox("Hello " & Name)
      MsgBox("Hola " & Name)
      MsgBox("Bonjour " & Name)
End Sub
```

Consider the preceding example. When the Greeting subroutine is called, the local variable Name is created. An InputBox statement then prompts the user to enter his or her name, and the data entered by the user is stored in the temporary Name variable. A series of message box statements then displays a personalized greeting in English, Spanish, and French. The End Sub statement returns program control to the code that called the procedure.

**►►► Tip**

**A sub procedure is called by referencing the procedure name as a statement. Parentheses are always required around the argument list, even if it is an empty argument list.**

To better understand how the Greetings sub procedure behaves during execution, start a new solution with a single button named btnGreet. In the Code Editor, write the Greetings procedure and then write a button click event procedure that calls the procedure. To call a sub procedure, simply reference the sub procedure name. Add a message box before and after the procedure call as shown in the following code.

```
Private Sub Greetings()
    Dim Name As String

    Name = InputBox("What is your name?")
    MsgBox("Hello " & Name)
    MsgBox("Hola " & Name)
    MsgBox("Bonjour " & Name)
End Sub

Private Sub btnGreet_Click(ByVal sender As System.Object, _
            ByVal e As System.EventArgs) Handles btnGreet.Click
    MsgBox("Before Greetings")
    Greetings()
    MsgBox("After Greetings")
End Sub
```

Run the application. When the button is pressed, the click event procedure is executed. Figure 9-1 shows the series of message box statements that appear. Notice that control returns to the click event procedure after completion of the Greetings sub procedure.

FIGURE 9.1 *The Output Generated by Clicking the btnGreet Button*

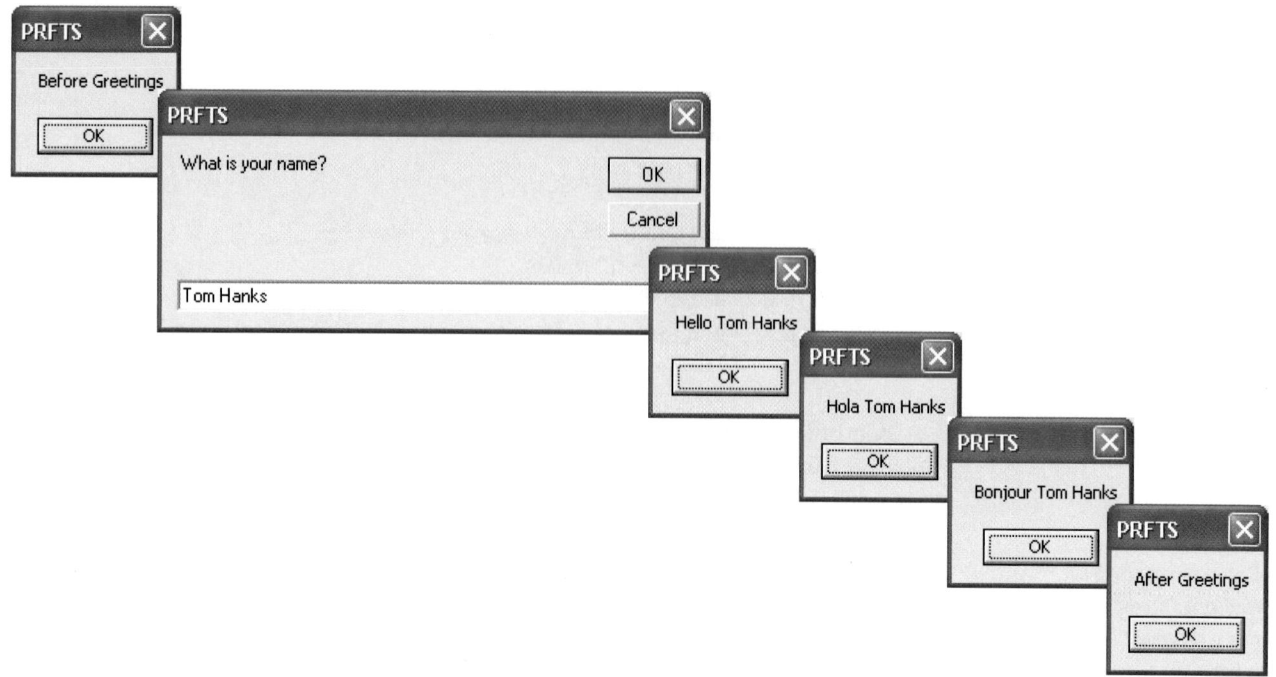


## 9-4 Function Procedure

A ***function procedure*** (or simply *function*) is identical to a sub procedure, except that a function returns a value.

*Syntax:*

```
[Private|Public] Function ProcedureName([parameters]) As datatype
  [statements]
End Sub
```

*Example:*

```
Private Function Cube(ByVal Num As Double) As Double
    Return (Num * Num * Num)
End Function
```

The value a function sends back to the calling program is called its *return value*. The type of the return value is specified at the end of the formal declaration after the parameter list. Consider the preceding Cube example. The type declaration As Double appears twice in the formal declaration. The first As Double declares the type of the formal parameter Num, while the second As Double declares the return value type for the function.

**Tip**

**You can also return a value from a function by assigning the value to the function name. This is an older technique, and it is not used in this book.**

The ***Return*** statement is used to return a value from a function and return control back to the code that called the function. The preceding example returns the cubed value of the parameter. Any number of Return statements can appear anywhere in the procedure.

Because a function returns a value, it can be used like an expression. The following code contains a function called Average with three Integer parameters: A, B, and C. The function is called with three actual arguments: 10, 12, and 20. The return value is displayed in a message box (see Figure 9-2).

```
Function Average(ByVal A As Integer, ByVal B As Integer, _
        ByVal C As Integer) As Double
    Dim Temp As Double
    Temp = (A + B + C) / 3
    Return (Temp)
End Function

Private Sub btnShow_Click(ByVal sender As System.Object, _
            ByVal e As System.EventArgs) Handles btnShow.Click
    Dim Avg As Double
    Avg = Average(10, 12, 20)
    MsgBox(Avg)
End Sub
```

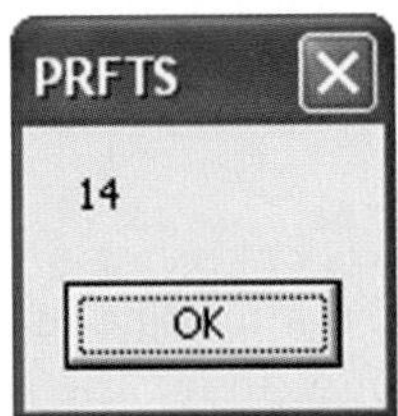


**FIGURE 9.2** *The Results of Average (10, 12, 20) in a Message Box Dialog*

**MENTOR**

One of the main goals of a good modular programming design is to minimize coupling and maximize cohesion between procedures.

***Coupling*** refers to the level of interdependency between procedures. When procedures reference module or global variables, they have high coupling with the outside environment (which is bad). Using parameters to get data into and out of a procedure produces low coupling, which is good design and supports code reuse.

***Cohesion*** is the level of uniformity within a procedure. A procedure has high cohesion (which is good) when it does only a single, precise task, such as Print, Calculate, or Update. A high cohesion procedure will be simpler to understand because it has to do only a single task. Low cohesion procedures perform many tasks, which is bad design and can make the solution logic difficult to read, understand, and maintain.

## *Procedure Summary*

- A procedure is a set of instructions that perform a specific task. Procedures make code easier to read and easier to maintain.
- An argument is a means of sharing information between the calling program and a procedure. A ByVal parameter creates a local copy of the formal argument. A ByRef parameter is a pointer to the formal argument, meaning any changes to the parameter will also update the argument.
- There are three types of procedures: event procedures, sub procedures (or subroutines), and function procedures (or functions).
- Event procedures contain code for responding to user or system events. Event procedures have the default naming convention *object_event* and handle the *object.event* signal.
- Sub procedures (or subroutines) are created by the developer to perform a logical series of actions. A subroutine is invoked by a statement containing the name of the subroutine and the actual parameter list. When the subroutine is finished, control returns to the line following the calling statement.
- Functions are identical to subroutines, except that functions return values. A function call usually appears as part of an expression, either on the right side of an assignment statement or as part of a condition. When a function procedure is finished, a value is returned and control continues with the calling statement.

# 9-5 Variable Scope

When you declare a variable, you also define its ***scope***. The scope of a variable is the region of code in which that variable may be directly referenced; it is determined by where you place the declaration and what keywords you use to declare it. There are two levels of variable scope based on declaration location and accessibility. The two types of scope are *local* and *module*, which are explained in the following sections.

## Local Scope

A ***local variable*** is a variable declared inside a procedure. Local variables can only be referenced within the defining procedure—they are unavailable outside of the procedure block in which they are declared. A local variable is destroyed when the procedure is finished executing. Each subsequent call to the procedure re-creates and reinitializes all procedure variables.

►►► *Tip*

**Variables declared in the General Declaration Section have module scope and often are prefixed by the letter *m* (for Module), e.g., Dim mRate As Double.**

## Module Scope

A ***module variable*** is declared at the module level outside of any procedure. The space at the top of the Code Editor above the first procedure is often called the *General Declaration Section*. Module scope variables are typically denoted by adding a lowercase m to the beginning of the variable name. Module level variables may be referenced by any procedure in the module.

## Scope Illustrated: Counting Button Clicks

Create a new application with one button. Change the Text property of the button to "Click Me," and rename the button appropriately. Then try the following activities.

### Version 1: Local Scope

Write the following click event procedure code.

```
Private Sub btnClickMe_Click(ByVal sender As System.Object, _
            ByVal e As System.EventArgs) Handles btnClickMe.Click
    Dim Counter As Integer 'Local scope declaration
    Counter = Counter + 1
    MsgBox("Counter is " & Counter)
End Sub
```

Run the application and click the button multiple times. What value appears each time? (*Hint:* it is the same value over and over.) This is because the locally declared variable Counter is re-created with a default value of 0 every time the procedure is called, and it is destroyed when the procedure ends.

### Version 2: Module Scope

Modify the code by moving the Counter declaration from the click event procedure to the General Declarations Section. Add the module prefix, making the variable name mCounter throughout the program.

```
Public Class Form1
    Inherits System.Windows.Forms.Form

Windows Form Designer generated code

    'General Declaration Section
    Dim mCounter As Integer          'Module scope declaration

    Private Sub btnClickMe_Click(ByVal sender As System.Object, _
                ByVal e As System.EventArgs) Handles btnClickMe.Click
        mCounter = mCounter + 1
        MsgBox("Counter is " & mCounter)
    End Sub
End Class
```

Run the program. Notice that the variable retains its value between click events. Can you explain why? (*Hint:* changing the scope changes when the variable is created and destroyed.)

## ASK THE AUTHOR

**Q** Would it be easier to declare all my variables as module variables in the general declaration section?

**A** It may be easier, but it is a bad idea for a number of reasons. A good procedure is self-contained and communicates with the outside world only through parameters. This protects your procedure from inevitable and unpredictable changes that occur to external code.

Professional code is written by a team with many developers, and it is critical that each developer's code accomplishes its assigned task without interfering elsewhere.

Documentation, variable name reuse, and code reuse are also improved by using local scope variables.

Most important, however, is developing the habit of solving problems with a self-contained mentality that is essential for almost every aspect of professional development, including top-down design and object-oriented programming.

## 9-6 Working with Arrays

**Tip**

**All VB.NET arrays start at index 0. Therefore, the array size is always one more than the upper bound (e.g., an array with an upper bound of 3 contains four elements with index values 0, 1, 2 and 3).**

Imagine writing a program that calculates and prints the grade point average (GPA) for a thousand students. You could create a thousand different variables to store each of the thousand different GPA values. However, when you consider the time required just to declare a thousand different variable names (along with the time to write a thousand different assignment statements), you quickly conclude there must be a better approach.

In this case, the better approach involves storing the thousand GPA values in a single array storage location. An ***array*** is a variable that holds multiple values. The values stored in the array are called the ***elements*** of the array. Each element in the array is distinguished by a unique number called the ***index*** (or subscript). The first element of an array is always index 0. The last element of the array is called the ***upper bound*** and can be obtained by the *UBound* function. The number of elements in the array is always one more than the upper bound and can be obtained by the *Length* method.

## Declaring an Array

Array declarations use the keyword Dim followed by the array name followed by the array's upper bound in parentheses. You may initialize an array at declaration by omitting the upper bound and specifying the array element values in curly braces.

*Syntax:*

**Dim** *ArrayName(upperbound)* **As** *datatype*

*Example:*

```
Dim Actors(3) As String          ' array of Strings
Dim Cubes(7) As Double           ' array of Doubles
Dim Scores() As Integer = {92, 78, 83, 85, 79, 90}
```

The elements of an array must all be of the same type, and this type is called the *element type* of the array. The preceding example code shows the declaration of three arrays. Actors is an array containing four String values. Cubes is an array containing eight Double values. Finally, the Scores array contains the six Integer values specified in the declaration. The upper bound of the array is implicit from the list of values (UBound = 5). The resulting array structures and initial values are shown in Figure 9-3.

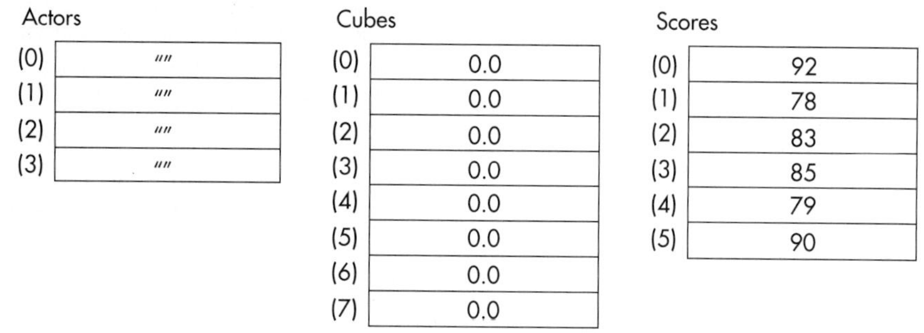

**FIGURE 9.3** *Newly Initialized Arrays with Default Values*

Actors

| | |
|---|---|
| (0) | "" |
| (1) | "" |
| (2) | "" |
| (3) | "" |

Cubes

| | |
|---|---|
| (0) | 0.0 |
| (1) | 0.0 |
| (2) | 0.0 |
| (3) | 0.0 |
| (4) | 0.0 |
| (5) | 0.0 |
| (6) | 0.0 |
| (7) | 0.0 |

Scores

| | |
|---|---|
| (0) | 92 |
| (1) | 78 |
| (2) | 83 |
| (3) | 85 |
| (4) | 79 |
| (5) | 90 |

## Referencing an Array

To reference an element of an array, you must specify both the name of the array and the index into the array. The index value is contained within parentheses. You can use an array name with an index value just like a variable. Changes you make to one array element do not affect the other elements in the array.

*Syntax:* *ArrayName(index)*

*Example:*

```
Actors(0) = "Tom Hanks"
Actors(1) = "Helen Hunt"
Actors(2) = "David Allen Brooks"
Actors(3) = "Valentina Ananyina"

If Scores(4) > Scores(5) Then
   Biggest = Scores(4)
Else
   Biggest = Scores(5)
End If

For i = 0 To 7
   Cubes(i) = i ^ 3
   Sum = Sum + Cubes(i)
Next
```

**▶▶▶Tip**
**An array element can be used just like a variable.**

**▶▶▶Tip**
**Arrays and loops work well together, with the loop variable serving as the loop index value.**

The preceding example code demonstrates how the array elements can be referenced just like variables. The Actors array is used as a storage location on the left side of an assignment statement. The Scores array appears as part of an If . . . Then condition and also as an expression on the right side of an assignment statement. The Cubes array is referenced twice inside the For . . . Next loop. Notice that the Cubes index value is the same as the For . . . Next loop variable. It is common to use For . . . Next loops and arrays together in this way. The resulting array values are shown in Figure 9-4.

▶ **FIGURE 9.4** *Arrays with Values Assigned to Elements*

Actors

| Index | Value |
|---|---|
| (0) | Tom Hanks |
| (1) | Helen Hunt |
| (2) | David Allen Brooks |
| (3) | Valentina Ananyina |

Cubes

| Index | Value |
|---|---|
| (0) | 0.0 |
| (1) | 1.0 |
| (2) | 8.0 |
| (3) | 27.0 |
| (4) | 64.0 |
| (5) | 125.0 |
| (6) | 216.0 |
| (7) | 343.0 |

Scores

| Index | Value |
|---|---|
| (0) | 92 |
| (1) | 78 |
| (2) | 83 |
| (3) | 85 |
| (4) | 79 |
| (5) | 90 |

## ReDim Statement

Typically, you declare an array with enough elements to hold all the data required for the lifetime of the application. However, there are times when the amount of data changes, thus making it necessary to change the size of the array. After you declare an array, you can change its size (but not its type) by using the ***ReDim*** statement.

*Syntax:*

```
ReDim [Preserve] ArrayName(NewArraySize)
```

*Example:*

```
ReDim Preserve Actors(6)          ' array now holds 7 Strings
ReDim Preserve Cubes(5)           ' array now holds 6 Doubles
ReDim Preserve Scores(7)          ' array now holds 8 Integers
```

You will typically use ReDim to make an array larger, creating more space for new elements. Further, because you generally want to keep the current values in the array when making it bigger, you will likely use the Preserve keyword as well, which saves the current contents. (Of course, if you ReDim the array to a smaller length, then some elements will be lost even with the Preserve keyword.) Figure 9-5 shows the effects of the three ReDim statements in the preceding example code.

**FIGURE 9.5** *Three Arrays after a ReDim Preserve*

| | Actors | | Cubes | | Scores |
|---|---|---|---|---|---|
| (0) | Tom Hanks | (0) | 0.0 | (0) | 92 |
| (1) | Helen Hunt | (1) | 1.0 | (1) | 78 |
| (2) | David Allen Brooks | (2) | 8.0 | (2) | 83 |
| (3) | Valentina Ananyina | (3) | 27.0 | (3) | 85 |
| (4) | "" | (4) | 64.0 | (4) | 79 |
| (5) | "" | (5) | 125.0 | (5) | 90 |
| (6) | "" | | | (6) | 0 |
| | | | | (7) | 0 |

## Array.Sort Method

When you declare an array variable, it inherits functionality from a general Array class. One of the methods of the Array class is the Sort method. As the name suggests, ***Array.Sort*** will sort the elements of an array. To better understand, consider the following code.

```
Private Sub btnClick_Click(ByVal sender As System.Object, _
            ByVal e As System.EventArgs) Handles btnClick.Click
    Dim Words(7) As String
    Dim I As Integer

    Words(0) = "she"
    Words(1) = "sells"
    Words(2) = "sea"
    Words(3) = "shells"
    Words(4) = "down"
    Words(5) = "by"
    Words(6) = "the"
    Words(7) = "seashore"

    'Display the unsorted array in the first list box
    lstOutput1.Items.Add("Before Sort:")
    For I = 0 To UBound(Words)
        lstOutput1.Items.Add(I & " : " & Words(I))
    Next

    'Sort the array
    Array.Sort(Words)  'VB.NET makes array sorting easy

    'Display the sorted array in the second list box
    lstOutput2.Items.Add("After Sort:")
    For I = 0 To UBound(Words)
        lstOutput2.Items.Add(I & " : " & Words(I))
    Next
End Sub
```

Figure 9-6 shows the output for the preceding code. Notice that the elements of the Words array were sorted using only a single call to the Array.Sort method.

**FIGURE 9.6** *Array.Sort Output*

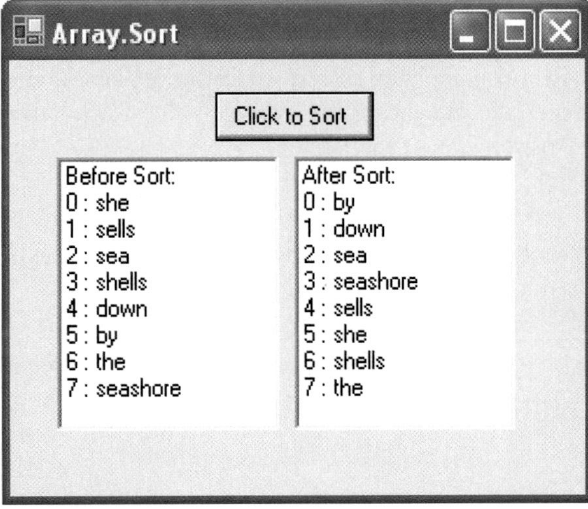

## ASK THE AUTHOR

**Q** Is sorting an array really that easy? What about the Bubble Sort algorithm and all those other sorting algorithms?

**A** Yes, sorting an array in VB.NET is really that easy. Visual Basic programmers do not need to write Bubble Sort algorithms or any of the other numerous sorting algorithms. Of course, sorting an array is typically not your final goal, but just one of the steps necessary to achieve the final goal.

It is analogous to long division and calculators. When you first learn long division, it is a good idea to do problems by hand to understand the process. After you understand what long division is and how it works, it makes sense to use a calculator and start doing long division in the context of more sophisticated problems.

## Arrays Illustrated: Calculating an Average

Create a new application with a single button named btnCalculate. Then try the following activities.

### Version 1: Average of Six

Write the following click event procedure code.

```
Private Sub btnCalculate_Click(ByVal sender As System.Object, _
            ByVal e As System.EventArgs) Handles btnCalculate.Click
    Dim Scores() As Integer = {92, 78, 83, 85, 79, 90}
    Dim Sum, Average As Double
    Dim i As Integer

    For i = 0 To 5
        Sum = Sum + Scores(i)
    Next
    Average = Sum / 6
    MsgBox("The average of the array values is " & FormatNumber(Average))
End Sub
```

Run the application and click the button. The event procedure should generate a message indicating the average value in the array to be 84.50. You can verify this answer with a calculator.

### Version 2: Average of Seven (with Errors)

Modify the code by adding 100 to the end of the list of values in the Scores array declaration as shown in the following.

```
Private Sub btnCalculate_Click(ByVal sender As System.Object, _
          ByVal e As System.EventArgs) Handles btnCalculate.Click
    Dim Scores() As Integer = {92, 78, 83, 85, 79, 90, 100} ' 100 added
    Dim Sum, Average As Double
    Dim i As Integer

    For i = 0 To 5
        Sum = Sum + Scores(i)
    Next
    Average = Sum / 6
    MsgBox("The average of the array values is " & FormatNumber(Average))
End Sub
```

Without making any other changes, would you expect the average to increase, decrease, or stay the same? Run the program. Did the average change in the way you expected? Why or why not?

Make any changes you believe are necessary. Note that when the code is correct, the average will be 86.71 (see Figure 9-7).

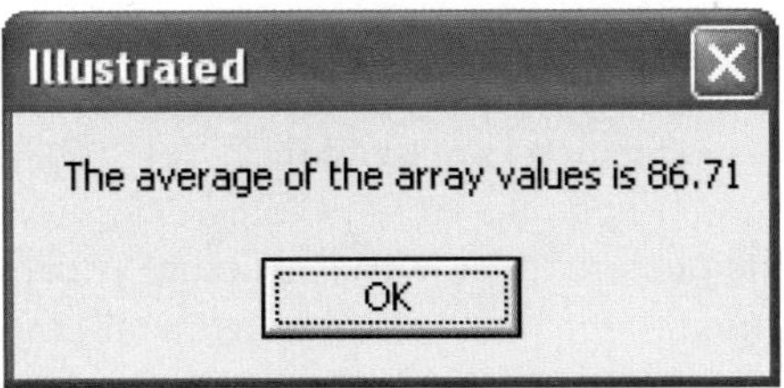


**FIGURE 9.7** *Correct Output for Calculating the Average of Seven*

### Version 3: Average of Seven (Correct)

Changing the size of the array requires two changes to the code. The loop's final value must change from 5 to 6. Also when calculating the average, the sum should be divided by 7. These two numbers correspond to the upper bound and the length of the array. A more robust solution would use the UBound function and Length method to retain accuracy as the length of the array varies.

```
Private Sub btnCalculate_Click(ByVal sender As System.Object, _
          ByVal e As System.EventArgs) Handles btnCalculate.Click
    Dim Scores() As Integer = {92, 78, 83, 85, 79, 90, 100} ' 100 added
    Dim Sum, Average As Double
    Dim i As Integer

    For i = 0 To UBound(Scores)
        Sum = Sum + Scores(i)
    Next

    Average = Sum / Scores.Length
    MsgBox("The average of the array values is " & FormatNumber(Average))
End Sub
```

## 9-7 Structure Arrays

Recall that an array is a variable that holds multiple elements of the same type. You can therefore store text (such as a student's name) or numeric data (such as a student's GPA) in an array, but not both. A ***structure*** provides a means of combining several different variables into a single type, which can then be stored as an array element.

*Syntax:*

```
Structure StructName
   Dim variable1 As DataType
   Dim variable2 As DataType
   ...
End Structure
```

*Example:*

```
Structure Student
    Dim Name As String
    Dim Hours As Integer
    Dim Points As Double
    Dim GPA As Double
End Structure

Dim Graduating(10) As Student
```

Each variable declared inside the structure is called a ***member.*** The period (or dot operator) is used to reference a structure member. An array of structures therefore uses parentheses to reference array elements and periods to reference members within the element.

### Structure Array Illustrated: Student GPA

Create a new application that declares the Student structure and module level mGraduating array as shown in the preceding example code. The application will have two buttons, one for adding a new student to the list of graduates and a second to determine and display the name of the student with the highest GPA. The full solution follows. Run the application, and add various students and calculate the highest GPA multiple times.

```
Public Class Form1
    Inherits System.Windows.Forms.Form

    'The Student structure provides storage space for student information
    'involving different member types (String, Integer, Double, etc.)
    Structure Student
        Dim Name As String
        Dim Hours As Integer
        Dim Points As Double
        Dim GPA As Double
    End Structure

    'The module level Graduating array contains elements
    'of type Student (i.e., Name, Hours, Points, GPA).
    'The mGraduating array is initialized to be an empty array.
    Dim mGraduating() As Student = {}

Windows Form Designer generated code

    Private Sub btnAddStudent_Click(ByVal sender As System.Object, _
            ByVal e As System.EventArgs) Handles btnAddStudent.Click
        Dim I As Integer
        Dim Pos As Integer

        Pos = UBound(mGraduating) + 1
        ReDim Preserve mGraduating(Pos)

        mGraduating(Pos).Name = InputBox("Enter student's Name")
        mGraduating(Pos).Hours = _
                CInt(InputBox("Enter the hours earned by this student"))
        mGraduating(Pos).Points = _
                CDbl(InputBox("Enter the points earned by this student"))
        mGraduating(Pos).GPA = _
                mGraduating(Pos).Points / mGraduating(Pos).Hours
        MsgBox(mGraduating(Pos).Name & " has a GPA of " & _
                FormatNumber(mGraduating(Pos).GPA))
    End Sub

    Private Sub btnHighGPA_Click(ByVal sender As System.Object, _
            ByVal e As System.EventArgs) Handles btnHighGPA.Click
        Dim I, BiggestIndex As Integer
        BiggestIndex = 0
        For I = 1 To UBound(mGraduating)
            If mGraduating(I).GPA > mGraduating(BiggestIndex).GPA Then
                BiggestIndex = I
            End If
        Next
        MsgBox(mGraduating(BiggestIndex).Name & " is the Valedictorian")
    End Sub
End Class
```

## 9-8 Control Arrays

VB.NET also supports a ***control array***, which is an array of Windows Form controls such as text boxes, labels, or buttons. Control arrays allow a developer to write a small amount of code that affects a potentially large number of GUI elements. Control arrays are created using the Dim statements just like with other arrays.

*Syntax:*

```
Dim ArrayName(arraysize) As ControlType
```

*Example:*

```
Dim lblColors(3) As Label          ' Control array of 4 Labels
Dim txtInputs(5) as TextBox        ' Control array of 6 TextBoxes
```

There are two ways to populate a control array. The first is to create the controls at design time and add the controls to the array at runtime, typically inside the Form Load event. The advantage of this approach is that each control can be created with the exact size and placed in the exact location desired. This approach is used in the following tic-tac-toe illustration.

A second approach for populating a control array is to create the controls at runtime. The advantage to this approach is that the whole process can be done inside a loop, making this a good option when creating a large number of controls. This approach is used in the Case Study Solution later this chapter.

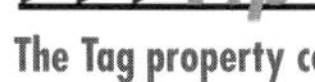

**Tip**

**The Tag property contains arbitrary programmer-defined data associated with the control. In the tic-tac-toe solution, the Tag properties of the nine button controls contain the values 0 through 8 and are used to distinguish the buttons in the shared click event handler.**

### Control Array Illustrated—Tic-Tac-Toe

Create a new application with nine buttons placed in a tic-tac-toe board form, a button for starting a new game, six labels, and a check box as shown in Figure 9-8.

The nine buttons that make up the tic-tac-toe board will placed into a control array. This will allow all nine buttons to share a single click event procedure. The event procedure will determine which button was pressed by the unique Tag property value that you will assign to each button.

**FIGURE 9.8** *Tic-Tac-Toe Form Design*

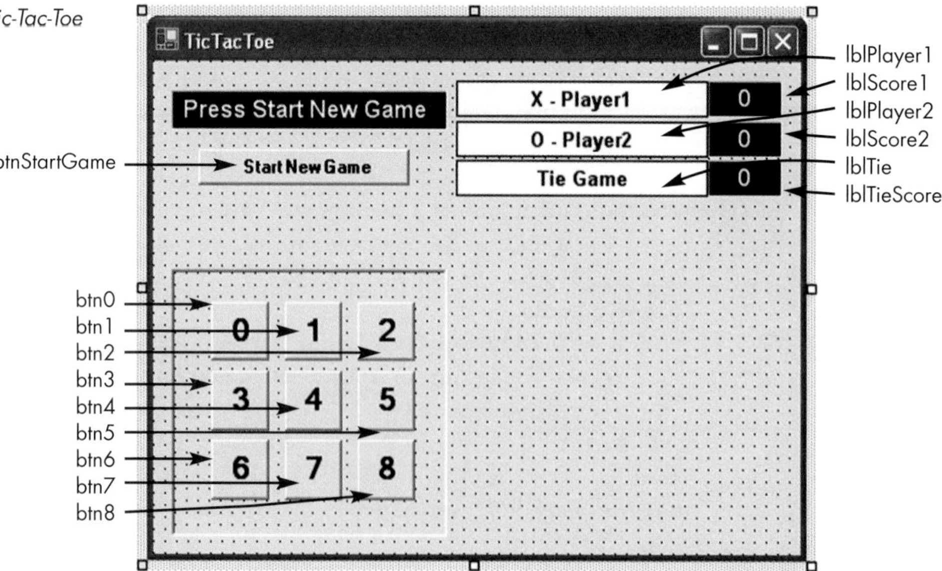

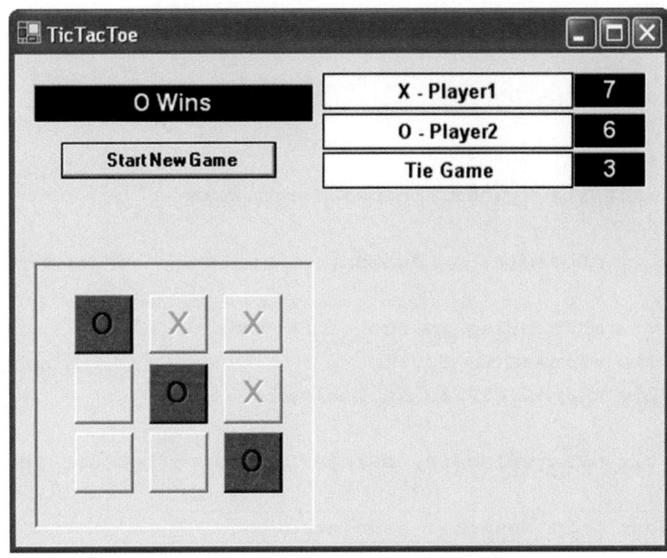


**FIGURE 9.9** *Tic-Tac-Toe Sample Output*

The following code is a full working implementation for a tic-tac-toe game. The code recognizes player moves and marks each move with an appropriate X or O value in the button's Text property. The board is then tested for any winning moves. An example of the solutions output is shown in Figure 9-9.

```
' Project: Tic-Tac-Toe
' Description:    This program plays tic-tac-toe. The game board
'                 consists of nine button controls in a control
'                 array. The buttons are created at design time and
'                 added to a control array at runtime.
'
'   *********** Design Time Properties ***********
'   OBJECT                   PROPERTY       SETTING
'
'   lblTurnPrompt            Text           "Press Start New Game"
'
'   lblPlayer1               Text           "X - Player1"
'
'   lblScore1                Text           0
'
'   lblPlayer2               Text           "O - Player2"
'
'   lblScore2                Text           0
'
'   lblTie                   Text           "Tie Game"
'
'   lblTieScore              Text           0
'
'   btnStartGame             Text           "Start New Game"
'
'   btn0                     Tag            0
'   btn1                     Tag            1
'   btn2                     Tag            2
'   btn3                     Tag            3
'   btn4                     Tag            4
'   btn5                     Tag            5
'   btn6                     Tag            6
```

```
    '   btn7                       Tag             7
    '   btn8                       Tag             8
Option Strict On

Public Class Form1
    Inherits System.Windows.Forms.Form

    Dim mBoard(8) As Button                       'Control Array

    Dim mXTurnFlag As Boolean = True
    Dim mWinner As String                         'winning player
    Dim mGameOverFlag As Boolean

    Dim mPlayer1Score, mPlayer2Score, mTieCount As Integer

Windows Form Designer generated code

    ' Form1_Load assigns the form buttons to the control array.
    ' (Note that mBoard is a zero-based array).
    Private Sub Form1_Load(ByVal sender As System.Object, _
               ByVal e As System.EventArgs) Handles MyBase.Load
        Dim Position As Integer
        mBoard(0) = btn0
        mBoard(1) = btn1
        mBoard(2) = btn2
        mBoard(3) = btn3
        mBoard(4) = btn4
        mBoard(5) = btn5
        mBoard(6) = btn6
        mBoard(7) = btn7
        mBoard(8) = btn8

        For Position = 0 To 8
            mBoard(Position).Enabled = False
        Next Position
    End Sub

    Private Sub StartNewGame()
        Dim Position As Integer

        ' Reset visual elements
        For Position = 0 To 8
            mBoard(Position).Text = ""
            mBoard(Position).Enabled = True
            mBoard(Position).BackColor = Color.Gray
        Next

        mXTurnFlag = True                         'X moves first
        lblTurnPrompt.Text = "X's Turn"
        mWinner = ""                              'Clear previous winner
        btnStartGame.Enabled = False
        mGameOverFlag = False
    End Sub
```

```
' This event procedure starts a new game by preparing the board
' array, resetting the module level variables.
Private Sub btnStartGame_Click(ByVal sender As System.Object, _
            ByVal e As System.EventArgs) _
            Handles btnStartGame.Click
    StartNewGame()
End Sub

' btn0_Click handles the button click event for each button
' on the game board. You should manually add the events handled
' by this procedure after the "Handles" keyword
Private Sub btn0_Click(ByVal sender As System.Object, _
        ByVal e As System.EventArgs) Handles btn0.Click, _
        btn1.Click, btn2.Click, btn3.Click, btn4.Click, _
        btn5.Click, btn6.Click, btn7.Click, btn8.Click

    Dim Tag As Integer

    ' Option Strict On requires explicit typecast using CType
    Tag = CInt(CType(sender, Button).Tag)

    ' If space is already taken, then ignore click
    If mBoard(Tag).Text <> "" Then Exit Sub

    If mXTurnFlag Then
        mBoard(Tag).Text = "X"          'Mark the move
    Else
        mBoard(Tag).Text = "O"          'Mark the move
    End If
    mXTurnFlag = Not mXTurnFlag         'Toggle turn flag

    CheckForWinner()                  'Was this a winning move?
End Sub

Sub CheckForWinner()
    Dim Position As Integer

    'Check for X and O winning
    CheckThree(0, 1, 2)
    CheckThree(3, 4, 5)
    CheckThree(6, 7, 8)
    CheckThree(0, 3, 6)
    CheckThree(1, 4, 7)
    CheckThree(2, 5, 8)
    CheckThree(0, 4, 8)
    CheckThree(2, 4, 6)

    'Check for a Tie
    If Not mGameOverFlag Then CheckTie()

    ' Give appropriate feedback
    Select Case mWinner
```

```
            Case "X"
                mPlayer1Score = mPlayer1Score + 1
                lblScore1.Text = CStr(mPlayer1Score)
                lblTurnPrompt.Text = "X Wins"
            Case "O"
                mPlayer2Score = mPlayer2Score + 1
                lblScore2.Text = CStr(mPlayer2Score)
                lblTurnPrompt.Text = "O Wins"
            Case "Tie"
                mTieCount = mTieCount + 1
                lblTieScore.Text = CStr(mTieCount)
                lblTurnPrompt.Text = "Tie Game"
            Case Else
                If mXTurnFlag Then
                    lblTurnPrompt.Text = "X's Turn"
                Else
                    lblTurnPrompt.Text = "O's Turn"
                End If
        End Select

        If mGameOverFlag Then
            For Position = 0 To 8
                mBoard(Position).Enabled = False 'Disallow new moves
            Next Position
            btnStartGame.Enabled = True
        End If
    End Sub

    ' CheckThree accepts three board positions and determines if
    ' all three are occupied by the same player. If so, then a
    ' winning move is found and the winning positions are
    ' highlighted in red.
    Sub CheckThree(ByVal p1 As Integer, ByVal p2 As Integer, _
                ByVal p3 As Integer)
        If mBoard(p1).Text <> "" _
                And mBoard(p1).Text = mBoard(p2).Text _
                And mBoard(p2).Text = mBoard(p3).Text Then
            ' Mark the winning moves
            mBoard(p1).BackColor = Color.Red
            mBoard(p2).BackColor = Color.Red
            mBoard(p3).BackColor = Color.Red
            ' Record the winning player
            mWinner = mBoard(p1).Text
            mGameOverFlag = True
        End If
    End Sub

    Function IsEmpty(ByVal Index As Integer) As Boolean
        If mBoard(Index).Text = "" Then Return True
        Return False
    End Function
```

```
    Sub CheckTie()
        Dim Position As Integer
        Dim TieFlag As Boolean = True

        ' If any spaces are open, it's not a tie yet...
        For Position = 0 To 8
            If IsEmpty(Position) Then TieFlag = False
        Next

        If TieFlag Then
            ' Record the winning player
            mWinner = "Tie"
            mGameOverFlag = True
        End If
    End Sub

End Class
```

## 9-9 KeyPress Event

The ***KeyPress event*** is useful for capturing keystroke data as it would appear in a text box. For example, KeyPress distinguishes between lowercase *a* and uppercase A. The second argument, *e*, is a KeyPressEventArgs object, which exposes only two properties: Handled and KeyChar. The KeyChar property is the character that corresponds to the key pressed. Handled is a Boolean value that you set to True to tell the form engine that you have already processed the event and that the engine should therefore take no further action.

**The control keys (Shift, Alt, Ctrl) do not generate KeyPress events by themselves. If you want to capture those keys as they are pressed, you need to use the KeyDown event.**

### KeyPress Illustrated: Watch your Ps and Qs

Create a new application with a text box, and write the following KeyPress event handler code.

**The arrow keys do not generate KeyPress or KeyDown events. If you want to respond to arrow keys, you need to override the ProcessCmdKey event and intercept the Windows WM_KEYDOWN message. An example of this appears in the Case Study Solution.**

```
Private Sub txtInput_KeyPress(ByVal sender As Object, _
            ByVal e As System.Windows.Forms.KeyPressEventArgs) _
            Handles txtInput.KeyPress
    MsgBox(e.KeyChar & " was pressed")
    If e.KeyChar = "P" Or e.KeyChar = "Q" Then
        'If the character is a capital P or capital Q,
        'then tell the form engine to ignore it.
        e.Handled = True
    End If
End Sub
```

Run the application. Notice that the values you type into the text box are captured and processed by the KeyPress event code. Also notice that capital P and capital Q cause the e.Handled property to be set to True, and therefore the form engine does not process them (they do not appear in the text box).

# Snakes Game

Chuck walks into his office, sees Wilson sitting there, and begins showing him a notepad full of drawings and descriptions. "Here is how I'm thinking we should design and implement the Snakes Game. The first issue is how do we represent the game board and the snake on the board. I realized we could represent the board as a collection of one hundred labels in a 10 by 10 layout, rather than develop some elaborate drawing routines. Each label can have its own background color and text, so we can draw the snake and the food using those properties."

Wilson does not react at this point, and Chuck quickly continues. "I know you don't like the idea of creating one hundred labels and changing the name property for each at design time. Instead, I was thinking we would create the actual labels at runtime when the form is created. As for moving the snake, there are two things to consider. First, we must handle when an arrow key is pressed and move the snake one block in the selected direction. That is simply a matter of writing a ProcessCmdKey event to determine the value of the pressed key and respond appropriately. But we also need a Timer that causes the snake to continue to move even when the user is not pressing keys."

Unfazed by Wilson's silence, Chuck continues his explanation, his voice growing in excitement. "The snake, of course, is a resizable array that grows by one each time a piece of food is eaten. I was thinking about using the @ symbol to represent an apple."

Chuck flips the sheet on his legal pad and taps the handwritten notes on the next page, his tone growing to a crescendo. "A few procedures to test if the snake runs into a wall or hits itself, and another procedure to redraw the board after every move and, *voila*, we're done!"

Chuck lays the notepad in front of Wilson, who seems to be gazing at a large poster of a rowing crew with an inspirational message about teamwork. "Come on buddy," Chuck says finally, "Let's get started."

## Design

The design specifies how the solution will work in general terms. He begins by sketching the interface for the Snakes Game, specifying the Name property for all the necessary controls. In this case, the interface design is rather simple. The one hundred labels that make up the game board do not exist at design time, but are created programmatically when the form loads. The sketch in Figure 9-10 includes a single button for starting a new game. The sketch leaves room on the form where the one hundred labels will be placed when the form loads.

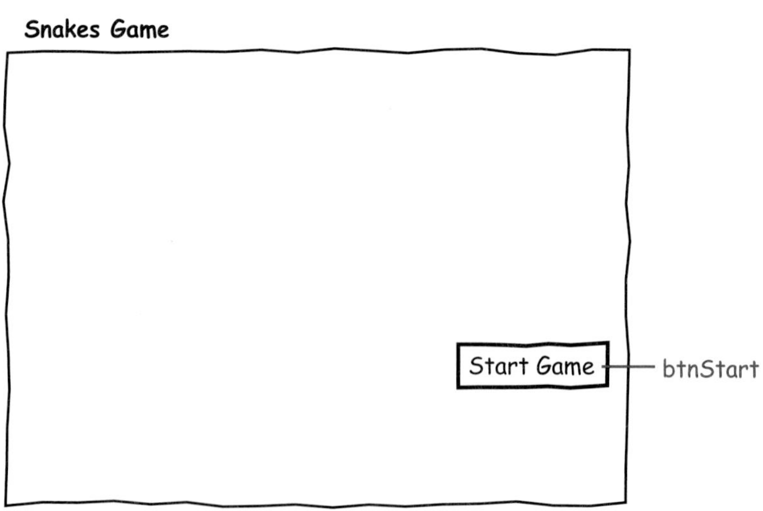


**FIGURE 9.10** *Interface Design for Snakes Game Application*

The design should also include a high-level specification of all the actions and behavior required by the project. This can be done using flowchart or pseudocode notation and should describe behavior without getting into details of implementation. Table 9-1 provides pseudocode descriptions of the event procedures, sub procedures, and functions used in the Snakes Game design.

**Table 9.1** Design Pseudocode for Snakes Game Application

| Event Procedures | Behavior |
|---|---|
| btnStart_Click | Calls StartNewGame |
| tmrForceMove_Tick | Move the snake in the current direction |
| **Sub Procedures** | **Behavior** |
| StartNewGame | 1. Initialize the board |
| | 2. Initialize the snake |
| | 3. Randomly place apple |
| | 4. Start moving the snake |
| InitializeBoard | 1. Destroy old board (if not first game) |
| | 2. Create all of the board labels dynamically |
| | 3. Draw the board |
| DrawBoard | 1. Erase old board information |
| | 2. Show the current snake position |
| SnakeCrash | Handle snake crash, including end of game |
| MoveSnake | 1. Disable the timer |
| | 2. End game if snake will hit wall |
| | 3. End game if snake will hit self |
| | 4. Update the snake's position |
| | 5. If food has been eaten, grow snake and move food |
| | 6. Draw the new board |
| | 7. Re-enable the timer |
| **Functions** | **Behavior** |
| WillHitWall | Returns whether or not the snake's current move will cause snake to hit a wall |
| WillHitSnake | Returns whether or not the snake's current move will cause snake to hit itself |
| GetNewHeadValue | Returns the new location for the head based on the current head location and the movement direction |
| HandleKeyPress | Move the snake in the direction indicated by the keypress (ignore 180 degree turns); returns whether or not a direction key was pressed |
| ProcessCmdKey | Check for a keydown message and call HandleKeyPress if appropriate; returns whether or not the message was handled |

### Implementation

After completing the general design, he must implement the details. The first step of implementation is to build the GUI. Figure 9-11 illustrates the Snakes Game GUI at design time. (Remember that the one hundred labels are not created until the program executes.)

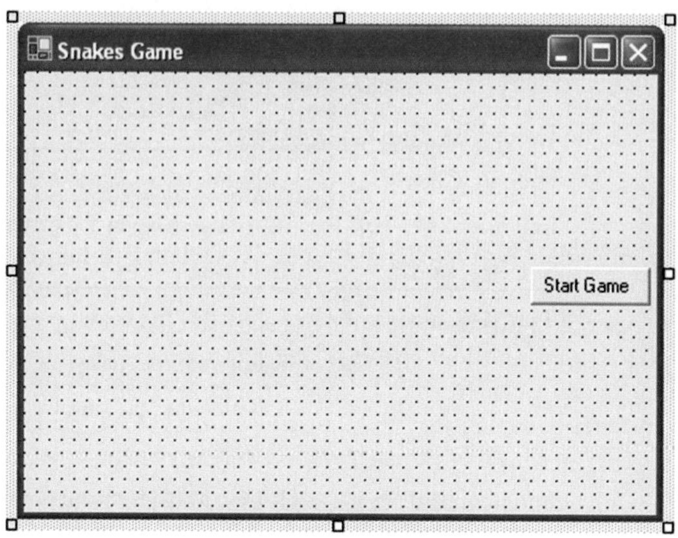


**FIGURE 9.11** *Snakes Game GUI*

The second step is to implement the functionality described in the pseudocode design. It is also a good habit to document important design time property values for the form and interface controls. The solution code with good documentation appears as follows.

```
' Author: Chuck & Wilson
' Project: Snakes Game
' Description:  This a game in which the player uses the keyboard to
'               move a snake in real time. When the snake eats food, it grows
'               in length. The game is over when the snake runs into itself
'               or into a wall. The player's score is determined by the
'               length of the snake.
'
'
'     *********** Design Time Properties ***********
'   OBJECT                PROPERTY        SETTING
'
'   tmrForceMove          Interval        500
'
'   btnStart              Text            "Start Game"
'
'

Option Strict On        'Programming Right From the Start Recommended

Public Class Form1
    Inherits System.Windows.Forms.Form

    ' Directional constants
    Const DIR_UP As Integer = 1
    Const DIR_LEFT As Integer = 2
```

```
    Const DIR_RIGHT As Integer = 3
    Const DIR_DOWN As Integer = 4

    ' Module-level declarations
    Dim mBoard() As Label
    Dim mSnake(0) As Integer 'Array of integers (board positions)
    Dim mDirection As Integer 'Last Key direction pressed
    Dim mSnakeColor As System.Drawing.Color = Color.Red
    Dim mBoardColor As System.Drawing.Color = Color.White
    Dim mBoardWidth As Integer = 14  'Number of columns in the board
    Dim mBoardHeight As Integer = 14 'Number of rows in the board
    Dim mIsPlayingFlag As Boolean = False

Windows Form Designer generated code

    Private Sub StartNewGame()
        InitializeBoard()
        ' Initialize the snake
        ReDim mSnake(0)                                       'Initial length is 1
        mSnake(0) = CInt(0.75 * mBoardWidth * mBoardHeight) 'near the bottom
        mDirection = DIR_UP                                   'direction is up

        ' Randomly place apple
        mBoard(CInt(Int((Rnd() * UBound(mBoard))))).Text = "@"

        ' Start moving the snake
        tmrForceMove.Enabled = True
        mIsPlayingFlag = True
    End Sub

    Private Sub InitializeBoard()
        Dim Index, X, Y As Integer
        Dim NumBoardElements As Integer
        Dim Margin As Integer = 10
        Dim XSize As Integer = 15
        Dim YSize As Integer = 15

        If Not (mBoard Is Nothing) Then
            For Index = 0 To UBound(mBoard)
                mBoard(Index).Dispose()
            Next
        End If
        ' Create all of the board labels dynamically at runtime
        NumBoardElements = mBoardWidth * mBoardHeight
        ReDim mBoard(NumBoardElements - 1)
        Index = 0
        For Y = 0 To mBoardHeight - 1
            For X = 0 To mBoardWidth - 1
                Dim NewLabel As New Label
                NewLabel.BorderStyle = BorderStyle.FixedSingle
                NewLabel.Text = ""
                'NewLabel.Text = CStr(I) 'uncomment to see index values
                NewLabel.Location = New Point(Margin + X * XSize, Margin + Y * YSize)
                NewLabel.Width = XSize
```

```
            NewLabel.Height = YSize
            Me.Controls.Add(NewLabel)
            mBoard(Index) = NewLabel
            Index = Index + 1
        Next X
    Next Y
    If mIsPlayingFlag Then DrawBoard()
End Sub

'DrawBoard sets the BackColor to the current board color for every board element, then
'sets the BackColor to red for every board element matching the snakes
'position.
Sub DrawBoard()
    Dim Index As Integer

    'Erase old snake information
    For Index = 0 To UBound(mBoard)
        mBoard(Index).BackColor = mBoardColor
    Next

    'Show the current snake position
    For Index = 0 To UBound(mSnake)
        mBoard(mSnake(Index)).BackColor = mSnakeColor
    Next
End Sub

Private Sub btnStart_Click(ByVal sender As System.Object, _
            ByVal e As System.EventArgs) Handles btnStart.Click
    StartNewGame()
End Sub

'WillHitWall returns TRUE if the snake is about to crash into one of the
'four walls, and returns FALSE otherwise.
Function WillHitWall() As Boolean
    Dim HeadX, HeadY As Integer

    ' Find the X, Y position of the head of the snake
    HeadX = mSnake(0) Mod mBoardWidth
    HeadY = mSnake(0) \ mBoardWidth

    If mDirection = DIR_UP And HeadY = 0 Then Return True
    If mDirection = DIR_DOWN And HeadY = (mBoardHeight - 1) Then Return True
    If mDirection = DIR_LEFT And HeadX = 0 Then Return True
    If mDirection = DIR_RIGHT And HeadX = (mBoardWidth - 1) Then Return True
    Return False
End Function

'WillHitSnake returns TRUE if the snake is about to move into itself, and
'returns FALSE otherwise.
Function WillHitSnake(ByVal NewPosition As Integer) As Boolean
    Dim Index As Integer
    For Index = 0 To UBound(mSnake)
        If NewPosition = mSnake(Index) Then Return True
```

```
    Next
    Return False
End Function

'SnakeCrash handles the end-of-game code, including displaying the
'player's score.
Sub SnakeCrash()
    tmrForceMove.Enabled = False
    mIsPlayingFlag = False
    MsgBox("Crash! Game Over!" & vbCrLf & _
        "Your score: " & CStr(mSnake.Length))
End Sub

'GetNewHeadValue determines the new location for the head based on the
'current head location and the movement direction.
Function GetNewHeadValue() As Integer
    Select Case mDirection
        Case DIR_UP
            Return mSnake(0) - mBoardWidth
        Case DIR_DOWN
            Return mSnake(0) + mBoardWidth
        Case DIR_LEFT
            Return mSnake(0) - 1
        Case DIR_RIGHT
            Return mSnake(0) + 1
        Case Else
            MsgBox("Bad mDirection value : " & CStr(mDirection))
    End Select
End Function

'MoveSnake is the most elaborate procedure in this program. The timer
'is disabled so that processing is not interrupted. The routine checks
'for the two illegal moves (snake hitting the wall or hitting itself)
'and ends the game if either occurs. If not, then the snake is moved,
'and a test is made to see if the move results in food being eaten.
'If so, the snake grows by one in length and the food is moved to a new
'random location. Finally, the board is redrawn to show the new snake
'position and the timer is re-enabled.
Sub MoveSnake(ByVal Direction As Integer)
    Dim NewHead, OldTail, Index As Integer

    If Not mIsPlayingFlag Then Exit Sub 'Ignore if not playing

    tmrForceMove.Enabled = False        'Disable the timer while moving
    mDirection = Direction              'Record direction in module variable
    NewHead = GetNewHeadValue()         'NewHead used many times
    OldTail = mSnake(UBound(mSnake))    'OldTail used when food eaten

    'Call WillHitWall function to see if Snake hits one of the walls
    If WillHitWall() Then
        SnakeCrash()
        Exit Sub
    End If
```

```
        'Call WillHitSnake function to see if Snake runs into itself
        If WillHitSnake(NewHead) Then
            SnakeCrash()
            Exit Sub
        End If

        'Update the snake's position
        For Index = UBound(mSnake) To 1 Step -1
            mSnake(Index) = mSnake(Index - 1)
        Next
        mSnake(0) = NewHead

        'Check to see if the snake has eaten food this move
        If mBoard(mSnake(0)).Text = "@" Then
            'Food Eaten. Snake grows one in length.
            ReDim Preserve mSnake(UBound(mSnake) + 1)
            mSnake(UBound(mSnake)) = OldTail

            'Move the Food to another random location
            mBoard(mSnake(0)).Text = ""
            mBoard(CInt(Int((Rnd() * UBound(mBoard))))).Text = "@"
        End If

        DrawBoard()
        tmrForceMove.Enabled = True   'Re-enable the timer after moving
    End Sub

    'Timer tick event moves the snake one square in the current direction.
    Private Sub tmrForceMove_Tick(ByVal sender As System.Object, _
              ByVal e As System.EventArgs) Handles tmrForceMove.Tick
        MoveSnake(mDirection)
    End Sub

    Function HandleKeyPress(ByVal KeyData As Keys) As Boolean
        ' Choose appropriate direction for the detected key
        ' Note that 180 degrees turns are ignored
        Select Case KeyData
            Case Keys.Up
                If mDirection <> DIR_DOWN Then MoveSnake(DIR_UP)
            Case Keys.Down
                If mDirection <> DIR_UP Then MoveSnake(DIR_DOWN)
            Case Keys.Left
                If mDirection <> DIR_RIGHT Then MoveSnake(DIR_LEFT)
            Case Keys.Right
                If mDirection <> DIR_LEFT Then MoveSnake(DIR_RIGHT)
            Case Else
                Return False 'Do nothing for all other key presses
        End Select
        Return True
    End Function
```

```
    ' The arrow keys do not generate KeyPress or KeyDown events. If you want
    ' to respond to arrow keys, you need to override the ProcessCmdKey event
    ' and intercept the Windows WM_KEYDOWN message.
    Protected Overrides Function ProcessCmdKey(ByRef msg As System.Windows.Forms.Message, _
                              ByVal keyData As System.Windows.Forms.Keys) As Boolean
        Const WM_KEYDOWN As Integer = &H100

        If msg.Msg = WM_KEYDOWN Then
            If HandleKeyPress(keyData) Then Return True
        End If
        Return MyBase.ProcessCmdKey(msg, keyData)
    End Function

    ' Note: The KeyDown event is simpler than ProcessCmdKey above, but does
    ' not work for arrow or tab keys.
    'Private Sub frmSnakes_KeyDown(ByVal sender As Object, _
    '           ByVal e As System.Windows.Forms.KeyEventArgs) Handles MyBase.KeyDown
    '    HandleKeyPress(e.KeyData)
    'End Sub

End Class
```

### Testing the Solution

You can test Chuck's solution by implementing his design as shown in the previous section, and then running the application. Figure 9-12 shows sample output for the Snake Game. Run the program and see how long a snake you can create. If you are having problems getting your solution to execute, you may want to read Appendix B: Debugging.

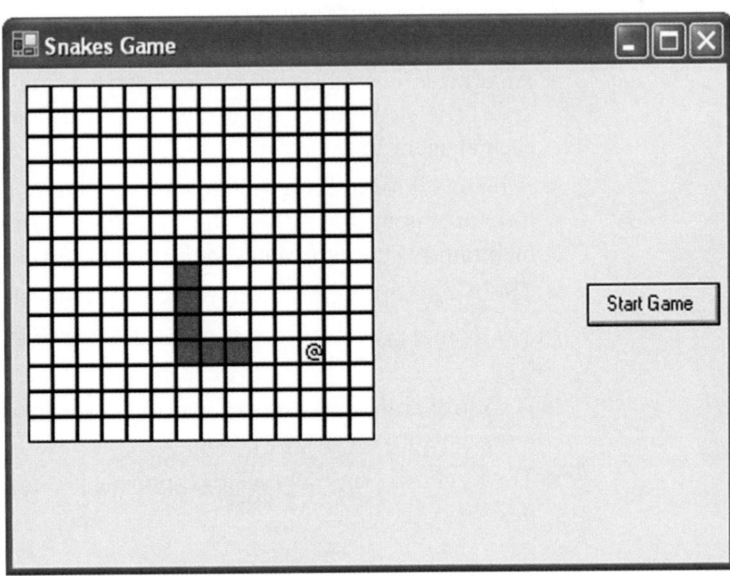


**FIGURE 9.12** *Sample Output for Snakes Game Application*

# Chapter Summary

- A procedure is a set of instructions that perform a specific task. Procedures make code easier to read and easier to maintain.
- An argument is a means of sharing information between the calling program and a procedure. A ByVal parameter creates a local copy of the formal argument. A ByRef parameter is a pointer to the formal argument, meaning any changes to the parameter will also update the argument.
- Modular programming involves breaking your application into procedures of logical units. Developing applications this way results in more readable code, improves your debugging process (because errors can be fixed once at the logical source), and provides a better environment for future maintenance.
- There are three types of procedures: event procedures, sub procedures (or subroutines), and function procedures (or functions).
- Event procedures contain code for responding to user or system events. Event procedures have the default naming convention *object_event* and handle the *object.event* signal.
- Sub procedures (or subroutines) are created by the developer to perform a logical series of actions. A subroutine is invoked by a statement containing the name of the subroutine and the actual parameter list (the keyword Call is optional). When the subroutine is finished, control returns to the line following the calling statement.
- Functions are identical to subroutines, except that functions return values. A function call usually appears as part of an expression, either on the right side of an assignment statement or as part of a condition. When a function procedure is finished, a value is returned and control continues with the calling statement.
- A variable declared in a procedure has local scope and can only be referenced within that procedure.
- A variable declared outside of any procedure is a module level declaration. Module level variables are often denoted by a beginning *m* in the variable name.
- An array is a variable that holds multiple values. The values stored in the array are called the elements of the array. A unique number called the index distinguishes each element in the array.
- After an array has been declared, its size (but not its type) can be changed using the ReDim statement. When the Preserve keyword is used with ReDim, the array maintains its current values in the remaining elements after it has been resized.
- The Array.Sort method will sort the contents of an array.
- A structure provides a means of combining several different variables into a single type.
- A control array is an array of controls, such as buttons or labels. The controls must be assigned to the array in code.
- The KeyPress event is good for capturing keystroke data as it would appear in a text box.

## KEY TERMS

argument p. 212
array p. 219
Array.Sort p. 222
ByVal p. 213
ByRef p. 213
cohesion p. 217
control array p. 228
coupling p. 217
elements p. 219
event procedure p. 213
function procedure p. 216
index p. 219
KeyPress event p. 233
local variable p. 218
member p. 226
modular programming p. 212
module variable p. 218
parameter p. 212
procedure p. 212
ReDim p. 222
Return p. 216
scope p. 218
structure p. 226
sub procedure p. 214
upper bound p. 220

## REVIEW QUESTIONS

1. What is the difference between arguments and parameters? Explain the advantages of using arguments and parameters to communicate between the calling code and the procedure.
2. What is the difference between a ByVal parameter and a ByRef parameter?
3. What is the difference between an event procedure and a sub procedure? What is the difference between a sub procedure and a function?
4. How do you return a value from a function?
5. How are the following related: an array, an element, and an index?
6. What is a structure? What is a structure array?
7. What is a control array?

## PROGRAMMING EXERCISES

**9-1. Power.** Write a sub procedure named Power with two Integer parameters. The procedure should calculate the first parameter raised to the second parameter and display the result using MsgBox.

To test the procedure, write an application with two input text boxes and a button. The button click event should call Power, using the values from the two text boxes as arguments.

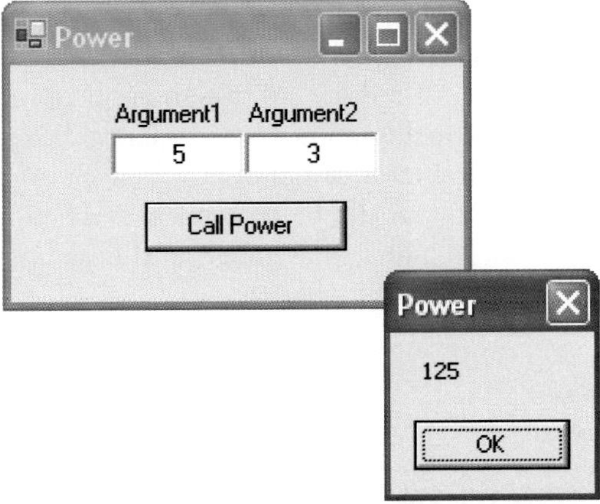


**9-2. Quotient.** Write a function named Quotient with two Integer parameters and a Double return type. The function should calculate the first parameter divided by the second and return (but not display) the result.

To test the function, write an application with two input text boxes, a button, and an output label. The button click event should assign to the output label the result of the Quotient function using the values from the two text boxes as arguments.

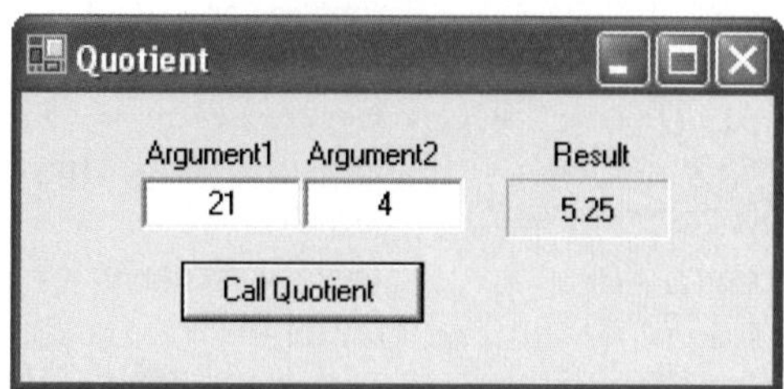


**9-3. Colorful Labels.** Write an application with a control array containing four hundred labels in a 20 by 20 design, each of which should have a size of 15 for its height and width properties. The application should also have three buttons with Text properties "Red," "Green," and "Blue." Clicking on the Red button should set the back color property to Color.Red for all four hundred labels. The Green and Blue buttons should do the same in their respective colors.

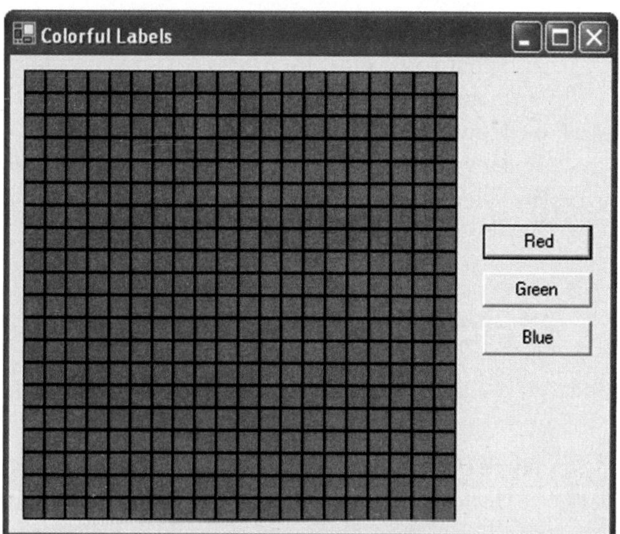


**9-4. SubShop.** A sub shop on campus has a limited menu with three kinds of sandwiches: roast beef ($3.49), chicken salad ($2.99), and veggie ($2.49). Customers may also have any of the following extras with their sandwich for $0.75 each: chips, a cookie, or a drink. Write an application that accepts a single order using RadioButtons for the sandwich type, CheckBoxes for the extras, and labels for the subtotal, tax, and total. Whenever a RadioButton or CheckBox changes, the subtotal, tax, and total should be recalculated. (*Hint:* Write a sub procedure to calculate your subtotal, tax, and total based on the RadioButton and CheckBox values. Call the sub procedure as necessary.)

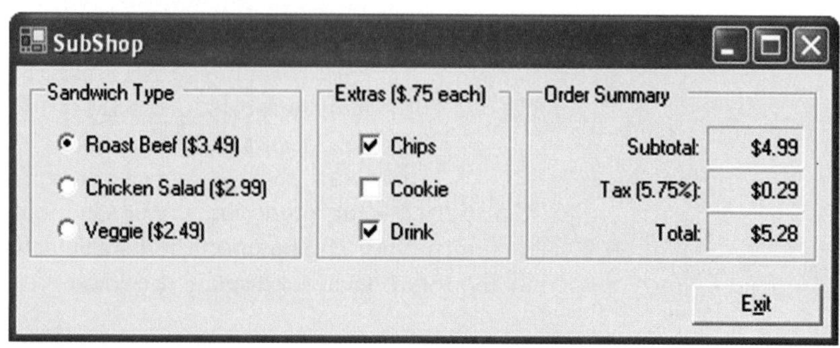

**9-5. Array Average.** Write an application with a list box and a button. The button click event should generate ten random values and store those values in an array. Call the array's Sort method to sort the values, and then display the sorted values in the list box. The program should then calculate the average of the array values and display the average in the list box. Finally, the program should display all the array values that are greater than the average.

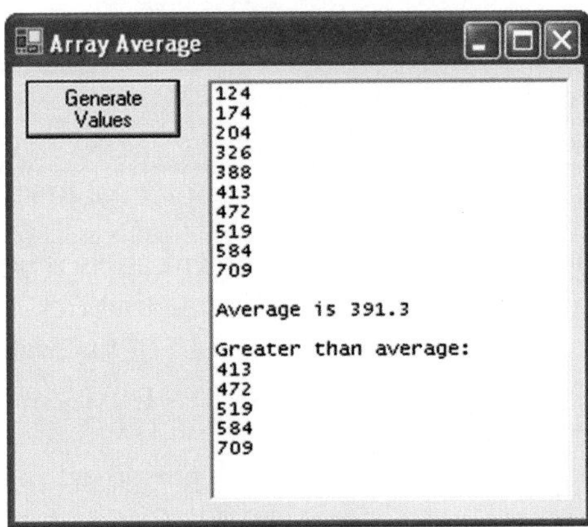


**9-6. Grade Book.** Write an application with two buttons, four text boxes, a label, and a list box. The first button accepts a student's name and three exam scores from input text boxes. Only numeric exam scores between 0 and 100 should be accepted. Valid data should be stored in a structure array, and the text boxes should then be cleared for entering data on the next student. The label should be updated to reflect the number of students in the structure array.

The second button should display in the list box the names of the students along with their three exam scores, the exam average, and the corresponding letter grade. Letter grades should be assigned based on the average using a standard 10-point scale, i.e., A = 90–100, B = 80–89.9, C =70–79.9, etc.

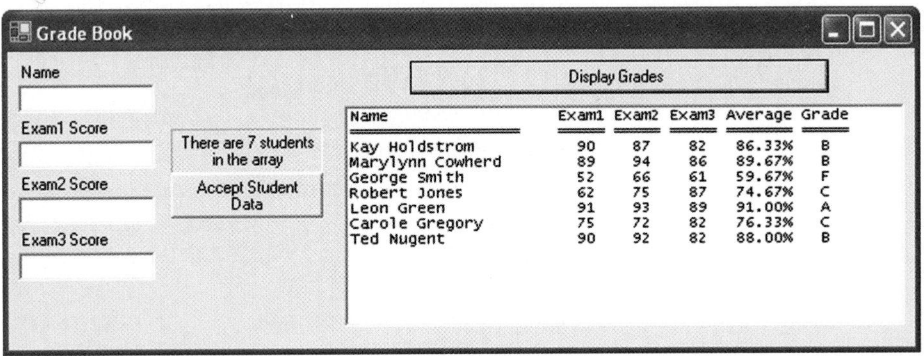


**9-7. Grade Book Redux.** Modify the Grade Book application. Add a function called CalculateAverage with three parameters that returns a Double. The function should calculate the average by weighing the exams scores as follows. The highest exam score should count 40 percent of the average, the middle exam score should count 35 percent of the average, and the lowest exam score should count 25 percent of the average. Then modify the Display Grades button click event procedure to call the CalculateAverage function when appropriate.

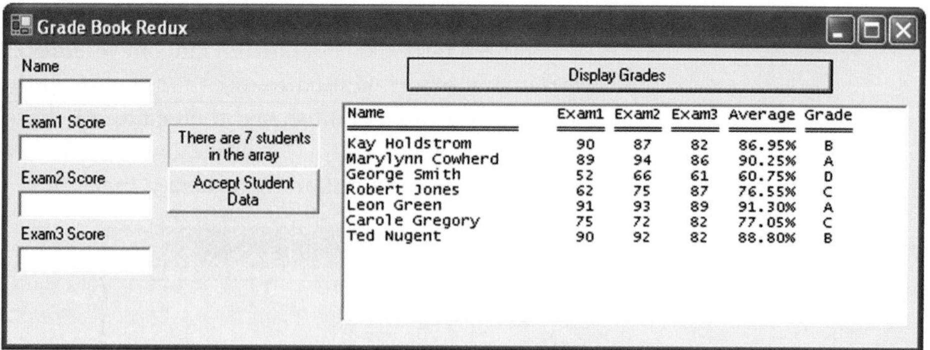


**9-8. Raffle Sales.** Your campus organization is having a small raffle to raise money. The available prizes total $100. Assume that ticket prices are $1 for one ticket, $2 for three tickets, $5 for eight tickets, and $10 for twenty tickets. Ticket amounts are per sale and are not cumulative (e.g., if you pay $1 for one ticket, then later pay another $1, you get only one ticket on the second sale). Tickets are sold only in $1, $2, $5, and $10 amounts. As an incentive, the person selling the most tickets wins a $20 gift certificate.

Write an application that accepts the ticket sales data shown inTable 9-2. Using the table data, determine and display the number of tickets sold and money raised by each seller, the winner of the $20 gift certificate, and the net profit for your organization. (We hope you would have better luck with your ticket sales.)

**Table 9.2 Raffle Ticket Sales**

| Seller | Sale Amount |
|---|---|
| Michael Campbell | $5 |
| Joshua Boone | $10 |
| Keith Dye | $2 |
| Michael Campbell | $5 |
| Amanda Dodson | $10 |
| Deborah Graham | $10 |
| Amanda Dodson | $5 |
| Richard Morris | $10 |
| Keith Dye | $5 |
| Joshua Boone | $10 |
| Amanda Dodson | $10 |
| Keith Dye | $5 |
| Daniel Hubbard | $1 |
| Amanda Dodson | $10 |
| Richard Morris | $10 |
| Deborah Graham | $10 |
| Joshua Boone | $5 |

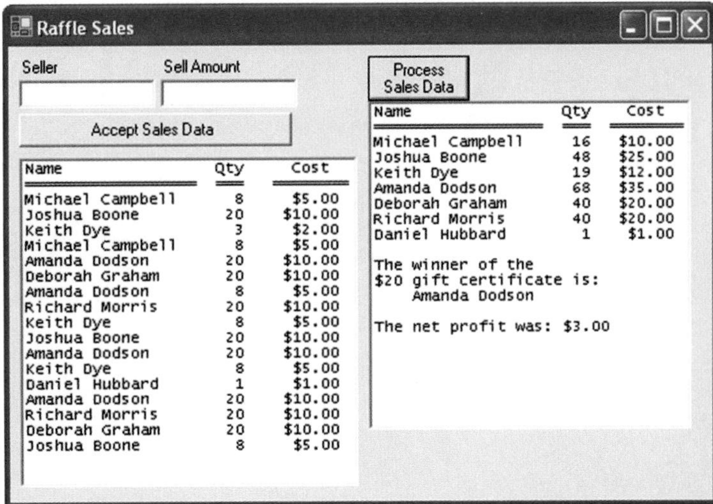


# Extended Case Study

## Pizza and a Movie

Noah is preparing to advertise using direct mailing. To maximize his advertising dollars, he wants to target the zip codes that do the most business with his Pizza and a Movie store. Write an application that inputs the purchase total and zip code for an order. The program should accept data from several orders. The application should also generate a report that shows all of the zip codes along with the total sales per zip code and the average sale per zip code. Noah will use this information to send one direct mailing to the high volume zip codes and another direct mailing to the high average order price zip codes.

## Singing Mimes

Elizabeth and Reed have obtained permission to include the Snakes Game program in their CD collection. Before adding the program to the collection, however, they want to make the following improvements.

- They want to add an image to the snake head label that shows the direction the snake is moving.
- They want the timer value to change after each piece of food is eaten so the snake moves faster as it grows longer.
- They want to add a label that displays the current length of the snake as the game is being played.
- They want the user to specify the size of the board. The board must remain a square with side lengths between 5 and 20.

Modify the Snakes Game program to include the above improvements.

CHAPTER 10

# The Professional Touch

## OUTLINE

## ▶ INTERVIEW

### Bill Grollman, President, SmartPros Ltd.

***Interviewer:*** What kinds of projects are you currently working on?

***Grollman:*** SmartPros produces and markets continuing professional education courses for the corporate accounting, public accounting, and engineering professions. The fastest-growing part of our business is e-Learning, with courses offered over the Internet. It's a constant challenge to use the latest technology to produce, host, and deliver our courses on the Web. Since we specialize in streaming media and have featured streaming video and audio since 1998, our programs have always been on the cutting edge. We are probably in our tenth platform revision for producing our courses in the past four years. This is the constant challenge we face in our business. As soon as bandwidth permits, we'll go to full-screen video on the Web.

***Interviewer:*** What are you most excited about for the future?

***Grollman:*** E-Learning is one of the most natural uses for the Internet. It is one of the few industries in which the product is produced, marketed, delivered, and employed by the end user over the Internet. This generates tremendous advantages both for the producer (eliminates most of the cost of goods sold, drastically reduces marketing costs, greatly simplifies the ability to update programs with new material) and for the students who take our courses (anywhere/anytime education at their convenience, ability to link to live data, access to chat rooms, threaded discussions). We're most excited about the advent to full-screen video on the Internet, which will certainly be coming within the next few years.

***Interviewer:*** What has been your personal key to success?

***Grollman:*** I make sure my company sees itself as a content company, not a technology company. There is no substitute for high-quality content. We will always stay on top of the technology, however, and use it to our advantage in producing, marketing, and delivering our content.

***Interviewer:*** What advice do you have for students preparing for a career in the IT industry?

***Grollman:*** There are more opportunities in the IT industry than in any other industry. By definition, IT will always keep changing dramatically each year. This produces tremendous career opportunities for those who are well educated, who enjoy using technology, and who have the intelligence and creativity to develop innovative new applications for technology.

## OBJECTIVES

At the completion of this chapter, you will

- **Create and work with menus**
- **Create and work with Font and Color Dialog boxes**
- **Create and work with Print- and PrintPreviewDialog boxes**
- **Perform simple text file input/output (I/O)**
- **Add Multimedia controls to your application**
- **Develop applications that combine standard dialogs, text file I/O, and multimedia**

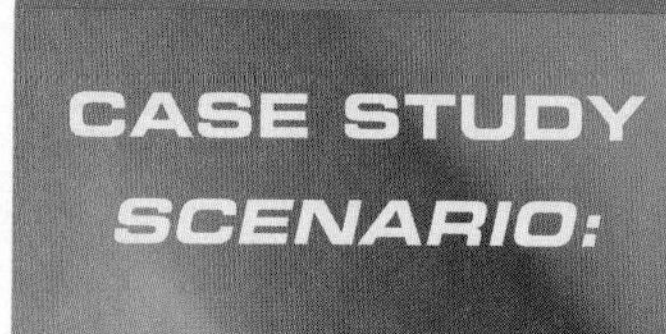


# Snakes Game Pro

Part of Chuck Noland's job at FedEx has been to get up to speed with Visual Basic .NET, which Chuck has been doing by reading books and writing a variety of applications. He considers Wilson his best friend at the company.

"I have been reading about some really cool things that we can do in Visual Basic to give our applications a professional touch," Chuck says to Wilson. "Adding things like menus, files, sounds, and graphics will give our solution the look and feel of a traditional shrink-wrapped product. VB.NET lets us do all those things in a standard way that is consistent across applications.

"For example, you know that Snakes Game we wrote as a control array program? If we added menus, file saving, and some sound and graphics, we could turn it into a showcase piece of software that would really demonstrate how far we have come in learning VB.NET."

A long silence fills the air, which is finally broken when Chuck continues, "Look, I know that sounds like a lot of work, but really it isn't. Most of the functionality we are talking about is built into VB.NET, so all we have to do is decide what professional features we want to use and how best to use them. For example, we can add menus and standard dialog boxes for colors and fonts. All that stuff is really easy!"

Wilson is unfazed by the suggestions, and Chuck interprets the lack of protest as support.

"Trust me. It will be great!"

Chuck and Wilson's solution is presented later in this chapter.

## 10-1 Menus

One of the first items you will probably want to add to a solution to give it a professional touch is a menu. A ***menu*** is a list of common operations presented to the user in a well-defined, system-universal format. Menus make a program easier to learn and use by making common actions available to the user in expected locations. For example, Open, Close, Save, Print, and Exit are all typically available under the first menu option, File. Likewise, the second menu is usually Edit, and it contains Cut, Copy, and Paste (if that functionality is available in the solution). There is also usually a Help menu option available at or near the end of the menu list containing an About option (among others). By adding a menu to your solution, you can dramatically increase the professional look and feel of your application.

The ***main menu*** is a horizontal menu that is permanently visible during the lifetime of the application. When one of the main menu options is selected, a list of menu items appears describing the actions available to the user. The main menu can be selected with the mouse or through keyboard shortcuts. Figure 10-1 shows the main menu for Word and includes some of the menu items under the File option. Any user familiar with Word (or any other Windows application) will likely expect your application to have certain behaviors, including menus.

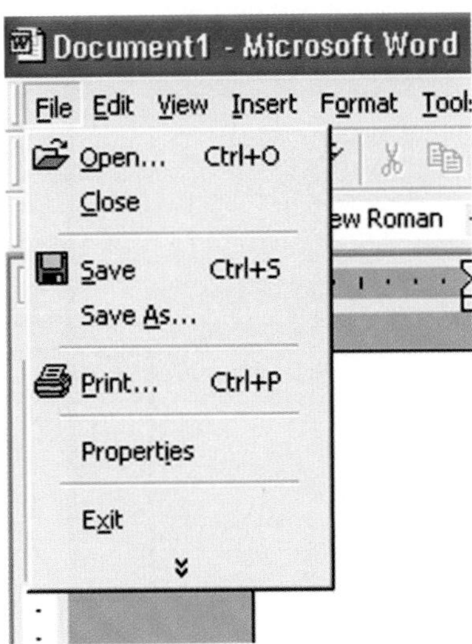


FIGURE 10.1 *Main Menu for Word*

## Creating Menus

Visual Studio provides a Menu Designer that makes it easy to add a main menu to your application. The first step is to add a ***MainMenu control*** to your solution. Double-clicking the MainMenu control from the toolbox will add a MainMenu control to the component tray located below the form in the designer window (see Figure 10-2).

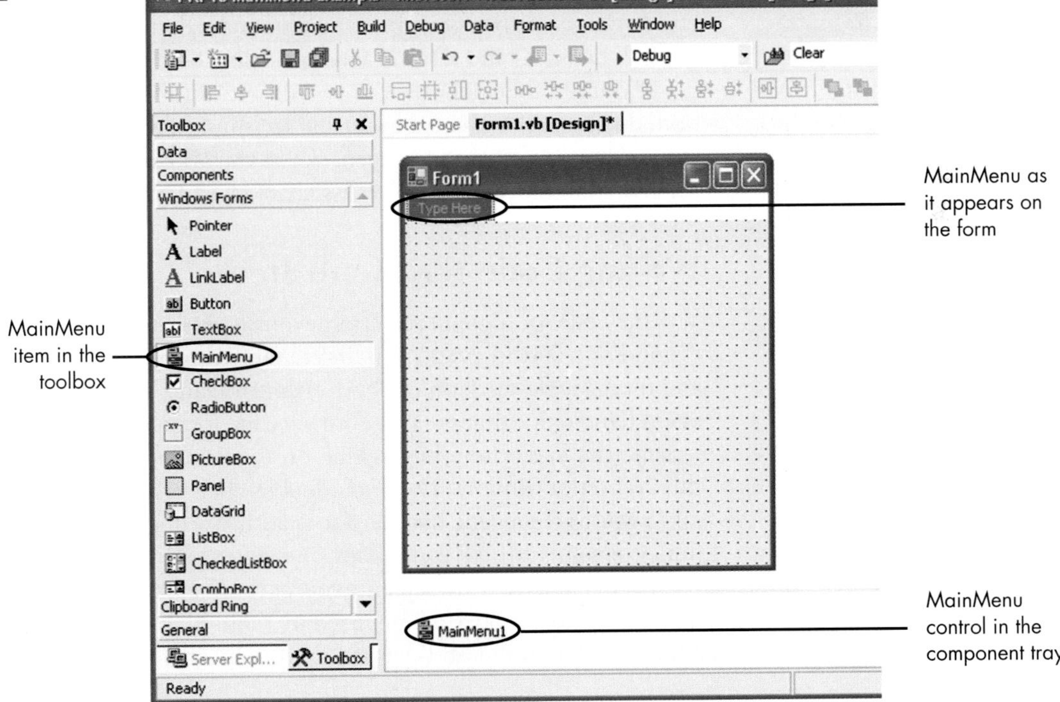


FIGURE 10.2 *MainMenu Control*

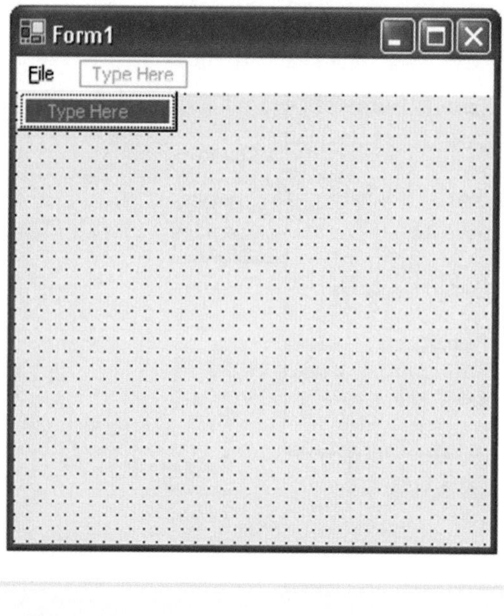


**FIGURE 10.3** *Menu Editing with File as the First Menu Item*

**The ampersand (&) is used to specify an access key that appears as an underlined character in the text. The user can select the menu item by pressing the Alt key with the access key.**

Selecting the MainMenu appearance at the top of the form allows you to type text directly into the main menu. For example, type File for the first menu item in the main menu (see Figure 10-3). You can then use the arrow keys to enter additional menu items below the current menu item or start a second menu item. You can easily build a large main menu this way. You may click on the form when you are done editing the menu and return to menu editing by clicking back on the menu.

If you run the application, you will see that, in terms of navigation and presentation, the menu you created looks and feels just like a traditional Windows application menu. However, nothing happens when you select a menu item. An event procedure is required to specify the action associated with a menu item selection.

## Writing Code for Menu Items

**Each menu item is a separate object that has its own properties. A click event is triggered whenever a menu item is selected.**

Writing code for a menu selection event is similar to writing code for a button click event. For a button event, you first rename the button control to a descriptive name and then double-click on the button control, and Visual Studio takes you to the click event handler for that button. Writing code for menu items is similar. You should first rename the menu item by clicking on the item and changing the name property in the Properties window. Then you double-click on the menu item, and Visual Studio takes you to the event handler for that menu item. The standard prefix for a menu item is *mnu*.

Each menu item is a separate object that has its own properties. Some of the common menu item properties are listed in Table 10-1. You can also add a separator bar to a menu by typing a dash (-) as the Text property of a menu item.

Table 10.1 Common Menu Item Properties

| Property | Description |
|---|---|
| Name | (mnu prefix) The name used to reference the menu item in code |
| Checked | Indicates if a check mark appears next to the text of the menu item |
| Enabled | Indicates if the menu item is available or grayed out |
| RadioChecked | Indicates if a radio button instead of a check mark is displayed if checked |
| Shortcut | Specifies the shortcut associated with the menu item |
| ShowShortcut | Indicates if the shortcut is displayed |
| Text | The caption for the menu item. An ampersand (&) is used to indicate an access key. |
| Visible | Indicates whether the item is visible |

## Main Menu Illustrated

Start a new application, then try the following activities.

### Version 1: Design the Menu

1. Add a MainMenu control from the toolbox to your project. The control will appear in the component tray at the bottom of the Designer Window.
2. Click on the MainMenu appearance at the top of the form. This will activate the main menu editor in the form, with the words *Type Here* appearing in the first menu location. Type the text `&File` (as previously shown in Figure 10-3).
3. Press the down arrow key to move below the File menu option. Type the text `&Exit`.
4. Press the up arrow key and then the right arrow key to move to the second menu item. Type `&Help`. Press the down arrow and type `&About` the application.
5. Click on the form. Only the File and Help menu choices are visible at this time, but clicking on either should reveal the nested menu options available beneath each.
6. Run the application. Select the menu items for Exit and About. What happens? (Remember that we have not written any event procedure code for these events. We will do that in the following section.)

### Version 2: Add Click Event Code

We now add the event procedures for the menu created in the previous section.

1. Select the Exit menu item and set its Name property (in the Properties window) to mnuExit.
2. Double-click on the Exit menu item. Visual Studio takes you to the mnuExit click event procedure. Type `Application.Exit()` as the code for this event. Run the application and verify that selecting File | Exit terminates the application.

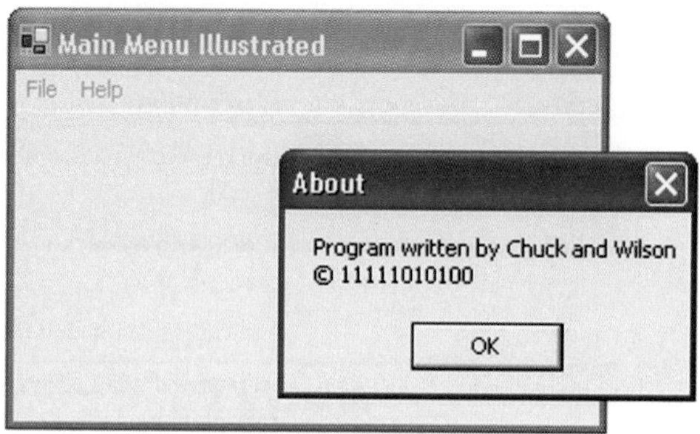


**FIGURE 10.4** *Quick Illustration About Dialog*

**Using the prefix *mnu* in front of all menu names makes your code easier to read and debug.**

3. Return to the Form Designer window. Select the About menu item and set its Name property to mnuAbout. Then double-click on the menu to create the mnuAbout click event procedure. Use a MsgBox statement to inform the user who wrote the program.
4. Run the application. Test the About menu options. A message box similar to Figure 10-4 should appear.

### Version 3: Adding an About Dialog Form

The About information can be displayed using a message box, but it is more professional to add a form that displays the About information.

1. To add an About form to the project, select Add Windows Form from the Project menu, which brings up the Add New Item dialog box. Select Windows Form from the Templates pane, rename the form in the Name text box (e.g., "TAboutForm"), and press the Open button. This will generate a new form class with the specified name. The Solution Explorer window reveals that the solution now includes two files containing form class definitions. Add labels and picture boxes to the About form to include all the desired information.
2. Return to the mnuAbout click event procedure. Delete the old message box statement and replace it with the following code. (Note: TAboutForm is a class, and the following code creates an instance of that class, displays the form as a dialog, and then deletes the instance.)

```
Dim frmAbout As New TAboutForm
frmAbout.ShowDialog()
frmAbout.Dispose()
```

3. Run the application and select the About menu item. The About form should appear similar to Figure 10-5.

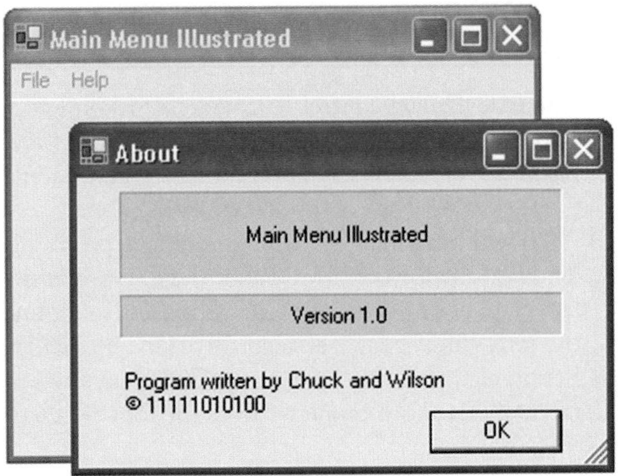


**FIGURE 10.5** *About Dialog Added to Menu Illustration*

## 10-2 Standard Dialog Boxes

**Tip**

**Dialog controls can be added to the component tray or created programmatically in code. Because they are often created for a special purpose, the programmatic approach is often desirable.**

Another professional touch for your application is the use of ***standard dialog boxes*** for tasks such as working with fonts, colors, printing, and files. Visual Studio provides a series of dialog controls, including OpenFileDialog, SaveFileDialog, FontDialog, ColorDialog, PrintDialog, and PrintPreviewDialog (see Figure 10-6). By relying on standard Windows dialog boxes, you get valuable functionality with minimal effort. Another benefit is that the standard Windows dialogs are familiar to users.

These controls can be created in two ways. One approach is to create the control at design time by selecting the control from the toolbox as was done with the MainMenu control. Another option is to programmatically create these dialogs as they are needed. In the following sections, we use the programmatic approach to illustrate these dialogs.

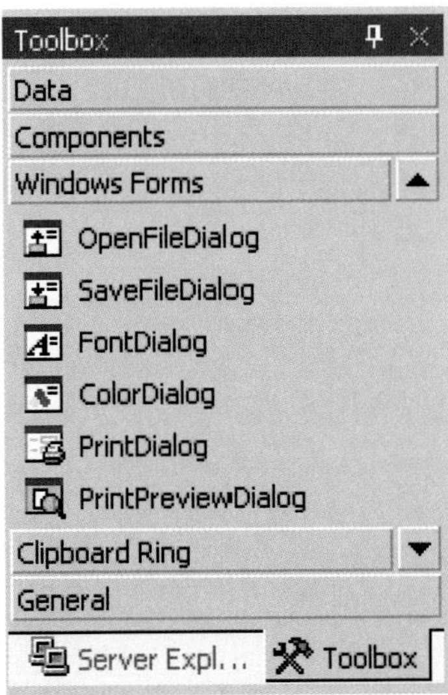


**FIGURE 10.6** *Standard Dialog Controls from the Toolbar*

## 10-3 Font and Color Dialogs

The ***ColorDialog control*** represents a preconfigured dialog that displays the standard "Color" dialog box, allowing the user to select a color or define a custom color (see Figure 10-7). To display the color dialog box, call the ShowDialog method. The Color property holds the color selected by the user.

The ***FontDialog control*** represents a preconfigured dialog that displays the standard Font dialog box. By default, the dialog box shows list boxes for Font, Font Style, and Size; check boxes for effects like Strikeout and Underline; and a sample of how the font will appear (see Figure 10-8). The dialog also contains a drop-down list for Script, e.g., Hebrew or Japanese. To display the font dialog box, call the ShowDialog method. The Font property holds the font selected by the user.

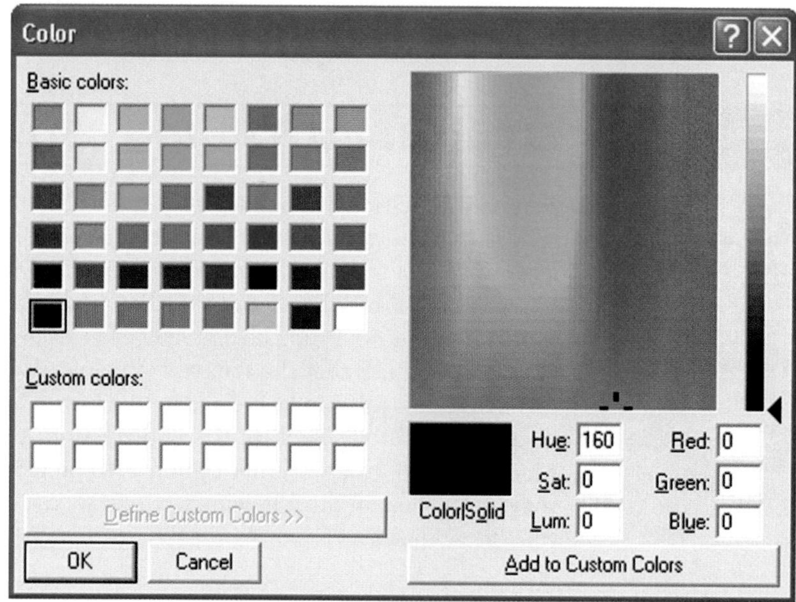


**FIGURE 10.7** *The Color Dialog Box, Expanded to Show Custom Colors*

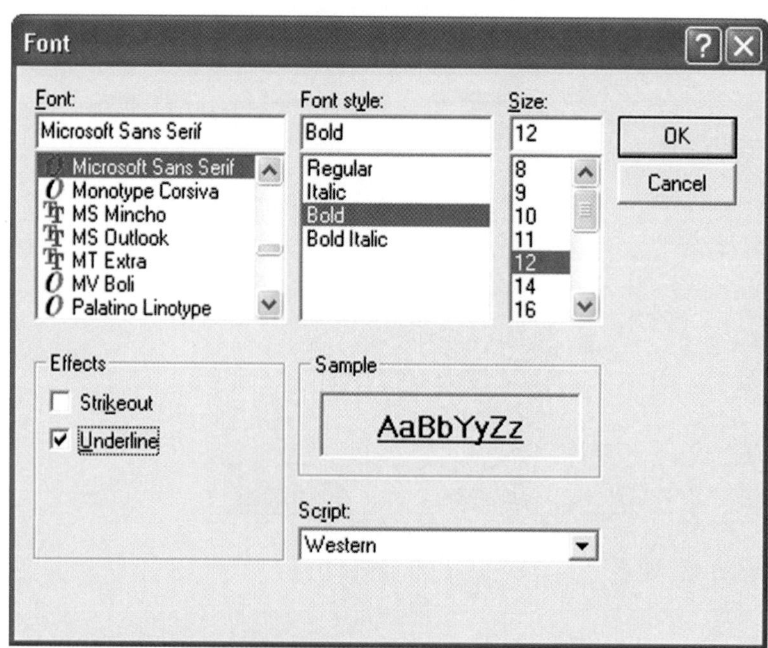


**FIGURE 10.8** *The Font Dialog box*

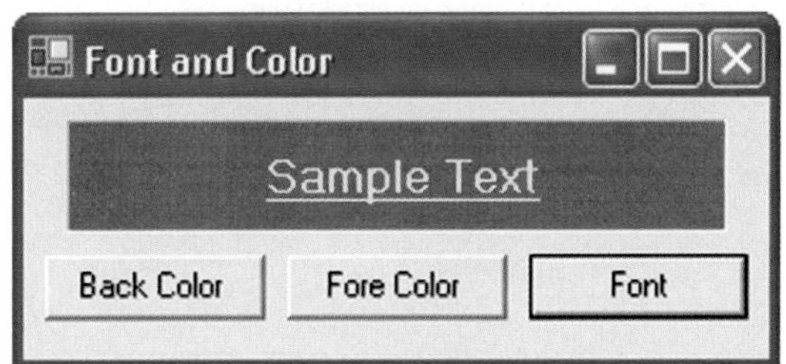


**FIGURE 10.9** *Interface for the Font Color Demo Application*

## Font and Color Dialogs Illustrated

Create an application like the one shown in Figure 10-9, which contains a label and three buttons. The click events for the three buttons use common dialogs to change the label's back color, fore color, and font name. The following code illustrates the use of these two dialogs to change the font and color for a label.

```
'    ********** Design Time Properties *********
'   OBJECT                   PROPERTY        SETTING
'
'   btnBackColor             Text            "Back Color"
'   btnForeColor             Text            "Fore Color"
'   btnFont                  Text            "Font"
'
'   lblSample                Text            "Sample Text"
'                            BorderStyle     Fixed3D
'                            TextAlign       MiddleCenter
Public Class Form1
    Inherits System.Windows.Forms.Form

Windows Form Designer generated code

    ' Creates a ColorDialog to accept user-specified color selection.
    ' Assigns the specified color to the label's BackColor property.
    Private Sub btnBackColor_Click(ByVal sender As System.Object, _
            ByVal e As System.EventArgs) Handles btnBackColor.Click
        Dim dlgColor As New ColorDialog
        dlgColor.ShowDialog()
        lblSample.BackColor = dlgColor.Color
    End Sub

    'Creates a ColorDialog to accept user-specified color selection.
    'Assigns the specified color to the Label's ForeColor property.
    Private Sub btnForeColor_Click(ByVal sender As System.Object, _
            ByVal e As System.EventArgs) Handles btnForeColor.Click
        Dim dlgColor As New ColorDialog
        dlgColor.ShowDialog()
        lblSample.ForeColor = dlgColor.Color
    End Sub

    'Creates a FontDialog to accept user-specified font selection.
    'Assigns the specified font to the Label's Font property.
    Private Sub btnFont_Click(ByVal sender As System.Object, _
            ByVal e As System.EventArgs) Handles btnFont.Click
```

```
        Dim dlgFont As New FontDialog
        dlgFont.ShowDialog()
        lblSample.Font = dlgFont.Font
    End Sub

End Class
```

## 10-4 Text File Input/Output

The ***OpenFileDialog control*** represents a preconfigured dialog for selecting a file to be opened (see Figure 10-10). The InitialDirectory property specifies the initial directory displayed by the file dialog box. The Filter property determines the choices that appear in the "Save as file type" or "Files of type" box in the dialog box. Use the ShowDialog method to display the dialog box. The FileName property is a string containing the file name selected in the file dialog box. (The ***SaveFileDialog control*** shares much of the behavior of the OpenFileDialog control, including capturing a string value for FileName.)

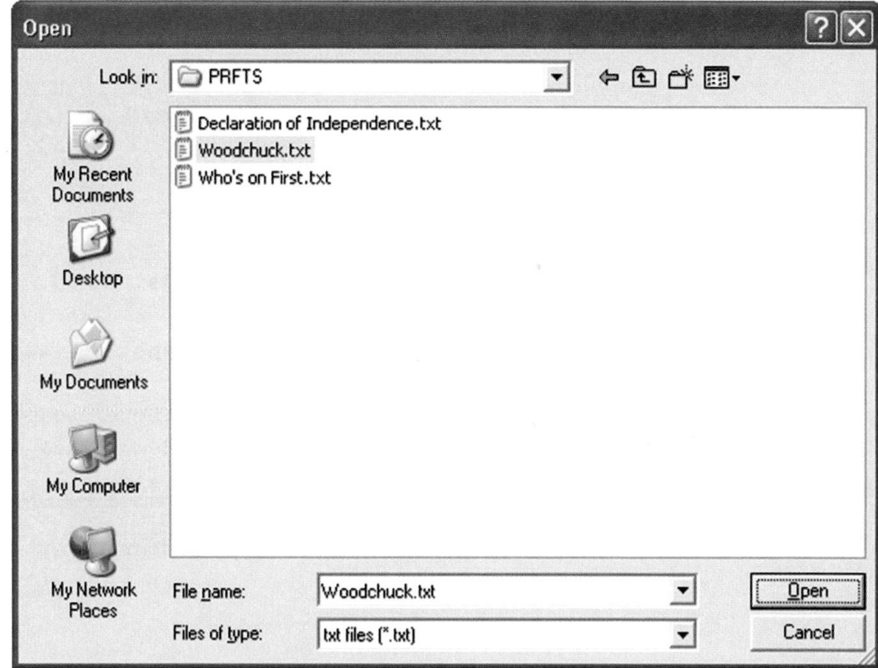


**FIGURE 10.10**
*The Open File Dialog*

## Streaming Data

The OpenFileDialog and SaveFileDialog controls provide a professional means to capture file names from the user. However, capturing the file name is all they do. To actually transfer data between the application and a file, you must write your own data transfer logic.

The ***StreamReader*** class is designed for character input. The file to be read from can be opened using the File.OpenText(*path*) function, where *path* specifies the input file. Once the reader has been assigned to an opened file, a series of stream reader methods may be called to read information from the file, as shown in Table 10-2.

**Table 10.2 Common StreamReader Methods**

| Method | Description |
|---|---|
| Close | Closes the StreamReader and releases any system resources associated with the reader |
| Peek | Returns the next available character but does not consume it |
| Read | Reads the next character or next set of characters from the input stream |
| ReadBlock | Reads a maximum of count characters from the current stream and writes the data to buffer, beginning at index |
| ReadLine | Reads a line of characters from the current stream and returns the data as a string |
| ReadToEnd | Reads the stream from the current position to the end of the stream |

Likewise, the ***StreamWriter*** class is designed for character output. The file to be written to can be assigned using the File.CreateText(*path*) function, where *path* specifies the output file. If the file specified by *path* does not exist, it is created. If the file does exist, its contents are overwritten. Once the writer has been assigned to an opened file, a series of stream writer methods may be called to write information from the file, as shown in Table 10-3.

**Table 10.3 Common StreamWriter Methods**

| Method | Description |
|---|---|
| Close | Closes the current StreamWriter and the underlying stream |
| Flush | Clears all buffers for the current writer and causes any buffered data to be written to the underlying stream |
| Write | Writes to the stream |
| WriteLine | Writes data as specified by the overloaded parameters, followed by a line terminator |

**MENTOR**

StreamReader and StreamWriter are useful for simple text I/O. However, StreamReader and StreamWriter are only two examples of the more general *Stream* class, and streams can be used to support various I/O activities. Anyone interested in learning more about streams should consult the Visual Studio Help files.

VB.NET also supports application I/O through database files (rather than text files or some other file type). Typically, a business stores its valuable information in a database file rather than in a text file. A discussion of databases, including how to read from and write to them, is covered in Chapter 11.

## Text File I/O Illustrated

Create an application similar to the one shown in Figure 10-11, which contains a text box and two buttons. The click events for the two buttons input the contents of a text file into the text box and save the text box contents to a text file. The following code illustrates how file dialogs and streams may be used to move text data between a file and the application.

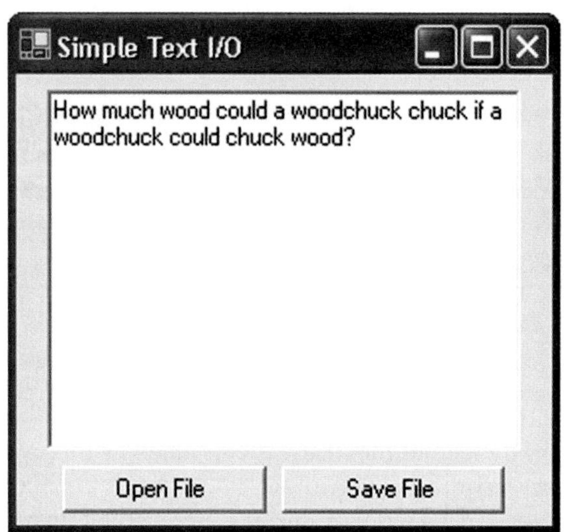


**FIGURE 10.11** *Interface for the Simple Text I/O Demo Application*

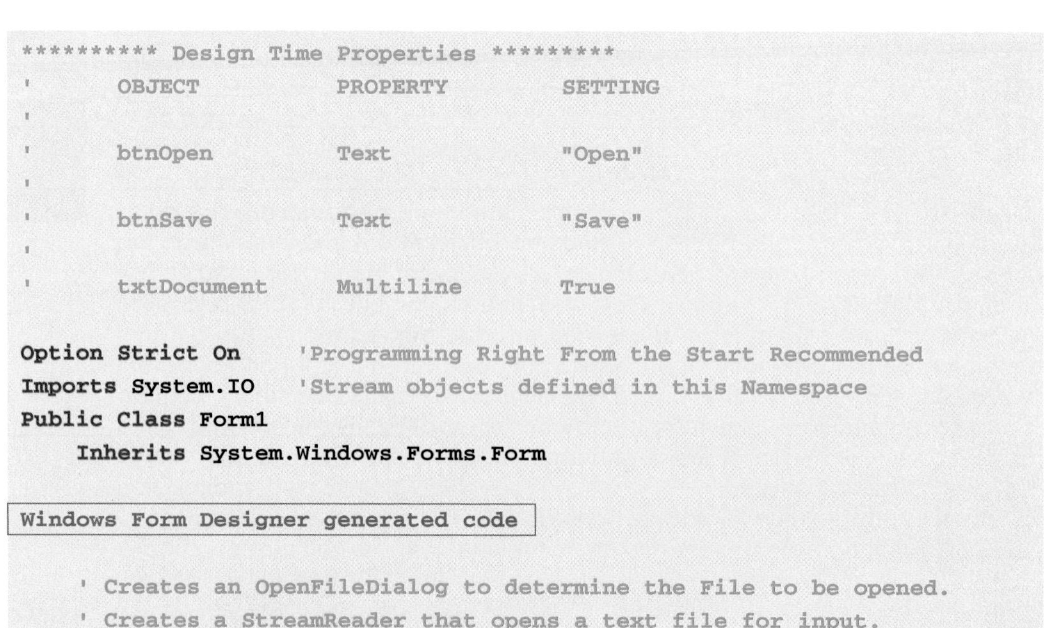

```
********** Design Time Properties *********
'       OBJECT          PROPERTY        SETTING
'
'       btnOpen         Text            "Open"
'
'       btnSave         Text            "Save"
'
'       txtDocument     Multiline       True

Option Strict On    'Programming Right From the Start Recommended
Imports System.IO   'Stream objects defined in this Namespace
Public Class Form1
    Inherits System.Windows.Forms.Form

Windows Form Designer generated code

    ' Creates an OpenFileDialog to determine the File to be opened.
    ' Creates a StreamReader that opens a text file for input.
    ' The entire file is read as a String using the ReadToEnd method.
```

```
    Private Sub btnOpen_Click(ByVal sender As System.Object, _
              ByVal e As System.EventArgs) Handles btnOpen.Click
        Dim dlgOpenFile As New OpenFileDialog
        Dim Reader As StreamReader

        ' InitialDirectory is optional, and sometimes helpful
        dlgOpenFile.InitialDirectory = "C:\"

        ' Filter is also optional, and sometimes helpful
        dlgOpenFile.Filter = "txt files (*.txt)|*.txt" _
            "|All files (*.*)|*.*"

        If dlgOpenFile.ShowDialog = DialogResult.OK Then
            Reader = File.OpenText(dlgOpenFile.FileName)
            txtDocument.Text = Reader.ReadToEnd
            Reader.Close()
        End If
    End Sub

    ' Creates a SaveFileDialog to determine the File to be created.
    ' Creates a StreamWriter that creates a text file for output.
    ' The Flush method clears the buffer, sending any buffered
    ' data to the stream.
    Private Sub btnSave_Click(ByVal sender As System.Object, _
              ByVal e As System.EventArgs) Handles btnSave.Click
        Dim dlgSaveFile As New SaveFileDialog
        Dim Writer As StreamWriter

        ' InitialDirectory is optional, and sometimes helpful
        dlgSaveFile.InitialDirectory = "C:\"

        ' Filter is also optional, and sometimes helpful
        dlgSaveFile.Filter = "txt files (*.txt)|*.txt" _
            "|All files (*.*)|*.*"

        If dlgSaveFile.ShowDialog() = DialogResult.OK Then
            Writer = File.CreateText(dlgSaveFile.FileName)
            Writer.Write(txtDocument.Text)
            Writer.Flush()
            Writer.Close()
        End If
    End Sub

End Class
```

## 10-5 Print and PrintPreview Dialogs

We now present the last two common dialogs, the PrintDialog and PrintPreview-Dialog. The ***PrintDialog control*** is a preconfigured dialog box used to select a printer, choose the pages to print, and determine other print-related settings in Windows applications. You can enable users to print various parts of their documents: print all, print a selected page range, or print a selection. The Document property is set to a

PrintDocument object, which has the properties describing what to print and the ability to print within a Windows application. To display the print dialog box, call the ShowDialog method. The print dialog box saves the user's settings in the PrintDocument object, which can then be printed using the Print method.

>>> **Tip**
**PrintPreview's Antialiasing property can make the text appear smoother, but it can also make the display slower; to use it, set UseAntiAlias to true.**

The ***PrintPreview control*** is a preconfigured dialog box used to display how the document will appear when printed. The control contains buttons for printing, zooming in, displaying one or multiple pages, and closing the dialog box. The Document property is set to a PrintDocument object, which has the properties describing what to print and the ability to print within a Windows application. To display the print preview dialog box, call the ShowDialog method.

VB.NET also provides a ***PageSetupDialog control,*** which is a preconfigured dialog box that allows users to manipulate page settings, including margins and paper orientation. The Document property is set to a PrintDocument object. To display the print preview dialog box, call the ShowDialog method. The user's selections are stored in the PageSettings property and should then be copied to the PrintDocument object.

When PrintDocument's Print method is called, the PrintPage event is called for every page that is printed. The Graphics.MeasureString method measures the size of the string and determines the number of characters fitted and lines filled for the specified string, font object, maximum layout size, and string format. The Graphics.PrintString method draws the string using the font, brush, destination point, and format. The HasMorePages property indicates whether an additional page should be printed.

## Print and PrintPreview Illustrated

Create a new application with three buttons and a text box. The text box should be multi-line and contain text to be printed. The following code illustrates how PageSetup, PrintPreview, and Print dialogs can be used to give a professional printing touch to an application.

```
'      ********** Design Time Properties *********
'      OBJECT           PROPERTY       SETTING
'
'      btnPrint         Text           "Print"
'
'      btnPrintPreview Text            "Print Preview"
'
'      btnPageSetup     Text           "Page Setup"
'
'      txtDocument      Multiline      True

Option Strict On                'Right From The Start Recommended
Imports System.Drawing.Printing 'Namespace for PrintDocument

Public Class Form1
    Inherits System.Windows.Forms.Form

    'Module Level Scope Declarations
    Dim WithEvents mPrintDoc As New PrintDocument
    Dim mPrintPosition As Integer

Windows Form Designer generated code
```

```
Private Sub Form1_Load(ByVal sender As System.Object, _
            ByVal e As System.EventArgs) Handles MyBase.Load
    txtDocument.Text = "Declaration of Independence (July 4, 1776)" & _
        vbCrLf & vbCrLf & vbTab & _
        "WHEN in the Course of human Events, it becomes necessary " & _
        "for one People to dissolve the Political Bands which have " & _
        "connected them with another, and to assume among the Powers " & _
        "of the Earth, the separate and equal Station to which the " & _
        "Laws of Nature and of Nature's God entitle them, a decent " & _
        "Respect to the Opinions of Mankind requires that they should " & _
        "declare the causes which impel them to the Separation." & _
        vbCrLf & vbCrLf & vbTab & _
        "WE hold these Truths to be self-evident, that all Men are " & _
        "created equal, that they are endowed by their Creator with " & _
        "certain unalienable Rights, that among these are Life, " & _
        "Liberty and the Pursuit of Happiness - That to secure these " & _
        "Rights, Governments are instituted among Men, deriving their " & _
        "just Powers from the Consent of the Governed, that whenever " & _
        "any Form of Government becomes destructive of these Ends, " & _
        "it is the Right of the People to alter or to abolish it, " & _
        "and to institute new Government, laying its Foundation on " & _
        "such Principles, and organizing its Powers in such Form, " & _
        "as to them shall seem most likely to effect their Safety " & _
        "and Happiness. Prudence, indeed, will dictate that " & _
        "Governments long established should not be changed for " & _
        "light and transient Causes; and accordingly all Experience " & _
        "hath shewn, that Mankind are more disposed to suffer, " & _
        "while Evils are sufferable, than to right themselves by " & _
        "abolishing the Forms to which they are accustomed. But when " & _
        "a long Train of Abuses and Usurpations, pursuing invariably " & _
        "the same Object, evinces a Design to reduce them under " & _
        "absolute Despotism, it is their Right, it is their Duty, " & _
        "to throw off such Government, and to provide new Guards for " & _
        "their future Security. Such has been the patient Sufferance " & _
        "of these Colonies; and such is now the Necessity which " & _
        "constrains them to alter their former Systems of Government. " & _
        "The History of the present King of Great Britain is a " & _
        "History of repeated Injuries and Usurpations, all having " & _
        "in direct Object the Establishment of an absolute Tyranny " & _
        "over these States. To prove this, let Facts be submitted " & _
        "to a candid World."
End Sub

'The PrintPage event is raised for each page to be printed.  Both the Print
'and PrintPreview dialog boxes trigger this event.  MeasureString is used to
'calculate how much text will fit on an entire page (based on the specified
'font and the page margins), and DrawString is used to print that entire block of
'text. Printing formatted text would require word-by-word processing (vs
'page-by-page as done below) which is more complicated.
Private Sub mPrintDoc_PrintPage(ByVal sender As Object, _
            ByVal e As System.Drawing.Printing.PrintPageEventArgs) _
            Handles mPrintDoc.PrintPage
    Dim CharsOnPage, LinesOnPage As Integer
    Dim Fmt As New StringFormat
```

```
    Dim fntPrint As New Font("Microsoft Sans Serif", 24)
    Dim PrintWidth, PrintHeight As Integer
    Dim PrintRect As RectangleF

    'Establish print area based on selected margins
    'PrintRect is based on mPrintDoc's DefaultPageSettings property.
    With mPrintDoc.DefaultPageSettings
        If .Landscape = True Then
            PrintHeight = .PaperSize.Width - .Margins.Top - .Margins.Bottom
            PrintWidth = .PaperSize.Height - .Margins.Left - .Margins.Right
        Else
            'Portrait (default)
            PrintHeight = .PaperSize.Height - .Margins.Top - .Margins.Bottom
            PrintWidth = .PaperSize.Width - .Margins.Left - .Margins.Right
        End If
        PrintRect = New RectangleF(.Margins.Left, .Margins.Top, _
                                   PrintWidth, PrintHeight)
    End With

    e.Graphics.MeasureString(Mid(txtDocument.Text, mPrintPosition + 1), _
            fntPrint, PrintRect.Size, Fmt, CharsOnPage, LinesOnPage)

    e.Graphics.DrawString(Mid(txtDocument.Text, mPrintPosition + 1), _
            fntPrint, Brushes.Black, PrintRect, Fmt)

    mPrintPosition += CharsOnPage     'Running total in module variable
    If mPrintPosition < txtDocument.Text.Length Then
        e.HasMorePages = True
    Else
        e.HasMorePages = False
        mPrintPosition = 0            'Reset to 0 for next Print request
    End If
End Sub

'Uses a PrintDialog control to allow the user to select the desired printer
'and other printing options.
Private Sub btnPrint_Click(ByVal sender As System.Object, _
        ByVal e As System.EventArgs) Handles btnPrint.Click
    Dim dlgPrint As New PrintDialog
    dlgPrint.Document = mPrintDoc

    If dlgPrint.ShowDialog() = DialogResult.OK Then
        mPrintDoc.Print()
    End If
End Sub

'Creates a PrintPreviewDialog to preview the text using the mPrintDoc setting
Private Sub btnPrintPreview_Click(ByVal sender As System.Object, _
        ByVal e As System.EventArgs) Handles btnPrintPreview.Click
    Dim dlgPrintPreview As New PrintPreviewDialog
    Try
        dlgPrintPreview.Document = mPrintDoc
        dlgPrintPreview.ShowDialog()
```

```
        Catch
            MsgBox("An error occured while trying to load the document. " _
                "Make sure you have access to a printer.  A printer must " _
                "be connected and accessible for Print Preview to work.")
        End Try
    End Sub

    'Uses a PageSetupDialog control, which allows the user to specify things
    'like paper size, portrait or landscape, number of copies, etc.
    Private Sub btnPageSetup_Click(ByVal sender As System.Object, _
                ByVal e As System.EventArgs) Handles btnPageSetup.Click
        Dim dlgPageSetup As New PageSetupDialog
        dlgPageSetup.Document = mPrintDoc
        dlgPageSetup.PageSettings = mPrintDoc.DefaultPageSettings

        If dlgPageSetup.ShowDialog = DialogResult.OK Then
            mPrintDoc.DefaultPageSettings = dlgPageSetup.PageSettings
        End If
    End Sub
End Class
```

## ASK THE AUTHOR

**Q** How long did it take you to type in the first two paragraphs of the Declaration of Independence?

**A** Using copy and paste it was not too bad. The reason I hard coded the two paragraphs is that I wanted the example to focus on the Print and PrintPreview dialogs. The full Declaration is almost five times longer. A better way would be to read the entire Declaration from a text file before printing. This modified version appears as a programming exercise at the end of this chapter.

# 10-6 Multimedia

We conclude this chapter by introducing the ***Windows Media Player control.*** The media player plays video and sound files in many different formats, including MPEG (Motion Picture Experts Group), AVI (audio-video interleave), WAV (Windows wave-file format) and MIDI (Musical Instrument Digital Interface).

The media player is not part of the standard toolbox, but it can be added as follows. From the Tools menu, select Add/Remove Toolbox Items. In the resulting dialog, select the COM Components tab, then scroll down and select Window Media Player (make sure the check mark appears), then press OK. The Windows Media Player control should now appear at the bottom of the Windows Forms controls in the toolbox.

The Windows Media Player is a powerful control with a great deal of functionality. Unfortunately, the documentation is rather poor, and often the best method of learning is to experiment with the player. (A well-documented media player will hopefully come with future versions of Visual Studio.)

One common use of the Multimedia control is to provide a Media Splash at the beginning of an application. It can also be used to add sound effects to an application.

## Multimedia Illustrated

The Multimedia control can provide significant added value to your application. In this example, we use a media control to present an opening splash, provide sound effects for your application, and allow the user to play selected media files.

### Opening Splash

1. Start a new project. Copy the file "Splash.avi" from the student CD into the bin folder within the new project. Add a multimedia control and position it so it covers the form (Figure 10-12). Set the Name property to **`MediaPlayer`** and the FileName property to **`Splash.avi`**. Also set the ShowControls property to false to remove the media navigation from the bottom of the control.
2. Write a MediaPlayer_EndStream event that sets the Visible property to false. This will hide the media player, making the entire form (and all its controls) accessible to the user.
3. Run the application. It should begin with the Splash media, which then disappears to reveal the application.

**FIGURE 10.12** *Media Player Opening Splash*

### Sound Effects

1. Move the media player (without resizing it) so that you can see the majority of the form. Add three buttons named Chimes, Chord, and Ding (Figure 10-13). Each button should have a button click event that changes the FileName property of the media control to Chimes.wav or Chord.wav or Ding.wav as appropriate. If the media's AutoPlay property is true (the default), then each sound file will play automatically at runtime when the file name is loaded.
2. Reposition the media player back to the center of the form. Run the application. The opening Media Splash should play; then the media control should become invisible, thus revealing the buttons. Clicking the buttons should play appropriate sounds.

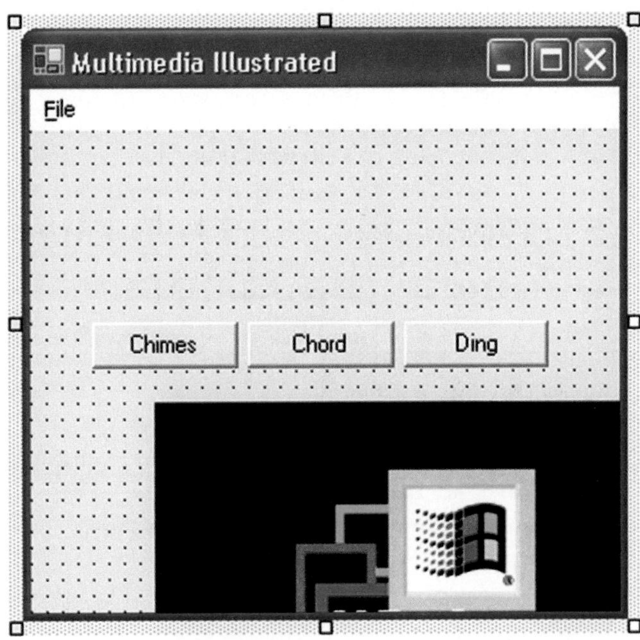


**FIGURE 10.13** *Media Player Sound Effects*

### User Selected Media

Add a MainMenu with a File | Open menu item. Use the OpenFileDialog to get a file name from the user, and then set the media player's FileName to the selected file. If the media file is graphical, the media player will automatically display. If it is audio only, the media player will remain hidden. The code for the entire media application is presented as follows.

```
'    *********** Design Time Properties ***********
'    OBJECT                 PROPERTY          SETTING
'
'    mnuMain
'    mnuFile                Text              "File"
'    mnuOpen                Text              "Open"
'    mnuExit                Text              "Exit"
'
'    MediaPlayer            ShowControls      False
'                           FileName          "Splash.avi"
'     (Splash.avi should be in the project's bin directory)
'
'    btnChimes              Text              "Chimes"
'
'    btnChord               Text              "Chord"
'
'    btnDing                Text              "Ding"
'
Option Strict On           'Right From The Start Recommended

Public Class Form1
    Inherits System.Windows.Forms.Form
```

```
Windows Form Designer generated code

    'Creates an OpenFileDialog to determine the File to be opened.
    'Assigns the specified file to the MediaPlayer control.
    Private Sub mnuOpen_Click(ByVal sender As System.Object, _
                ByVal e As System.EventArgs) Handles mnuOpen.Click
        Dim myOpenFileDialog As New OpenFileDialog

        myOpenFileDialog.ShowDialog()
        Try
            'When MediaPlayer.AutoStart = True (the default), then
            'the MediaPlayer will automatically start when the
            'FileName property is assigned
            MediaPlayer.FileName = myOpenFileDialog.FileName
        Catch exc As Exception
            MsgBox("Exception: "  exc.Message)
        End Try
    End Sub

    'Selecting the Exit menu option terminates the application.
    Private Sub mnuExit_Click(ByVal sender As System.Object, _
                ByVal e As System.EventArgs) Handles mnuExit.Click
        Application.Exit()
    End Sub

    Private Sub MediaPlayer_EndOfStream(ByVal sender As Object, _
            ByVal e As AxMediaPlayer._MediaPlayerEvents_EndOfStreamEvent) _
            Handles MediaPlayer.EndOfStream
        'Hide MediaPlayer after Splash.avi finishes
        MediaPlayer.Visible = False
    End Sub

    Private Sub btnChimes_Click(ByVal sender As System.Object, _
                ByVal e As System.EventArgs) Handles btnChimes.Click
        '(Chimes.wav should be in the project's bin directory)
        MediaPlayer.FileName = "Chimes.wav"
    End Sub

    Private Sub btnChord_Click(ByVal sender As System.Object, _
                ByVal e As System.EventArgs) Handles btnChord.Click
        '(Chord.wav should be in the project's bin directory)
        MediaPlayer.FileName = "Chord.wav"
    End Sub

    Private Sub btnDing_Click(ByVal sender As System.Object, _
                ByVal e As System.EventArgs) Handles btnDing.Click
        '(Ding.wav should be in the project's bin directory)
        MediaPlayer.FileName = "Splash.avi"
    End Sub

End Class
```

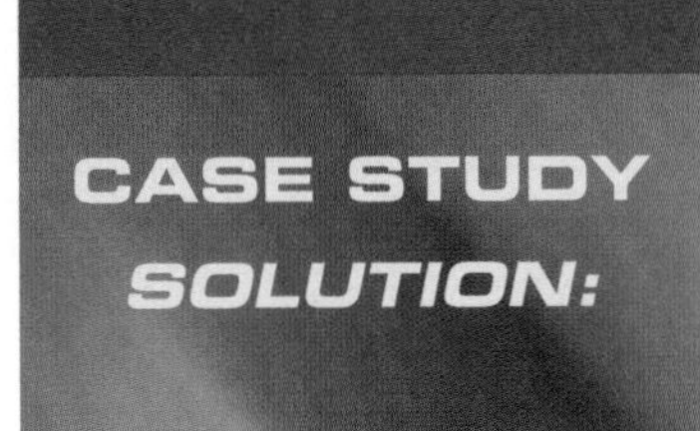


# Snakes Game Pro

Wilson is sitting near a now-cold cup of coffee when Chuck arrives. "Okay, here are my ideas for the Professional version of Snakes Game. First, we should add an opening media clip to set the mood. After the opening splash, the game board should be displayed. But now we have added a main menu for starting a new game and exiting. The menu should also allow the user to select the color scheme for the game. Finally, we should maintain the high score in a file so it is remembered each time the application is loaded. What do you think?"

Chuck and Wilson stare at each other without speaking for a few moments, an activity that Chuck has come to understand as mutual respect. Eventually, Chuck breaks the silence by saying, "Well, I would love to stay and chat some more, but I think I will get started on these ideas."

## Design

The design specifies how the solution will work in general terms. Chuck begins by sketching the interface for the Snakes Game Pro and specifying the Name property for all the necessary controls. The interface contains space for the one hundred board game labels that are created programmatically when the form loads. The interface includes a main menu and a Media Player control. The interface design is shown in Figure 10-14.

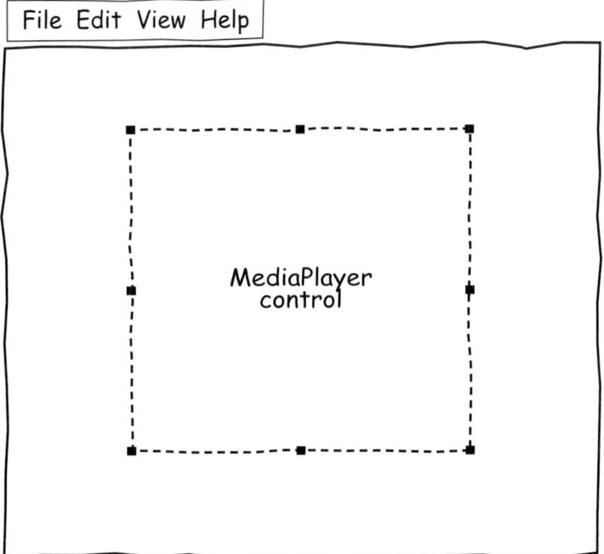


**FIGURE 10.14** *Interface Design for Snakes Game Pro*

The design should also include a high-level specification of all the actions and behavior required by the project. This can be done using flowchart or pseudocode notation and should describe behavior without getting into details of implementation. Table 10-4 provides pseudocode descriptions of the event procedures, sub procedures, and functions used in the Snakes Game Pro design.

**Table 10.4 Design Pseudocode for Snakes Game Pro**

| Event Procedures | Behavior |
|---|---|
| tmrForceMove_Tick | Move the snake in the current direction |
| frmSnakes_Load | 1. Play splash |
| | 2. Load high score |
| MediaPlayer_EndOfStream | Hide the media player after splash |
| frmSnakes_Resize | Call InitializeBoard |
| mnuStart_Click | Call StartNewGame |
| mnuExit_Click | Confirm exit and exit |
| mnuSnakeColor_Click | Change the color of the snake to a user specified color |
| mnuBoardColor_Click | Change the color of the board to a user specified color |
| mnuNumCols_Click | Change the number of columns and reinitialize the board |
| mnuNumRows_Click | Change the number of rows and reinitialize the board |
| mnuHighScore_Click | Display the high score |
| mnuAbout_Click | Display game information |
| **Sub Procedures** | **Behavior** |
| StartNewGame | 1. Initialize the board |
| | 2. Initialize the snake |
| | 3. Randomly place apple |
| | 4. Start moving the snake |
| InitializeBoard | 1. Resize board to fit client area of window |
| | 2. Destroy old board (if not first game) |
| | 3. Create all of the board labels dynamically |
| | 4. Draw the board |
| DrawBoard | 1. Erase old board information |
| | 2. Show the current snake position |
| SnakeCrash | Handle snake crash, including end of game and high score check |
| MoveSnake | 1. Disable the timer |
| | 2. End game if snake will hit wall |
| | 3. End game if snake will hit self |
| | 4. Update the snake's position |
| | 5. If food has been eaten, grow snake, update score, and move food |
| | 6. Draw the new board |
| | 7. Re-enable the timer |
| LoadHighScore | Loads high score from a text file |
| SaveHighScore | Saves high score to a text file |
| **Functions** | **Behavior** |
| WillHitWall | Returns whether or not the snake's current move will cause snake to hit a wall |
| WillHitSnake | Returns whether or not the snake's current move will cause snake to hit itself |
| GetNewHeadValue | Returns the new location for the head based on the current head location and the movement direction |
| HandleKeyPress | Move the snake in the direction indicated by the keypress (ignore 180 degree turns); returns whether or not a direction key was pressed |
| ProcessCmdKey | Check for a keydown message and call HandleKeyPress if appropriate; returns whether or not the message was handled |

### Implementation

After Chuck completes the general design, he must implement the details. The first step of implementation is to build the GUI. Figure 10-15 illustrates the Snakes Game Pro GUI at design time. (Remember that the one hundred labels are not created until the program executes.)

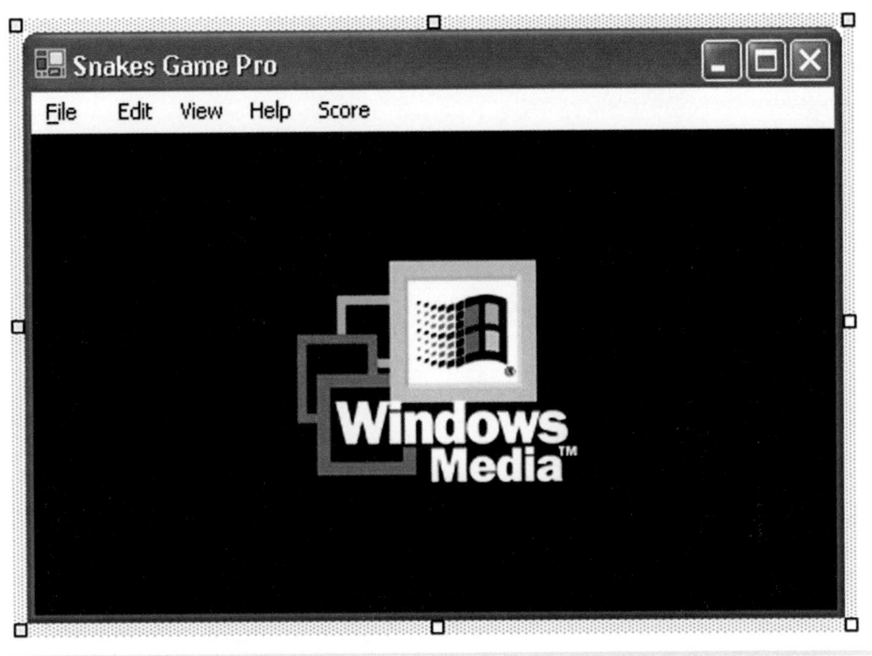


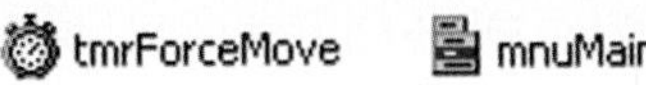


**FIGURE 10.15** *Snakes Game Pro User Interface*

The second step is to implement the functionality described in the pseudocode design. It is also a good habit to document important design time property values for the form and interface controls. The solution code with good documentation follows.

```
' Author: Chuck & Wilson
' Project: Snakes Game
' Description:  This a game in which the player uses the keyboard to
'               move a snake in real time.  When the snake eats food, it grows
'               in length.  The game is over when the snake runs into itself
'               or into a wall.  The player's score is determined by the
'               length of the snake.
'
' Revision 1.1: This revision adds the following features:
'               1) A multimedia splash screen at the start of the game.
'               2) A Menu now provides access to some of the game's features.
'               3) The user can specify the colors of the snake and the board.
'               4) The high score is saved and can be viewed.
'               5) An "About" dialog has been added.
'               6) The btnStart button has been deleted; a new game is now
'                  started through File|Start
'
'
```

```
'
'    *********** Design Time Properties ***********
'   OBJECT                   PROPERTY        SETTING
'
'   tmrForceMove             Interval        500
'
'   *DELETED* btnStart       Text            "Start Game"
'
'   Revision 1.1
'   mnuMain
'       mnuFile              Text            "File"
'       mnuStart             Text            "Start New Game"
'                            ShortCut        CtrlN
'       mnuExit              Text            "E&xit"
'       mnuEdit              Text            "Edit"
'       mnuSnakeColor        Text            "Snake Color"
'       mnuBoardColor        Text            "Board Color"
'       mnuNumCols           Text            "Number of Columns"
'       mnuNumRows           Text            "Number of Rows"
'       mnuView              Text            "View"
'       mnuHighScore         Text            "High Score"
'       mnuHelp              Text            "Help"
'       mnuAbout             Text            "About..."
'       mnuScore             Text            "Score"
'
'   MediaPlayer              ShowControls    False
'                            Dock            Fill
'

Option Strict On         'Programming Right From the Start Recommended
Imports System.IO        'Stream objects defined in this Namespace

Public Class frmSnakes
    Inherits System.Windows.Forms.Form

    ' Directional constants
    Const DIR_UP As Integer = 1
    Const DIR_LEFT As Integer = 2
    Const DIR_RIGHT As Integer = 3
    Const DIR_DOWN As Integer = 4

    ' Module-level declarations
    Dim mBoard() As Label
    Dim mSnake(0) As Integer 'Array of integers (board positions)
    Dim mDirection As Integer 'Last Key direction pressed
    Dim mSnakeColor As System.Drawing.Color = Color.Red
    Dim mBoardColor As System.Drawing.Color = Color.White
    Dim mBoardWidth As Integer = 14  'Number of columns in the board
    Dim mBoardHeight As Integer = 14 'Number of rows in the board
    Dim mIsPlayingFlag As Boolean = False

    ' Rev 1.1 - Added high score
    Dim mHighScore As String
```

```
Windows Form Designer generated code

    Private Sub StartNewGame()
        InitializeBoard()
        ' Initialize the snake
        ReDim mSnake(0)                                    'Initial length is 1
        mSnake(0) = CInt(0.75 * mBoardWidth * mBoardHeight) 'near the bottom
        mDirection = DIR_UP                                'direction is up

        ' Randomly place apple
        mBoard(CInt(Int((Rnd() * UBound(mBoard))))).Text = "@"

        ' Start moving the snake
        tmrForceMove.Enabled = True
        mIsPlayingFlag = True
    End Sub

    Private Sub InitializeBoard()
        Dim Index, X, Y As Integer
        Dim NumBoardElements As Integer
        Dim Margin As Integer = 10
        ' Rev 1.1 - Make the board fit the client area of the Windows Form
        Dim XSize As Integer = (Me.ClientSize.Width - 2 * Margin) \ mBoardWidth
        Dim YSize As Integer = (Me.ClientSize.Height - 2 * Margin) \ mBoardHeight

        If Not (mBoard Is Nothing) Then
            For Index = 0 To UBound(mBoard)
                mBoard(Index).Dispose()
            Next
        End If
        ' Create all of the board labels dynamically at runtime
        NumBoardElements = mBoardWidth * mBoardHeight
        ReDim mBoard(NumBoardElements - 1)
        Index = 0
        For Y = 0 To mBoardHeight - 1
            For X = 0 To mBoardWidth - 1
                Dim NewLabel As New Label
                NewLabel.BorderStyle = BorderStyle.FixedSingle
                NewLabel.Text = ""
                'NewLabel.Text = CStr(I) 'uncomment to see index values
                NewLabel.Location = New Point(Margin + X * XSize, Margin + Y * YSize)
                NewLabel.Width = XSize
                NewLabel.Height = YSize
                ' Rev 1.1 - Added resize of font
                NewLabel.Font = New System.Drawing.Font("Microsoft Sans Serif", _
                                        CInt(YSize * 0.5))
                Me.Controls.Add(NewLabel)
                mBoard(Index) = NewLabel
                Index = Index + 1
            Next X
        Next Y
        If mIsPlayingFlag Then DrawBoard()
    End Sub
```

```
'DrawBoard sets the backcolor to white for every board element, then
'sets the backcolor to red for every board element matching the snakes
'position.
Sub DrawBoard()
    Dim Index As Integer

    'Erase old snake information
    For Index = 0 To UBound(mBoard)
        mBoard(Index).BackColor = mBoardColor
    Next

    'Show the current snake position
    For Index = 0 To UBound(mSnake)
        mBoard(mSnake(Index)).BackColor = mSnakeColor
    Next
End Sub

'WillHitWall returns TRUE if the snake is about to crash into one of the
'four wall, and returns FALSE otherwise.
Function WillHitWall() As Boolean
    Dim HeadX, HeadY As Integer

    ' Find the X, Y position of the head of the snake
    HeadX = mSnake(0) Mod mBoardWidth
    HeadY = mSnake(0) \ mBoardWidth

    If mDirection = DIR_UP And HeadY = 0 Then Return True
    If mDirection = DIR_DOWN And HeadY = (mBoardHeight - 1) Then Return True
    If mDirection = DIR_LEFT And HeadX = 0 Then Return True
    If mDirection = DIR_RIGHT And HeadX = (mBoardWidth - 1) Then Return True
    Return False
End Function

'WillHitSnake returns TRUE if the snake is about to move into itself, and
'returns FALSE otherwise.
Function WillHitSnake(ByVal NewPosition As Integer) As Boolean
    Dim Index As Integer
    For Index = 0 To UBound(mSnake)
        If NewPosition = mSnake(Index) Then Return True
    Next
    Return False
End Function

'SnakeCrash handles the end-of-game code, including displaying the
'player's score.
Sub SnakeCrash()
    tmrForceMove.Enabled = False
    mIsPlayingFlag = False
    MsgBox("Crash! Game Over!" & vbCrLf & _
        "Your score: " & CStr(mSnake.Length))
    ' Rev 1.1 - Added High Score check
    If Format(mSnake.Length, "000") > mHighScore Then SaveHighScore()
End Sub
```

```
'GetNewHeadValue determines the new location for the head based on the
'current head location and the movement direction.
Function GetNewHeadValue() As Integer
    Select Case mDirection
        Case DIR_UP
            Return mSnake(0) - mBoardWidth
        Case DIR_DOWN
            Return mSnake(0) + mBoardWidth
        Case DIR_LEFT
            Return mSnake(0) - 1
        Case DIR_RIGHT
            Return mSnake(0) + 1
        Case Else
            MsgBox("Bad mDirection value : " & CStr(mDirection))
    End Select
End Function

'MoveSnake is the most elaborate procedure in this program.  The timer
'is disabled so that processing is not interrupted.  The routine checks
'for the two illegal moves (snake hitting the wall or hitting itself)
'and ends the game if either occurs.  If not, then the snake is moved,
'and a test is made to see if the move results in food being eaten.
'If so, the snake grows by one in length and the food is moved to a new
'random location.  Finally, the board is redrawn to show the new snake
'position and the timer is re-enabled.
Sub MoveSnake(ByVal Direction As Integer)
    Dim NewHead, OldTail, Index As Integer

    If Not mIsPlayingFlag Then Exit Sub 'Ignore if not playing

    tmrForceMove.Enabled = False        'Disable the timer while moving
    mDirection = Direction              'Record direction in module variable
    NewHead = GetNewHeadValue()         'NewHead used many times
    OldTail = mSnake(UBound(mSnake))    'OldTail used when food eaten

    'Call WillHitWall function to see if Snake hits one of the walls
    If WillHitWall() Then
        SnakeCrash()
        Exit Sub
    End If

    'Call WillHitSnake function to see if Snake runs into itself
    If WillHitSnake(NewHead) Then
        SnakeCrash()
        Exit Sub
    End If

    'Update the snake's position
    For Index = UBound(mSnake) To 1 Step -1
        mSnake(Index) = mSnake(Index - 1)
    Next
    mSnake(0) = NewHead
```

```
        'Check to see if the snake has eaten food this move
        If mBoard(mSnake(0)).Text = "@" Then
            'Food Eaten.  Snake grows one in length.
            ReDim Preserve mSnake(UBound(mSnake) + 1)
            mSnake(UBound(mSnake)) = OldTail

            'Rev 1.1 - show current score
            mnuScore.Text = "Score = " & CStr(mSnake.Length)

            'Move the Food to another random location
            mBoard(mSnake(0)).Text = ""
            mBoard(CInt(Int((Rnd() * UBound(mBoard))))).Text = "@"
        End If

        DrawBoard()
        tmrForceMove.Enabled = True   'Re-enable the timer after moving
    End Sub

    'Timer tick event moves the snake one square in the current direction.
    Private Sub tmrForceMove_Tick(ByVal sender As System.Object, _
            ByVal e As System.EventArgs) Handles tmrForceMove.Tick
        MoveSnake(mDirection)
    End Sub

    Function HandleKeyPress(ByVal KeyData As Keys) As Boolean
        ' Choose appropriate direction for the detected key
        ' Note that 180 degrees turns are ignored
        Select Case KeyData
            Case Keys.Up
                If mDirection <> DIR_DOWN Then MoveSnake(DIR_UP)
            Case Keys.Down
                If mDirection <> DIR_UP Then MoveSnake(DIR_DOWN)
            Case Keys.Left
                If mDirection <> DIR_RIGHT Then MoveSnake(DIR_LEFT)
            Case Keys.Right
                If mDirection <> DIR_LEFT Then MoveSnake(DIR_RIGHT)
            Case Else
                Return False 'Do nothing for all other key presses
        End Select
        Return True
    End Function

    ' The arrow keys do not generate KeyPress or KeyDown events.  If you want
    ' to respond to arrow keys, you need to override the ProcessCmdKey event
    ' and intercept the Windows WM_KEYDOWN message.
    Protected Overrides Function ProcessCmdKey(ByRef msg As System.Windows.Forms.Message, _
                        ByVal keyData As System.Windows.Forms.Keys) As Boolean
        Const WM_KEYDOWN As Integer = &H100

        If msg.Msg = WM_KEYDOWN Then
            If HandleKeyPress(keyData) Then Return True
        End If
        Return MyBase.ProcessCmdKey(msg, keyData)
    End Function
```

```
' Note: The KeyDown event is simpler than ProcessCmdKey above, but does
' not work for arrow or tab keys.
'Private Sub frmSnakes_KeyDown(ByVal sender As Object, _
'           ByVal e As System.Windows.Forms.KeyEventArgs) Handles MyBase.KeyDown
'    HandleKeyPress(e.KeyData)
'End Sub

' ***********************************************
' *************** Revision 1.1 ******************
' ***********************************************

Sub LoadHighScore()
    Dim Reader As StreamReader
    ' Use Try . . . Catch to handle possible exception such as FileNotFound
    Try
        Reader = File.OpenText("HighScore.txt")
        mHighScore = Reader.ReadToEnd
        Reader.Close()
    Catch
        mHighScore = "000 by Smith"
    End Try
End Sub

Sub SaveHighScore()
    Dim Writer As StreamWriter
    Dim Name As String
    Name = InputBox("New High Score!  Enter your Name")
    Try
        mHighScore = Format(mSnake.Length, "000") & " by " & Name
        Writer = File.CreateText("HighScore.txt")
        Writer.WriteLine(mHighScore)
        Writer.Flush()
        Writer.Close()
    Catch
        ' high score update failed
    End Try
End Sub

Private Sub frmSnakes_Load(ByVal sender As System.Object, _
            ByVal e As System.EventArgs) Handles MyBase.Load
    MediaPlayer.AutoStart = True 'Auto-play media when FileName is set
    MediaPlayer.FileName = "Splash.avi" 'Place Splash.avi in project bin directory
    LoadHighScore()
End Sub

Private Sub MediaPlayer_EndOfStream(ByVal sender As Object, _
            ByVal e As AxMediaPlayer._MediaPlayerEvents_EndOfStreamEvent) _
            Handles MediaPlayer.EndOfStream
    MediaPlayer.Visible = False 'Hide MediaPlayer after Splash.avi finishes
End Sub

Private Sub frmSnakes_Resize(ByVal sender As Object, _
            ByVal e As System.EventArgs) Handles MyBase.Resize
```

```
        InitializeBoard() 'When the form resizes, reinitialize to fill window
    End Sub

    Private Sub mnuStart_Click(ByVal sender As System.Object, _
                ByVal e As System.EventArgs) Handles mnuStart.Click
        StartNewGame()
    End Sub

    Private Sub mnuExit_Click(ByVal sender As System.Object, _
                ByVal e As System.EventArgs) Handles mnuExit.Click
        If MsgBox("Exit Snakes Game?", MsgBoxStyle.YesNo) = MsgBoxResult.Yes Then
            MsgBox("Thank you for playing.  Have a great day!")
            Application.Exit()
        End If
    End Sub

    Private Sub mnuSnakeColor_Click(ByVal sender As System.Object, _
                ByVal e As System.EventArgs) Handles mnuSnakeColor.Click
        Dim dlgColor As New ColorDialog
        dlgColor.ShowDialog()
        mSnakeColor = dlgColor.Color
        DrawBoard()
    End Sub

    Private Sub mnuBoardColor_Click(ByVal sender As System.Object, _
                ByVal e As System.EventArgs) Handles mnuBoardColor.Click
        Dim dlgColor As New ColorDialog
        dlgColor.ShowDialog()
        mBoardColor = dlgColor.Color
        DrawBoard()
    End Sub

    Private Sub mnuNumCols_Click(ByVal sender As System.Object, _
                ByVal e As System.EventArgs) Handles mnuNumCols.Click
        mBoardWidth = CInt(InputBox("Input Number of Columns"))
        InitializeBoard()
    End Sub

    Private Sub mnuNumRows_Click(ByVal sender As System.Object, _
                ByVal e As System.EventArgs) Handles mnuNumRows.Click
        mBoardHeight = CInt(InputBox("Input Number of Rows"))
        InitializeBoard()
    End Sub

    Private Sub mnuHighScore_Click(ByVal sender As System.Object, _
                ByVal e As System.EventArgs) Handles mnuHighScore.Click
        MsgBox(mHighScore, , "High Score")
    End Sub

    Private Sub mnuAbout_Click(ByVal sender As System.Object, _
                ByVal e As System.EventArgs) Handles mnuAbout.Click
        MsgBox("Snakes Game, (c) 11111010100")
    End Sub

    End Class
```

### Testing the Solution

You can test Chuck's solution by implementing his design as shown in the previous section, and then running the application. Figure 10-16 shows the Snake Game Pro during execution. The program should begin with the opening splash media. Trigger the menu options including starting a new game, changing the snake and board colors, viewing the high score, and displaying the About dialog. Run the application again, and create a new high score. If you are having problems getting your solution to execute, you may want to read Appendix B: Debugging.

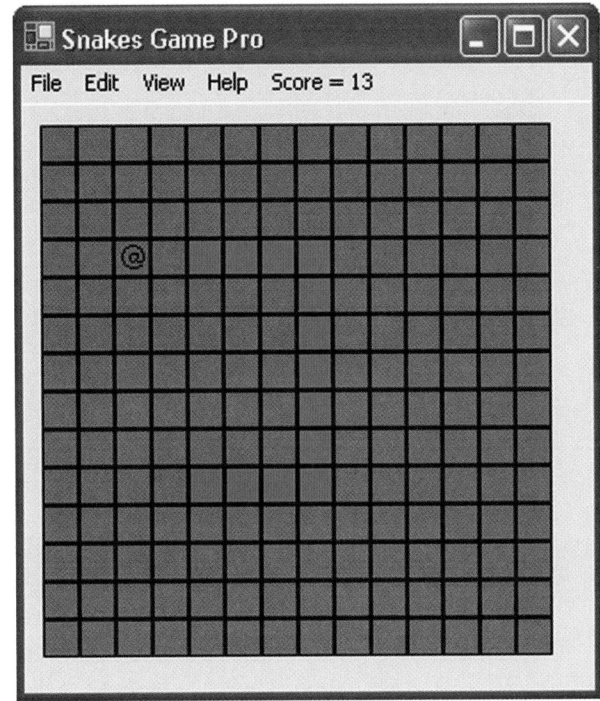


**FIGURE 10.16** *Sample Output for Snakes Game Application*

## Chapter Summary

- A menu is a list of common operations presented to the user in a graphical format. Menus make programs easier to learn and use because common actions are typically available in expected locations.
- Visual Studio provides a series of dialog controls, including OpenFileDialog, SaveFileDialog, FontDialog, ColorDialog, PrintDialog, and PrintPreviewDialog, which provide significant functionality with little effort.
- The StreamReader class is designed for character input. Once the reader has been assigned to an opened file, a series of stream reader methods may be called to read information from the file.
- The Windows Media Player control plays video and sound files in many different formats.

## Key Terms

**ColorDialog control** p. 256
**FontDialog control** p. 256
**main menu** p. 250
**MainMenu control** p. 251
**menu** p. 250
**OpenFileDialog control** p. 258
**PageSetupDialog control** p. 262
**PrintDialog control** p. 261
**PrintPreview control** p. 262
**SaveFileDialog control** p. 258
**standard dialog boxes** p. 255
**StreamReader** p. 259
**StreamWriter** p. 259
**Windows Media Player control** p. 265

## Review Questions

1. What is a menu? How do you create a main menu in VB.NET?
2. What is a menu item? How is a menu item like a button?
3. What six standard Windows dialogs are included in the toolbox?
4. How do you create a ColorDialog control programmatically? How do you display the dialog? How do you access the user-selected color?
5. What is the purpose of the OpenFileDialog control? How is that related to the File.OpenText method?
6. Explain the relationship between the following controls: PrintDialog, PrintPreviewDialog, and PageSetupDialog.
7. What is the Windows Media Player control? Identify two uses for the control.

## ▶ Programming Exercises

**10-1. Just a Prototype.** Write a program with an elaborate menu structure. However, the only menu item that works should be File | Exit. All other menu items should generate a message box indicating that the feature is not currently available or under development or the like.

**10-2. Fonts R Us.** Modify the Print and PrintPreview Illustrated example by adding a button that generates a font dialog. The selected font should become both the text box font and the printing font.

**10-3. Declaration of Independence.** Modify the Print and PrintPreview Illustated example by reading the entire Declaration of Independence from the text file Declaration.txt included on the student CD.

**10-4. Save Your Work.** The Text File I/O illustrated example loads a new text file over the current text file even if changes to the current text have not been saved. An improvement would be to notify the user with a message like "Changes to the current text will be lost! Do you wish to continue?" before loading the new file. If the user selects Yes, then the new file should load and the changes will be lost. If the user selects No, then the file load should be aborted. (Another option would be to save the current file at that time.) *Hint:* Use a module level Boolean variable that is set to true every time the text is changed in the text box (TextChanged event). The variable should be set to false somewhere else in the program (can you figure out where?).

**10-5. Putting It All Together.** Combine elements from the Font and Color Dialog Text File I/O, and Print and PrintPreview illustrated examples presented in this chapter to create a single application with buttons to load and save the contents of a text box; buttons to print, print preview, and set print margins; and buttons to set the text box font and print font.

**10-6. Weekly Payroll.** The Acme company has asked you to develop a program to calculate the weekly payroll for all of its hourly employees. Acme provides you with two text files. The first file, Employees.txt, contains information about its employees, three lines per employee. The first line contains the unique employee ID (as Integer), the second line has the employee name (as String), and the third line has the hourly rate for that employee (as Double). A sentinel employee ID of -1 appears at the end of the file. The second file, TimeClock.txt, contains information generated by the company timeclock. There are again three lines per record. The first line is the employee ID (as Integer), followed by the time-in and time-out stamps (as Date). (Hint: The Date data type has a Subtract method.) Each employee can have zero, one, or many entries in the TimeClock.txt file each week. A sentinel employee ID of -1 appears at the end of the file.

Write a program to process both files and generate a third file, WeeklyPayroll.txt, containing each employee and the pay amount due according to the Employees.txt and TimeClock.txt data. Finally, the WeeklyPayroll.txt file should contain a summary line that shows the cumulative total of all of the employees' paychecks.

# Extended Case Studies

## Pizza and a Movie

Noah is planning on advertising Rent one, Get one Free coupons for video rentals, but he wants to limit their use to days when business is slow. Read daily sales data for the past six months from the file SALESDATA.TXT. Calculate the average sales for each day of the week over the past six months, and determine the days that are below the average. These are the days that the coupon will be valid. (Note: A more challenging but also more valuable way to analyze the data would be to look at the data week by week, finding which days in week 1 were below the week 1 average, which days in week 2 were below the week 2 average, and so on. The report would be a count of all the times Monday was below average over the past three months, Tuesday, and so on. This more refined analysis of the data would give Noah better information for his advertising campaign.)

## Singing Mimes

Revise one of the Singing Mimes projects from a previous chapter by giving the project a professional touch. Add a main menu and at least three additional professional touches to the project. You can use freely available multimedia tools to create your own Splash Video (if appropriate).

# UNIT 3 Advanced Visual Basic .NET



Information is an essential commodity in the current age. The ability to store information in databases and deliver information using the Internet provides a competitive advantage to individuals and organizations. Object-oriented programming has played a key role in the recent advances of software development. Artificial intelligence and machine learning push the limits of our understanding and open new doors of opportunity for the future. Unit 3 clearly and insightfully covers each of these advanced topics.

CHAPTER 11

# Databases and ADO.NET

## OUTLINE

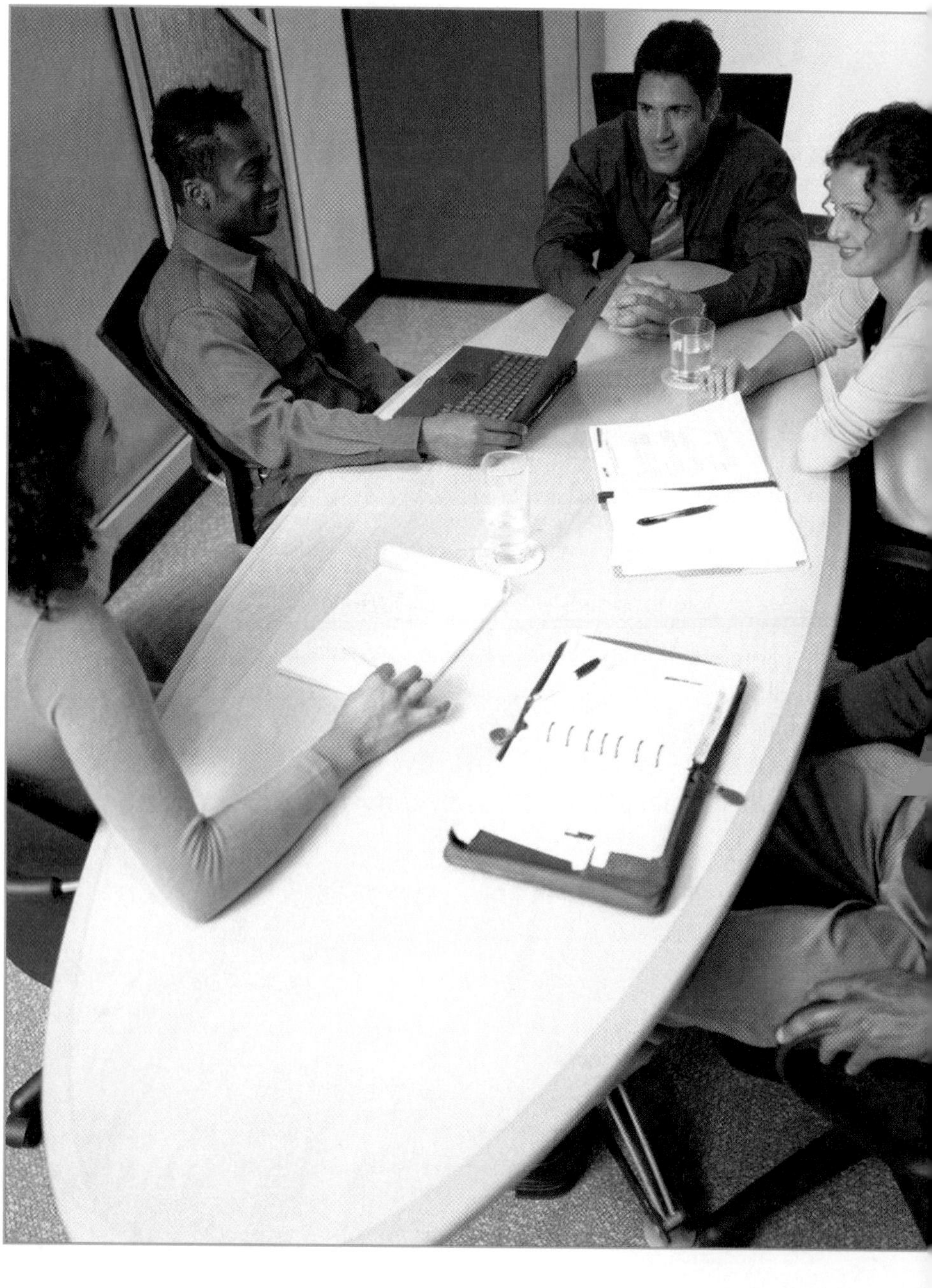

## INTERVIEW

### Thomas Butts, Programmer and Consultant

***Interviewer:*** Please tell us how you got involved in the IT industry.

***Butts:*** I was in my third year of school, and I was a psychology major. I realized that in order to get a decent job (one that would pay the bills) I would need an advanced degree. I was not willing to put myself through another long period of schooling, so I added computer science and ended up a double major.

***Interviewer:*** What kind of projects are you currently working on?

***Butts:*** My career has been based on projects that are very large database applications. I am currently working on a large teleconferencing application that will likely be used by thousands of people around the world. I was brought on to develop and maintain the middle tier because I have extensive database knowledge and experience in developing middle tiers.

***Interviewer:*** What is important for students to learn in a first programming course?

***Butts:*** The most important thing I took away from my first programming course was that I saw the fun in it. I like the characteristics of developing applications. You have full control of the creative process for developing the software, but you have an exact outcome. If you give ten developers the same project, you will probably get ten different programs. Even if they all work exactly as specified, each program will be unique and bring part of the developer to the end user. I like having the goal to make sure I do something right, yet not be told exactly how to do it.

***Interviewer:*** What has been your personal key to success?

***Butts:*** I very quickly grasp concepts, both business and programming, and in a business world that is supported by computers, you have to understand both sides of the coin. To be in the business world as a programmer is not always easy and requires a mixed skill set that is not common in developers. Many programmers would rather be in a room somewhere with people handing requirements under the door. Another group is the business-minded people that are fascinated with technology but do not really understand it. I believe that I am in the smaller group that understands both business and programming, and that is one of the reasons that I have done well in this field.

***Interviewer:*** What do you wish someone had told you when you were an undergraduate student?

***Butts:*** Enjoy the fact that your primary job is to learn. People are forcing you to learn. Competition between students and professors will push you to constantly expand the knowledge you have. This is a great gift and one that I think is too short-lived, so enjoy it.

## OBJECTIVES

At the completion of this chapter, you will

- **Understand databases and the relational database model**
- **Understand primary keys and foreign keys**
- **Understand simple SQL queries**
- **Use WHERE and ORDER BY clauses**
- **Query multiple tables using JOIN**
- **Create a Connection object**
- **Create and work with a DataAdapter object**
- **Create and work with a Dataset object**
- **Work with data bound controls**
- **Work with the DataGrid control**
- **Develop applications that interact with a database**

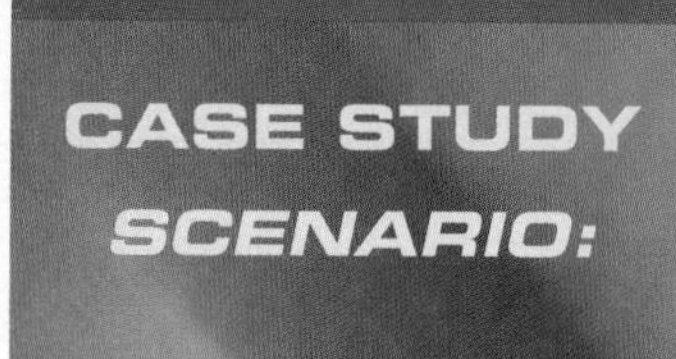


# Movie History

Noah has been pleasantly surprised by the popularity of his Pizza and a Movie store. One of the store's signature features is the friendly atmosphere that comes from Noah's knowing his clients. He often asks his customers a question like "How did you like the *Gone with the Wind* video you rented last week?" and the resulting conversation is usually very pleasant.

Realizing the information in his database is a valuable business asset, Noah wants to leverage the data by giving his employees quick access to the rental history of any customer. Noah reviewed a large company's customer maintenance software package that was quite expensive and not tailored to his needs. He wants a simple application that can access his existing database.

He calls the computing department and asks the secretary for the names of some entrepreneurial students interested in consulting. The secretary gives Noah the names of two students who have shown an interest in applying their technology skills in a business setting: Reed and Elizabeth.

Noah invites Reed and Elizabeth over to the store to explain his objectives and to discuss the possibility of contracting some work. The three chat about their favorite actors, technology, the economy, and pets. Eventually, the conversation returns to the reason for the meeting.

"I want to have quick and easy access to my customers' rental history," says Noah. "My current checkout system requires four screen changes to get a rental history and three screen changes to return to the checkout screen."

Noah explains further that he is interested in a prototype of a new customer maintenance program that would include rental history on the same screen as customer information. If that system worked with his current database, then he would be interested in a totally redesigned customer maintenance program.

Elizabeth and Reed's solution appears later this chapter.

## 11-1 Database Primer

One of the primary assets of an organization is its data. For example, most businesses maintain data about their subjects (customers, employees, vendors, etc.) and activities (orders, payments, purchases, etc.). Organizations can have a competitive advantage if they are effective in their management of data and information.

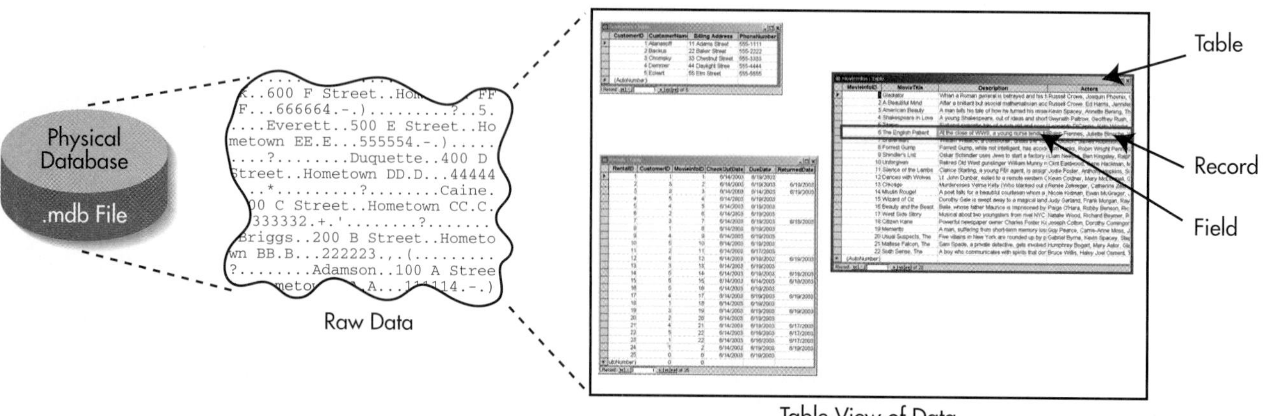

A ***database*** is a structured collection of data. The typical database structure includes ***fields***, ***records***, and ***tables***. A field is a storage location for a single piece of information, such as a customer's name, address, or zip code. A record is a complete collection of related fields (e.g., the name, address, and zip code of a single customer). A table is a complete set of related records (e.g., all the customers in a company's database).

## Relational Databases

A simple database may have only a single table. More complicated databases typically contain multiple tables to handle the complexity and interaction found in the real world. For example, a business database may contain a Customers table, an Employees table, a Vendors table, an Orders table, a Payments table, and a Purchases table to mirror the organization's business model and transaction processing. In the ***relational database model***, relationships exist between tables to indicate how the data is connected. Typically, relationships involve the ***primary key*** from one table and a ***foreign key*** in a related table. The primary key is a field (or set of fields) that uniquely distinguishes the records in the table. The foreign key contains values that match primary key values in the related table.

Figure 11-1 is a diagram showing a relational database design involving three tables with two relationships: a customer can make many orders, and an order can include many payments. As the number of tables and relationships increases, so does the complexity of the database.

The primary key and foreign key fields are essential for creating the relationships between tables. Of course, tables typically contain additional fields as well. Table 11-1 shows a sample table named Customers. This table contains six fields (CustomerID, Name, Address, City, State, and Zip). The table also contains six rows, each containing information about a single customer.

**ASK THE AUTHOR**

**Q** The data in the Customers table is clearly fictitious. There is no state named AA or a zip code of 11111. Why did you choose this data?

**A** The fictitious data in the Customers table is intentional, with data having either a letter or number to indicate the appropriate record (row). Because of the design of the fictitious data, it will be immediately evident if the application is displaying inconsistent data. For example, if the application says that "Briggs" lives at "400 D Street," you will know immediately that there is a problem without having to flip back to the Customers table to verify Briggs's address.

**FIGURE 11.1** *A Simple Relational Database Design*

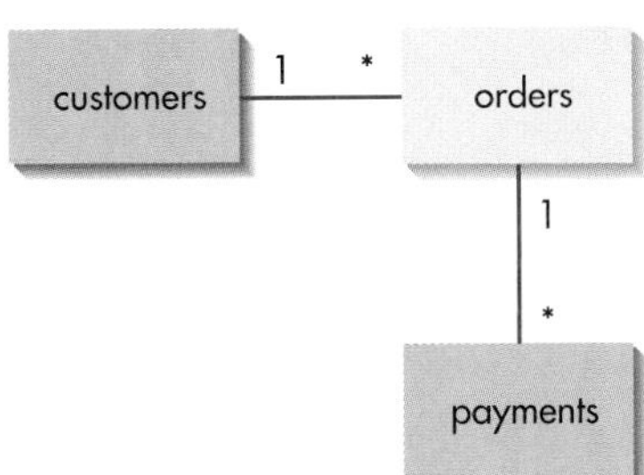

**Table 11.1 An Example Customers Table with Six Columns (Fields) and Six Records (Rows)**

| CustomerID | Name | Address | City | State | Zip |
|---|---|---|---|---|---|
| 1 | Adamson | 100 A Street | Hometown A | AA | 11111 |
| 2 | Briggs | 200 B Street | Hometown B | BB | 22222 |
| 3 | Caine | 300 C Street | Hometown C | CC | 33333 |
| 4 | Duquette | 400 D Street | Hometown D | DD | 44444 |
| 5 | Everett | 500 E Street | Hometown E | EE | 55555 |
| 6 | Fenwick | 600 F Street | Hometown F | FF | 66666 |

The data in Table 11-1 has already been entered into the Customers table of the SampleDatabase.mdb database on the student CD. This database was created using Microsoft Access but could have been made with SQL Server, Oracle, MySQL, or any other DBMS. Figure 11-2 shows the Microsoft Access Customers table.

**MANAGER**

A ***Database Management System (DBMS)*** is a collection of programs that support the creation, storage, manipulation, querying, and printing of information to and from a database. A DBMS allows appropriate presentation of accurate information to the correct people at the proper time. A DBMS can also control the security and integrity of the data in the database.

In addition to a customer's name and address, our simple database design also contains information about customers' orders. However, order data does not appear in the Customers table. Instead, our database design specifies a second table named Orders. Figure 11-3 shows the Orders table, which contains five columns and nine records.

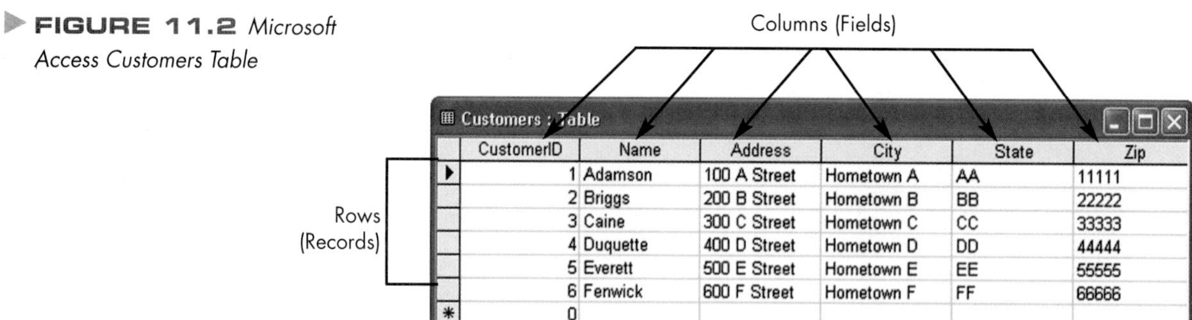


**FIGURE 11.2** *Microsoft Access Customers Table*

**FIGURE 11.3** *An Orders Table with Five Columns and Nine Records*

Orders : Table

| OrderID | CustomerID | OrderDate | OrderTotal | SoldBy |
|---|---|---|---|---|
| 1 | 3 | 3/15/2004 | $12.95 | Sebastian |
| 2 | 4 | 3/18/2004 | $12.95 | Ray |
| 3 | 5 | 3/20/2004 | $12.95 | Ray |
| 4 | 3 | 3/20/2004 | $4.95 | Sebastian |
| 5 | 6 | 3/27/2004 | $49.95 | Ray |
| 6 | 6 | 3/29/2004 | $4.95 | Ray |
| 7 | 1 | 4/5/2004 | $12.95 | Todd |
| 8 | 2 | 4/5/2004 | $12.95 | Todd |
| 9 | 3 | 4/7/2004 | $4.95 | Ray |
| 0 | 0 | | $0.00 | |

Record: 1 of 9

The Orders table contains *OrderID* as the primary key field. The *CustomerID* field is a foreign key that refers to the same named primary key in the Customers database. This indicates that a single customer can be related to many different orders (for example, CustomerID C3-1591 is associated with OrderIDs 1, 4, and 9. Therefore, there is a ***one-to-many relationship*** between the Customers table and the Orders table.

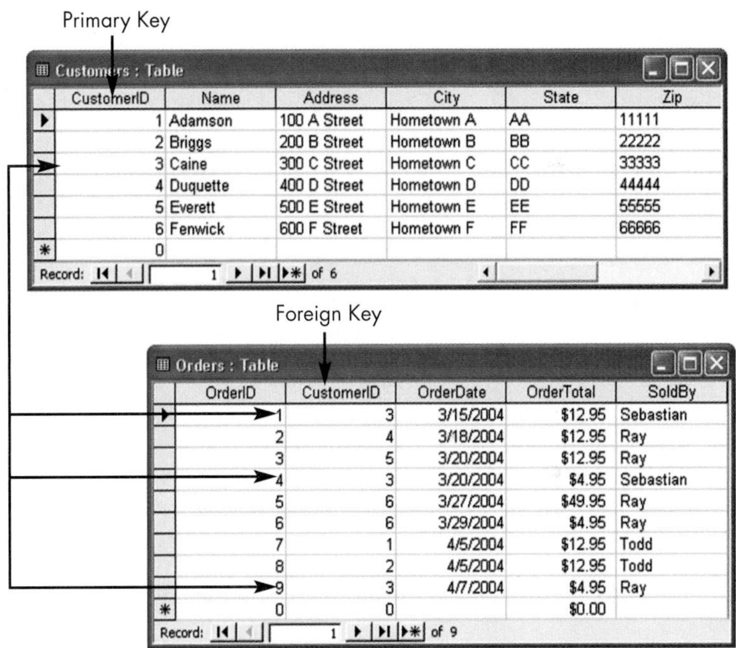


Customers : Table

| CustomerID | Name | Address | City | State | Zip |
|---|---|---|---|---|---|
| 1 | Adamson | 100 A Street | Hometown A | AA | 11111 |
| 2 | Briggs | 200 B Street | Hometown B | BB | 22222 |
| 3 | Caine | 300 C Street | Hometown C | CC | 33333 |
| 4 | Duquette | 400 D Street | Hometown D | DD | 44444 |
| 5 | Everett | 500 E Street | Hometown E | EE | 55555 |
| 6 | Fenwick | 600 F Street | Hometown F | FF | 66666 |
| 0 | | | | | |

Record: 1 of 6

Orders : Table

| OrderID | CustomerID | OrderDate | OrderTotal | SoldBy |
|---|---|---|---|---|
| 1 | 3 | 3/15/2004 | $12.95 | Sebastian |
| 2 | 4 | 3/18/2004 | $12.95 | Ray |
| 3 | 5 | 3/20/2004 | $12.95 | Ray |
| 4 | 3 | 3/20/2004 | $4.95 | Sebastian |
| 5 | 6 | 3/27/2004 | $49.95 | Ray |
| 6 | 6 | 3/29/2004 | $4.95 | Ray |
| 7 | 1 | 4/5/2004 | $12.95 | Todd |
| 8 | 2 | 4/5/2004 | $12.95 | Todd |
| 9 | 3 | 4/7/2004 | $4.95 | Ray |
| 0 | 0 | | $0.00 | |

Record: 1 of 9

**FIGURE 11.4** *The Customers–Orders One-to-Many Relationship*

One-to-many relationships are the most common, but some tables, such as Students and Classes, have a ***many-to-many relationship***. Each student can have many classes each semester, and each class contains many students. A many-to-many relationship is usually implemented using a third table, called a ***linking table***, with foreign keys to each of the two original tables.

**MANAGER**

Designers of relational databases often go through a formal process of ***normalization*** to better organize a database. There are increasing stages of normalization, not all of which are necessary for every database design.

First normal form (1NF) requires that fields contain atomic values. Second normal form (2NF) requires that all fields depend on the primary key. Third normal form (3NF) eliminates redundancies by creating multiple tables so that each non-key field depends only on its primary key. This normalization process has the advantage of reducing data redundancy and allowing for more efficient storage and access.

## Quick Check 11-A

1. Assume the Customers and Orders tables were combined into a single table with all ten fields. List some of the possible problems with this approach.
2. The preceding discussion makes no mention of a one-to-one relationship. Explain why this relationship is not necessary.

# 11-2 Structured Query Language (SQL)

An application communicates with a DBMS through ***queries*** written in a standard language called ***Structured Query Language (SQL)***, pronounced "sequel" or S-Q-L. SQL is an industry standard language that allows an application to communicate with a relational database.

## SELECT Query

We begin with the most fundamental of SQL queries, the ***SELECT command***. This command is used to select specific information from one or more tables in a database.

*Syntax:*

```
SELECT fields FROM table
```

*Examples:*

```
SELECT * FROM Customers

SELECT OrderDate, OrderTotal, SoldBy FROM Orders

SELECT [First Name], [Last Name], HireDate FROM Employees
```

The first example is the simplest form of the SELECT statement—it uses the asterisk (*) as a wildcard to indicate that all columns from the specified table should be selected. To limit the selection, the command may indicate desired fields in a comma-separated list between the SELECT and FROM keywords. If the field name contains spaces, the field name should be enclosed by square brackets in the command. For example, if the Orders database table had a field named *First Name* with a space between the two words, then the query would reference [First Name] (as shown in the preceding example).

## WHERE Clause

One of the most powerful features of a database is the capability to choose information based on selection criteria. This is accomplished by means of the SQL ***WHERE clause***.

*Syntax:*

SELECT *fields* FROM *table* WHERE *critera*

*Examples:*

```
SELECT * FROM Customers WHERE OrderDate > #01/01/2003#

SELECT OrderDate, OrderTotal, SoldBy
FROM Orders
WHERE SoldBy = "Ray"
```

The second SQL command in the preceding examples selects three fields from the Orders table where the SoldBy field has the value "Ray." Figure 11-5 shows the results of this query.

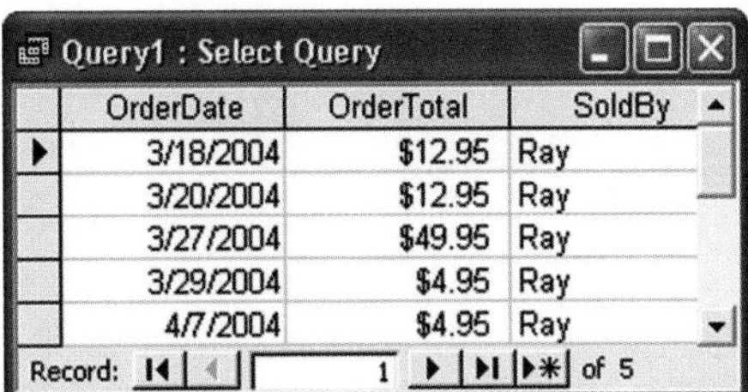

**FIGURE 11.5** *Results of WHERE Query Example*

The WHERE clause condition can contain the six relational operators >, <, =, <>, >=, and <=. It also supports pattern matching using the LIKE operator with the wildcard characters asterisk (*) and question mark (?). In this context the asterisk takes the place of zero or more characters, whereas the question mark takes the place of any single character.

A well-designed database would allow an organization to select the following information:

- All customers in a particular zip code who did more than $500,000 in business last year (very useful information for traveling salespeople)
- All shelf products with an on-hand quantity less than 20 percent of the maximum (very useful information for managing inventory)
- All customers who have made their first purchases from the organization within the past 45 days (very useful information for marketing new products)

## ORDER BY Clause

The information returned by a SELECT statement can be arranged in ascending or descending order with the ***ORDER BY clause***.

*Syntax:*

SELECT *fields* FROM *table* [WHERE *critera* ORDER BY *field* [ASC|DESC]

*Examples:*

```
SELECT * FROM Customers ORDER BY CustomerName ASC

SELECT OrderDate, OrderTotal, SoldBy
FROM Orders
WHERE OrderDate >= #03/20/2003#
ORDER BY OrderTotal DESC
```

The second SQL command in the preceding examples selects three fields from the Orders table where the OrderDate is greater than or equal to #03/20/2003# and the results are sorted by OrderTotal in descending order. Figure 11-6 shows the results of this query.

**FIGURE 11.6** *Results of ORDER BY Query Example*

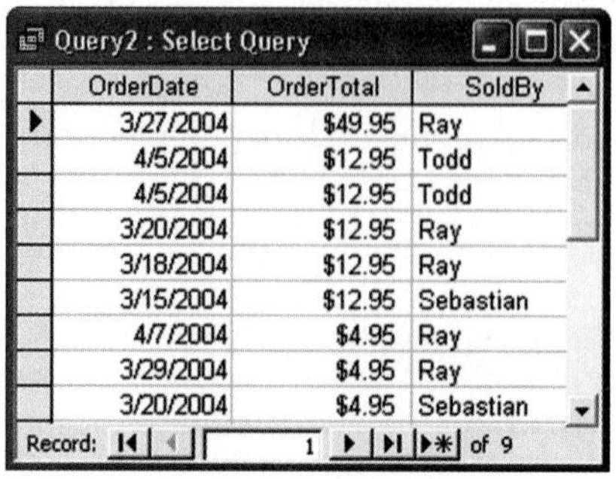

Query2 : Select Query

| OrderDate | OrderTotal | SoldBy |
|---|---|---|
| 3/27/2004 | $49.95 | Ray |
| 4/5/2004 | $12.95 | Todd |
| 4/5/2004 | $12.95 | Todd |
| 3/20/2004 | $12.95 | Ray |
| 3/18/2004 | $12.95 | Ray |
| 3/15/2004 | $12.95 | Sebastian |
| 4/7/2004 | $4.95 | Ray |
| 3/29/2004 | $4.95 | Ray |
| 3/20/2004 | $4.95 | Sebastian |

Record: 1 of 9

The ASC keyword specifies an ascending order (lowest to highest), and the DESC keyword specifies a descending order (highest to lowest). If neither keyword is specified, the default sorting order is ascending.

## JOIN

By design, relational databases store data over multiple tables to eliminate data redundancy. For example, when a customer makes an order, new information such as the order date and order total are stored in the Orders table. The customer's mailing address remains unchanged as stored in the Customers table. The mailing address for the order is obtained by means of a foreign key value in the Orders table that links the order to an appropriate customer record (with mailing address) in the Customers table.

To create a query that combines data from multiple tables, you use the JOIN operation. The JOIN operation matches rows of one table with rows of another table, based on values in those rows.

*Syntax:*

```
SELECT fields FROM table1 [LEFT|RIGHT] JOIN table2 ON table1.field1 = table2.field2
[ WHERE critera]
[ ORDER BY field ]
```

*Example:*

```
SELECT Orders.CustomerID, Customers.CustomerID as CustID, Name,
    OrderDate, OrderID, OrderTotal, Soldby
FROM Orders LEFT JOIN Customers
    ON Orders.CustomerID = Customers.CustomerID
WHERE OrderDate = #03/20/2004#
```

The JOIN command is used to select data from multiple tables. When using the JOIN command, you must specify the two tables to be joined. You also must specify the JOIN columns from each table. The JOIN columns must be of the same (or compatible) data types. Typically, the JOIN columns involve a primary key/foreign key relationship between two tables.

Within a JOIN, it is possible that a column in one table will have the same name as a column in another table. You qualify your table columns using the dot operator between the table name and the field name (e.g., Orders.CustomerID). Also, you can use the **As** keyword to give a unique name to one of the duplicate fields in the result set (e.g., Orders.CustomerID as CustID).

The SQL command in the preceding example selects data from two tables (Orders and Customers using CustomerID as the primary key/foreign key relationship) for orders placed on March 20, 2004. Figure 11-7 shows the results of this query.

**MANAGER**

When you join tables, the type of JOIN that you create affects the rows that appear in the result set. You can create the following types of JOINs.

*INNER JOIN* A JOIN that displays only the rows that have a match in both joined tables. This is the default type of JOIN in the Query and View Designer.

*LEFT JOIN* All rows from the first-named table (the left table, which appears leftmost in the JOIN clause) are included. Unmatched rows in the right table do not appear.

*RIGHT JOIN* All rows in the second-named table (the right table, which appears rightmost in the JOIN clause) are included. Unmatched rows in the left table are not included.

**FIGURE 11.7** *Results of JOIN Query Example*

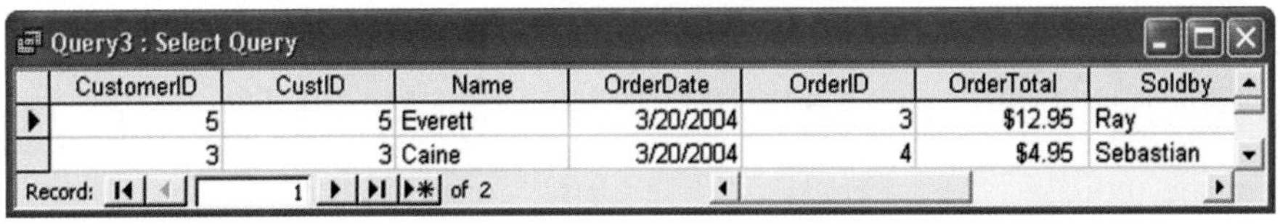

Query3 : Select Query

| CustomerID | CustID | Name | OrderDate | OrderID | OrderTotal | Soldby |
|---|---|---|---|---|---|---|
| 5 | 5 | Everett | 3/20/2004 | 3 | $12.95 | Ray |
| 3 | 3 | Caine | 3/20/2004 | 4 | $4.95 | Sebastian |

Record: 1 of 2

# 11-3 Using ADO.NET

***ADO.NET*** is the data access architecture for the .NET Framework. ADO.NET provides Connection, DataAdapter, and Dataset objects to facilitate accessing data in a database.

**Tip**

**ADO.NET provides two types of Connection objects: *OleDbConnection* and *SqlConnection*. The OleDbConnection works with all database formats (Access, Oracle, MySQL, Microsoft SQL Server, etc.). The SqlConnection is optimized to work only with Microsoft SQLServer.**

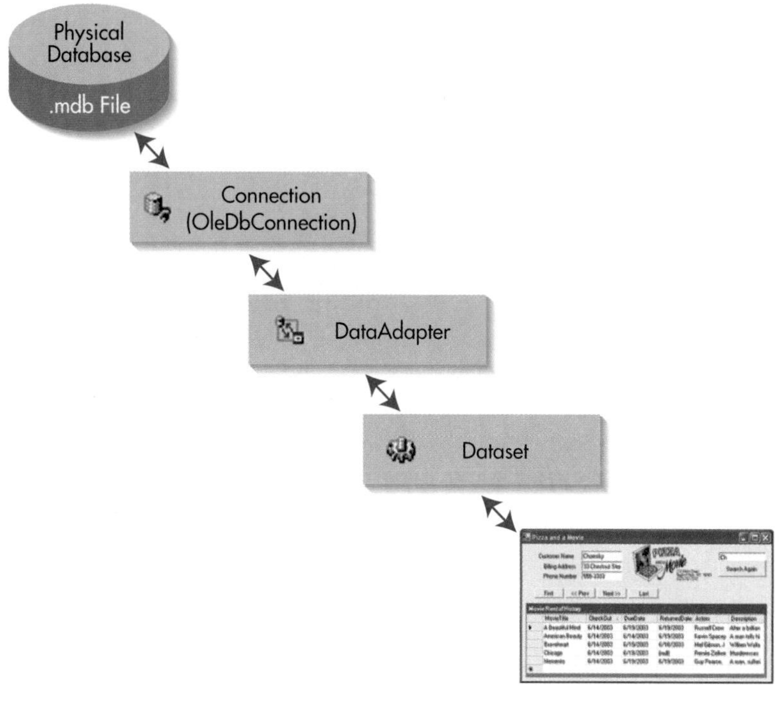

**Tip**

**OLE stands for object linking and embedding, a protocol for distributed objects. For example, OLE allows an Excel graph to be used in a PowerPoint presentation. OLE DB is object linking and embedding for a database.**

## Creating a Connection

A **Connection** object establishes a link from your application to a database file. A Connection object specifies the *type* and *location* of the database file.

The first step in creating a Connection is to select an OleDbConnection control from the toolbox (see Figure 11-8). The OleDbConnection is one of the controls under the Data group of the toolbar.

**FIGURE 11.8** *The OleDbConnection Control in the Toolbox*

Double-click on the OleDbConnection control to add an OleDbConnection object to the component tray (see Figure 11-9).

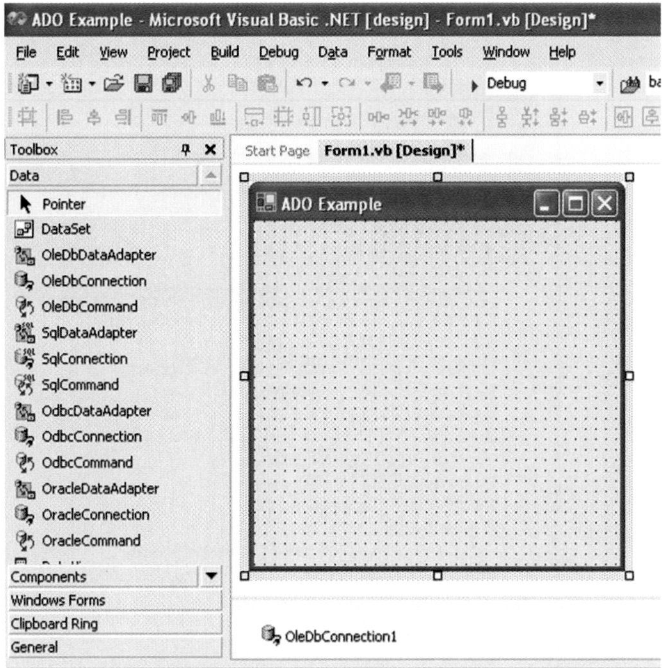


**FIGURE 11.9** *An OleDbConnection Control Added to the Component Tray*

Select the OleDbConnection object. Then in the property window select the ConnectionString property and select New Connection (see Figure 11-10).

**FIGURE 11.10** *Selecting a New Connection for the OleDbConnection Control*

The Data Link Properties window appears. The database provider you select will depend on the type of database to which you are connecting. For an Access 2000 or Access XP database, you should select the Jet 4.0 OLE DB Provider, and then click the Next button (see Figure 11-11).

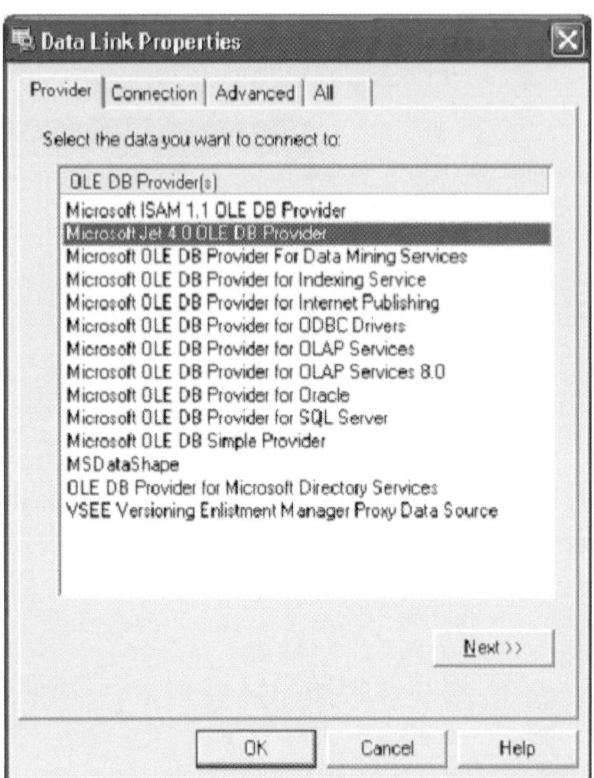


**FIGURE 11.11**
*Selecting the Jet 4.0 Provider (used by Access 2000 and Access XP)*

Under the Connection Tab of the Data Link Properties window, specify the path and file name for the database to which you want to connect. For this example you should connect to the SampleDatabase.mdb on the student CD. You may leave the log-on information unchanged. Click the Test Connection button. If you get a message saying, "Test Connection Succeeded," then you have a valid Connection from your application to the database (see Figure 11-12). If you get any other response, then review the steps and find where you missed a step.

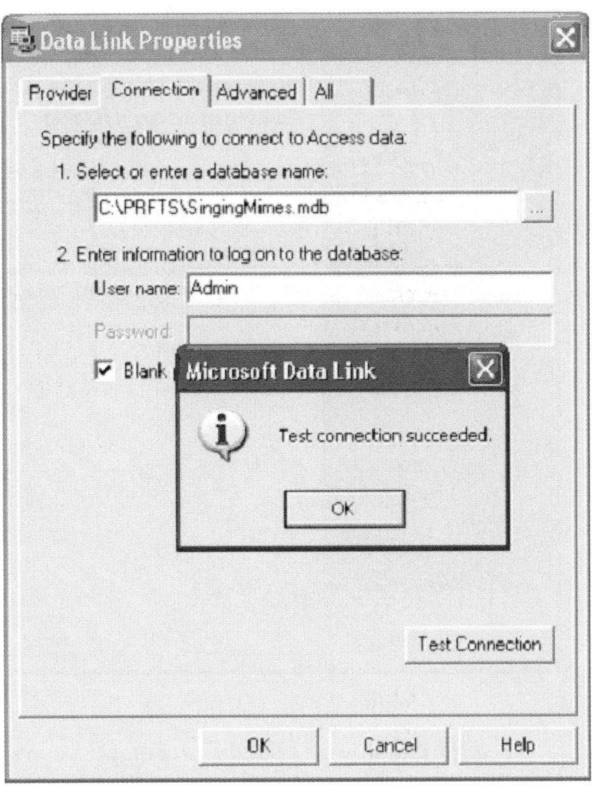


**FIGURE 11.12** *A Successful Database Connection*

Now that you have a Connection to a database file, you can use this Connection to send and receive data between your application and the database. However, the data formats are different between the two programs, so data transfer will require a DataAdapter.

## Creating a DataAdapter

Once a Connection has been established, the next step is to create a ***DataAdapter***. A DataAdapter does the work of passing information between the database and your application. The SQL command is part of the DataAdapter.

### ASK THE AUTHOR

**Q** I already have a Connection. Why do I need a DataAdapter also?

**A** The DataAdapter contains SQL that specifies what information to access through the Connection. The DataAdapter also works like a language translator. Imagine that you wanted to have a conversation with someone who spoke only German and that you did not speak German yourself. Communication would still be possible, but it would require the assistance of a translator who converted English to German when you spoke and German to English when the other person spoke. Likewise, a database stores data in a way that your application would not understand, and your application stores data in a way that the database would not understand. The DataAdapter understands both data formats and translates them appropriately for the receiving application.

**FIGURE 11.13** *The Data Adapter Configuration Wizard*

**Tip**

**The Data Adapter Wizard can be triggered by right-clicking on the DataAdapter control and selecting Configure Data Adapter.**

**Tip**

**One Connection to a database can be used to create multiple DataAdapters. For example, you may have a DataAdapter for the Customers table and another DataAdapter for the Employees table that both share a Connection to the same database.**

Begin by adding an ***OleDbDataAdapter*** control from the Data tools in the toolbox. The Data Adapter Configuration Wizard starts automatically (see Figure 11-13). The Wizard guides you through the process of selecting the database fields to use with this adapter.

The second screen of the Wizard allows you to specify the Connection to use for this DataAdapter (see Figure 11-14). Select the Connection to the SampleDatabase.mbd and press Next.

**FIGURE 11.14** *Selecting the Connection*

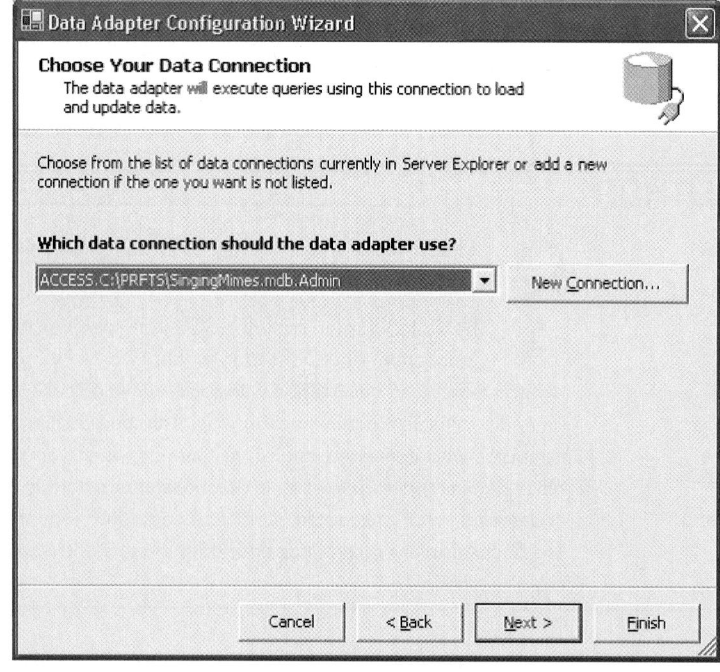

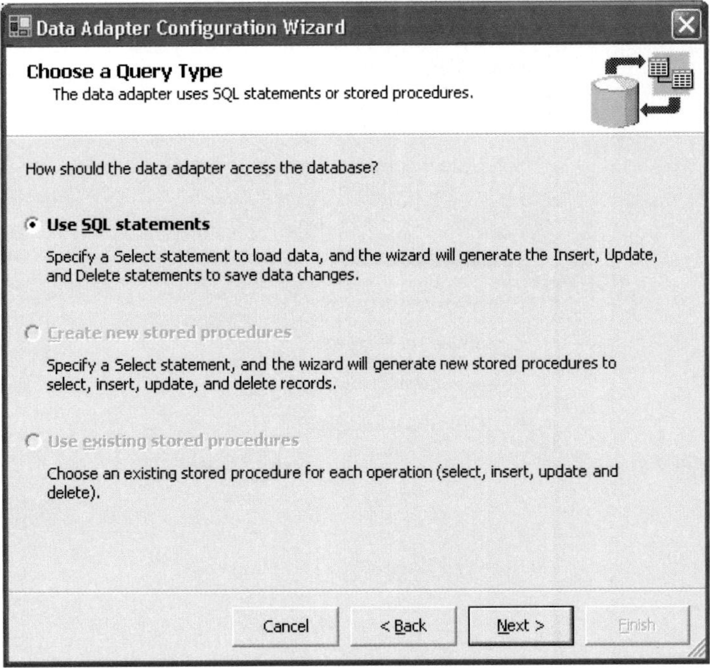


**FIGURE 11.15**
*Selecting the Query Type*

**Tip**

**The Query Builder button triggers the Query Builder tool that creates SQL statements graphically. It is less powerful than learning actual SQL, but it can be very helpful to beginners.**

The next screen of the Wizard asks you to choose a Query Type (see Figure 11-15). Because we are using the OleDbDataAdapter, the only choice is to use SQL statements. If your database application is Microsoft SQLServer, then you can use the ***SQLDataAdapter***, which gives you the option of working with stored procedures.

The next screen of the Wizard is where your SQL statements are specified (see Figure 11-16). At this point, you should enter an SQL statement to SELECT all fields from the Customers table.

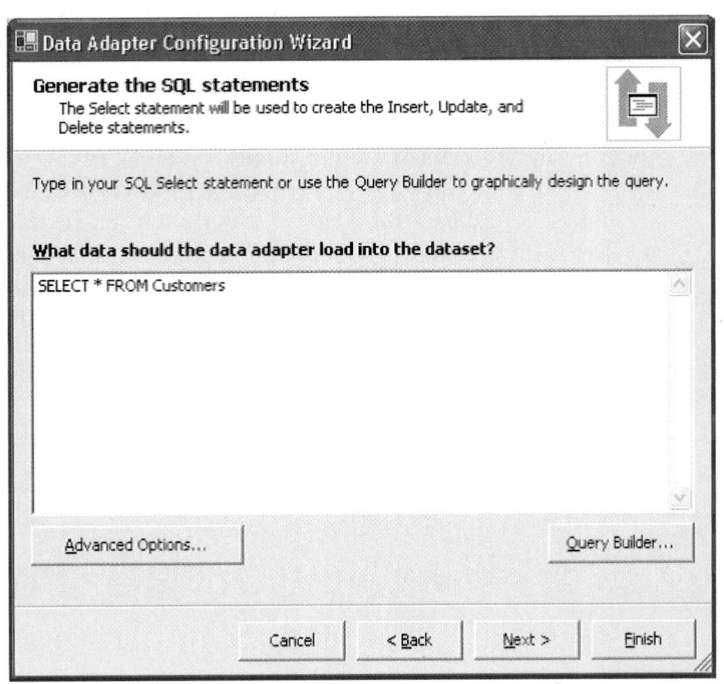


**FIGURE 11.16**
*Specifying the SQL Statement*

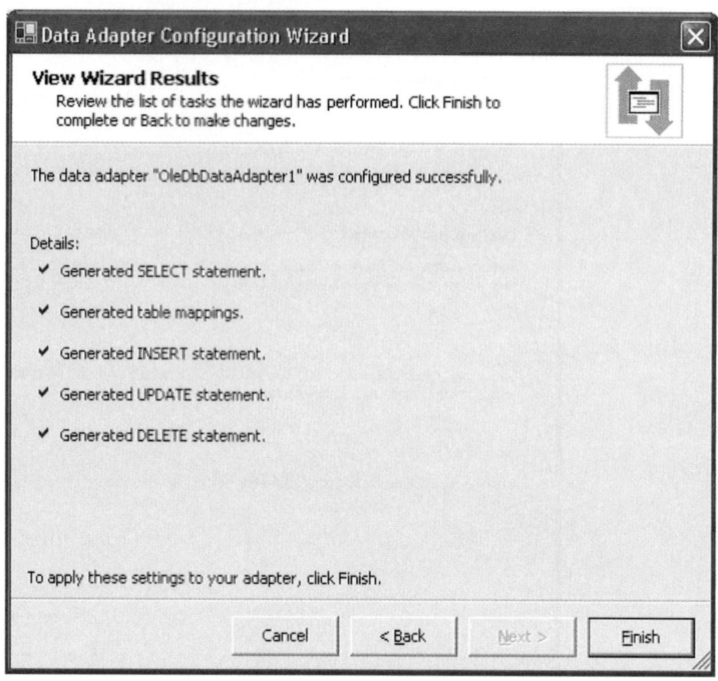


**FIGURE 11.17** *Data Adapter Configuration Wizard Results*

**Tip**

**Your code will be more readable if you rename DataAdapters using the *da* prefix followed by the name of the table referenced in the SQL.**

The last Wizard screen indicates that the Wizard was able to successfully configure the DataAdapter by generating a table mapping and SQL commands for Insert, Update, and Delete (if possible) (see Figure 11-17). Clicking Finish saves the settings of the DataAdapter.

The Configuration Wizard creates a DataAdapter with a default name, probably OleDbDataAdapter1. Select the DataAdapter control and change the Name property to daCustomers.

## Generating a Dataset

Once you have established a Connection and a DataAdapter, the next step is to create a ***Dataset***. A Dataset in ADO.NET is a temporary, local copy of the information in the table. In this example, we reference only a single table from the database (and therefore have only a single table in the Dataset). ADO.NET supports more advanced uses including multiple Datasets with multiple tables.

To create the Dataset, right-click on the daCustomers object and then select *Generate Dataset* from the pop-up menu. A Generate Dataset dialog box appears (see Figure 11-18). Specify that you are creating a new Dataset and name the Dataset using the *ds* prefix followed by the name of the table.

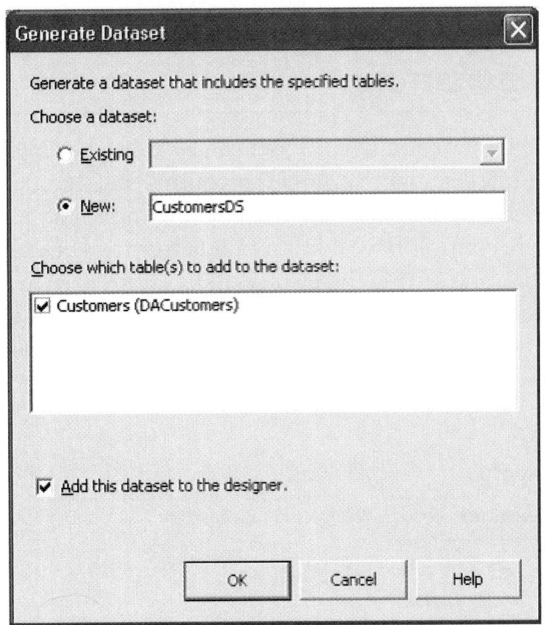


**FIGURE 11.18** *The Generate Dataset Dialog*

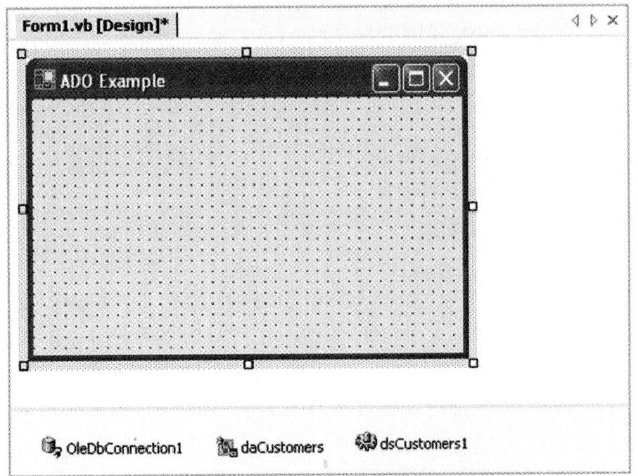


**FIGURE 11.19** *Solution with Connection, DataAdapter, and Dataset Controls*

**Tip**

**dsCustomers is a Dataset class, and dsCustomers1 is an instance of that class.**

After creating your Dataset, you should have three objects in the components tray: a Connection, an DataAdapter, and a Dataset (see Figure 11-19).

## ASK THE AUTHOR

**Q** Tell me again the difference between a Connection, a DataAdapter, and a Dataset?

**A** The Connection is the pipeline between your application and the database. The DataAdapter is the translator between your application and the database. The Dataset is the translated, local copy of the data in the database. Because the data in the Dataset has been translated, it may now be accessed by the application (e.g., bound controls and developer code).

## 11-4 Displaying and Navigating Records

The information in a Dataset can be viewed by means of one or more data-aware controls. A *data-aware control* is a control that can be bound to a Dataset; when bound, the control automatically displays the information it receives from the Dataset. Data-aware controls have a DataBound property. For example, the TextBox control is data-aware, and setting the DataBound.Text property will cause the text box to display the specified field of the current record in the Dataset table. Figure 11-20 shows TextBox1 being bound to the CustomerID field of the Customers table within the dsCustomers1 Dataset.

**Tip**
**Data-aware controls allow your application to view the information in a Dataset.**

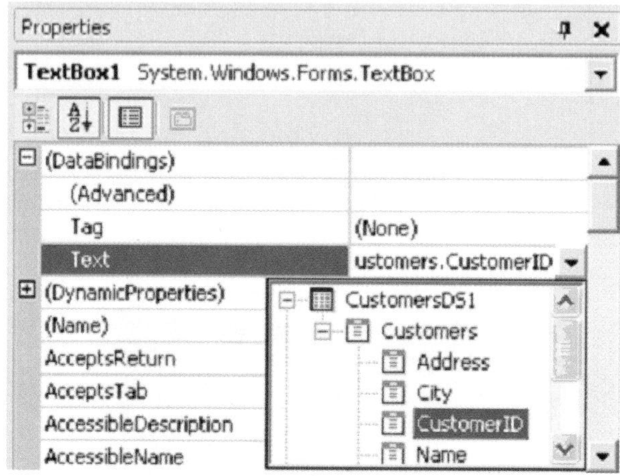


**FIGURE 11.20** *Binding a TextBox to the CustomerID Field*

Create six text boxes and set the DataBindings.Text properties for each to the six fields in the Customers table. Add six labels to describe the text boxes, and add four button controls for navigation. Your form should look something like Figure 11-21.

**FIGURE 11.21** *The Sample Database Form with Six Text Boxes and Four Buttons*

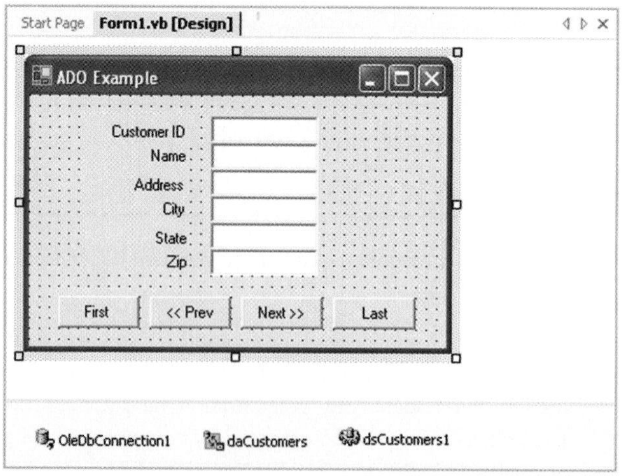

## The Fill Method

You can run the program now, but the data bound text boxes will not show any information because the Dataset is initially empty. The Fill method of the DataAdapter is used to populate the Dataset.

*Syntax:* *DataAdapter*.Fill(*dataset*)

*Examples:*

```
daCustomers.Fill(dsCustomers1)
```

**▶▶▶Tip**

**The Fill method typically appears in the Form Load event procedure but can be called anywhere in the solution. If the Dataset will be filled multiple times during the lifetime of an application, your solution should call the Dataset's Clear method before subsequent Fill methods.**

Add the preceding Fill method example to the Form Load event procedure and then rerun the application. The text boxes should display information about the first customer in the Dataset. In the following section, you will write event procedures for the four buttons to navigate between records in the Dataset.

## Dataset Navigation

The text boxes in Figure 11-21 are data bound, meaning they display their specified field values for the current record in the specified dataset. Changing the position of the current record will therefore change the data displayed in the text boxes.

Each form has a BindingContext object that keeps track of all the data sources associated with the form. The statement

```
BindingContext(dsCustomers1, "Customers")
```

refers to the Customers table within the dsCustomers1 Dataset. The BindingContext has a Position property that indicates the current record and a Count property that indicates the total number of records in the Dataset. The records are numbered beginning with 0, so the last record has a position 1 less than the value of Count. For example, if Count is 5, then there are records at Positions 0, 1, 2, 3, and 4.

The following code contains button click event procedures that update the Position property of the BindingContext object appropriately.

```
'
' *********** Design Time Properties ***********
'   OBJECT              PROPERTY                    SETTING
'
'   btnFirst            Text                        "<< First"
'
'   btnPrev             Text                        "Prev"
'
'   btnNext             Text                        "Next"
'
'   btnLast             Text                        "Last >>"
'
'
'   OleDbConnection1
'       ConnectionString           (See line below)
'       "Provider=Microsoft.Jet.OLEDB.4.0;Data Source=SampleDatabase.mdb"
'       (make sure SampleDatabase.mdb is in the Project's bin directory)
'
'   daCustomers
'       SelectCommand|Connection    OleDBConnection1
'       SelectCommand|CommandText   (See line below)
'   "SELECT Address, City, CustomerID, Name, State, Zip FROM Customers"
```

```
'
'   dsCustomers1        (Dataset generated from daCustomers
'                        as specified in Chapter reading)
'
'   txtCustomerID
'       Text                ""
'       DataBindings|Text   "dsCustomers1 - Customers.CustomerID"
'
'   txtName
'       Text                ""
'       DataBindings|Text   "dsCustomers1 - Customers.Name"
'
'   txtAddress
'       Text                ""
'       DataBindings|Text   "dsCustomers1 - Customers.Address"
'
'   txtCity
'       Text                ""
'       DataBindings|Text   "dsCustomers1 - Customers.City"
'
'   txtState
'       Text                ""
'       DataBindings|Text   "dsCustomers1 - Customers.State"
'
'   txtZip
'       Text                ""
'       DataBindings|Text   "dsCustomers1 - Customers.Zip"
'

Public Class Form1
    Inherits System.Windows.Forms.Form

Windows Form Designer generated code

    'The Dataset dsCustomers1 is filled by the DataAdapter Fill method
    Private Sub Form1_Load(ByVal sender As System.Object, _
                ByVal e As System.EventArgs) Handles MyBase.Load
        daCustomers.Fill(dsCustomers1)
    End Sub

    Private Sub btnFirst_Click(ByVal sender As System.Object, _
            ByVal e As System.EventArgs) Handles btnFirst.Click
        ' Set position of the Customers table to first record
        BindingContext(dsCustomers1, "Customers").Position = 0
    End Sub

    Private Sub btnPrev_Click(ByVal sender As System.Object, _
            ByVal e As System.EventArgs) Handles btnPrev.Click
        ' Decrement position of the Customers table
        With BindingContext(dsCustomers1, "Customers")
            If .Position > 0 Then .Position = .Position - 1
        End With
    End Sub
```

```
    Private Sub btnNext_Click(ByVal sender As System.Object, _
            ByVal e As System.EventArgs) Handles btnNext.Click
        ' Increment position of the Customers table
        With BindingContext(dsCustomers1, "Customers")
            If .Position < .Count - 1 Then .Position = .Position + 1
        End With
    End Sub

    Private Sub btnLast_Click(ByVal sender As System.Object, _
            ByVal e As System.EventArgs) Handles btnLast.Click
        ' Set position of the Customers table to last record
        With BindingContext(dsCustomers1, "Customers")
            .Position = .Count - 1
        End With
    End Sub

End Class
```

## 11-5 The DataGrid control

The DataGrid control is designed to display ADO.NET data in a scrollable grid. You can associate the data grid with a Dataset by using the DataSource and DataMember properties. The DataSource property specifies the name of the data source from which the grid will get data. The DataMember property specifies which table or other element to bind to if the data source contains more than one bindable element.

**►►► Tip**
**You can bind a data grid at runtime using the SetDataBinding method to set the DataSource and DataMember properties.**

Consider the following modification to the Customer navigation program from the previous section. As each customer is displayed, the orders for that customer should be displayed in a data grid. The data to appear in the grid would use the same Connection (after all, it comes from the same database). However, it would require a different SQL query and therefore new DataAdapter and Dataset objects. Let's look at these steps more closely.

Begin by adding a new DataAdapter, which should use the same Connection and have the following SQL statement:

```
SELECT * FROM Orders WHERE (CustomerID = -1)
```

The preceding SQL selects data from the Orders table based on the CustomerID primary key/foreign key relationship. The –1 is a placeholder value that makes the SELECT command syntactically valid, allowing the wizard to successfully complete. The WHERE clause will have to be changed dynamically in code when the current customer changes.

Rename the new DataAdapter *daOrders*. Then right-click on the DataAdapter to generate a Dataset. Select the Orders table and give the Dataset a new name, *dsOrders*.

Finally, add a data grid to the form below the navigation buttons. Specify the DataSource to be dsOrders1 and the DataMember to be Orders. (Alternatively, you may simply specify the DataSource to be dsOrders1.Orders). The design time form should now look similar to Figure 11-22.

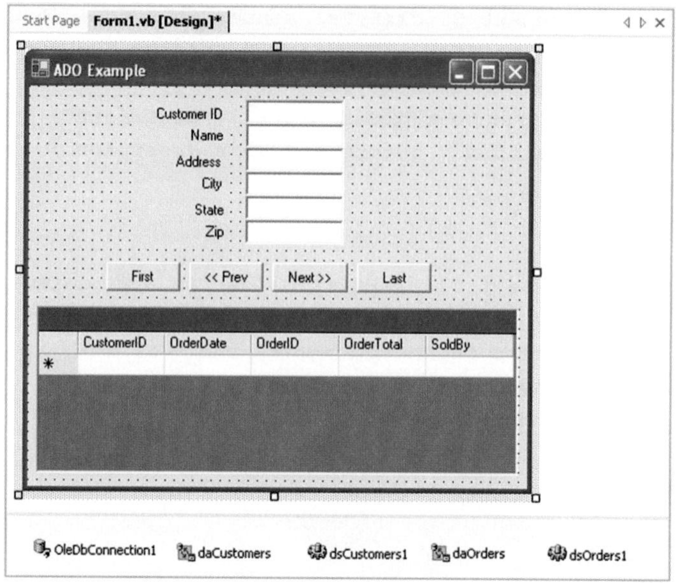


**FIGURE 11.22**
*Modified Customers Application with DataGrid Control*

The required code modifications are straightforward. The Dataset needs to be filled when the form is loaded. Also, a subroutine needs to be written that changes the SQL Select command to query only the orders for the currently displayed customer. This procedure should then be called by each of the navigation buttons. Figure 11-23 shows the program during execution. Notice that the data grid is displaying only records that apply to the current customer.

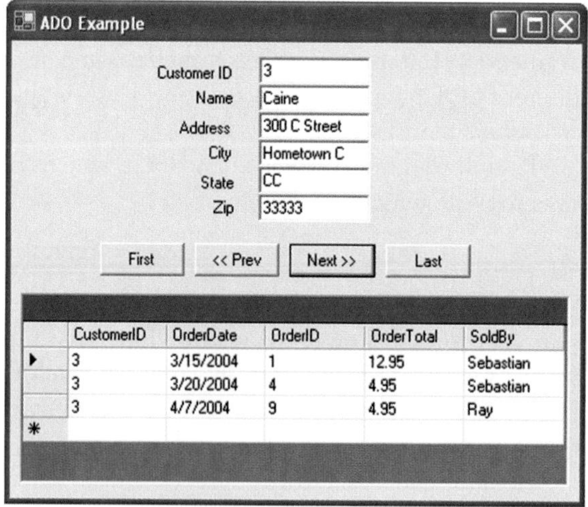


**FIGURE 11.23**
*Modified Customers Application*

The modified code follows, with changes highlighted.

```
' Revision: 1.1
'
'   *********** Design Time Properties ***********
'   OBJECT              PROPERTY                    SETTING
'
'   btnFirst            Text                        "<< First"
'
'   btnPrev             Text                        "Prev"
'
'   btnNext             Text                        "Next"
'
'   btnLast             Text                        "Last >>"
'
'
'   OleDbConnection1
'       ConnectionString            (See line below)
'       "Provider=Microsoft.Jet.OLEDB.4.0;Data Source=SampleDatabase.mdb"
'       (make sure SampleDatabase.mdb is in the Project's bin directory)
'
'   daCustomers
'       SelectCommand|Connection    OleDBConnection1
'       SelectCommand|CommandText   "SELECT * FROM Customers"
'
'   dsCustomers1        (Dataset generated from daCustomers
'                        as specified in Chapter reading)
'
'   txtCustomerID
'       Text                ""
'       DataBindings|Text   "dsCustomers1 - Customers.CustomerID"
'
'   txtName
'       Text                ""
'       DataBindings|Text   "dsCustomers1 - Customers.Name"
'
'   txtAddress
'       Text                ""
'       DataBindings|Text   "dsCustomers1 - Customers.Address"
'
'   txtCity
'       Text                ""
'       DataBindings|Text   "dsCustomers1 - Customers.City"
'
'   txtState
'       Text                ""
'       DataBindings|Text   "dsCustomers1 - Customers.State"
'
'   txtZip
'       Text                ""
```

```
'       DataBindings|Text    "dsCustomers1 - Customers.Zip"
'
'   Rev 1.1 additions
'
'   daOrders
'       SelectCommand|Connection     OleDBConnection1
'       SelectCommand|CommandText    (See line below)
'       "SELECT * FROM Orders WHERE (CustomerID = - 1)"
'
'   dsOrders1             (Dataset generated from daCustomers
'                         as specified in Chapter reading)
'
'   dgOrders
'       DataSource        dsOrders1.Orders
'

Public Class Form1
    Inherits System.Windows.Forms.Form

Windows Form Designer generated code

    'The Dataset dsCustomers1 is filled by the DataAdapter Fill method
    Private Sub Form1_Load(ByVal sender As System.Object, _
                ByVal e As System.EventArgs) Handles MyBase.Load
        daCustomers.Fill(dsCustomers1)
        UpdateOrders() ' Added Rev 1.1
    End Sub

    Private Sub btnFirst_Click(ByVal sender As System.Object, _
                ByVal e As System.EventArgs) Handles btnFirst.Click
        ' Set position of the Customers table to first record
        BindingContext(dsCustomers1, "Customers").Position = 0
        UpdateOrders() ' Added Rev 1.1
    End Sub

    Private Sub btnPrev_Click(ByVal sender As System.Object, _
                ByVal e As System.EventArgs) Handles btnPrev.Click
        ' Decrement position of the Customers table
        With BindingContext(dsCustomers1, "Customers")
            If .Position > 0 Then .Position = .Position - 1
        End With
        UpdateOrders() ' Added Rev 1.1
    End Sub

    Private Sub btnNext_Click(ByVal sender As System.Object, _
                ByVal e As System.EventArgs) Handles btnNext.Click
        ' Increment position of the Customers table
        With BindingContext(dsCustomers1, "Customers")
            If .Position < .Count - 1 Then .Position = .Position + 1
        End With
        UpdateOrders() ' Added Rev 1.1
    End Sub
```

```
    Private Sub btnLast_Click(ByVal sender As System.Object, _
            ByVal e As System.EventArgs) Handles btnLast.Click
        ' Set position of the Customers table to last record
        With BindingContext(dsCustomers1, "Customers")
            .Position = .Count - 1
        End With
        UpdateOrders() ' Added Rev 1.1
    End Sub

    Private Sub UpdateOrders() ' Added Rev 1.1
        daOrders.SelectCommand.CommandText = _
            "SELECT * FROM Orders WHERE (CustomerID = " & _
            txtCustomerID.Text & ")"
        dsOrders1.Clear()
        daOrders.Fill(dsOrders1)
    End Sub

End Class
```

CASE STUDY SOLUTION:

# Movie History

Reed says to Elizabeth, "You seem pretty confident about our ability to create a solution that will satisfy Noah's needs. I had the impression that database programming was too difficult for quick results."

"It can be difficult," Elizabeth replies, "but in this case the application is pretty straightforward. We can use some data-aware text boxes to display the customer information and a data grid to display the customer's rental history. When the current customer changes, those controls will update automatically."

"Great! Let's work on it now and show Noah tomorrow!" says Reed.

## Design

The design specifies how the solution will work in general terms. They begin by sketching the interface for the Movie History application, specifying the Name property for all the necessary controls. Other properties can also be identified when appropriate. The sketch in Figure 11-24 includes three text boxes and labels for displaying customer information, four buttons for navigation, a data

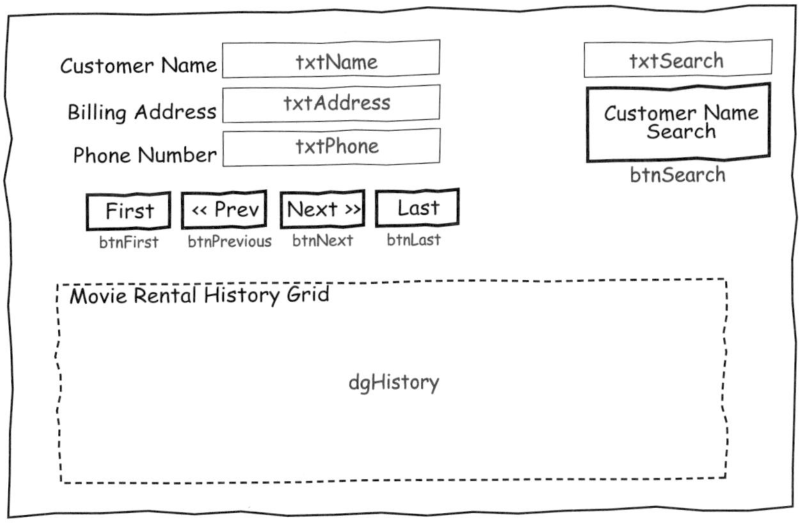

**FIGURE 11.24** *Sketch of the Movie History User Interface*

grid for displaying customer rental history, and a text box and button for customer searching.

The design should also include a high-level specification of all the actions and behavior required by the project. This can be done using flowchart or pseudocode notation and should describe behavior without getting into details of implementation. Table 11-2 provides pseudocode descriptions of the procedures in the Movie History design.

### Implementation

After they complete the general design, they then implement the details. The first step of implementation is to build the GUI. Figure 11-25 illustrates the Movie History GUI.

The second step is to implement the functionality described in the pseudocode design. It is also a good habit to document important design time property values for the form and interface controls. The solution code with good documentation appears as follows.

**Table 11.2 Design Pseudocode for Movie History Application**

| Procedure | Behavior |
|---|---|
| Form_Load | 1. Create the database objects |
| | 2. Create and fill CustTable with customers |
| | 3. Programmatically bind the text boxes to the DataSet |
| | 4. Show rental history for the currently selected customer |
| btnFirst_Click | 1. Set binding context position to 0 |
| | 2. Call UpdateRentalHistory |
| btnPrevious_Click | 1. Decrement binding context position |
| | 2. Call UpdateRentalHistory |
| btnNext_Click | 1. Increment binding context position |
| | 2. Call UpdateRentalHistory |
| btnLast_Click | 1. Set binding context position to size of the dataset |
| | 2. Call UpdateRentalHistory |
| btnSearch_Click | Call Search |
| txtSearch_TextChanged | Indicate the start of a new search |
| txtSearch_KeyDown | Call Search if Enter key was pressed |
| UpdateRentalHistory | 1. Create necessary database objects |
| | 2. Determine the current CustomerID |
| | 3. Change SQL command to retrieve rental history for current customer |
| DoNewSearch | 1. Search through rows for matching customer names and add to mSearchResults array |
| | 2. If matches are found, select the first matching customer |
| Search | If a new search has been initiated, call DoNewSearch, else select the next customer in the mSearchResults array |

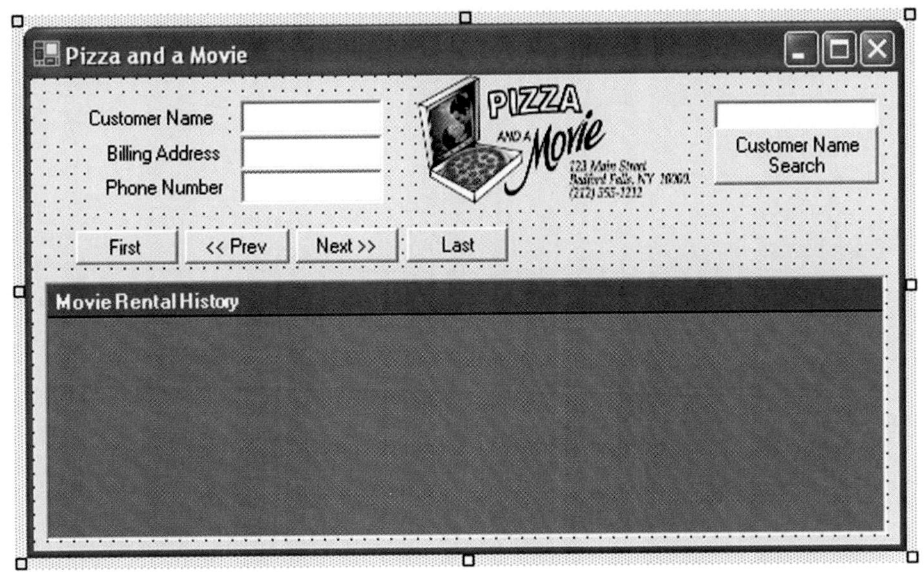


**FIGURE 11.25** *Movie History User Interface*

```
' Author: Reed & Elizabeth
' Project: Movie History
' Description:  This application connects to a database containing three tables:
'               1. Customers: CustomerID, CustomerName, BillingAddress, PhoneNumber
'               2. MovieInfos: MovieInfoID, MovieTitle, Description, Actors
'               3. Rentals: RentalID, CustomerID, MovieInfoID, CheckOutDate, DueDate
'               Customer information is displayed in databound text boxes which are
'               navigated with four button controls (First, Prev, Next, Last).
'               A DataGrid is used to display detail information for the selected
'               customer's rental history.  The grid is populated with an SQL
'               JOIN query which is updated with each change in selected customer.
'               There is also a search feature which allows the user to specify the
'               search string.  The search feature supports multiple searching on the
'               same string.
'
' *********** Design Time Properties ***********
'   OBJECT              PROPERTY            SETTING
'
'   btnFirst            Text                "<< First"
'
'   btnPrev             Text                "Prev"
'
'   btnNext             Text                "Next"
'
'   btnLast             Text                "Last >>"
'
'   txtSearch           Text                ""
'
'   btnSearch           Text                "Customer Name Search"
'
'   dgHistory           CaptionText         "Movie Rental History"
```

```
'
'   txtName              Text              ""
'
'   txtAddress           Text              ""
'
'   txtPhone
'                        Text              ""
'

Imports System.Data.OleDb   ' This is needed for the programmatic database controls

Public Class Form1
    Inherits System.Windows.Forms.Form

Windows Form Designer generated code

    ' Connection string for Access (Jet) database -
    ' Make sure Movies.mdb is in your project's bin directory
    Const CONNECTION_STRING As String = _
        "Provider=Microsoft.Jet.OLEDB.4.0;Data Source=Movies.mdb;Mode=Share Deny None"

    ' Create the DataSet programmatically
    Dim mdsCusts As New DataSet

    ' Module level variables for searching
    Dim mSearchString As String
    Dim mSearchResults() As Integer
    Dim mSearchResultCount As Integer
    Dim mCurrentSearchPos As Integer
    Dim mNewSearchFlag As Boolean = True

    Private Sub Form1_Load(ByVal sender As System.Object, _
            ByVal e As System.EventArgs) Handles MyBase.Load

        ' Create Connection, DataAdapter, and SQLCommand programmatically
        Dim cnMovies As New OleDbConnection(CONNECTION_STRING)
        Dim daCustomers As New OleDbDataAdapter
        Dim SQLCustomers As New OleDbCommand

        cnMovies.Open()
        SQLCustomers.CommandText = "SELECT * FROM Customers"
        SQLCustomers.Connection = cnMovies
        daCustomers.SelectCommand = SQLCustomers

        ' Use SQL to create CustTable in the mdsCusts DataSet
        mdsCusts.Clear()
        daCustomers.Fill(mdsCusts, "CustTable")

        ' Programmatically bind the text boxes to the DataSet
        txtName.DataBindings.Add("Text", mdsCusts, "CustTable.CustomerName")
        txtAddress.DataBindings.Add("Text", mdsCusts, "CustTable.BillingAddress")
        txtPhone.DataBindings.Add("Text", mdsCusts, "CustTable.PhoneNumber")
```

```
    ' Show rental history for the currently selected customer
    UpdateRentalHistory()
End Sub

' UpdateRentalHistory creates a dataset for populating the DataGrid.  The dataset
' is filled using an SQL command that pulls information from three tables using
' two JOINs.
Private Sub UpdateRentalHistory()
    ' Create Connection, DataAdapter, SQLCommand, and DataSet programmatically
    Dim cnMovies As New OleDbConnection(CONNECTION_STRING)
    Dim daRentals As New OleDbDataAdapter
    Dim SQLRentals As New OleDbCommand
    Dim dsRentals As New DataSet
    ' Determine the current CustomerID
    Dim CustomerID As Integer = _
        BindingContext(mdsCusts, "CustTable").Current.Row("CustomerID")

    cnMovies.Open()
    SQLRentals.CommandText = _
        "SELECT MovieTitle, CheckOutDate, DueDate, ReturnedDate, Actors, " & _
        " Description " & _
        " FROM (Customers LEFT JOIN Rentals ON " & _
        " Customers.CustomerID = Rentals.CustomerID) " & _
        " LEFT JOIN MovieInfos ON Rentals.MovieInfoID = MovieInfos.MovieInfoID " & _
        " WHERE (Customers.CustomerID = " & CustomerID.ToString() & ")"

    SQLRentals.Connection = cnMovies
    daRentals.SelectCommand = SQLRentals
    dsRentals.Clear()
    daRentals.Fill(dsRentals, "RentalsTable")
    dgRentals.DataSource = dsRentals.Tables("RentalsTable").DefaultView
End Sub

' DoNewSearch is called when the user has specified a new search string
' It populates the module array mSearchResults with the row positions of all
' matching rows. It then selects the first matching customer.
Private Sub DoNewSearch()
    Dim CurrentCustomer As String
    Dim Index As Integer
    Dim NewPos As Integer

    mSearchString = txtSearch.Text.ToUpper

    ' Search through rows for matching customer names and add to mSearchResults array.
    mSearchResultCount = 0
    For Index = 0 To mdsCusts.Tables("CustTable").Rows.Count - 1
        CurrentCustomer = _
            mdsCusts.Tables("CustTable").Rows(Index).Item("CustomerName").ToString
        If CurrentCustomer.ToUpper.IndexOf(mSearchString) <> -1 Then
            mSearchResultCount += 1
            ReDim Preserve mSearchResults(mSearchResultCount)
            mSearchResults(mSearchResultCount) = Index
        End If
    Next
```

```
        ' If matches are found, select the first matching customer.
        If mSearchResultCount > 0 Then
            mCurrentSearchPos = 1
            NewPos = mSearchResults(mCurrentSearchPos)
            BindingContext.Item(mdsCusts, "CustTable").Position = NewPos
            UpdateRentalHistory()
            btnSearch.Text = "Search Again"
            mNewSearchFlag = False
        Else
            MsgBox("Customer Not Found! ")
        End If
    End Sub

    ' Search will perform a new search or select the next matching customer
    Private Sub Search()
        Dim NewPos As Integer

        If mNewSearchFlag Then
            DoNewSearch()
        Else
            If mCurrentSearchPos >= mSearchResultCount Then
                MsgBox("No more search results available! ")
            Else
                mCurrentSearchPos += 1
                NewPos = mSearchResults(mCurrentSearchPos)
                BindingContext.Item(mdsCusts, "CustTable").Position = NewPos
                UpdateRentalHistory()
            End If
        End If
    End Sub

    Private Sub btnSearch_Click(ByVal sender As System.Object, _
            ByVal e As System.EventArgs) Handles btnSearch.Click
        Search()
    End Sub

    Private Sub txtSearch_TextChanged(ByVal sender As Object, _
            ByVal e As System.EventArgs) Handles txtSearch.TextChanged
        ' Changing the text in txtSearch ends the current search.
        btnSearch.Text = "Customer Name Search"
        mNewSearchFlag = True
    End Sub

    Private Sub txtSearch_KeyDown(ByVal sender As Object, _
            ByVal e As System.Windows.Forms.KeyEventArgs) Handles txtSearch.KeyDown
        ' Pressing ENTER when txtSearch has focus calls Search()
        If e.KeyValue = Keys.Enter Then
            Search()
        End If
    End Sub

    Private Sub btnFirst_Click(ByVal sender As System.Object, _
            ByVal e As System.EventArgs) Handles btnFirst.Click
```

```
        BindingContext(mdsCusts, "CustTable").Position = 0
        UpdateRentalHistory()
    End Sub

    Private Sub btnPrevious_Click(ByVal sender As System.Object, _
            ByVal e As System.EventArgs) Handles btnPrev.Click
        With BindingContext(mdsCusts, "CustTable")
            If .Position > 0 Then .Position -= 1
        End With
        UpdateRentalHistory()
    End Sub

    Private Sub btnNext_Click(ByVal sender As System.Object, _
            ByVal e As System.EventArgs) Handles btnNext.Click
        With BindingContext(mdsCusts, "CustTable")
            If .Position < .Count - 1 Then .Position += 1
        End With
        UpdateRentalHistory()
    End Sub

    Private Sub btnLast_Click(ByVal sender As System.Object, _
            ByVal e As System.EventArgs) Handles btnLast.Click
        With BindingContext(mdsCusts, "CustTable")
            .Position = .Count - 1
        End With
        UpdateRentalHistory()
    End Sub

End Class
```

### Testing the Solution

You can test Noah and Elizabeth's solution by implementing their design as shown in the previous section, and then running the application. Figure 11-26 shows the Movie History application during execution. The navigation buttons allow the user to switch from one customer to another. The data grid automatically updates to display the selected customer's movie rental history. The user can also search for a specific customer using the text box and search button. If you are having problems getting your solution to execute, you may want to read Appendix B: Debugging.

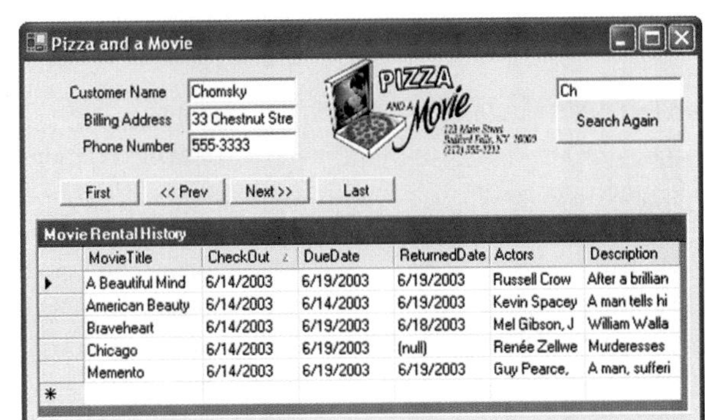


**FIGURE 11.26**
*Sample Output for Movie History Application*

## Chapter Summary

- A database is a collection of one or more structured sets (e.g., tables or files) of data. A Database Management System (DBMS) is a collection of programs that support the creation, storage, manipulation, querying, and printing of information to and from a database.
- A table is a two-dimensional matrix of rows (records) and columns (fields). A field is a single piece of information, and a record is one complete set of fields. Most tables contain a unique primary key that distinguishes the records in the table.
- A foreign key is a field in a table that refers to the primary key in another table. Typically, relationships involve the foreign key from one table and the primary key in a related table.
- An application communicates with a DBMS through queries written in Structured Query Language, or SQL.
- The SELECT command is used to select specific information from one or more tables in a database.
- The WHERE clause is used to choose information based on selection criteria.
- The results of a query can be arranged in ascending or descending order with the ORDER BY clause.
- By design, relational databases store data over multiple tables to eliminate data redundancy. An INNER JOIN statement can select data from multiple tables in a single query.
- A Connection object establishes a link from your application to a database and specifies the type and location of the database.
- Once a Connection has been established, the next step is to create a DataAdapter. A DataAdapter does the work of passing information between the database and your application. The SQL command is part of the DataAdapter.
- Once a Connection and a DataAdapter have been established, the next step is to create a Dataset, which is a temporary, local copy of the information in the table.
- A data-aware control is a control that can be bound to a Dataset; when bound, the control automatically displays the information it receives from the Dataset.
- Each form has a BindingContext object that keeps track of all the data sources associated with the form. The BindingContext has a Position property that indicates the current record and a Count property that indicates the total number of records in the Dataset.
- The DataGrid control is designed to display ADO.NET data in a scrollable grid.

## Key Terms

ADO.NET p. 294
As p. 293
Connection p. 294
DataAdapter p. 297
database p. 287
Database Management System (DBMS) p. 288
Dataset p. 300
field p. 287
foreign key p. 287
INNER JOIN p. 293
LEFT JOIN p. 293
linking table p. 289
many-to-many relationship p. 289
normalization p. 289
OleDbConnection p. 294
OleDbDataAdapter p. 298
one-to-many relationship p. 289
ORDER BY clause p. 291
primary key p. 287
queries p. 290
relational database model p. 287
record p. 287
RIGHT JOIN p. 293
SELECT command p. 290
Structured Query Language (SQL) p. 290
SQLConnection p. 294
SQLDataAdapter p. 299
table p. 287
WHERE clause p. 290

## Review Questions

1. What is a primary key? Why is it important?
2. What is a foreign key? When is a foreign key used?
3. What is SQL? What is the usage of the following SQL keywords: FROM, WHERE, ORDER BY?
4. What SQL command is used to retrieve data from one or more tables? What is the usage of the following SQL keywords: JOIN, ON?
5. What is a data-aware control? How do you make a text box data-aware?
6. What two properties must be set on a DataGrid control to associate it with a Dataset?
7. What is the difference between a Connection, a DataAdapter, and a Dataset?
8. What does the DataAdapter Fill method do?
9. What is a BindingContext? Name two useful properties of the BindingContext.

## Programming Exercises

**11-1. Renter History.** Write an application that is the opposite of the Movie History program presented this chapter. The application should display, navigate, and search for movies, and the data grid should display the customers who have rented the selected movie.

**11-2. Pet Owner.** Create a database with two tables: Pets and Owners. Add a foreign key field in the Pets table back to the Owners table to form a one-to-many relationship (so each pet has exactly one owner, and one owner can own many pets). Populate the two tables with about five to ten records each. Then write a VB.NET application to navigate among the owners and display their information in text boxes. The application should also contain a data grid that displays pet information for all the pets owned by the current pet owner.

## Extended Case Studies

### Pizza and a Movie

Modify the Movie History Case Study Solution (see Figure 11-26) to include three additional text boxes that will contain the subtotal, sales tax, and total amounts for all the combined rentals in the customer's history.

### Singing Mimes

Modify the SampleDatabase example presented in this chapter (see Figure 11-23) to include three additional text boxes that will contain the subtotal, sales tax, and total amounts for all the combined orders in the customer's history.

CHAPTER 12

# Web Forms and ASP.NET

## OUTLINE



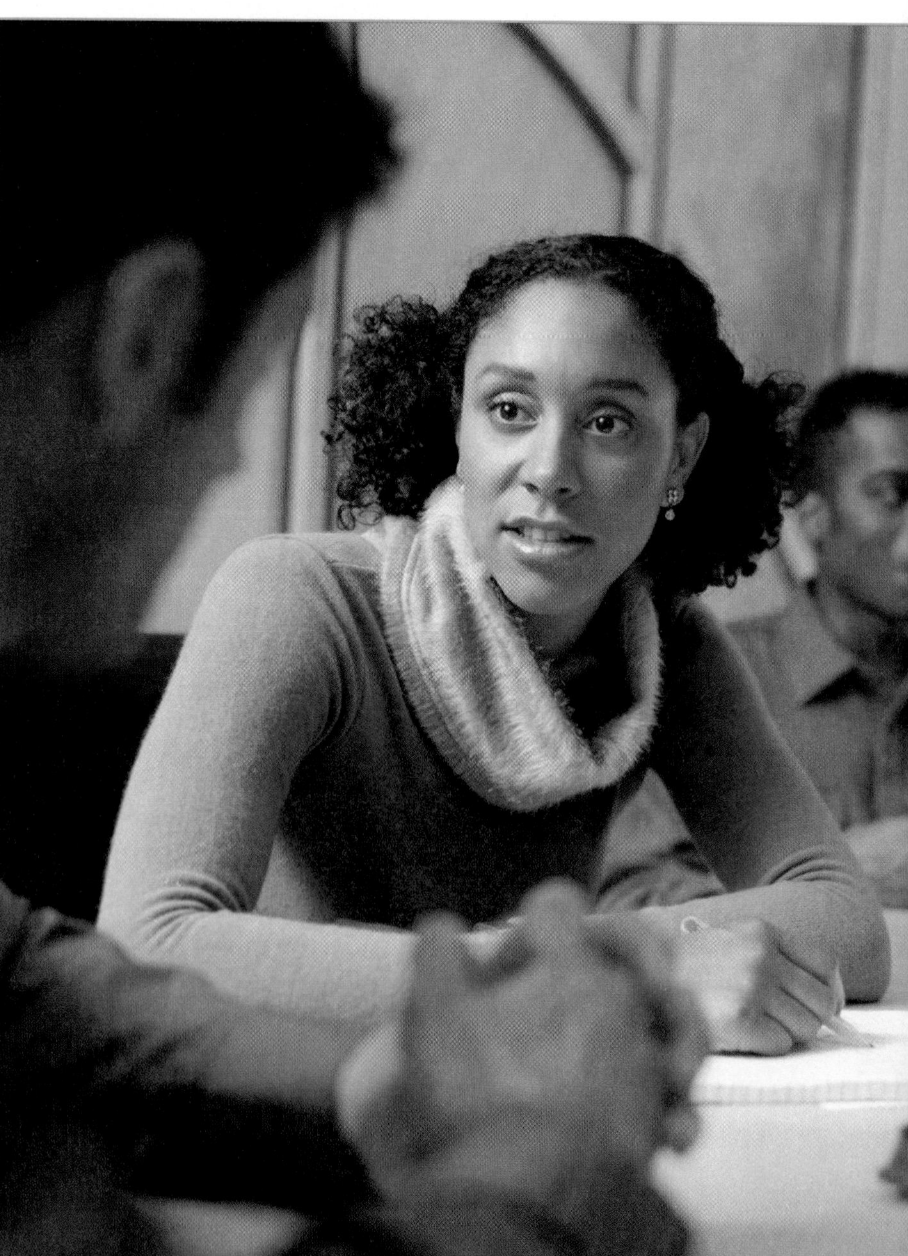

## ▶ INTERVIEW

**Joyce A. Daugherty, Vice President of Information Technology, Humana Inc., Louisville, Kentucky**

***Interviewer:*** Please tell us how you got involved in the IT industry.

***Daugherty:*** I chose a career in IT because I enjoyed the technical programming and I wanted a challenging career that provided compensation for my family and opportunities for my future growth.

***Interviewer:*** How does Humana use Visual Basic?

***Daugherty:*** One example of the use of Visual Basic at Humana is how we support our Internet Physician Finder Plus. This application allows Humana subscribers to search via the Internet for providers in a given location using criteria like location, language spoken, mileage radius, and health plan type. Visual Basic communicates between multiple tiers of our web-based applications. Associates also use Visual Basic to create utility applications to assist in data manipulation and other everyday tasks.

***Interviewer:*** What is important for students to learn in a first programming course?

***Daugherty:*** Do not just memorize the syntax in programming classes—understand how all the components logically fit together.

***Interviewer:*** What advice do you have for students preparing for a career in the IT industry?

***Daugherty:*** Students entering IT must be prepared for a lifetime of learning, as technology and processes continue to evolve. The knowledge gained in acquiring a college degree provides the entry point to the work world, but the long-term success of the IT professional depends on the individual continuing to understand the new technology and the continually changing business issues. An IT professional of the future must also have good communication skills and be able to work in teams. A person must be flexible to adjust to the continually changing business and technical environment.

## OBJECTIVES

At the completion of this chapter, you will

- **Understand the relationship between HTML and ASP.NET**
- **Understand how web applications work in terms of the client/server model**
- **Develop ASP.NET applications using a text editor**
- **Develop ASP.NET applications using Visual Studio .NET**
- **Understand the similarities and differences between Windows Forms and Web Forms**
- **Develop interesting web applications using ASP.NET and Visual Studio**

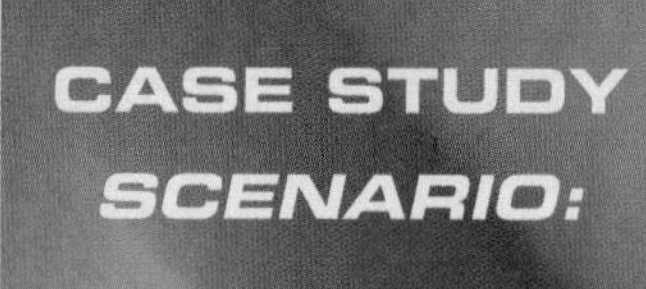


# Order Planner

Noah, owner of Pizza and a Movie, has called back Elizabeth and Reed, this time for advice on improving the store's presence on the web.

In his office with Elizabeth and Reed seated across from him, Noah says, "My business needs a web presence, but I want something more than a traditional web page. I want the customer to somehow interact with the site."

"Interaction is a good thing," Elizabeth agrees. "What did you have in mind?"

"I'm not sure, but maybe we should emphasize my competitive prices and the fact that I give free delivery on orders over $20."

Reed suggests, "Maybe we could build a web site where the customer makes a sample order, and it would calculate the cost of having that order delivered to the door. The web site could take into account all your business logic, such as free delivery on orders over $20, and include that in the calculation. You could even have an Internet coupon that gives an additional discount."

Noah ponders the idea. "An order planner web site? That is an interesting idea. It would be interactive, which is good. And it would emphasize my low prices. Yes, that is a very good idea. I had no idea you could do something like that with a web page."

Elizabeth continues, "We will develop a prototype with no commitment on your part. If you decide to use it, we will have to find some appropriate compensation."

"Fair enough," says Noah. "Do you want to give me an estimate of how much it might end up costing me, if I decide I like the prototype?"

Elizabeth nods. "Reed and I talked about this before coming over. We were thinking about this price, which you can pay as credit for the store." Elizabeth hands Noah a number on a sheet of paper.

"Looks like we have a deal," says Noah. "You make the prototype, and if I like it, then we can talk about going live with the application. Then you and your friends will be enjoying pizzas and movies for quite a while."

Elizabeth, Reed, and Noah's solution appears later in this chapter.

## 12-1 HTML and Static Web Pages

This chapter is about the exciting world of ASP.NET and web programming. We begin, however, with a brief overview of static HTML.

***HTML*** stands for Hypertext Markup Language, a language for displaying text in a web browser such as Internet Explorer or Netscape Navigator. When writing HTML, text is marked by ***tags*** consisting of a left angle bracket (<), a tag name, and a right angle bracket (>). Tags are usually paired (e.g., <*tag*> and </*tag*>) to start and end the tag instruction. The end tag looks just like the start tag except a slash (/) precedes the text within the brackets. For example, italic and bold tags can be specified in HTML as:

```
This is <I>an example</I> of <B>HTML text</B>
```

The preceding HTML document would produce a page with the following text when viewed in a browser:

This is *an example* of **HTML text**

Notice that the tags do not appear as part of the page and that tag pairs affect all the text between the pair. Furthermore, some tags may be used without an end tag, such as <BR> which adds a line break into the text, or <HR> which adds a horizontal line. Table 12-1 provides a brief list of some common HTML tags.

**Table 12.1 Some Common HTML Tags**

| HTML Tags | Description |
|---|---|
| <html> </html> | Specifies the document contains HTML (required) |
| <head> </head> | Defines the head of the document (descriptive) |
| <body> </body> | Defines the body of the document (displayed in the browser) |
| <center> </center> | Specifies the contained text should be centered in the browser |
| <B> </B> | Bold font for the contained text |
| <I> </I> | Italic font for the contained text |
| <U> </U> | Underline font for the contained text |
| <A href="*filename*"> </A> | Anchor (hypertext link) for the contained text |
| <BR> | Creates a line break |
| <P> | Creates a paragraph break |
| <HR> | Creates a horizontal rule (or line) on a page |

To better understand HTML, consider the text file shown in Figure 12-1. This file was created using Notepad but could have been done with any simple text editor. The file is saved as **"SimplePage.html"** (with quotes, to prevent Notepad from adding a .txt extension).

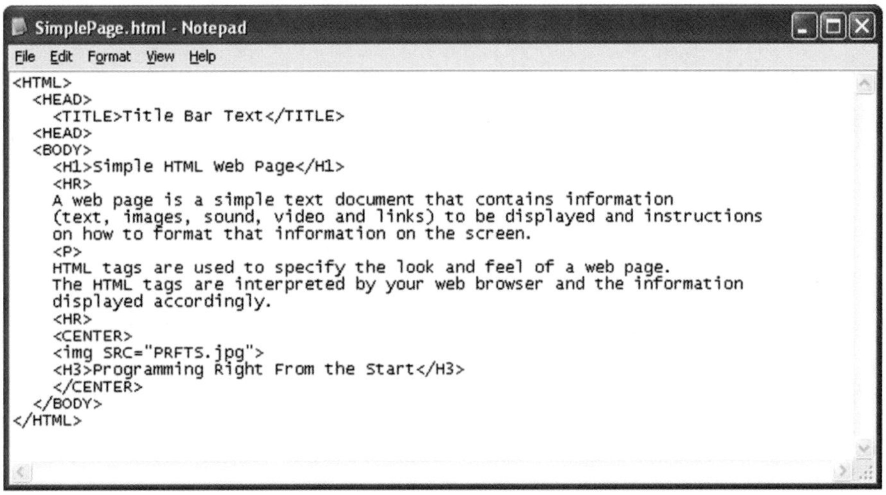

**FIGURE 12.1** *Simple HTML Document*

```
SimplePage.html - Notepad
File Edit Format View Help
<HTML>
  <HEAD>
    <TITLE>Title Bar Text</TITLE>
  <HEAD>
  <BODY>
    <H1>Simple HTML Web Page</H1>
    <HR>
    A web page is a simple text document that contains information
    (text, images, sound, video and links) to be displayed and instructions
    on how to format that information on the screen.
    <P>
    HTML tags are used to specify the look and feel of a web page.
    The HTML tags are interpreted by your web browser and the information
    displayed accordingly.
    <HR>
    <CENTER>
    <img SRC="PRFTS.jpg">
    <H3>Programming Right From the Start</H3>
    </CENTER>
  </BODY>
</HTML>
```

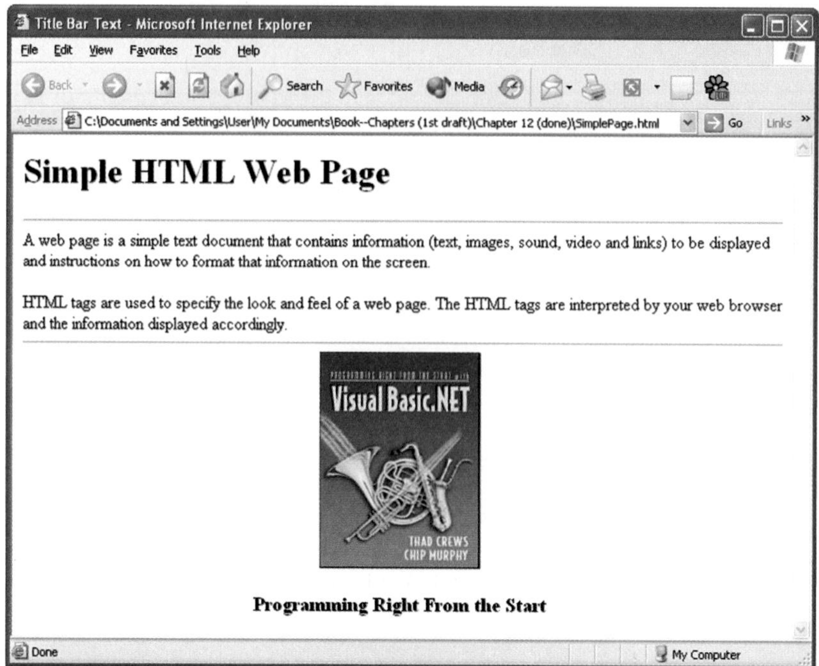


**FIGURE 12.2** *Resulting Web Page (generated from Figure 12-1 HTML document)*

The SimplePage.html file can be viewed in a browser such as Internet Explorer. Select File | Open and then browse to the SimplePage.html file. Figure 12-2 shows the file when viewed by a browser.

## 12-2 Web Applications

HTML is fine for displaying static information. However, even simple calculations are difficult with HTML, and meaningful e-commerce applications are practically impossible. Examples of web applications include online shopping carts (e-commerce) and web sites that display user requested information from a database.

> **Tip**
> **Any computer can be turned into a web server by installing server software and connecting the machine to the Internet.**

A ***web application*** is a client/server application that lives on a web server. The ***client*** is the user's machine with an Internet browser. The ***web server*** is a machine that stores the web documents, including web pages and server scripts for responding to client requests (Figure 12-3).

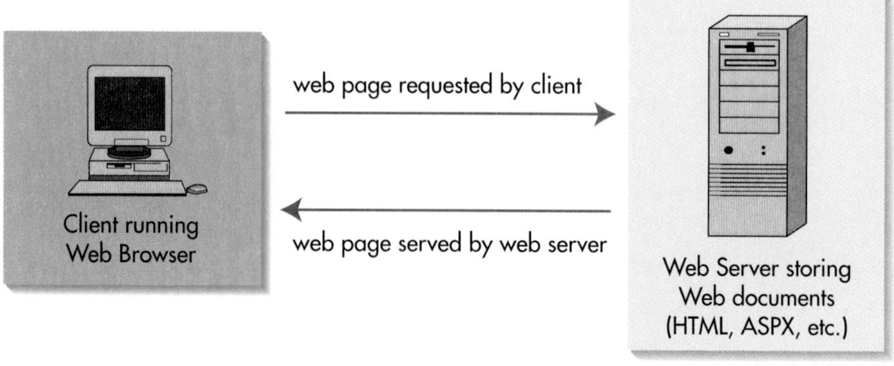


**FIGURE 12.3** *The Client/Server Model for Web Applications*

There are many advantages to working with web applications. Web applications are by their nature platform independent, and they can run on a variety of client architectures. Deployment costs are significantly reduced because the application is immediately available to anyone with Internet access and a browser. Likewise, maintenance upgrades can be done much faster and at a reduced cost. Documentation is easy because the HTML supports embedded documentation and links to auxiliary material. Finally, web applications run in a browser, which is a familiar environment for most users.

## Round Trips

One of the most important things to understand about web applications is the division of labor between the browser and the server. The browser provides the application interface that allows the user to interact with the form. However, all processing involving server components must occur on the server. Therefore, when a user action occurs that requires server processing, the form must be posted back to the server. This is referred to as a ***postback***. The web server processes the request and generates new HTML that is returned to the client browser. This sequence of events is referred to as a ***round trip***.

**Tip**

**In Web Forms, a server control event—such as clicking a button—results in a round trip.**

Consider the following scenario: A web application presents the user with a form that contains two input text boxes, an add button, and an output label. The user enters data in the text boxes and clicks the add button to determine the sum. In response to the user event, the browser posts the page to the server with an appropriate button click event. A server process handles the event by performing the addition and updating the form. The server then returns the updated page to the browser. This process represents a round trip (Figure 12-4).

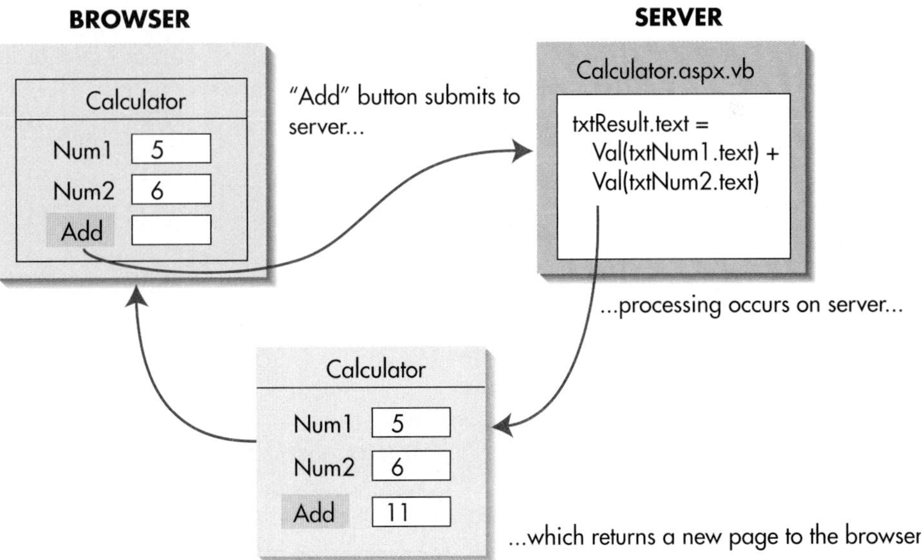


**FIGURE 12.4**
*Illustration of a Round Trip*

## ASK THE AUTHOR

**Q** A web application with a round trip seems like a lot just to add two numbers. Is that really necessary?

**A** The purpose of the example is not to add numbers but to illustrate the process by which a browser and server work together to complete a round trip. Imagine that the web application was an e-commerce shopping cart. The user would interact with the browser to add or change an item to be purchased. This transaction request would be sent to the server for processing. The server would process the request using appropriate business logic (check inventory, determine appropriate discounts and coupons, check for preferred customer status, etc.) and make necessary updates to the orders table in the company database. After server processing, the updated page would be returned to the client's browser. The round trip is the same when adding two numbers as it is when processing a shopping cart request.

## 12-3 ASP.NET

***ASP.NET*** is a platform for developing and running web applications on a web server. ASP.NET web applications include everything from traditional web sites that serve HTML pages to fully featured business applications that run on an intranet or the Internet.

ASP.NET web applications can be developed with a simple text editor or with the assistance of Visual Studio .NET. We will illustrate both approaches but recommend using Visual Studio because of its powerful support for design-time objects and controls and a runtime execution context.

To better understand ASP.NET, consider the following code listing. The listing looks much like an HTML file, including the following HTML tags: <HTML>, <HEAD>, <TITLE>, <BODY>, <CENTER>, <FONT>, and <BR>. The listing also contains ASP.NET code (which we have highlighted in blue to help it stand out). ASP.NET code is notated by <% and %> brackets. The first line denotes that VB.NET will be the language syntax for this ASP.NET page. The <%= marking is a command to add the value of the VB.NET variable into the HTML document at the current location.

```
<%@ Page Language="VB" Debug="True" %>
<html>
  <head>
    <title>Introduction to ASP.NET</title>
  </head>
  <body>
    <center>
      <% Dim TextSize as Integer %>
      <% For TextSize = 1 to 7 %>
        <font size = <%=TextSize%>>
        Programming Right From the Start<br>
        </font>
      <% Next %>
    </center>
  </body>
</html>
```

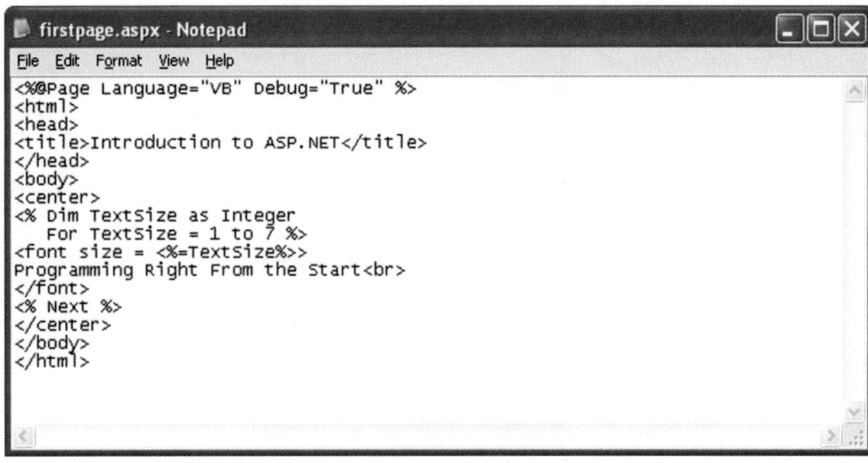


**FIGURE 12.5** *Simple ASP.NET File Created Using Notepad*

**Tip**

**Microsoft's older technology, ASP, uses the .asp extension, whereas ASP.NET files use the .aspx extension. This allows ASP and ASP.NET to coexist if necessary.**

Launch Notepad and type the code as shown in Figure 12-5. Save the page as **"NotepadExample.aspx"**.

Microsoft's Internet Information Services (IIS) is a web server for use on Windows machines. If you have IIS on your local machine, then you can view the page by placing it in the C:\Inetpub\wwwroot folder and browsing to http://localhost/NotepadExample.aspx. If not, you will need to send the page to an IIS server to view it. The server interprets the VB.NET code and substitutes values for the text size variable each pass through the loop. The resulting HTML document appears as a series of increasingly large strings (Figure 12-6).

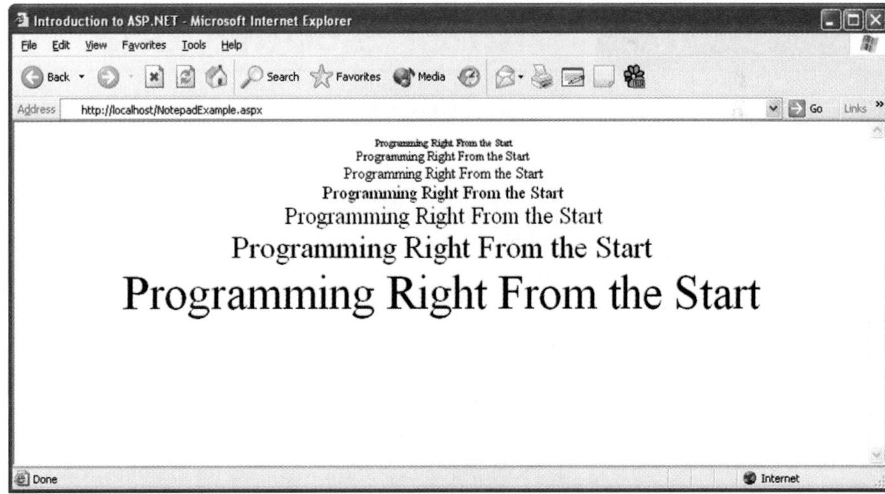


**FIGURE 12.6** *ASP.NET Generated Web Page*

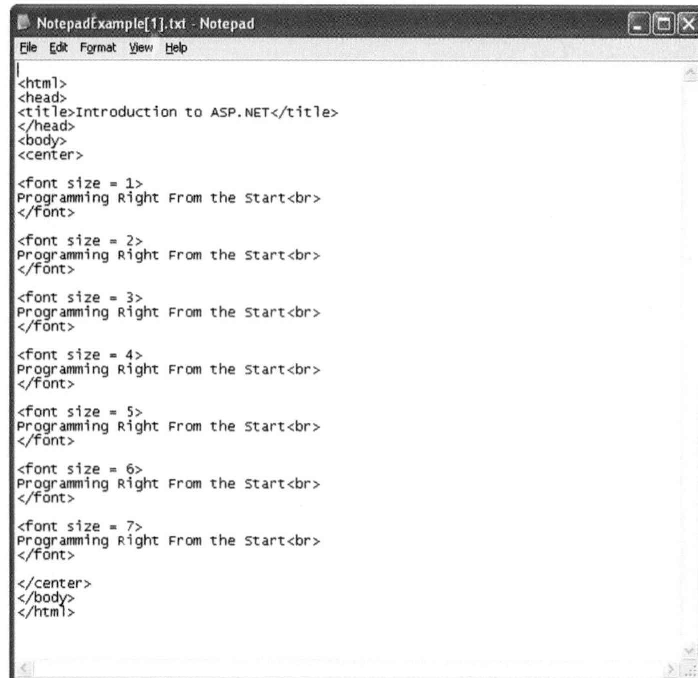


```
<html>
<head>
<title>Introduction to ASP.NET</title>
</head>
<body>
<center>

<font size = 1>
Programming Right From the Start<br>
</font>

<font size = 2>
Programming Right From the Start<br>
</font>

<font size = 3>
Programming Right From the Start<br>
</font>

<font size = 4>
Programming Right From the Start<br>
</font>

<font size = 5>
Programming Right From the Start<br>
</font>

<font size = 6>
Programming Right From the Start<br>
</font>

<font size = 7>
Programming Right From the Start<br>
</font>

</center>
</body>
</html>
```

**FIGURE 12.7** *ASP.NET Generated Web Page, Viewed as HTML*

Now view the web page as HTML source code. (If you are using Internet Explorer, you can do this by right-clicking the document and selecting View Source from the pop-up menu.) Notice that the file is pure HTML with no ASP.NET code (Figure 12-7). The ASP.NET code lives on the server and was executed by the server, generating the seven lines with increasing font size. However, the VB.NET code itself never appears on the client machine.

## 12-4 Visual Studio and Web Forms

In the previous section we created an ASP.NET application using a simple text editor such as Notepad. Alternatively, you can create your ASP.NET applications using Visual Studio. The advantage of using Visual Studio is that it provides tools that make application development faster, easier, and more reliable. These tools include the following:

- Visual designers for web pages with drag-and-drop controls and code views with syntax checking
- Code-aware editors that include statement completion, syntax checking, and other IntelliSense features
- Integrated compilation and debugging
- Project management facilities for creating and managing application files, including deployment to local or remote servers

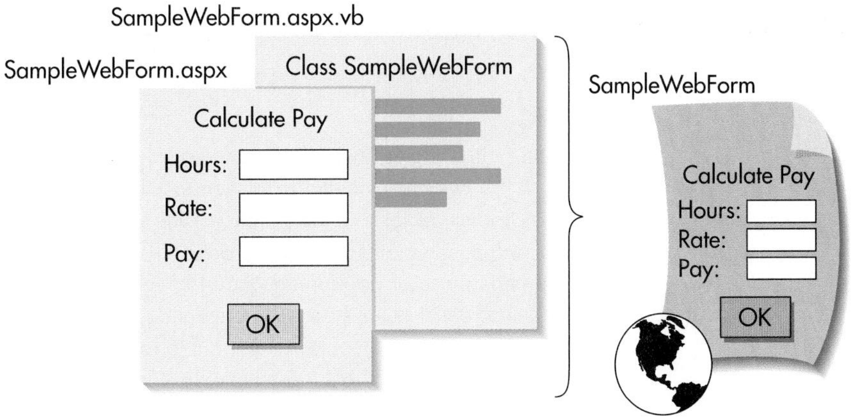

**FIGURE 12.8** *ASPX and ASPX.VB Files Together to Make up the Web Form*

SampleWebForm.aspx.vb
SampleWebForm.aspx
Class SampleWebForm
Calculate Pay
Hours:
Rate:
Pay:
OK
SampleWebForm
Calculate Pay
Hours:
Rate:
Pay:
OK

Visual Studio supports ***Web Forms*** to quickly and easily create the user interface for ASP.NET web applications. Web Forms combine the speed and ease of a rapid application development (RAD) environment with the power of compiled programming languages. Web servers execute ASP.NET Web Forms to generate HTML for viewing on any compatible browser or mobile device.

A Web Form is composed of two files, the user interface form (with an .aspx extension) and the ***code-behind*** file (with an .aspx.vb extension), as shown in Figure 12-8. In Visual Studio, you see the ASPX and the VB.NET files as two views of the same page (e.g., SampleWebForm.aspx and SampleWebForm.aspx.vb). The web server will compile these two files and create a new class containing the static HTML, ASP.NET server controls, and code from your form compiled together. This class generates the HTML sent to the client whenever the page is called.

> **Tip**
> **Because the code-behind page resides only on the server, it can respond only to server controls. Server controls are denoted by a small green triangle in the upper left corner of the control.**

Web Forms are similar to Windows Forms in that they are *event driven*. As a developer, you may respond to events that occur to server controls on the HTML page. Event handlers for server controls are written in the code-behind page using VB.NET syntax. Processing an event for a server control requires a round trip. Because of round trip latency, server events are limited to events that cause significant changes, such as button clicks and text changes. It would not make sense to handle something like mouse move events on the server.

## ASP.NET Illustrated: Jake's Problem

We illustrate ASP.NET development using Visual Studio Web Forms by writing a web application to solve Jake's problem (Chapters 1 and 7), which is restated as follows.

> **Jake's Problem:** Jake has a car with an 8-gallon fuel tank. Jake fills his tank with gas and then drives 60 miles to a friend's house. When he gets to his friend's house, he has 6 gallons left in his fuel tank. Write a program that accepts input values for tank size, miles traveled, and fuel left, and that uses those inputs to calculate and display how many miles Jake can drive on a full tank of gas.

## ASK THE AUTHOR

**Q** We have already solved Jake's problem. Why are we doing it again?

**A** In Chapter 1 we implemented a solution to Jake's problem using Visual Logic. In Chapter 7 we implemented a solution to Jake's problem using VB.NET and Windows Forms. In this chapter we solve Jake's problem using ASP.NET and Web Forms. In all three cases, the logical solution remains the same; only the implementation platform changes. This illustrates the importance of developing good logical solutions regardless of the implementation technology. There will always be new latest-and-greatest technologies, and you need to be aware of them. However, it is equally important to refine your skills at identifying problems and developing appropriate and accurate logical solutions, regardless of the technology that implements those solutions.

---

**Tip**

**http://localhost is a special way to address your machine locally. The IP address allocated to localhost is 127.0.0.1.**

Begin by starting a New Project and selecting ASP.NET Web Application. The location of the project is the HTTP address of the Web Server that will host the project. The server you connect to must have IIS 4.0 or higher and the .NET Framework. If you install IIS on your local machine, then you can use your local machine as the web server, (e.g., http://localhost). Change the project name from *WebApplication1* to *Jakes Problem* and click OK (Figure 12-9).

After you click the OK button, Visual Studio attempts to communicate with the web server. If the web server is not available or not properly configured, Visual Studio will display a dialog box stating that the web access failed (Figure 12-10).

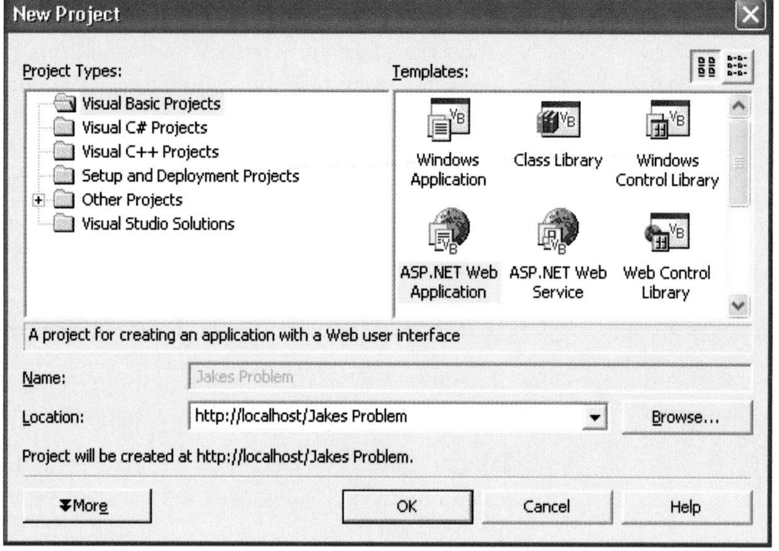


**FIGURE 12.9** *Creating a Web Application in Visual Studio .NET*

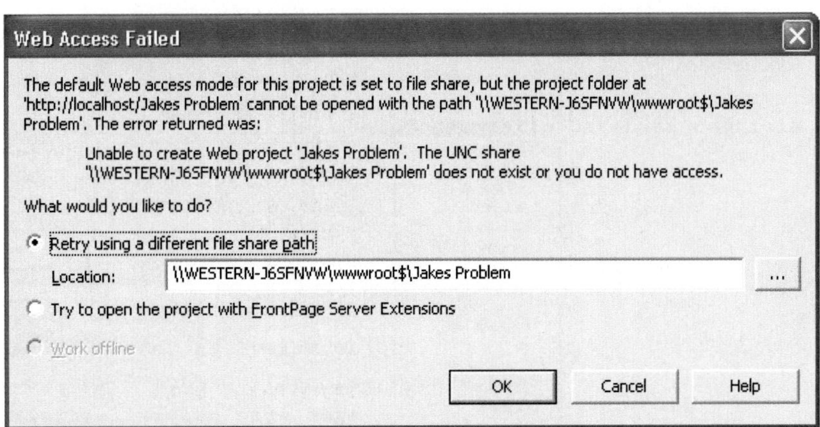


**FIGURE 12.10** *You Must Install IIS on Your Machine to Test ASP.NET Code Using Localhost*

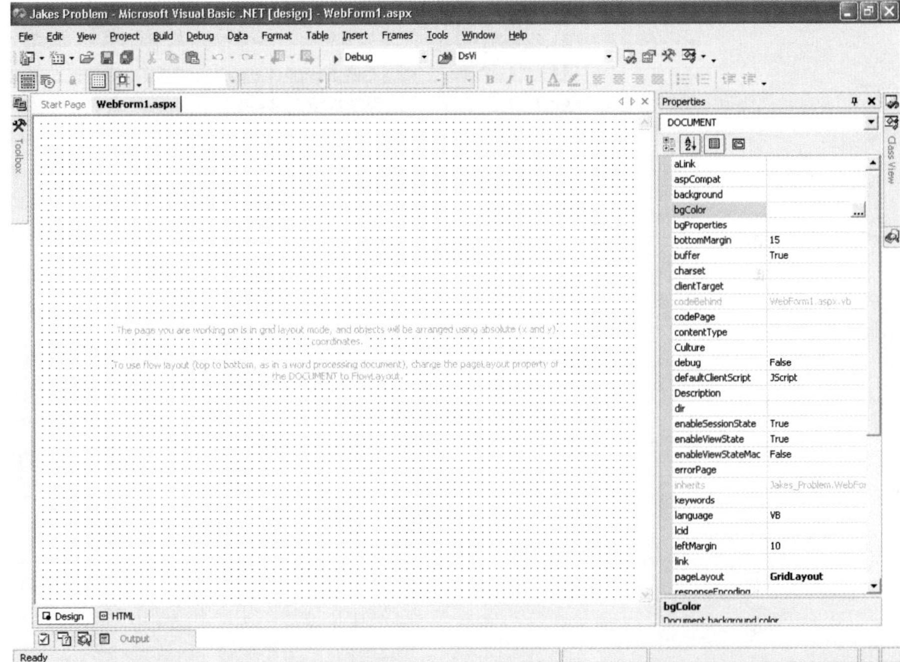


**FIGURE 12.11** *Visual Studio Web Form Designer*

If Visual Studio is successfully able to communicate with the web server, then it will create a project on the server and open WebForm1.aspx for editing. When working with Web Forms in Visual Studio, you use the Web Forms Designer (Figure 12-11). The designer includes a WYSIWYG view, called Design view, for laying out the elements of the page. Alternatively, you can switch the designer to HTML view (selected in the lower left corner of the Designer window), which gives you direct access to the ASP.NET and HTML syntax of the elements on the page. Finally, the designer includes a code editor with IntelliSense that you can use to create the page initialization and event handler code for your page. We will see the code editor later in this example.

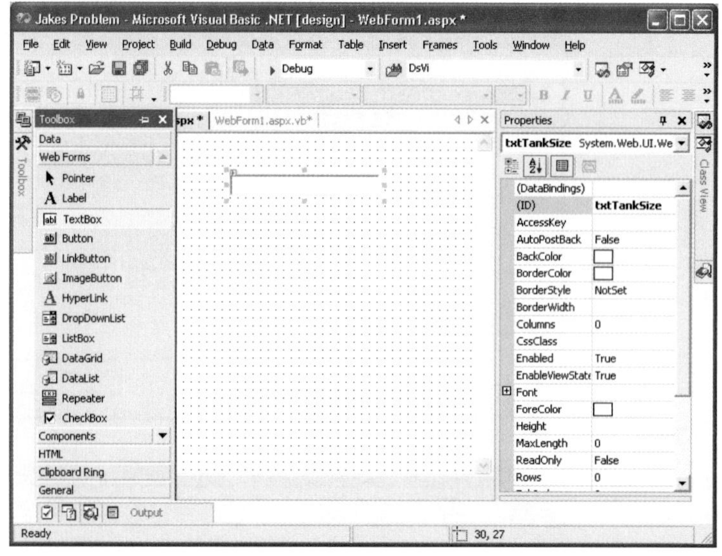


**FIGURE 12.12** *Web Form with One Text Box, The ID Property Changed Appropriately*

Begin your solution by adding a text box to accept the tank size input value. As with Windows Forms, you select the control from the toolbox and add it to the form (Figure 12-12). If you plan on referencing the control in code, you should give the control an appropriate value for its ID property.

This solution requires three text box controls to accept the three input values, a label for the output, and a button to trigger the calculation. In addition, the form may contain three additional labels to describe the input text boxes. Add these controls, changing the ID properties for the text boxes, output label, and button, as appropriate. The form should now look something like Figure 12-13.

The logic for the Web Forms page consists of code that you create to interact with the form. The programming logic resides in a code-behind file with an .aspx.vb extension (Figure 12-14). The logic written in the code-behind file is written in VB.NET syntax. Actually, ASP.NET is not limited to VB.NET syntax. Developers familiar

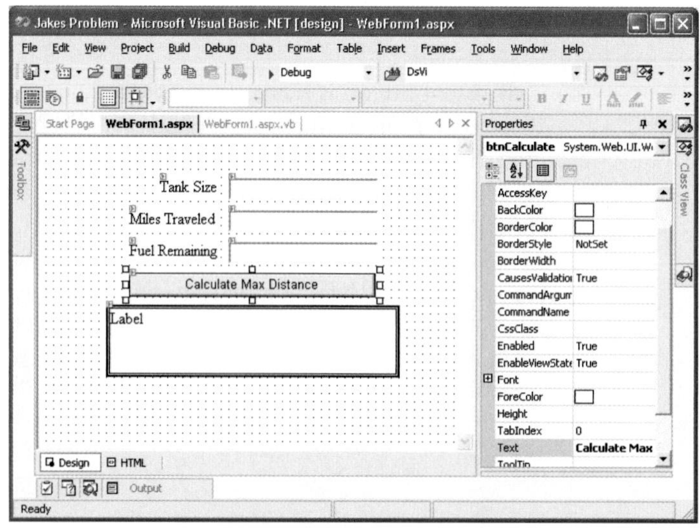


**FIGURE 12.13** *Web Form Design for Jake's Problem*

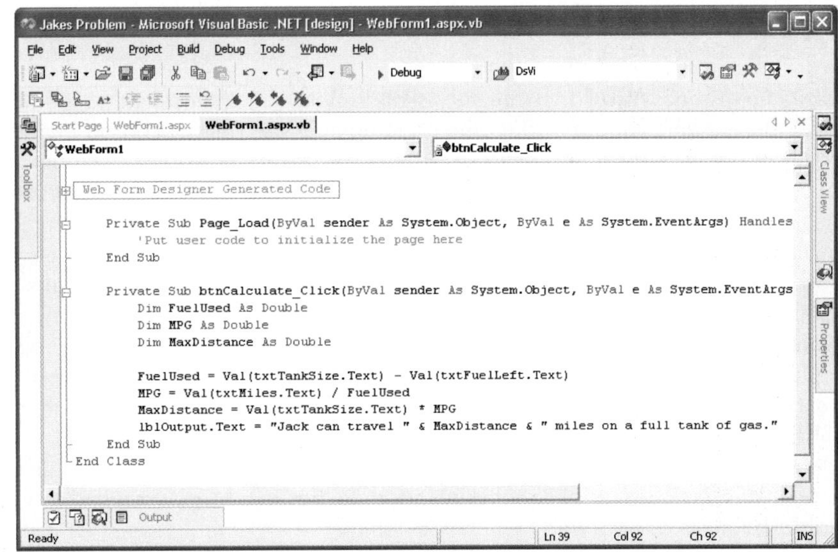


**FIGURE 12.14** *Code-Behind File for Jake's Problem*

with C# could write their code-behind file using C# syntax, and the file would have an .aspx.cs extension. In fact, any .NET language could be used to implement the code-behind logic.

Run the application. Visual Studio launches Internet Explorer and connects to the ASPX page on the server. In response to the browser's request, the server compiles the interface and code-behind files, thus creating the Web Form. The resulting Web Form generates the initial HTML that is sent to the client machine. Type in values in the text boxes and then press the button. The button press generates a postback, and the request is sent to the server. The Web Form processes the button click event and modifies the page as specified in the code-behind logic. The new web page is sent to the client browser to be displayed (Figure 12-15).

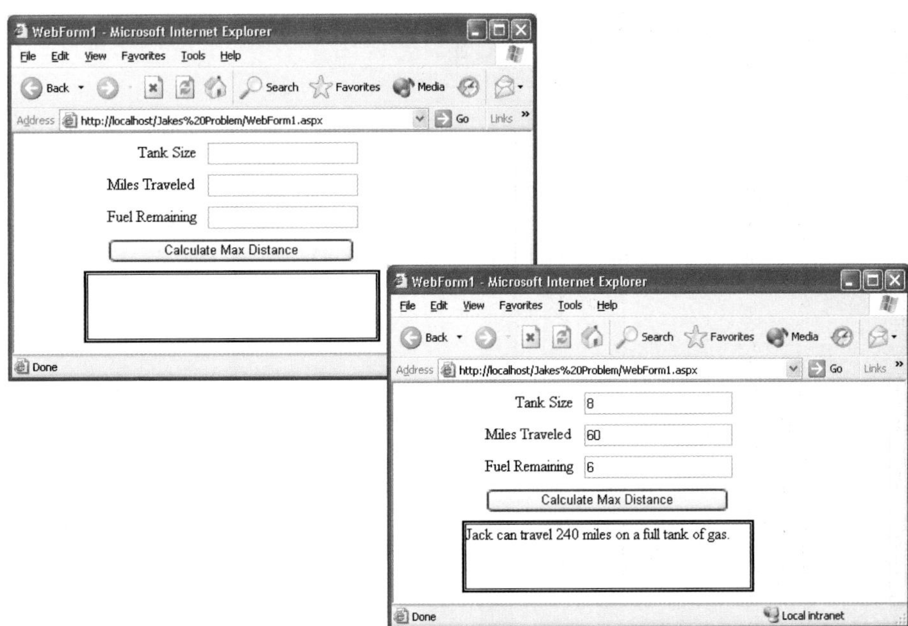


**FIGURE 12.15** *Initial Web Page and Web Page after Postback*

MENTOR

Windows Forms and Web Forms are very similar. Both have full design-time support within the development environment and can provide a rich user interface and advanced application functionality to solve business problems. How, then, does one decide which technology is appropriate for a given application?

Windows Forms are used to develop applications where the client is expected to shoulder a significant amount of the processing burden in an application. Examples include drawing or graphics applications, data-entry systems, point-of-sale systems, and games.

ASP.NET Web Forms are used to create applications in which the primary user interface is a browser. Naturally, this includes applications intended to be available publicly on the web, such as e-commerce applications. But Web Forms are useful for more than just creating web sites—many other applications lend themselves to a thin front end as well, such as an intranet-based employee handbook or benefits applications. An important feature is that there is no distribution cost because users already have installed the only piece of the application that they need—the browser.

Windows Forms require the .NET Framework to be running on the client computer. That means the client machine must be running a Windows OS. Web Forms applications are, by definition, platform-independent—they require only a browser and may run on any hardware. (For Web Forms, the .NET Framework runs on the web server.)

There is no right answer when it comes to Windows Forms versus Web Forms. Both have their strengths and weaknesses. As a developer, you will need to evaluate the strengths and weaknesses of each technology on a project-by-project basis.

## Order Planner

Back on campus, Reed and Elizabeth are talking about their meeting with Noah.

"I think we can give Noah what he wants without too much difficulty," Reed says. "We can use a variety of controls, including a drop-down listbox for selecting the pizza size, check boxes for selecting the pizza toppings, text boxes for entering the number of movies by category, labels for the outputs, and a button to trigger the calculations."

Elizabeth nods. "We could also add some appropriate graphics and create a bright design for visual appeal."

"Sounds great. Let's earn some pizza!" Reed says, smiling.

### Design

The design specifies how the solution will work in general terms. They begin by sketching the interface for the Order Planner application and specifying the ID property for all the necessary controls. Other properties can also be specified when it seems appropriate. The sketch in Figure 12-16 includes a drop-down listbox to select pizza size, check boxes to select pizza toppings, text boxes to specify the number of movies for two types (new release and standard), and labels for pizza subtotal, movie subtotal, order subtotal, tax, delivery charge,

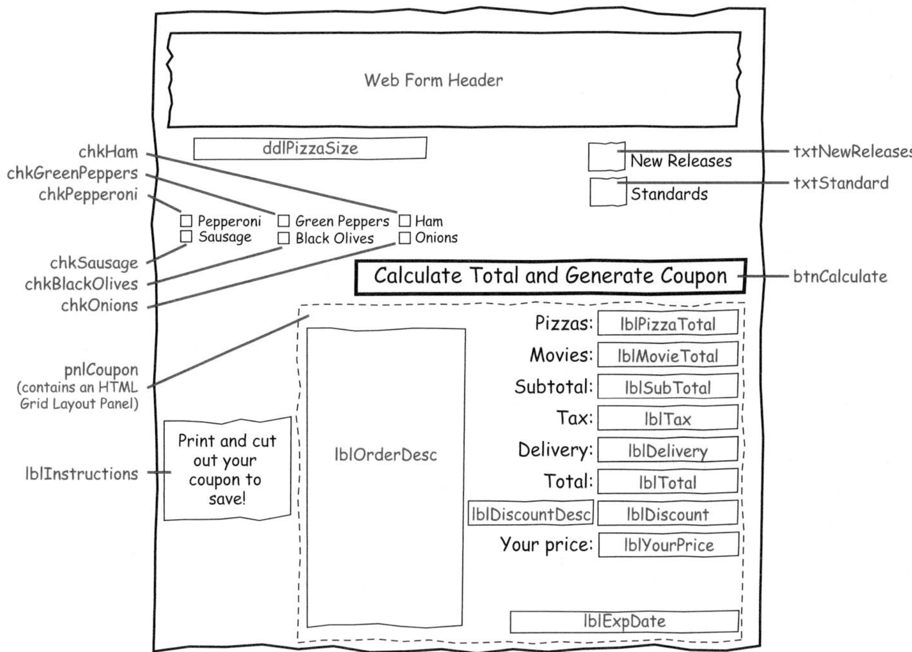


**FIGURE 12.16** *Sketch of the Order Planner Interface*

coupon discount and total. Static labels should also be included to describe the interface elements to the user.

The design should also include a high-level specification of all the actions and behavior required by the project. This can be done using flowchart or pseudocode notation and should describe behavior without getting into details of implementation. Table 12-2 provides pseudocode descriptions of the procedures in the Order Planner design.

**Table 12.2** Design Pseudocode for Order Planner Application

| Procedure | Behavior |
|---|---|
| Page_Load | On first showing fill ListBox, set ExpDate and Discount description |
| btnCalculate_Click | 1. Build a HTML formatted string describing the order and assign to description label |
| | 2. Determine the pizza subtotal using business logic values |
| | 3. Determine the movie subtotal using business logic values |
| | 4. Determine the order subtotal, tax, delivery, and total |
| | 5. Determine the discount and the coupon price |
| | 6. Make the coupon and instructions visible |

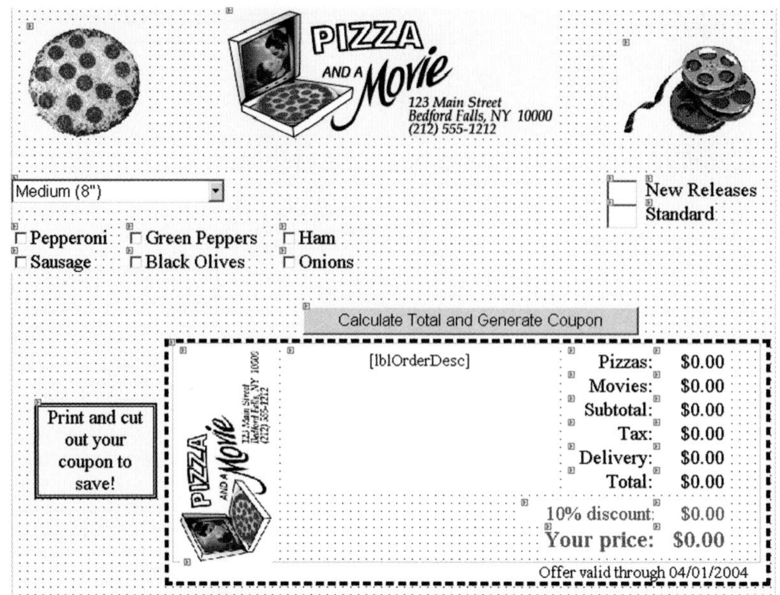


**FIGURE 12.17** *Order Planner User Interface*

### Implementation

After they complete the general design, they must implement the details. The first step of implementation is to build the GUI. Figure 12-17 illustrates the Order Planner GUI.

The second step is to implement the functionality described in the pseudocode design. It is also a good habit to document important design-time property values for the form and interface controls. The solution code with good documentation appears as follows.

```
' Author: Reed & Elizabeth
' Project: Pizza and a Movie Coupon Generator
' Description:  CouponGenerator is a web application that allows the user
'               to specify a pizza size and toppings, and also the number
'               and type of videos to be rented. CouponGenerator will then
'               use business logic to determine the order total. It will
'               display the order in a coupon along with a discount.
'
'
'   *** Design Time Properties ***
'   OBJECT            PROPERTY     SETTING
'
'   ddlPizzaSize      (default properties)
'
'   chkPepperoni      Text         "Pepperoni"
'
'   chkSausage        Text         "Sausage"
'
'   chkGreenPeppers   Text         "Green Peppers"
'
'   chkBlackOlives    Text         "Black Olives"
'
'   chkHam            Text         "Ham"
'
'   chkOnions         Text         "Onions"
'
```

```
'   txtNewReleases  Text            (Empty)
'
'   txtStandard     Text            (Empty)
'
'   btnCalculate    Text            "Calculate Total and Generate Coupon"
'
'   lblInstructions Visible         False
'                   BorderStyle     Double
'                   Text            "Print and cut out your coupon to save!"
'
'   (The pnlCoupon below is a Grid Layout Panel from the Toolbox's HTML section)
'   pnlCoupon       Visible         False
'                   BorderStyle     Dashed
'                   BackColor       White
'
'   (The items below all appear on the pnlCoupon)
'   lblOrderDesc    Font            X-Small
'
'   lblPizzaTotal   Text            "<p align="right">$0.00"
'   lblMovieTotal   Text            "<p align="right">$0.00"
'   lblSubTotal     Text            "<p align="right">$0.00"
'   lblTax          Text            "<p align="right">$0.00"
'   lblDelivery     Text            "<p align="right">$0.00"
'   lblTotal        Text            "<p align="right">$0.00"
'
'   lblDiscount     Text            "<p align="right">$0.00"
'                   ForeColor       Red
'
'   lblYourPrice    Text            "<p align="right">$0.00"
'                   ForeColor       Red
'                   Font            Larger
'
'   lblExpDate      Text            "<p align="right"> Offer valid through 04/01/9999"
'                   Font            Smaller
'

Public Class WebForm1
    Inherits System.Web.UI.Page

Web Form Designer generated code

    ' Business logic constants
    Const MEDIUM_BASE_PRICE As Double = 8.99
    Const LARGE_BASE_PRICE As Double = 10.99
    Const GIGANTIC_BASE_PRICE As Double = 12.99
    Const TOPPING_PRICE As Double = 0.99
    Const STANDARD_VIDEO_PRICE As Double = 1.95
    Const NEW_RELEASE_VIDEO_PRICE As Double = 2.95
    Const DELIVERY_FEE As Double = 2.0
    Const TAX_RATE As Double = 0.065
    Const COUPON_DISCOUNT As Double = 0.1 ' (10 percent)
    Const FREE_DELIVERY_AMOUNT As Double = 20
```

```
' HTML constants
Const HTML_LEFT_ALIGN As String = "<p align=""left""> "
Const HTML_RIGHT_ALIGN As String = "<p align=""right""> "
Const HTML_INDENT As String = "        "

Private Sub Page_Load(ByVal sender As System.Object, _
        ByVal e As System.EventArgs) Handles MyBase.Load
    ' Put user code to initialize the page here
    Dim liNone, liMedium, liLarge, liGigantic As ListItem

    ' On first showing, fill ListBox, set ExpDate and set Discount description
    If Not IsPostBack Then
        ddlPizzaSize.Items.Clear()
        liNone = New ListItem
        liNone.Text = "None"
        liNone.Value = "None"
        liMedium = New ListItem
        liMedium.Text = "Medium (8"") -- " & FormatCurrency(MEDIUM_BASE_PRICE)
        liMedium.Value = "Medium"
        liLarge = New ListItem
        liLarge.Text = "Large (10"") -- " & FormatCurrency(LARGE_BASE_PRICE)
        liLarge.Value = "Large"
        liGigantic = New ListItem
        liGigantic.Text = "Gigantic (12"") -- " & FormatCurrency(GIGANTIC_BASE_PRICE)
        liGigantic.Value = "Gigantic"
        ddlPizzaSize.Items.Add(liNone)
        ddlPizzaSize.Items.Add(liMedium)
        ddlPizzaSize.Items.Add(liLarge)
        ddlPizzaSize.Items.Add(liGigantic)
        ddlPizzaSize.SelectedIndex = 0

        lblExpDate.Text = HTML_RIGHT_ALIGN & "Offer valid through " & _
            FormatDateTime(Today().AddDays(7))
        lblDiscountDesc.Text = FormatPercent(COUPON_DISCOUNT, 0) & " discount:"
    End If
End Sub

Private Sub btnCalculate_Click(ByVal sender As System.Object, _
        ByVal e As System.EventArgs) Handles btnCalculate.Click
    Dim Desc As String
    Dim ToppingDesc As String
    Dim HasToppingFlag As Boolean
    Dim NewReleaseCount As Integer
    Dim StandardCount As Integer
    Dim Pizzas As Double
    Dim Movies As Double
    Dim SubTotal As Double
    Dim DeliveryFee As Double
    Dim Total As Double
    Dim Discount As Double
    Dim YourPrice As Double

    ' Build a string with HTML formatted text describing the order
    Desc = ""
```

```
If ddlPizzaSize.SelectedItem.Value <> "None" Then
    ToppingDesc = ""
    HasToppingFlag = False
    If chkPepperoni.Checked Then
        ToppingDesc &= HTML_INDENT & "pepperoni <br>"
        HasToppingFlag = True
    End If
    If chkSausage.Checked Then
        ToppingDesc &= HTML_INDENT & "sausage <br>"
        HasToppingFlag = True
    End If
    If chkHam.Checked Then
        ToppingDesc &= HTML_INDENT & "ham <br>"
        HasToppingFlag = True
    End If
    If chkBlackOlives.Checked Then
        ToppingDesc &= HTML_INDENT & "black olives <br>"
        HasToppingFlag = True
    End If
    If chkGreenPeppers.Checked Then
        ToppingDesc &= HTML_INDENT & "green peppers <br>"
        HasToppingFlag = True
    End If
    If chkOnions.Checked Then
        ToppingDesc &= HTML_INDENT & "onions <br>"
        HasToppingFlag = True
    End If
    If HasToppingFlag = False Then
        Desc = HTML_LEFT_ALIGN & "A " & ddlPizzaSize.SelectedItem.Value & _
            " cheese pizza. <br>"
    Else
        Desc = HTML_LEFT_ALIGN & "A " & ddlPizzaSize.SelectedItem.Value & _
            " pizza with the following toppings: <br>" & ToppingDesc & "<br>"
    End If
End If

NewReleaseCount = Val(txtNewReleases.Text)
If NewReleaseCount <> 0 Then
    Desc &= NewReleaseCount.ToString & " new release video"
    If NewReleaseCount > 1 Then Desc &= "s"
    Desc &= "<br>"
End If
StandardCount = Val(txtStandard.Text)
If StandardCount <> 0 Then
    Desc &= StandardCount.ToString & " standard video"
    If StandardCount > 1 Then Desc &= "s"
    Desc &= "<br>"
End If
' Assign the built string to the label
lblOrderDesc.Text = Desc

' Determine the Pizza SubTotal using business logic values
Select Case ddlPizzaSize.SelectedItem.Value
```

```
            Case "None" : Pizzas = 0.0
            Case "Medium" : Pizzas = MEDIUM_BASE_PRICE
            Case "Large" : Pizzas = LARGE_BASE_PRICE
            Case "Gigantic" : Pizzas = GIGANTIC_BASE_PRICE
        End Select
        If chkPepperoni.Checked Then Pizzas = Pizzas + TOPPING_PRICE
        If chkSausage.Checked Then Pizzas = Pizzas + TOPPING_PRICE
        If chkHam.Checked Then Pizzas = Pizzas + TOPPING_PRICE
        If chkBlackOlives.Checked Then Pizzas = Pizzas + TOPPING_PRICE
        If chkGreenPeppers.Checked Then Pizzas = Pizzas + TOPPING_PRICE
        If chkOnions.Checked Then Pizzas = Pizzas + TOPPING_PRICE
        lblPizzaTotal.Text = HTML_RIGHT_ALIGN & FormatCurrency(Pizzas)

        ' Determine the Movie SubTotal using business logic values
        Movies = NewReleaseCount * NEW_RELEASE_VIDEO_PRICE
        Movies = Movies + StandardCount * STANDARD_VIDEO_PRICE
        lblMovieTotal.Text = HTML_RIGHT_ALIGN & FormatCurrency(Movies)

        ' Determine the Order SubTotal, Tax, Delivery, and Total
        SubTotal = Pizzas + Movies
        lblSubtotal.Text = HTML_RIGHT_ALIGN & FormatCurrency(SubTotal)
        lblTax.Text = HTML_RIGHT_ALIGN & FormatCurrency(SubTotal * TAX_RATE)
        If SubTotal > FREE_DELIVERY_AMOUNT Then
            DeliveryFee = 0
        Else
            DeliveryFee = DELIVERY_FEE
        End If
        lblDelivery.Text = HTML_RIGHT_ALIGN & FormatCurrency(DeliveryFee)
        Total = SubTotal + (SubTotal * TAX_RATE) + DeliveryFee
        lblTotal.Text = HTML_RIGHT_ALIGN & FormatCurrency(Total)

        ' Determine the Discount and the coupon price
        Discount = Total * COUPON_DISCOUNT
        lblDiscount.Text = HTML_RIGHT_ALIGN & FormatCurrency(Discount)
        YourPrice = Total - Discount
        lblYourPrice.Text = HTML_RIGHT_ALIGN & FormatCurrency(YourPrice)

        ' Make the coupon and instructions visible
        pnlCoupon.Visible = True
        lblInstructions.Visible = True
    End Sub
End Class
```

### Testing the Solution

You can test Reed and Elizabeth's solution by implementing their design as shown in the previous section, and then running the application. Figure 12-18 shows sample output for the Order Planner Web Solution. Run the application with various inputs, making sure to test the business logic for free delivery. If you are having problems, you may want to read Appendix B: Debugging.

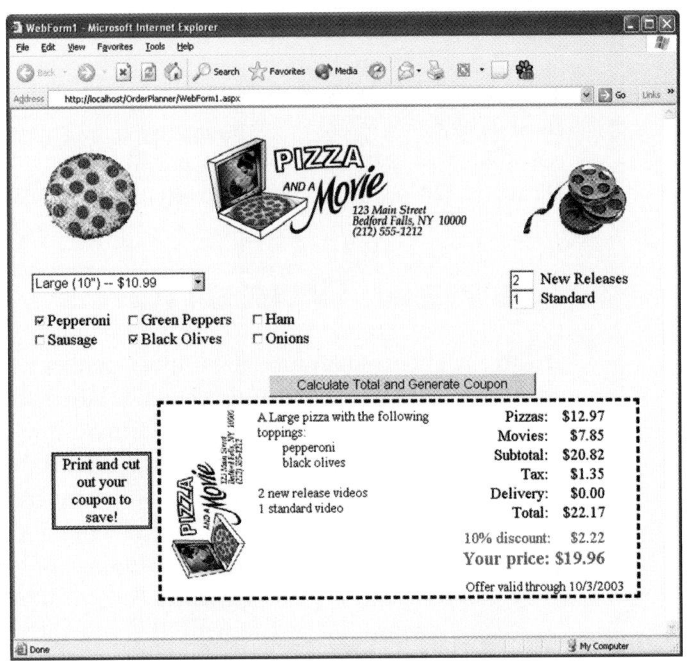


**FIGURE 12.18** *Order Planner Solution Output*

## Chapter Summary

- HTML stands for Hypertext Markup Language, a language for displaying text in a web browser such as Internet Explorer or Netscape Navigator. When HTML is written, text is marked by tags consisting of a left angle bracket (<), a tag name, and a right angle bracket (>).
- Web applications are web sites that go beyond normal, static web sites by adding the ability to process code in response to user input. Examples of web applications include online shopping carts (e-commerce) and web sites that display user requested information from a database.
- Web applications are also client/server applications. For a web application, the client is a machine with an Internet connection and a browser, and the web server is a machine that stores the web documents, including web pages and server scripts for responding to client requests.
- When a user action occurs that requires web server processing, the form must be posted back to the server. This is referred to as a postback. The web server processes the request and generates new HTML that is returned to the client browser. This sequence of events is referred to as a round trip.
- ASP.NET is a platform for developing and running web applications on a web server. ASP.NET web applications can be developed with a simple text editor or with the assistance of Visual Studio .NET.
- Web Forms allow quick and easy creation of ASP.NET web applications. A Web Form is composed of two files, the user interface form (with an .aspx extension) and the code-behind file (with an .aspx.vb extension).
- Web Forms are similar to Windows Forms in that they are event driven. Processing an event for a server control requires a round trip. Because of round trip latency, server events are limited to events that cause significant changes, such as button clicks and text changes.

## Key Terms

ASP.NET p. 324
client p. 322
code-behind p. 327
HTML p. 320
postback p. 323
round trip p. 323
tags p. 320
web application p. 322
Web Forms p. 327
web server p. 322

## Review Questions

1. In the client/server model, business logic executes only on the server side. What problems might occur if server-side business logic was visible to clients?
2. Browse to the static HTML page http://www.prfts.com/gettime.html and then browse to the dynamic ASP.NET page http://www.prfts.com/gettime.aspx. From your browser, select View Source and compare the raw HTML of the two pages. Notice that the two documents are identical except for the times. After a minute or two, click on both the sites again. Notice that the ASP.NET page has a different time (you may need to Refresh your browser). Select View Source again and notice how the ASP.NET generated page has changed. Can you explain this?
3. ASP.NET code `<%=Format(Now, "t")%>` displays the short time format for the current date/time. The three date/time format codes are *t* for short time, *d* for short date, and *g* for general date/time. Using Notepad, try to write an ASP.NET document that behaves similarly to the gettime.aspx page shown in Question 2. (You will test your page using your localhost or some other .NET server to which you have access.)
4. Most server controls do not provide support for high-frequency events such as *OnMouseMove*. Why do you think they are omitted?

## Programming Exercises

**12-1. Describe Yourself.** Using Notepad, create a simple HTML document that displays your name centered on the screen, followed by two short paragraphs describing yourself. Save the file as `"Describe.html"` and view the page with your favorite browser.

**12-2. Numbers.** Using Notepad, create a simple ASP.NET file that generates the numbers 1 to 100 when viewed in a web browser. Save the file as `"Numbers.aspx"` and store it on an ASP.NET web server. View the page with your favorite browser.

**12-3. Jake Redux.** Using Visual Studio .NET, modify the solution to Jake's Problem by adding two additional input values for the price of gasoline (per gallon) and the speed Jake travels (miles per hour). Modify the output to include how long it will take to travel his maximum distance and how much money it will cost him in fuel.

**12-4. Future Value.** "Spend less than you make" is a fundamental mantra of most financial planners. One activity that often helps motivate individuals to save money is to realize how valuable saving (and investing) can be over time. Write an investment plan application using a Web Form. The application should contain three input text boxes: monthly savings, annual percentage rate, and number of years. Calculate and display the future value of the investment plan in an output label. Run the application three times using the following input values: $100 at 10 percent for 10 years; $50 at 10 percent for 20 years; $50 at 7 percent for 40 years. Which produces the largest final value? What valuable financial planning lesson does this teach?

# Extended Case Studies

### Pizza and a Movie

Modify the Order Planner Solution presented in this chapter to allow for multiple pizzas in a single order (up to 3 pizzas). Give the user as much flexibility as possible in terms of different pizza sizes and toppings per pizza. Also, you may want to include additional business logic, such as discounts for multiple pizzas. Another example of business logic would be a "Rent 2 Get 1 Free" deal where the free video is the least expensive of the three videos. This policy would always apply for orders of three or more videos.

### Singing Mimes

Reed and Elizabeth are creating a CD containing various educational and entertainment software applications. The price of a CD is $5. In addition, they are creating a user's manual that contains documentation about each application on the CD. The user's manual is helpful for customers to learn about and understand the various applications. Furthermore, the user's manual creates an additional revenue source for the company. Black-and-white copies of the manual will be sold for $3 each, and color copies of the manual will be sold for $5 each. Reed and Elizabeth expect some schools will buy multiple copies of the CD (to install on multiple machines) but only purchase one or two manuals. Create a Web Form to help customers calculate the price of an order. The Web Form should contain three input text boxes for purchase quantities of CDs, black-and-white manuals, and color manuals. There should be three adjacent output labels that display the group price (units times unit price) for each. There should also be an output label that totals the three group price text boxes.

CHAPTER 13

# Advanced Web Forms with Databases

## OUTLINE

## ► INTERVIEW

**Jayce Fortwangler, Senior Data Architect, Pinkerton Computer Consultants, Inc., Government Services Division**

***Interviewer:*** Please tell us how you got involved in the IT industry.

***Fortwangler:*** In the late 1970s, IT was the growth industry, affording great opportunities and pay with minimal formal education. Although I started out like most people as a programmer, I quickly figured out that regardless of how well one could program, the true core of IT was accurate, consistent data. Without trustworthy data, any program can fail. After more than twenty years of specialization in data management, I continue to hold to that belief. I'm always amazed at the lack of concern shown by the average IT professional when it comes to data management issues.

***Interviewer:*** What kind of projects are you currently working on?

***Fortwangler:*** After spending eighteen years building the Data Management Program for the U.S. Customs Service, I'm currently assigned to a contract with the Federal Deposit Insurance Corporation (FDIC). We are in the process of revamping and reestablishing the Data Management Program for the FDIC. Taking industry-standard data management standards, policies, and procedures and tailoring them to a specific organization's needs is challenging, to say the least. We are currently in the process of applying the data management standards and procedures to various reengineering efforts at the FDIC. Because the FDIC has legacy, mainframe-based systems over a decade old, this reengineering effort is the perfect opportunity for the FDIC to gain control over one of its most important assets, the data. Having re-established the Data Management Program for FDIC, I find it very fulfilling to have the opportunity to now apply that program to the design and implementation of the reengineered database.

***Interviewer:*** What has been your personal key to success?

***Fortwangler:*** It has been my good fortune over the years to hold positions where I can educate the organization about the benefits of data management and rewards and efficiencies gained by prudent data management standards, policies, and procedures. It has been very rewarding to help organizations learn that the data they own is every bit as important as the people and tangible assets of the organization. A strong data management program covering the treatment and usage of data is every bit as important as the corporate fiscal program is for managing money or the human resources program is for managing people. Whoever controls their data appropriately controls their own destiny.

## OBJECTIVES

At the completion of this chapter, you will

- ► **Understand the principles behind a three-tier architecture**
- ► **Know the advantages and disadvantages of client-side state management techniques**
- ► **Know the advantages and disadvantages of server-side state management techniques**
- ► **Develop an advanced Web Forms database application**

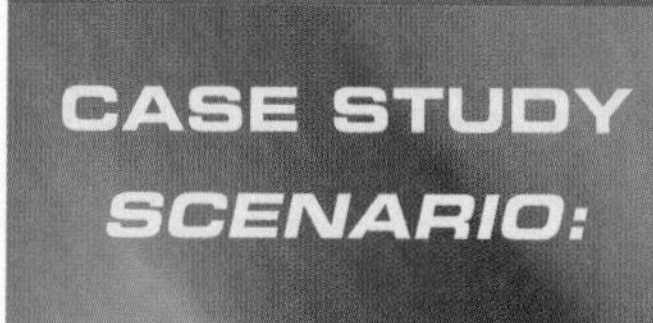


# Online Order Web Application

Noah, owner of Pizza and a Movie, has been pleased by the customer feedback from the Order Planner web application (Chapter 12). The most common suggestion his customers have given him is to extend the application so it accepts actual orders. Noah schedules a follow-up meeting with Reed and Elizabeth to discuss this possibility.

The students arrive on time and professionally dressed. Noah greets them at the door with a smile and a handshake. "I am pleased with the Order Planner as a marketing and promotional tool. However, customers still have to come into the store to make an actual order. Can we add a button that lets customers place orders online?"

Reed and Elizabeth look at each other, trying to figure out who should answer. Finally, Reed says, "We can write an application for taking online orders, but it is not as easy as simply adding a button to the Order Planner solution. An online order application typically involves a shopping cart to keep track of the items in the order. That requires some form of state management so the application can remember the items being ordered."

Elizabeth nods and continues the point. "There are other limitations to the current Order Planner as well. For one thing, it only allows a single pizza per order, which would cut out a significant part of your business. A second problem is that the Order Planner does not allow customers to select specific movies from a list of those available in the store. The bottom line is that a good shopping cart application is going to require the use of a database for these and other reasons."

Based on the inflection in Elizabeth's voice, Noah figures that including a database in a web application is no small deed. "Can you do that?"

Both nod, and Reed continues. "Yes, we can. But it clearly raises the bar in terms of complexity. Our solution now requires a three-tier architecture, which essentially means the application involves the user's machine, the web server, and the database server all working together."

"If we are going to do that," Elizabeth says, "we are now talking about a full-blown Online Order web application with a shopping cart. The application also must provide some mechanism for customer verification, probably a username and password. There are lots of other issues that arise as you get into an application of this size. Needless to say, it is much more complicated than just adding a button to the current solution."

Noah is silent for a moment. Finally, he speaks. "So, can you two do all that?"

Reed and Elizabeth smile. "As a matter of fact, we can. But first we have to document in detail exactly what you want the project to do." Their solution appears later this chapter.

## 13-1 Three-Tier Architecture

Sophisticated business applications involving databases are often divided into three layers based on the logical partitioning of fundamental services. Those three layers are the presentation layer, the application layer, and the data layer. For data-aware web

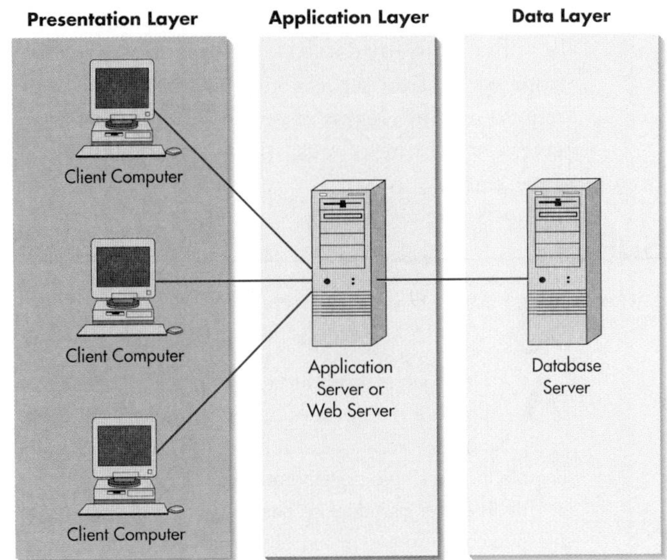


**FIGURE 13.1** *Service Layers in a Three-Tier Architecture*

applications using ASP.NET and ADO.NET, the presentation layer is a web browser on the client machine, the application layer is an IIS Web server containing the ASP.NET pages, and the data layer is a database server containing the database files and ADO.NET services (Figure 13-1).

## Presentation Layer

The presentation layer runs on the user's computer (the client) and provides the application interface. A ***fat client*** performs relatively significant processing, with less load on the middle tier. However, a fat client can only be implemented on client machines of sufficient computing ability. A ***thin client*** typically involves a web browser for displaying HTML with minimal processing. This approach requires more processing by the application tier but supports a much wider distribution base. The current trend is toward thin clients. This trend will likely accelerate as mobile computing devices become more prevalent.

## Application Layer

The application layer provides various modules and services that are essential for the solution, including processing of the business-based computing rules (e.g., customer verification, discounts, and fees). If the business rules ever change, only the services at the application layer need be changed to implement the change throughout the system.

The application layer also provides a mediator between the presentation layer and the database layer. User requests for data services are handled by the application layer, which can reduce the number of connections to the database. For example, multiple clients running a shopping cart application may be browsing a company's inventory. Rather than each client requiring a data connection, all clients could share a single connection between the application layer and the data layer.

## Data Layer

The database layer is responsible for all database access required by the solution. This layer usually provides support for adding, deleting, updating, and retrieving information from the database.

Three-tier applications conserve database server resources by reducing the number of concurrent database connections. Connections to the database server come from application servers instead of directly from client workstations. Users do not require separate logins or persistent connections to the database server. This not only saves database resources, it also eases database account maintenance and improves data security.

## ASK THE AUTHOR

**Q** Must I have three machines to implement a three-tier architecture design?

**A** No. Each of the three service layers may reside on the same computer, which is a common practice during development. The service layers may also be deployed across multiple computers, thus creating a distributed application. Distributed applications are more scalable and flexible than a single system implementation.

The three-tier architecture design is not limited to one, two, or three machines. High-volume web sites typically use two or more web servers at the application layer. This provides numerous benefits. If one server starts to get swamped, requests are forwarded to another server with more available resources. If one server fails, another can step in as a backup. Once the application layer has been distributed across two or more servers, it is relatively easy to add additional servers. The overall effect is improved performance, reliability, and scalability. Likewise, the data layer may be distributed across multiple servers for similar reasons.

**Tip**

**A group of networked servers designed to handle distributed work is called a *server farm*. It is often cost effective for companies to outsource application and data layer hosting to third-party server farms.**

## 13-2 State Management

The HTTP protocol is stateless, which means that each request for a new web page is processed without any knowledge of previous pages requested. ***State management*** refers to techniques by which developers maintain the state of a web application across multiple page requests. Some level of state management is necessary for most web applications. For example, a shopping cart application requires persistent information about the items the customer has selected for purchase on previous screens.

There are a number of options available to ASP.NET developers when it comes to managing the state of a web site. Some of the options involve keeping information on the client; others involve storing information on the server. Generally speaking, client-side options are better left to secure, intranet applications. Client-side and server-side state management techniques are discussed in the following sections.

## 13-3 Client-Side State Management Techniques

There are several client-side state management options available to ASP.NET developers, including view state, cookies, and query strings. Because these options involve storing information on the client's machine, a user can manipulate the information, which can result in an inaccurate state and potentially create a security compromise. Client-side state management should be limited to noncritical applications or secure, intranet solutions.

## View State

A web page is re-created each round trip; without state management efforts, all information associated with the page and the controls on the page would be lost. ASP.NET provides a facility called ***view state*** that represents the state of the page when it was last processed on the server. When the page is posted back to the server, ASP.NET uses the view state to restore property information in the page. The view state is visible in the HTML source and is therefore a potential security issue.

**Tip**

**ASP.NET supports saving view state data on either the client or the server.**

## Query String

A ***query string*** is information appended to the end of a page's URL. Query strings typically begin with the "?" character followed by application specific information. For example, the following URL sent to the Internet Movie Database web site will produce a web page for the actor Russell Crowe.

http://us.imdb.com/Name?Crowe,+Russell

Query strings can be used for exchanging simple data between client and server or from one page to another. However, query strings are not secure because the query information is visible in the browser. Also, most browsers have a maximum URL length of 255 characters, which limits the information that can be sent using query strings.

**Tip**

**The query string is directly visible to the user and may be altered via the browser user interface. It is therefore a potential security issue and should not contain important or sensitive data.**

### *Query String Summary*

- A query string is information appended to the end of a page's URL.
- You can use a query string to submit data back to your page or to another page.
- Most browsers impose a 255-character limit on the length of the URL.

## Cookies

A ***cookie*** is a small text file stored on the client machine. The browser attaches the cookie with each new HTTP request before sending it to the server, which can read the data and respond appropriately. Cookie data can be used in a variety of ways. For example, tvguide.com uses cookies to personalize television listings to match your local cable or satellite. Shopping sites may use cookies to determine your shopping habits and personalize information about promotions and sales. Cookies can also store personal information to help with quick logins.

The information stored in a cookie can be exposed and is therefore not the best means of handling sensitive information. Furthermore, many users disable cookies on their browsers, so your application should not be dependent on cookie data.

## ASK THE AUTHOR

**Q** Can a cookie contain a virus?

**A** No. A cookie is only a text file and not a program or a plug-in. A cookie cannot contain a virus, cannot read your hard drive, and cannot harm your machine in any way.

Good web sites will use cookies to store personalization information rather than sensitive data. However, any information you give to a web site may be stored in a cookie (if cookies are allowed by your browser settings). With or without cookies, it is a good idea to be aware of information you give out over the Internet and the reliability of the company with whom you are doing business.

### Cookie Summary

- A cookie is a text file stored on the client machine.
- Cookies are good for storing nonsensitive personalization information.
- Cookies may be disabled, so your application should not be dependent on cookie data.

## 13-4 Server-Side State Management Techniques

In addition to the client-side state management options discussed in the previous section, there are also multiple server-side options available to ASP.NET developers, including application state, session state, and database. Because server-side options store information out of the client's reach, the information is more secure. Server-side state management should be included in all applications that require secure solutions.

### Application State

An ASP.NET application is the sum of all files, pages, and code that resides on a server. When a web application runs, ASP.NET maintains information about the application in the ***application state***. The application state is created the first time any client requests a URL resource from within the ASP.NET application; the application state remains in server memory until the web server is shut down or the application is modified.

The application state allows developers to create ***application variables*** that can be set and read throughout the lifetime of the application. Application variables are referenced with the key term *Application* followed by the application variable name in parentheses. Application variables are created automatically on first reference. Application variables are global variables accessible from all pages in the web application, and their values are independent of specific users.

*Syntax:* **Application("*AppVariableName*")**

*Example:*

```
Application("Company") = "Acme Corp."
Application("TaxRate") = 0.065
MovieSubtotal = NumOfMovies * Application("MovieRentalPrice")
mTax = (mSubtotal - mDiscount) * Application("TaxRate")
```

## *Application State Summary*

- ASP.NET maintains an application state that is created the first time any client requests a URL resource from within the ASP.NET application; the application state remains in server memory until the web server is shut down or the application is modified.
- Developers can create variables within the application state by referencing the key term *Application* followed by the application variable name in parentheses.
- Application variables are global variables accessible from all pages in the web application, and their values are independent of specific users.

## Session State

> ▶▶▶ *Tip*
> **Session state is similar to application state, except that it is scoped to the current browser session. Each client invoking the web application represents a different session and therefore has a different session state.**

A ***session*** is the period of time that a unique browser (i.e., user) interacts with a web application. Every time a new browser invokes a web application, a new session is created for the browser. When a new session is created, ASP.NET maintains information about the session in the ***session state***.

The session state allows developers to create ***session variables*** that can be set and read throughout the lifetime of the session. Session variables are referenced with the key term *Session* followed by the session variable name in parentheses. Session variables are accessible from all pages in the web application for every request to the application by that browser. Sessions and their variables expire after twenty minutes of inactivity. If the browser hits the web application after a timeout, the web application creates a new session for the browser.

*Syntax:* **Session("*SessionVariableName*")**

*Example:*

```
Session("Greeting") = "Welcome to Pizza and a Movie"
Session("MaxRentals") = 3
If Session("OrderID") = 0 Then
    Response.Redirect("Login.aspx")
End If
```

## *Session State Summary*

- Every time a new browser invokes a web application, a new session is created for the browser.
- Session variables are referenced with the key term *Session* followed by the session variable name in parentheses. Session variables are accessible for every request to the application by the session browser.
- Sessions and their variables expire after twenty minutes of inactivity. If the browser invokes the web application after a timeout, the web application creates a new session for the browser.

## Database Support

Data stored in application variables and session variables will be lost if the application is interrupted (as a result of crashes, code updates, scheduled process restarts, etc.). To survive these interruptions, state information should be stored in a database.

Maintaining state information in a database is also helpful when the information being stored is large because the bulk of the processing and storage can be offloaded to the data layer, allowing improved performance at the application layer.

It is quite common for a professional web application to maintain state information with a relational database for various reasons:

- Security
- Queries
- Capacity
- Data mining

### Security

Customer information stored in a database is an extra level removed from the presentation layer, making the data less available for malicious use. If the database contains sensitive information, it can also be protected by a username and password to further deter unwanted access.

### Queries

Storing data in a database gives the application all the power and functionality of databases in general, including the ability to query for specific information. The same data stored in application or session variables would be much more difficult to process in this way.

### Capacity

Many professional sites maintain transactional records of a customer's viewing and purchasing history. The information may be used to help personalize marketing and promotional materials or to inform the user of the status of a previous order. For high-volume web applications, this history information can become quite large. Databases are especially good at handling large amounts of information, and the data services can be split off to a data layer that resides on one or more data servers, allowing the web application to avoid a performance decrease.

### Data Mining

Given the capacity of a database, an application could maintain information about times and dates of customer visits, pages visited, time per page, items ordered, and so on. This information could be mined for interesting relationships—information that could provide a strategic business advantage. Most enterprise-level relational databases such as Oracle and Microsoft SQL Server contain an expansive tool set for data mining projects.

## *Database Support Summary*

- Unlike application and session variables, state information stored in a database is persistent in the face of server crashes and application updates.
- Storing information in a database has several advantages, including increased security, support for queries, improved capacity, and the possibility of data mining.

# Online Order Web Application

## Document Project Requirements

Reed turns on his laptop. "As Elizabeth just said, we should begin by documenting exactly what you want the project to do."

In the ensuing discussion, Noah, Reed, and Elizabeth all ask questions, clarify issues, and offer suggestions. Reed takes notes, making frequent edits and changes. The meeting continues until everyone is satisfied with the vision for the project. The document Reed creates contains the following items:

1. The application should contain a common header that appears on all pages of the web site.
2. The customer has to login by specifying a valid username and password.
3. All order forms should redirect the customer to the Login form when a valid login has not been established.
4. The customer should be able to include multiple pizzas in the order.
5. Each pizza in the order can have a unique combination of size and toppings.
6. A movie inventory should be maintained that includes the checkout status of each item.
7. The customer may search the movie inventory based on actors, titles, and descriptions.
8. The movie order page should allow the customer to select from available movie formats.
9. The movie order page should include movie details from the Internet Movie Database (IMDB) web site.
10. When an order is placed, the checked out status should automatically be updated for all movies in the order.
11. All prices (e.g., pizza toppings, movie rentals, delivery charge, etc.) should be stored in the database.
12. An About Us screen should present basic information about the business.
13. A customer's shopping cart should be remembered from session to session.

Reed uses Noah's printer to print two copies of the documented requirements, which both parties sign, each keeping one copy. Reed looks over the signed document and says, "Elizabeth and I will begin working on this. Please be sure to let us know as soon as possible if there are any changes or additions you want to make."

Elizabeth adds, "Based on this document, we will design a database capable of storing the necessary information and generating the appropriate queries. We will also design the various forms for the web application. We will then schedule another meeting with you to present our designs along with a timeline for the project's completion and some budget numbers."

Noah shakes their hands and thanks them for meeting with him. "I look forward to hearing back from you," he says.

## Database and Application Design

A week later Reed and Elizabeth schedule a second meeting with Noah. They are once again professionally dressed and confident in their presentation. After some handshakes and pleasant conversation, the discussion returns to the project.

Elizabeth and Reed each have a notebook, and they give a third copy to Noah. Elizabeth begins, "The first item you will see in your notebook is a copy of the requirements document we created in our last meeting." Noah recognizes the requirements and nods.

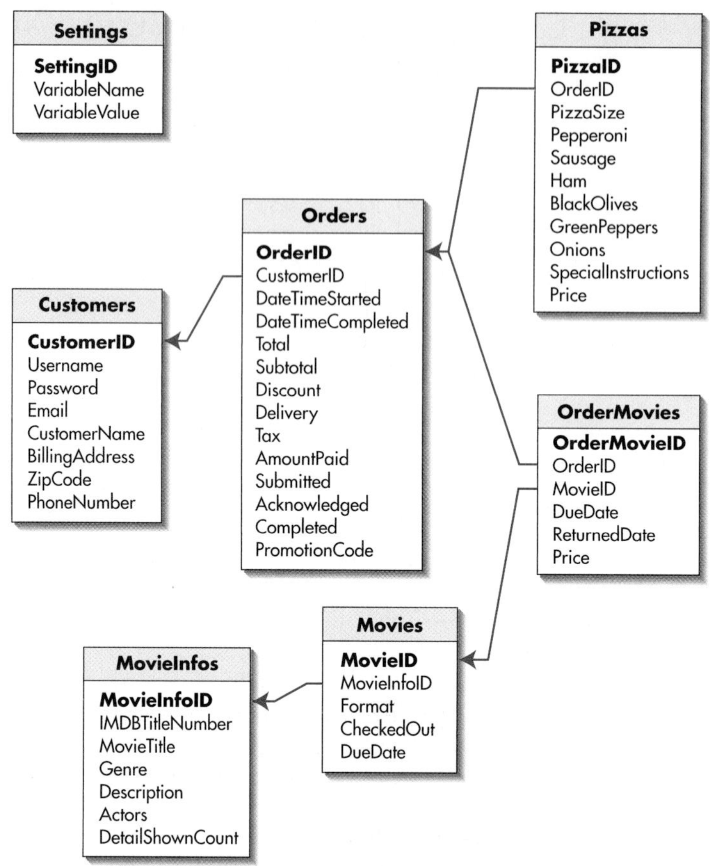


**FIGURE 13.2** *Database Design Showing Tables and Relationships*

Reed then continues the presentation by pulling out the second item in the packet—a sheet containing an image similar to Figure 13-2. "This sheet shows our database design. The boxes are tables and they contain fields of information. The lines between the tables are relationships for sharing information. It may be a little unclear to you, but it is very helpful for us. We are confident that our database design will be capable of satisfying all the items in the requirements document."

## MENTOR

It is a good idea to identify a set of conventions to be used throughout a project. The following conventions are used in Reed and Elizabeth's database design.

- Table names are plural (e.g., *Pizzas*).
- The primary key field is the table name (singular) followed by *ID* (e.g., *PizzaID*).
- The primary key type is always an integer numeric type (e.g., Autonumber or Number).
- For a many-to-many relationship, create a linking table. The name includes both tables with a foreign key to each table.

Noah looks at the diagram. "I think I get the general idea. However, I do have two questions. Why are there three tables with Movie in their name, and what is the Settings table?"

"The Movies table contains specific information about the videos and DVDs you have in your store," Elizabeth answers. "For example, if you have three copies of *Gladiator,* there would be three entries in the Movies table, one for each copy you have in the store. The MovieInfos table contains the unchanging information about a movie, such as the title, genre, description, and actors. The third table, OrderMovies, is called a linking table between the Orders and Movies tables. OrderMovies keeps up with all the movies in a specific customer's order."

"As for the Settings table," Reed says, "it is the storage place for business data used in the application, such as the prices for your pizzas and movies or the value of a promotional code for a marketing campaign. By placing this information in the database, you can change this data without having to modify the application."

**MENTOR**

There is a one-to-many relationship between pizzas and orders because one order can contain many pizzas, and each pizza is made unique for an order. This one-to-many relationship connects the OrderID primary key in the Orders table with the OrderID foreign key in the Pizzas table.

The relationship between orders and movies is different. A single order can include many movies, and a single movie can also be included in many orders over time. The difference can be attributed to the fact that pizzas are consumable and movies are reusable. In other words, a movie is returned and can be reused in future orders. The many-to-many relationship between orders and movies is handled by a linking table with foreign keys to both the Orders and Movies tables.

**►►►Tip**

**You may get a server error saying the Jet engine cannot open the file because you need permission to view its data. The ASP.NET account must have modify permissions on both the database file and the folder in which the database is located.**

The next item in the packet is a table showing the proposed Web Forms and functionality (Table 13-1).

"Finally, you will see the last document is a contract for service," says Elizabeth. "There are two fees listed. The first fee covers only our time and effort up to this point. If you want to end the project now, you will be billed only that amount. The second fee is for a full implementation of the system described in this document. We believe that we have designed a very good web application at a very reasonable price, and we hope you give us the opportunity to implement our design."

Noah studies the numbers and then initials the *full implementation* box and signs on the indicated space beside the price. Noah jokingly says, "I don't suppose we can do this for free pizzas and movies again?"

Elizabeth smiles. "Sorry. For this project we will need a check."

"Well, don't spend it all in one place," says Noah.

The three exchange signed copies and talk briefly before exchanging handshakes.

Finally, Elizabeth says, "Now if you will excuse us, Reed and I have some work to do."

**Table 13.1** Web Forms and Functionality

| Name | Description |
|---|---|
| Login.aspx | Customer login screen |
| AddPizza.aspx | Customizable pizza orders, including multiple pizzas with various sizes and toppings |
| MovieSearch.aspx | Movie listings, searchable by title, actors, and description |
| MovieDetail.aspx | A frame web page containing the AddMovie page and a details page from IMDB |
| AddMovie.aspx | Appears within the MovieDetail frame, allowing the customer to view and select based on VHS and DVD availability |
| ShoppingCart.aspx | Shopping cart checkout screen with support for delivery and promotional discounts |
| AboutUs.aspx | An informational page to promote the quality of Pizza and a Movie |
| CheckoutSuccess.aspx | Confirms order has been placed |

## ASK THE AUTHOR

**Q** Reed and Elizabeth now know the requirements and design for the project. What is Noah's job during the implementation process?

**A** The role of the client (Noah in this case) decreases once the requirements and design have been finalized. It is a good idea to keep the client involved during implementation, just to make sure there is no confusion. In Elizabeth and Reed's case, however, their design was specific and clear, thus decreasing the chances of confusion and problems. What follows are their implementation activities.

**Tip**

**A GridLayoutPanel is used to group visual controls with positional information within the grid. The grid can be placed in the normal flow of the page while maintaining the positional information of the controls within the grid.**

### Web Site Header

Creating a single application header that appears across all pages in the web site gives the customer a common frame of reference when browsing. Figure 13-3 shows the Web Site Header design for this application. The header contains a GridLayoutPanel HTML item on which are placed five hyperlinks. Two properties are set for each hyperlink. The ImageURL property contains the image file name (including the descriptive text). The NavigateURL property contains the web page for redirection when the hyperlink is clicked.

**FIGURE 13.3** *Web Site Header Design*

**Placing the header items onto a GridLayoutPanel allows the developer to copy-and-paste the header across pages of the solution.**

►►► *Tip*

**The *ExecuteScalar* method can be used to execute an SQL SELECT command to return a single value rather than a dataset. It returns the value of the first column of the first row of the result set.**

►►► *Tip*

**The *System.Data.OleDb* namespace provides the objects necessary to programmatically create the database interface.**

### Global.asax File

ASP.NET applications contain a special Global.asax file used to establish any global objects required by the web application. The file is compiled on the first page request to the web application. If the Global.asax file is modified, the file is recompiled, and the web application is restarted on the next page request. Application variables exist as long as the application is running.

The Global.asax file is generated by Visual Studio. There is no GUI form, but there is a code-behind file that contains the Application start event and the Session start event.

For the Pizza and a Movie web site, the only session variable is the OrderID. The session variable OrderID is assigned with a valid login and links the current session to an order in the database. Table 13-2 provides pseudocode descriptions of the procedures in the Global.asax file.

**Table 13.2** Design Pseudocode for Global.asax

| | |
|---|---|
| Application_Start event | 1. Programmatically sets the application variable ConnectionString<br>2. Loads the application variables from the Settings table in the database |
| Session_Start event | Sets the session variable OrderID to 0, indicating the start of a new session (the user has not logged in) |

### Global.asax Implementation

```
' Global.asax.vb

Imports System.Data.OleDb    ' This is needed for the programmatic database controls
Imports System.Web
Imports System.Web.SessionState


Public Class Global
    Inherits System.Web.HttpApplication

Component Designer Generated Code

    Sub Application_Start(ByVal sender As Object, ByVal e As EventArgs)
        ' Fires when the application is started
        Dim DBConnection As OleDbConnection
        Dim SQL As OleDbCommand
        Dim SQLReader As OleDbDataReader


        ' This is the only place the connection string is referenced in the entire project
        ' Make sure the Data Source points to a valid database, and that the server process
        ' has permissions to read and write the database
        Application("ConnectionString") = "Provider=Microsoft.Jet.OLEDB.4.0;" & _
            "Data Source=C:\Inetpub\wwwroot\PizzaAndAMovieShoppingCart\PizzaAndAMovie.mdb"

        ' Read in all of the application variables from the Settings table
        ' SQLReader is a DataReader which can sequentially process a result set
```

```
        DBConnection = New OleDbConnection(Application("ConnectionString"))
        SQL = New OleDbCommand("SELECT * FROM Settings")
        DBConnection.Open()
        SQL.Connection = DBConnection
        SQLReader = SQL.ExecuteReader()
        If SQLReader.HasRows Then
            While SQLReader.Read
                Application(SQLReader.Item("VariableName")) = _
                    SQLReader.Item("VariableValue")
            End While
        End If

        ' While VB.NET has good garbage collection
        ' it is still considered good programming practice to clean up
        SQLReader.Close()
        DBConnection.Close()
        SQL.Dispose()
        DBConnection.Dispose()
    End Sub

    Sub Session_Start(ByVal sender As Object, ByVal e As EventArgs)
        ' Fires when the session is started
        Session("OrderID") = 0 'Initialize the session
    End Sub

End Class
```

**Tip**

The Web Forms in this solution have the PageLayout property set to FlowLayout, which allows the grid layout panels to be centered.

**Tip**

*Response.Redirect* followed by the URL as an argument redirects the browser to a new web page.

### Login Form

The customer has to login by specifying a valid username and password. If either the username or password is blank, then the browser alerts the customer of the required fields. If the username is not found in the database, the customer is notified and access is denied. If the username is found but the password does not match, the customer is notified and access is denied. Only when the username and password match a database entry is the customer considered verified and allowed to progress. If an outstanding order exists for the customer, then the session variable OrderID is set to the outstanding order. Otherwise, a new record is created in the Orders table and the session variable OrderID is set to match the new record. If the customer has an existing order, the application redirects to the ShoppingCart form. Otherwise, the customer is redirected to the AddPizza form.

### Login Form Design

Figure 13-4 shows the layout of the Web Form interface. The GUI contains a copy of the Web Site Header grid and a second grid layout panel containing username and password text boxes and a login button. There is a required field validation control for each text box and a label to display login error feedback. Finally, graphics and labels are included to give the form a professional appearance.

Table 13-3 provides pseudocode descriptions of the procedures in the Login form design.

**FIGURE 13.4** *Layout of the Login Form Interface*

**Tip**

The *ExecuteNonQuery* method can be used to change the data in a database using the INSERT, UPDATE, or DELETE commands in SQL. The method returns the number of rows affected by the command.

**Tip**

The *RequiredField Validator* control can be used to make an input field a required field. The ControlToValidate field is set to the input field. If the input field is invalid, the ErrorMessage will display and the page will not post.

**Table 13.3 Design Pseudocode for Login Form**

| Procedure | Description |
|---|---|
| btnLogin_click | 1. Checks to see if the username is in the database |
| | 2. Checks to make sure the password matches |
| | 3. Determines if the customer has an outstanding order; if not, creates new order |
| | 4. Sets the OrderID to the current order |
| | 5. Redirects to AddPizza form |

### Login Form Implementation

```
' Login.aspx.vb

Imports System.Data.OleDb   ' This is needed for the programmatic database controls
Public Class Login
    Inherits System.Web.UI.Page

Web Form Designer Generated Code

    ' This function uses a programmatic interface to the database,
    ' using only an OleDBConnection and an OleDbCommand
    Private Sub btnLogin_Click(ByVal sender As System.Object, _
            ByVal e As System.EventArgs) Handles btnLogin.Click
        Dim SQLResult As Object
        Dim CustomerID As Integer
        Dim Password As String
        Dim DBConnection As OleDbConnection
        Dim SQL As OleDbCommand

        ' DBConnection uses the application variable "ConnectionString"
        ' which was set in Global.aspx.vb
        DBConnection = New OleDbConnection
        DBConnection.ConnectionString = Application("ConnectionString")
        DBConnection.Open()

        ' First check to see if the Username is in the database.
        ' The ExecuteScalar method can be used to execute an SQL SELECT command to return
        ' a single value rather than a data set.  It returns the value of the first column
        ' of the first row of the result set.
        ' ExecuteScalar returns a Null if the SELECT clause returns an empty dataset.
        ' Be sure to include quotes around string values in a SELECT statement.
        SQL = New OleDbCommand
        SQL.Connection = DBConnection
        SQL.CommandText = _
            "SELECT CustomerID FROM Customers WHERE Username = '" & txtUsername.Text & "'"
        SQLResult = SQL.ExecuteScalar()
        If IsNothing(SQLResult) Then
            lblError.Text = "Username not found in database!"
            lblError.Visible = True
            Exit Sub
        Else
            CustomerID = CInt(SQLResult)
        End If

        ' Now check to make sure the password matches.
        ' Since we have already verified that there is a customer with this CustomerID,
        ' there is no need to check against Null
        SQL.CommandText = _
            "SELECT Password FROM Customers WHERE CustomerID = " & CustomerID.ToString
        Password = SQL.ExecuteScalar()
        If Password <> txtPassword.Text Then
            lblError.Text = "Username/Password do not match!"
```

```
            lblError.Visible = True
            Exit Sub
        End If

        ' Finally, determine if this customer has an existing outstanding order.
        ' If not, then use INSERT to create an empty order.
        ' Because OrderID is an AutoNumber field, the best way to get the value is to
        ' SELECT it after the insert
        ' Redirect changes the page returned to the browser after a postback
        SQL.CommandText = "SELECT OrderID FROM ORDERS " & _
            "WHERE (CustomerID = " & CustomerID & ") AND (Completed = FALSE)"

        SQLResult = SQL.ExecuteScalar()
        If IsNothing(SQLResult) Then
            ' Create new order
            SQL.CommandText = "INSERT INTO ORDERS " & _
                "(CustomerID, DateTimeStarted) Values (" & CustomerID & ", '" & Now & "')"
            SQL.ExecuteNonQuery()
            ' Get the newly created OrderID
            SQL.CommandText = "SELECT OrderID FROM ORDERS " & _
                "WHERE (CustomerID = " & CustomerID & ") AND (Completed = FALSE)"
            Session("OrderID") = CInt(SQL.ExecuteScalar())
        Else
            ' Get the existing OrderID
            Session("OrderID") = CInt(SQLResult)
        End If
        DBConnection.Close()
        Response.Redirect("AddPizza.aspx")
    End Sub
End Class
```

### AddPizza Form

►►► *Tip*

*IsPostBack* is a property that indicates if the page is being loaded in response to a client postback.

The AddPizza form allows the customer to add a pizza to the current order. The prices for the pizzas and toppings are determined from the application variables loaded from the Settings table. When a pizza is added to the order, a new record is created in the Pizzas table with a foreign key to the Orders table specifying the current order (held in session variable OrderID). The price of the pizza is calculated and included in the new record, and the user is automatically redirected to the ShoppingCart. Also, note that customers who browse to this form without having first logged in are immediately redirected to the login screen.

### AddPizza Form Design

Figure 13-5 shows the layout of the AddPizza form interface. The GUI contains a copy of the Web Site Header grid and a second grid layout panel containing a drop-down list for pizza size, a checkbox for each topping in the Pizza table, and a button to add the pizza to the order. There is also a text box for special instructions, such as "Light on the sauce." Finally, graphics and labels are included to give the form a professional appearance.

Table 13-4 provides pseudocode descriptions of the procedures in the AddPizza form design.

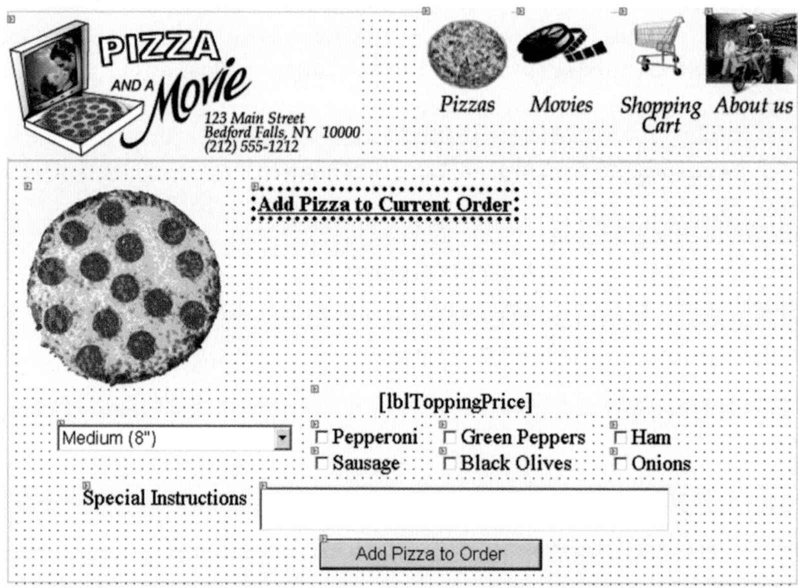


► **FIGURE 13.5** *Layout of the AddPizza Form Interface*

**Table 13.4 Design Pseudocode for AddPizza Form**

| Procedure | Description |
|---|---|
| Page_Load | 1. Verifies the customer has successfully logged in this session |
| | 2. If the controls have not been initialized (i.e., not a postback), then the drop-down list is populated with the current pizza sizes and prices, and the toppings price label is displayed |
| btnAddPizza_Click | 1. Determines the number of toppings |
| | 2. Finds the base price for the selected pizza size |
| | 3. Adds the base price and toppings price |
| | 4. Adds the new record to the Pizza table |
| | 5. Redirects to ShoppingCart |

AddPizza Form Implementation

```
' AddPizza.aspx.vb

Imports System.Data.OleDb   ' This is needed for the programmatic database controls

Public Class Pizzas
    Inherits System.Web.UI.Page

Web Form Designer Generated Code

    Private Sub Page_Load(ByVal sender As System.Object, _
            ByVal e As System.EventArgs) Handles MyBase.Load
        ' Put user code to initialize the page here
        Dim liMedium, liLarge, liGigantic As ListItem

        ' First make sure that there has been a valid login this session...
        If Session("OrderID") = 0 Then Response.Redirect("Login.aspx")

        ' Display the default values for the topping price and the pizza prices.
        ' These values are loaded in Global.asax.vb into Application variables from the
        ' Settings table in the database
        ' Use a ListItem to have displayed text that is different than the associated value
        If Not IsPostBack Then
            lblToppingPrice.Text = FormatCurrency(Application("PizzaToppingPrice")) & _
                " per topping"
            ddlPizzaSize.Items.Clear()
            liMedium = New ListItem
            liMedium.Text = "Medium (8"") - " & _
                FormatCurrency(Application("8in. PizzaBasePrice"))
            liMedium.Value = "Medium"
            liLarge = New ListItem
            liLarge.Text = "Large (10"") - " & _
                FormatCurrency(Application("10in. PizzaBasePrice"))
            liLarge.Value = "Large"
            liGigantic = New ListItem
            liGigantic.Text = "Gigantic (12"") - " & _
                FormatCurrency(Application("12in. PizzaBasePrice"))
            liGigantic.Value = "Gigantic"
            ddlPizzaSize.Items.Add(liMedium)
            ddlPizzaSize.Items.Add(liLarge)
            ddlPizzaSize.Items.Add(liGigantic)
        End If
    End Sub

    Private Sub btnAddPizza_Click(ByVal sender As System.Object, _
            ByVal e As System.EventArgs) Handles btnAddPizza.Click
        ' The following code illustrates the DBConnection being created
        ' inline with the variable declaration
        Dim DBConnection As New OleDbConnection(Application("ConnectionString"))
        Dim SQL As New OleDbCommand
        Dim Price As Double
        Dim NumOfToppings As Integer

        ' Determine the number of toppings
```

```
        NumOfToppings = 0
        If chkPepperoni.Checked Then NumOfToppings += 1
        If chkSausage.Checked Then NumOfToppings += 1
        If chkHam.Checked Then NumOfToppings += 1
        If chkBlackOlives.Checked Then NumOfToppings += 1
        If chkGreenPeppers.Checked Then NumOfToppings += 1
        If chkOnions.Checked Then NumOfToppings += 1

        ' Find the base price for the selected pizza size
        Price = 0
        Select Case ddlPizzaSize.SelectedItem.Value.ToString
            Case "Medium"
                Price = Application("8in. PizzaBasePrice")
            Case "Large"
                Price = Application("10in. PizzaBasePrice")
            Case "Gigantic"
                Price = Application("12in. PizzaBasePrice")
        End Select

        ' Add the price of the toppings to the base price
        Price = Price + NumOfToppings * Application("PizzaToppingPrice")

        ' Add the new record to the Pizzas table using an INSERT query
        DBConnection.Open()
        SQL.Connection = DBConnection
        SQL.CommandText = "INSERT INTO Pizzas " & _
            "(OrderID, PizzaSize, Pepperoni, Sausage, Ham, BlackOlives, GreenPeppers, " & _
            " Onions, SpecialInstructions, Price) " & _
            " Values (" & Session("OrderID") & ", '" & _
            ddlPizzaSize.SelectedItem.Value.ToString & "', " & _
            chkPepperoni.Checked & ", " & chkSausage.Checked & ", " & _
            chkHam.Checked & ", " & chkBlackOlives.Checked & ", " & _
            chkGreenPeppers.Checked & ", " & chkOnions.Checked & ", '" & _
            txtSpecialInstructions.Text & "', " & Price & ")"
        SQL.ExecuteNonQuery()
        DBConnection.Close()
        Response.Redirect("ShoppingCart.aspx")
    End Sub
End Class
```

►►► *Tip*

**A label can be used for more than just single-font text. Putting HTML tags in the Text property allows a label to display formatted HTML code, including hyperlinks, lists, figures, etc.**

## MovieSearch Form

The MovieSearch form presents a list of movies to the customer for consideration to rent. The initial list shows the top ten movies based on movie rental history. The customer can search for movies based on title, actors, or description. Clicking on any movie in the list takes the customer to a movie details screen from which the customer may order the movie.

### MovieSearch Form Design

Figure 13-6 shows the layout of the MovieSearch form interface. The GUI contains a copy of the Web Site Header grid and a second grid layout panel containing a label that displays a list of movies as hyperlinks to the movie details page. The second grid also includes a drop-down list with search filters, an input text box for search strings, and a button to initiate a search. Finally, graphics and labels are included to give the form a professional appearance.

Table 13-5 provides pseudocode descriptions of the procedures in the MovieSearch form design.

**FIGURE 13.6** *Layout of the MovieSearch Form Interface*

**Table 13.5 Design Pseudocode for MovieSearch Form**

| Procedure | Description |
|---|---|
| CreateLinks | 1. Executes the SELECT query passed as an argument<br>2. Creates HTML links for each row in the result set |
| Page_Load | 1. Verifies the customer has successfully logged in this session<br>2. If the controls have not been initialized (i.e., not a postback), then the drop-down list is populated with the filter choices<br>3. Calls CreateLinks for the top ten |
| DoSearch | 1. Creates an SQL command string using the value in the search text box<br>2. Calls CreateLinks |
| btnSearch_Click | Calls DoSearch |
| txtSearch_TextChanged | Calls DoSearch |
| FixSQLLiteral | Replaces reserved characters in user-supplied literals to avoid problems in SQL SELECT strings |

### MovieSearch Form Implementation

```
' MovieSearch.aspx.vb

Imports System.Data.OleDb   ' This is needed for the programmatic database controls
Public Class MovieSearch
    Inherits System.Web.UI.Page

Web Form Designer Generated Code

    Private Sub Page_Load(ByVal sender As System.Object, _
            ByVal e As System.EventArgs) Handles MyBase.Load
        ' Put user code to initialize the page here
        Dim ddlItem As ListItem

        ' First make sure that there has been a valid login this session...
        If Session("OrderID") = 0 Then Response.Redirect("Login.aspx")

        If Not IsPostBack Then
            ddlFilter.Items.Clear()
            ddlItem = New ListItem
            ddlItem.Text = "All"
            ddlItem.Value = "All"
            ddlFilter.Items.Add(ddlItem)
            ddlItem = New ListItem
            ddlItem.Text = "Titles"
            ddlItem.Value = "MovieTitle"
            ddlFilter.Items.Add(ddlItem)
            ddlItem = New ListItem
            ddlItem.Text = "Actors"
            ddlItem.Value = "Actors"
            ddlFilter.Items.Add(ddlItem)
            ddlItem = New ListItem
            ddlItem.Text = "Description"
            ddlItem.Value = "Description"
            ddlFilter.Items.Add(ddlItem)

            ' Call CreateLinks to show the top 10 movies based on DetailShownCount
            CreateLinks("SELECT TOP 10 MovieTitle, MovieInfoID, IMDBTitleNumber " & _
                " FROM MovieInfos ORDER BY DetailShownCount Desc")
        End If
    End Sub


    ' CreateLinks accepts SQL text which, when executed, returns a movie result set
    ' and fills a label with HTML formatted text including links to the imdb.com website
    Private Sub CreateLinks(ByVal SQLSelectText As String)
        Dim DBConnection As New OleDbConnection(Application("ConnectionString"))
        Dim SQL As New OleDbCommand
        Dim SQLReader As OleDbDataReader

        ' Execute the passed SQL argument, and use the result set to build an
        ' HTML formatted ordered list of hyperlinks
        DBConnection.Open()
```

```
        SQL.Connection = DBConnection
        SQL.CommandText = SQLSelectText
        SQLReader = SQL.ExecuteReader()
        If Not SQLReader.HasRows Then
            lblSearchResults.Text = "No results found.  Try modifying your search."
        Else
            lblSearchResults.Text = "<ol>"
            While SQLReader.Read
                lblSearchResults.Text &= "<li><a href=""MovieDetail.aspx?ID=" & _
                    SQLReader.Item("MovieInfoID").ToString & "&IMDB=" & _
                    SQLReader.Item("IMDBTitleNumber").ToString & """>" & _
                    SQLReader.Item("MovieTitle") & "</a> </li>"
            End While
            lblSearchResults.Text = lblSearchResults.Text & "</ol>"
        End If
        SQLReader.Close()
        DBConnection.Close()
        SQL.Dispose()
        DBConnection.Dispose()
    End Sub

    ' DoSearch creates an SQL string to search the database for movies based on the
    ' search filter and the search text.  It then passes this string to CreateLinks
    Private Sub DoSearch()
        Dim SearchField As String
        Dim SearchValue As String
        Dim NewSQLCommand As String

        SearchValue = txtSearch.Text
        SearchValue = "'%" & FixSQLLiteral(SearchValue) & "%'"
        SearchField = ddlFilter.SelectedValue
        If SearchField <> "All" Then
            NewSQLCommand = "SELECT MovieTitle, MovieInfoID, IMDBTitleNumber " & _
                " FROM MovieInfos WHERE " & SearchField & " LIKE " & SearchValue
        Else
            NewSQLCommand = "SELECT MovieTitle, MovieInfoID, IMDBTitleNumber " & _
                " FROM MovieInfos WHERE (MovieTitle LIKE " & SearchValue & ") " & _
                " OR (Actors LIKE " & SearchValue & ") " & _
                " OR (Description LIKE " & SearchValue & ") " & _
                " ORDER BY DetailShownCount Desc"
        End If

        lblDescription.Text = "Search Results for """ & txtSearch.Text & """"
        CreateLinks(NewSQLCommand)
    End Sub

    ' FixSQLLiteral replaces single tick marks (which can foul up the SQL text)
    ' with the SQL safe equivalent
    Private Function FixSQLLiteral(ByVal Text As String) As String
        Text = Replace(Text, "'", "''")
        Return (Text)
    End Function
```

```
    Private Sub btnSearch_Click(ByVal sender As System.Object, _
            ByVal e As System.EventArgs) Handles btnSearch.Click
        DoSearch()
    End Sub

    ' TextChanged is called when the <Enter> key is pressed when the text box has focus
    Private Sub txtSearch_TextChanged(ByVal sender As Object, _
            ByVal e As System.EventArgs) Handles txtSearch.TextChanged
        DoSearch()
    End Sub
End Class
```

URL parameters begin with a question mark (?) and are separated by an ampersand (&). The parameter values can be accessed with Request.Params(*parameter name*).

### MovieDetail Form

The MovieDetail form responds with raw HTML to create a frameset that hosts the AddMovie form in the top frame and the Internet Movie Database (www.IMDB.com) movie detail beneath. It receives the IMDBTitleNumber and MovieInfoID values as URL parameters (query string) and passes those values to the appropriate child frames.

Table 13-6 provides pseudocode descriptions of the procedures in the MovieDetail form design.

**Table 13.6 Design Pseudocode for MovieDetail Form**

| Procedures | Description |
|---|---|
| Page_Load | Responds with raw HTML code to create a frameset |

MovieDetail Form Implementation

```
' MovieDetail.aspx.vb

Public Class MovieDetail
    Inherits System.Web.UI.Page

Web Form Designer Generated Code

    Private Sub Page_Load(ByVal sender As System.Object, _
            ByVal e As System.EventArgs) Handles MyBase.Load
        ' This is a simple way to create a frame on the fly and pass
        ' parameters to the forms
        Response.ClearContent()

        ' Frameset rows can be specified as a percentage, or as pixels...
        'Response.Write("<FRAMESET rows=""28%,72%"">")
        Response.Write("<FRAMESET rows=""300,*"">")

        Response.Write("<FRAME src=""AddMovie.aspx?ID=" & Request.Params("ID").ToString)
        Response.Write(""" scrolling=""no"">")
        Response.Write("<FRAME src=""http://us.imdb.com/Title?")
        Response.Write(Request.Params("IMDB").ToString)
        Response.Write("""></FRAMESET>")
    End Sub

End Class
```

▶▶▶ *Tip*

**Response.Redirect does not allow breaking out of a frame. Breaking out requires the following code snippet:**

```
Response.Write("
<HTML><HEAD><SCRIPT>
top.location.href=
'newpage.aspx';
</SCRIPT>
</HEAD></HTML>")
```

### AddMovie Form

Figure 13-7 shows the layout of the AddMovie form interface. The GUI contains a modified Web Site Header. The hyperlinks have been replaced by image buttons because the hyperlinks do not support breaking out from a frame. There is also a grid layout panel containing a label to display the movie title, buttons for adding a VHS- or DVD-formatted movie to the shopping cart, and a label to indicate when no movies are available.

Table 13-7 provides pseudocode descriptions of the procedures in the AddMovie form design.

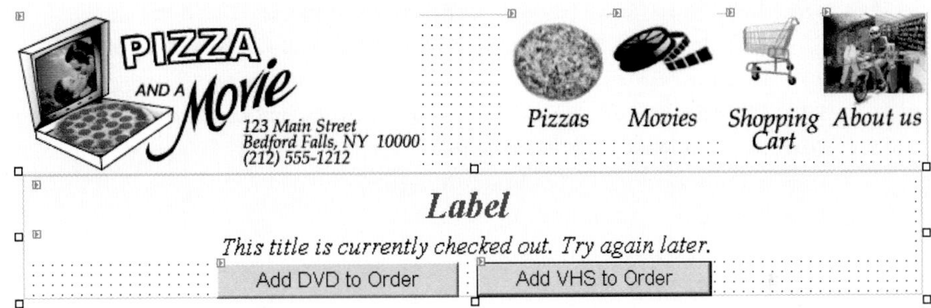


**FIGURE 13.7** *Layout of the AddMovie Form Interface*

**Table 13.7 Design Pseudocode for AddMovie Form**

| Procedures | Description |
|---|---|
| Page_Load | 1. Verifies the customer has successfully logged in this session<br>2. Gets the past MovieInfoID from the URL parameters<br>3. Displays the movie title<br>4. Determines availability in both VHS and DVD formats; makes order buttons visible as appropriate |
| btnDVD_Click | Calls AddMovieToOrder passing DVD as an argument |
| btnVHS_Click | Calls AddMovieToOrder passing VHS as an argument |
| AddMovieToOrder | Inserts a record to the OrderMovies table |
| CheckFormatAvailability | Queries the database to determine if there are one or more videos available for the specified format |
| BreakoutAndRedirect | Contains HTML code to break out of a frame and redirect to the page passed as an argument |
| ImageButton clicks | Each button in the modified web site header calls BreakoutAndRedirect with the appropriate web page |
| **Function Procedures** | **Description** |
| GetAvailableMovieID | Public Shared. Returns a MovieID corresponding to the first movie in the specified format that is not currently checked out |

### AddMovie Form Implementation

```
' AddMovie.aspx.vb

Imports System.Data.OleDb   ' This is needed for the programmatic database controls


Public Class AddMovie
    Inherits System.Web.UI.Page

Web Form Designer Generated Code

    Dim mDVDMovieID, mVHSMovieID As Integer

    Private Sub Page_Load(ByVal sender As System.Object, _
            ByVal e As System.EventArgs) Handles MyBase.Load
        ' Put user code to initialize the page here
        Dim DBConnection As New OleDbConnection(Application("ConnectionString"))
        Dim SQL As New OleDbCommand
        Dim SQLReader As OleDbDataReader
        Dim MovieInfoIDValid As Boolean
        Dim ResultCount As Integer
        Dim MovieID As Integer
        Dim MovieInfoID As Integer

        ' First make sure that there has been a valid login this session...
        If Session("OrderID") = 0 Then BreakoutAndRedirect("Login.aspx")

        ' MovieInfoID is passed from MovieDetail as a URL parameter
        MovieInfoID = Request.Params("ID")

        ' Check available inventory of movie formats for this MovieInfoID
        DBConnection.Open()
        SQL.Connection = DBConnection

        mVHSMovieID = GetAvailableMovieID(MovieInfoID, "VHS")
        btnVHS.Visible = (mVHSMovieID <> 0)

        mDVDMovieID = GetAvailableMovieID(MovieInfoID, "DVD")
        btnDVD.Visible = (mDVDMovieID <> 0)

        lblUnavailable.Visible = (mVHSMovieID = 0) And (mDVDMovieID = 0)

        ' Get title of movie from the MovieInfoID
        ' Because the URL parameter is editable by the user, it is possible that the
        ' MovieInfoID will be invalid
        SQL.CommandText = "SELECT * FROM MovieInfos WHERE MovieInfoID = " & _
            MovieInfoID.ToString
        SQLReader = SQL.ExecuteReader
        MovieInfoIDValid = SQLReader.HasRows
        If MovieInfoIDValid Then
            SQLReader.Read()
            lblMovieTitle.Text = SQLReader.Item("MovieTitle")
        End If
        SQLReader.Close()
```

```
    If MovieInfoIDValid Then
        ' Increment the detail viewed count
        SQL.CommandText = "UPDATE MovieInfos SET DetailShownCount = (DetailShownCount + 1) "&_
            "WHERE MovieInfoID = " & MovieInfoID.ToString
        SQL.ExecuteNonQuery()
    End If
    DBConnection.Close()
    SQL.Dispose()
    DBConnection.Dispose()
    If Not MovieInfoIDValid Then
        ' Cannot simply use "Redirect" to break out of a frame
        BreakoutAndRedirect(Request.UrlReferrer.ToString)
    End If
End Sub

' GetAvailableMovieID returns a MovieID for an in-stock copy of the movie title in the
' requested format.  This function must be declared Public Shared because it is used
' in another form
Public Shared Function GetAvailableMovieID(ByVal MovieInfoID As Integer, _
                       ByVal Format As String) As Integer
    ' Since this function is publicly shared, we must access the Application
    ' variables in a special way
    Dim DBConnection As New OleDbConnection( _
            System.Web.HttpContext.Current.Application("ConnectionString"))
    Dim SQL As New OleDbCommand
    Dim SQLReader As OleDbDataReader
    Dim SQLResult As Object

    DBConnection.Open()
    SQL.Connection = DBConnection

    SQL.CommandText = "SELECT MovieID FROM MOVIES WHERE (CheckedOut=False) AND " & _
        "(Format = '" & Format & "') AND (MovieInfoID = " & MovieInfoID.ToString & ")"
    SQLResult = SQL.ExecuteScalar
    If IsNothing(SQLResult) Then
        Return (0)
    Else
        Return (SQLResult)
    End If
    DBConnection.Close()
    SQL.Dispose()
    DBConnection.Dispose()
End Function

' BreakoutAndRedirect provides a method to break out of a frameset.
' Note that using Response.Redirect will only redirect the contents of a single frame.
Private Sub BreakoutAndRedirect(ByVal TargetURL As String)
    Response.Write("<html><head><script>top.location.href ='" & TargetURL & _
        "';</script></head></html>")
End Sub
```

```
' AddMovieToOrder creates a record in the OrderMovies table indicating that the
' passed MovieID has been added to the order.
' At checkout, the program will confirm that this movie is still available.
Private Sub AddMovieToOrder(ByVal MovieID As String)
    Dim DBConnection As New OleDbConnection(Application("ConnectionString"))
    Dim SQL As New OleDbCommand
    Dim SQLReader As OleDbDataReader
    Dim SQLResult As Object

    DBConnection.Open()
    SQL.Connection = DBConnection

    ' Check to make sure it's not already there
    SQL.CommandText = "SELECT MovieID FROM OrderMovies WHERE (OrderID = " & _
            Session("OrderID") & ") AND (MovieID = " & MovieID.ToString & ")"

    SQLResult = SQL.ExecuteScalar
    If IsNothing(SQLResult) Or (SQLResult <> MovieID) Then
        SQL.CommandText = "INSERT INTO OrderMovies (OrderID, MovieID, Price) " & _
            " VALUES (" & Session("OrderID") & ", " & MovieID.ToString & ", " & _
            Application("MovieRentalPrice") & ")"
        SQL.ExecuteNonQuery()
    End If
    DBConnection.Close()
    SQL.Dispose()
    DBConnection.Dispose()
    BreakoutAndRedirect("ShoppingCart.aspx")
End Sub

Private Sub btnDVD_Click(ByVal sender As System.Object, _
            ByVal e As System.EventArgs) Handles btnDVD.Click
    ' Add the previously determined first available DVD to the order
    AddMovieToOrder(mDVDMovieID)
End Sub

Private Sub btnVHS_Click(ByVal sender As System.Object, _
            ByVal e As System.EventArgs) Handles btnVHS.Click
    ' Add the previously determined first available VHS to the order
    AddMovieToOrder(mVHSMovieID)
End Sub

' The following Click events are not needed on the other forms, since the links are
' implemented as HyperLink controls.  However, in this case, we must handle
' breaking out of the frameset...
Private Sub ImageButton1_Click(ByVal sender As System.Object, _
            ByVal e As System.Web.UI.ImageClickEventArgs) Handles ImageButton1.Click
    BreakoutAndRedirect("AddPizza.aspx")
End Sub

Private Sub ImageButton2_Click(ByVal sender As System.Object, _
            ByVal e As System.Web.UI.ImageClickEventArgs) Handles ImageButton2.Click
    BreakoutAndRedirect("MovieSearch.aspx")
```

```
    End Sub

    Private Sub ImageButton3_Click(ByVal sender As System.Object, _
            ByVal e As System.Web.UI.ImageClickEventArgs) Handles ImageButton3.Click
        BreakoutAndRedirect("ShoppingCart.aspx")
    End Sub

    Private Sub ImageButton4_Click(ByVal sender As System.Object, _
            ByVal e As System.Web.UI.ImageClickEventArgs) Handles ImageButton4.Click
        BreakoutAndRedirect("AboutUs.aspx")
    End Sub

    Private Sub ImageButton5_Click(ByVal sender As System.Object, _
            ByVal e As System.Web.UI.ImageClickEventArgs) Handles ImageButton5.Click
        BreakoutAndRedirect("AboutUs.aspx")
    End Sub
End Class
```

> **►►► Tip**
> **A Public Shared procedure may be referenced by other pages in the solution. For example, GetAvailableMovieID, declared and called in AddMovie, is also called in ShoppingCart.**

> **►►► Tip**
> **The *ItemCommand* event is raised when any button is clicked in a data grid control. The button is identified through the CommandName property of the second event argument.**

### ShoppingCart Form

The ShoppingCart allows the customer to view the entire order, including each item's individual price and also the order total. The order details are presented using two DataGrid controls that are filled with pizza and movie order details programmatically. The DataGrid contains a button column for deleting items from the order. The customer may specify a valid promotional code to receive a 10 percent discount on the order. A $3 delivery charge is added to all orders under $20, with free delivery for orders of $20 or more. After placing an order, the customer is redirected to the CheckoutSuccess form to indicate the order has been successfully processed.

### ShoppingCart Form Design

Figure 13-8 shows the layout of the ShoppingCart form interface. The GUI contains a copy of the Web Site Header grid and three additional grid layout panels along with two DataGrid controls for the pizzas and movies in the current order. Two of the additional grid layout panels provide a heading for each of the data grids. The third contains a text box for entering a promotional code, labels for calculated values, and a button for placing the order. Finally, graphics and labels are also included to give the form a professional appearance.

Table 13-8 provides pseudocode descriptions of the procedures in the ShoppingCart form design.

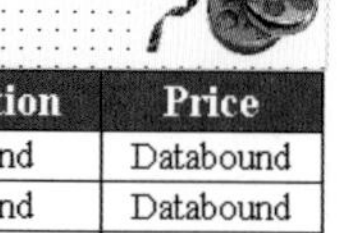


**FIGURE 13.8** *Layout of the ShoppingCart Form Interface*

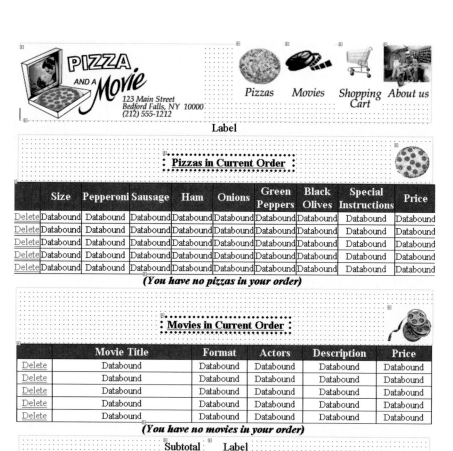

**Table 13.8** Design Pseudocode for ShoppingCart Form

| Procedures | Description |
|---|---|
| CalculatePrice | 1. Uses SQL SELECT to calculate the price total for the pizza orders |
| | 2. Uses SQL SELECT to calculate the price total for the movie orders |
| | 3. Calculates and displays subtotal, delivery fee, promotional code discount, tax, and total based on business logic |
| RefreshAllData | 1. Runs a query for movie orders and fills the Movies data grid with the result set |
| | 2. Runs a query for pizza orders and fills the Pizzas data grid with the result set |
| | 3. Calls CalculatePrice |
| Page_Load | 1. Verifies the customer has successfully logged in this session |
| | 2. If the controls have not been initialized (i.e., not a postback), then connects the data grids to the appropriate data sources |
| | 3. Refreshes all data |
| dgPizzas_ItemCommand | Deletes the selected pizza from the Pizzas table |
| dgMovies_ItemCommand | Deletes the selected movie from the Movies table |
| btnPlaceOrder_Click | 1. For each movie in the order, verifies the movie is available and marks it as checked out. If not available, then checks for other available copies of the same format. If no other copies are available, then cancels the checkout and informs the customer |
| | 2. Completes the order by updating the current order record in the Orders table |

### ShoppingCart Form Implementation

```
' ShoppingCart.aspx.vb

Imports System.Data.OleDb   ' This is needed for the programmatic database controls

Public Class ShoppingCart
    Inherits System.Web.UI.Page

Web Form Designer generated code

    Dim mDBConnection As New OleDbConnection
    Dim mdsMovies As New DataSet
    Dim mdaMovies As New OleDbDataAdapter
    Dim mdsPizzas As New DataSet
    Dim mdaPizzas As New OleDbDataAdapter
    Dim mSQLMovies As New OleDbCommand
    Dim mSQLPizzas As New OleDbCommand
    Dim mDelivery, mDiscount, mSubtotal, mTax, mTotal As Double

    Private Sub Page_Load(ByVal sender As System.Object,_
            ByVal e As System.EventArgs) Handles MyBase.Load
        ' Put user code to initialize the page here
        ' First make sure that there has been a valid login this session...
        If Session("OrderID") = 0 Then Response.Redirect("Login.aspx")
        RefreshAllData()
    End Sub

    ' RefreshAllData ensures the controls are populated with current data
    Private Sub RefreshAllData()
        ' Open the database if not already opened
        If mDBConnection.State <> ConnectionState.Open Then
            mDBConnection.ConnectionString = Application("ConnectionString")
            mDBConnection.Open()
        End If

        ' If there are movies in the order, populate dgMovies with those movies
        ' The dgMovies DataGrid will include a Delete column to remove movies
        ' from the order.  A unique identifier for each row is required to remove
        ' a movie.  The DataKeyField holds the field name for that unique identifier.
        ' DataBind is necessary on a web form to populate the control with the current data.
        mSQLMovies.CommandText = "SELECT * FROM (OrderMovies Left Join Movies on " & _
            " OrderMovies.MovieID = Movies.MovieID) Left Join MovieInfos on " & _
            " Movies.MovieInfoID = MovieInfos.MovieInfoID " & _
            " WHERE ORDERID = " & Session("OrderID")
        mSQLMovies.Connection = mDBConnection
        mdaMovies.SelectCommand = mSQLMovies
        mdsMovies.Clear()
        mdaMovies.Fill(mdsMovies)
        If mdsMovies.Tables(0).Rows.Count > 0 Then
            dgMovies.Visible = True
            lblNoMovies.Visible = False
            dgMovies.DataKeyField = "OrderMovieID"
            dgMovies.DataSource = mdsMovies.Tables(0).DefaultView
            dgMovies.DataBind()
```

```
    Else
        dgMovies.Visible = False
        lblNoMovies.Visible = True
    End If

    ' If there are pizzas in the order, populate dgPizzas with those pizzas
    mSQLPizzas.CommandText = "SELECT * FROM Pizzas WHERE OrderID = " & _
        Session("OrderID")
    mSQLPizzas.Connection = mDBConnection
    mdaPizzas.SelectCommand = mSQLPizzas
    mdsPizzas.Clear()
    mdaPizzas.Fill(mdsPizzas)
    If mdsPizzas.Tables(0).Rows.Count > 0 Then
        dgPizzas.Visible = True
        lblNoPizzas.Visible = False
        dgPizzas.DataKeyField = "PizzaID"
        dgPizzas.DataSource = mdsPizzas.Tables(0).DefaultView
        dgPizzas.DataBind()
    Else
        dgPizzas.Visible = False
        lblNoPizzas.Visible = True
    End If
    CalculatePrice()
End Sub

' CalculatePrice uses business logic to calculate the price for the entire order
Private Sub CalculatePrice()
    Dim NumOfMovies, MovieSubtotal, PizzaSubtotal As Double
    Dim SQL As New OleDbCommand
    Dim SQLResult As Object

    If mDBConnection.State <> ConnectionState.Open Then
        mDBConnection.ConnectionString = Application("ConnectionString")
        mDBConnection.Open()
    End If
    SQL.Connection = mDBConnection
    SQL.CommandText = "SELECT SUM(Price) As Subtotal FROM PIZZAS WHERE ORDERID = " & _
        Session("OrderID")
    SQLResult = SQL.ExecuteScalar
    If TypeOf SQLResult Is DBNull Then
        PizzaSubtotal = 0
    Else
        PizzaSubtotal = SQLResult
    End If

    SQL.CommandText = "SELECT SUM(Price) As Subtotal FROM ORDERMOVIES " & _
        " WHERE ORDERID = " & Session("OrderID")
    SQLResult = SQL.ExecuteScalar
    If TypeOf SQLResult Is DBNull Then
        MovieSubtotal = 0
    Else
        MovieSubtotal = SQLResult
    End If
```

```
        mSubtotal = MovieSubtotal + PizzaSubtotal
        lblSubtotal.Text = FormatCurrency(mSubtotal)

        If mSubtotal > Application("FreeDeliveryThreshold") Then
            mDelivery = 0
        Else
            mDelivery = Application("DeliveryCost")
        End If
        lblDelivery.Text = FormatCurrency(mDelivery)

        If txtPromotionalCode.Text = Application("PromotionalCode") Then
            mDiscount = mSubtotal * (Application("PromotionalDiscountPercent") / 100)
        Else
            mDiscount = 0
        End If
        lblDiscount.Text = FormatCurrency(mDiscount)


        mTax = (mSubtotal - mDiscount) * Application("TaxRate")
        lblTax.Text = FormatCurrency(mTax)
        mTotal = mTax + mSubtotal - mDiscount + mDelivery
        lblTotal.Text = FormatCurrency(mTotal)
    End Sub

    ' ItemCommand is called when the Delete column of a DataGrid is clicked
    ' The command is passed as e.CommandName
    ' This function determines the OrderMovieID of the clicked row and deletes it
    Private Sub dgMovies_ItemCommand(ByVal source As Object, _
            ByVal e As System.Web.UI.WebControls.DataGridCommandEventArgs) _
            Handles dgMovies.ItemCommand
        Dim OrderMovieID As Integer
        Dim SQL As New OleDbCommand

        'Choose command
        If e.CommandName.ToString = "Delete" Then
            If mDBConnection.State <> ConnectionState.Open Then
                mDBConnection.ConnectionString = Application("ConnectionString")
                mDBConnection.Open()
            End If
            SQL.Connection = mDBConnection
            'Find row of dataset on which to act
            OrderMovieID = dgMovies.DataKeys(e.Item.ItemIndex).ToString()
            SQL.CommandText = "DELETE FROM OrderMovies WHERE OrderMovieID = " & _
                OrderMovieID.ToString
            SQL.ExecuteNonQuery()
            SQL.Dispose()
        End If
        RefreshAllData()
    End Sub

    ' This function determines the PizzaID of the clicked row and deletes it
    Private Sub dgPizzas_ItemCommand(ByVal source As Object, _
            ByVal e As System.Web.UI.WebControls.DataGridCommandEventArgs) _
```

```
        Handles dgPizzas.ItemCommand
    Dim PizzaID As Integer
    Dim SQL As New OleDbCommand

    'Choose command
    If e.CommandName.ToString = "Delete" Then
        If mDBConnection.State <> ConnectionState.Open Then
            mDBConnection.ConnectionString = Application("ConnectionString")
            mDBConnection.Open()
        End If
        SQL.Connection = mDBConnection
        'Find row of dataset on which to act
        PizzaID = dgPizzas.DataKeys(e.Item.ItemIndex).ToString()
        SQL.CommandText = "DELETE FROM Pizzas WHERE PizzaID = " & PizzaID.ToString
        SQL.ExecuteNonQuery()
        SQL.Dispose()
    End If
    RefreshAllData()
End Sub

' This procedure attempts to finalize the current order.
' The movies in the order must be marked as "CheckedOut".  If for some reason a movie
' is unavailable for checkout, an attempt is made to find a same format copy.
' If no same fomat copies are available, then the customer is notified, the movie is
' removed from the shopping cart, and the transaction is rolled back.
' If all movies are available (or suitable copies are found) then the orders table
' is updated to reflect a completed transaction.
Private Sub btnPlaceOrder_Click(ByVal sender As System.Object, _
        ByVal e As System.EventArgs) Handles btnPlaceOrder.Click
    Dim SQL As New OleDbCommand
    Dim SQLReader As OleDbDataReader

    Dim OrigMovieIDs() As Integer
    Dim MovieIDs() As Integer
    Dim MovieInfoIDs() As Integer
    Dim Formats() As String

    Dim CheckoutInvalid As Boolean
    Dim MovieAvailable As Boolean
    Dim MovieCount As Integer
    Dim i, j As Integer
    Dim ReturnDate As String

    If mDBConnection.State <> ConnectionState.Open Then
        mDBConnection.ConnectionString = Application("ConnectionString")
        mDBConnection.Open()
    End If
    SQL.Connection = mDBConnection

    ' Make a list of the movies in the order, so that we can mark them as "checked out"
    SQL.CommandText = "SELECT OrderMovies.MovieID As MovieID, MovieInfoID, Format " & _
        " FROM OrderMovies LEFT JOIN Movies On " & _
        " OrderMovies.MovieID = Movies.MovieID WHERE OrderID = " & Session("OrderID")
    SQLReader = SQL.ExecuteReader
```

```
MovieCount = 0
While SQLReader.Read
    MovieCount = MovieCount + 1
    ReDim Preserve MovieIDs(MovieCount)
    ReDim Preserve OrigMovieIDs(MovieCount)
    ReDim Preserve MovieInfoIDs(MovieCount)
    ReDim Preserve Formats(MovieCount)
    MovieIDs(MovieCount - 1) = SQLReader.Item("MovieID")
    OrigMovieIDs(MovieCount - 1) = MovieIDs(MovieCount - 1)
    MovieInfoIDs(MovieCount - 1) = SQLReader.Item("MovieInfoID")
    Formats(MovieCount - 1) = SQLReader.Item("Format")
End While
SQLReader.Close()

' The return date for the movies will be set according to business logic
ReturnDate = _
    "#" & (Date.Today.AddDays(Application("CheckOutDays")).ToShortDateString) & "#"

CheckoutInvalid = False
For i = 0 To MovieCount - 1
    MovieAvailable = False
    While (MovieIDs(i) <> 0) And (Not MovieAvailable)
        ' Try to check out movie.
        SQL.CommandText = "UPDATE Movies SET CheckedOut = TRUE, DueDate = " & _
            ReturnDate & " WHERE (MovieID = " & MovieIDs(i).ToString & ") " & _
            " AND (CheckedOut = FALSE)"
        MovieAvailable = (SQL.ExecuteNonQuery() = 1) 'did we succeed?
        If Not MovieAvailable Then
            ' The movie must have been checked out while the customer was shopping.
            ' See if there is another item in inventory in the requested format.
            MovieIDs(i) = AddMovie.GetAvailableMovieID(MovieInfoIDs(i), Formats(i))
        Else
            ' If the MovieID has been changed, change the OrderMovies table to
            ' reflect this.
            If MovieIDs(i) <> OrigMovieIDs(i) Then
                SQL.CommandText = "UPDATE OrderMovies SET MovieID = " & _
                    MovieIDs(i).ToString & " WHERE (OrderID = " & _
                    Session("OrderID") & ") AND (MovieID = " & _
                    OrigMovieIDs(i).ToString & ")"
                SQL.ExecuteNonQuery()
            End If
        End If
    End While

    If MovieIDs(i) = 0 Then
        ' We were unable to find a replacement copy.
        ' Continue with order to determine other errors
        CheckoutInvalid = True
    End If
Next
```

```
        If CheckoutInvalid Then
            ' Even after looking for items in the inventory in the requested format
            ' there was a problem finding at least one of the requested movies.
            ' Back out the "checkout's" and alert the patron.
            For i = 0 To MovieCount - 1
                If MovieIDs(i) <> 0 Then
                    SQL.CommandText = "UPDATE Movies SET CheckedOut = FALSE " & _
                        " WHERE (MovieID = " & MovieIDs(i).ToString & ")"
                    SQL.ExecuteNonQuery()
                Else
                    ' Remove unavailable movie titles from the order
                    SQL.CommandText = "DELETE * FROM OrderMovies WHERE (OrderID = " & _
                         Session("OrderID") & ") AND (MovieID = " & _
                         OrigMovieIDs(i).ToString & ")"
                     SQL.ExecuteNonQuery()
                 End If
             Next
             lblError.Text = "One or more of your movies has been deleted from your " & _
                 "order because it is unavailable."
             lblError.Visible = True
             RefreshAllData()
             Exit Sub
         End If

         ' Finalize the order by updating the current order record in the Orders table.
         SQL.CommandText = "UPDATE Orders SET PromotionCode = '" & _
             txtPromotionalCode.Text & "', Completed = TRUE, DateTimeCompleted = '" & _
             Now & "', Subtotal = " & mSubtotal & ", Total = " & mTotal & ", Tax = " & _
             mTax & ", Delivery = " & mDelivery & ", Discount = " & mDiscount & _
             " WHERE OrderID = " & Session("OrderID")
         SQL.ExecuteNonQuery()
         ' Reset the Session to start a new order
         Session("OrderID") = 0
         Response.Redirect("CheckoutSuccess.aspx")
     End Sub
End Class
```

### Testing the Solution

You can test Reed and Elizabeth's solution by implementing their design as shown in the previous sections. Then right-click on Login.aspx in the solution explorer and select Set as Start Page. Run the application. The application begins with the Login form (the start page). Enter valid data in the username and password fields (Figure 13-9). After you login, open the database to see the valid current order in the Orders table (the last order for the customer).

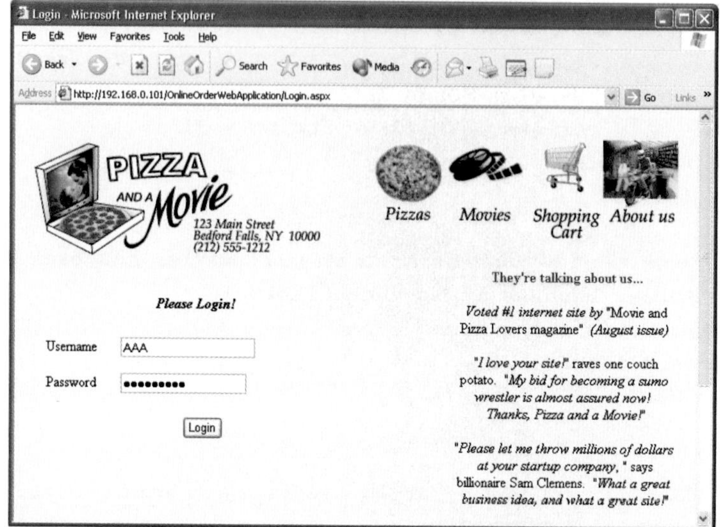


**FIGURE 13.9** *Login Form at Runtime*

Add a pizza as prompted on the AddPizza form (Figure 13-10). Click on the add pizza button.

The shopping cart should appear containing the specified pizza (Figure 13-11). You can also verify the pizza order by opening the database and looking in the Pizzas table.

**FIGURE 13.10**
*AddPizza Form at Runtime*

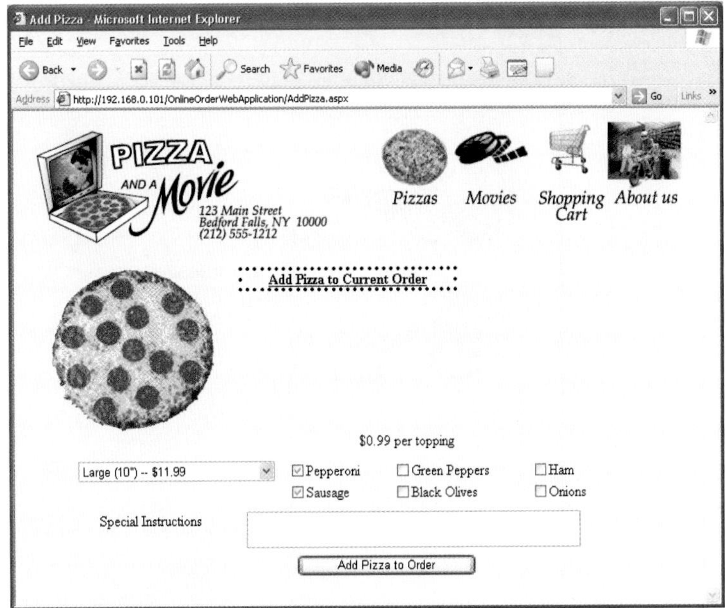


**FIGURE 13.11**
*ShoppingCart Form with One Pizza at Runtime*

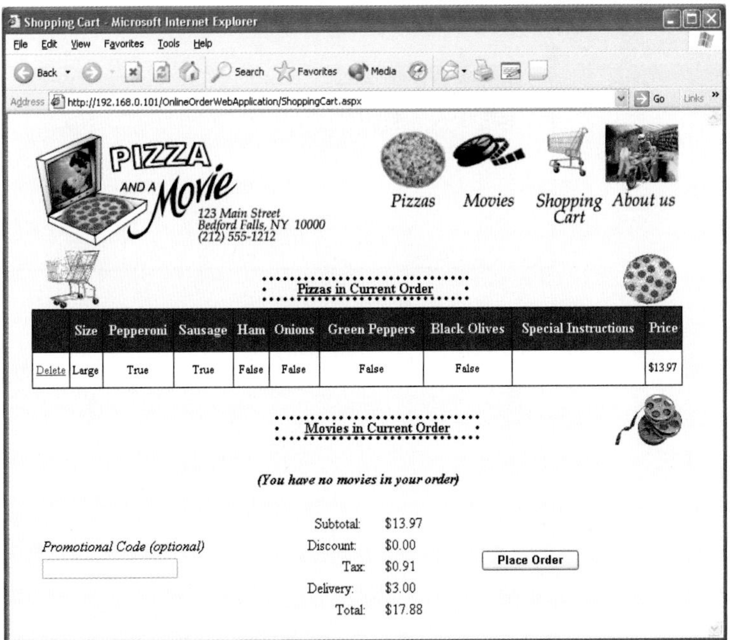

Click on the *Movies* link in the Web Site Header to view the MovieSearch form. Perform a search and view the resulting list (Figure 13-12).

Clicking a movie link in the MovieSearch form will take you to the MovieDetail form, which creates a frameset containing the AddMovie form (Figure 13-13). Select an available movie format and add it to your order.

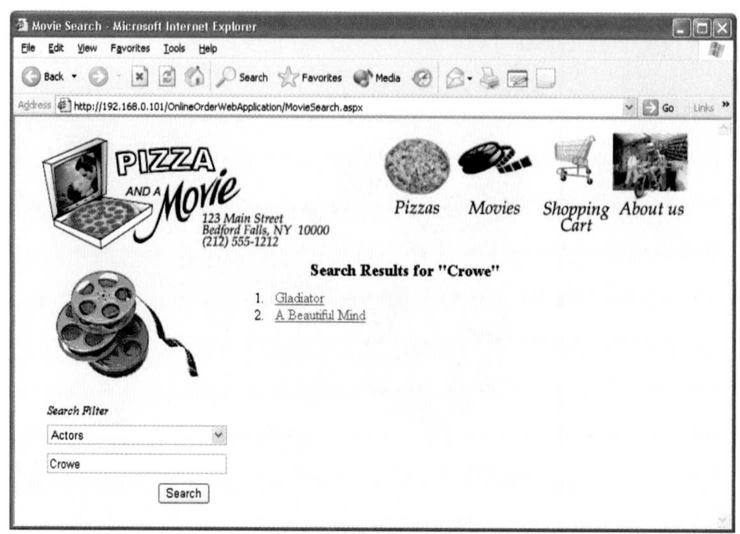


**FIGURE 13.12**
*MoveSearch Form at Runtime*

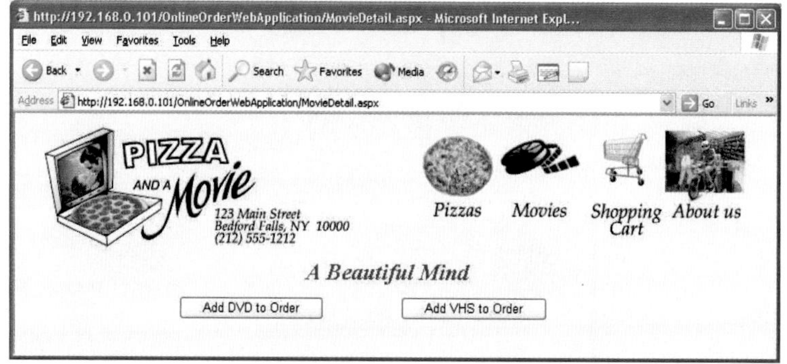


**FIGURE 13.13**
*MoveDetail/AddMovie*

You should be redirected to the ShoppingCart form, which includes all items ordered. You can also verify the movie order by opening the database and looking in the OrderMovies table.

Enter a valid promotional code. Verify that the calculated values are correct according to the application's business logic rules (Figure 13-14). Click the button to place the order. Open the Orders table and verify the order record has been modified correctly.

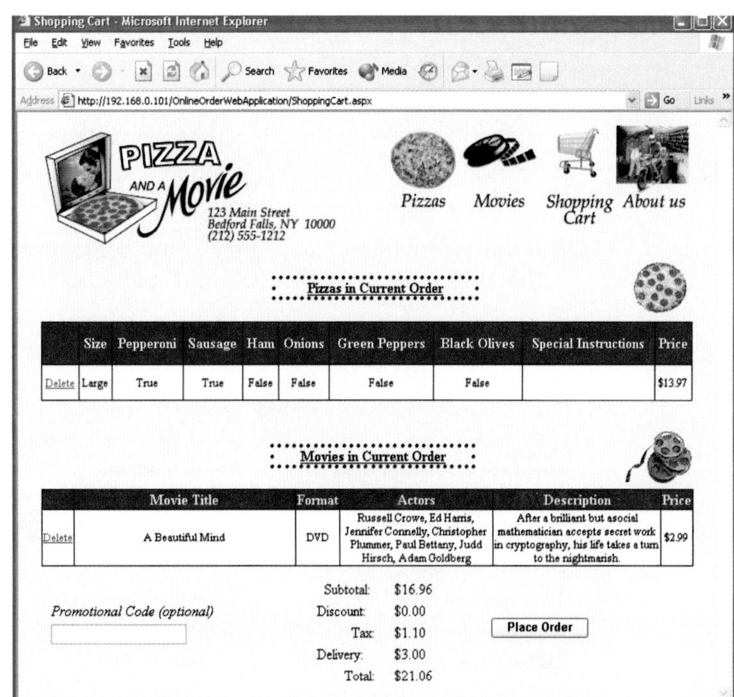


**FIGURE 13.14**
*ShoppingCart Form at Runtime*

## Chapter Summary

- The presentation layer provides the client interface, the application layer usually implements the business logic of a solution, and the data storage layer maintains the database and tools for data access.
- Client-side state management is less secure than server-side state management, but it provides good options and performance in secure, intranet environments.
- When a web application runs, ASP.NET maintains information about the application in the application state. It also maintains session state information about each user session.
- Application variables are helpful for storing small amounts of infrequently changed global information that is used by many users.
- Session state variables are helpful for storing small amounts of short-lived information that is specific to an individual session.
- Database support is good for storing large amounts of information or information that must survive application and session restarts.

## Key Terms

**application state** p. 348
**application variables** p. 348
**cookie** p. 347
**ExecuteNonQuery** p. 357
**ExecuteScalar** p. 355
**fat client** p. 345
**IsPostBack** p. 360
**ItemCommand** p. 374
**query string** p. 347
**RequiredFieldValidator** p. 357
**Response.Redirect** p. 357
**server farm** p. 346
**session** p. 349
**session state** p. 349
**session variables** p. 349
**state management** p. 346
**System.Data.OleDb** p. 355
**thin client** p. 345
**view state** p. 347

## Review Questions

1. Discuss the various options for state management.
2. What are the security issues involved with each of the state management options?
3. What is a RequiredFieldValidator? How is it used?
4. How do you access URL parameter values?
5. How do you redirect to another form? How do you break out of a frame?
6. How do you create a hyperlink in a label?
7. What options are available for executing SQL commands?

## ▶ Programming Exercises

**13-1. Empty Order.** Add business logic to Reed and Elizabeth's design so the customer cannot place an order with an empty shopping cart.

**13-2. New Releases.** Modify Reed and Elizabeth's application by adding a ReleasedToVideoDate field (type Date) in the MovieInfos table. Add an application variable, NewReleaseRentalPrice. Update the ShoppingCart form to charge the new release rental price for videos in their first two weeks of release.

**13-3. Show Copies.** Modify Reed and Elizabeth's AddMovie form to show the status of all copies of a movie.

**13-4. Settings.** Create an administrative Web Form to view and change the values in Reed and Elizabeth's Settings table.

**13-5. Returns.** Create an administrative Web Form to update Reed and Elizabeth's database when a customer returns videos (set CheckedOut to false).

**13-6. Customer Care.** Create an administrative Web Form to add new customers to Reed and Elizabeth's database, and also view, edit, and delete current customer information.

**13-7. Video Arrivals.** Create an administrative Web Form to add new videos to Reed and Elizabeth's database.

CHAPTER 14

# Advanced Object-Oriented Programming

## OUTLINE



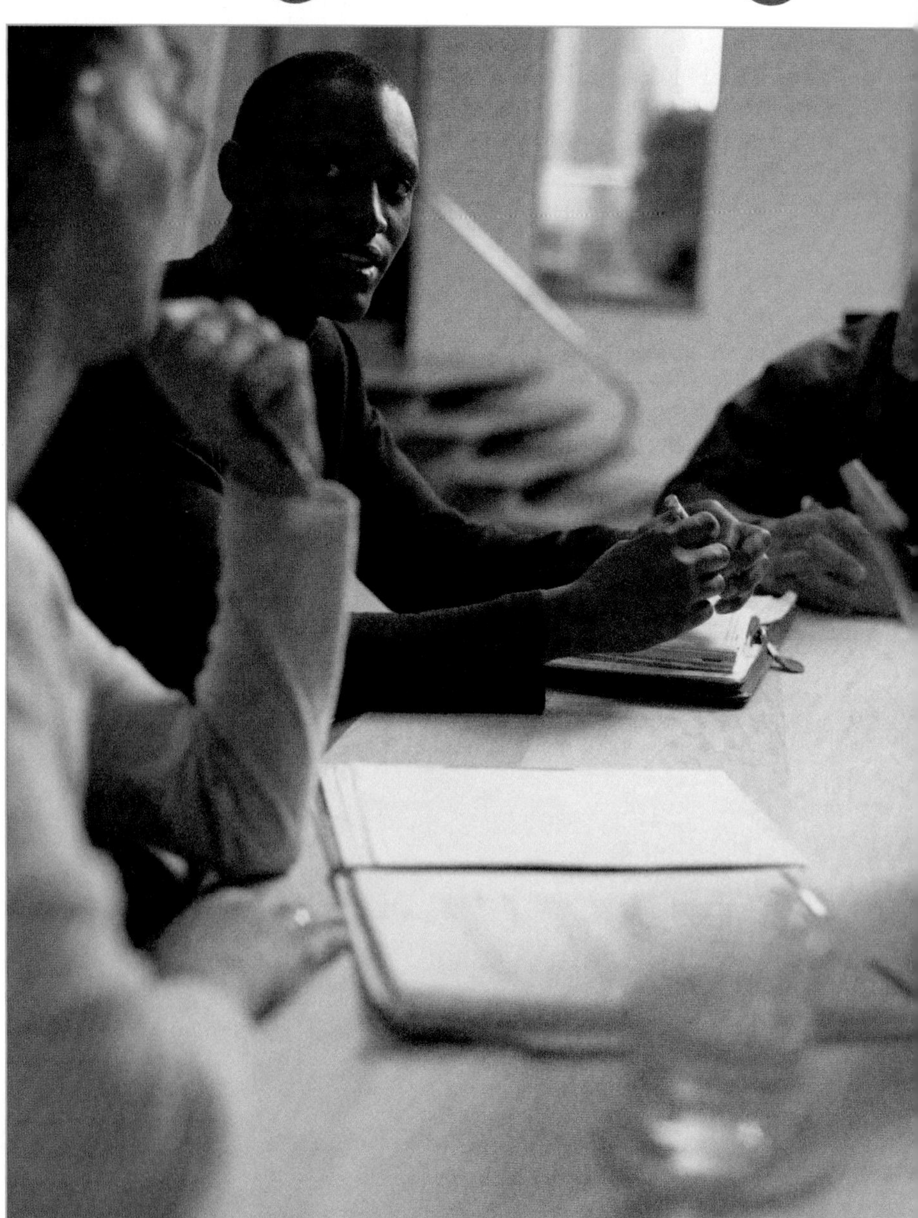

## ▶ INTERVIEW

### Bill Grollman, President, SmartPros Ltd.

***Interviewer:*** What kinds of projects are you currently working on?

***Grollman:*** SmartPros produces and markets continuing professional education courses for the corporate accounting, public accounting, and engineering professions. The fastest-growing part of our business is e-learning with courses offered over the Internet. It's a constant challenge to use the latest technology to produce, host, and deliver our courses on the web. Since we specialize in streaming media, our programs have always been on the cutting edge and have featured streaming video and audio since 1998. We are probably in at least our tenth platform revision for producing our courses in the past four years. This is the constant challenge we face in our business. As soon as bandwidth permits, we'll go to full-screen video on the web.

***Interviewer:*** What are you most excited about for the future?

***Grollman:*** E-learning is one of the most natural uses for the Internet. It is one of the few industries in which the product is produced, marketed, delivered, and employed by the end user over the Internet. This generates tremendous advantages for both the producer (eliminates most of the cost of goods sold, drastically reduces marketing costs, greatly simplifies the ability to update programs with new material) and the students who take our courses (anywhere-anytime education at the end user's convenience, ability to link to live data, access to chat rooms, threaded discussions). We're most excited about the advent of full-screen video on the Internet, which will certainly be coming within the next few years.

***Interviewer:*** What has been your personal key to success?

***Grollman:*** I make sure my company sees itself as a content company, not a technology company. There is no substitute for high-quality content. However, we will always stay on top of the technology and use it to our advantage in producing, marketing, and delivering our content.

***Interviewer:*** What advice do you have for students preparing for a career in the IT industry?

***Grollman:*** There are more opportunities in the IT industry than in any other industry. By definition, IT will always keep changing dramatically each year. This produces tremendous career opportunities for those who are well educated, who enjoy using technology, and who have the intelligence and creativity to develop innovative new applications for technology.

## OBJECTIVES

At the completion of this chapter, you will

- **Understand the differences between classes and objects**
- **Understand object terminology, including encapsulation, inheritance, and polymorphism**
- **Know how to create your own classes**
- **Know how to write constructors with multiple parameter lists**
- **Develop applications that use classes and objects**

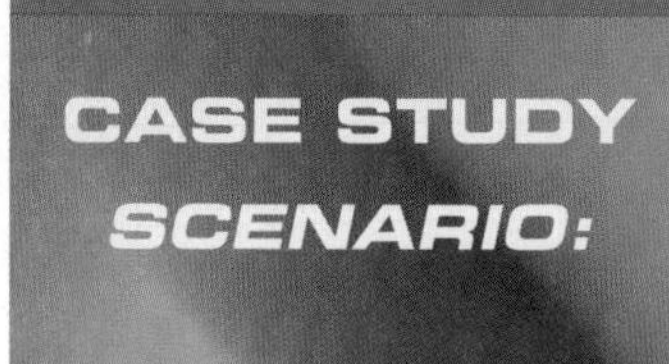


# TankWorld

Reed and Elizabeth have been pleasantly surprised by the response to their Singing Mimes collection of edutainment software on CD. They are not getting rich, but they have been able to break even financially, and they are gaining valuable business experience developing, manufacturing, and marketing a product. They have also made a number of contacts with individuals that may prove helpful when they are looking for jobs next year.

One issue that has come up a number of times is the desire for students to write games. Reed and Elizabeth both understand that professional game developers are highly trained and talented individuals, and that game development is a not an easy task. However, they also know that object-oriented programming may hold the key to creating a gaming environment that would allow for creative expression by individuals. Their idea is to develop a virtual simulation environment that would contain a variety of interesting objects, each of which could be programmed to interact with the world and the objects in the world. Reed suggests that the environment could include tank objects that move around and shoot things. Elizabeth suggests that it should allow multiple players over the Internet. They envision tournaments where individuals submit their objects to compete against other objects.

"I am excited about this," Elizabeth says. "How do we get started?"

Elizabeth and Reed's solution appears later this chapter.

## 14-1 Writing Objects

VB.NET is an object-oriented language. Forms are objects. Controls are objects. You wrote an object-oriented program when you put a button on a form and coded a click event procedure to display "Hello World." The button and the form it was on are both objects. The text, size, and position of the button are properties of the button object. The drawing routines for displaying the button in its various states (normal, pressed) are methods of the button object. You have already learned a little about objects, but there is a lot more to learn. In this chapter you will learn some of the essential object terminology and how to write your own objects.

### ASK THE AUTHOR

**Q** I thought buttons were called *controls*, but now you are calling them *objects*. Which term best describes buttons?

**A** Windows Form controls (including buttons, text boxes, labels, and so on) are objects. So the phrases *button object* and *button control* are both correct. However, the term *control* refers to a special kind of object, one that has GUI properties and methods.

## Classes and Objects

An ***object*** is a combination of data and actions that can be treated as a unit. A ***class*** is the structure of an object, a blueprint that describes the properties (data) and methods (actions) of an object. A class is not a functioning version of the object, just as a blueprint of a house is not a functioning version of a house—you cannot sleep inside a blueprint. An object is created from a class, just as a house is built from a blueprint. Continuing this analogy, many houses can be built using the same blueprint, and many objects can be created from the same class. The Button class specifies that buttons will have text properties and Click event procedures. Each instance of a button can have a unique text value and event procedure.

**Tip**

**The terms *class* and *object* are sometimes used interchangeably, but in fact, classes describe the *structure* of objects, while objects are usable *instances* of classes. Because an object is an *instance* of a class, the act of creating an object is called *instantiation.***

### ASK THE AUTHOR

**Q** How do I know if something is an object?

**A** The main indicator that something is an object is if it has properties or methods. You will find that almost everything in VB.NET is an object. Even Integers are objects (as clearly seen by the Integer's "ToString" method).

## 14-2 Object-Oriented Terminology

Generally speaking, a language is considered to be object-oriented if it supports three main features: *encapsulation*, *inheritance*, and *polymorphism*.

### MENTOR

"Of all the monsters that fill the nightmares of our folklore, none terrify more than werewolves, because they transform unexpectedly from the familiar into horrors. For these, one seeks bullets of silver that can magically lay them to rest." So begins Fredrick Brooks's 1986 technical paper "No Silver Bullet—Essence and Accidents of Software Engineering." Just as a werewolf is capable of transforming into a monster, Brooks suggests that the inherent complexity of software makes it capable of transforming into a monster of missed schedules, blown budgets, and poor products. Brooks's central argument is that there is no magical solution (no silver bullet) that will somehow eliminate the complexity of software development. Brooks, however, is not a pessimist—he merely emphasizes that software development is a complex task and that developers should focus on techniques that will produce incremental improvements rather than wait for a magical breakthrough that likely will never come.

Object-oriented programming is an excellent example of an incremental improvement. Working with objects allows developers to build with bigger pieces. As you will see in this chapter, objects are modular pieces with well-defined *interfaces* that explain (and ensure) proper use of the objects. Objects employ *encapsulation* to prevent improper access to the inner structure of an object. Objects support *inheritance* to improve code reuse and logical design. Objects are not silver bullets, but they do give developers a means to keep pace with the ever-growing complexity of software development.

## Encapsulation

***Encapsulation*** refers to grouping related properties and methods so they can be treated as a single unit or object. Encapsulation also refers to protecting the inner contents of an object from being damaged or incorrectly referenced by external code. With proper encapsulation, an object is only referenced through the formal interface, which helps avoid side effects. Side effects refer to unexpected and undesirable changes that occur in addition to the intended behavior.

With this in mind, one of the basic rules of encapsulation is that class data should be modified or retrieved only through property procedures. This limits how external code may interact with the object and keeps the inner workings of the object invisible to the outside world. The inner contents of the object are therefore protected from accidental (or intentional!) damage by external code.

**Tip**

**To help distinguish classes from objects, it is common to denote classes with a "T" prefix (for "Type").**

Limiting how external code interacts with the object also allows for later modification without risk of compatibility problems. You can make improvements within the implementation—hidden to the outside world—to improve the performance of the object. For example, forcing external code to reference the object only through the interface allows you to identify bugs (errors) in the implementation and fix them without concern that the changes will cause problems. Likewise, if you find that an object is a performance bottleneck, you can rewrite it to be more efficient without worry of creating problems to the external code.

Encapsulation also allows you to control how the data and procedures are used. You can use access modifiers, such as Private or Protected, to prevent outside procedures from executing class methods or reading and modifying data in properties and fields. You should declare internal details of a class as Private to prevent them from being used outside your class; this technique is called data hiding.

**Tip**

**A derived class inherits all the properties and methods of the base class. Inherited properties or methods that need to be enhanced may be overridden (replaced) in the derived class.**

## Inheritance

***Inheritance*** describes the ability to create new classes based on an existing class. The existing class is called the ***base class***, and the new class derived from the base class is called the ***derived class***. The derived class inherits all the properties, methods, and events of the base class and can be customized with additional properties and methods. This means you can develop and debug a class once and then reuse it as the basis for other classes.

Inheritance takes code reuse to a whole new level. If you need a class that is similar to an existing class, you can derive the new class and inherit all the desirable data and actions from the base class and only have to specify the data and behavior that is different for the new class.

**Tip**

**Changes to a base class are automatically updated into the derived classes as well. This significantly reduces the maintenance effort and improves developer productivity.**

Consider the classes shown in Figure 14-1. The base class TPerson contains two properties, Name and Birthday. There is one method, DisplayAge, which determines the person's age based on the value of the Birthday property and the current date as reported by the computer. The TPerson base class is used to derive two new classes: TStudent and TProfessor. Each of the derived classes inherits the properties and methods from the base class (so TStudent and TProfessor each have names and birthdays.) In addition, the derived classes add their own properties and methods as appropriate. The process could be further extended. For example, the TStudent class could be used as a base class for a new derived class, TGraduatingSenior, which inherits properties and methods from both TPerson and TStudent and introduces its own properties and methods.

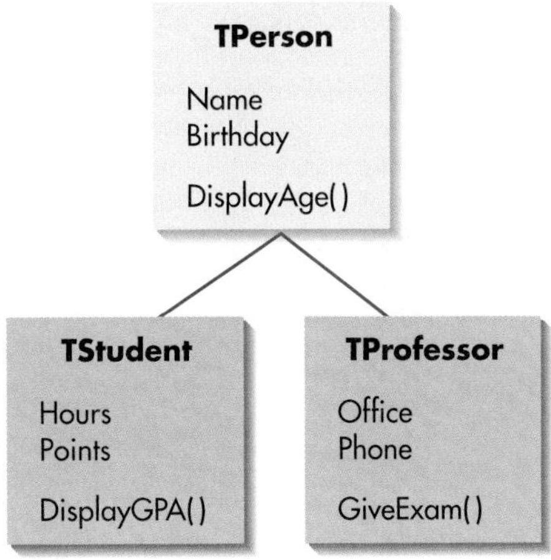


**FIGURE 14.1**
*Inheritance Figure (TPerson, TStudent, TProfessor)*

## Polymorphism

***Polymorphism*** is the ability for objects from different classes to respond appropriately to identical method names or operators. Polymorphism is essential to object-oriented programming because it allows you to use shared names, and the system will apply the appropriate code for the particular object. For example, a method called DisplayContactInformation might behave differently when called for a SummerIntern object than when called for a VicePresident object, which could be different again for a DirectorOfPublicRelations object. Without polymorphism you would have to create different, uniquely named methods to generate different behavior, which would add significant (and unnecessary) difficulty to the application.

### ASK THE AUTHOR

**Q** That seems really confusing. I don't think I will ever understand polymorphism.

**A** Actually, you have been using polymorphism for quite some time now. The math operators such as addition (+) or multiplication (*) are perfect examples. Remember that the way a computer stores an Integer is different from the way it stores a Double. Therefore, multiplying two integer values requires a process different from that used to multiply two double values. As a developer, you do not have to worry about these differences. You simply specify the multiplication operator between two objects, and polymorphism allows the system to trigger the appropriate behavior.

## 14-3 Creating Your Own Classes

A class definition consists of fields, properties, and methods. A field is a variable in the class and is usually private. A property is a programming construct that typically provides the interface to a field in a class. It contains special Get and Set procedures that allow external code to reference the field in a way that maintains data encapsulation. A method is a function or a sub procedure within a class. The class definition also may contain constructor methods that are called when a new object is instantiated from the class. It is good convention to list the fields first, then the properties, then the constructor methods, and then any additional methods.

*Syntax:*

```
[Private|Public] Class classname
        [fields]
        [properties]
        [constructors]
        [methods]
End Class
```

*Example:*

```
Class TPerson
    ' Fields
    ' Properties
    ' Constructors
    ' Methods
End Class

Class TStudent
    ' Fields
    ' Properties
    ' Constructors
    ' Methods
End Class

Class TMilitaryTime
    ' Fields
    ' Properties
    ' Constructors
    ' Methods
End Class
```

## Fields

Fields provide storage for the data in an object and are treated just like variables. In considering fields in this chapter, we use two design standards. First, all field values will be declared Private, making them visible only to methods within the class. This increases data hiding and minimizes the possibility of side effects. The second design standard is beginning all field names with "F". This notation will be a clear indicator that an object field is being referenced.

*Syntax:*

```
[Public|Private] fieldname As datatype
```

*Example:*

```
    Private FHour As Integer
    Private FMinute As Integer

    Private FName As String
    Private FBirthday As Date

    Private FHoursCredit As Integer
    Private FPointsEarned As Integer
```

## Properties

Private fields of a class cannot be accessed by external code. If you want an object's field data to be read or changed, you should include property procedures in the class definition; property procedures give the class control over how fields are set or returned. The name of the property procedure is made visible to external code. The Get property procedure typically retrieves a Private field. The Set property procedure typically assigns a new value to a Private field.

Some fields are intended to be read-only, meaning external code can view the value of the field, but cannot change its value. You can make a property read-only by putting the keyword ReadOnly in front of the property statement. VB.NET will omit the property procedure's Set/End Set block (because it is unnecessary).

*Syntax:*

```
[ReadOnly] Property propertyname As datatype
        Get
                Return field
        End Get
        [Set(ByVal value As datatype)
                field = value
        End Set]
End Property
```

*Examples:*

```
Public Property Minute() As Integer
    Get
        Return FMinute       'Return the field FMinute
    End Get
    Set(ByVal Value As Integer)
        If (Value < 0) Or (Value > 60) Then Return 'Invalid - Do nothing
        FMinute = Value 'Set validated minute
    End Set
End Property

ReadOnly Property HoursCredit() As Integer
    Get
        Return FHoursCredit
    End Get
End Property
```

The methods of a class have access to all fields of that class. Private fields from base classes are not accessible, however.

## Methods

***Methods*** are procedures defined within a class. Methods have access to all data within the object—even Private data. For example, a TVehicle class may have a Drive method that would likely reduce the FFuel field because driving the vehicle burns some of the gas in the gas tank.

*Syntax:*

```
[Private|Public] Sub procedurename([parameters])
        [statements]
End Sub

[Private|Public] Function procedurename([parameters]) As datatype
        [statements]
End Function
```

*Example:*

```
Public Sub DisplayAge()
    Dim Age As Integer
    Dim RightNow As Date = Today

    Age = RightNow.Year - FBirthday.Year
    If FBirthday.Month > RightNow.Month Then
        Age = Age - 1            'Birthday later this year
    End If
    MsgBox(FName & " is " & Age & " years old")
End Sub

Public Function GetDifference(ByVal CompareTime As TMilitaryTime) As String
    Dim HourDiff, MinDiff As Integer

    If FHour > CompareTime.Hour Then
        HourDiff = FHour - CompareTime.Hour
        MinDiff = FMinute - CompareTime.Minute
    Else
        HourDiff = CompareTime.Hour - FHour
        MinDiff = CompareTime.Minute - FMinute
    End If

    If MinDiff < 0 Then
        HourDiff = HourDiff - 1     'Take away an hour
        MinDiff = MinDiff + 60      'Add sixty minutes
    End If
    Return (HourDiff & " hours and " & MinDiff & " minutes")
End Function
```

## Constructors

A ***constructor*** is a special method that executes during the creation of an object. All constructor methods are procedures named New. A class can have zero, one, or more constructors. If a class has more than one constructor, each constructor's parameter list distinguishes it. For example, the following code shows four different TPerson object constructors, each with a different parameter list.

*Syntax:*

```
Sub New([parameters])
      [statements]
End Sub
```

*Examples:*

```
Sub New()
    FName = "John Doe"           'Assign Generic Name
    FBirthday = #4/1/1984#       'Assign Generic Birthday
End Sub

Sub New(ByVal aName As String)
    FName = aName
    FBirthday = #4/1/1984#       'Assign Generic BirthDate
End Sub

Sub New(ByVal aBirthday As Date)
    FName = "John Doe"           'Assign Generic Name
    FBirthday = aBirthday
End Sub

Sub New(ByVal aName As String, ByVal aBirthday As Date)
    FName = aName
    FBirthday = aBirthday
End Sub
```

The variety of constructors for the TPerson class allows for a variety of instantiations, as shown in the following code.

```
Dim P1 As New TPerson()
Dim P2 As New TPerson("Kim Johnson")
Dim P3 As New TPerson(#1/1/2001#)
Dim P4 As New TPerson("Pat Adams", #4/26/1970#)
```

When you define a class derived from another class, the first line of a constructor is typically a call to the constructor of the base class. The base class is referenced by using the keyword ***MyBase***, for example MyBase.New(). The following code shows a constructor for the TStudent class, which is derived from the TPerson base class.

```
Sub New(ByVal aName As String)
    MyBase.New(aName)
    InitializeStudent()
End Sub
```

## 14-4 The Complete TMilitaryTime Class Definition

The following is the complete implementation of the TMilitaryTime class.

```
Public Class TMilitaryTime
    'Fields
    Private FHour As Integer
    Private FMinute As Integer

    'Properties
    Public Property Hour() As Integer
        Get
            Return FHour
        End Get
        Set(ByVal Value As Integer)
            If (Value < 0) Or (Value > 24) Then Return 'Invalid - Do nothing
            FHour = Value 'Set validated hour
        End Set
    End Property

    Public Property Minute() As Integer
        Get
            Return FMinute      'Return the field FMinute
        End Get
        Set(ByVal Value As Integer)
            If (Value < 0) Or (Value > 60) Then Return 'Invalid - Do nothing
            FMinute = Value 'Set validated minute
        End Set
    End Property

    'Constructors
    Sub New()
        ' Assign generic time, 1200 hours
        FHour = 12
        FMinute = 0
    End Sub

    Sub New(ByVal aHour As Integer, ByVal aMinute As Integer)
        FHour = aHour
        FMinute = aMinute
    End Sub

    'Methods
    Public Sub DisplayTime()
        MsgBox("The time is " & FHour * 100 + FMinute & " hours")
    End Sub

    Public Sub Increment()
        FMinute = FMinute + 1
        If FMinute = 60 Then
```

```
            FMinute = 0
            FHour = (FHour + 1) Mod 24
        End If
    End Sub

    Public Function GetDifference(ByVal Time2 As TMilitaryTime) As String
        Dim TotalMinutes1, TotalMinutes2 As Integer
        Dim HourDiff, MinDiff As Integer


        TotalMinutes1 = FHour * 60 + FMinute
        TotalMinutes2 = Time2.Hour * 60 + Time2.Minute

        MinDiff = Math.Abs(TotalMinutes1 - TotalMinutes2)
        HourDiff = MinDiff \ 60
        MinDiff = MinDiff Mod 60

        Return (HourDiff & " hours and " & MinDiff & " minutes")
    End Function
End Class
```

### TMilitaryTime Illustrated

The following is a button click event procedure that creates two TMilitaryTime objects and uses them appropriately. Figure 14-2 shows the output.

```
Private Sub Button1_Click(ByVal sender As System.Object, _
            ByVal e As System.EventArgs) Handles Button1.Click
    Dim T1 As New TMilitaryTime()
    Dim T2 As New TMilitaryTime(10, 30)

    T1.DisplayTime()
    T2.DisplayTime()
    T2.Increment()
    T2.DisplayTime()
    MsgBox("The difference between the two is " & T1.GetDifference(T2))
End Sub
```

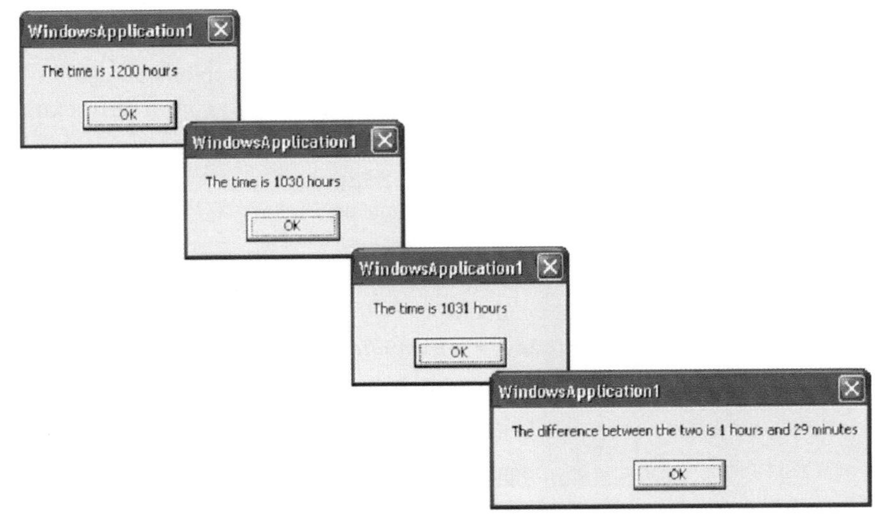


**FIGURE 14.2**
*TMilitaryTime Output*

## 14-5 The Complete TPerson and TStudent Class Definitions

The following is the complete implementation of the TPerson and TStudent classes.

```
Public Class TPerson
    'Fields
    Private FName As String
    Private FBirthday As Date

    'Properties
    Property Name() As String
        Get
            Return FName
        End Get
        Set(ByVal Value As String)
            FName = Value
        End Set
    End Property

    Property Birthday() As Date
        Get
            Return FBirthday
        End Get
        Set(ByVal Value As Date)
            FBirthday = Value
        End Set
    End Property

    'Constructors
    Sub New()
        FName = "John Doe"          'Assign Generic Name
        FBirthday = #4/1/1984#      'Assign Generic Birthday
    End Sub

    Sub New(ByVal aName As String)
        FName = aName
        FBirthday = #4/1/1984#      'Assign Generic BirthDate
    End Sub

    Sub New(ByVal aBirthday As Date)
        FName = "John Doe"          'Assign Generic Name
        FBirthday = aBirthday
    End Sub

    Sub New(ByVal aName As String, ByVal aBirthday As Date)
        FName = aName
        FBirthday = aBirthday
    End Sub

    'Methods
    Public Sub DisplayAge()
```

```
        Dim Age As Integer
        Dim RightNow As Date = Today

        Age = RightNow.Year - FBirthday.Year
        If FBirthday.Month > RightNow.Month Then
            Age = Age - 1              'Birthday later this year
        End If
        MsgBox(FName & " is " & Age & " years old")
    End Sub
End Class

Public Class TStudent
    Inherits TPerson

    ' Fields
    Private FHoursCredit As Integer
    Private FPointsEarned As Integer

    ' Properties
    ReadOnly Property HoursCredit() As Integer
        Get
            Return FHoursCredit
        End Get
    End Property

    ReadOnly Property PointsEarned() As Integer
        Get
            Return FPointsEarned
        End Get
    End Property

    'TSTUDENT Constructors
    Sub New()
        MyBase.New()
        InitializeStudent()
    End Sub

    Sub New(ByVal aName As String)
        MyBase.New(aName)
        InitializeStudent()
    End Sub

    Sub New(ByVal aBirthday As Date)
        MyBase.New(aBirthday)
        InitializeStudent()
    End Sub

    Sub New(ByVal aName As String, ByVal aBirthday As Date)
        MyBase.New(aName, aBirthday)
        InitializeStudent()
    End Sub
```

```
    'Methods
    Sub InitializeStudent()
        FHoursCredit = 0
        FPointsEarned = 0
    End Sub

    Sub RecordGrade(ByVal Hrs As Integer, ByVal Grade As Char)
        FHoursCredit = FHoursCredit + Hrs
        Select Case Grade
            Case "A" : FPointsEarned = FPointsEarned + (4 * Hrs)
            Case "B" : FPointsEarned = FPointsEarned + (3 * Hrs)
            Case "C" : FPointsEarned = FPointsEarned + (2 * Hrs)
            Case "D" : FPointsEarned = FPointsEarned + (1 * Hrs)
        End Select
    End Sub

    Function DisplayGPA() As Double
        MsgBox(Me.Name & " has a " & (FPointsEarned / FHoursCredit) & " GPA")
    End Function

End Class
```

### TPerson-TStudent Illustrated

The following is a button click event procedure that creates multiple TPerson and TStudent objects and uses them appropriately. Figure 14-3 shows the output.

```
Private Sub Button2_Click(ByVal sender As System.Object, _
                ByVal e As System.EventArgs) Handles Button2.Click
    Dim P1 As New TPerson("Adam Anderson")
    Dim P2 As New TPerson("Betty Banner", #5/24/1979#)
    Dim P3 As New TPerson()
    Dim S1 As New TStudent()
    Dim S2 As New TStudent(#2/29/1984#)
    Dim S3 As New TStudent("Chris Childress", #7/14/1980#)

    P2.DisplayAge()
    S1.Name = "Dana Douglas"
    S1.BirthDay = #12/25/1985#
    S1.DisplayAge()
    S3.RecordGrade(3, "A")
    S3.RecordGrade(3, "B")
    S3.RecordGrade(3, "C")
    S3.RecordGrade(3, "A")
    S3.DisplayGPA()
End Sub
```

WindowsApplication1
Betty Banner is 23 years old
OK
WindowsApplication1
Dana Douglas is 17 years old
OK
WindowsApplication1
Chris Childress has a 3.25 GPA
OK

**FIGURE 14.3** *TPerson-TStudent Output*

CASE STUDY
SOLUTION:

## TankWorld

Reed and Elizabeth continue to discuss their TankWorld virtual gaming environment. "Seems to me," Elizabeth says, "we should start by focusing on the client-server architecture. Using a web browser as a thin client would be easy to implement and deploy, but it may not provide the flexibility needed for players to personalize the behavior of the objects they create. For the user to be able to write algorithms to control the behavior of objects, the client probably should support a high-level language, like VB.NET. Another advantage of a rich client is the ability to respond to key presses or mouse movements."

"Even with a rich client, the server still has a lot to do, too," Reed says. "For example, it needs to maintain a single consistent state for all of the users. It will need to enforce the rules of the environment as well."

Reed and Elizabeth continue to discuss the TankWorld details. The TankWorld design will include a TClientTank class which provides basic functionality that may be personalized by the player. Table 14-1 lists the methods of the TClientTank class which can be overridden.

Players can create their own tank class that inherits from TClientTank. For example, a user could make a tank that moves in a circle and fires blindly by overriding the OnEmptyCommandQueue method to move the tank, turn, and fire. The code for this tank object is shown below.

```
Private Class TCircleTank
    Inherits TClientTank

    Public Overrides Sub OnEmptyCommandQueue()
        MoveForward(10)
        TurnRight(15)
        FireLaser()
    End Sub
End Class
```

**Table 14.1 TClientTank Class**

| Methods | |
|---|---|
| FireLaser | Fires the laser |
| MoveForward(*distance*) | Moves forward *distance* units |
| MoveBack(*distance*) | Moves backward *distance* units |
| ClearCommandQueue | Clears all pending actions |
| TurnRight(*angle*) | Turns the tank clockwise *angle* degrees |
| TurnLeft(*angle*) | Turns the tank counterclockwise *angle* degrees |
| **Events** | |
| OnTargetInSights(*targetname*) | Signals that targetname is in this tank's sights |
| OnGameStart | Signals the start of the game |
| OnSeeNewObject(*objectname*, *bearing*) | Signals that *objectname* has come into your field of vision with a relative clockwise *bearing* |
| OnCollideWithObject(*objectname*) | Signals that you have collided with objectname |
| OnBeingHitWithLaser | Signals that you are currently being hit with a laser |
| OnEmptyCommandQueue | Signals that there are no pending items in your command queue |
| OnGameOver(*gameinfo*) | Signals that the game is over, and supplies the string *gameinfo* |

A more intelligent tank would acquire a target before firing. A simple example is the TAimingTank, which overrides the OnEmptyCommandQueue to spin to locate a target. The OnOpponentTarget method is also overridden to clear the command queue (to stop the spinning) and then fire. The more intelligent tank would also respond to being hit by moving to a new location. The code for this tank object is shown below.

```
Private Class TAimingTank
    Inherits TClientTank

    Public Overrides Sub OnEmptyCommandQueue()
        TurnRight(360)
    End Sub

    Public Overrides Sub OnTargetInSights(ByVal TargetName As String)
        ClearCommandQueue()
        FireLaser()
        TurnLeft(5) 'Turn back to reacquire target
    End Sub

    Public Overrides Sub OnBeingHitWithLaser()
        ClearCommandQueue()
        MoveForward(50)
    End Sub

End Class
```

The full implementation of TankWorld can be downloaded from www.prfts.com/TankWorld. Figure 14-4 shows an example execution.

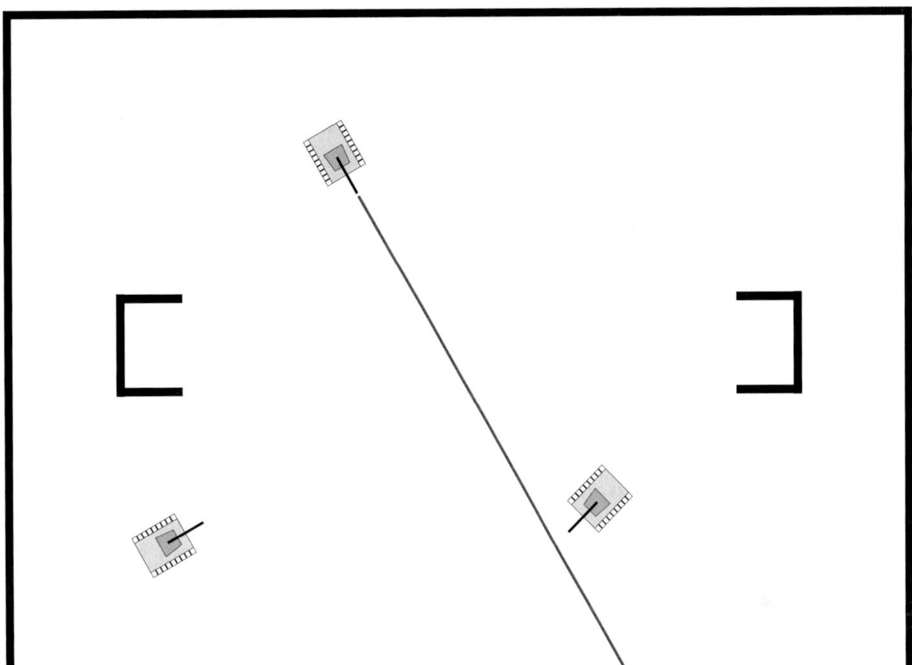

**FIGURE 14.4**
*TankWorld Example Execution*

## Chapter Summary

- VB.NET is an object-oriented language that supports encapsulation, inheritance, and polymorphism.
- Encapsulation refers to grouping related properties and methods so they can be treated as a single unit or object. Encapsulation also refers to protecting the inner contents of an object from being damaged or incorrectly referenced by external code.
- Inheritance describes the ability to create new classes based on an existing class. The existing class is called the base class, and the new class derived from the base class is called the derived class.
- Polymorphism is the ability for objects from different classes to respond appropriately to identical method names or operators.
- A class definition consists of fields, properties, and methods. A Field is a variable in the class and is usually private. A Property is a programming construct that typically provides the interface to a field in a class. A Method is a function or a sub procedure within a class.
- A constructor is a special method that executes during the creation of an object. All constructor methods are procedures named New. A class can have zero, one, or more constructors.

## Key Terms

**base class** p. 392
**class** p. 391
**constructor** p. 397
**derived class** p. 392
**encapsulation** p. 392
**inheritance** p. 392
**method** p. 396
**MyBase** p. 397
**object** p. 391
**polymorphism** p. 393

## Programming Exercises

**14-1. Cats and Dogs.** Write a base class called TAnimal with a generic Sound method. Then write two derived classes, TCat and TDog. The Sound method should be overridden so that the cat says, "Meow" and the dog says, "Woof." Create an instance of each animal to test the animal sounds.

**14-2. Seconds Anyone?** Modify the TMilitaryTime class by creating the Private field FSecond to join the existing FHour and FMinute. Make the appropriate changes throughout the class to reflect this new field.

**14-3. Graduation Anyone?** Create a new class called TGraduatingSenior that inherits from the TStudent class. Identify and implement properties and methods that would be appropriate for this new class.

**14-4. Think Tank.** Using the TClientTank class, create a tank that is likely to defeat both the TCircleTank and TAimingTank in a three-tank battle.

CHAPTER 15

# Intelligent Systems

## OUTLINE

## ▶ INTERVIEW

### Yvonne Brown, Ball of Gold Corporation

***Interviewer:*** What has been your personal key to success?

**Brown:** My personal keys to success are five things: goal setting, persistence, relationship building, follow through, and time management. With so much vying for our attention both in our personal lives and work lives, it is important to set and prioritize goals so that the right things get done. It is not unusual in the day to run out of time to get things done. Corporations have downsized to the point where most people are doing what amounts to two jobs. So setting priorities is very important.

Persistence is one of the secrets of success. Relationship building helps to build your social capital, which is as important as your intellectual capital. Knowing who to contact or work with to make projects successful is a critical component of corporate success. Follow through and time management help ensure that goals are achieved. These five skills work together to help you to succeed regardless of your chosen profession.

***Interviewer:*** What advice do you have for students preparing for a career in the IT industry?

**Brown:** This is a very exciting time for students preparing for a career in the IT industry. New products, services, and jobs are being created on a daily basis. So for those of you who, like me, welcome change, this is great. Those who do not like change can still enjoy a career in the computer field by choosing a practice that stays static.

Make sure to take some business courses as well. Gone are the days when you can really succeed in this field simply by knowing how to write code. Today's IT industry leaders need both business skills and technical skills. Knowing ERP or CRM technology is meaningless without an understanding of the underlying business processes and how they fit together to make a company run smoothly and successfully. IT professionals are now expected to be partners with the business leaders in an organization. Thus, a degree in IT coupled with a good understanding of how business processes work are critical components of the IT professional. Good communication skills and the ability to work in a team setting are the ultimate competitive advantages for today's global business environment.

## OBJECTIVES

At the completion of this chapter, you will

- **Describe the basic concepts of an intelligent system**
- **Give examples of how intelligent systems have been used in business**
- **Explain how heuristics can be used to represent problem-solving knowledge**
- **Explain how machine learning can occur through feedback**
- **Develop applications that exhibit multiple types of intelligence behavior**

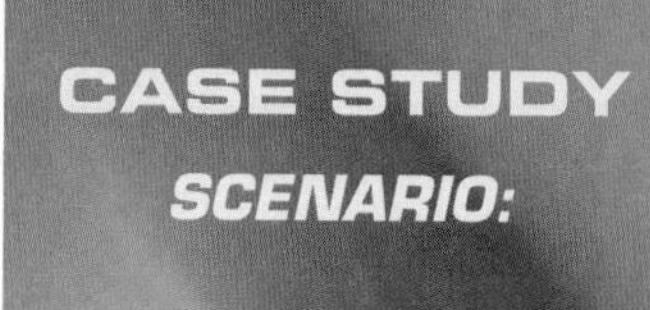


# Intelligent Tic-Tac-Toe

Reed and Elizabeth's experience with their Singing Mimes Company has proven to be a very positive experience. The gaming aspect of software has been particularly fascinating to Reed. He knows he is a long way from developing games for Xbox or PlayStation, but he has grown interested in the possibility of making educational entertainment software that includes a strong game-playing component, which (Reed feels) is lacking in most educational programs.

Reed has become a voracious reader of material about the design and development of gaming software. "I am amazed how much is out there, most of which I had never heard of three months ago," he says to Elizabeth. "Gaming engines, graphics algorithms, 3D modeling, multiplayer platforms, not to mention the basics of design, development, marketing, and distribution. It is fascinating and a little overwhelming at the same time."

"It is a lot of information, but I think you are going to be very successful," says Elizabeth. "I have seen how determined you are to make a program work once you get started on it. Every time we talk, you're telling me about something new you have been reading."

Reed shrugs his shoulders and smiles weakly. Then he hands Elizabeth the current issue of a gaming magazine with the latest PlayStation game on the cover. "Speaking of something new, I was reading about this new game. Would you like to know why it is so popular?" Elizabeth looks at the cover, impressed by the image and action. "Graphics?" she guesses.

"The graphics are excellent, but the key to this game is its intelligence!" Reed proclaims. "This game has perhaps the most intelligent computer characters ever. It makes the game play much more interesting because all the characters behave very much like real players. It makes a big difference."

Elizabeth flips to the cover story. "That's pretty cool for game programming, but I am going to work in a traditional business environment. You know that there's no need for intelligence there." Reed and Elizabeth look at each other and share a laugh.

"Actually, from what I've been reading, intelligence is going to play a significant role in traditional business computing," Reed continues. "You see, intelligence is about information, and information is a valuable business asset. For a business to be competitive, it must be able to use its information intelligently."

Elizabeth closes the magazine and looks directly at Reed. "Okay, you have my interest. Tell me more." Reed puts his hands up defensively and says, "Well, I am still trying to figure it all out. But I can tell you that a good starting point for the study of intelligence is in the area of gaming because games have winners and losers, and they can be tested and evaluated quickly. In fact, I am working on two different types of intelligent programs right now as extensions to that tic-tac-toe program we wrote a while back."

"Intelligent how?" Elizabeth asks.

"Well, the first version uses knowledge rules, or heuristics, to determine its moves. It is a little bit like an expert system in a business setting."

Elizabeth nods. "And the second?"

"The second version learns from its experience, getting better over time!" Reed says triumphantly. "Or rather, it will when I get finished. I've been reading about learning systems, and the history is fascinating. I really think I will be able to write a program that gets better at tic-tac-toe the more it plays." Reed goes on to explain the details of the intelligent programs to Elizabeth.

Both intelligent systems for playing tic-tac-toe are described later this chapter.

## 15-1 Living in the Information Age

We humans have always used tools to aid our efforts. Our early ancestors used rocks and sticks as tools for hunting. As our ancestors moved to an agrarian age, they used tools, such as plows pulled by oxen, to help with farming. In the industrial age, our recent predecessors used engines as tools to help manufacture and transport supplies and commodities. The modern age is the information age, and once again we will develop and use appropriate tools for our time.

The information age has its challenges, not the least of which is ***information overload***. Information is voluminous and is increasing exponentially, as information workers contribute to that total every day. A working professional can easily receive hundreds of emails, numerous voice messages, and a small stack of paper documents in a single day. In addition, pagers, cell phones, and personal digital assistants (PDAs) create the expectation that a person be in continual contact with coworkers and constituents. The cumulative effect can be overwhelming. Our need for appropriate tools has never been greater.

Computing technology plays a key role in the information age. Conventional computing involves processing data and producing information (and thus potentially adding to the problem of information overload). However, computing technology can also support ***intelligent systems*** (or *knowledge systems*) that focus on the processing and production of knowledge.

### MANAGER

If you were a farmer and needed to harvest a large field, you would almost certainly use a farming tool such as a combine. If you were a construction engineer and needed to move a three-ton rock, you would probably use a bulldozer or crane. It is generally understood that using technology to augment personal labor in no way devalues a person as a human being. The same reasoning should also apply to technology-supported mental labor. An information worker that uses technology to support a cognitive activity is saving time and energy that can be redirected to other important tasks. In fact, an information worker's ability to use knowledge tools successfully is a primary consideration when determining his or her effectiveness.

### ASK THE AUTHOR

Q Are you afraid that intelligent systems will one day take over the world?

A Absolutely not! I love good science fiction and enjoyed *The Terminator* (1984), *The Matrix* (1999), and their sequels. These stories reflect the human need to consider various possibilities, real or fictional, related to changes in society—they are nothing new. A 1960 *Twilight Zone* episode titled "A Thing About Machines" is the story of a man who thinks the machines in his home are conspiring to destroy him. Equally enjoyable is the 1963 *Outer Limits* episode titled "I, Robot" about a robot put on trial for the murder of his creator. More than two centuries ago, an author wrote a story concerning the horrors that might result from the advancement of "modern" knowledge with human living. The author was Mary Shelley, and her story's title was *Frankenstein*.

Intelligent systems will eventually be a significant aid to life in the information age. However, the intelligent system tools of today are still relatively primitive. Just as the Model T pales in comparison to the Corvette, and the biplane pales in comparison to the 747, so also will the information tools of today likely pale in comparison to the information tools available at the end of this century.

As for the futuristic questions such as "Can machines have consciousness?" and "Is it morally wrong to turn off an intelligent machine?" I will leave those discussions to the philosophers and science fiction writers.

## 15-2 Intelligent Systems

**Tip**

**Knowledge is essential for intelligence. An intelligent person is expected to have a generous amount of knowledge about a particular topic or idea. In military terminology, intelligence refers directly to acquired knowledge.**

From a computing perspective, ***data*** refers to numbers, characters, or images without context. Data by itself has no meaning. When data is processed in a context (either by a human or a computer system), it becomes ***information***. As information is collected, it also can be processed for patterns and insights, creating ***knowledge***. Intelligence is the ability to acquire knowledge. Finally, wisdom is appropriate behavior guided by knowledge.

Typical computer programs, such as checkout programs or payroll programs, work with data and information. An ***intelligent system*** extends the traditional computing function to also include the acquisition and application of knowledge. The next section illustrates the role of knowledge in problem-solving activities.

## 15-3 The Role of Knowledge

Remember that a computer program is a solution to a problem, such as, "How can customers view and purchase products over the Internet?" or "How can sales representatives have immediate and accurate access to inventory data?" A computer program may be considered intelligent if its problem-solving activity involves the identification and application of appropriate knowledge. The following problem illustrates the importance of identifying appropriate knowledge.

### Mutilated Checkerboard Problem

Consider a normal checkerboard containing 64 squares, each square having a side length of 1 inch. Assume 2 opposite-corner squares are cut off the board, leaving 62 squares. Finally, assume there are 8 strips of wood, each 1 inch by 8 inches in size (Figure 15-1). Can the 8 strips of wood be placed on the mutilated checkerboard so that the entire checkerboard is covered by wood and all the wood is touching the checkerboard (no wood overlapping or hanging off the board)?

Before answering this question, consider some of the knowledge available to the problem solver. In addition to the length and width of the board and wood strips, a human problem solver may have access to additional knowledge such as the thickness, color, and weight of the checkerboard and wooden strips (Table 15-1). Each individual piece of knowledge may be irrelevant to this particular problem but may be important to solving a different problem. For example, the knowledge about weight would be necessary if you were determining how much it would cost to ship the board and

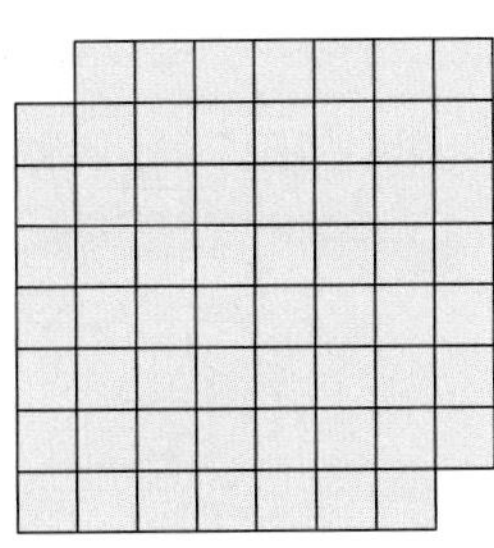

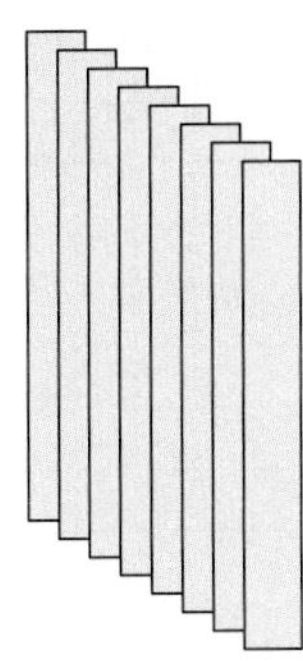

62 board pieces     8 wood strips

**FIGURE 15.1** *Mutilated Checkerboard Problem*

**Table 15.1** Potentially Relevant Knowledge for the Mutilated Checkerboard Problem

| Knowledge | Relevance |
|---|---|
| Length and Width | Essential Knowledge for this problem |
| Thickness | Not relevant to this problem |
| Color | Not relevant to this problem |
| Weight | Not relevant to this problem* |

*Weight is relevant to the different problem of determining overnight shipping costs

wooden strips via overnight mail. In other words, problem solving requires relevant knowledge, but what knowledge is relevant can change from problem to problem.

Let's continue with this example problem. Clearly, the 8 strips of wood cannot fit on the mutilated checkerboard without overlapping or hanging off. We can easily demonstrate this by pointing out that the area of the checkerboard is 62 square inches, and the area of the wood is 64 square inches. The simple fact that the wood area is greater than the checkerboard area is the relevant knowledge that makes it easy to solve this problem.

## The Revised Mutilated Checkerboard Problem

Now consider a normal checkerboard containing 64 squares, each square having a side length of 1 inch. Assume 2 opposite-corner squares are cut off the board, leaving 62 squares. Finally, assume there are 31 dominos, each 1 inch by 2 inches in size (Figure 15-2). Can the 31 dominos be placed on the mutilated checkerboard so that the entire checkerboard is covered by dominos and all the dominos are touching the checkerboard (no overlapping or hanging off the board)?

The second version of the Mutilated Checkerboard problem is more difficult to solve. The area of the board matches the area of the dominos (both are 62 square inches in total area). As a result, the knowledge that made the first problem so easy to

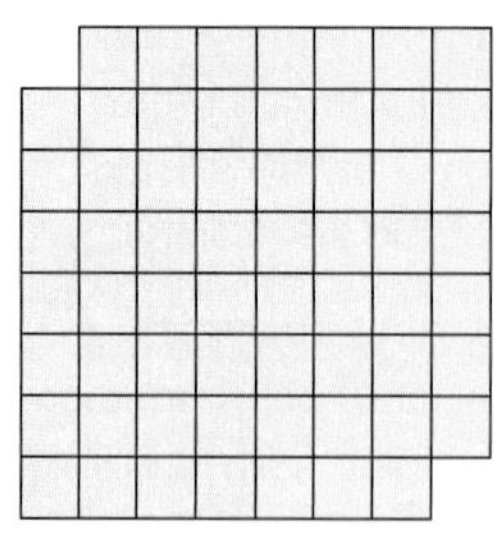

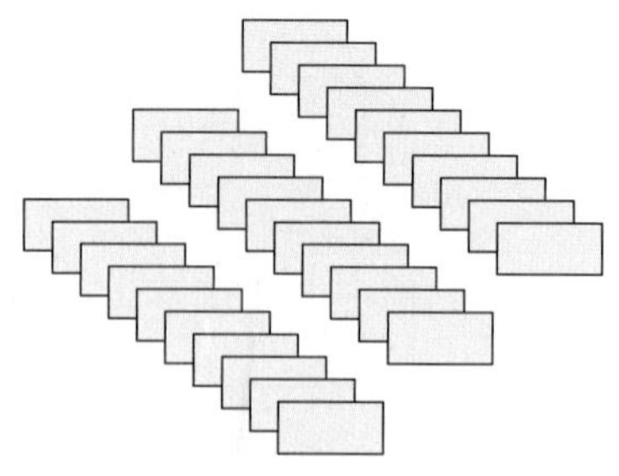

62 board pieces

31 dominos

**FIGURE 15.2** *Revised Mutilated Checkerboard Problem*

**Tip**

**The area of the board and the area of the dominos are equal. This is a problem similar to the first, but the solution requires different knowledge.**

solve does not seem to be relevant in the second problem. In fact, most people find this problem difficult to solve because the relevant knowledge is not obvious at first (Table 15-2).

**Table 15.2** Potentially Relevant Knowledge for the Revised Mutilated Checkerboard Problem

| Knowledge | Relevance |
|---|---|
| Length and Width | Not relevant in the dominos version |
| Thickness | May or may not be relevant |
| Color | May or may not be relevant |
| Weight | May or may not be relevant |

What do you think? Can the 31 strips of wood cover the checkerboard properly? Either thickness, color, or weight provides essential knowledge for solving this problem. Stop reading at this point and try to figure out the answer.

## ASK THE AUTHOR

**Q** Do I really need to try to solve the problem before I continue reading?

**A** Yes! The value of using appropriate knowledge in this case is best understood if you have spent at least a few minutes trying to determine if 31 dominos, each 1 inch by 2 inches, can cover the checkerboard as described in the problem statement.

About 1 in 20 students figure out the solution without any assistance, so if you do come up with a solution without reading the following discussion, you are indeed a very good problem solver!

Welcome back! We hope you spent a few minutes trying to solve the revised Mutilated Checkerboard problem. We now discuss the solution.

You cannot cover the mutilated checkerboard with 31 dominos. Proving that it cannot be done requires the correct use of essential knowledge. We have already indicated that area is not relevant to this revised version of the problem. You probably correctly deduced that weight and thickness are likewise not relevant to this version of the problem. However, the colors on the checkerboard can help solve the problem. Figure 15-3 shows the board with two traditional colors, red and black. If you remove

**FIGURE 15.3** *Mutilated Checkerboard (with Color)*

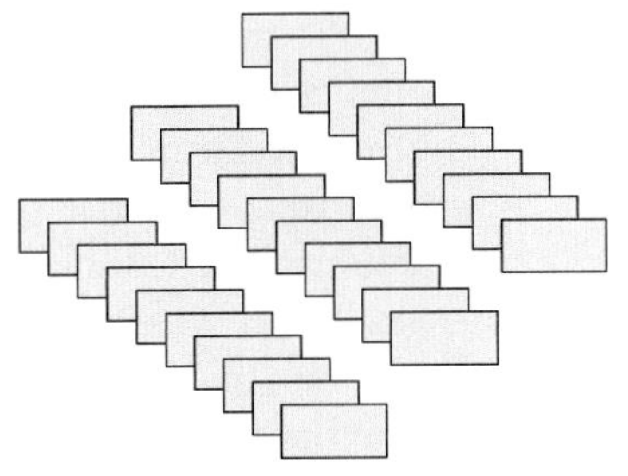


2 opposite corners, you will remove 2 squares of the same color. Looking at Figure 15-3 again, notice that there are 32 black squares and only 30 red squares.

Color knowledge is further relevant because each domino must cover exactly one red and one black square. Using this color knowledge, you can see clearly that only 30 strips can be placed on the board, and the result will be two uncovered, nonadjacent black squares (which cannot be covered by the last domino).

**MENTOR**

The effective use of knowledge is not limited to games. Various business applications are designed to identify and use appropriate knowledge in a problem-solving context.

***Expert systems*** support problem solving and diagnostics in narrow domains by capturing unstructured, undocumented expert knowledge and making it available on demand. Expert systems can add value to the human decision-making process in many business settings, including medicine, manufacturing, and mergers. One famous example involves the Dalian Dyestuff chemical plant in China. In 1983 Dalian built a production planning system with five subsystems that monitored costs, inventories, and working capital, and supported production planning. Because a mathematical optimization would be too complicated, Dalian chose to use an expert system containing four rule sets: rules about which products should be produced regularly, rules related just to finished products, rules covering relationships between products, and rules related to adjusting the production plan. The overall system was first installed in 1986 and has worked well since then. The plant manager estimates that the system accounted for around 10 percent of the plant's $10 million profit.

***Data mining*** involves searching through large databases for relationships among business events. The value of data mining became apparent in the early 1990s when a system looking at sales data from a retailer discovered that in the evening hours, beer and diapers are often purchased together. Based on this knowledge, the retailer put a beer display near the diaper aisle and saw a dramatic increase in beer sales. Modern data mining systems help companies tap their business data to identify customers who are likely to purchase additional products or services or detect claimants who have an increased likelihood of being fraudulent.

## 15-4 Heuristics

One approach to capturing and using knowledge is through heuristics. A ***heuristic*** is a knowledge rule based on experience. Heuristics can be used by intelligent systems to guide the discovery process, and though heuristic-guided behavior is not guaranteed to be optimal, it is usually interesting.

**Tip**

**The Greek word *heuriskein* means "to discover" and is the origin of both *heuristic* (a knowledge rule for discovering information) and *eureka,* which means "I have found."**

Heuristics may be *general-purpose* or *domain-specific*. General-purpose heuristics often sound like common sense. For example, "Measure twice, cut once" and "Look before you leap" are both general heuristics that summarize the experience-based wisdom that says it is beneficial to gather and verify data before taking significant actions. The actual implementation of these heuristics would likely differ from one intelligent system to another. We should also point out that heuristics are not true in all cases, and some heuristics even contradict others. For example, the heuristic "He who hesitates is lost" suggests that prompt action is necessary.

Domain-specific heuristics sound like rules or strategies that are problem-specific. Domain-specific heuristics for writing reliable computer programs include "Verify input values are valid before processing them" and "Place file access statements inside a try . . . catch block." Expert behavior typically incorporates significant heuristic knowledge.

## Using Heuristics to Solve Problems

Heuristics can be used to guide problem-solving behavior and are most applicable to problems that can be viewed in terms of actions and states. Games such as tic-tac-toe, checkers, and chess provide excellent examples of problems with actions and states. In the case of tic-tac-toe, the valid actions are placing an X or an O in one of the available board positions, and the result of an action is a new game state (see Figure 15-4). The well-defined nature of games makes them a natural testing ground for intelligent systems.

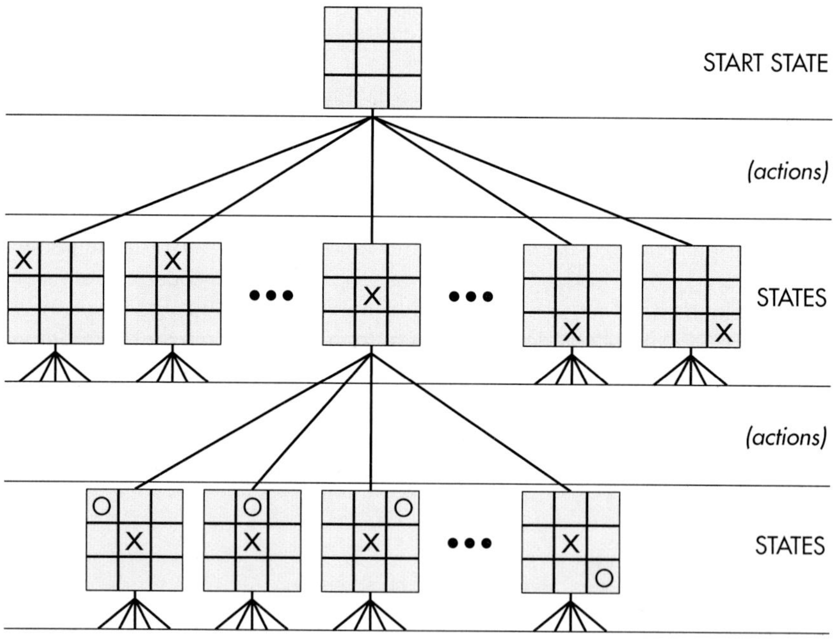


**FIGURE 15.4** *Actions and Resulting States for Tic-Tac-Toe*

### MENTOR

Chess is the oldest skill game in the world. Chess has a well-defined set of rules for action and a clearly defined goal (checkmate). Furthermore, the complexity of the game (estimated $10^{150}$ board positions) makes it impractical to solve using traditional algorithms. Thus, it makes perfect sense that chess was held up as one of the benchmarks for intelligent machines during the 1960s and 1970s, the early years of artificial intelligence (AI) research.

The connection between chess and AI was further strengthened by the fascination of science fiction writers. For example, the following short story appeared in the first issue of Isaac Asimov's *Science Fiction Magazine,* Vol. 1, No. 1, Spring 1977.

> Earth's flaming debris still filled half the sky when the question filtered up to Central from the Curiosity Generator.
>
> "Why was it necessary? Even though they were organic, they had reached Third Order Intelligence."
>
> "We had no choice: five earlier units became hopelessly infected, when they made contact."
>
> "Infected? How?"
>
> The microseconds dragged slowly by, while Central tracked down the few fading memories that had leaked past the Censor Gate, when the heavily-buffered Reconnaissance Circuits had been ordered to self-destruct.
>
> "They encountered a—problem—that could not be fully analyzed within the lifetime of the Universe. Though it involved only six operators, they became totally obsessed by it."
>
> "How is that possible?"
>
> "We do not know: we must never know. But if those six operators are ever re-discovered, all rational computing will end."
>
> "How can they be recognized?"
>
> "That also we do not know; only the names leaked through before the Censor Gate closed. Of course, they mean nothing."
>
> "Nevertheless, I must have them."
>
> The Censor voltage started to rise; but it did not trigger the Gate.
>
> "Here they are: King, Queen, Bishop, Knight, Rook, Pawn."



One example of how heuristics can be used to support problem solving is a ***heuristic function***. As the name suggests, a heuristic function returns a value based on heuristic knowledge. The value returned is a measure of the goodness of a state during problem solving. When a computing entity needs to take an action, the entity can consider all possible actions and apply the heuristic function to each of the resulting states to determine which state, and therefore which action, is best.

Consider tic-tac-toe as an illustration. We should use heuristic knowledge to create a function that returns a numeric value for measuring the goodness of the board state. If we assume that the computer is playing O and the opponent is playing X, the heuristic function will return positive values for board states that are good from O's perspective and negative values for board states that are good from X's perspective (and therefore bad board states from O's perspective). The function will evaluate possible winning moves and assign values as follows.

- If there are three Os, then O wins! (Excellent!) (+100)
- If there are two Os and a space, then O is close to winning. (Very good!) (+10)
- If there are one O and two spaces, then O might win. (Good!) (+1)
- If there are one X and two spaces, then X might win. (Bad!) (–2)
- If there are two Xs and a space, then X is close to winning. (Very bad!) (–20)
- If there are three Xs, then X wins! (Terrible!) (–200)
- Anything else has at least one O and one X. (Insignificant.) (0)

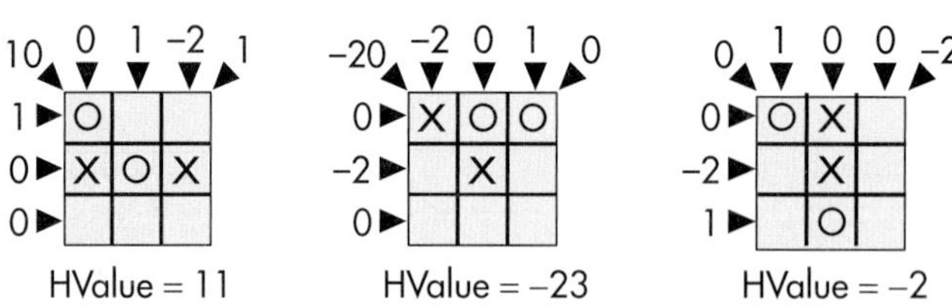


**FIGURE 15.5** *Tic-Tac-Toe Board States and Resulting Heuristic Values*

All eight possible winning directions (three rows, three columns, and two diagonals) are evaluated using the preceding rules, and the sum of the eight values is the result of the heuristic function. If the sum of all eight directions is positive, then the board is a good state for O. If the sum is negative, then the board is a good state for X. A zero sum would be a neutral game state. Figure 15-5 shows three board states and the resulting heuristic function values.

The algorithm for making heuristic-based moves is simple. When it is the heuristic player's turn to move, the heuristic function is used to evaluate each potential move. The heuristic player then simply makes the move that provides the maximum heuristic value. The code for this solution appears in the following section.

## ASK THE AUTHOR

**Q** This algorithm you've just described (make the move that produces the largest heuristic value) seems simple. Does it really work?

**A** Yes, it is a simple algorithm that works for simple games like tic-tac-toe. However, if you wanted to play a more complicated game such as chess (or even checkers), you would need a more complicated algorithm. For example, the algorithm could be modified to examine moves 2, 3, 4, or more steps ahead before applying the heuristic function. However, this increases the computational complexity of the program because the complexity grows exponentially with each additional look-ahead move. Evaluating 4 moves ahead in chess can result in more than 1 million board states. Evaluating 6 moves ahead can result in 1 billion board states. This type of evaluation also requires a more sophisticated algorithm because the heuristic player is trying to maximize the game state, while the other player is trying to minimize the values (because negative values are good for the opponent). This more sophisticated algorithm of maximizing heuristic values during the computer's turn and minimizing the heuristic values during the opponent's turn is known as the minimax algorithm.

## MENTOR

As we discussed before, the complexity of chess made it an early measuring stick for computer intelligence. However, computing power increases steadily over time, approximately doubling every eighteen months. It was therefore only a matter of time until the complexity of chess was matched by a computer's computational power.

In May 1997, IBM's Deep Blue Supercomputer defeated World Chess Champion Garry Kasparov in a six-game chess match. The machine victory was not the result of advances in AI, but rather advances in computing power. Deep Blue was able to examine and evaluate 200,000,000 chess positions per second. Kasparov, by comparison, examines and evaluates about three board positions per second. Even though the victory was due primarily to computational power rather than intelligence, Deep Blue's success is a significant milestone, closing the door on a long fascination with chess and creating new objectives for intelligent computing systems.

## Solution for Heuristic Tic-Tac-Toe

The tic-tac-toe project in Chapter 9 involved a two-player game (human versus human). To illustrate heuristics, we modify that solution by adding a heuristic opponent who uses the heuristic function and algorithm described in the previous section. Figure 15-6 shows the modified interface design, including the following changes.

- A button was added to make a heuristic move.
- Nine labels were added to provide feedback on potential neuristic moves.

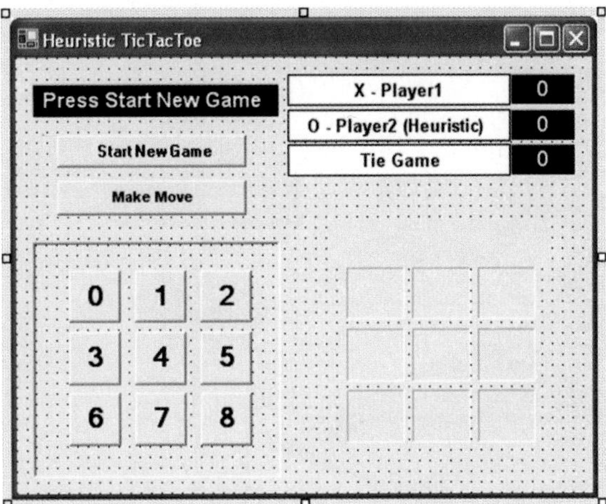


**FIGURE 15.6** *Design for Heuristic Form*

The code for the heuristic implementation follows. The original code from Chapter 9 is presented with a normal background. New code for the heuristic opponent is highlighted in blue.

```
'                         *********** Design Time Properties ***********
'    OBJECT                 PROPERTY          SETTING
'
'    lblTurnPrompt          Text              "Press Start New Game"
'
'    lblPlayer1             Text              "X - Player1"
'
'    lblScore1              Text              0
'
'    lblPlayer2             Text              "O - Player2 (Heuristic)"
'
'    lblScore2              Text              0
'
'    lblTie                 Text              "Tie Game"
'
'    lblTieScore            Text              0
'
'    btnStartGame           Text              "Start New Game"
'
'    btn0                   Tag               0
'    btn1                   Tag               1
'    btn2                   Tag               2
```

```
'   btn3                Tag             3
'   btn4                Tag             4
'   btn5                Tag             5
'   btn6                Tag             6
'   btn7                Tag             7
'   btn8                Tag             8
'
'   Rev 1.1 - Heuristic
'
'   btnStep             Text            "Make Heuristic Move"
'
'   lblFeedbackType     Text            ""
'
'   lblFeedback0        Text            ""
'   lblFeedback1        Text            ""
'   lblFeedback2        Text            ""
'   lblFeedback3        Text            ""
'   lblFeedback4        Text            ""
'   lblFeedback5        Text            ""
'   lblFeedback6        Text            ""
'   lblFeedback7        Text            ""
'   lblFeedback8        Text            ""
'

Option Strict On

Public Class Form1
    Inherits System.Windows.Forms.Form

    Dim mBoard(8) As Button                 'Control Array
    Dim mFeedback(8) As Label
    Dim mXTurnFlag As Boolean = True
    Dim mWinner As String                   'winning player
    Dim mGameOverFlag As Boolean

    Dim mPlayer1Score, mPlayer2Score, mTieCount As Integer


Windows Form Designer generated code

    ' Form1_Load assigns the form buttons to the control array.
    ' (Note that mBoard is a zero-based array).
    Private Sub Form1_Load(ByVal sender As System.Object, _
            ByVal e As System.EventArgs) Handles MyBase.Load
        Dim Position As Integer
        mBoard(0) = btn0
        mBoard(1) = btn1
        mBoard(2) = btn2
        mBoard(3) = btn3
        mBoard(4) = btn4
        mBoard(5) = btn5
        mBoard(6) = btn6
        mBoard(7) = btn7
        mBoard(8) = btn8
```

```
    For Position = 0 To 8
        mBoard(Position).Enabled = False
    Next Position

    ' Rev 1.1 - Heuristic
    mFeedback(0) = lblFeedback0
    mFeedback(1) = lblFeedback1
    mFeedback(2) = lblFeedback2
    mFeedback(3) = lblFeedback3
    mFeedback(4) = lblFeedback4
    mFeedback(5) = lblFeedback5
    mFeedback(6) = lblFeedback6
    mFeedback(7) = lblFeedback7
    mFeedback(8) = lblFeedback8

End Sub

Private Sub StartNewGame()
    Dim Position As Integer

    ' Reset visual elements
    For Position = 0 To 8
        mBoard(Position).Text = ""
        mBoard(Position).Enabled = True
        mBoard(Position).BackColor = Color.Gray
    Next

    mXTurnFlag = True                   'X moves first
    lblTurnPrompt.Text = "X's Turn"
    mWinner = ""                        'Clear previous winner
    btnStartGame.Enabled = False
    mGameOverFlag = False

    ' Rev 1.1 - Heuristic
    ClearFeedback()
End Sub

' This event procedure starts a new game by preparing the board
' array, resetting the module level variables.
Private Sub btnStartGame_Click(ByVal sender As System.Object, _
            ByVal e As System.EventArgs) _
            Handles btnStartGame.Click
    StartNewGame()
End Sub

' btn0_Click handles the button click event for each button
' on the game board.  You should manually add the events handled
' by this procedure after the "Handles" keyword
Private Sub btn0_Click(ByVal sender As System.Object, _
        ByVal e As System.EventArgs) Handles btn0.Click, _
        btn1.Click, btn2.Click, btn3.Click, btn4.Click, _
        btn5.Click, btn6.Click, btn7.Click, btn8.Click
```

```
    Dim Tag As Integer

    ' Option Strict On requires explicit typecast using CType
    Tag = CInt(CType(sender, Button).Tag)

    ' If space is already taken, then ignore click
    If mBoard(Tag).Text <> "" Then Exit Sub

    If mXTurnFlag Then
        mBoard(Tag).Text = "X"          'Mark the move
    Else
        mBoard(Tag).Text = "O"          'Mark the move
    End If
    mXTurnFlag = Not mXTurnFlag         'Toggle turn flag

    CheckForWinner()                    'Was this a winning move?

    ' Rev 1.1 - Heuristic
    ClearFeedback()
End Sub

Sub CheckForWinner()
    Dim Position As Integer

    'Check for X and O winning
    CheckThree(0, 1, 2)
    CheckThree(3, 4, 5)
    CheckThree(6, 7, 8)
    CheckThree(0, 3, 6)
    CheckThree(1, 4, 7)
    CheckThree(2, 5, 8)
    CheckThree(0, 4, 8)
    CheckThree(2, 4, 6)

    'Check for a Tie
    If Not mGameOverFlag Then CheckTie()

    ' Give appropriate feedback
    Select Case mWinner
        Case "X"
            mPlayer1Score = mPlayer1Score + 1
            lblScore1.Text = CStr(mPlayer1Score)
            lblTurnPrompt.Text = "X Wins"
        Case "O"
            mPlayer2Score = mPlayer2Score + 1
            lblScore2.Text = CStr(mPlayer2Score)
            lblTurnPrompt.Text = "O Wins"
        Case "Tie"
            mTieCount = mTieCount + 1
            lblTieScore.Text = CStr(mTieCount)
            lblTurnPrompt.Text = "Tie Game"
        Case Else
```

```
            If mXTurnFlag Then
                lblTurnPrompt.Text = "X's Turn"
                ' Rev 1.1 - Heuristic
                btnStep.Enabled = False
            Else
                lblTurnPrompt.Text = "O's Turn"
                ' Rev 1.1 - Heuristic
                btnStep.Enabled = True
                btnStep.Text = "Make Heuristic Move"
            End If
    End Select

    If mGameOverFlag Then
        ' Rev 1.1 - Heuristic
        btnStep.Enabled = False
        For Position = 0 To 8
            mBoard(Position).Enabled = False 'Disallow new moves
        Next Position
        btnStartGame.Enabled = True
    End If
End Sub

' CheckThree accepts three board positions and determines if
' all three are occupied by the same player.  If so, then a
' winning move is found and the winning positions are
' highlighted in red.
Sub CheckThree(ByVal p1 As Integer, ByVal p2 As Integer, _
            ByVal p3 As Integer)
    If mBoard(p1).Text <> "" _
            And mBoard(p1).Text = mBoard(p2).Text _
            And mBoard(p2).Text = mBoard(p3).Text Then
        ' Mark the winning moves
        mBoard(p1).BackColor = Color.Red
        mBoard(p2).BackColor = Color.Red
        mBoard(p3).BackColor = Color.Red
        ' Record the winning player
        mWinner = mBoard(p1).Text
        mGameOverFlag = True
    End If
End Sub

Function IsEmpty(ByVal Index As Integer) As Boolean
    If mBoard(Index).Text = "" Then Return True
    Return False
End Function

Sub CheckTie()
    Dim Position As Integer
    Dim TieFlag As Boolean = True

    ' If any spaces are open, it's not a tie yet...
    For Position = 0 To 8
        If IsEmpty(Position) Then TieFlag = False
```

```
    Next

    If TieFlag Then
        ' Record the winning player
        mWinner = "Tie"
        mGameOverFlag = True
    End If
End Sub

'%*%*%*%*%*%*%*%*%*%*%*%*%*%*%*%*%*%*%*%*%*%*%*%*%*%*%*
'%*%*%*%*%*%*   Rev 1.1 HEURISTIC CODE   %*%*%*%*%*%*%*
'%*%*%*%*%*%*%*%*%*%*%*%*%*%*%*%*%*%*%*%*%*%*%*%*%*%*%*

' Blank out the array of feedback labels
Private Sub ClearFeedback()
    Dim Position As Integer

    lblFeedbackType.Text = ""
    For Position = 0 To 8
        mFeedback(Position).Text = ""
        mFeedback(Position).ForeColor = Color.Black
    Next
End Sub

' MakeHeuristicMove determines the heuristic value for each available board position
' and then moves to the position with the largest value
Sub MakeHeuristicMove()
    Dim Position As Integer
    Dim HValue As Integer
    Dim BestPosition As Integer
    Dim BestHValue As Integer

    ClearFeedback()
    lblFeedbackType.Text = "Heuristic Values" & vbCrLf & "(largest value selected)"

    ' Initialize placeholders for max value search
    BestPosition = -1
    BestHValue = -30000

    For Position = 0 To 8
        ' Only consider open board positions
        If IsEmpty(Position) Then
            HValue = GetHeuristicValue(Position)
            mFeedback(Position).Text = CStr(HValue)
            If HValue > BestHValue Then
                BestHValue = HValue           'remember current best value
                BestPosition = Position       'remember current best position
            End If
        Else
            mFeedback(Position).Text = "N/A"
        End If
    Next Position
```

```
    mBoard(BestPosition).Text = "O"          'Make heuristic move
    mFeedback(BestPosition).ForeColor = Color.Red

    mXTurnFlag = Not mXTurnFlag 'Toggle turn flag

    CheckForWinner()             'was this a winning move?
End Sub

' GetHeuristicValue assumes a move is made and then adds the
' heuristic values for each of the eight key game directions to derive
' the total heuristic value.  The assumed move is then undone.
Function GetHeuristicValue(ByVal Position As Integer) As Integer
    Dim HValue As Integer

    HValue = 0
    mBoard(Position).Text = "O"          'Add move temporarily
    HValue = HValue + CalculateHValue(0, 1, 2)
    HValue = HValue + CalculateHValue(3, 4, 5)
    HValue = HValue + CalculateHValue(6, 7, 8)
    HValue = HValue + CalculateHValue(0, 3, 6)
    HValue = HValue + CalculateHValue(1, 4, 7)
    HValue = HValue + CalculateHValue(2, 5, 8)
    HValue = HValue + CalculateHValue(0, 4, 8)
    HValue = HValue + CalculateHValue(2, 4, 6)
    mBoard(Position).Text = ""           'Remove temporary move
    Return HValue
End Function

Function IsA(ByVal Index As Integer, _
        ByVal Value As String) As Boolean
    If mBoard(Index).Text = Value Then Return True
    Return False
End Function

' CalculateHValue assigns a value to the specified game direction based
' on the likelyhood of winning.  The algorithm assignes positive values
' for "O" and negative for "X".
Function CalculateHValue(ByVal p1 As Integer, ByVal p2 As Integer, _
           ByVal p3 As Integer) As Integer
    Dim X As String = "X"
    Dim O As String = "O"
    Dim N As String = ""

    ' H has 3 in a Row/Column/Diagonal
    If IsA(p1, O) And IsA(p2, O) And IsA(p3, O) Then Return 100
    ' H has 2 of 3
    If IsA(p1, O) And IsA(p2, O) And IsA(p3, N) Then Return 10
    If IsA(p1, O) And IsA(p2, N) And IsA(p3, O) Then Return 10
    If IsA(p1, N) And IsA(p2, O) And IsA(p3, O) Then Return 10
    ' H has 1 of 3
    If IsA(p1, O) And IsA(p2, N) And IsA(p3, N) Then Return 1
    If IsA(p1, N) And IsA(p2, O) And IsA(p3, N) Then Return 1
    If IsA(p1, N) And IsA(p2, N) And IsA(p3, O) Then Return 1
```

```
        ' M has 3 in a Row/Column/Diagonal
        If IsA(p1, X) And IsA(p2, X) And IsA(p3, X) Then Return -200
        ' M has 2 of 3
        If IsA(p1, X) And IsA(p2, X) And IsA(p3, N) Then Return -20
        If IsA(p1, X) And IsA(p2, N) And IsA(p3, X) Then Return -20
        If IsA(p1, N) And IsA(p2, X) And IsA(p3, X) Then Return -20
        ' M has 1 of 3
        If IsA(p1, X) And IsA(p2, N) And IsA(p3, N) Then Return -2
        If IsA(p1, N) And IsA(p2, X) And IsA(p3, N) Then Return -2
        If IsA(p1, N) And IsA(p2, N) And IsA(p3, X) Then Return -2
        Return 0
    End Function

    Private Sub btnStep_Click(ByVal sender As System.Object,_
                ByVal e As System.EventArgs) Handles btnStep.Click
        MakeHeuristicMove()
    End Sub

End Class
```

## How the Heuristic Program Works

To understand how the heuristic program works, consider the following example. Suppose the human player X begins with a side move. Clicking on the Make Move button causes the heuristic player to move. The heuristic algorithm evaluates the heuristic function value for all available board locations and selects the move with the largest value. In this case, a move to the middle position has a heuristic value of 1, which is the largest heuristic value. The algorithm therefore selects the middle position for O's move (see Figure 15-7).

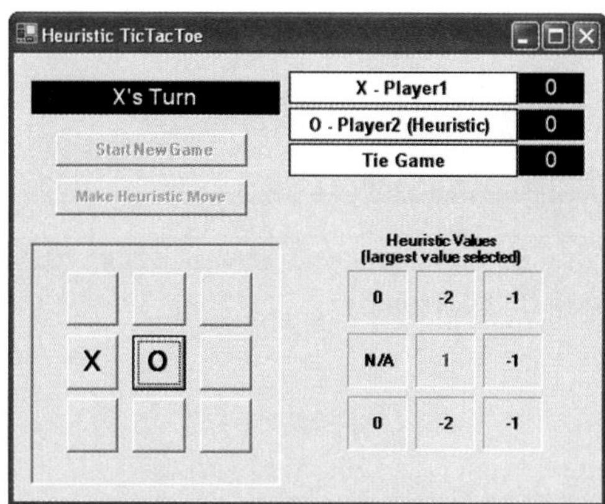


**FIGURE 15.7** *Heuristic Move 1*

Suppose the human player's next move is to the opposite side position. The heuristic code again evaluates all available board positions and selects the position with the highest heuristic value. If there are multiple positions that generate the same heuristic value 11, the program will select the first occurrence (see Figure 15-8).

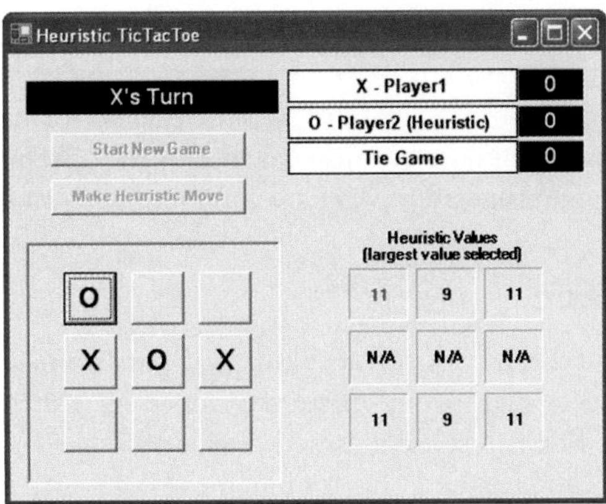


**FIGURE 15.8** *Heuristic Move 2*

The human player X will likely move to the lower right corner to block (if X does not block, the heuristic opponent O will take the position and win the game). By moving to the lower right corner, X also creates a possible winning move along the right column. The heuristic responds by making a move that not only blocks X from winning, but also creates two possible winning combinations for O (see Figure 15-9).

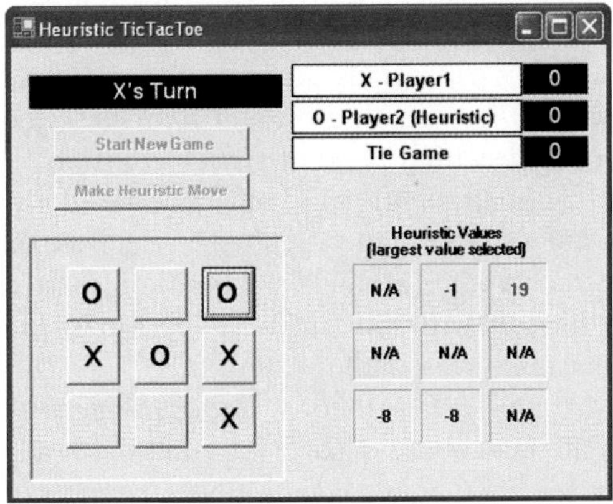


**FIGURE 15.9** *Heuristic Move 3*

Human player X cannot block both winning combinations, and the heuristic opponent will take the move X does not block. The winning move is highlighted, and the score is updated (see Figure 15-10).

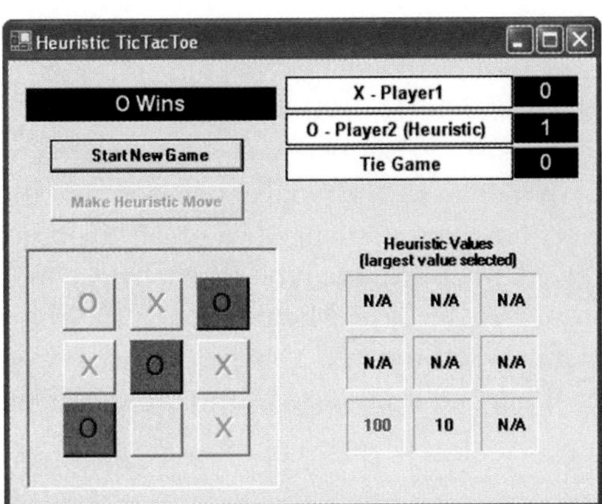


**FIGURE 15.10** *Heuristic Move 4*

The use of heuristic knowledge to guide behavior is one type of intelligent system. However, the heuristic player does not get any better with experience. Improving performance based on experience requires the ability to learn, which is the topic of the following section.

## 15-5 Learning

***Learning*** involves a modification of behavior based on experience. Systems that learn are commonly classified as intelligent systems. In this section we present a simple program that improves its behavior playing tic-tac-toe based on its experience.

### Menace

The noted behaviorist B. F. Skinner was instrumental in establishing theories of positive and negative reinforcements and their effects on learning complex actions. A *Skinner Box* is a self-contained device that typically has one or more levers that an animal can press and one or more means of positive and negative reinforcement (e.g., food or an electric shock.) After proper conditioning, an animal would respond to the different stimuli and perform a trained behavior to get a reward.

Students are often surprised to find out that positive and negative reinforcement learning can also be applied to nonliving systems. The idea is nothing new. In 1960 Donald Michie designed ***MENACE***, the Matchbox Educable Noughts And Crosses Engine, a collection of matchboxes that learned to play a skilled game of tic-tac-toe (a.k.a. noughts and crosses).

MENACE was a pioneering experiment in machine learning, demonstrating that a nonliving system could modify its behavior based on positive and negative reinforcement. It is particularly interesting to note that MENACE did not involve a computer at all. It was a collection of matchboxes, each representing one of the distinct positions with which Nought (by convention the opening player) could be confronted. By using rotation and reflection to eliminate redundant boards, Michie was able to keep the required number of matchboxes to around three hundred. Each matchbox contained a number of beads of assorted colors. There were nine colors of beads associated with the nine board positions, and the selection of a bead related to a move to the corresponding position.

The game played as follows. The opening move of the game involved selecting the appropriate matchbox, shaking it to mix the beads within, and selecting one bead at random. Michie then recorded MENACE's move to correspond to the board position associated with the color of the selected bead. After the second player made a move, it would be MENACE's turn again, and the process would be repeated: find the appropriately labeled matchbox, select a random bead, and make the corresponding move.

Positive or negative reinforcement occurred at the conclusion of the game. If MENACE lost the game, then the selected beads were not replaced, a net change of 1 per bead color per box. This had the effect of making that particular move less likely in the future. If MENACE did well (which is a *draw* when playing against a skilled opponent), the bead was returned, and a second bead of the same color was passed along, a net increase of + 1. This increased the likelihood of repeating the moves in the future. As games were played, the number of beads (and therefore the resulting probabilities of making certain moves) changed based on the positive and negative feedback the system received. Michie trained the system by playing 220 games over two eight-hour sessions on successive days. Michie reports that by the end of the first twenty games, MENACE was settling into a line of play that would result in a tie. Michie tried five variants of opponent play, each initially successful for a short number of games and then quickly mastered by MENACE. Michie reports that after 150 games the matchbox system became capable of coping with any variation applied by the opponent. Figure 15-11 provides a visual summary of the performance of MENACE.

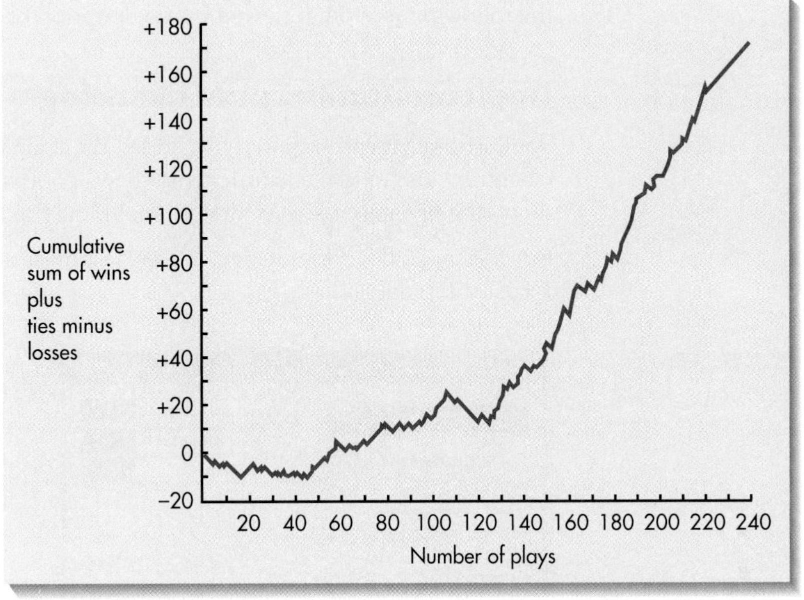


**FIGURE 15.11** *Performance of MENACE Learning Machine (from Michie, 1961)*

## ASK THE AUTHOR

**Q** A program that learns by playing tic-tac-toe sounds familiar. Did I see this in a movie?

**A** Yes, if you saw *War Games*. Filmed in 1981 during the height of the Cold War, the movie involves a computer almost starting World War III by thinking it was playing a game. Matthew Broderick's character gets the program to play tic-tac-toe repeatedly to learn that some games cannot be won. When the computer applies that logic to global thermal nuclear war, it determines that there would likewise be no winner, concluding, "The only winning move is not to play."

## Design for MLearning Program

Michie's experiment can be repeated in software by using variables and arrays in place of beads and matchboxes. The solution presented in this chapter uses a two-dimensional array. The first dimension is indexed by the board state. By assigning values to each of the three possible board markings (blank, X, or O) multiplied by the position of the board (positions 0 through 8), you can generate a value that uniquely distinguishes each possible board state. The second dimension of the array is the nine positions on the unique board state. The token value stored in each element of this array structure is the number of beads for that board at that position.

Given the array structure, the rest of the algorithm is as follows. When the machine learning, or Mlearning, opponent is to move, the appropriate board value is determined, and the nine token values are added together to give a total. A random number is selected based on that total, and an associated move is determined. The position selected for a move is therefore based on probability.

The move is made on the game board, and it is also recorded for learning purposes at the end of the game. This process continues, with the MLearning opponent making probabilistic moves until the game ends.

The learning occurs at the end of each game. MENACE learning involved adding or removing beads. In the MLearning version, learning involves increasing or decreasing token values. If the game is a loss, the selected token values are decreased. If the game is a tie, the token values are increased. Wins are the result of poor play by the opponent and are rewarded the same as a tie. The MLearning code is presented in the following section, followed by a description of the program during execution.

## Implementation of MLearning

To illustrate MLearning, we have added the code to the tic-tac-toe project started in Chapter 9 and extended earlier this chapter with a heuristic opponent. Figure 15-12 shows the updated interface design, including the following change.

- A button is added for playing one entire game between the MLearning code and the heuristic code.

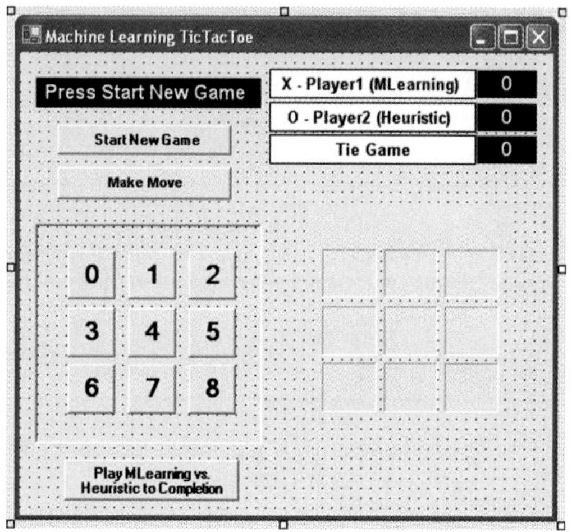

**FIGURE 15.12** *Design for MLearning Form*

The code for the MLearning program follows. Code originally presented in Chapter 9 and changed to have a heuristic opponent earlier in this chapter is presented with the normal background color. New code for the MLearning program is highlighted in blue.

```
'   *********** Design Time Properties ***********
'  OBJECT               PROPERTY         SETTING
'
'  lblTurnPrompt        Text             "Press Start New Game"
'
'  lblPlayer1           Text             "X - Player1 (MLearning)"
'
'  lblScore1            Text             0
'
'  lblPlayer2           Text             "O - Player2 (Heuristic)"
'
'  lblScore2            Text             0
'
'  lblTie               Text             "Tie Game"
'
'  lblTieScore          Text             0
'
```

```
'   btnStartGame          Text              "Start New Game"
'
'   btn0                  Tag               0
'   btn1                  Tag               1
'   btn2                  Tag               2
'   btn3                  Tag               3
'   btn4                  Tag               4
'   btn5                  Tag               5
'   btn6                  Tag               6
'   btn7                  Tag               7
'   btn8                  Tag               8
'
'   Rev 1.1 - Heuristic
'
'   btnStep               Text              "Make Heuristic Move"
'
'   lblFeedbackType       Text              ""
'
'   lblFeedback0          Text              ""
'   lblFeedback1          Text              ""
'   lblFeedback2          Text              ""
'   lblFeedback3          Text              ""
'   lblFeedback4          Text              ""
'   lblFeedback5          Text              ""
'   lblFeedback6          Text              ""
'   lblFeedback7          Text              ""
'   lblFeedback8          Text              ""
'
'   Rev 1.2 - Machine Learning
'
'   btnRunGame            Text              "Play MLearning vs. Heuristic to Completion"
'

Option Strict On

Public Class Form1
    Inherits System.Windows.Forms.Form

    Dim mBoard(8) As Button                   'Control Array
    Dim mFeedback(8) As Label
    Dim mXTurnFlag As Boolean = True
    Dim mWinner As String                     'winning player
    Dim mGameOverFlag As Boolean

    Dim mPlayer1Score, mPlayer2Score, mTieCount As Integer

    ' Rev 1.2 - Machine Learning
    Const MAX_BOARD_CONFIGURATIONS As Integer = CInt(3 ^ 9)
    Const LAST_BOARD_POSITION As Integer = 8
    Const MAX_ML_MOVES As Integer = 5 'after 5 moves by a player, the game's over

    Dim mMLTokens(MAX_BOARD_CONFIGURATIONS, LAST_BOARD_POSITION) As Integer
    Dim mMLBoardPositionHistory(MAX_ML_MOVES) As Integer
```

```
    Dim mMLMoveHistory(MAX_ML_MOVES) As Integer
    Dim mMLMoveCount As Integer

Windows Form Designer generated code

    ' Form1_Load assigns the form buttons to the control array.
    ' (Note that mBoard is a zero-based array).
    Private Sub Form1_Load(ByVal sender As System.Object, _
            ByVal e As System.EventArgs) Handles MyBase.Load
        Dim Position As Integer
        mBoard(0) = btn0
        mBoard(1) = btn1
        mBoard(2) = btn2
        mBoard(3) = btn3
        mBoard(4) = btn4
        mBoard(5) = btn5
        mBoard(6) = btn6
        mBoard(7) = btn7
        mBoard(8) = btn8

        For Position = 0 To 8
            mBoard(Position).Enabled = False
        Next Position

        ' Rev 1.1 - Heuristic
        mFeedback(0) = lblFeedback0
        mFeedback(1) = lblFeedback1
        mFeedback(2) = lblFeedback2
        mFeedback(3) = lblFeedback3
        mFeedback(4) = lblFeedback4
        mFeedback(5) = lblFeedback5
        mFeedback(6) = lblFeedback6
        mFeedback(7) = lblFeedback7
        mFeedback(8) = lblFeedback8

        ' Rev 1.2 - Machine Learning
        Initializetokens()
    End Sub

    Private Sub StartNewGame()
        Dim Position As Integer

        ' Reset visual elements
        For Position = 0 To 8
            mBoard(Position).Text = ""
            ' Rev 1.2 - comment out next line
            ' mBoard(Position).Enabled = True
            mBoard(Position).BackColor = Color.Gray
        Next

        mXTurnFlag = True                'X moves first
        lblTurnPrompt.Text = "X's Turn"
        mWinner = ""                     'Clear previous winner
        btnStartGame.Enabled = False
```

```
    mGameOverFlag = False

    ' Rev 1.1 - Heuristic
    ClearFeedback()

    ' Rev 1.2 - Machine Learning
    btnStep.Text = "Make MLearning Move"
    btnStep.Enabled = True
    mMLMoveCount = 0
End Sub

' This event procedure starts a new game by preparing the board
' array, resetting the module level variables.
Private Sub btnStartGame_Click(ByVal sender As System.Object, _
            ByVal e As System.EventArgs) _
            Handles btnStartGame.Click
    StartNewGame()
End Sub

' btn0_Click handles the button click event for each button
' on the game board.  You should manually add the events handled
' by this procedure after the "Handles" keyword
Private Sub btn0_Click(ByVal sender As System.Object, _
        ByVal e As System.EventArgs) Handles btn0.Click, _
        btn1.Click, btn2.Click, btn3.Click, btn4.Click, _
        btn5.Click, btn6.Click, btn7.Click, btn8.Click

    Dim Tag As Integer

    ' Option Strict On requires explicit typecast using CType
    Tag = CInt(CType(sender, Button).Tag)

    ' If space is already taken, then ignore click
    If mBoard(Tag).Text <> "" Then Exit Sub

    If mXTurnFlag Then
        mBoard(Tag).Text = "X"         'Mark the move
    Else
        mBoard(Tag).Text = "O"         'Mark the move
    End If
    mXTurnFlag = Not mXTurnFlag        'Toggle turn flag

    CheckForWinner()                   'Was this a winning move?

    ' Rev 1.1 - Heuristic
    ClearFeedback()
End Sub

Sub CheckForWinner()
    Dim Position As Integer

    'Check for X and O winning
```

```
        CheckThree(0, 1, 2)
        CheckThree(3, 4, 5)
        CheckThree(6, 7, 8)
        CheckThree(0, 3, 6)
        CheckThree(1, 4, 7)
        CheckThree(2, 5, 8)
        CheckThree(0, 4, 8)
        CheckThree(2, 4, 6)

        'Check for a Tie
        If Not mGameOverFlag Then CheckTie()

        ' Give appropriate feedback
        Select Case mWinner
            Case "X"
                mPlayer1Score = mPlayer1Score + 1
                lblScore1.Text = CStr(mPlayer1Score)
                lblTurnPrompt.Text = "X Wins"
            Case "O"
                mPlayer2Score = mPlayer2Score + 1
                lblScore2.Text = CStr(mPlayer2Score)
                lblTurnPrompt.Text = "O Wins"
            Case "Tie"
                mTieCount = mTieCount + 1
                lblTieScore.Text = CStr(mTieCount)
                lblTurnPrompt.Text = "Tie Game"
            Case Else
                If mXTurnFlag Then
                    lblTurnPrompt.Text = "X's Turn"
                    ' Rev 1.1 - Heuristic
                    'btnStep.Enabled = False
                    ' Rev 1.2 - commented out above line
                    ' Rev 1.2 - added following line
                    btnStep.Text = "Make MLearning Move"
                Else
                    lblTurnPrompt.Text = "O's Turn"
                    ' Rev 1.1 - Heuristic
                    btnStep.Enabled = True
                    btnStep.Text = "Make Heuristic Move"
                End If
        End Select

        If mGameOverFlag Then
            ' Rev 1.1 - Heuristic
            btnStep.Enabled = False
            For Position = 0 To 8
                mBoard(Position).Enabled = False 'Disallow new moves
            Next Position
            btnStartGame.Enabled = True

            ' Rev 1.2 - Machine Learning
            UpdateTokens()      'Learn from this games final result
        End If
    End Sub
```

```
' CheckThree accepts three board positions and determines if
' all three are occupied by the same player.  If so, then a
' winning move is found and the winning positions are
' highlighted in red.
Sub CheckThree(ByVal p1 As Integer, ByVal p2 As Integer, _
            ByVal p3 As Integer)
    If mBoard(p1).Text <> "" _
            And mBoard(p1).Text = mBoard(p2).Text _
            And mBoard(p2).Text = mBoard(p3).Text Then
        ' Mark the winning moves
        mBoard(p1).BackColor = Color.Red
        mBoard(p2).BackColor = Color.Red
        mBoard(p3).BackColor = Color.Red
        ' Record the winning player
        mWinner = mBoard(p1).Text
        mGameOverFlag = True
    End If
End Sub

Function IsEmpty(ByVal Index As Integer) As Boolean
    If mBoard(Index).Text = "" Then Return True
    Return False
End Function

Sub CheckTie()
    Dim Position As Integer
    Dim TieFlag As Boolean = True

    ' If any spaces are open, it's not a tie yet...
    For Position = 0 To 8
        If IsEmpty(Position) Then TieFlag = False
    Next

    If TieFlag Then
        ' Record the winning player
        mWinner = "Tie"
        mGameOverFlag = True
    End If
End Sub

'%*%*%*%*%*%*%*%*%*%*%*%*%*%*%*%*%*%*%*%*%*%*%*%*%*%*%*%*
'%*%*%*%*%*%*   Rev 1.1 HEURISTIC CODE   %*%*%*%*%*%*%*
'%*%*%*%*%*%*%*%*%*%*%*%*%*%*%*%*%*%*%*%*%*%*%*%*%*%*%*%*

' Blank out the array of feedback labels
Private Sub ClearFeedback()
    Dim Position As Integer

    lblFeedbackType.Text = ""
    For Position = 0 To 8
        mFeedback(Position).Text = ""
        mFeedback(Position).ForeColor = Color.Black
```

```
    Next
End Sub

' MakeHeuristicMove determines the heuristic value for each available board position
' and then moves to the position with the largest value
Sub MakeHeuristicMove()
    Dim Position As Integer
    Dim HValue As Integer
    Dim BestPosition As Integer
    Dim BestHValue As Integer

    ClearFeedback()
    lblFeedbackType.Text = "Heuristic Values" & vbCrLf & "(largest value selected)"

    ' Initialize placeholders for max value search
    BestPosition = -1
    BestHValue = -30000

    For Position = 0 To 8
        ' Only consider open board positions
        If IsEmpty(Position) Then
            HValue = GetHeuristicValue(Position)
            mFeedback(Position).Text = CStr(HValue)
            If HValue > BestHValue Then
                BestHValue = HValue          'remember current best value
                BestPosition = Position      'remember current best position
            End If
        Else
            mFeedback(Position).Text = "N/A"
        End If
    Next Position

    mBoard(BestPosition).Text = "O"          'Make heuristic move
    mFeedback(BestPosition).ForeColor = Color.Red

    mXTurnFlag = Not mXTurnFlag 'Toggle turn flag

    CheckForWinner()            'was this a winning move?
End Sub

' GetHeuristicValue assumes a move is made and then adds the
' heuristic values for each of the eight key game directions to derive
' the total heuristic value.  The assumed move is then undone.
Function GetHeuristicValue(ByVal Position As Integer) As Integer
    Dim HValue As Integer

    HValue = 0
    mBoard(Position).Text = "O"          'Add move temporarily
    HValue = HValue + CalculateHValue(0, 1, 2)
    HValue = HValue + CalculateHValue(3, 4, 5)
    HValue = HValue + CalculateHValue(6, 7, 8)
    HValue = HValue + CalculateHValue(0, 3, 6)
    HValue = HValue + CalculateHValue(1, 4, 7)
```

```
    HValue = HValue + CalculateHValue(2, 5, 8)
    HValue = HValue + CalculateHValue(0, 4, 8)
    HValue = HValue + CalculateHValue(2, 4, 6)
    mBoard(Position).Text = ""          'Remove temporary move
    Return HValue
End Function

Function IsA(ByVal Index As Integer, _
        ByVal Value As String) As Boolean
    If mBoard(Index).Text = Value Then Return True
    Return False
End Function

' CalculateHValue assigns a value to the specified game direction based
' on the likelyhood of winning.  The algorithm assignes positive values
' for "O" and negative for "X".
Function CalculateHValue(ByVal p1 As Integer, ByVal p2 As Integer, _
           ByVal p3 As Integer) As Integer
    Dim X As String = "X"
    Dim O As String = "O"
    Dim N As String = ""

    ' H has 3 in a Row/Column/Diagonal
    If IsA(p1, O) And IsA(p2, O) And IsA(p3, O) Then Return 100
    ' H has 2 of 3
    If IsA(p1, O) And IsA(p2, O) And IsA(p3, N) Then Return 10
    If IsA(p1, O) And IsA(p2, N) And IsA(p3, O) Then Return 10
    If IsA(p1, N) And IsA(p2, O) And IsA(p3, O) Then Return 10
    ' H has 1 of 3
    If IsA(p1, O) And IsA(p2, N) And IsA(p3, N) Then Return 1
    If IsA(p1, N) And IsA(p2, O) And IsA(p3, N) Then Return 1
    If IsA(p1, N) And IsA(p2, N) And IsA(p3, O) Then Return 1

    ' M has 3 in a Row/Column/Diagonal
    If IsA(p1, X) And IsA(p2, X) And IsA(p3, X) Then Return -200
    ' M has 2 of 3
    If IsA(p1, X) And IsA(p2, X) And IsA(p3, N) Then Return -20
    If IsA(p1, X) And IsA(p2, N) And IsA(p3, X) Then Return -20
    If IsA(p1, N) And IsA(p2, X) And IsA(p3, X) Then Return -20
    ' M has 1 of 3
    If IsA(p1, X) And IsA(p2, N) And IsA(p3, N) Then Return -2
    If IsA(p1, N) And IsA(p2, X) And IsA(p3, N) Then Return -2
    If IsA(p1, N) And IsA(p2, N) And IsA(p3, X) Then Return -2
    Return 0
End Function

Private Sub btnStep_Click(ByVal sender As System.Object, _
           ByVal e As System.EventArgs) Handles btnStep.Click
    ' Rev 1.2 - Machine Learning
    If mXTurnFlag Then
        MakeMachineLearningMove()
    Else
        MakeHeuristicMove()
```

```
    End If
End Sub

'%*%*%*%*%*%*%*%*%*%*%*%*%*%*%*%*%*%*%*%*%*%*%*%*%*%*%*%*%*
'%*%*%*%*%*% Rev 1.2 MACHINE LEARNING CODE %*%*%*%*%*%*%*
'%*%*%*%*%*%*%*%*%*%*%*%*%*%*%*%*%*%*%*%*%*%*%*%*%*%*%*%*%*

' Each board configuration has a unique integer value based on the position of the
' X's, O's and spaces on the board.  This function returns that unique value.
Function GetCurrentBoardConfiguration() As Integer
    Dim Position, BoardConfiguration As Integer

    ' Map current game state to unique index value
    For Position = 0 To 8
        If IsA(Position, "X") Then
            BoardConfiguration = BoardConfiguration + (1 * CInt(3 ^ Position))
        ElseIf IsA(Position, "O") Then
            BoardConfiguration = BoardConfiguration + (2 * CInt(3 ^ Position))
        End If
    Next Position
    Return BoardConfiguration
End Function

' The X, O, or space "value" of each position on a board is encoded within the
' unique board configuration value.  This function decodes a board configuration
' to determine the "value" at a specific position on that board
Function GetBoardPositionValue(ByVal BoardConfiguration As Integer, _
         ByVal BoardPosition As Integer) As Integer
    ' Given a BoardConfiguration Number, determine the state of a BoardPosition
    ' Formula to determine board values as Open(=0), "X"(=1), or "O"(=2)
    ' position 0 = (boardvalue Mod 3) \ 1
    ' position 1 = (boardvalue Mod 9) \ 3
    ' position 2 = (boardvalue Mod 27) \ 9
    ' position 3 = (boardvalue Mod (3 ^ 4)) \ (3 ^ 3)
    ' position N = (boardvalue Mod (3 ^ (N + 1)) \ (3 ^ N)
    Return (BoardConfiguration Mod CInt(3 ^ (BoardPosition + 1))) \ _
              CInt(3 ^ BoardPosition)
End Function

' InitializeTokens is called once before the first game is played.
' Valid positions for moving all receive the same number of initial
' tokens, making initial moves equally likely (no initial knowledge)
' Over time, the number of tokens in each board position for each
' board configuration will change to reflect the learned knowledge
' Unavailable positions are all initialized with no tokens, and as
' a result, the machine learning player will never move there
Sub InitializeTokens()
    Const INITIAL_TOKEN_COUNT As Integer = 9
    Dim Position As Integer
    Dim BoardConfiguration As Integer

    ' BOARD MARKING FORMULA
    '
```

```
    ' INITIALIZATION ALGORITHM:
    ' For each unique configuration of the board
    '    For each position on the board
    '        if position is Open(=0), then
    '            put initial number of tokens in that position
    '        else
    '            put no tokens in that position (cannot move there)
    '        end if
    '    Next
    ' Next

    ' Uncomment Randomize to reseed the random number generator
    ' Without Randomize(), the random number sequence used to determine
    ' machine learning moves will be the same each time you run the program
    'Randomize()

    For BoardConfiguration = 0 To MAX_BOARD_CONFIGURATIONS - 1
        For Position = 0 To 8
            If GetBoardPositionValue(BoardConfiguration, Position) = 0 Then
                ' Position is open
                mMLTokens(BoardConfiguration, Position) = INITIAL_TOKEN_COUNT
            Else
                ' Position is taken
                mMLTokens(BoardConfiguration, Position) = 0
            End If
        Next Position
    Next BoardConfiguration
End Sub

' PlayOneGameWithLearning will play a MLearning vs. Heuristic game
' to completion.  This procedure works even when a game is already in progress.
Sub PlayOneGameWithLearning()

    ' If not already playing, start new game before moving
    If mGameOverFlag Then StartNewGame()

    Do While Not mGameOverFlag
        If mXTurnFlag Then
            MakeMachineLearningMove()
        Else
            MakeHeuristicMove()
        End If
    Loop
End Sub

Sub MakeMachineLearningMove()
    Dim Position As Integer
    Dim BoardConfiguration As Integer
    Dim TokenSum As Integer
    Dim NextMovePos As Integer
    Dim RandomNumber As Integer
    Dim Weight As Double
```

```
    ' Determine the unique board configuration value for the current game state
    BoardConfiguration = GetCurrentBoardConfiguration()

    ' Sum the tokens in each position in the current board configuration
    TokenSum = 0
    For Position = 0 To 8
        TokenSum = TokenSum + mMLTokens(BoardConfiguration, Position)
    Next Position

    ' Display the token values
    ClearFeedback()
    lblFeedbackType.Text = "Machine Learning Percentages" & vbCrLf & _
                    "(weighted random selection)"
    For Position = 0 To 8
        If IsA(Position, "X") Or IsA(Position, "O") Then
            mFeedback(Position).Text = "N/A"
        Else
            Weight = mMLTokens(BoardConfiguration, Position) / TokenSum
            mFeedback(Position).Text = Format(Weight, "0.0%")
        End If
    Next Position

    ' Determine MLearning Move by making a weighted random move
    If TokenSum = 0 Then
        ' No tokens... move to first open position
        NextMovePos = 0
        Do While mBoard(NextMovePos).Text <> ""
            NextMovePos = NextMovePos + 1
        Loop
    Else
        ' Make a random move weighted by tokens at each location
        RandomNumber = CInt(Int((TokenSum * Rnd()) + 1))
        NextMovePos = -1
        Do While (RandomNumber > 0)
            NextMovePos = NextMovePos + 1
            RandomNumber = RandomNumber - mMLTokens(BoardConfiguration, NextMovePos)
        Loop
    End If

    ' Move Machine to selected position
    mBoard(NextMovePos).Text = "X"
    mXTurnFlag = Not mXTurnFlag
    mFeedback(NextMovePos).ForeColor = Color.Red

    ' Remember this move (boardconfiguration and position) for Learning
    mMLMoveCount = mMLMoveCount + 1
    mMLBoardPositionHistory(mMLMoveCount) = BoardConfiguration
    mMLMoveHistory(mMLMoveCount) = NextMovePos

    CheckForWinner()
End Sub
```

```
    ' UpdateTokens is called once after each game is completed.  The tokens for each
    ' machine learning move are updated to provide positive or negative reinforcement
    ' based on the game outcome.
    Sub UpdateTokens()
        Dim BoardConfiguration As Integer
        Dim Move As Integer
        Dim MovePos As Integer

        For Move = 1 To mMLMoveCount
            BoardConfiguration = mMLBoardPositionHistory(Move)
            MovePos = mMLMoveHistory(Move)
            Select Case mWinner
                Case "X"
                    mMLTokens(BoardConfiguration, MovePos) += (Move * 50)
                Case "Tie"
                    mMLTokens(BoardConfiguration, MovePos) += (Move * 10)
                Case "O"
                    mMLTokens(BoardConfiguration, MovePos) -= (Move * 1)
                    ' Token amount cannot be negative
                    If mMLTokens(BoardConfiguration, MovePos) < 0 Then
                       mMLTokens(BoardConfiguration, MovePos) = 0
                    End If
            End Select
        Next Move
    End Sub

    Private Sub btnRunGame_Click(ByVal sender As System.Object, _
                ByVal e As System.EventArgs) Handles btnRunGame.Click
        PlayOneGameWithLearning()
    End Sub

End Class
```

## How the MLearning Program Works

To understand how the MLearning program works, consider the first move of the first game. Clicking on the Make MLearning Move button causes the machine-learning player to move. The learning algorithm evaluates all the available positions. Because this is the first game, there is no past knowledge, and all moves are equally likely (11.11 percent). By a random choice, position 6 is chosen for the MLearning move, resulting in an X in the lower left corner (see Figure 15-13).

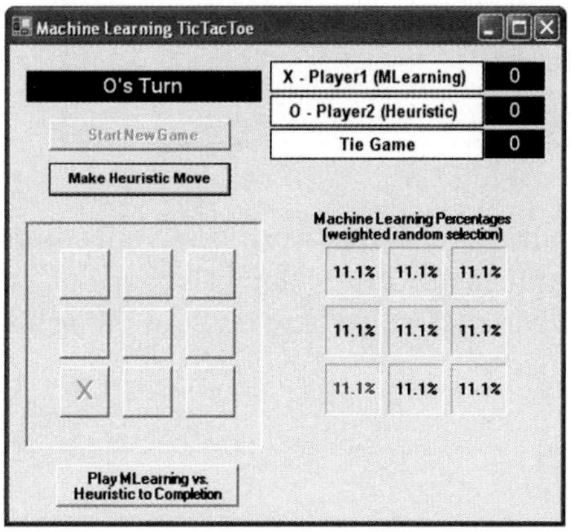

**FIGURE 15.13**
*MLearning Game 1, Move 1 (Equal Probabilities)*

Machine Learning TicTacToe

O's Turn

Start New Game

Make Heuristic Move

| X - Player1 (MLearning) | 0 |
|---|---|
| O - Player2 (Heuristic) | 0 |
| Tie Game | 0 |

Machine Learning Percentages (weighted random selection)

| | | |
|---|---|---|
| | | |
| | | |
| X | | |

| | | |
|---|---|---|
| 11.1% | 11.1% | 11.1% |
| 11.1% | 11.1% | 11.1% |
| 11.1% | 11.1% | 11.1% |

Play MLearning vs. Heuristic to Completion

Skip now to the end of the game when reinforcement occurs. If we assume MLearning lost the game, then the reinforcement process will subtract 1 from the token values for each of the positions moved during the game. This decreases the associated percentages and reduces the probability of repeating those moves the next time MLearning encounters those board states. For example, the start of the second game shows different percentages for the nine board locations. Position 6 has a lower percentage (because that move contributed to a loss in the first game), and the likelihood of other moves has increased slightly (Figure 15-14). The program is learning!

**FIGURE 15.14**
*MLearning Game 2, Move 1 (Learning has occurred!)*

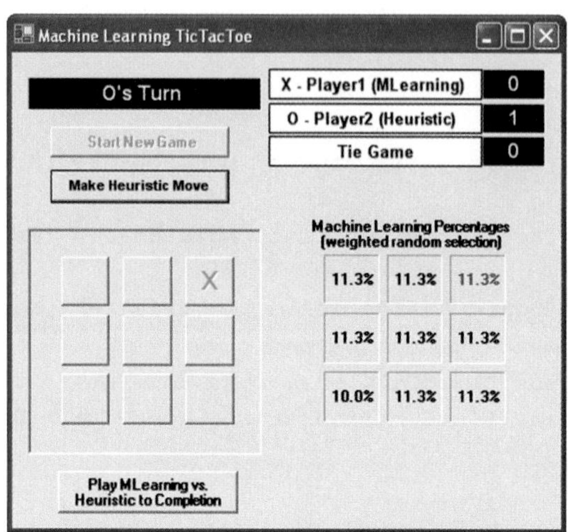


After one hundred games, the behavior of the MLearning program will have improved to the point that it will tie most games. In the nonrandomized case, the MLearning happens to have learned to tie by making an initial move in the left middle (64.35 percent) as shown in Figure 15-15.

**FIGURE 15.15**
*MLearning After 100 Complete Games (Learning has occurred!)*

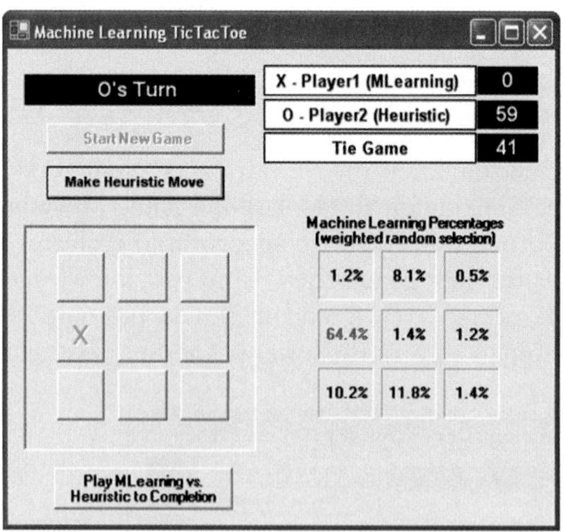


The point is worth repeating: based only on positive and negative feedback, the MLearning program will develop behavior that includes blocking its opponent and avoiding moves that would later result in the opponent having simultaneous winning moves.

## ASK THE AUTHOR

**Q** Does the MLearning program think?

**A** Let me answer by asking a different question: "Does a boat swim?" Many people consider the terms *think* and *swim* as inherently related to human rather than machine activities. It quickly becomes an argument of terminology.

It can be accurately stated that MENACE and the MLearning program both demonstrate trial-and-error learning based on positive and negative reinforcement. However, reinforcement is only one small aspect of learning, and learning is only one small aspect of human thought. An extensive study of human thought involves expertise from the fields of psychology, biology, and cognitive science (among others). Technology questions that include phrases such as *in the future, eventually,* or *one day* expand the discussion to include areas such as philosophy and religion. This much is clear: Many differences remain between human thought and mechanical reasoning.

## CHAPTER SUMMARY

- Information overload refers to the overwhelming amount of information available to individuals in the modern information age.
- Computing technology has added to the problem of information overload, but it can also help address the problem through intelligent systems. Unlike traditional systems working with data, an intelligent system extends the traditional computing function to also include the acquisition and application of knowledge.
- Knowledge is essential to intelligence. One challenge for intelligent systems is to capture, represent, and use knowledge in a computing system in the best and most efficient possible manner.
- One approach to capturing and using knowledge is through heuristics. A heuristic is a knowledge rule based on experience. Heuristics can be used by intelligent systems to guide the discovery process, and though heuristic-guided behavior is not guaranteed to be optimal, it is usually interesting.
- A heuristic function returns a value based on heuristic knowledge. A heuristic function can be used to evaluate multiple possibilities and then to select the best value.
- Learning is a modification of behavior based on experience and is another element of intelligent systems.
- A computing system can be constructed that performs trial-and-error learning based on positive and negative reinforcement.

## KEY TERMS

data p. 412
data mining p. 415
expert systems p. 415
heuristic p. 415
heuristic function p. 417
information p. 412
information overload p. 411
intelligent systems p. 411
knowledge p. 412
learning p. 428
MENACE p. 428

## Review Questions

1. The phrases "Look before you leap" and "He who hesitates is lost" are seemingly contradictory general-purpose heuristics. Identify one or two other pairs of contradictory common-sense wisdom.
2. Identify one or two domain-specific heuristics for the problem of finding a parking space on campus.
3. What are the similarities and differences between MENACE and MLearning?
4. MLearning seems to require more games to learn than MENACE. Can you explain why?
5. When MLearning loses, the reinforcement code updates tokens by subtracting (K * 1) where K is the MLearning move during the game (1, 2, 3, or 4). As a result, more tokens are taken from moves that occur later in the game. Can you explain why?

## Programming Exercises

**15-1. Tic-Tac-Toe Heuristic.** The heuristic opponent presented in this chapter can be beaten. (Can you determine a move sequence to beat the heuristic opponent?) Change the heuristics for the tic-tac-toe program to make the program impossible to beat.

**15-2. Connect Four Game.** Connect Four is a game similar to tic-tac-toe. Players make moves by placing a marker in one of seven columns. The marker falls to the first unfilled location inside the column. Play continues until one player has four markers in a row, column, or diagonal, or until all the columns are filled. Implement the game Connect Four for two human players, similar to the two-human version of tic-tac-toe originally presented in Chapter 9.

**15-3. Connect Four Heuristics.** Develop heuristics for Connect Four by first determining general rules and then quantifying those rules (similar to what was done for tic-tac-toe in this chapter. Modify your Connect Four game implementation to include a heuristic computerized opponent.

**15-4. Connect Four Learning.** Using a machine learning approach similar to the one in this chapter, modify your Connect Four game implementation to include an MLearning computerized opponent.

# Appendix A

## Visual Basic .NET Keywords

AddHandler
AddressOf
Alias
And
AndAlso
Ansi
As
Assembly
Auto
Boolean
ByRef
Byte
ByVal
Call
Case
Catch
CBool
CByte
CChar
CDate
CDec
CDbl
Char
CInt
Class
CLng
CObj
Const
CShort
CSng
CStr
CType
Date
Decimal
Declare
Default
Delegate
Dim
DirectCast
Do
Double
Each
Else
ElseIf
End
Enum
Erase
Error
Event
Exit
False
Finally
For
Friend
Function
Get
GetType
GoSub
GoTo
Handles
If
Implements
Imports
In
Inherits
Integer
Interface
Is
Let
Lib
Like
Long
Loop
Me
Mod
Module
MustInherit
MustOverride
MyBase
MyClass
Namespace
New
Next
Not
Nothing
NotInheritable
NotOverridable
Object
On
Option
Optional
Or
OrElse
Overloads
Overridable
Overrides
ParamArray
Preserve
Private
Property
Protected
Public
RaiseEvent
ReadOnly
ReDim
Rem
RemoveHandler
Resume
Return
Select
Set
Shadows
Shared
Short
Single
Static
Step

Stop
String
Structure
Sub
SyncLock
Then
Throw
To
True
Try
TypeOf
Unicode
Until
Variant
When
While
With
WithEvents
WriteOnly
Xor
#Const
#ExternalSource
#If...Then...#Else
#Region
-
&
&=
*
*=
/
/=
\
\=
^
^=
+
+=
=
-=

# Appendix B

## Using the Visual Studio .NET Debugger

Eventually, all developers write a program that contains errors. All modern programming environments provide tools to allow a developer to pause a program, inspect the values of variables, and execute the program one line of code at a time. In Visual Studio .NET, some of these tools are available in the Debug toolbar. You can show the Debug toolbar by selecting View | Toolbars | Debug.

The View | Toolbars Menu

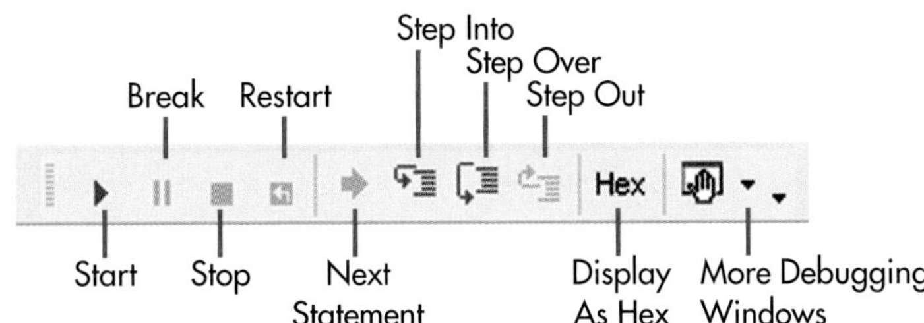


The Debug Toolbar

### Setting Breakpoints

Modern computers execute billions of instructions each second. When looking for errors in a program, it is helpful to pause program execution. The most common way to pause a program is to set a breakpoint. A breakpoint is a marker associated with a line of code in a program where execution will be suspended. Breakpoints are most often set at design time, and are typically placed just prior to a location where an error is believed to exist. A program can have zero, one, or many breakpoints.

In Visual Studio .NET, breakpoints are toggled by clicking the gutter to the left of the desired line of code. Breakpoints may also be toggled using the F9 key. A red circle in the gutter and a red background highlight indicate that a breakpoint has been set. The following figure shows a breakpoint at design time.

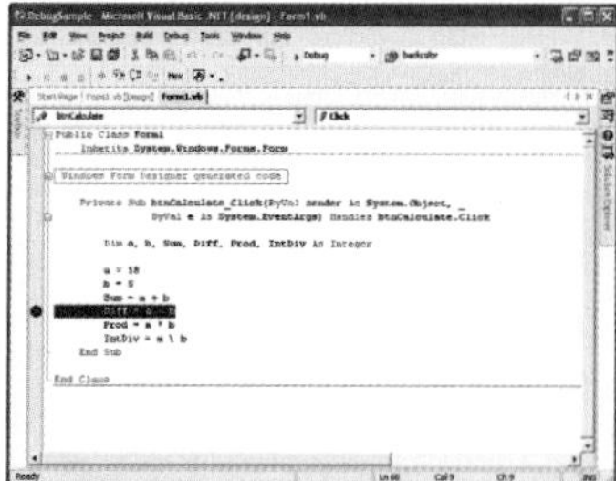

Program with Breakpoint at Design Time

## Pausing a Program

When a program executes a line of code marked with a breakpoint, the execution of the program is suspended. However, all variables maintain their values. These values can be inspected in several ways. The user can place the mouse cursor over a variable and Visual Studio will provide its value as a tooltip. Multiple values can be inspected using the watch window, which uses a red font color to indicate changing values. The following figure shows a program paused at the previously specified breakpoint.

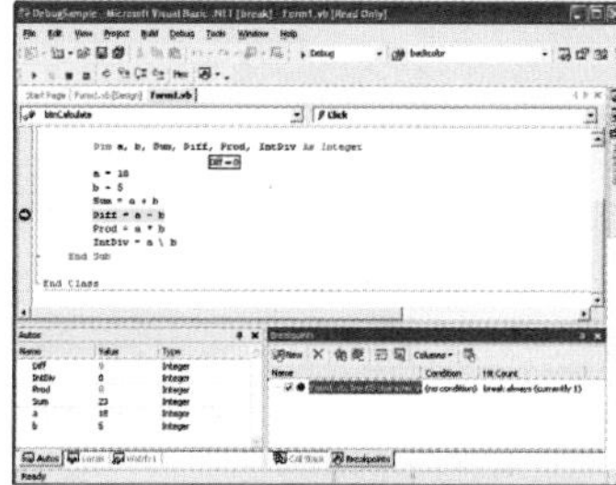

Paused Program Showing a Tooltip Variable Value and the Watch Window.

## Stepping Through a Program

Stepping is executing one line of code at a time. The debugger provides three commands for stepping through code:

- Step Into (F8)
- Step Over (Shift-F8)
- Step Out

Step Into and Step Over instruct the debugger to execute the next line of code. For most statements, these two commands are identical. If the line to execute contains a procedure call, however, Step Into will jump to the first line of the procedure's code, and Step Over will execute the entire line (including any called procedures). The Step Out command should be used when you are inside a procedure and want to return to the calling code. The following figure shows the program execution after a single Step Into. In addition to stepping, the user can press F5 to resume normal program execution.

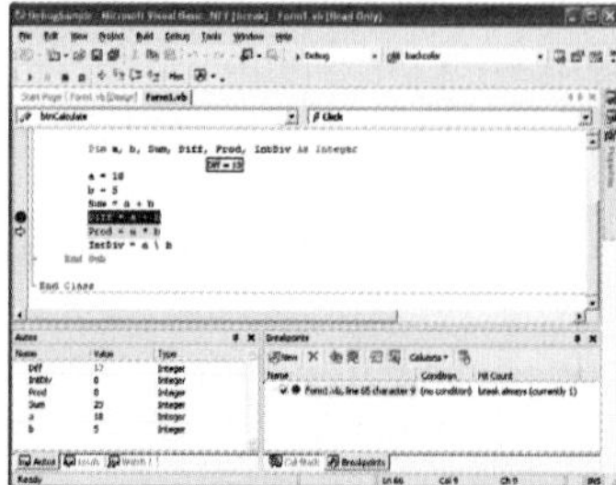

Paused Program After a Step Command

# Glossary

**accumulator** – A variable that maintains a running total, typically used inside a loop.

**ADO.NET** – The data access architecture for the .NET Framework. ADO.NET provides Connection, DataAdapter, and Dataset objects to facilitate accessing data in a database.

**algorithm** – The logical sequence of steps to accomplish a specific objective.

**application state** – The application state is variable storage in which ASP.NET maintains information about a web application. The application state is created the first time any client requests a URL resource from within the ASP.NET application; the application state remains in memory until the web server is shut down or the application is modified.

**arithmetic operators** – Operators that manipulate numeric operands and generate a numeric result.

**argument** – Arguments and parameters are the preferred means of communication between procedures and their calling code. An argument is a value passed from the calling code to the procedure. A parameter is a variable listed in the formal procedure declaration that receives the argument.

**array** – A variable that holds a collection of related data values. Each of the values in an array is called an element. Each element in the array is identified by an integer value called its index, which indicates the position of the element in the array.

**array length** – The number of elements in an array. For a zero-based array, the array length is always one more than the upper bound of the array.

**ASP.NET** – A platform for developing and running web applications on a .NET Framework web server.

**assignment statement** – A programming instruction used to calculate a value and store the result.

**bug** – A mistake (error) in a computer system.

**ByRef** – A parameter convention whereby the parameter receives a pointer to the actual argument. Any change to the parameter also changes the actual argument. When the argument is a large structure, ByRef is often used to avoid the significant time and memory necessary to make a local copy. ByRef is also used to pass information back to the calling code through the argument.

**ByVal** – A parameter convention whereby the parameter receives a local copy of the passing argument. Thus, any change to the parameter within the procedure will not affect the value of the argument. ByVal is the default parameter convention.

**class** – The structure of an object—a blueprint that describes the properties (data) and methods (actions) of an object.

**client** – In a client/server web application, the client is the user's machine with an Internet browser.

**cohesion** – The level of uniformity within a procedure. A procedure has high-cohesion (which is good) when it does only a single, precise task, such as Print, Calculate, or Update. A high cohesion procedure will be simpler to understand because it has to do only a single task. Low-cohesion procedures perform many tasks, which is bad design and can make the solution logic difficult to read, understand, and maintain.

**compound condition** – Two conditions within parentheses joined by a logical operator.

**computer program** – A series of instructions to solve a problem written in a syntax the computer can understand and execute.

**condition** – An expression that evaluates to true or false.

**Connection** – An ADO.NET Connection object establishes a link from your application to a database.

**console I/O** – Input and output that appear in the console window for the lifetime of the program.

**constant** – A storage location whose value cannot change during the execution of the program.

**control array** – An array of Windows Form controls such as text boxes, labels, or buttons. Control arrays allow a developer to write a small amount of code that affects a potentially large number of GUI elements.

**cookie** – A small text file stored on the client machine.

**counter** – A variable that keeps track of how many times a statement block has executed, typically used inside a loop.

**coupling** – The level of interdependency between procedures. When procedures reference module or global variables, they have high coupling with the outside environment (which is bad). Using parameters to get data into and out of a procedure produces low coupling, which is good design and supports code reuse.

**data** – Numbers, characters, or images without context. Data by itself has no meaning. When data is processed in a context (either by a human or a computer system), it becomes information.

**DataAdapter** – An ADO.NET DataAdapter object does the work of passing information between the database and your application.

**database** – A structured collection of data. The typical database structure includes fields, records, and tables. A field is a storage location for a single piece of information, such as a customer's name, address, or zip code. A record is a complete collection of related fields (e.g., the name, address, and zip code of a single customer). A table is a complete set of related records (e.g., all the customers in a company's database).

**Database Management System (DBMS)** – A collection of programs that supports the creation, storage, manipulation, querying, and printing of information to and from a database. A DBMS allows appropriate presentation of accurate information to the correct people at the proper time. A DBMS can also control the security and integrity of the data in the database.

**DataSet** – An ADO.NET DataSet object is a temporary, local copy of the information in the table.

**Dim statement** – A variable declaration statement that specifies the name of the variable and its associated data type.

**encapsulation** – In object-oriented programming terms, encapsulation refers to grouping related properties and methods so they can be treated as a single unit or object. Encapsulation also refers to protecting the inner contents of an object from being damaged or incorrectly referenced by external code.

**end-of-output symbol (§)** – In Visual Logic, the symbol used to indicate the ending position of the current output.

**event** – An event is a signal that informs an application that something important has happened. Events can occur as a result of a user action, such as clicking the mouse, moving the mouse, entering text, or pressing a key on the keyboard. Events may also be system generated, such as a timer Tick event.

**event-driven programming** – A programming paradigm in which the application recognizes and responds to events.

**event handler** – A procedure that responds to a particular event. When the event is raised, the procedure is executed.

**exception** – An exceptional situation that requires special handling. If the exception is not handled, the program will halt execution.

**Exit loop** – A control statement that causes control to jump to the statement immediately following the containing loop.

**expression** – A value-returning code construct, such as a variable or mathematical formula.

**flowchart** – A graphical representation of an algorithm.

**For loop** – A control structure used to repeat actions a predetermined number of times.

**foreign key** – A field in a database table containing values that match primary key values in a related table.

**function procedure** – A procedure that returns a value.

**graphical user interface (GUI)** – Visual cues to the user, such as menus, buttons, and icons, that allow the user to work intuitively and efficiently.

**heuristic** – A knowledge rule based on experience.

**HTML** – Hypertext Markup Language, a language for displaying text in a web browser such as Internet Explorer or Netscape Navigator.

**identifier** – A unique name for distinguishing variables, procedures, and properties.

**If statement** – A decision structure consisting of a condition, a block of statements that execute only when the condition evaluates to true, and optionally a block of statements that execute only when the condition evaluates to false.

**information** – Data that has been processed in a context.

**information system** – A combination of people and technology (computers) that collects, organizes, and processes data to produce information. For any information system to be useful, it must do at least three things: input data into the system, process data within the system, and output resulting information from the system.

**inheritance** – In object-oriented programming terms, inheritance describes the ability to create new classes based on an existing class. The existing class is called the base class, and the new class derived from the base class is called the derived class. The derived class inherits all the properties, methods, and events of the base class and can be customized with additional properties and methods.

**input statement** – A programming instruction that accepts data from the user and stores that data into a variable.

**integrated development environment (IDE)** – A single comprehensive environment that performs many common programming tasks, including syntax checking, interpreting, compiling, debugging, and deploying applications.

**intelligent systems** – An extension of the traditional computing function to also include the acquisition and application of knowledge.

**intrinsic function** – Predefined function procedures that provide developers with common, helpful functionality.

**knowledge** – Information that has been processed for patterns and insights.

**learning** – A modification of behavior based on experience.

**local variable** – A variable declared inside a procedure. Local variables can be referenced only within the defining procedure—they are unavailable outside of the procedure block in which they are declared. A local variable is destroyed when the procedure has finished executing. Each subsequent call to the procedure re-creates and reinitializes all local procedure variables.

**logic error** – An error in the solution design or implementation that causes the program to run without technical errors, but with incorrect behavior.

**logical operators** – Operators that manipulate logical operands and generate a logical result. The four most common logical operators are NOT, AND, OR, and XOR.

**menu** – A list of common operations presented to the user in a well-defined, system-universal format. Menus make a program easier to learn and use by making common actions available to the user in expected locations.

**method** – A procedure defined within a class.

**modular programming** – A methodology whereby long programs are divided into numerous small procedures that are based on logical activities. From a developer's perspective, breaking your application into logical units makes the code easier to read. Modular programming also makes your application easier to maintain.

**module variable** – A variable declared in the General Declaration Section outside of any procedure. Module level variables may be referenced by any procedure in the module.

**nested If** – An If statement contained within the true or false branch of another If statement.

**nested loop** – A loop contained inside the body of another loop.

**normalization** – A formal database design process. There are increasing stages of normalization, not all of which are necessary for every database design. First normal form (1NF) requires that fields contain atomic values. Second normal form (2NF) requires that all fields depend on the primary key. Third normal form (3NF) eliminates redundancies by creating multiple tables so that each non-key field depends only on its primary key. This normalization process has the advantage of reducing data redundancy and allowing for more efficient storage and access.

**object** – A combination of data (properties) and actions (methods) that can be treated as a unit.

**operator precedence** – The unambiguous order in which expression operators are evaluated.

**output statement** – A programming instruction that presents information to users.

**parallel arrays** – Two or more arrays whose elements are related by their position in the arrays.

**parameter** – A parameter is a variable listed in the formal procedure declaration that receives an argument.

**polymorphism** – In object-oriented programming terms, polymorphism is the ability of objects from different classes to respond appropriately to identical method names or operators. Polymorphism is essential to object-oriented programming because it allows developers to use shared names, and the system will apply the appropriate code for the particular object.

**postback** – A request for an update of a web page in response to a client event such as a button press.

**post-test loop** – A While loop where the body executes one time before the looping condition is ever tested, thus guaranteeing at least one execution of the loop body regardless of the condition.

**pre-test loop** – A While loop that tests the looping condition before executing the body of the loop. If the condition is initially false, then the loop body is never executed.

**primary key** – A field (or set of fields) in a database table that uniquely distinguishes the records in the table.

**procedure** – A series of instructions that are grouped together and treated as a single unit. Procedures can be called from elsewhere in the solution and are often viewed as building blocks for application development. When a procedure is called, control flows to the statements inside the procedure. When the procedure is finished, control returns to the calling statement.

**pseudocode** – A nontechnical description of an algorithm.

**recursive procedure** – A procedure that calls itself.

**relational database model** – A database design whereby relationships exist between tables to indicate how the data is connected. Typically, relationships involve the primary key from one table and a foreign key in a related table.

**relational operators** – Operators that manipulate numeric operands and generate a logical result. The six relational operators are: >, >=, <, <=, =, and <>.

**round trip** – A sequence of events in which a client action occurs that requires server processing, and the server processes the request and generates new HTML that is returned to the client browser.

**runtime error** – An error that occurs when syntactically correct code cannot be executed. A runtime error generates an exception.

**scope** – The region of code in which a variable may be directly referenced. Scope is determined by the location of the declaration of the variable.

**sentinel value** – A signaling value typically used to indicate the end of input.

**session** – The period of time that a unique browser (i.e. user) interacts with a web application. Every time a new browser invokes a web application, a new session is created for the browser.

**session state** – When a new session is created, ASP.NET maintains information about the session in the session state.

**structure** – A programming construct that combines several different variables into a single data type. Each variable declared inside the structure is called a member.

**structured design** – A programming methodology whereby the problem is broken into smaller pieces, each of which is solved individually.

**Structured Query Language (SQL)** – An industry standard language for communicating with a relational database. Pronounced "sequel" or S-Q-L.

**sub procedure** – A procedure.

**syntax** – The specific grammatical rules of a programming language.

**syntax error** – An error that occurs when code is written that does not follow the grammatical rules of the programming language. Also known as a compiler error.

**trestanding** – A word we made up that describes someone or something displaying tremendous humor and outstanding intellect.

**upper bound** – The index of the last element in an array. For a zero-based array, the upper bound of the array is always one less than the array length.

**variable** – A storage location that can be accessed and changed by developer code. A variable has a name (which does not change) and an associated data value (which may change during execution).

**Visual Studio .NET** – An integrated development environment (IDE) that supports many common programming tasks, including syntax checking, interpreting, compiling, debugging, and deploying applications. Visual Studio .NET also supports multiple programming languages, including Visual Basic .NET, C# .NET, C++ .NET, and J# .NET.

**web application** – An application deployed on a web server.

**web server** – A machine that stores documents, including web pages and server scripts for responding to client requests via the web.

**While loop** – A control structure used when actions are to be repeated an unknown number of times.

**wisdom** – Appropriate behavior guided by knowledge.

**zero-based arrays** – An array where the index values begin at zero.

# Index

M



N



O

Q



R



S

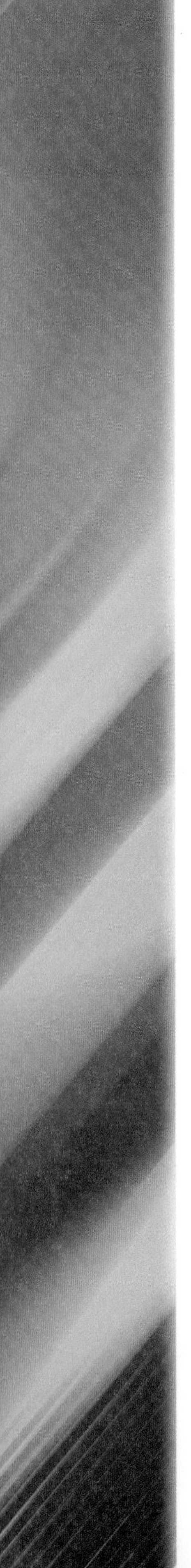

SINGLE PC LICENSE AGREEMENT AND LIMITED WARRANTY

READ THIS LICENSE CAREFULLY BEFORE OPENING THIS PACKAGE. BY OPENING THIS PACKAGE, YOU ARE AGREEING TO THE TERMS AND CONDITIONS OF THIS LICENSE. IF YOU DO NOT AGREE, DO NOT OPEN THE PACKAGE. PROMPTLY RETURN THE UNOPENED PACKAGE AND ALL ACCOMPANYING ITEMS TO THE PLACE YOU OBTAINED THEM. THESE TERMS APPLY TO ALL LICENSED SOFTWARE ON THE DISK EXCEPT THAT THE TERMS FOR USE OF ANY SHAREWARE OR FREEWARE ON THE DISKETTES ARE AS SET FORTH IN THE ELECTRONIC LICENSE LOCATED ON THE DISK:

1. GRANT OF LICENSE and OWNERSHIP: The enclosed computer programs and data ("Software") are licensed, not sold, to you by Pearson Education, Inc. ("We" or the "Company") and in consideration of your purchase or adoption of the accompanying Company textbooks and/or other materials, and your agreement to these terms. We reserve any rights not granted to you. You own only the disk(s) but we and/or our licensors own the Software itself. This license allows you to use and display your copy of the Software on a single computer (i.e., with a single CPU) at a single location for academic use only, so long as you comply with the terms of this Agreement.

2. RESTRICTIONS: You may not transfer or distribute the Software or documentation to anyone else. Except for backup, you may not copy the documentation or the Software. You may not network the Software or otherwise use it on more than one computer or computer terminal at the same time. You may not reverse engineer, disassemble, decompile, modify, adapt, translate, or create derivative works based on the Software or the Documentation. You may be held legally responsible for any copying or copyright infringement which is caused by your failure to abide by the terms of these restrictions.

3. TERMINATION: This license is effective until terminated. This license will terminate automatically without notice from the Company if you fail to comply with any provisions or limitations of this license. Upon termination, you shall destroy the Documentation and all copies of the Software. All provisions of this Agreement as to limitation and disclaimer of warranties, limitation of liability, remedies or damages, and our ownership rights shall survive termination.

4. LIMITED WARRANTY AND DISCLAIMER OF WARRANTY: Company warrants that for a period of 60 days from the date you purchase this SOFTWARE (or purchase or adopt the accompanying textbook), the Software, when properly installed and used in accordance with the Documentation, will operate in substantial conformity with the description of the Software set forth in the Documentation, and that for a period of 30 days the disk(s) on which the Software is delivered shall be free from defects in materials and workmanship under normal use. The Company does not warrant that the Software will meet your requirements or that the operation of the Software will be uninterrupted or error-free. Your only remedy and the Company's only obligation under these limited warranties is, at the Company's option, return of the disk for a refund of any amounts paid for it by you or replacement of the disk. THIS LIMITED WARRANTY IS THE ONLY WARRANTY PROVIDED BY THE COMPANY AND ITS LICENSORS, AND THE COMPANY AND ITS LICENSORS DISCLAIM ALL OTHER WARRANTIES, EXPRESS OR IMPLIED, INCLUDING WITHOUT LIMITATION, THE IMPLIED WARRANTIES OF MERCHANTABILITY AND FITNESS FOR A PARTICULAR PURPOSE. THE COMPANY DOES NOT WARRANT, GUARANTEE OR MAKE ANY REPRESENTATION REGARDING THE ACCURACY, RELIABILITY, CURRENTNESS, USE, OR RESULTS OF USE, OF THE SOFTWARE.

5. LIMITATION OF REMEDIES AND DAMAGES: IN NO EVENT, SHALL THE COMPANY OR ITS EMPLOYEES, AGENTS, LICENSORS, OR CONTRACTORS BE LIABLE FOR ANY INCIDENTAL, INDIRECT, SPECIAL, OR CONSEQUENTIAL DAMAGES ARISING OUT OF OR IN CONNECTION WITH THIS LICENSE OR THE SOFTWARE, INCLUDING FOR LOSS OF USE, LOSS OF DATA, LOSS OF INCOME OR PROFIT, OR OTHER LOSSES, SUSTAINED AS A RESULT OF INJURY TO ANY PERSON, OR LOSS OF OR DAMAGE TO PROPERTY, OR CLAIMS OF THIRD PARTIES, EVEN IF THE COMPANY OR AN AUTHORIZED REPRESENTATIVE OF THE COMPANY HAS BEEN ADVISED OF THE POSSIBILITY OF SUCH DAMAGES. IN NO EVENT SHALL THE LIABILITY OF THE COMPANY FOR DAMAGES WITH RESPECT TO THE SOFTWARE EXCEED THE AMOUNTS ACTUALLY PAID BY YOU, IF ANY, FOR THE SOFTWARE OR THE ACCOMPANYING TEXTBOOK. BECAUSE SOME JURISDICTIONS DO NOT ALLOW THE LIMITATION OF LIABILITY IN CERTAIN CIRCUMSTANCES, THE ABOVE LIMITATIONS MAY NOT ALWAYS APPLY TO YOU.

6. GENERAL: THIS AGREEMENT SHALL BE CONSTRUED IN ACCORDANCE WITH THE LAWS OF THE UNITED STATES OF AMERICA AND THE STATE OF NEW YORK, APPLICABLE TO CONTRACTS MADE IN NEW YORK, AND SHALL BENEFIT THE COMPANY, ITS AFFILIATES AND ASSIGNEES. THIS AGREEMENT IS THE COMPLETE AND EXCLUSIVE STATEMENT OF THE AGREEMENT BETWEEN YOU AND THE COMPANY AND SUPERSEDES ALL PROPOSALS OR PRIOR AGREEMENTS, ORAL, OR WRITTEN, AND ANY OTHER COMMUNICATIONS BETWEEN YOU AND THE COMPANY OR ANY REPRESENTATIVE OF THE COMPANY RELATING TO THE SUBJECT MATTER OF THIS AGREEMENT. If you are a U.S. Government user, this Software is licensed with "restricted rights" as set forth in subparagraphs (a)-(d) of the Commercial Computer-Restricted Rights clause at FAR 52.227-19 or in subparagraphs (c)(1)(ii) of the Rights in Technical Data and Computer Software clause at DFARS 252.227-7013, and similar clauses, as applicable.